Comments from scholars, users, reviewers and readers of the 1st Edition

Towey is clearly a very gifted writer, and able to take his readers through dense and complex theological issues with assurance and clarity. In the highways and byways of Christian history, and the maze of doctrines, and theological and moral issues, he is as sure a guide as one could hope for.

Martyn Percy, Dean of Christ Church, Oxford

Look no further, students of Christian theology. In one volume Anthony Towey offers a masterful guide to Christianity from its biblical beginnings to its postmodern present. Prepare to encounter people, events and ideas that have sealed fates, shaped history, and stirred the hearts and minds of generations. With erudition, enthusiasm and humour, he has produced that rare thing: a compendium of Christian theology to make the brain hum and the heart sing.

Julie Clague, University of Glasgow, UK

Towey writes engagingly. He refreshingly takes the student of theology into areas that will allow them to sense the richness, complexity, problems and wonders of the Christian tradition.

Gavin D'Costa, University of Bristol

This is a faithful, intelligent, accessible and witty introduction to theology. Its biblical, historical approach lets students know where theology came from and what data it must deal with.

Gerald O'Collins, SJ., Gregorian University, Rome

The greatest challenge when teaching theology to undergraduate students is that of translating what is, for so many today, a new language and alien concepts into something that is accessible and which can be understood. Towey achieves this without ever over-simplifying or diminishing the content.
Eamonn Fitzgibbon Director of the Irish Institute for Pastoral Studies

Wide ranging and comprehensive, a recommended primer for the student of Christian Theology.
Gerard Mannion, Georgetown University, Washington DC

I have been using this book for the diocesan on-going formation (master's level) programme since publication, and for other, less formal, courses I teach at parish level. I shall certainly continue to use it myself, and urge my students so to do.
Steve Porter, Diocese of San Bernardino, CA

I have found Anthony Towey's book hugely useful. It is so easy to access and so entertaining that undergraduates are able to cope with it. His presentation makes theology come alive and relevant – a real achievement to my mind.
Kate Williamson, University of Brighton, UK

An outstanding primer – the recommended introductory text on our diaconate formation programme.
Ashley Beck, Archdiocese of Southwark, UK

Scholarly quips sparkle throughout this 500-page compendium of Christian theology, making it an accessible and user-friendly read. In *Evangelii Gaudium* Pope Francis says that Christian joy is essential if the Church is to rediscover the original source of evangelisation in the contemporary world; Anthony Towey believes this same joy is essential to the study of theology. *An Introduction to Christian Theology* is an excellent primer for students and teachers, who will further benefit as multi-media resources linked to the text are made available on the web. Highly recommended, Anthony Towey has set a new standard in an important field.
Diana Klein in *The Tablet*

There is an important self-effacing quality to Towey's approach: this book helps to equip the reader to be a better reader of the primary texts of the Christian tradition and in particular a wiser reader of Scripture. Throughout, Towey proves a reliable guide.
Ashley Cocksworth in *Theology*

The arguments of this book are divided into four main parts: the ancient heritage, New Testament, classical period and contemporary era. The reasons for that structure consist in the historical approach followed by the author who succeeds in presenting a clear and detailed exposition of the whole subject.

Alessandro Giostra in *Reviews in Religion and Theology*

[This] is a work of impressive ambition: an academic sojourn beginning deep in ancient Judaism and ending with contemporary debates. For all the lightness of style, there is the deeper signature of a serious pedagogical intent: the thoroughgoing concern for narrative; the taming of technical vocabulary by etymological recourse; the explanation of subtle schools of thought in simple, but not simplistic, ways; the provision of a useful glossary and an extensive study guide replete with various scholarly sources.

Paul McHugh in *International Studies in Catholic Education*

We have not quite reached the point where the blog will replace the book entirely, but it is coming and this book itself shows awareness of the constantly changing range of thoughts about how reality works – A kickstart to anyone who wishes to pursue the conversation of theology.

Euan Marley OP in *New Blackfriars*

Towey's introduction is *customer*-oriented. It is reader-friendly. Every chapter has its own index, a short introduction and summary, to make it easier to sum up what has already been said. There is a useful glossary as well. The fact that Towey invites his readers to think one step further with him when it comes to this topic is a pleasant and welcome trait in his introduction to systematic theology.

Benjamin Dahlke in *ET Studies*, Leuven

In his foreword, Towey writes: 'Theology is "thoughtful conversation about God"' and this book is written for anyone who would like to be more acquainted with Christian thinking in a formal sense. On the basis of my brief 'chat' with Anthony Towey, I plan to have a much longer conversation.

Dermot Lamb, in *Open House*

'Big book, big evil' complained Callimachus, the ancient Greek librarian. This book is a big book, over 500 pages. A big evil it is not, however. It is clearly set out, with good use of maps, a good list of references and further reading, an excellent glossary and a timeline. Besides undergraduates, this would be an ideal and up-to-date single theology text book for sixth formers, any adult undertaking a course of studies in theology, and indeed any jaded cleric or catechist.

David Gibbons in *The Pastoral Review*

The author is one of the best lecturers I have ever heard. His aphorisms are legendary in this university so it is no wonder that his writing is as fresh, thought-provoking and often plain provoking as his personal presence in the classroom. This will be a leading textbook in the field at undergraduate and MA level for decades to come.

Trevor G. Stammers, Centre for Bioethics &
Emerging Technologies, SMU, London

A top book by Dr Towey. This book is a great place to start, and to refer back to. Even for those who have been reading Theology for a while, this book gives a refreshing approach.

Dan MacNamara, Scripture Union

A fabulous introduction to Christian Theology, easy to read, lively witty style, and doesn't go around the houses. It will be helpful for both the student and average parishoner alike and in fact anyone who has an interest in God.

Fiona Ozyer-Key, Maltby, UK

An Introduction to Christian Theology

Second Edition

An Introduction to Christian Theology

Second Edition

By
Anthony Towey

Bloomsbury T&T Clark
An imprint of Bloomsbury Publishing Plc

t&tclark

LONDON • NEW YORK • OXFORD • NEW DELHI • SYDNEY

Bloomsbury T&T Clark

An imprint of Bloomsbury Publishing Plc

Imprint previously known as T&T Clark

50 Bedford Square
London
WC1B 3DP
UK

1385 Fifth Avenue
New York
NY 10018
USA

www.bloomsbury.com

BLOOMSBURY, T&T CLARK and the Diana logo are trademarks of
Bloomsbury Publishing Plc

First published 2013
This version published 2018

British Library Cataloguing-in-Publication Data
A catalogue record for this books is available from the British Library.

ISBN: HB: 978-0-5676-7820-1
PB: 978-0-5676-7819-5
ePub: 978-0-5676-7821-8
epdf: 978-0-5676-7822-5

Library of Congress Cataloging-in-Publication Data

Cover image © The Martyrs' Picture by Durante Alberti,
1581 Photograph by Anthony Milner

Typeset by Deanta Global Publishing Services, Chennai, India
Printed and bound in Great Britain

Contents

Acknowledgements

I suppose these must start with my mother and father, Mary and Luke, who first got me thinking about God. Good Gospel names for wonderful people – and a mention to all my family and relatives near and far who made 'thoughtful conversation about God' a lively ingredient of my upbringing. Hats should be doffed to various teachers in schools and clergy in parishes that suffered indefatigable quizzing for answers. To brothers and sisters, students and mentors among various cherished communities, St Mary Magdalene, Maltby, De La Salle and All Saints, Sheffield, The Maltfriscans, London School of Economics, VEC, Gregorian and Biblicum in Rome, St Bede's and St. Bernard's Rotherham, Kirkedge, Hallam Diocese, Shuxi, Manchester Met., Loreto, CTA and St Mary's University College, London – a privileged life among the wise, the kind and the witty.

In the immediate production of this tome, I must thank Georgina, Thomas, Anna, Katie and Subitha at T&T Clark/Bloomsbury for their confidence and Michael Hayes for his necessary nagging. I thank Tarcisius Mukuka and Stephanie Modak for their prodigious efforts in helping me tame the project along with Mark Murphy, Pia Matthews and Ashley Beck. I must also thank Tony Milner, Peter Tyler, Kathleen O'Gorman, George Skelton, my sister Evleen and Tom Mann for reading and commenting on various sections of the manuscript as well as Samantha Chant, Christina Bartkowiak and Carol Lourdas. All faults are mine, all blessings be theirs.

Generally at this point, acknowledgements always get a little dewy-eyed as the author ultimately thanks his/her beloved and promises never to undertake such a mad project again. Káren, you are a total star – but hey – you knew that before you met me. Thanks for maintaining a joyful swirly ambience during the course of the writing and buying me a shed to finish it in. Can I come back in now?

Anthony M.G. Towey,
Strawberry Hill

Foreword

Theology is 'thoughtful conversation about God', and this book is written for anyone who would like to be more acquainted with Christian thinking in a formal sense, whether for personal, professional or academic reasons. It requires no prior knowledge of the subject, but the consequence is that you may have to fasten your seat belt for a white-water ride through several thousand years of 'God speculation' from the dawn of humanity to the present day.

Knowing the direction of travel might help, and the way this book is designed is quite straightforward. Rather than taking a thematic approach, the analysis is basically historical, and divided into four phases:

- The Ancient Heritage – the Hebrew and Greek scriptures which include the Creation accounts, Abraham, Moses, the Prophets, Kings and Wisdom literature.
- The New Testament – the Jesus event and the theological understanding of this in the Gospels, as well as Acts, Paul, John and Revelation.
- The Classical Period – this includes both the early centuries when central creeds and doctrines were debated and defined as well as the theological creativity and contestations which led to the divisions within Christianity observable today.
- The Contemporary Era – which begins by exploring some of the philosophical and scientific challenges faced by Christian Theology in the Modern period before discussing creative areas of dialogue which have opened up in more recent times.

Although this approach means many detours into detail have to be forsaken, the advantage is it gives the work something of a 'one-stop' quality. When someone is beginning the study of this subject, they are often required to acquire four separate things, a Bible, an introduction to Biblical Studies, an introduction to classical or doctrinal Theology and sometimes a set of supplementary texts in a Reader. The strength of this book is that it collates all these aims in one volume, and serves as a primer for each. In other words, it is a book which may either save you money or make you go out and buy four more!

When this work was commissioned, I was told: 'Your language can't be simple enough'. Having taught the subject at every level and to every age group, I was pretty confident this would be easy, but I now realize why that was said. There is such a thing as sacred jargon, and while it is impossible to avoid using specialized terms, I have tried to explain them in the flow of the text, and if all else fails, there is a glossary. Though 'readability' has demanded that citations, notes and bibliographies be deliberately selective, the aim of the work is that by the end, the reader will understand why Christian Theology has the shape it does, will be familiar with its key sources, and believer or not, be able to apply some of its insights to contemporary challenges. Enjoy the adventure.

AMGT

Foreword to the Second Edition

It is a privilege to be able to write a few words contextualizing the second edition of *Introduction to Christian Theology: Biblical, Classical, Contemporary*. I have been edified by the comments and reviews following its first publication in 2013, particularly regarding the comprehensive scope of the work and the clarity of the text. My task in preparing the second edition was to retain those characteristics while taking on *some* of the suggestions which fellow scholars, educators and readers have made.

In retaining 'Theology as thoughtful conversation about God' as the key *motif*, I began to agree that the most glaring omission from the first edition was the absence of a section devoted to prayer and spirituality. On reflection it did seem a little odd – perhaps even rude – that I had not included 'conversation *with* God' as part of the picture! Hence it is with some fear and trembling that I have added a distinct chapter entitled 'Dialogues in Prayer' towards the end of the main text. Although this does run the risk of making a big book even bigger, apart from some updating and minor re-phrasing, this constitutes the main *print* modification.

My second focus this time around has been on helping the many teachers, students and general readers who have enquired regarding ancillary media options in support of the text. Since the work is deliberately patterned so that it can be used as a course book, this takes the form of a series of short recorded introductions and chapter by chapter presentation slides supporting each of the topics. I do hope these distinct contributions will help the book to come alive even more and provoke further 'God-conversation!' The electronic media will be accessible through the Bloomsbury web portal from Spring 2018.

While limiting change in this way does mean that the text retains a predominantly 'Northern' and 'Western' theological purview, the reader is encouraged to pursue their own pathways of exploration. As well as excerpts from ancient texts and original thinkers supporting each chapter, there are also suggestions for further theological exploration at every turn.

Withal, I would like to thank Anna Turton and her colleagues at Bloomsbury for their support throughout this second iteration of the project and colleagues as well as students past and present at St. Mary's University for all their encouragement.

Lastly I must mention my beloved Káren. On the one hand for allowing me to build *another* shed to write in and on the other for gifting me with the wonderful joy that is our daughter Bethany Rosarii. In love I dedicate this work to them.

Anthony M.G. Towey,
Strawberry Hill

Abbreviations

Old Testament

Genesis - Gen
Exodus - Ex
Leviticus - Lev
Numbers - Num
Deuteronomy - Deut

Tobit - Tob
Judith - Jdt
Esther - Esth 1
Maccabees - 1 Macc
2 Maccabees - 2 Macc

Lamentations - Lam
Baruch - Bar
Ezekial - Ezek
Daniel - Dan

Joshua - Josh
Judges - Judg
Ruth - Ruth
1 Samuel - 1 Sam
2 Samuel - 2 Sam
1 Kings - 1 Kings
2 Kings - 2 Kings
1 Chronicles - 1 Chr
2 Chronicles - 2 Chr
Ezra - Ezra
Nehemiah - Neh

Job - Job
Psalms - Ps
Proverbs - Prov
Ecclesiastes - Ecc
Song of Songs - Song
Canticles - Cant
Wisdom - Wis
Sirach - Sir

Isaiah - Isa
Jeremiah - Jer

Hosea - Hos
Joel - Joel
Amos - Am
Jonah - Jon
Micah - Mic
Nahum - Nah
Habakkuk - Hab
Zephaniah - Zeph
Haggai - Hag
Zechariah - Zech
Malachi - Mal

New Testament

Matthew - Matt
Mark - Mark
Luke - Luke
John - John
Acts of the Apostles - Acts
Romans - Rom
1 Corinthians - 1 Cor
2 Corinthians - 2 Cor
Galatians - Gal
Ephesians - Eph
Philippians - Phil
Colossians - Col
1 Thessalonians - 1 Thess
2 Thessalonians - 2 Thess

1 Timothy - 1 Tim
2 Timothy - 2 Tim
Titus - Titus
Philemon - Philemon
Hebrews - Heb
James - Jas
1 Peter - 1 Pet
2 Peter - 2 Pet

1 John - 1 John
2 John - 2 Jn
3 John - 3 Jn
Jude - Jude
Revelation - Rev

BCE – Before Common or Christian Era
CE – Common or Christian Era

LXX – Septuagint/Greek version of
TaNaK – Hebrew Scripture
ST – 'Summa Theologiae'
LW – Luther's Works

Referencing in the Main Text

See page 429 for referencing protocols. Please note the abbreviation 'cf.' means 'compare' and is used to nuance the argument of the main text.

Part 1
Introduction

1

Thoughtful Conversation about God

While not everyone may consider themselves to be a religious person there is a way in which the natural inclination of human beings to communicate and ask questions gives rise to the study of Theology.

a) Theology: Thoughtful conversation about God

Theology, like many technical terms in our language, comes from a Greek root – *Theos* – meaning 'God' and *logos*, which signifies 'word', 'reason', 'meaning'. Theology then may usefully be understood as 'thoughtful conversation about God' – an exploration of 'God-words', 'God-reasonings', 'God-meanings'. Obviously, some people do more of this than others, some people even make a living out of it, but everyone who can communicate can *do* it.

So how did Theology or 'God conversations' begin? Some argue that 'God-words' can only truly be said to have begun when God spoke them. This view proposes that Theology follows on from 'revelation' – an explicit self-communication of God, such as that which Judaism believes was given through Moses in the Ten Commandments, as Christianity believes was given through Jesus in the Gospels, or as Islam proclaims was given to Mohammed when writing the Qur'an. Expressed in the form of sacred texts, beliefs, rituals and teachings, revelation forms the 'raw material' for the Theology of a particular religious tradition.

While this view might envisage the nature of Theology originally being 'from on high', another would imagine God conversations emerging 'from below'. Several theories attempt to explain the emergence of religion, but it is not implausible to imagine primitive humanity gazing at the sky and wondering whether that great big hot yellow thing should be worshipped because it was a welcome alternative to an Ice Age, or be cursed for parching their burning throat. This dimension of contemplation, which finds expression in religious terms, is sometimes classified as a type of 'Natural Theology'. Understood in this sense, like her ancient sisters Philosophy and Science, one could propose that Theology begins with a *sense of wonder*. Fascination, observation, thinking, reflection, theorizing – these all form part of the human reaction to the experience of life and give rise to human knowledge expressed in all its forms.

Though the 'revealed' or 'natural' origins of the subject may be a matter of some debate, it is worth noting that what sets Theology apart from other disciplines is that the magnetic north of theological reflection points towards the following thesis:

'Reality is best understood as God-based'.

Theologians and believers of every stripe may argue about how this might be best expressed or lived out, but it can serve as a useful working hypothesis in this book. Clearly, some will disagree with this proposal. Some might not be religious at all. Yet already, by voicing that very disagreement, the conversation of Theology has begun. And it started a long time ago.

b) Theology: A basic human conversation

The proposal of Theology that *reality is God based* is ancient and certainly not the sole preserve of any culture or epoch. Whether one considers it misguided or not, one has to acknowledge that enduring speculation about 'God' is a basic human question. This is evidenced by the testimony of the earliest cultures for which we have written records in Mesopotamia (present-day Iran and Iraq) and from Ancient Egypt. Egyptian thinking is partly preserved by their written record of 'hieroglyphics' or 'priest-symbols' of the day. Certainly by 3000 BCE, Egypt had a highly developed theological/cosmological understanding of reality, which has long drawn interest from numerous Christian scholars since it was oriented around a dying and rising sun – a cosmic pattern which has been paralleled with the death and resurrection of Jesus.

If we note that 'religion' – from the Latin word *re-ligare* – means 'to bind together', we are perhaps less surprised to find that 'Priests', 'Priestesses', 'Prophets', 'Shamans' and other designated mediators between 'God' and humanity have played a central role in tribal communities from the dawn of history. As such, it is priests rather than prostitutes who can lay some claim to being the 'oldest profession', although they do have competition from accountants. The earliest archives from the royal houses of Mesopotamia almost 5000 years ago are enlivened by colourful prophetic oracles and ritual instructions, but such spiritual annals are more than balanced by the huge archives of tedious financial records.

Meanwhile, it may be important to note that priests as undoubtedly the 'first theologians' were in large part also the world's 'first philosophers' and 'first scientists'. The English word for 'science' is simply based on the Latin verb *scire* – 'to know' – and the ancients did not carve up their knowing or understanding of reality in the same manner as we do today. The mistaken view that presently imagines philosophers, theologians and scientists to be mutual enemies simply did not exist then, and the process by which these disciplines acquired distinct identities in Western culture will form part of the exploration of this book. For now, it is merely important to note that they were part of the same intellectual awakening at the dawn of civilization, which saw humanity trying to articulate an understanding of reality.

Originally, those who studied the 'movements' of the stars in the heavens were just as likely to be the ones interpreting them and writing the horoscopes of the Pharaoh. Temples were centres of learning as well as ritual in much the same way that monasteries, cathedrals and church colleges gave rise to the modern university system in Western Europe. History attests that Christian, Islamic and Jewish theologians fostered the intellectual heritage of the West for centuries after the collapse of the cultures of Greece and Rome. They did this not out of an interest in antique books, but rather because their love of Theology involved a love of learning in general. Indeed theologians would claim that the common purpose of all investigation leads to ultimate questions such as the existence of God and the meaning of life, which provide the very texture of Theology.

As evidence of this, theologians point out that scientists and philosophers inevitably find themselves confronting theological questions. Best-selling books about God in the English-speaking world have been written by Richard Dawkins, a professional scientist (*The God Delusion*, 2006), and Antony Flew, an atheist philosopher turned believer (Flew and Varghese, *There is a God*, 2007).

Neither of these authors has had a formal theological training, but it is as if they cannot stay away from the subject matter proper to Theology. In this light, one can perhaps understand Wolfhart Pannenberg's comment that humanity is 'incurably religious' (Pannenberg, 1991, p. 157) and the arrogant claim made by theologians that their subject is the 'Mother' or 'Queen' of Sciences. Why? Because Theology involves the core human questions of origin, life and destiny – topics which are of interest to everyone and frame the whole spectrum of human conversation.

c) Theology: A confused conversation?

Since Theology involves basic questions of humanity and meaning, a sceptic might quibble that it has not been a very successful pursuit as its endeavours have yielded confusion rather than coherence. Various religions manifest differences between each other and witness to multiple interpretations within their own communities of faith. Clearly, neither 'revealed' nor 'natural' Theology has yielded unanimity of meaning among believers. Besides the groupings of the major world religions, there are countless less well known belief systems each claiming a particular, unique understanding of God. Given the level of confusion, one could legitimately make an argument either against the existence of God or that there are actually quite a number of Deities genuinely vying for attention. Likewise, it may call into question the quality of theological reflection across all religions and all ages, given that between them all the efforts of numerous theologians clearly haven't resolved the 'God question' to universal satisfaction.

Matters are hardly improved by the difficulties that all religions acknowledge in speaking about God. As if to derail the theological enterprise from the start, it can be argued that God and words don't really go together well. Mystics in all religions bemoan the limitations of human utterances, which can never adequately capture the dumbfounding nature of divinity. Rarely short of a winning line, even St. Paul speaks of religious encounter in terms of 'things that are not to be told' (2 Cor 12:4). In so doing, he echoes the strong Jewish tradition of the 'unspeakability' or 'ineffability' of God intimated by the synagogue reading of the Torah where the name for God, the sacred 'YHWH', is deemed too holy to voice and *Adonai* – Hebrew for 'My Lord' is used instead.

Yet, while theologians readily acknowledge the problem of adequately describing the mystery of God, the phenomenon of religion demands our attention and in the broad view, its core proposals are surprisingly coherent. Mainstream religions propose that human beings have genuine significance in relation to God and moral duties in relation to one another. Detachment regarding many aspects of life seems to be encouraged while family and nurturing responsibilities are affirmed. Cultic dispositions of gratitude and the marking of life moments by rituals are common. Furthermore, a notion of cosmic goodness and justice is a resilient feature of the major religions alongside conceptions of eternal life.

Likewise, since Theology proposes to connect the mystery of human reality with God, then it is clear that the great human dramas of love and hate, birth and death, war and peace form part of its concerns. The question of how humanity should relate to God and indeed the whole dialogue of life itself are open to theological conversation. And in this view, the astonishment must lie in the fact that such huge families of faith have gathered for centuries bound in allegiance to the major world religions. What on earth keeps them together?

d) Theology: A conversation about meaning

The widespread phenomenon of religious allegiance appears to be due to theologians of whatever religious description providing 'systems of meaning' or 'worldviews' applicable to human life. Far from being contributors to confusion, theologians offer through these great stories a context of life, love and eternity, which give each individual a value, a place and personal significance within a cosmic matrix of understanding. For example, within Christianity, a fundamental part of the 'narrative' is that each individual is a 'Child of God' – which immediately endows everyone with a special dignity, a particular importance.

Religions are not unique in this. A secular example would be 'The American Dream', which invites everyone in the 'Land of the Free' to strive for 'success' because 'everything is possible'. One can easily see how that simple narrative can give a certain direction to society and encourage 'upward mobility'. Other systems such as Marxism likewise offer a context for the individual to operate within and derive significance through participating in the common struggle to revolutionize society in the name of equality.

The technical term for these 'mega-stories' is 'meta-narratives'. Religious versions tend to be more encompassing than secular alternatives. They speak not only to the most intimate situations such as personal sin but also to the broadest of social perspectives such as the destiny of the whole world. In some ways, much of the rest of this book will be a description of how the meta-narrative of Christian Theology has emerged from its ancient roots through to its contemporary expression today. Hence, at this juncture, we might usefully ask, 'Where do we find this mega-story and how do we engage more closely in the conversation that is Christian Theology?' The response inevitably demands that we review the constituent elements of this faith matrix in its public and personal dimensions.

e) Theology: A conversation across time

Analysing the Christian mega-story in its public dimension involves engaging with a series of sources which we can summarize under the headings of '3 C's and 3 T's'.

- The **Canon** is the 'rule' or 'collection' of scriptures commonly called the Bible, which contains cherished writings gathered over many centuries. Subsequent chapters will discuss how this compendium came to be put together and finalized, but for now it is sufficient to say that the hallowed scrolls of the ancient Law of Moses, along with other Prophetic and Wisdom writings, provided the religious vocabulary for the various Jesus movement authors in their attempts to explain or theologize the Christ event.
- The **Creeds** can be understood as shorthand summaries of this revelation. Some creeds seem to have originated in the context of prayer, such as the celebration of Christian initiation of Baptism, while others were deliberately formulated at the great councils of the early Christian centuries.
- The early **Councils of the Church** were gatherings of leaders who confronted theological and practical controversies of the time and left a definitive legacy of writings which have been recognized as authoritative by Christian thinkers throughout the centuries.

These first three sources of faith are understood by all Christians to *reveal* a privileged understanding of God and God's purposes for humanity and it stands to reason that the student of Theology must thoughtfully engage with them. While general God conclusions might be drawn from *Natural*

Theology – by observing creation and so forth, these holy writings and summaries of doctrine are understood to contain specific truths which are *revealed* by God. For Christians, these sources of faith are human and divine realities, that is, they are God's own self-communication as revealed through inspired – 'spirit prompted' – human beings using speech, imagery, rituals, symbols, words, ink and parchment. This mediation through human agency is important to note and is part of the fascination of theological investigation. For none of these public sources of faith fell from the sky, but are instead the fruit of thoughtful conversations, meditations and even arguments about God at key moments in history among the believing community.

If 'Canon, Creed and Councils' are at the heart of Christian revelation, what prevents it being merely a descriptive chapter in the history of religious thought? Here is where tradition theologians and time must be considered as vivifying dialogue partners in the thoughtful conversation that is Christian Theology.

- **Tradition** is an umbrella term which comprises the wider experience of the Christian community, its way of life, customs, rituals, practices and so forth. Not everything always gets written down (John 21:25), and the rich historical expression of Christian faith, its patterns of worship and patterns of behaviour have been an essential theological consideration. Appeal to what has happened in the past is often encountered when disagreements emerge, such as whether infants should be baptized or not? Can divorce be allowed? What do we mean by sanctity of life? While 'tradition' might not always provide an immediate solution to a problem, G. K. Chesterton remarked that it does serve to keep theologians mindful of a group that are too readily ignored, namely, 'the dead!' (Chesterton, [1908] 1996, p. 63).
- **Theologians** are the important fifth source to be added. While those who came to write the biblical texts retain a privileged theological position, many of the great early leaders of the Church made important contributions to Christian understanding. Study of these early theologians from the first 600 years of Christianity is called *Patristics* – derived from the Latin word for 'Fathers'. Later theologians such as Aquinas, Luther and Calvin have also profoundly shaped Christian thinking, and consideration of key figures on into the present will be noted during the course of this work.
- **Time** is last to be considered. The theological vitality of Christianity in every age is framed in the dialogue between believers and the events of every era. These 'signs of the times' are in a sense the sixth and final source. In every era, new concerns take centre stage and become part of theological conversation. A recent example would be the concerns regarding global warming. How should Christians respond to this crisis? The result has been a number of studies which analyse this issue in the light of biblical and other theological sources.

f) Theology as an open conversation

Canon, Creed and Councils, tradition, theologians and time – all these are articulations of the *content* of Christian faith – sometimes called *fides quae* – the faith *which* is believed. This public faith is distinct from personal faith or *fides qua* – the faith *by which* someone believes, signifying the sort of conviction that would lead someone to request Baptism and formal community belonging. Since St Anselm (1033–1109 CE) famously defined Theology as 'faith seeking understanding', one school of thought insists personal conviction is a pre-requisite for the proper study of Christian thinking, whereas another has countered that faith is actually a hindrance to theological inquiry.

In an attempt to referee this dispute, we can note that because the sources of the Christian 'meta-narrative' are open to all, even if someone does not particularly assent to personal faith in God, they can still 'do' Theology – making connections and seeking meanings based on their scholarship or insight. Taking this a stage further, since there is no certainty regarding the existence of God, it might be argued that a non-believer is actually better placed to study Theology on account of their being 'unbiased' and therefore more objective than one who has a committed faith.

In considering this argument, it is important to acknowledge that theologians have never been actually able to *prove* God's existence in a manner which has ever guaranteed acceptance by all of the people all of the time. Even in the traditionally theocentric – 'God-centred' – culture of ancient Israel, more than once do we find a psalm beginning with the sideswipe, 'Fools say in their hearts "There is no God"' (Ps 14:1; 53:1). Atheism was around even in biblical times and in any case, the relationship implied by personal faith cannot be forced on anyone. Instead, what theologians may more modestly propose are arguments and evidence which support the view that belief in God is *reasonable*.

But are believing theologians biased? Do they have vested interests in affirming divine reality such that any scientific or philosophical challenge to that position is not honestly appraised? After all, if believing theologians perceive themselves to be in a relationship with a God, they aren't going to want to upset their deity by *really* questioning God's existence. As an example, the twentieth-century philosopher and atheist Bertrand Russell (1872–1970) was unimpressed that the first part of the famous *Summa Theologiae* of Thomas Aquinas (1225–1274) asks '*utrum deus sit*' – 'Is there a God?' Russell was equally unmoved that Aquinas then gives cogent reasons why God is not self-evident to humanity (ST Ia Q2 Art3). According to Russell's *History of Western Philosophy*, Thomas had already decided what the right answer was, so there was little true philosophical spirit in his work (Russell, [1945] 1984, p. 463).

Unfortunately, there is no inherent logic in seeing believers as biased and unbelievers as somehow clear of any prejudice. It ill behoves anyone, whether atheist or otherwise, to claim for themselves some kind of unique intellectual neutrality or maturity which believers do not share. Russell himself laboured for many years with his friend Alfred North Whitehead on *Principia Mathematica*, and after three-hundred pages of logic was able to assert that $1 + 1 = 2$ (Whitehead & Russell, 1927, p. 362). It does not detract from the quality of his reasoning to reckon on him already knowing the answer. A 'fervent' atheist takes a negative standpoint on God's existence which is as much an act of faith as that of the believer.

Since theists and atheists can be somewhat notorious for argumentative passion, there may be an attraction towards the middle position of the 'agnostic' (from the Greek *a-gnosis* – 'one who does not know'). It might be claimed that the agnostic theologian is in the best place to study God-logic since they are neither avowed believers nor non-believers. However, if the believer or atheist is to be disallowed on the grounds of conviction, it would seem odd to presume that those who are undecided are any wiser. Recording an 'open verdict' is a perfectly acceptable *ending* to a judicial or theological enquiry but until arguments are weighed back and forth, personal neutrality may be the result of ignorance, poor reasoning or sheer lack of curiosity. In the final analysis, an agnostic absence of conclusion should not be granted any privileged position because of its supposed lack of bias. If Theology at the raw level is open to everybody, then the opinions of agnostics are to be respected neither more nor less than any other.

g) Theology and personal faith

Staying with these considerations a little longer, I think that part of the problem here is confusion regarding the nature of faith understood as not being 'realistic' or not properly grounded like other dimensions of our knowing. The fact is that most of our knowing is based on some sort of trust to which we give assent. One of the philosophical greats, Plato (423–347 BCE), anchored his system in an undefined notion of goodness and even Descartes (1596–1650), a master of doubt, was forced at least to trust himself with the famous words, *cogito ergo sum*, 'I think therefore I am'. Hence in his *Grammar of Assent*, John

Henry Newman (1801–1890) pointed out that trust is effectively fundamental to any concept of ourselves, knowledge or common sense:

> We all believe without any doubt that we exist, that we have individuality and identity all our own; that we think, feel and act in the home of our own minds. Nor is the act of assent limited to our self-consciousness . . . We accept and hold with an unqualified assent that the earth, considered as a phenomenon, is a globe; that all its regions see the sun by turns; that there are vast tracts on it of land and water; that there are really existing cities on definite sites which go by the names of London, Paris, Florence and Madrid. We are sure that Paris or London, unless suddenly swallowed up by an earthquake or burned to the ground, is today just what it was yesterday, when we left it. (Newman, [1870] 1979, pp. 167–68)

While many of the everyday things that we take for granted are based on an act of implicit trust without which we can't really function, it might be worth noting one or two other aspects of *fides qua* – 'personal faith'– before moving on.

- Even if it is accepted that faith in God takes its place as a dimension of knowledge within the familiar experience of common trust, it must also be accepted that not everyone experiences this sense of trust in a divine being. This has led to the much discussed view that faith is not a human action but is itself a gift of God – a key question in Christian Theology.
- Meanwhile, where personal faith is present, it is not surprising that it is of a nature that is both intensely personal and difficult to communicate. The great poets struggle to frame the mysteries of love, the mathematician uses the concept of infinity but cannot express it, and the string-theorist posits cosmological relations even if they cannot be measured. When personal faith is translated into Christian Theology, it is similarly limited and at best offers insights into God by *analogy* or *likeness*.
- Thirdly, personal faith in God tends to be an *involving* type of knowledge – it is the point where psychologically the individual begins to be intertwined with another – no matter how distant or inexpressible. In his famous work *I and Thou*, the Jewish theologian Martin Buber likens this to inhabiting two different worlds, one personal, one impersonal ([1923] 2004, p. 13). The upshot is that if the basic theological proposal suggests that *reality is God based*, then the development of the hypothesis in the Judeo-Christian tradition is that *reality is God loved*.

As a last point on this matter, it is worth noting that personal faith or doubt, indeed God-convictions of any persuasion, can lend an intensity to theological conversations that are absent in other areas of academic study. Many years of teaching have at least taught me that! Whether someone is a believer or not, the idea of faith may be unsettling for all sorts of emotional rather than intellectual reasons, which therefore demands respect. If there is any consolation, it is that the basic trust required in any relationship is not just a risk peculiar to religious faith, it is ultimately a universal risk of human life, knowledge and love.

h) Theology as history, interpretation and paradox

While one can argue that studying Theology without any personal faith is akin to studying Shakespeare without ever seeing a play, the invitation of this textbook is that in the first instance, theological enquiry should be understood as a conversation as wide as humanity itself. Perhaps the verb used in Anselm's definition *fides quaerens intellectum* – 'faith seeking understanding' – might be helpful here since the seeking, questioning, critical dimension of the heart and mind make Theology alive. It is important to understand Christian Theology in this sense as an *activity*, not the straightforward teaching of belief sometimes called *catechetics*. Theology is not repetition nor is it merely 'talking about Jesus with bigger words'. Like any inquiry or path of knowledge, Christian Theology questions its source materials and is engaged in a permanent, ever-new critical and creative dialogue with lived experience.

In this light, the methodology proposed by this book is threefold. In the first instance, it is straightforwardly *historical* insofar as it will be attentive to the key sources and contextual origins that gave rise to Christian thinking. Because the Christian 'mega-story' or 'meta-narrative' is rooted in the worldview of a scriptural tradition, this book will begin by exploring key themes from both Hebrew and Greek writings which provide the immediate context of the Gospel narratives and doctrinal developments thereafter. Theology books that do not begin with these texts risk being 2-D rather than 3-D.

At a second level, this book will emphasize the importance of interpretation or *hermeneutics*. While this can be simply a question of method (such as in discussing different approaches to the study of biblical texts), sensitivity to the importance of interpretation is absolutely key to explaining the core theological issues under review. As an obvious example, the book will note that the distinction between Judaism and Christianity which is fairly obvious today emerged not because of a different scriptural tradition, but because of a *different interpretation* of the biblical evidence leading to *different theologizing* of the Jesus event. To a large extent, exactly the same process will mark the differences between denominations within Christianity – they may be understood as different 'interpretation communities' cohering around different theological priorities and core markers of belonging.

Thirdly, and less straightforwardly, the method adopted here demands a preliminary acceptance of the possibility of *paradox*. A paradox is an apparent contradiction, which is resolved by deeper reflection. This is not meant to be at all duplicitous, but if the reader can grasp that the reconciliation of opposites is in the DNA of Christian Theology, then much of what follows will be less confusing. After all, a religious system which proposes a virgin birth, a God-man, a death and resurrection and a Triune God is not looking to build its house on the even-numbered side of the street. If it is any consolation, scientists tell us that sub-atomic physics is similarly paradoxical, so maybe such theological 'reconciliation of opposites' is deeply realistic! 'Both/and' thinking is crucial to Christian reasoning, and paradox is one of its governing principles. So, mindful of history, interpretation and paradox, the study now turns to review the sources of Christian Theology, the first of these being the Canon of Scripture – the Bible.

Summary

Summarizing the journey that has been undertaken in this chapter, we have seen that Theology is a study originating in the very dawn of human consciousness and involves the proposal that reality is ultimately God-based. Through Theology, major faiths propose 'meta-narratives' of meaning for life which in Christian thinking find expression in authoritative texts such as the Canon of Scripture, the Creeds and the Councils of the Church. In principle, theological study of these sources is an activity open to all, and the procedure adopted by this book is an approach mindful of history, contextual interpretation and paradox.

Part 2
Theology of Creation and Covenant

1. The Old Testament World

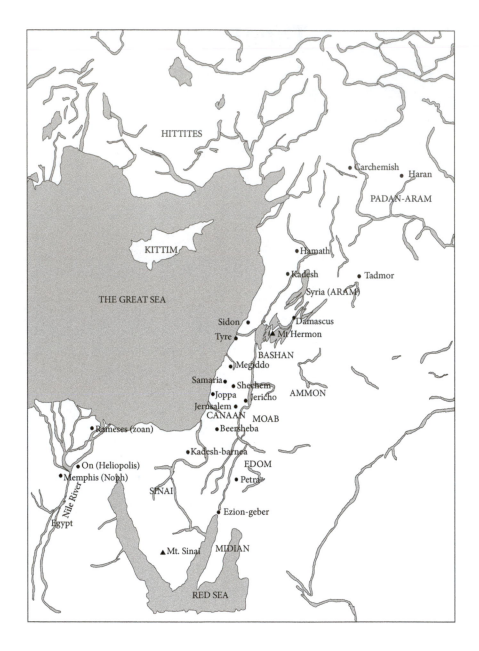

2

Genesis: God, Creation and Humanity

If Theology is 'thoughtful conversation about God' then it is clear that we have to engage with its sources intelligently. Theologically, the Bible is to be considered as both divine and human word. The Bible is a collection, a 'little library' of books which are the pre-eminent sources of Christian thinking. Among these varied writings are the brilliant creation poems of Genesis 1-3 which combine ancient cosmology with 'aetiology' – stories designed to explain 'why things are the way they are.' It is not scientific writing as that is understood it today, nor does it present itself as philosophically rigorous. It does, however, purport to shine a light on creation, humanity and God. And these first passages of the Bible exemplify the demanding but enjoyable nature of the challenge.

a) The Bible: An inspired library

If Theology is 'thoughtful conversation about God' and the Bible is a key constituent of Christian thinking, then it stands to reason that the budding theologian must engage with this source intelligently, and to do so it may be helpful to consider its 'divine and human' designation.

On the one hand, the proposal of Christian Theology is that the Bible is *revelation* insofar as God's nature, our nature and the purpose of our existence are communicated to us through it. All biblical scriptures are inspired, or 'God-breathed' (2 Tim 3:16) – there is a holy, divine dimension to the words which in turn can only be properly understood through the Spirit (2 Pet 1:20-21). Hence the classical understanding of biblical inspiration has God key to both the authorship of the Bible and the reading of it, both its origin and its interpretation, both its expression and its effects.

On the other hand, the text is also very human – a factor which likewise must demand theological attention. 'Bible' comes from the Greek *biblia* – meaning 'little books' – and it cannot be stressed enough that the Bible is not a monograph but rather a library of different scrolls or 'volumes' – which comes from the Latin *volvo* meaning 'roll/rotate'. Furthermore, the majority of these 'volumes' or 'books' are themselves collections of smaller oral stories, prayers, oracles and accounts which were written down and collated by known and unknown authors and editors over many centuries. Nowhere in mainstream Christian Theology is it claimed that the Bible is the product of one author in the same way that the Qur'an may be attributed to Mohammed, still less received on golden tablets as Joseph Smith claimed is the case for *The Book of Mormon*. Instead, while the 'canon' or collection of scrolls which constitute what is commonly called the Bible are understood in Christian Theology to have been *inspired* by God, they have been *inscribed* by humans. The collection is therefore a source of faith which is at once divine and human – theologically bearing the transforming power of the unchanging word of God, sociologically bearing the human thumbprints of a multiplicity of ages and cultures.

Paradoxically, while dealing with the human dimension of the biblical text can be troubling to some, it is important to realize that this apparent contradiction is entirely consistent with the 'theo-logic' at the heart of Christianity. After all, the designation of Jesus as both divine and human is Christianity's pivotal mystery and to be consistent with this central theme, the Bible must be, of necessity, conceived as a divine-human entity. It does not denigrate the holiness of the text to affirm that it has a human component.

What it does rule out when doing Theology, however, is a thoughtless fundamentalism or literalism in relation to the Bible which ignores its long history of coming to be.

Historically, the library that we call the Bible is the product of the events, the memories, the traditions and the rituals of the various communities which gave rise to these documents. Whether used in prayer or study, today's Bible is a collection of varied writings entrusted not just by the original authors but a gift endowed also by the scribes and scholars, ancient and modern, who have painstakingly copied, preserved or translated these hallowed scrolls for the edification of others. The budding theologian must happily embrace the fact that in capturing the numerous oral accounts, these scriptures have passed through many hands. Any critical edition of the Bible will be evidence of this and will demonstrate the variations in original sources and alternative translations which will enable the thoughtful reader to see the subtle, hazy edges of the text. Biblical fundamentalism is possible, but it is not a properly theological option since it does not think through the human expression of the divine word. To put it another way, if anyone likes their religion ultra-neat and tidy, they would be well advised to fly solo, avoid the Bible and ditch the community adventure of Christian Theology with immediate effect.

Equally problematic is a scepticism borne out of an unthinking approach to the nature of the texts being considered. Classically, this happens when a passage from the Bible is approached without thought being given to what *type* of book is being read. While in a library, different types of literature are kept apart, the Bible as printed today glues different types of books together in one binding. Within the collection there are prophecies, prayers and poetry; there are annals, legends and family trees; there are proverbs, parables and miracles; there are battles, rituals and fables. This variety in the library of the scriptures should alert readers to approach these texts thoughtfully. No one would go into a library and try to gather insights into car maintenance from books in the poetry section nor seek insights into cookery among the crime writers.

Unfortunately, the Bible is often mistakenly read with thoughtless literalism. This 'one size fits all' approach can be problematic. No child learning English history will think that King Richard the Lionheart actually had the heart of a big scary cat, yet all too often a literal reading of poems and parables without any sensitivity to metaphor and imagery leads to confusion. The upshot is that otherwise intelligent people may decide that descriptions of many headed beasts and apocalyptic horsemen in the Book of Revelation render the Bible incredible and unworthy of serious consideration. To avoid this pitfall, some effort must be made by anyone interested in serious engagement with Christian Theology to have a basic sensitivity to the nature and origin of biblical texts and how they have impacted upon later thinking. Nowhere is this more important than in the first chapters of Genesis to which we now turn.

b) In the beginning

If we start at the very beginning (which is a very good place to start), then we read:

> In the beginning when God created the heavens and the earth, the earth was a formless void and darkness covered the face of the deep, while a wind from God swept over the face of the waters. Then God said, 'Let there be light' and there was light. (Gen 1:1-3)

If a sense of wonder is the beginning of all knowledge, then it is no surprise that a meditation on cosmic origins is placed at the beginning of the collection of scriptures we call the Bible. To be clear from the outset, the ancient Hebrews were not the only people to have considered the question of the origin of the Universe. It was a point of speculation common in other ancient cultures and has been an enduring fascination for scientists, theologians and philosophers of all ages. In our own time, an unnecessary tension between scientific theories of cosmic origins and biblical literature has emerged, controversies which are more fully discussed in Chapter 20 below. For now, it is important to begin by considering how an intelligent reading of Genesis contributes to 'thoughtful conversation' about God. It will literally throw us in at the 'deep end' since in these few but famous lines, a whole Theology of God, creation and humanity emerge from the watery cosmic depths.

The first three chapters of Genesis offer two distinct poems about creation and human origins. Gen 1:1-2:4 presents a vivid picture of God's creative action. It is written in the epic genre of *cosmogony* ('cosmos'– 'explanation') which, though typical of the ancient world, yields timeless theological truths. While other ancient cultures depicted the origins of the Universe as the result of a fight between gods or as a consequence of the carving open of a great sea monster, Genesis has God's creative action taking place in the formless void of a dark watery deep (cf. Pritchard, 2011, p. 67). God is immediately introduced as the Creator of heaven and earth (1:1) and is seen to be Master of the terrifying *tohu bohu* – the primal chaos that will be ordered by God's Word (1:2). The darkness covered watery deep is significant because in the consciousness of Israel, the sea was a place of terror – full of wild waves and monsters. (Note how the Exodus from Egypt had to take place via dry land and why even the fishermen friends of Jesus were never quite at home on the Sea of Galilee.) The scene is completed by the presence of the *ruah elohim* – the 'Spirit' or 'Storm' of God that hovers over this mayhem. Then God speaks:

'Let there be light' – and there was light. (Gen 1:3)

God's word is presented as absolute, effective and good. Separating the light and darkness is the first moment of ordering, and the naming of the cosmic realities designates God's authority over them (1:4-5). The primordial chaos is thus transformed by the power of God's word. God's word not only brings light, it is light – it creates the space, the vault within which life is possible. Theologically, the biblical text proposes that the creation you are able to see is only there because God has spoken it into being and you can only perceive it in the light which he has also voiced. If the core theological idea suggests *reality is God based,* these first verses of revelation detail *how* – through God's *word.* As such, the word of God is more real than anything you experience, anything you encounter, anything you know or anything that lands on your head with a clunk. God's word is more real than you, since you are a personal outcome of God's creative word-based cosmos. With God's word comes light and the created order which includes time. God is the transcendent master of that created order – the supernatural Lord of the natural.

Now, if these first paragraphs of Theology have you reaching for a lifebelt so as not to drown in your own version of the primordial deep, do not panic. Whether believer or unbeliever, the theological proposal that reality is based on a *word* is quite difficult for the modern mindset to grasp. After all, we are hard-headed moderns schooled in atomic physics and astronomical theories which over the past century have ranged from 'Steady State' cosmos thinking, through to the 'Big Bang' and 'Multi-Universe' theories of more recent times. Yet, all of us presume a certain order to the interactions of the cosmos and principles which govern its operation. In that sense, the theological proposal here is not so far removed – the poem in Genesis suggests that the recognizable logic (*logos*) of the universe is organized by the logic of God.

Moreover, while most people do not experience words in the same way as they sense metal or wood, all nonetheless experience the power of words to transform for good or for ill. Words can bring comfort, words can bring discomfort, words may not just advocate change but actually change us. We have all felt physically different through hearing the essentially non-physical words of another and have at times had the blushes, the heart flutters, the stomach upsets and headaches to prove it. Words can change reality and in linguistics, there is a useful distinction made between 'describing words' and 'action words'. Blessings, curses and transformative words are a key part of religious ritual but they also apply in secular life – if the president declares war, the country is at war! When the minister declares 'I now pronounce you man and wife', the couple are married – for better or for worse! These are called *performative* speech acts – they make happen what they say. The journalists who then report the breaking news about the war or the wedding (or both!) are merely *describing* or *narrating* the situation that has come about.

c) A dam-burst of theology

In this light, it is clear that Genesis 1 outlines the performative speech act *par excellence* and it may be worth summarizing a number of enduring Christian theological conclusions that have been drawn from these first few lines of the Bible:

- God is Creator. The *omnipotent* 'all powerful' nature of God is evidenced.
- God is Transcendent. God is not *part* of creation, God *configures* creation.
- Creation is Holy. God sees creation and designates it as *good*.
- Creation includes Time. As author of light, God is author of time, there is no 'before'. The subsequent passing of an evening and a morning indicates this – the first day.
- Creation bears witness to God. The cosmos can be seen as an original canvas of the artist, an original revelation of God since creation comes about because of God's word.

In terms of connections, we can also note that this short passage:

- Connects 'Revealed' with 'Natural' Theology. Divine truth which can only be known through God's self-communication ('Revealed Theology') intersects here with 'Natural Theology' (thinking about God based on experience of creation).
- Connects God's Word with Transformation. If the cosmos is transformed by God's word, so will humanity be transformed. The Words of God at the heart of the Torah will be foundational for the chosen people and likewise the voicing of God's word by the prophets.
- Connects the Bible with the Word of God. If God's Word is the foundation of the universe, then the Bible as the Word of God can also be understood as a creative force and venerated as *sacred* scripture.

Yet, all these connections are not felt to be so significant as the links that this book will go on to make between God, Creation and Humanity in the subsequent verses. Possibly only fundamentalists insist on the 'days' of creation signifying a literal sense of 24 hours. Others who wish to map Genesis onto phases of evolution derived from Darwin's theories may understand the 'days' as 'ages' and occasionally cite 2 Pet 3:8 'that with the Lord one day is like a thousand years, and a thousand years are like one day.' Both approaches risk missing the more important thrust of this cosmic poetry which leads through the various divine actions to the point where humanity is brought forth, male and female, in God's image. Western thinking tends to emphasize our individual nature, but there is a theological texture here of complementarity – two together, a plurality imaging God. There is also a tendency to imagine God as male – but as the biblical text indicates, God is beyond gender and beyond our human categories. We may be in God's image but our imagining of God is always inadequate (Gen 1:27).

The verses following this are usually remembered for their 'be fruitful and multiply' theme, but they are also a bit of a shock since they seem to indicate a terrible truth for all lovers of flesh – be it hamburgers or hot dogs: 'See, I have given you every plant yielding seed that is upon the face of all the earth, and every tree with seed in its fruit; you shall have them for food' (1:29). Theologically, vegetarians appear to be on the money since man and woman are expected to share this blessing with the beasts, birds and creeping things and anything with the breath of life in it. Revealing God's essential benevolence, humanity is given a share of God's authority in dominion over and stewardship of the earth, but the often overlooked culmination of Creation is the day of rest which can also be understood as a divine gift. The Sabbath is part of the blessing. To live life and be too hard-pressed to contemplate its goodness risks the madness of frenzy and is not to live life as God intended. In short, the Sabbath sums up that reality is not just God *based*, not just at root a *divine relationship*, but that *chill-out* time is essential.

d) Introducing Adam and Eve

The second poem of creation and human origins runs from Gen 2:5-3:24, where we see a different picture of God and a more intimate view of humanity. The vivid story of Adam and Eve is one of the most misunderstood passages of the Bible and to this day, heated arguments about 'whether it actually happened' still survive, particularly in fundamentalist churches and on the internet – not quite the most recommended places for theological conversation. But far from being a 'myth' which can be dismissed, the story of Adam and Eve is *disconcertingly true*. It typifies a type of literature common in the ancient world known as 'aetiology' – vivid explanations as to 'why things are the way they are'. Like parables, the key to the writing does not lie in the factual force of the story. For example, listeners rarely worry about exactly where, when or even whether the Good Samaritan performed his heroics in Jesus' famous parable from Luke 10:25-37 – the challenge to break down ethnic and religious barriers is clear. In a similar fashion, a thoughtful reading of the poems of Genesis 2 and 3 reveal rich theological themes which, through the prism of ancient writing, sheds piercing light on our alienation from our God, our earth and ourselves.

In this second description of beginnings, God prepares an earth pregnant with life, but it seems to hint that a human being might be of some help to till the soil (2:5). Here there is an echo of the Mesopotamian myth which says that man was created to till the earth because the Gods were so lazy (Pritchard, 2011, p. 33). God doesn't seem to have that motive here, and nature is arguably in harmony with the project as a mist rises from the earth to water the land. God's action in verse 7 is to create human beings and most translations will say that 'God created man from the dust of the earth' – or some such thing. Perhaps to frame our thinking a little better we need to note that the Hebrew says that God created *Adam* from the *Adamah* – there is hardly any difference between the name for man and the word for red-brown soil. To drive this home, it might be better to translate this as:

'God fashioned Clod Man from the ground'.

The next time you are frustrated with a fellow human being, remember this description. Understood as a crowd of clod folk, human limitations are a little more understandable since theologically we are little groundlings of humble, earthy origin. It is at this point, however, that God then adds a divine dimension – breathing into its nostrils the 'breath of life', Clod Man becomes a living *nephesh* – 'soul/being' (2:7). Thus, humanity has an earthiness shot through with divine life. The groundling is placed in a garden at Eden, which is imaged as the source of the rivers which water the known world of the time. God plants two special trees in the garden, the Tree of Life and the Tree of Knowledge, and God gives a command that the fruit of all the trees can be eaten, but not the fruit of the Tree of Knowledge (2:8-17).

Famously, God then decides that it is not good for Adam to be alone and creates a series of creatures which are named by man, but are not suitable to be an *ezer k'negdo* – 'helpmate like unto himself'. One can imagine the ancient storyteller painting a picture of a glum Cloddite confronted with an array of animals, goats, rhinos – whatever, leaving the listeners awaiting the next instalment (2:18-20).

The turning point then comes when God makes Clod Man fall into a deep sleep which is like a death (2:21). Adam seems to be almost split in half – a self-separation. Woman is created and as soon as she is brought forth, Adam bursts into life, bursts into language, bursts into relationship: 'This at last is bone of my bones and flesh of my flesh' (2:23). This may not seem particularly poetic to modern ears, but it is sassy, rhythmic Hebrew. So not only was Adam the original rap artist, it is of deep theological significance that the first human words are a love song. The emergence of human personality, language and relationship all happen under the auspices of love. And as if to emphasize love's power, the writer goes on to remark that this mutually magnetic force is what causes men and women to leave home and to become one flesh – imaging a cosmic return to oneness that has been lost by the original separation (2:24).

e) The poem of the fall

Unfortunately, the happy picture of the innocent couple is ruptured in the next phase of the story. The vivid account of the disobedience of humanity ('The Fall') describes how the woman is persuaded to eat the fruit of the Tree of Knowledge by a devious reptile (3:1-2). The image of the winged reptile or dragon is very common in ancient cultures and even today remains a feature of innumerable flags, shields and crests. As a consequence, it is often proposed by anthropologists ('humanity analysts') that somehow this creature symbolizes something deep within us, perhaps what modern psychology might link to the unbounded recklessness of our subconscious. In this account, the woman is persuaded to eat the forbidden fruit in order to become 'like the Gods' – the irony being that she *already is* like God if not quite the *same* as God. She shares the divine breath of life and she lives in communion with God in a beautiful place in unthreatened harmony with her partner.

Regrettably, the curiosity of the woman, her appetite and desire get the better of her so she takes and eats the fruit (3:6). This, of course, resonates very strongly with the experience of any of us who have been unable to control a desire or appetite, whether physical or emotional. Hence in the language of 'myth', the writer is describing an uncomfortable 'truth' that most of our problems come from our inability to say no to our appetites – whether that is for an unwise desire for food, drink, sex, power, violence or revenge.

The woman then shares the fruit with the man and they suddenly recognize themselves as vulnerable and naked (3:7). Among interpretations of this pivotal moment, sexual awakening is often mentioned. Adult humans are conscious of their physicality in a way that prior to puberty they are unaware of. The notion of the fruit being connected with sexual knowledge would also fit neatly, given the common use of the Hebrew word *YD'* 'to know' as a reference to sexual intercourse. Furthermore, by reading ahead we are aware that part of the punishment will be the denial of the fruit of the Tree of Life. By discovering the secret of life-giving power inherent in sex, humans gain an image of themselves through their children. In this sense, humans become 'God-like' but must pay the price of being subject to mortality.

It is worth saying that sexual knowledge is not the only connotation here. Knowing 'good and evil' could also be understood as knowing everything from top to bottom. Adam and Eve have tried to mimic God's omniscience – God's all-knowing nature – and this would also fit the context. It might also be worth bearing in mind that in Genesis 1, the fruitfulness of man and woman is part of the blessing of creation and in that sense, the composite biblical text does not propose that sexuality carries these overtones or associations with disobedience.

f) The loss of communion

Though there are no hints in the Hebrew, since *malum* in Latin can mean 'apple' or 'evil thing', the fruit has been thus identified and symbolized as such for millennia – most recently and successfully by a leading computer company! Whatever the nature of the fruit, the act of disobedience is not seen as a good thing and unfortunately, a troubling chain of events is set in motion. The drama has the couple covering themselves before each other with the famous fig leaves and hiding from God among the trees of the garden (3:7-8). The call 'Where are you?' may be thought to demonstrate ignorance on the part of God thus challenging the idea of God's omniscient 'all knowing' nature, but it is just as likely to be a literary device in the story to build up the tension. There is no doubt that God is definitely more 'anthropomorphic' – 'human-shaped' or 'human-like' in this account by comparison with Chapter 1, but the pathos of God's cry is to emphasize the breaking down of the communion between humanity and God. Note the wonderfully human avoidance of responsibility whereby the man blames God and the woman blames the snake:

> But the Lord God called to the man, and said to him, "Where are you?" He said, "I heard the sound of you in the garden, and I was afraid, because I was naked; and I hid myself." He said, "Who told you that you were naked? Have you eaten from the tree of which I commanded you not to eat?" The man said, "The woman

whom you gave to be with me, she gave me fruit from the tree, and I ate." Then the Lord God said to the woman, "What is this that you have done?" The woman said, "The serpent tricked me, and I ate." (Gen 3:9-13)

Not only does the text here hold up a mirror to the way we actually are when things go wrong, it continues with a series of curses that have clear 'aetiological' – 'why things are as they are' – roots. The serpent or dragon is now going to slither around and crawl on its belly – it has been deprived of legs and its spitting action is interpreted as an eating of dust (3:14). From being in cahoots with the woman, the snake will now be at war with her children. While later Christian writers will link this text with Mary and the enmity between her son Jesus and Satan, here the aetiology is explaining an obvious feature of hot climates where snakes that bite the heels of humans are likely to have their heads crushed (3:15). Snakes are one thing, but unfortunately for the man and woman there are problems much nearer home.

g) The battles of the sexes

The first of the woman's curses is well known – the traumatic pain of childbirth articulates the life-giving but always life-risking experience of motherhood. The account is emphasizing the haunting paradox of childbirth – that it has for most of human history been the most lethal physical thing a woman could undergo. Psychologically, the less well-known curse introduces the 'Battle of the Sexes' and is as follows:

Your desire shall be for your husband, and he shall rule over you. (Gen 3:16)

Whatever their provenance, be it social conditioning, genetic programming or the chemistry of physiology, gender behavioural differences can be complementary, contradictory, fascinating and amusing, as the phenomenal success of books such as *Men are from Mars, Women are from Venus* have demonstrated (Gray, 1992). However, the very popularity of such observational bestsellers underlines an enduring truth which the biblical text is keenly aware of, namely, that the harmony between the sexes is threatened. Indeed the problem it identifies is that power and the predominant retention of that by men is seen as a fundamental issue which humanity is destined to struggle with. In this light, the often harrowing consequences of male domination or 'patriarchy' (much of which is witnessed in biblical testimony) become a concern for all theologians, feminist and non-feminist alike.

Meanwhile for man, the curse for his disobedience will be that the soil from which he is taken and has yielded the fruits to sustain his life, will now be his grave and consume him in death. Again the aetiological themes are strong. The fertility of the land in a rural society is a constant and often losing battle. Work is hard. The Clod creature having received the breath of life will now return to being just earth again. The groundling who should feel so at one with earth and in harmony with it has now become its enemy instead of its custodian. In a deep sense, the text is describing the alienation and the estrangement of humans from their own nature (3:18-19).

Both these themes – the alienation of the sexes and the alienation of humanity from its environment are the subject of important contemporary theological reflection which we will consider in Chapters 22 and 23. At this juncture, it serves for now to accent the immediate consequences that follow on from the loss of friendship between humanity and God because the biblical text quickly shows them to be disastrous at family, tribal, human and cosmic levels. Hence, although God gives some protection to the couple by making them proper clothes (3:21), the catalogue of mayhem begins with them being expelled from Eden and deprived of access to the Tree of Life, the fruit of immortality so that they should *not* become 'like one of us' (3:22). Once more, a contrast with the first creation account can be discerned whereby if in Genesis 1 humanity is created in the *image* of God, by the end of Genesis 3 they may be said to no longer bear God's *likeness*.

Theologically, the depiction of 'The Fall' of Adam and Eve and its consequences has been of MASSIVE significance. It has not only conditioned the way theologians have viewed who and what we are as human beings, but as will be outlined in later chapters, the loss of this original state of bliss will be used to explain the work of Christ and the entire destiny of the cosmos.

h) East of Eden

The picture of the exiled Adam and Eve marks the start of a tumbling sequence of violence that ends with God 'de-creating' the world in the flood. The first family endures the first homicide, when Abel is killed by Cain (Gen 4:1-16). In a paradox that will be repeated time and again, it is the younger rather than the elder that is favoured by God and in the case of these two, the one representing the rootless wandering tribesman offering a sheep is preferred to the settled landowning farmer offering crops. Cain is found out because Abel's life blood calls from the ground. How? Because alongside breath, blood was understood to be the 'life' agent of a human, or indeed, any creature. The idea that life was borne in the blood can help the modern reader understand the reasoning behind some of the dietary laws of Israel since to drink the blood of an animal would be tantamount to taking on the life and likeness of an animal. It is worth noting that this 'life-blood' imagery will prove central to the symbolism that will characterize various scriptural covenant rituals, including the communion rite at the heart of Christian worship.

Within a short generation span, Lamech (one of Cain's descendents) is threatening seventy-seven fold vengeance on his enemies (Gen 4:24) and God despairs of the violence of human beings and is grieved to the heart (Gen 6:5-7; 11). God regrets bringing about his creation but determines to save Noah who has found favour in his sight (Gen 6:9). In the composition of the famous flood account which follows, God reverses the process of Genesis 1, the editors presenting it to us as a kind of 'de-creation' (Gen 7:1-24). The vault which God had created to separate the waters above and below the earth is opened and for forty days and nights rain falls. Forty denotes a time of transformation, and in this period the earth is cleansed while by means of Noah's ark, humans and creatures alike are spared. Much is made of the similarities between this biblical episode and similar ancient myths such as Utnapishtim in the Epic of Gilgamesh or the Sumerian flood hero Atrahasis. There are numerous intriguing parallels alongside key theological differences, for example, in the latter, humanity was not imperilled because of violence but for being too noisy and keeping the gods awake! (cf. McClain Carr, 1996, pp. 242–3)

Once the waters recede, God makes a b^{e}rit [BRT] – a 'covenant'– with Noah (Gen 8:20-9:17). The idea of covenant runs through the different books of the Bible, giving them a theological connection even while they differ in appearance. Covenant is a mutually binding agreement, normally 'sealed' by a sign or ritual. For Noah and for humanity, the *agreement* is that God will not inundate the earth again, the *ritual* is the food offering made by Noah and the *sign* is the rainbow. The earthly tranquillity does not last long though and in a pattern that characterizes the Bible, the sealing of a covenant is often followed by catastrophe. In a drama that acts as a mirror to the scene in the garden, the men of Babel decide to make a name for themselves and build a tower to heaven, presumably to be more God-like (Gen 11:1-9). Just as in Eden, this 'man-made' attempt to be more like God goes horribly wrong and the Lord confuses their languages. The word 'babble' comes directly from this passage which serves as another example of aetiology, accounting for the linguistic disunity which so plagues human beings. Every tourist has probably had an awkward 'lost in translation' moment, but language divisions which have split clans, tribes and cultures have had more tragic consequences through prejudice and war. Theologically, the Christian response to this division will eventually be provided in the story of Pentecost (Acts 2:1-36).

i) Postscript: Authors, editors and *Star Wars*

The Babel episode ends what might be called the 'pre-history' in Genesis, the fabulous cosmic phase which sees God acting in relation to the whole of humanity and the whole of his creation. Since Genesis is the first of the five Books of Moses, there has been a long tradition that Moses himself was given a privileged vision of the dawn of humanity, and that he passed on the grand narrative of God's chosen people from the Garden of Eden to the threshold of the Promised Land. This view is extremely rare among modern scholars who would suggest that a number of different authors have been involved in contributing to the actual written text. Though it is impossible to identify who these scribes may have actually been, scholars commonly talk of at least three, if not four, important contributors designated as the Yahwist, the Elohist, the Deuteronomist and the Priest (J, E, D and P respectively).

So, for example, Gen 1-3 is normally considered to be from two separate sources. Due to distinctive characteristics of written style, vocabulary and theological emphasis, Gen 1:1-2:4 is considered to be from the Priestly source and Gen 2:5-3:24 from the Yahwist source – designated 'J' from the German spelling. An entire world of argument surrounds both this 'Documentary Hypothesis' and the dating of the activity of these authors and compilers which need not delay us here. Suffice to say, most scholars envisage that the body of literature that makes up this 'Pentateuch' (from the Greek meaning 'five') was only finally collated, gathered and reached something like its current form once the tumults of Judaic history had subsided around 450 BCE, which is possibly as much as a thousand years later than the time of Moses (Ska, 2006, pp. 96–164).

This is not to say that these writings do not capture *oral* accounts that are extremely ancient, or to undermine the notion that the Bible is *inspired*. Oral tradition passed on from one generation to the next was *the* form of transmission. Though we take literacy and literature for granted, the skills of reading and writing only became a widespread aspiration in developed countries during the last century. In this context, we can perhaps better understand the way that through generations of retelling, these writings adopt varied textures and layers of understanding which are woven together in the scriptures. The result is a lyrical tapestry imaging God and humanity which has held audiences spellbound for millennia.

Indeed the reason these early stories of Genesis continue to be fascinating is that at their very heart they have the classic bestseller theme that runs through the most successful literary and movie franchises. The golden thread that links *Star Wars, Lord of the Rings* and *Harry Potter* is a theme as old as the *Myth of Gyges* of Plato, as old as humanity itself, namely:

> The drama of a gifted individual learning to choose good.

This drama is attractive to us because it is lived out by everyone in the everyday. We may never meet Luke or Leia, Frodo or Arwen, Harry or Hermione, but we identify with the comradeship, sacrifice, doubts and courage represented by the heroes of these great stories. Although we are not doing battle on an interstellar level, we imperceptibly understand these values as cosmic and they soak down into our decisions about whether to take a year helping the poor or whether to jump the queue/skip the line in Starbucks. It is another example of the involving nature of Theology since we are all embroiled in this drama as gifted individuals with the cosmic power of our creative choices which will serve ourselves and others for good or for ill. The human inclination to choose ill – 'Original Sin' – is the major theological concept drawn from such considerations. Not only does it constitute the most plainly obvious theological truth according to G. K. Chesterton; a literary genius like Flannery O'Connor regards it as *the* essential component of storytelling.

At the risk of repetition, the centre of this 'decision drama' is the theological truth at the core of the account of the Fall – the symbolic design is merely meant to draw the listener/reader into the plot. In forcing the listener to consider his or her choices, the text is meant to become true or real in the story of the present rather than sought in its deliberately fantastic picture of the past. Only as Genesis 1-11 concludes does the narrative begin a transition to what we might recognize as normality. The immense lifespans of the first humans become shorter and the famous family tree formula is invoked to plot the bloodline of Shem, one of Noah's sons. His lineage eventually leads us to Abraham (Gen 11:10-32) and with him the narrative of Genesis will begin to take more recognizable, less fabulous shape. But the choice-challenge of the cosmic drama is not forgotten, rather, it becomes focused once more on the destiny of one man and his family.

Summary

The Bible is a collection of writings sacred to Christianity which witnesses to truths concerning the nature of God and the human condition. It is regarded as inspired, sacred and holy, yet it also bears the marks of its human compilers and authors. This collection of writings begins with two accounts of Creation written in the poetic genre of their time. Though these neither present themselves as Science or History, they are theologically very rich in their reflections on God, humanity and creation. Troublingly, these ancient tales also convey uncomfortable truths about the human condition as familiar themes of dissatisfaction, envy and violence follow on from the poem of 'The Fall'. The cosmic hero drama of 'choosing good' underpins the 'pre-history' of these first biblical chapters and in this sense they should be understood as 'mythical' – not because they are fanciful – but because they are permanently true, conveying the basic wisdom by which humanity has always lived (cf. Campbell, [1949] 1993, pp. vii–viii).

3

The Torah: Covenant, Exodus and the Law

Theologically, the arrangement of the writings that make up the rest of the Bible may be understood as the story of the attempt to restore the harmony lost in the Garden. To that end, the various biblical books are gathered under the umbrella theme of an enduring 'covenant' relationship that God establishes with Israel. While being deliberately organized in distinct 'old' and 'new' covenant collections, thoughtful reference to the original Hebrew heritage is presupposed by Christian Bibles. In particular the monotheism of Abraham and the Moses narratives of Exodus and Sinai provide essential background to any understanding of Christian Theology.

a) The Bible and Christian interpretation

Intelligent engagement with biblical texts will inevitably arouse questions surrounding their origins. The historian of the text is like a biblical detective arriving on the scene and asking:

What language is this and in what *way* or *style* is it written?
Who could have written this and *when* might they have done it?
Which is the most original text and *whether* it has been altered by a later editor?

All these are shot through with *why* was it written – the core question which underpins the motive and meaning in the text.

One simple way of getting a handle on this is to think of three worlds when considering a biblical text:

- The world behind the text – the intentions and motives of the author, the life-context of the original hearers, the events that generated the writing, etc. Generally, these can be called historical considerations.
- The world within the text – the actual way the text is written, the vocabulary and meaning of particular words, style, narrative, poetry, plot pattern and so forth. Generally, these may be considered under the umbrella of language and textual considerations.
- The world in front of the text – how the text impacted upon subsequent listeners, how it affected the 'theologic' of later listeners, the way in which it came to be understood over time. Generally, these may be considered as interpretation questions or *hermeneutics*. (Cf. Kille, 2002, p.129)

Just like in modern policing, biblical scholars draw on a multiplicity of skills to hone their craft – linguistic, literary, historical, archaeological, anthropological, sociological and psychological to name but a few. Some practitioners prefer one method over another and down the years certain approaches have dominated particular periods. Students new to theological studies are sometimes needlessly perturbed by differences of opinion on biblical matters. But as fictional and real-life detective works demonstrate, disagreements about clues, leads and evidence are part of the fascination in problem-solving. Re-interpreting the clues in the light of new evidence inevitably yields nuanced conclusions, and the hope here is that the reader can not only be part of the courtroom jury, but also gain some insight into investigative techniques.

So, for example, if the *origins* of the text are understood in the language and grammar of *history*, the *effects* of the text are often understood through biblical reading and *interpretation*. Very often, this is in the grammar of *symbolism*. To give just one instance, current scholarly views on the history of the people of Israel's escape from Egypt are far from unanimous. Some would claim the biblical text is historically accurate while others are much more sceptical (cf. Davies, 2004, pp. 23–40). What no biblical scholar disputes, however, is that the story of Moses and the children of Israel miraculously escaping from Pharaoh eventually came to *symbolize* God's liberating action on behalf of the chosen people. To this day, the imagery of the *Exodus* – the escape from Egypt – dominates the central celebration of the Passover festival in Judaism. With its various symbols, this ritual is designed to relive the *past* such that Israel's descendents in the *present* experience Exodus for themselves, calling to mind the saving power of God (cf. Larsson, 1999).

As a disclaimer, it is important that the reader allows that there is neither the time nor space to explore all three 'worlds'. We cannot hope to chart all the changing tides of opinion in historical method nor can this text pursue the detail of every translation, interpretation or symbolic meaning attributed to the Bible. A deliberate attempt will be made, where possible, to make some mention of the original context and history of key biblical passages, characters and events. Likewise, there will be attention to literary style and occasional scrutiny of particular words. Generally though, the focus will ultimately be on *hermeneutics* – the subsequent interpretation of key biblical texts in later Christian thinking. Although this is not entirely satisfactory, it remains faithful to the overall stated methodology of this textbook and will perhaps spark the interest of readers to engage in some of their own biblical detective work.

Meanwhile, at the risk of stating the obvious, it is profoundly significant that Christian Bibles are divided into the 'Old' and 'New' Testaments. 'Testament' or 'covenant' means 'mutually binding agreement', and Christian bibles present the covenant relationship between God and humanity in two phases. The first phase of 'salvation history' is expressed through the theological traditions of the 'chosen people' – the generations of Abraham, Jacob, Moses and the judges, kings, prophets and priests who succeeded them down through subsequent centuries. The second phase is the event of Jesus which is recorded and pondered upon in the books of the 'New' Testament.

Since the very layout of Christian Bibles marks this distinction, a fundamental task of this book will be to outline how the writings of the 'New' Testament emerged as an interpretation of the 'Old' Testament in the light of the Jesus event. This is more understandable if one thinks of Christians as Jews with a Jesus tradition rather than as a completely separate family of faith. In other words, those who theologized about Jesus (e.g. Paul, John, Luke) drew conclusions about who he was and what had been accomplished by him using vocabulary and symbolism drawn from their original Jewish religious beliefs. This approach was famously summarized by St. Augustine as 'The New is in the Old concealed, the Old is in the New revealed' (cf. *Dei Verbum* IV:16). Inevitably, this has long risked rendering the rich theologies present in Genesis, Exodus and the like to mere curtain raisers for the Jesus event which reveals the 'true' meaning of the older text. However, it at least avoids the common error in textbooks which is to begin Christian Theology without any reference to the Judaic roots from which it emerged and to which this study now turns.

b) Abraham and monotheism

Theologically, Abraham is one of the most important figures in religious history. Jews, Christians and Muslims are sometimes designated the 'Abrahamic Faiths' since they trace their monotheism – belief in only one God – back to this ancient figure. In the biblical tradition, Abraham is from Ur in the region of Chaldea, the south of present-day Iraq. From the outset it needs to be acknowledged that there are difficulties anchoring Abraham in objective historical terms since there are no traces of a tradition of Abraham outside the biblical texts. That said, both the lifestyle depicted and the names associated with the Abraham narratives 'fit' that part of the world in those days (approximately 2000 BCE). The initial picture of Abraham as a wandering nomad sees him tracking to the South and West through Canaan, into Egypt because of famine and back out again towards the 'Promised Land'. Abraham is constantly building altars and invoking the name of God – YHWH (cf. Gen 12:7; 13:18). However, this does not exempt Abraham from strife or indicate that he was a perfect person. There is trouble from a Pharaoh who is besotted with Sarah, Abraham's wife, with the biblical account observing that God's power intervenes to put a stop to the hanky panky, rather than her non-valiant husband (Gen 12:10-20).

Abraham's call from God and his responses are sealed by a series of covenants which include the promise that he will be the father of an 'uproar of nations' and his descendants 'will be as numerous as the stars of heaven' (Gen 26:4). Looked at scientifically, this seemed far-fetched – Abraham is depicted as being a little 'past the age' and his wife is barren. Moreover, present-day cosmology numbers galaxies by the million, never mind stars. Here again we are in the realm of resonant symbolism where the main theological assertion is that faith in the promises of God will accomplish the unexpected. This theme is outlined in further detail below, but it might be worth noting that history attests that the heirs of Abraham have indeed been an 'uproar of nations' and since over 3,000,000,000 Jews, Christians and Muslims together number about half the current human race, they at least constitute some kind of galactic number.

Dedication to God is the first theological glory of Abraham. By invoking the Lord he begins to re-connect a fractured humanity with the Creator God. This does not exempt him from life's difficulties. Within his own family there is rivalry with his nephew Lot (Gen 13:1-14). He finds himself in battles with one group of kings and yet makes friends with others (cf. Gen 14:1-16; 21:22-34). These tumults are not without abiding theological repercussions even today, especially the promise of the land 'from the river of Egypt to the great river' in Gen 15:18-21. This seems to include an invitation to subjugate indigenous peoples at God's behest – a promise felt by some Jewish groups to be a theological mandate for Israel's political sovereignty in the region today.

The major problem facing Abraham is the lack of an heir. To be without children is to have no future. This is the drama depicted in the intriguing tale whereby advancing years lead Sarah to offer her Egyptian servant girl Hagar to Abraham as a surrogate mother to provide him with a son (Gen 16:1-15). Unfortunately, this leads to a testy relationship between the two women and Hagar is forced to leave the camp before returning for the birth of Ishmael, whose name means 'May God Hear'. In the ensuing narrative, God's relationship with Abraham in covenant is renewed and the practice of circumcision adopted (Gen 17:10). Although a non-religious view might argue that this genital modification perhaps had more to do with male hygiene in sandy deserts than a command of God, the *understanding* of this symbol in Israel became a sign of belonging, a sign of being chosen – the sign of covenant.

Subsequently, there is the mysterious visit of YHWH by the Oak of Mamre, which has the unusual imagery of God depicted as three divine beings whom Abraham addresses in the singular (Genesis 18:1-8). *Hermeneutically* ('interpretationally') this will be later seen in Christian Theology as a pre-figurement of the revelation of the Triune God or 'Trinity'. 'Exegetically'– from within the ancient narrative – it is more likely that what is understood here is that YHWH appears with two angels who are later to wreak havoc on the ill-fated town of Sodom. At this point, their visit leads to the promise that within the year, Sarah will have a child, which makes her laugh (Gen 18:12). When challenged about this, Sarah denies the charge, but later in a stylish play on words she will call her son 'Isaac', which means laughter (Gen 21:5-6). Isaac is the first of a number of unexpected births that otherwise barren women are blest with in the scriptures. Angelic visitation followed by birth is a feature in the birth of Samson (Judg 13:3), and of course the birth of Jesus in the New Testament (Luke 1:31).

c) Fraternal rivalry from Isaac to Joseph

Abraham's descendants are thus understood as the chosen people, the tribes in a special relationship of covenant with God. The stories of these descendants are among the most colourful in the Bible. His two sons, Isaac and Ishmael, take different paths. Ishmael is sent away due to continuing tensions between Sarah and Hagar but is promised an important destiny as a great nation (Gen 21:9-20). Though historically these matters are hard to trace, Ishmael's descendants came to be identified as the Arabian tribes of the great Saudi peninsula. This is significant since it explains the continuity that Muslims see in the initial revelation of the one God to Abraham with what for them is the final revelation of God to the Prophet Mohammed. Though Jews, Christians and Muslims are united in this belonging to God, we should not be too surprised that their relationships have not always been harmonious, since family disagreements constitute a *major* biblical theme.

For example, Isaac marries Rebekah and they have two sons, Esau and Jacob. Once more the spectre of brotherly rivalry emerges and in a pattern often seen in the Bible, it is the younger one who comes out best to inherit the mantle as head of the family (Genesis 25-27). The story of Jacob is a colourful tale of love, trickery and family conflict. Jacob is a slippery character who wrestles with God and is renamed 'Israel' – 'God's little struggler' (Gen 32:28). Likewise, the fate of Jacob's own family gives testimony to the same phenomenon of 'non-brotherly love'. Of his twelve sons, Joseph is the favoured son who is rejected and sold into slavery by his brothers. Then, through his ability to interpret dreams, Joseph becomes an important man in Egypt and the saviour of his family when they are forced out of Canaan because of famine (Gen 45-51). Two significant points may be noted here:

> The fact that Joseph does not take revenge on his brothers illustrates an interesting aspect of the relationship between fraternal anger and the family bond. Despite the cleansing of the Flood, anger is often unleashed without restraint against those not of the clan (see Gen 34:1-31). Although the problematic family of King David is something of an exception (cf. 2 Sam 13:21; 28), parties wronged by their own family such as Esau and Joseph *tend* to withhold the ultimate vengeance. In this light, the mitigation of anger because of ties of kinship can be seen to be a step in the right ethical direction and it is a picture mirrored in the understanding of God likewise being committed to a particular family – the Twelve tribes of Israel. Secondly, however, it does allow God to be much less concerned with the fortunes of other peoples, as Exodus and the Book of Joshua will demonstrate.

d) Moses and YHWH: The rebel meets the holy

The recurring theme of the weak one unexpectedly becoming powerful is classic theological paradox. Not only does it make for good storylines, it also enables the biblical narrators to stress that it is the favour of God that counts rather than any human privilege or status. The Book of Genesis ends with all the optimism of a reconciled family. Jacob's sons – whose offspring will become the future Twelve tribes – have been reconciled and their status made secure by their influential brother. Unfortunately, things would not remain serene for long. Almost lulling the reader into a narrative trap, Exodus lists the names of the sons of Jacob and tells how they were fruitful, multiplied and filled the land, before chillingly announcing: 'Now a new king arose over Egypt, who did not know Joseph' (Ex 1:8).

In most ancient and in many contemporary societies, the phenomenon of *patronage* – protection of groups by powerful individuals is a key reality of life. The writer alerts the reader that this will no longer be so for the children of Israel – this new Pharaoh owes nothing to these people. To the Egyptians, the descendants of Jacob/Israel are not unlike immigrants in our own day, often begrudged and tolerated at best. They do the menial jobs that the natives won't do. In Israel's case, this means labouring hard to build the great store cities of Pithom and Raam'ses (Ex 1:11). Pharaoh will eventually set higher productivity targets asking for more bricks to be made with less material (see Ex 5:8). This is not a problem confined to the past, as even today many an office, factory, college or school has some kind of Pharaoh like this, and echoing the ancient Israelites, the cries of the people rise up just like theirs (Ex 5:15).

A more fundamental problem is that the Hebrews are multiplying disconcertingly quickly as far as the Egyptians are concerned – a sign of a lack of sophistication to the locals. They are suspicious of the loyalty of these migrants and subconsciously facing a threat to their culture and their future (Ex 1:12). Pharaoh reacts with unfair legislation and a sinister threat to restrict the birth rate by infanticide of the Hebrew children (Ex 1:15-22). Quick thinking on the part of the mother of Moses sees him saved from this fate. She puts him in his famous basket which floats past Pharaoh's daughter who takes a shine to him and comes to hire his own mother to act as his nursemaid (Ex 2:6-10). Once again we have the cosmic drama of covenant coming down to an individual who will prove gifted but also flawed.

Through this miraculous deliverance, the drama of the story has Moses growing up with privileged connections, but unfortunately he blows it. Clearly possessed with a hot temper, he sees a Hebrew being bullied by an Egyptian and in an act of ethnic solidarity, kills the man (Ex 2:11-15). The next day, he gets involved again, this time in a fight between two Hebrews, but his assistance is not appreciated and they make reference to his homicide of the previous day. Moses is shocked to realize that the matter has become known and flees to the wilderness to escape the vengeance of Pharaoh. There he takes a lowly position as a shepherd and perhaps the only bright spot is that following a heroic gesture at a well, he is given the hand of Zipporah in marriage (Ex 2:16-22). Since women were tasked with drawing water, wells tended to have certain romantic connotations and they also play a part in the romances of Isaac and Jacob (cf. Genesis 24 and 29). Not quite speed dating and maybe not as easy as the internet, but when it comes to love stories in the Bible, 'where there's a well there's a way'.

It is while tending the sheep one day that Moses sees a strange sight, a thorny bush aflame but not being destroyed (Ex 3:1-3). The verses that follow are among the most theologically potent sentences of the Bible. To begin with, the flames have been interpreted by theologians and mystics as the fire of God's love – creative but not destructive. That said, as shall be clear from other biblical texts, fire is a classic sign of *theophany* – 'God-manifestation'– and it is no surprise that Moses must take off his sandals as he is informed that this is 'holy ground' (Ex 3:5). The removal of footwear is one of many cultural signals practised in a religious context as a sign of the sacred, the presence of the holy. With literary skill, the picture of Moses tiptoeing towards the flames, attracted yet scared, captures the idea of God often described as the *mysterium fascinans et tremendum* – God is 'fascinating and awesome', 'alluring but terrifying', 'attractive but fearful'.

The notion of the Holy, the notion of 'Divinity as Other', then takes another twist in the spoken exchanges between God and Moses. In the *theophany*, Moses is given the instruction to return to Egypt and free the children of Israel from their slavery (Ex 3:7-12). We sometimes pass too quickly over these verses and think that because Moses is having a conversation with God then it should be all plain sailing. Moses should do as he is told with a cool conviction and get on with it. The drama of the narrative, however, demands that we be mindful of the fact that not only is he wanted for murder there, he was sent on his way by his own people with the snide comment 'who made you a ruler and judge over us?' (Ex 2:14). Given his dubious birth status as a foundling and the fact that he apparently has a speech impediment (Ex 4:10), we are once more confronted with a thickening plot in which the spotlight is falling on a weak, flawed, yet ultimately heroic figure, confronting the power of Pharaoh.

Not unreasonably, Moses needs to have more credentials for this mission than a tall tale of a talking shrub. The Gods of the ancients normally had some speciality or other. The Canaanite God Ba'al was often depicted as a Thunder God just as Thor had a similar role in the Norse pantheon from which English speakers get the name for Thursday (Thor's day). Dagon among the Philistines was a fish God, which, given the fact they were coastal peoples of the sea, was not surprising. Egypt had sun and fertility Gods and the later cultures of Greek and Rome would have numerous specialist deities such as Aphrodite/Venus for love and Poseidon/Neptune for the sea. Against this background, it seems reasonable that Moses should ask God to declare who He is and perhaps even throw in what his speciality as a deity might be. In response, God probably left Moses both reassured and perplexed in equal measure. God reassuringly declares himself the God of Moses' family, the God of Abraham, Isaac and Jacob, but perplexingly declares Himself *'Ehyeh 'asher 'Ehyeh*.

e) The divine name

'Ehyeh 'asher 'Ehyeh is usually translated as 'I AM WHO AM'. The roots of this name for God seem to be anchored in the Hebrew verb 'to be' and connect with the familiar name – YHWH – used throughout most of the Bible. YHWH is the sacred 'tetragrammaton' – 'the four letters' – the name of God so holy that it remains unutterable in Jewish worship. Although normally translated as 'I AM WHO AM', grammatically it can also read as 'I WILL BE WHO I WILL BE'. Both of these names are elusive and both are soaked in theological possibilities. Taking the first, if God is the God who 'Is', then 'is-ness' is YHWH's speciality. As God of all that is, God is not just a God of thunder or of fish, this God is the God of *everything*. This is a God worthy of worship. And though the second reading of 'I will be who I will be' perhaps connotes a 'mind your own business' or 'I will please myself' elusiveness, it can equally be read as an *iterative* or 'continuing presence' indicating that God will always be with Moses and the chosen people (cf. Van Kooten, 2006).

Understood as the self-disclosure of God, this is *revelation* in the primary sense. While exegetically, the text can be read as a simple confirmation for Moses that he belongs to the tribe that has been chosen by YHWH God, it is no surprise that hermeneutically other theological interpretations of the sacred name match this picture with that of the Cosmic God of Genesis 1 and open up the broad horizon of a God who is universal – a God of everything and God of everyone. Perhaps even more intriguingly, there is a further step that may be taken which involves a nuanced reading of the sacred name. The proposal is that YHWH makes the closest sound that could be written to represent human breath (Waskow, 1996, p. 161). In this understanding, the holy name is permanently on the lips of humanity. It may be recalled that the groundling Adam receives life when the breath of God is breathed into him (Gen 2:7). Likewise in this reading, the 'breath name' of YHWH is intimately close and essential to human beings, a name we live by, a name a baby speaks even before it knows itself, our first and our last utterance. Once more the possible theological consequences are numerous, opening a picture of a humanity not only created in the image of God but participating in a constant hymn of life to the Creator in whom 'we live and move and have our being' (Acts 17:28).

f) Exodus

The subsequent account of the Exodus from Egypt by the Hebrews is arguably the focal point of all Jewish history. The theological commemoration of this moment in the *Seder Meal* which Jewish households continue to celebrate each year embosses this consciousness on every generation. It is an event rich in symbolism depicted vividly in the biblical account. Despite the difficulties involved in cross-referencing these moments with the annals of Egyptian lore, the biblical picture is that Exodus constitutes the pivotal 'nation forming' experience of the people of Israel.

Moses goes down to Egypt with his kinsman Aaron as his spokesperson armed with a magical wand and a clear mission statement: 'Let my People Go!' (Ex 4:15-5:1). Moses and Aaron then take on the Egyptians at their own game. In the ancient world, to be versed in 'Egyptian arts' was to be familiar with wizardry. In a classic case of 'meeting people where they are at', a struggle worthy of Harry Potter's Hogwarts ensues between Moses and the magicians of Egypt. In producing serpents, rivers turning to blood and smelly frogs, the honours are fairly even (Ex 7-8:14), but Moses has a clear victory when he produces gnats from dust (Ex 8:18). The plagues are deliberately garish and disgusting, but each time Pharaoh gets to the brink of agreeing to let the people go, he goes back on his word (Ex 8:32). Paradoxically, this stubbornness seems to be both predicted and produced by God (Ex 4:21). Ultimately, it proves disastrous as the plagues intensify with flies, livestock deaths, boils, hail, famine, locusts and darkness, leading ultimately to the threat to the Egyptians' firstborn (Ex 11:5). Unlike the Egyptians, the Hebrews have been protected by the ritual freedom meal which includes bread to sustain them on their dangerous journey. The blood of the shared lamb is sprinkled on the doorposts to safeguard their lives from death so that the Lord will 'pass over' (Ex 12:23).

Although the death of the Egyptian first born might be seen as fair dues for a cruel oppression, the continuing theme of innocent death in the Bible which begins with the murder of Abel bears some theological reflection. It is given vivid expression in the story of Abraham, who on the brink of slaying his son as an offering to God sees instead a ram caught in a thicket offered as a replacement (Gen 22:1-18). Historically, we know that part of the picture of life in the ancient world was the sacrifice of children to appease Gods. The traditions of the Philisitines included child sacrifice and likewise the local Gods of Canaan, Chemosh and Moloch seem to have required this (2 Kings 23:10). We can reasonably surmise, therefore, that what is being depicted within the biblical tradition through the story of Abraham and the story of Passover is the *rejection* of child sacrifice. The slaughter of the innocent human is to be replaced by the slaughter of the young, symbolically innocent lamb.

To modern minds sensitive to animal suffering this may not seem like a major advance, but we must be wary of judging past generations. After all, it can be argued that we remain deaf to the sufferings of the young in our own day, be they the overworked juveniles in the sweatshops of capitalism, the malnourished children around the globe or the innocent unborn. It is also important to note that these symbols of Exodus are not merely re-enacted by Jews in the *Seder Meal*, but are clearly transposed into the Christian understanding of Eucharist where the elements of bread and wine become the saving meal – the Holy Communion. In the story itself the people are led by God as a pillar of cloud by day and a pillar of flame by night (Ex 13:21). Pharaoh decides to give chase with well-known catastrophic consequences. The Hebrews with their traditional terror of the water as a place of monsters and chaos confront their fear and pass through. The Egyptians are caught up in the returning tidal flow and are drowned (Ex 14:28-31).

g) Habiru and ritual identity

At this point, it is perhaps worth re-iterating that there are real difficulties in anchoring this material with the kind of cross-referenced objectivity that might be desired in order for historians to unanimously declare the details of Exodus as fact. Periodic attempts are made to link the plagues and the passage through the sea with natural phenomena such as volcanes and tsunamis, but once more the time distance involved means that such matters cannot be proved with any satisfaction. When biblicists look to Egyptian historians for some kind of corroboration of the Exodus, there is a fundamental silence. Some argue this is proof that there was no such event, others that it is inevitable that in a totalitarian regime, any information of a military defeat would be suppressed. Although there seems almost no 'middle ground,' one thought-provoking suggestion goes as follows.

Exodus seems to deliberately use 'Hebrew' in its description of the multiplication of the tribes in Egypt. This can be linked with the generic word *Habiru* or *Apiru* which was used throughout the ancient Near East as a term for *nomadic or semi-nomadic, rebellious, outlaws, raiders, servants or slaves, migrant labourers* from around 2000–1200 BCE. There probably isn't a modern-day equivalent, though parallels could be drawn with immigrant or Romany groups. In some ways, this may fit the picture of early Israel viewed as an underprivileged, ethnically different social group fighting for their rights in Egypt. Then, through the activities of a rebel leader, they become cohesive enough to emigrate. Protagonists of this view sometimes point to the act of plundering the Egyptians as an act in keeping with the general reputation of 'Habiru' (Ex 12:35-36).

In this explanation of the events, the emigration of a group that were basically nomadic anyway would be seen as an incident of social unrest and not figure greatly in the big picture of Egyptian history (cf. Bright, 2000, pp. 93–6). Interestingly, the most notable external corroboration of Israel's existence at this time offers what some consider a type of confirmation of this picture. The 1210 BCE commemorative stone of the Pharaoh Merneptah (the *Merneptah Stele*) describes the nations that are part of Egypt's picture of the near East. Israel is described as being without 'seed' – perhaps meaning without land – which would again fit the picture of a wandering, nomadic group. The welding of this group into a coherent nation would not happen overnight. The process by which this took place, with its inherent difficulties, is the raw material for the stories of the forty years in the wilderness, once more using the symbolic number depicting transformation.

Whatever the difficulties encountered in cross-referencing the Exodus with outside confirmation, there is no doubt that the event becomes central to the collective identity of Israel. It is through ritual that the people are to re-experience this drama each year (Ex 12:17). In capturing this epic moment, this meal becomes a sign of identity, a sign of covenant. The symbolism expresses the self-understanding of the Hebrews as the chosen people of YHWH, an identity which involves struggle, slavery, liberation, ritual and journeying. All the characteristics of a covenant relationship of both trusting and tussling with God and each other are here. But at the cornerstone of the relationship is that YHWH is a God who acts, who intervenes in history, who brings the mighty down from their thrones and sets prisoners free.

h) Ten words of freedom

As the biblical compilation makes abundantly clear, freedom from a superpower is one thing, freedom to live rightly is another. The wanderings, incessant grumblings and dramas depicted in the remaining books of the Torah are pre-occupied with the struggles of Moses and the people of Israel on their way to the Promised Land. The books of Leviticus, Numbers and Deuteronomy deal with religious customs, the wandering in the desert and 'the second law', respectively. Since the cohering theme of this collection of writings is the giving of the Law to Moses, all these books – including Genesis – have become known by the collective name Torah – 'Law'.

At the heart of the Law revealed to Moses is the *Decalogue* or 'Ten Words' of Exodus 20. Since this rudimentary moral code is commonly called the 'Ten Commandments', there is a risk that the context of deliverance in which these guiding principles are issued may be forgotten. Theologically, they can be seen as *part of the liberation*, not *constrictions on freedom* as modern libertarian culture tends to perceive them. Among the most famous passages of the Bible, these 'Ten Words' have proved to be an enduring contribution to the ethical consciousness of humanity and are an excellent focus for theological conversation. The injunctions of Ex 20:1-17 which are restated in Deut 5:1-21 are as follows: YHWH is to be the God of this people – no other – and Israel must avoid making 'images' that can become false objects of worship. The use of God's name is to be reserved and the Sabbath is to be held holy, not by a particular act of worship but by giving everyone rest, slaves and animals included. Parents are to be honoured, murder, adultery and theft are forbidden as well as false testimony regarding the actions of others. Jealousy of any kind is to be avoided (Ex 20:1-17 cf. Deut 5:6-21).

Particularly in an individualistic age, these rules may appear restrictive and domineering on the part of a God who seems to want a lot of attention and threatens vengeance on anyone who disagrees and on their family (Ex 20:5)! In the first instance, this can partly be explained by the strong sense of communal identity in kinship cultures – in the fleshly, psychic and social sense people *were* their family rather than 'lone egos' in the way that we understand ourselves. Arguably, since human nature has not changed much, these words have been found to have a permanent relevance. False attachments and any false imagery of ourselves or of others are potentially destructive. The enslavement, particularly of the poor, is a wrong which the Sabbath rest sought to reverse at least once a week. Family and marital strife, theft, violence and the perversion of the course of justice are hardly desirable features in societies of any epoch and many of these disorders are actually fuelled by what might be identified as the 'original' sin of jealousy. While one might acknowledge that the medical treatment of lepers in the Torah or rules on menstruation appear locked in the time frame of a more primitive lifestyle, these 'Ten Words' have a proven, enduring relevance and are rooted in covenant principles:

- God establishes the covenant with Israel freely.
- The covenant involves mutual belonging and mutual respect.
- The covenant is to serve Israel's freedom and preserve their sense of kinship.
- The patterning of life should be a constant reminder of covenant.
- Reneging on the covenant has consequences which may go beyond the present generation.

A formal renewal of covenant which follows includes the sprinkling of blood upon the tribes to symbolize the oneness of their life as God's chosen people (Ex 24:3-8). This covenant symbolism is followed by a sacred meal where God sits, eats and drinks with Moses and the elders (Ex 24:11). Later Christian ritual will take up such themes in its sacramental understanding of Holy Communion. Unfortunately, readers familiar with the biblical text will recall that as Moses and God work out some of the finer details of the Law, the people become impatient (Ex 25-31). The narrative eventually depicts Moses descending the mountain with these words only to find the Israelites already making an image of a God – the 'golden calf' (Ex 32:1-35). Though many a preacher has interpreted this as a foreshadowing of contemporary money worship, exegetes would suggest it was connected with one of the ancient Cannanite depictions of Ba'al (cf. Collins, 2004, 1221–37). In response, Moses grinds the calf to dust and makes the people taste their infidelity and the people suffer a plague for their sin (Ex 32:20; 35).

i) Moses and Torah

Unfortunately for Moses though, he doesn't make it to the Promised Land. He's given a glimpse, but no more. Moses is the flawed yet chosen leader of a flawed yet chosen race. He is the one who forges the notion of nationhood and its consciousness as the chosen people of YHWH. Moses introduces the rituals that will pattern the worship of Israel. He is the one who has seen the face of God and lived. Moses is the one who promises that the people will not be without the guidance of God, that they will be led by a prophet like him (Deut 18:15). Yet though Moses is depicted as being all this and more in the consciousness of Israel, he is not blessed with the task of leading them into the Promised Land – that falls to Joshua his warrior aide (Deut 31:14-23). Moses instead passes away, though his grave is unknown (Deut 34:5-6).

His theological legacy, however, remains absolutely key to understanding Judeo-Christian thinking. As noted above, apart from the Book of Genesis, the figure of Moses dominates the accounts which come to be known collectively as the Torah. Theologically, the scrolls of the Torah, these 'Five Books of Moses,' talk of a covenant relationship with God understood through:

- Genesis – Creation, Flood, Patriarchs, Egypt.
- Exodus – Liberation and the Ten Commandments.
- Leviticus – 'The Priest Book' – Rituals and laws.
- Numbers – Stories of the sojourn in desert.
- Deuteronomy – The 'Second Law' – further details and articulations of the Moses saga.

As noted above, since Moses so dominates the scrolls which make up the Torah, there has been a long tradition that Moses himself authored this whole sweep of writings from Genesis to Deuteronomy, but this view has become extremely rare among biblical scholars who instead suggest a number of different authors to have been involved in contributing to the actual written text. In effect, the Torah is understood as a compilation of sacred traditions compiled over many centuries perhaps beginning during the reign of David (c.950 BCE) and only being completed after the Babylonian exile around 450 BCE. Archaeology demonstrates that the Hebrew language itself seems only to have gradually developed into its biblical form across the many centuries in question and any image of Moses sitting down with the ancient equivalent of a word processor producing the biblical books we are familiar with today is fanciful in the extreme. The emergence of the eventual text that became *canonical* was originally *oral* and took the best part of a millennium to find its way into written form. In this context, we can perhaps better understand the way that through generations of retelling, these writings include varied textures and layers of understanding. Woven together, sometimes seamlessly and sometimes less smoothly, these scriptures collectively retain the epic style in which they were first spoken and present an extremely rich understanding of God and humanity which have remained sacred to the Children of Abraham and held audiences spellbound for millennia.

Summary

Theologically, the Creator God of the early chapters of Genesis comes into focus in the stories of Abraham, Isaac and Moses as YHWH, an imageless God who is both elusive and intimate. YHWH is a God in covenant – in a mutual relationship with this chosen people – expressed in ritual and signs of belonging such as circumcision and the rejection of child sacrifice. Paradoxically, YHWH God is ready to act and to intervene in the lives of the people such as in Exodus, but wishes to be recalled by inaction, 'not doing - just being' in the covenant sign of Sabbath. YHWH sets free the children of Israel and through Moses issues 'Ten Words' of covenant freedom – the Decalogue. This 'saving-belonging' impacts on the Theology of the Hebrews articulated in legalistic and storied imagery throughout the Torah – the first five books of the Bible.

4

Nebi'im: Prophets, Kings and Covenant

The collected writings of 'Nebi'im' – 'The Prophets' – constitute the second section of the TaNaK, the Hebrew scriptures. It is not surprising that Christian Bibles divide these writings differently into historical books and prophetic books since this section contains the vivid story of the rise and fall of the Hebrew monarchy as well as the collection of oracles and deeds attributed to specific prophets. The centre point of the drama remains the covenant which by and large the Kings are prone to abuse and the Prophets are keen to defend. Theologically, these books are hugely influenced by the work of the historian known only to us as 'The Deuteronomist.' The major tragedies of the epoch are the forced exiles suffered first by Israel and then by Judah which the Deuteronomist regards as deserved punishments for the infidelity of the people. After the exiles, leadership devolves to priestly figures as the land struggles under domination by a series of foreign powers, namely Persia, Greece and Rome. The desire for liberation from these overlords becomes expressed in prayer and prophetic yearning for a new intervention by God at the hand of a new leader, a new anointed one, a new 'Messiah.'

a) Theology of covenant

The Hebrew scriptures sacred to all Jews are divided into *Torah* (The Law), *Nebi'im* (The Prophets) and *Ketubim* (The Writings). In Christian Bibles, these divisions are also present but the *Nebi'im* are divided into 'Early Prophets' (now more commonly called 'Historical Books'), and 'Later Prophets' placed after the collection of *Ketubim* – the 'Writings' or 'Wisdom Literature.' It is definitely a risky simplification to collapse all the varied theologies articulated in these scriptures under the single heading of 'covenant' but in designating them the 'Old Testament' or 'Old Covenant' that is exactly what traditional Christian Theology has done. It can be considered reasonable since the varied texts written over a period spanning perhaps a thousand years ultimately recount the myriad ramifications of the mutual relationship between YHWH and the chosen people, which is the essence of covenant.

Though history and archaeology can neither confirm nor contradict the epic story of Exodus, symbolically, the escape, the desert, the receiving of the Law and the reaching of the Promised Land together constitute an image which is key to Jewish religious consciousness, even to the present day. Theologically, the account of this relationship, this covenant, is reliant upon the original power and initiative of God who 'establishes' or 'cuts' covenants with Israel's ancestors (see Gen 9:17, Ex 6:4, Gen 15:18, Ex 24:8). God's affection is therefore the key ingredient of this saving relationship.

Though the covenant is not Israel's idea, certain groups within society may be regarded as particular custodians of covenant, namely the political, prophetic and priestly castes. Just as Moses had exercised tribal and prophetic authority, his scriptural heirs are effectively the kings and the prophets respectively who are often depicted as being in conflict with regard to the covenant as we shall see below. Aaron and the tribe of Levi on the other hand seem to have had a priestly role, mediating between God and the people through religious ritual, rulings and wisdom. Although the Hebrew term *mashiah*, meaning 'anointed one', was usually used to describe a kingly figure, all three 'power archetypes' eventually came to be associated with the notion of 'God's anointed one' from which the term 'Messiah' is derived. As the history of the chosen people unfolds, these different groups jostle for authority and almost take turns in pre-eminence until at a particular period, the longing for a 'complete' *mashiah* reaches critical intensity.

b) Covenant and violence

After the death of Moses, the authority over the people of Israel passes to Joshua, Son of Nun. The Hebrew verb *ysh'* means 'to save' and the name Joshua, like Jesus, is derived from this (cf. Matt 1:21). It might be argued that there the similarity ends. Whatever symbolic connections might be made by later theological reflection to connect these two figures, the bloody conquest of the land depicted in the Book of Joshua is one of the most controversial sections of the scriptures and stands in stark contrast to the fundamentally non-violent message of the Gospels.

In the first instance, it is worth noting that the stories of Joshua are widely seen as a somewhat exaggerated part of 'the foundation legend' of Israel. Instead of a bloody series of battles, the argument runs that Canaan was more gradually infiltrated by the wandering tribes of Hebrews/Habiru who worshipped YHWH. Over time, these tribes asserted dominance over the land and eventually centralized political control in and around Jerusalem. 'Gradual infiltration' hardly constitutes an exciting tale, so in this view, the spectacular narrative of conquest is much more a reminder to listeners and readers to keep themselves from being *impure*, rather than being an account of actual events.

To some extent, though, this lets God off the hook. 'YHWH *Sabaoth*' means 'Lord of Armies' and the biblical picture of a God that stops the sun going down so that he can better target Amorites with hailstones might be wisely feared but hardly loved (Josh 10:1-15). Moreover, part of the theological reasoning here is the notion of *herem* – 'the ban' – since in these accounts, people put under the ban are to be eliminated, including women and children (Josh 10:16-48). Certainly, there are ways of reading 'the ban' symbolically as the personal challenge to be rid of the things that lead one astray from God. This is echoed in Islam's understanding of the personal struggle with oneself being the chief meaning of 'jihad'. The conquest of the land can be read as the conquest of ourselves, to live out our promise, to be more fully who we are in covenant with God. Troublingly however, the most obvious reading is that a righteous war has no constraint. And anyone who has lived post-Crusades, post-colonialism, post-Hiroshima/Nagasaki or post-9/11 knows the horror of that.

That such biblical episodes give religion and God a bad name is not a new idea. Marcion (85–160 CE) was an early Christian theologian who thought that such texts showed that the God of Jesus Christ was not the same as the God of the Old Testament (see below Section 12g). Marcion's view was ultimately rejected by the mainstream because the majority of Christian theologians saw these stories as part of the *unfolding* of a covenant history which eventually revealed the heart of God in Jesus as non-violent love. A bit like the Theory of Evolution, Israel's understanding of God develops and in this foreshadowing stage, YHWH's methods were depicted crudely in a manner that could be understood by primitive peoples.

Human consciousness may indeed be the problem here. Warrior imagery has a deep appeal and heroism in every generation has all too often been forced to have its most vivid expression in the context of war. We shall return to this topic in subsequent chapters, but it seems early Christians had no doubt that the Gospel 'Good News' disarmed both Joshua and Joshua's God in the revelation of Jesus. Sadly, as history attests, far too many Christian political and religious leaders have been more Joshua than Jesus. Mindful of colonial conquests and ethnic cleansing, we might repent that the blood of Indians, Africans and Native Americans soak the foundations of so many prosperous Western nations. Likewise, we might reflect that the abiding Israel/Palestine conflict remains an open wound that is inextricably linked to the land and to this part of the scriptural text.

Unfortunately, if the biblical reader is looking for respite after the wars of Joshua, there isn't much in the Book of Judges (cf. Birch, 2005, pp. 173–214). It begins with allusions to Joshua's renewal of covenant, and the settlement of the different tribes in their own section of the land. The problem of having a federal type tribal league means that the Israelites have to rely on a series of charismatic figures to unite them when threatened by other Canaanite kings and warlords. Ehud, Deborah, Barak, Gideon and Samson take turns in beating the odds and the opposition with the help of YHWH. There is disorder in the land, however, and the gruesome rape and dismemberment of a Levite's concubine triggers further tribal conflict (20:2). The 'judgement on Judges' summarizes the anarchy: 'In those days there was no king in Israel; all the people did what was right in their own eyes' (21:25).

c) Covenant and kingship

In the sequence of the biblical books, the chaotic, tragic and comic scenes of Judges then give way to more ordered but nonetheless memorable narratives in the Books of Samuel. The boy Samuel – meaning 'Hearer of God'– becomes a prophet at a young age and eventually leader of the people (1 Sam 3:19-20). After a promising start, he begins to suffer a similar level of grumbling to Moses as the tribes increasingly demand a king to protect them from their enemies. Samuel's view is rather that they should rely on God and his reply is worth quoting at some length:

> He said, 'These will be the ways of the king who will reign over you: he will take your sons and appoint them to his chariots and to be his horsemen, and to run before his chariots; and he will appoint for himself commanders of thousands and commanders of fifties, and some to plough his ground and to reap his harvest, and to make his implements of war and the equipment of his chariots. He will take your daughters to be perfumers and cooks and bakers. He will take the best of your fields and vineyards and olive orchards and give them to his courtiers. He will take one-tenth of your grain and of your vineyards and give it to his officers and his courtiers. He will take your male and female slaves, and the best of your cattle and donkeys, and put them to his work. He will take one-tenth of your flocks, and you shall be his slaves. And in that day you will cry out because of your king, whom you have chosen for yourselves; but the Lord will not answer you in that day.' (1 Sam 8:11-18)

Here we see depicted clearly the acknowledgement of skewed power relationship arising from fear – in this case, the fear of other nations. YHWH does not approve, but tolerates it. Yet the warning is clear that political power always takes advantage of the common people – a theme that the prophets continue to critique in the covenant life of Israel even in their treatment of David, the most famous of Israel's kings.

David is recalled in the theological tradition of Israel as the archetypal king. In traditional biblical fashion however, this includes the paradox of his lowly birth. He is the youngest son of Jesse, a shepherd, a lad with no prospects but chosen by God (1 Sam 16:13). He is brave, confronting Goliath and conquering him through wit and faith more than by strength (1 Sam 17:45-49). Through a series of complicated civil conflicts, David succeeds Saul as King of Israel (2 Sam 5:3). On the one hand, David is depicted as having poetic and musical gifts with many of the psalms being attributed to him. His expressive devotion to YHWH is most famously witnessed when he dances in the streets before the Ark of the Covenant as it was returned to Jerusalem (2 Sam 6:5). On the other, David is also guilty of the most crass abuse of lust, power and greed when he arranges the death of Bathsheba's husband, the brave and loyal Uriah, so that he can possess her (2 Sam 11:15). The text does not shirk one whit from the horror of this, and the challenge to this power abuse led by the Prophet Nathan is a brilliant exemplar of the Hebrew capacity for self-criticism (2 Sam 12:1-9).

In the sad aftermath, the first child of David and Bathsheba's adultery dies and a later misdemeanour leads to pestilence afflicting the land (2 Sam 24:15). Although it seems that the people and the child suffer rather than David, insofar as the king is a symbol for the whole people there is once more the theological resonance that sin has consequences. Though ostensibly united, the country is rarely at peace during David's reign, his household is fraught with strife, including the civil war and rebellion of his son Absalom. That said, the reign of David becomes embossed on the consciousness of Israel as a kind of ideal period and part of this reasoning must lie in his unifying political action and particularly the conquest of Jerusalem. Through his cunning conquest of this Jebusite stronghold on Mount Zion, David endowed the people with a centre of political, economic and administrative gravity which in time acquired richly symbolic significance (2 Sam 5:6-9).

Since monarchical palaces were centres of innovation and scholarly activity, it has long been suggested that it was around David's time that 'J' (from the German spelling of 'Jahwist' in Wellhausen's JEDP theory - see above, 2i) began to collect and compile the traditions of Israel's cosmic and patriarchal origins. Like the great tales of how Rome was founded, the legends of early Britannia, or the depiction of great figures of the American War of Independence, 'foundation stories' serve to give a sense of nationhood, a shared history, unity and purpose. Key notions of creation, Abraham's covenant, Jacob and the chosen-ness of Israel are woven throughout the origin stories attributed to the 'Yahwist' which would all help David's political propaganda. That said, their near-Eastern imagery leads others to suggest they are more likely to have connection with the period of exile in Babylon and the Persian empire (cf. Irwin, 1944, pp. 160–73 and Ska, 2006, pp. 127–64). Whether *historically* they were compiled and edited much later, *theologically* these accounts have proved to be of inestimable importance in the eventual 'meta-narratives' of the Judeo-Christian 'universe of meaning'.

d) Covenant and the prophets

It was left to Solomon to fulfil his father's dream of building a temple to God, the significance of which cannot be underestimated (1 Kings 6:1ff). As custodian of the covenant, this is another biblical text which demonstrates the *religious* importance of the *political* leader since the site of the Temple at Jerusalem has provided a focus for worship of YHWH to the present day. Solomon, despite his wisdom, was susceptible to feminine charms and the foreign religious practices of his many wives and concubines (1 Kings 11:1-3). Inevitably there are consequences, which in this case follow the death of Solomon when his son Rehoboam unwisely maltreats the Northern tribes causing rebellion under the leadership of Jeroboam, and the Kingdom is divided (1 Kings 12:1-16). Subsequently, the larger Northern Kingdom which establishes the town of Samaria as its capital becomes referred to as 'Israel', while 'Judah' is the name of the smaller Southern Kingdom centred around Jerusalem.

The deliberately theological style of the Book of Kings is plainly evident at this point. Dwelling at Shechem, the account has Jeroboam deliberately setting up an altar at Bethel to weaken both the religious and political links between the Northern tribes and Jerusalem (1 Kings 12:26-33). In keeping with the theological concerns of the writer, these actions are immediately challenged by a double-barrelled prophetic assault which foretells doom upon Jeroboam's dynasty (1 Kings 13:1-14:20). In this epoch of Israel and Judah (950–587 BCE), the success or otherwise of the kings as custodians of the covenant is measured by the narrator and entire reigns are summed up in grateful praise or damning indictments. (Contrast the fine picture of Hezekiah in 2 Kings 18:1-8 with that of his wicked son Manasseh in 2 Kings 21:1-4.) The overriding theme is that infidelity to YHWH and oppression of the poor will ultimately be punished, a conclusion which crystallizes around the painful double experience of invasion and exile (2 Kings 24-25).

With the establishment of separate kingdoms, the biblical text presents the prophets as the connecting principle of covenant. Although there is a tendency for modern readers to think of prophets as foretellers of the future, it is perhaps more helpful to think of them as truth tellers on behalf of God. These *nebi'im* are depicted as chosen instruments of YHWH to guide his people. The power of their words as spokespersons for God is not quite the same as the voice of God which calls forth creation in Genesis 1, but they nonetheless have a transformational power. Prophets change the way people think, their words are effective – almost creative. In the modern era, we might think of figures such as Gandhi, Martin Luther King or Nelson Mandela, figures who against all odds brought about remarkable political change on behalf of the oppressed. They literally changed the consciousness of entire nations through the power of their words. In the biblical context, empowered with the *ruah elohim* that hovered over the primordial waters, the prophets who followed Moses had a similar counter-cultural role. Their unenviable task was to keep the Hebrew 'tumult' and their leaders faithful to the covenant with YHWH.

The depiction of prophets flourishing around 900 BCE is particularly vivid. From 1 Kings 17:1 to 2 Kings 13:20, the two great figures of Elijah ('My God is YHWH') and Elisha ('My God hears') dazzle from the text. Set in the context of the Northern Kingdom around Samaria, Elijah confronts the impious and unjust King Ahab and his corrupt wife Jezebel. Their false prophets of the Canaanite God Baal are humiliated and summarily despatched by the victorious combination of Elijah and YHWH at Mount Carmel (1 Kings 18:20-40). Elijah eventually passes on his prophetic gift to his successor Elisha before mysteriously disappearing in a whirlwind (2 Kings 2:11). Interestingly, because these two cycles of texts include healings, concern for the poor and widows, nature miracles and heavenly intervention, it is possible that the stories of Elijah and Elisha provide the most obvious template for the way in which the Gospel accounts present Jesus (cf. Poirer, 2009 and Croatto, 2005).

e) Injustice and infidelity

Be that as it may, within the more immediate theological context the radical challenges to the social order voiced by the prophets are likewise taken up outside the historical narratives typified by the oracles of Amos. Situated around 750 BCE, he is concerned about the infidelity of the people to the covenant manifested by the worshipping of other gods and their unjust practices towards one another. A change is called for lest judgement befall the nation and Amos in particular is devastating in his critique. Eventually Amaziah, the priest of Bethel, asks Amos to stop prophesying since 'the land is not able to bear all his words' (Amos 7:10). He receives short shrift:

> Hear this, you that trample on the needy, and bring to ruin the poor of the land, saying, "When will the new moon be over so that we may sell grain; and the sabbath, so that we may offer wheat for sale? We will make the ephah small and the shekel great and practise deceit with false balances, buying the poor for silver and the needy for a pair of sandals, and selling the sweepings of the wheat." The LORD has sworn by the pride of Jacob: Surely I will never forget any of their deeds. Shall not the land tremble on this account, and everyone mourn who lives in it, and all of it rise like the Nile, and be tossed about and sink again, like the Nile of Egypt? (Amos 8:4-8)

This option for the poor was theologically significant. The vulnerable members of society, widows, strangers and orphans were part of the particular concerns of the prophets. The social critiques of the prophets called to mind the purpose of Sabbath – to enable *all* to take rest from labour, especially the poor. The jubilee tradition of Israel which demanded a cancellation of debts every fifty years formed part of this picture (Lev 25:1-27:34).

Similarly vocal against the iniquities of the Northern Kingdom, Hosea acted out the infidelity of Israel by marrying a prostitute (Hos 1:2). The cultural impurity of the people and their penchant for offering raisin cakes to other gods were mirrored back to them vividly by Hosea's action and by his deliberate naming of his children as reproaches to Israel (Hos 1:3-10). As Jeremiah and Ezekiel would later demonstrate, such symbolic acts formed part of the vocabulary of the prophets driving home the message not just by words but by being a living sign of God's challenge. Meanwhile, Hosea's words mingle judgement with yearnings for reconciliation and promises of mercy. 'When Israel was a child I loved him . . . I led them with cords of human kindness, with bands of love' (Hos 11:1-4).

Unfortunately, the theological implication is that the continued infidelity of the people led to the conquest of the Northern Kingdom (Hos 11:5-12). This shattering event was understood to be a vindication of words of the prophets, and the collections of oracles by Amos, Hosea and others were conserved and transmitted finding their way ultimately into written form. This preservation of what are essentially collections of self-criticism is not unique to Israelite religion but remains of deep theological significance. While the straightforward link between infidelity and disaster may jar in the modern mindset, the classic pattern involving the rejection of both the message and the prophet to the eventual detriment of the people constitutes part of the theological sub-structure of the Christian Gospels.

f) Invasion and salvation

In 722 BCE, after a series of campaigns begun by Tigleth-Pileser III, invading Assyrian armies from the North finally subdued Israel and conquered its capital Samaria (2 Kings 15:29-17:5). This crushing occupation was exacerbated by the forced deportation of the local inhabitants and the deliberate repopulation of the area with undesirable Assyrian settlers. This 'dilution' of the purity of the local Hebrew religion and the gene pool of its inhabitants led to long-standing suspicion of Samaritans on the part of the people of Judah. As the text reports:

> So they worshipped the Lord, but they also served their own gods, after the manner of the nations from among whom they had been carried away. To this day they continue to practise their former customs. They do not worship the Lord and they do not follow the statutes or the ordinances or the law or the commandment

that the LORD commanded the children of Jacob, whom he named Israel. (2 Kings
17:33-34)

Not long afterwards, in 701 BCE, another fearsome Assyrian invasion under
Sennacherib besieged Jerusalem. All seemed lost until suddenly . . . they
turned and went back home.

Here we are at a classic nexus of History and Theology. There is little
doubt that Jerusalem and Judah retained their independence and integrity at
this dramatic point in history. The biblical account attributes this to the
direct intervention of God. King Hezekiah consults the Prophet Isaiah who
tells him not to be afraid. Before hostilities are engaged, the text recounts
that Sennacherib's army is decimated by an angel while encamped around
Jerusalem and they go home defeated (cf. 2 Kings 19:1-36; Isa 36:1-37:38). In
contrast, while the Assyrian version of events has King Hezekiah trapped
like a 'caged bird' and eventually paying a secret tribute which satisfied the
invaders, the Greek version by Herodotus attributes the retreat to an
infestation of mice in the Assyrian camp (cf. Pritchard, 2011, p. 246;
Herodotus, *Histories*, 2.141).

In war, 'the first casualty is truth' and it is difficult at this distance to take
sides. On a personal note, I can vividly remember reading about the 1982
Falklands/Malvinas war between Britain and Argentina while in Italy. One of
the newspapers gave up trying to reconcile the reports and placed the different
versions from London and Buenos Aires in separate columns down either
side of the page leaving the reader to make up their own mind. History is
rarely a straightforward recitation of facts, it always betrays accents influenced
by the philosophical, sociological and psychological standpoint of its authors.
Here, and most importantly, the theological interpretation of these events in
Judah was that the Northern Kingdom had been punished for its sins, but
somehow Jerusalem, Mount Zion, was impregnable because of the presence
of God in the Temple of YHWH. Though this interpretation gave colour and
conviction to the cult of YHWH in Jerusalem, it was perhaps the worst thing
that could have happened to its kings. Possibly rendered smug by the demise
of their Northern neighbours, the descendants of Hezekiah are one after
another depicted as being corrupt and unfaithful to God, each receiving
damning obituaries by the writer of the Book of Kings. The one exception is
Josiah, a figure so distinct from the others that he merits separate consideration.

g) Josiah and the Deuteronomist

A monarch from the age of 8, two pivotal chapters in 2 Kings 22-23 depict the reforms of Josiah which clamp down on worship of other Gods, child sacrifice and other abominations and decisively centre the cult on Jerusalem. The Feast of Passover is celebrated with renewed solemnity and a new commitment to covenant. These reforms seem to be triggered by the discovery of an ancient copy of the Law while the Temple is being refurbished (2 Kings 22:8). Now anyone who has ever found themselves moving or repairing a house has probably found themselves pausing to muse on an old artefact, book or even a newspaper. This discovery was something of an entirely different order and has generally been identified as the whole or some part of what is now called the Book of Deuteronomy. Although this is more informed speculation than certainty, it supports the argument that the huge stretch of Israel's history from the settling of the land as recounted in Joshua to virtually the end of the Book of Kings was collected and edited at this time. Rather unimaginatively, this anonymous historian is called 'The Deuteronomist' – the 'D' of the four-source JEDP theory (Vogt, 2006, pp. 1–32).

Josiah made it his mission to centralize the religious practices of Israel on Jerusalem. Besides being a reformer of the cult, he also seems to have had a reputation for justice and fairness, Jer 22:15-16 rebukes Josiah's son for not being like his father who gave the poor a fair trial. Sadly, however, things did not go entirely well. Josiah overstretched himself militarily and was killed at Megiddo in 609 BCE doing battle with Neco, the King of Egypt. Theologically, it is very significant to read the reasons given for this misfortune. The 'Deuteronomist' explains:

> The Lord said, "I will remove Judah also out of my sight, as I have removed Israel; and I will reject this city that I have chosen, Jerusalem, and the house of which I said, My name shall be there." (2 Kings 23:27)

This summary clearly lays the blame at the feet of Josiah's disreputable ancestors (2 Kings 23:26). Worse still, his heirs (Jehoahaz, Eliakim and Zedekiah) had a torrid time caught between the local superpowers of Egypt and Babylon (2 Kings 24:1-20). Eventually after a partial invasion and expulsion of leaders in 598 BCE, King Nebuchadnezzer of Babylon defeated Judah and after killing Zedekiah's sons in front of him, had his eyes put out, placed him in chains and took him to Babylon (2 Kings 25:5-7).

Although the exile in Babylon did not mark the end of monarchical influence in Israel, the predominant failure of kings to live up to covenant expectations certainly characterizes the theological judgement made upon them in the Bible. Although the pre-eminent figure of David maintained the lustre of 'anointedness', the more usual heroes in the Deuteronomist's editorial collection were the prophets. And it was their warnings that appear, theologically at least, to have enabled the people to survive the shattering blow of losing their symbols of covenant – the Promised Land, Jerusalem and the Temple where God dwelt on earth.

h) Theology of exile

Isaiah, Jeremiah and Ezekiel are the three major prophets that bestride the shuddering events which saw Judah at first survive extinction (Isaiah) but then suffer the ignominy of its own defeat (Jeremiah) and experience the bitterness of captivity (Ezekiel). Isaiah was active around Jerusalem at the time of the siege of the city, and was consulted by King Hezekiah (Isa 37:21). Isaiah would seem to have been a priest of the temple where he received a vivid prophetic calling (Isa 6:1-13). The oracles of Isaiah are very extensive and most scholars would argue that there are three phases of writing by different authors (Chapters 1–39, 40–55 and 56–66) which cover this whole period but have been edited as one scroll. Christian Theology sets great store by Isaiah since they contain visionary oracles which were later applied to Jesus (e.g. Isa 7:14). In particular, the 'Songs of the Servant of YHWH' are of key importance since they depict an image of one chosen by God who ultimately inexplicably suffers for the sake of others (Isa 42:1-4; 49:1-6; 50:4-9; 52:13-53:12).

It is difficult for those of us who have never suffered war, destruction and displacement to imagine the situation faced by the defeated remnant of Judah. Desolate, poor and powerless, a portion of the people remained in the land. Separated from their kinfolk, another portion were far away in Babylon where, as the famous psalm recounts, they sat and wept in recollection of their homeland (Ps 137:1-3).

Any sense that they were a special people privileged by God with especial protection had to be rethought in the light of events. The theological historiography begun by 'the Deuteronomist' may have been completed at this time and likewise the collections of oracles and sayings of key prophetic figures. The very different styles of Jeremiah and Ezekiel nonetheless shared the same view that only a renewed sense of purpose and covenant commitment would give the people a future, a home in Zion (Renz, 1999, pp. 77–103). In yet another paradox of tragedy leading to new birth, biblical scholars identify the exilic period as a highly significant moment in the crystallization of Israel's self-understanding. This rebirth of religious identity would prove essential since the following centuries were to pass without political independence or the national self-expression that the people craved.

i) Colonization and later prophecy

To bring this chapter to a close, the received biblical text is unambiguous that the best prophets and kings were those zealous for covenant and the religious and ethnic purity of the people. 'Syncretism' – the polluting of the true faith by mixing ethnically or by embracing strange beliefs, was a no-no. Yet for six centuries following the exile, Israel was an occupied province of Empire of first Persia (538–333 BCE), then Greece (333–68 BCE), and then Rome (68–70 CE). As a result, Judean faith in YHWH did not evolve in a historical vacuum, and despite the concerns of the ruling priestly caste to maintain purity and exclusivity, there are clear points of contact between biblical traditions and other cultures. Like the old saying goes: 'You can chase the wolf from the door but he might still come in through the window'.

First, it can be argued that the creation legends and cosmic theologies of their Babylonian captors prompted Hebrew theologians to review faith in YHWH in a way that was more global, more universal, more inclusive of all peoples. The first chapter of Genesis, normally attributed to the author 'P' might be a case in point with its picture of a cosmic universal God rather than the more tribal traditions of YHWH present in other parts of the biblical epic. In turn, the interaction with Assyrian, Babylonian and Persian cultures may explain the 'cross-referencing' of Hebrew traditions such as the story of Noah with Babylonian and Sumerian flood legends. In such a fashion then, it can be argued that the Exile may have paradoxically served both to *focus* and to *broaden* the theological perspectives of the worshippers of YHWH.

Secondly, while the critique of the prophets and the urgings of the priests continued to exhort the people to fidelity and right worship of God, a tendency to imagine an overthrow of this oppression through decisive action on God's part became a key motif. 'The Day of the Lord' (*Yôm YHWH*), which in Amos' time had been a day of judgement for Israel, increasingly becomes a day of transformation in favour of Israel, a decisive time when the present order of things will be radically altered and the superpowers overthrown (cf. Amos 5:18 and Zeph 1:14-18). These pictures of prophetic possibility were in the later period allied to cosmic notions of dark and light, good and evil, influenced by Persian thinking.

Though neither of these factors wholly explain the rise of 'apocalyptic literature' (which will be discussed below, Section 5k), symbolic imagery became very much part of the religious imagination of Judah. By situating the present in the context of a cosmic struggle, God's vindication of Israel in the face of its oppressors became an increasing feature of YHWH Theology, which in turn would look to its traditional 'messianic' categories of prophecy, kingship and even priesthood for deliverance.

Summary

The core theme of the Nebi'im *is covenant, the mutual relationship between Israel and God which is safeguarded in different ways by the power figures in the story of Israel. The historical trajectory covered by these writings sees Israel experience the prophetic, charismatic leadership of the tribal federation, the kingship of the monarchy, the pain of exile and the prophetic oracles of the colonial period following the return. In this section of the Hebrew scriptures, the combined influence of the prophets and the Deuteronomist-historian is immense, equipping the people with a theological understanding of the tragedies that had befallen them. Despite many years of foreign colonial oppression, a sustained religious hope for a delivering 'anointed one' was maintained in Israel – a Day of the Lord when God would intervene to save his people.*

Ketubim: Priests, Poets, Wisdom

The third great division of the TaNaK is known as the 'Writings', a collection mostly comprised of prayers, poems and proverbs. Also classified as 'Wisdom' literature, it can be characterized as the contemplative response to God by his people. The 'direct action' of God is referred to but it is the way the faith in YHWH is lived that takes centre stage. The main actors in the collection are the sages and the priests. True, many of the psalms are attributed to David and many of the Proverbs are attributed to Solomon, but the context for much of the collection seems to be later. The presence of Daniel within the Writings draws attention to the important development of apocalyptic literature which is the proximate theological background to the New Testament.

a) *Ketubim* and theology

The *ketubim* or 'writings' that form the third major subdivision of the Old Testament may be characterized as the contemplative response to the God of the chosen people. A core theme in 'the writings' is the hunger for understanding or 'wisdom' (*hokmah* in Hebrew or *sophia* in Greek). As a result, the *ketubim* are often collectively referred to as the 'Wisdom Literature' of the Bible. That said, any presumption that these writings might be either a collection of dry philosophical meditations or a bland set of commentaries on common sense would be mistaken. They constitute a varied collection and the musings of the writers map the terrain of human experience. 'All of human life is here' and indeed the *ketubim* include some of the most treasured passages of the scriptures, as well as some of the most violent, fabulous and garish.

One of the problematic aspects of the writings is that they are presented differently in the great Judeo-Christian traditions. The Hebrew collection of writings includes books of the historical type (Ezra, Nehemiah and Chronicles), poetry (Psalms, Lamentations and Song of Songs), wisdom (Job, Proverbs and Ecclesiastes), as well as fabulous stories (Ruth, Esther and Daniel). As we shall see below, at various turns, Christian tradition has not only come to redistribute these books in a different order, but the main distinct branches of Christianity (Catholic, Protestant and Orthodox) have all ended up with slightly different views on which of these books should actually be in their biblical canon (cf. section 12h below, Murphy, 2002, pp. 1–14 and Crenshaw, 2010, pp. 1–23).

b) Priestly power and the Second Temple

Religious authority in Israel was not the exclusive preserve of patriarchs, prophets or even kings. Across religions in general, priests tend to have a mediator role with God through ritual prayer and offerings. This is prevalent in so many cultures that a Latin tag identifies the basic bargain/deal-making/exchange mentality behind such thinking: *Do ut Des* – 'I give so that you [God] might give back'. As such, these masters of ritual acquire central importance in various cultures and the traditions of Israel are no exception.

In the Torah, the theological importance of priesthood first appears with the mysterious figure of Melchizedek in Gen 14:18-21. Abraham, fresh from defeating a number of kings, receives a blessing from this 'priest of God most High' and gives him a tithe – both signs that the tribal leader is somehow inferior to this religious leader. In the drama of the Exodus, there is no question that Moses is the hero but he is presented as needing a spokesman and ritual leader, Aaron of the priestly tribe of Levi who has magical powers (Ex 7:1-11:10).

After the Exodus, the narrative continues with the ritual matters which dominate the 'priest's book' of Leviticus and the presentation of Aaron in the Torah is suggestive of a role which came to be a powerful office in the life of the nation, namely the High Priest. Aaron is depicted as having the especial favour of God (Num 17:8), and after the wanderings in the desert and the entering of Canaan, those of Aaron's tribe, the Levites, were given duties at local altars rather than any allotted land. In return, the other tribes were to give them tithes – a tenth of everything – to sustain their families. Unfortunately, since their tasks tended to be literally ritualistic, they do not seem to have figured too highly in the historical editorials of the tribes and tribulations from Conquest to Exile compiled by the Deuteronomist. To correct this, it would appear that a Levite sympathizer wrote the Books of Chronicles which repeat almost all of the episodes of the Books of Kings but with added priestly pop-ups at key moments, cf. 2 Kings 22:21-22 and 2 Chron 35:1-19. Since this was in all likelihood during an epoch of priestly dominance, it is no surprise that most scholars situate this compilation some time after the return from exile in Babylon.

The restoration of freedom was granted to the exiles by King Cyrus of Persia. In the interminable conflicts that plagued the Near East, Persia conquered Babylon and Cyrus issued an Edict of Liberation in 538 BCE. The biblical text presents King Cyrus as an instrument of God, acting in fulfilment of the scriptures. The Book of Ezra begins with Cyrus making what amounts to a confession of faith in YHWH which seems rather unlikely (Ezra 1:2). That said, the understanding fostered among the returning exiles was that God had forgiven them their wrongdoing under the kings of Israel and Judah, and that a time of restoration, like a new Exodus, was at hand. Unfortunately, the triumphant picture that this might conjure up did not match the realities of refugees who straggled homewards. The returning exiles had to rebuild their sense of community and their sense of nationhood. *Religion* was literally their 're-binding' or 're-connecting' and the painstaking depiction of this recovery in the books of Ezra and Nehemiah evidence this. Despite a lack of resources, Nehemiah endeavours to rebuild the walls of Jerusalem in the face of grumpy opposition. His enemy Sanballat the Horonite is especially scathing:

> He [Sanballat] said in the presence of his associates and of the army of Samaria, "What are these feeble Jews doing? Will they restore things? Will they sacrifice? Will they finish it in a day? Will they revive the stones out of the heaps of rubbish—and burnt ones at that?" (Neh 4:2)

In a somewhat self-righteous but nonetheless determined fashion, Nehemiah defies his detractors and presses on with his sacred task of restoration. Ultimately, it is the re-laying of the cornerstones of covenant described when Ezra solemnly reads from the Law of YHWH that constitutes the more significant part of the rebuilding programme (Neh 8:1-18).

With some inevitability, the about turn in fortunes was not good news for everyone. The religious restoration was ethnic as well as liturgical and the desire to purify the nation demanded that those who had taken foreign wives were guilty of transgression (Ezra 10:3). The dismissal of all foreign wives and children from such unions seems excessive to the modern mind, but within the context of the collection of biblical writings, there is a certain consistency here. The concern to identify bloodlines and the painstaking family lists is all too reminiscent of the genealogies of the Torah and the intolerance of foreigners and their practices is hardly unique to Ezra. Zeal, concern for right worship and commitment to the Law, though all born of a worthy motivation not to short-change YHWH, were part of a picture that saw religious authority come to dominate this period of Judean history. Although this inevitably left its theological mark such that the 'writings' predictably include strong themes encouraging religious observance, the poetry and wisdom of the tradition went beyond conformity to the Law and articulated all the raw emotion of Israel as '*Israelim*' – 'God's strugglers' in covenant.

c) *Ketubim* and prayer

Poetic books by their nature tend to be less constrained than historical writings. To illustrate the extremes of emotion depicted in the *ketubim*, one can cite texts drawn from the Book of Psalms. Many of these famous poetic prayers and hymns are traditionally ascribed to the hand of King David, who was known to be a musician and known to be particularly expressive in his worship. When the Ark of the Covenant was returned to Jerusalem from captivity among the Philistines, David danced so delightedly that his wife was embarrassed – a marital scene possibly repeated throughout history, though probably not so often for religious reasons (2 Sam 6:13-20).

Although most scholars would not exclude the idea of David's court being the origin of a number of the psalms, there would not be an automatic consensus that the description 'Psalm of David' means it was written by the archetypal sovereign of the twelve tribes. Since their composition and regular recitation were part of the religious activity of the numerous priests, prophets and Levites attached to the royal court or to the Temple, it is difficult to be certain on details of authorship or dates. Withal, it is one of the specific riches of the psalms that they appear to capture songs of Israel and Judah spanning a number of centuries reflecting varied circumstances of celebration and catastrophe, days of festival and of failure.

A few examples may help illustrate the point. Psalm 1 describes where true happiness lies – away from gossip and tittle-tattle, rooted in the Law and in righteousness, 'like trees planted by streams of water'. Anxiety is the enemy in a number of psalms, famously exemplified by Psalm 23 'The Lord is my shepherd . . . even though I walk through the darkest valley, I fear no evil'. In many places, the beauty of the Law as a gift of God to Israel is celebrated – 'The Law of the Lord is perfect, it revives the soul' (Ps 19:7), in others there is a celebration of God's majesty and creation such as Ps 104:1 – 'Bless the Lord, O my soul . . . You are clothed with honour and majesty, wrapped in light as with a garment'.

Although the psalms are ostensibly categorized as prayers, there is a raw honesty of expression that would rarely be articulated in most contemporary Christian worship. The psalmist cries, 'My God my God, why have you forsaken me' in Ps 22:1 while the author of Ps 137:9 is so angry about the destruction of Jerusalem by Nebuchadnezzar and the exile of the people that they look forward to a day when they can smash the heads of Babylonian babies. Two psalms ascribed to David depict stunning levels of self-reflection (Psalm 50 and Psalm 55) which lament wrongdoing and betrayal, respectively.

The collection itself has internal currents such as the 'Songs of Ascent' numbered 120-134. Traditionally these songs are understood to be those sung by the pilgrims as they traversed the hilly approaches to Jerusalem – Mount Zion – to worship at the Temple. The intensity of praise filled emotion of these psalms is, if anything, surpassed in the last five psalm songs, each of which begins with a resounding '*Halleluyah*' 'Praise to YHWH'. Perhaps fittingly, the entire collection almost tumbles over itself in a litany of praise as it ends:

> Praise him with the sound of trumpet,
> Praise him with lyre and harp,
> Praise him with tambourines and dancing,
> Praise him with strings and pipes,
> Praise him with clashing cymbals,
> Praise him with resounding cymbals
> Let everything that has breath praise the Lord.
> Praise the Lord! (Ps 150:3-6)

Since the Psalms seem so varied and sporadic, theologians can be tempted to ignore their importance which is a mistake for several reasons. First, it may surprise some that the New Testament quotes the Psalms more than any other book in the Old Testament. Moreover, the Psalms illustrate a well-known theological principle of *lex orandi lex credendi* which loosely translated means that 'doctrine follows on from prayer' (see Section 13c). Lastly, in the course of Christian history, the Psalms have remained markedly at the centre of church worship in all denominations (cf. Mays, 1994, Reardon, 2000, Firth and Johnstone, 2005). Not only have they been a key part of the patterns of monastic life, they also remain at the heart of contemporary worship and provide a common vocabulary for Jewish and Christian prayer.

d) *Ketubim* as Proverbs

The Book of Proverbs is another collection, this time of wise sayings and life observations interspersed with some significant poems about wisdom itself. Some of the lines from Proverbs have made their way into common parlance such as 'Pride goes before a fall' (16:19) and 'A soft answer turns away wrath' (15:1). Yet one might be grateful that other observations in the text are not quite so popular. Given that this is 'wisdom' literature, 'fools' come in for particularly heavy criticism. Their castigations vary from the somewhat violent, 'A whip for the horse, a bridle for the donkey and a rod for the back of fools' (26:3), to the somewhat distasteful, 'Like a dog that returns to its vomit, is a fool who reverts to his folly' (26:11), to the somewhat politically incorrect, 'Like a gold ring in a pig's snout is a beautiful woman without good sense' (11:22).

The theological stance of Proverbs is that wisdom begins with the *yr't* YHWH – the 'fear' or 'respect' for God (1:7). Thus set in right relationship, the task for the good person is to obey the commands (*mishpatim*) of the law inherent in that belonging which is the essence of right living. One can see the family resemblance of the Psalms with the Proverbs from their opening lines and a comparison of Psalm 1 with Proverbs 1 is helpful. Both offer an invitation to be at rights with God, to learn what wisdom and discipline are, to treat all with fairness and thereby to avoid folly and its negative consequences. There is a strong sense of justice and concern for the poor throughout Proverbs, for example, 'A false balance is an abomination to the Lord, but an accurate weight is his delight' (11:1) and 'Do not rob the poor because they are poor, or crush the afflicted at the gate' (22:22). Elsewhere, Proverbs exhorts us to listen to parents, to be loyal friends and to be good neighbours. Such persistent reminders to be sensible are garnished by more poetic moments:

> Three things are too wonderful for me;
> four I do not understand:
> the way of an eagle in the sky,
> the way of a snake on a rock,
> the way of a ship on the high seas,
> and the way of a man with a woman. (Prov 30:18-19)

In terms of Christian Theology, one might pick out three things of particular interest about the Proverbs.

- First, there is an intriguing 'personification' of 'wisdom' in Chapter 8:22ff which depicts Wisdom as present before the foundation of the world, 'at play' in the moment of creation, delighting in the 'sons of men' (Prov 8:31). This can be argued to ground 'Natural Theology' in the revelation of Scripture since it implies that God can be found through wisdom – through discerning, if you like, the touch of God in the created universe.
- A second twist is given through the depiction of 'wisdom personified'. In what may have been a blatant attempt to hold the attention of young men, Wisdom is depicted in Proverbs as a beautiful woman to be desired above all things (Prov 1:20ff). Whatever the motivation back then, in our own time this feminine identification of wisdom has been emphasized by modern theologians as a counter-balance to the generally masculine archetypes identified with divinity in the Judeo-Christian scriptures (cf. Sir 24:1-34 and Luke 7:35).
- Lastly, the importance of wisdom-proverb activity gathers further traction when one considers the use of memorable sayings as a teaching aid for right living. This wisdom technique, common in the Ancient Near East, has echoes in the pattern *and* content of Jesus' teaching. Compare Prov 25:6-7 with Luke 14:10 'Do not put yourself forward in the king's presence or stand in the place of the great; for it is better to be told, "Come up here", than to be put lower in the presence of a noble'. Likewise, Prov 25:21 'If your enemies are hungry, give them bread to eat; and if they are thirsty, give them water to drink', may be compared with the famous parable of the Good Samaritan (Luke 10:29-37).

It can be argued that the presentation of Jesus in his quick-witted disputations with Scribes and Pharisees in the Gospels locate Jesus as belonging to the wisdom tradition as well as the prophetic. The clearest indication given that Jesus himself recognized this is when he rebukes the Pharisees for their grumpy attitude. He uses a feminine image when chiding them saying 'Wisdom is vindicated by all her children' (Luke 7:35). This in turn leads a number of modern theologians to call for a de-emphasizing of gender even when speaking of Christ – which, needless to say, is one of the concerns of feminist theological discourse (see below, Section 22e).

e) *Ketubim* and suffering

The Book of Job may well be among the most ancient texts of the Bible. The Hebrew text of Job is full of words only used once in the entire scriptures. A 'one-off' word is called a *hapax legomenon* and there are so many in Job that most translators of this part of the Bible don't particularly need faith in God, but they do need to have faith in their dictionary. Moreover, just as there appear to be versions of the Noah story in other ancient cultures, there are Akkadian and Babylonian stories that seem to echo the troubles of Job who famously endures great suffering before having his fortunes restored (Pritchard, 2011, pp. 352–7). Whatever the pre-history of Job, the account that unfolds disturbs many of the theological patterns that generally prevail in the Bible. Here the mantra of 'Observe the Law, you will be blest' which is so characteristic of the Proverbs and Psalms seems to be contradicted. Indeed it might be best to think of Job as a 'minority report' – part of the counter-intuitive, paradoxical strand of Old Testament thinking.

The opening two chapters of the Book of Job begin with a scene from the Heavenly Court which is itself theologically puzzling (Job 1:6). First, YHWH seems to be chief among a number of Gods – this is usually called *Henotheism* rather than strict *Monotheism* which understands there to be just one God. Secondly, one might ask why Satan is allowed in to God's company at all, given his destructive, negative role in biblical scripture (Job 1:7-9). Furthermore, YHWH seems at ease in allowing Satan to wreak mayhem with animals and humans as a means to upset Job (Job 1:13-19). In fact, the only person close to Job to survive is his wife, who somewhat unsympathetically invites him to 'Curse God, and die!' (Job 2:9). Covered in the sores and welts of a second wave of Satan's tortures, Job is left on an ash heap. His three friends who arrive are so shocked at his sufferings, they remain silent for seven days and seven nights (Job 2:13).

There then follow the series of dialogues where Job defends his integrity before God and before the Law while his friends try and find out what he must have done to deserve this fate. Eventually a fourth visitor, the youthful and enthusiastic Elihu takes over the dialogue (Job 32:1ff). He is less sympathetic and with passion and poetry very much puts Job in his place before eventually God appears moved to respond.

Yet God's famous 'answer to Job' is not quite what the modern mind might expect (Job 38:1-41:34). God offers no explanation. God doesn't tell Job about his conversations with Satan and in this sense the literary device allows the reader more privileged information than Job. God basically reminds Job of his humanity, that he is of the earth, he is only a creature. God is God. Job was not there when the pillars of the earth were set in place or the sun was set in the sky (Job 38:4; 12). In the face of this theophany and statements of the 'Godness' of God, Job falls silent and repents of his impertinence. In a flurry of activity his fortunes are restored, he is blest with sons again, his unusually named daughters (Turtledove, Cassia and Mascara) are the most beautiful in the land and they all live happily ever after (Job 42:10-17).

And yet there is something nigglingly annoying about this 'solution'. In the contemporary context, hard wired as most of us seem to be with the need for *explanation*, the proposal here appears to emphasize *acceptance*. A matter of humanity accepting creatureliness, accepting the absurdity of life, accepting impotence in the face of events, accepting injustice, accepting the presence of evil, and accepting that God must know best. Theologically this 'triumph of impotence' will find echoes in the New Testament depiction of the suffering Christ, yet the seemingly random experience of human distress remains disconcerting and is one of the conundra discussed below in section 20d (cf. Cox, 1978 and Boss, 2010).

f) *Ketubim* and cynicism

While Job's realization of his own limitations leads him to return to the acknowledgement of God, the limitations observed by Qoheleth, 'The Preacher' sometimes called 'Ecclesiastes', elicit a more cynical conclusion. The authorship of this book tends to be situated early in the post-exilic period. Little is known of the author, but the 'wisdom' articulated by Qoheleth seems to crystallize around the message 'Life is as it is. Get on with it'. Qoheleth is not impressed by the achievements of humanity, most of which, including the writing of books (!), he dismisses as vanity and a waste of time (Ecc 1:2). Qoheleth seems to see disillusionment of the confident as part of his contribution to wisdom, not being impressed by wine, women, wealth or piety (Ecc 2:3, 8; 9:2).

Given this somewhat unremitting cynicism, one might be tempted to quietly ignore this section of the Bible and move on quickly to more positive passages, but Qoheleth's meditation on time is memorable and worth quoting at length:

> For everything there is a season, and a time for every matter under heaven:
> a time to be born, and a time to die;
> a time to plant, and a time to pluck up what is planted;
> a time to kill, and a time to heal;
> a time to break down, and a time to build up;
> a time to weep, and a time to laugh;
> a time to mourn, and a time to dance;
> a time to throw away stones, and a time to gather stones together;
> a time to embrace, and a time to refrain from embracing;
> a time to seek, and a time to lose;
> a time to keep, and a time to throw away. (Ecc 3:1-6)

Time . . . life . . . *is* these things. Life, understood as a series of events experienced rather than hours to be filled or dates on a calendar, reminds us that the Western worldview is hopelessly skewed towards the future since it tends to regard time as an empty category stretching out ahead (cf. Fox, 1999, pp. 191–213). It is a subtle distinction, but to be old in the Hebrew mind meant that you were 'full of days' – not tick-tocked out by appointments in an overloaded diary. Qoheleth would probably be amused by our chronic chronological obsessions. Echoing Job he endeavours to remind humanity that 'As they came from their mother's womb, so they shall go again, naked as they came; they shall take nothing for their toil, which they may carry away with their hands' (Ecc. 5:15).

g) *Ketubim* and love

Meanwhile, the *Shir Hashirim* or 'Song of Songs' is just about the polar opposite of the world-weary Qoheleth. It is introduced as the 'Song of Solomon' but again, there is no consensus about authorship. The canticle consists of a series of sensuous poems presented as a dialogue between lovers who delight in the beauty of creation and of each other. With wonderful imagery, the poems express some of the yearning, bewilderment, heartache, passion and desire that characterize being in love. And while not all of the poetry such as 'My beloved is like a gazelle' (Song 2:9) would be recommended for your next Valentine's card, there is no doubting the affirmation of romance throughout the text.

Two problems and two solutions tend to dominate the theological understanding of the text. The first 'problem' is that the poetry is adventurously erotic. From the first, alcohol is immediately dismissed as a B-list pleasure compared to physical tenderness. 'Let him kiss me with the kisses of his mouth! For your love is better than wine' (1:2), cries the woman as she invites her lover to 'lie between [her] breasts' (1:13). The groom replies with equal intensity: 'You have ravished my heart, my sister, my bride, you have ravished my heart with a glance of your eyes, with one jewel of your necklace' (4:9). There is something of a climax to all this passion articulated in the Fourth poem:

> My beloved thrust his hand into the opening,
> and my inmost being yearned for him.
> I arose to open to my beloved,
> and my hands dripped with myrrh,
> my fingers with liquid myrrh,
> upon the handles of the bolt. (Song 5:2-5)

The yearning of such intimacy, this bliss, becomes the driving force of the exchanges which depict love as the essence of fruitfulness and abundance, abandonment as desert-edness and be-wilderment.

The vivid nature of this poetry might appear at first glance to be theologically inconsistent with the more prudish tones articulated in the Torah. Aspects of sexual reality such as seminal discharge and menstrual blood-flow were seen as unclean (Lev 15:16-19) and one could be forgiven for reading texts such as Lev 18:1-30 less as an invitation to marital fidelity and more of a warning about sexual misconduct. A simple speculative explanation is that the poems were written by a woman, unfettered by the picky rules of religious males. That said, whatever the authorship, Song of Songs *is* consistent with the fundamental theological idea of the 'original blessing' expressed in the Genesis accounts (cf. Gen 1:27 and Gen 2:24). Understood in this way, the Song can be seen as expressing the inherent goodness of sexual love. After all, it is through the ecstasy of this pleasure that human beings begin life, and it is the divine pattern by which humanity imitates God as creator of image and likeness.

The second theological 'problem' is that God is not mentioned – at all. This depiction of a lover's paradise seems to exclude God and is one of the reasons why it can be argued that this 'book' of the Bible owes more to the traditions of Persian love poetry than the covenant traditions of Israel. Whatever the arguments of modern exegetes on the origin of the text, the 'solution' offered by traditional Jewish Theology is that far from being absent, God is intimately present in the text, as the lover, the bridegroom. In this view, the 'bride' is Israel – the chosen love.

This may seem fanciful, and perhaps the proposal that the lover's two breasts are Moses and Aaron might raise a smile. Theologically, however, it develops the tradition most vividly depicted by the Prophet Hosea – that Israel was the unfaithful spouse of the faithful YHWH (Hos 3:1). Later, in Christian Theology, this concept of bride and bridegroom is further grounded in the image of Christ. Jesus is the image of God as the groom, and the Church, the New Israel, is the bride. In this context, the notion of deathless love in the Song of Songs becomes significant:

> Set me as a seal upon your heart,
> as a seal upon your arm;
> for love is strong as death,
> passion fierce as the grave.
> Its flashes are flashes of fire,
> a raging flame.
> Many waters cannot quench love,
> neither can floods drown it.
> If one offered for love
> all the wealth of one's house,
> it would be utterly scorned. (Song 8:6-7)

h) *Ketubim* and welfare

Among the collection of the 'writings' the traditional Hebrew arrangement includes Ruth, Esther and Daniel which Christian Bibles distribute among the historical and prophetic sections. The Book of Ruth begins with the dilemma of Naomi, an exile in Moab, having lost not only her husband Elimelech, but also her two married sons, Chilion and Mahlon (1:1-5). She is left connected only to her daughters-in-law and decides to return to Bethlehem. Orpah opts to stay behind but in a famous declaration of loyalty, Ruth refuses to be separated from Naomi and says:

> "Do not press me to leave you or to turn back from following you! Where you go, I will go; where you lodge, I will lodge; your people shall be my people, and your God my God. Where you die, I will die - there will I be buried. May the Lord do thus and so to me, and more as well, if even death parts me from you!" (Ruth 1:16-17)

The two women return to Judah and in the narrative, their plight helps us understand some key 'welfare issues' in relation to the tribal society of ancient Israel-Judah. First, since they are poor, Ruth has to 'glean' pickings from the harvested grain of the fields of a man called Boaz (2:1-10). This tradition, that there should be leftovers for the benefit of the poor and the stranger, was one of the ways that tribal society cared for the marginalized. In a sense, this allowance for rough edges is symbolic of nature and countryside – the very opposite of the mechanized quest for efficiency that abounds in so-called advanced urban culture today. Secondly, after Boaz takes pity on Ruth and they have a night time tryst, the issue of her being a widow to his kinsman Mahlon brings up the rule of the 'Levirate' law. Under this ruling, male relatives were obliged to 'redeem' the widows of kinfolk to stop them falling into poverty, homelessness and prostitution (cf. Deut 25:5-10 and Ruth 3:1-18). Again, this short book shows us the mechanism whereby this is arranged. The 'City Gate' was where public matters were resolved and Boaz discusses the matter with his brother and the elders of the community. His brother is willing to take the land belonging to Mahlon but is not willing to redeem Ruth. Boaz is prepared to do both and with a symbolic removal and handing over of his sandal, he asks the assembled elders to witness and thereby formalize this exchange (cf. Lev 25:25 and Ruth 4:1-12).

Theologically, several themes are worth noting. Some of the force of the story is hidden in the names, for example, Ruth means 'friend' and her poor husband Mahlon's name means 'sick'. Another key thread seems to be the connection with the important family tree line of David. Naomi's husband was called Elimelech, meaning 'My God is my king' which is significant since Ruth marries Boaz who is the father of Obed, and 'Obed of Jesse, and Jesse of David' (4:22). It is for this reason that traditionally the book has been dated sometime around David's reign, perhaps 900 BCE. Intriguingly, other scholars note that the presence of Ruth's 'foreign blood' in the royal line seems clean contrary to the 'ethnic cleansing' ideas present in Ezra which demanded that non-Jewish wives be dismissed by the people (e.g. Claasens, 2012, p. 672). Their argument is that Ruth was precisely written as a lyrical response to Ezra which would place the text sometime after 500 BCE. In effect, Ruth is presented as a 'foreign Jewess', a convert to Judaism and like the positive view of the Persian King Cyrus, evidence that the Judean world view was not simplistically xenophobic.

i) *Ketubim* – triumph of the weak

The dominant role of women in the story and the enduring theme of *hesed*, 'loving kindness', are such strong features that Ruth has attracted considerable attention as another example of the often overlooked 'feminine side' of the biblical writings. The Book of Esther is similarly woven around a female character and despite its royal setting, her situation has echoes of that of Naomi and Ruth. An exiled Hebrew orphan in Persia raised by her Uncle Mordechai, Esther's situation is transformed when she wins what is effectively a beauty contest to be the wife of the King (Esth 2:17). Her status then becomes perilous when a persecution of all the Jews in the Empire is authorized by a wicked dignitary named Haman, who is infuriated by the refusal of her beloved uncle to offer him homage (3:2). Urging her kinfolk to fast and pray (4:16), Esther uses all her alluring charm to win the King round and in a dramatic about turn of fortunes, the persecution is mitigated, Haman is executed and Mordechai ultimately achieves high office in the King's own court (7:1-8:17).

This vivid story is hard to pin down in 'real-time' history since there is no record of such events in the Persian annals. One school of thought identifies the origin of this story as a Hebrew retelling of an ancient Babylonian myth concerning the Goddess Ishtar (Esther) and Marduk (Mordechai). More common opinion places this excerpt of writings after the exile, and possibly much later, since the picture presented is of a vulnerable but beautiful Jewess remaining faithful in the face of fierce persecution which could equally fit the Greek period.

The Book of Daniel betrays a similar theme and although it is classed among the prophetic books in Christian bibles, it is placed among the 'writings' in the Hebrew collection. The series of adventures which the young man Daniel goes on are set in the courts of the Kings of Babylon. Daniel, whose name means 'God is my strength', is wise beyond his years and like the young Joseph in the court of Pharaoh, he constantly outwits the native courtiers, prophets, soothsayers and magicians. Daniel is famous for surviving the lion's den (6:1-28) and his fearless witness in the face of mighty power is the repeated theme.

Daniel, too, is hard to pin down, and although more traditional scholarship is happy to place these gripping stories in the exilic period of history, it is likely that Babylon is being used in Daniel as a symbol of *any* oppressive power. The common consensus then is that his works belong to a later period, perhaps even as late as 150 BCE when Israel-Judah was under the heel of Greek oppression and *apocalyptic* literature was becoming a favoured form of theologizing.

j) *Ketubim* and apocalyptic

Apocalyptic writings are 'un-veiling' or 'revealing' literature. They take the 'triumph of the weak' literature seen in Ruth and Esther to a different level. Such writings make much use of symbols and fantastical imagery. They are deliberately cosmic, describing a wild unseen world of angels, demons and mysterious powers as the secret background which explains the tribulations of the faithful in the seen world. Much of Daniel fits this pattern as it contains vivid examples of symbolic oracles and supernatural activity and in this apocalyptic vein, he contributes two passages which will become very significant for Christian Theology. The first refers to a cosmic Son of Man – the name by which Jesus referred to himself:

> I watched in the night visions, I saw one like a son of man coming with the clouds of heaven. And he came to the Ancient One and was presented before him. To him was given dominion and glory and kingship, that all peoples, nations, and languages should serve him. His dominion is an everlasting dominion that shall not pass away, and his kingship is one that shall never be destroyed. (Dan 7:12-14)

In another passage, Daniel deals with resurrection themes – again, a central part of the Christian proclamation.

> At that time Michael, the great prince, the protector of your people, shall arise. There shall be a time of anguish, such as has never occurred since nations first came into existence. But at that time your people shall be delivered, everyone who is found written in the book. Many of those who sleep in the dust of the earth shall awake, some to everlasting life, and some to shame and everlasting contempt. Those who are wise shall shine like the brightness of the sky, and those who lead many to righteousness, like the stars for ever and ever. (Dan 12:1-3)

Imagining a life after death as reward for the righteous and vindication for those denied justice in their lifetimes was not the most common theological motif in the biblical tradition. An example is the prayer of Hezekiah, one of the few virtuous kings of the Deuteronomist's history (Isa 38:10-20, especially verse 18). Though this will merit further discussion later, death was commonly seen as a land of shadows inhabited by shadows, twilight multiplied by twilight with all the excitement of an empty underground car park. Apocalyptic literature began to change all that and fascination with figures from Israel's past who had apparently not died or had disappeared also gathered momentum (cf. Enoch [Gen 5:24], Melchizedek, [Gen 14:18-20], Elijah [2 Kings 2:12]). To be sure, the earlier prophetic tradition did not lack for vivid symbolism, cosmic imagery or revivification in the power of the Spirit (cf. Ezek 1:1-28; 37:1-15). Nevertheless, there are cogent arguments that particular colonial actions in this period help to explain the preponderance of this literature in the centuries prior to the Jesus event and that the notion of wise men as 'seers' helped to connect apocalyptic with the *ketubim* (cf. Knibb, 2009).

k) Colonization and messianic expectation

The conquests of Alexander the Great had brought Greek culture to a vast swathe of the Mediterranean and Near Eastern lands. As Greek language and thought became accordingly diffused, so certain Greek practices were destined to cause conflict in parts of the Empire. For example, while the Greek cult of the body may have led to increased fitness among Judean youths, the tradition of doing exercises in the nude was offensive to the locals, a matter made worse by the practice of attempting to reverse circumcision in order to conform (1 Macc 1:15).

Whatever the insults or risks associated with ancient plastic surgery (the mind boggles), a more serious concern for the Jewish faithful was the direct interference with the cult of YHWH in general and the Temple in particular. Some of the local rulers who had charge of Judea were notorious, and none more so than Antiochus Epiphanes IV. Shedding 'much blood' and speaking 'with arrogance', he desecrated the Temple by erecting statues of Zeus and Aphrodite in the sanctuary (1 Macc 1:10-64). Politically, these abominations in the House of God caused outright rebellion among a section of the population led by Judas Maccabeus and his insurgent army (1 Macc 3-5). Theologically, it seems reasonable to suppose they helped generate the religious response typified by the defiant tone of apocalyptic literature, which, as we shall show in the next chapter, began to crystallize into a hope that God would decisively enter into Israel's history once more.

That this is the presumed Theology of the Christian Bible is evidenced by the situating of the *Nebi'im* – the Prophetic books (including Daniel) at the end of the Old Testament instead of the *Ketubim* – the Writings which complete the Hebrew scriptures (cf. Myers and Rogerson, 1997, pp. 305–15). In so doing, Christian Theology places a prophecy from Malachi concerning the return of Elijah as the last oracle. Elijah was a popular figure in apocalyptic writings since he had disappeared in a whirlwind rather than died (2 Kings 2:12). In the oracle of Malachi, Elijah is the messenger who would herald judgement and reconciliation of the people in the great Day of the Lord.

> I will send you the prophet Elijah before the great and terrible day of the Lord comes. He will turn the hearts of parents to their children and the hearts of children to their parents, so that I will not come and strike the land with a curse. (Mal 4:5-6)

Ultimately, this oracle proves the link with the Gospel writers who all have reference to an Elijah figure in the early stages. Recast as John the Baptist, the Elijah figure is the herald of the decisive intervention of YHWH, the 'apocalypse', the 'unveiling' of God in the image of man – the 'Messiah' or 'Christ event' of Jesus the Nazarene.

Summary

The Wisdom writings contain a range of compositions which cover the experience of the faithful of YHWH in their prayer, their thinking, their love, their joy, their sorrow. Collated and collected during the Second Temple period following the Exile, they have the mark of priestly fingerprints in their retelling of the story of Israel-Judah. There is a directness to the language of the Psalms, Proverbs, Job and especially the somewhat cynical Qoheleth. The Song of Songs is not for the faint-hearted either and for different reasons, neither are the visions of Daniel. Especially significant for the New Testament are the personifications of Wisdom in Proverbs 8 and the 'Son of Man' vision in Daniel 7. Another world of theological speculation opens up in these writings, from which the expected Messiah will come.

Part 3
Theology of the Jesus Event

2. The New Testament World

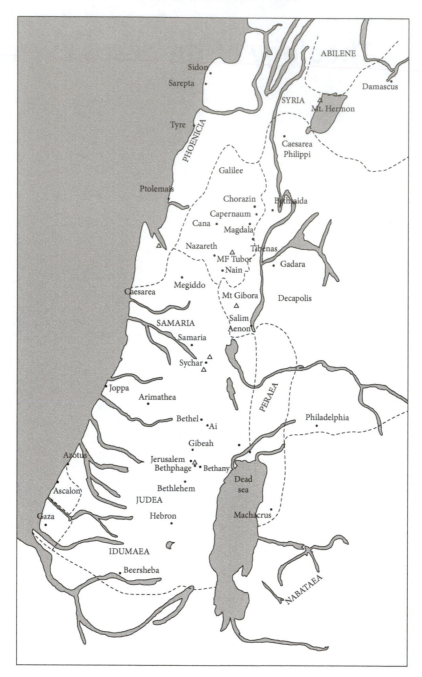

6

Gospels: Theology of Jesus as Messiah

The Gospels are theological reflections on the person or 'event' of Jesus of Nazareth written, so that people may believe that God has definitively interrupted history for the good of humanity. If the original Creation story begins with a Spirit or God-storm in the darkness (Gen 1:3), the Gospels are the equivalent of a theological earthquake. Familiarity with them can make them appear tame, but both their content and their context are decidedly 'edgy.' All begin differently but the entry point for each Gospel into the public life of Jesus is the ministry of the wild-man herald, John the Witness-Baptizer, whose water ritual remains the entry point into Christianity today. The four canonical Gospels intentionally differ in their style and their theological focus, in part because of the different sources available to their authors and in part because of their different audiences. Interpreting the words and deeds of Jesus in the vocabulary of their religious tradition, the Gospel writers identify Jesus as the Messiah, the Son of Man and Son of God.

a) Theology on the edge

Rehearsing some of the key theological components of Israelite-Judean faith that emerged over the two-thousand years or so of reflection depicted in the Bible from the time of Abraham, we might identify the following as being essential background to an analysis of the Gospels. Hebrew theologians had come to understand themselves as descendants of the twelve tribes belonging to YHWH the One God. While YHWH is the creator of all things and has sovereignty over the cosmos, humanity is made in God's image and is tasked with a custodial role on earth. YHWH is in a covenant of mutual commitment with Israel and has endowed the Law through Moses as guidance for right living, which includes concern for the poor. This covenant relationship is also expressed in household ritual and especially in worship at the Temple in Jerusalem where YHWH dwells on earth. YHWH is not disinterested in the fortunes of Israel. On the contrary, YHWH is a God who will interrupt history if necessary to discipline his people for their behaviour or to deliver them from their enemies.

And this was the rub. After five hundred years of being under the control of a series of powerful enemies there seemed to be no salvation, no saviour, no *yeshua* available. While the office of the High Priest did retain important religious authority, there was no David to conquer the colonial Goliath of Rome. There was no Elijah to confront the feckless puppet monarchs who governed the land on behalf of Caesar. There was no Day of the Lord to signal the end of domination by foreigners and the vindication of Israel by God, a day when living waters would flow from Jerusalem and the Lord would be king over the whole earth (Zech 14:8-9).

In these circumstances, theological imagination seems to have flourished. An example would be *The Similitudes of Enoch* which take their cue from Gen 5:24, which says 'Enoch walked with God; then he was no more, because God took him'. The mysterious nature of Enoch's non-dying and centuries of speculation ultimately yield the wondrous imagery of *The Similitudes* which include a cluster of titles that will resonate through the Gospels: The 'Righteous One' (1 Enoch 38:2), an enthroned 'Elect One' (1 Enoch 45:3) and a 'Messiah' who is a 'Son of Man' and 'pre-existent' (1 Enoch 48:2-6). This kind of super-hero goes beyond the normal depiction of leaders from Israel's past such as Moses, David or Joshua, but quite how such titles came to be apportioned to a carpenter from Nazareth can only be explained by the theological revolution-whirlwind that followed the Jesus event.

b) Qumran and messianic expectation

So what were the first signs of this Jesus-Theology storm? Well, if confirmation were needed that a kind of edgy cosmic theologizing was present at the time of Jesus, then the discovery of a library of texts at Qumran, on the margins of the Judean desert, has provided ample evidence. The general consensus is that these scrolls were collected by Jewish believers known as Essenes – 'pious ones' or 'healers' who lived a common life akin to the monasteries and convents of the later Christian tradition. They seem to have flourished in the years between 150 BCE–150 CE and though they never expanded beyond Palestine, they may have numbered as many as 4000 at the time of Jesus. While it is difficult to identify with any certainty exactly when particular texts were written, there is no doubt that this community had a strong expectation of God's imminent intervention. God would interrupt history through the agency of one or more 'messiahs' to effect the deliverance of the people.

As an example, a scroll from the first cave links all three 'power' motifs of messiahship by envisioning the coming of a prophet, along with priestly and kingly anointed ones (1QS 9:10-11). Another comprises a commentary on the blessings which Jacob imparted to his sons which promises that the 'sceptre (i.e. rule) shall come from Judah' (Gen 49:10). It speaks of 'The coming of the righteous Messiah, the Scion of David. For to him and his offspring are given the covenant of kingship over his people for everlasting generations' (4Q252 6:3-4). Yet even this text has not excited as much interest as the following extract taken from what has become known as Qumran's 'Messianic Apocalypse':

> For the heavens and the earth will listen to His Messiah and all that is in them will not swerve away from the commandments of the holy ones. Be strengthened in his service all you who seek the Lord! Shall you not find the Lord in this all you who hope in your hearts? For the Lord will seek out pious ones, and righteous ones He shall call by name. Over afflicted ones shall His Spirit hover, and faithful ones He shall renew with His power. He shall honour the pious on a throne of eternal kingship, freeing prisoners, giving sight to the blind, straightening up those bent over. For ever will I cling to those who hope, and with steadfast love He shall recompense; the fruit of a good deed will be delayed for no one. Wondrous things such as have never been before will the Lord do just as He said. For He shall heal the wounded, revive the dead, and proclaim good news to the afflicted; the poor He shall satiate, the uprooted He shall guide and on the hungry He shall bestow riches; and the intelligent, and all of them, shall be like holy ones. (4Q521 2 ii 4:1-14 see Fitzmyer, 2007, p. 96)

This text has so many Gospel echoes that it is difficult not to surmise some connection between the two (cf. Matt 11:1-19, Luke 7:18-30). Such parallels have led to speculation that the disciple group may have originated at Qumran and that maybe Jesus himself was an Essene or at least spent some time there. Certainly from the evidence of this text it would appear that the Gospel writers were at least familiar with the kind of teachings shared by this desert community. And if we are to look for a personal connection, it is intriguing that Matthew and Luke's version of this text is presented as Jesus' response to a question from someone he undeniably did spend time with – John the Baptizer.

c) John the Baptizer

Just as the entry point for Christian belonging is marked by Baptism, so the entry point for the proclamation of the Gospel is marked by each evangelist with reference to John the Baptist (Matt 3:1-6, Mark 1:2-6, Luke 3:1-6, John 1:19-23). This intriguing figure is presented in all four Gospels as a man on the edge, a man from the wilderness with a rigorous ascetic lifestyle. His trademark activity is fiery preaching followed by an invitation to a ritual drenching, an immersion of individuals in the Jordan River as an act of cleansing from their sin. Since elaborate water rituals were part of the pattern of community living at Qumran, and since the desert context and content of John's preaching also fit their geography and world-view, it is commonly held that the Baptist was either an Essene or at least strongly influenced by that tradition.

The Gospels unanimously identify John as a herald whose task is to announce the Messiah – each of them identify him as a voice 'cry[ing] out in the wilderness, "Prepare the way of the Lord"' (cf. Matt 3:3, Mark 1:3, Luke 3:4, John 1:23 and Isa 40:3). They also unanimously contend that something happened in the context of John's baptismal ministry which is decisive in the life of Jesus. This baptismal context identifies Jesus as *the* Chosen One revealing Father, Son and Spirit in the breaking of the waters (Matt 3:13-17, Mark 1:9-11, Luke 3:21-22 cf. John 1:33-34). Theologically these accounts echo the dawn of a new creation (cf. Gen 1:1) and the threefold symbolism marks a development in the understanding of God as triune – 'Trinity'. More modestly, however, since all the Gospels note that the arrest of John and his imprisonment is a trigger for Jesus' own mission and ministry, it may also indicate that Jesus was in fact a disciple of John and that he undertook to carry on the work of the Baptizer once the authorities had intervened (Matt 4:12, Mark 1:14, Luke 3:19-20, John 3:24).

While each Gospel holds to these core recollections of the Baptist, they do differ slightly in detail. Matthew and Mark remark on John's clothing of camel hair and his unusual diet of locusts and wild honey (cf. Matt 3:1-12, Mark 1:1-8). This imagery connects John with Elijah, the most dynamic of all the ancient prophets who did not experience death, like Enoch, and was taken from earth directly by God (2 Kings 1:8; 2:1-12). As noted above, in what are effectively the last words of the Old Testament prophets, Malachi had prophesied Elijah would return to prepare the people for the Day of the Lord (Mal 4:5). Luke takes a different tack and presents the reader with an account of John's birth and infancy identifying him as a descendent of the priestly line of Aaron and herald of Jesus, even as an unborn child leaping in the womb of his mother Elizabeth (Luke 1:1-45). The Fourth Gospel gives the strongest hint of Jesus and the Baptist working together since the first disciples seem to be drawn from John's circle while continuing to be actively engaged in the work of baptizing (John 1:19-51; 4:1-4).

The figure of John the Baptist is so familiar to us through scripture, art, theatre and film that the impact, urgency and danger of his edgy message can be lost. This man was pure trouble. By announcing that a *kairos* moment, a special 'appointed time' had arrived, he was snapping the people out of any *chronos*, tick-tock 'business as usual' slumber. The Day of the Lord is at hand – get ready – because the judgement is going to be fierce as a firestorm, a thrasher harvest, a permanent blaze. John was announcing all this without any official permission from the religious authorities in Jerusalem and if his message was problematic to them, his methods were even more so. Forgiveness of sins in Judah had become big business since it was linked to making the appropriate sacrifice in the Temple. This involved changing normal money into Temple money with a commission charge, buying an approved creature and paying for the services of the priest. Throwing forgiveness around like water was not good news for their vested interests. To make matters worse, John also criticized the marital arrangements of Herod Antipas, one of three puppet kings acting as local leaders under the Roman colonial governor Pontius Pilate, and was consequently imprisoned. From prison, the Gospels recount that he made enquiries regarding Jesus:

> "Are you the one who is to come, or are we to wait for another?" When the men had come to him, they said, 'John the Baptist has sent us to you to ask, "Are you the one who is to come, or are we to wait for another?"' Jesus had just then

cured many people of diseases, plagues, and evil spirits, and had given sight to many who were blind. And he answered them, "Go and tell John what you have seen and heard: the blind receive their sight, the lame walk, the lepers are cleansed, the deaf hear, the dead are raised, the poor have good news brought to them." (Luke 7:19-22)

In a pattern repeated in the life of Jesus (and indeed throughout history), by irritating both the political and religious authorities, John placed his life in mortal danger. During a night of revelry, Herod makes an ill-judged public promise to his step-daughter, whereupon his wife, whose status John has threatened, takes the opportunity to demand the Baptist's head on a platter. Herod reluctantly acquiesces, but it is sobering to think that someone designated as 'Elijah' and the 'greatest of the prophets' was ultimately beheaded because of an impressive lap-dance (Matt 11:11-12;14:1-12).

d) The Gospels of Christ

In theological narrative, the role John the Baptist fulfils in all the Gospels is to set the stage for the revelation that Jesus *is* the Anointed One, the promised Messiah. Rendered as 'Christ' in Greek, this appellation is so frequent throughout the New Testament that it almost functions as a surname. As we have seen, however, it is far from a banal identification of just another Nazarene. In the theological context of the time, it was a designation of dramatic political, prophetic and religious significance which included cosmic as well as earthly connotations.

It is important to emphasize that with regard to Jesus' messiahship, the Gospels are not neutral documents. On the contrary, as the writer of the Fourth Gospel makes explicit – 'these things are written so that you might believe' (John 20:31). This admission by the writer does not imply that the events they describe are untrue, only that the way they present and interpret these events constitute four narratives designed to lead the listener to a theological conclusion. The Gospels are designed to answer the key question posed at the time by the people, disciples, Pharisees, priests, leaders and imperial authorities: 'Who is this Man?' Moreover, since *Euangelion,* or 'Good News' was a term used for announcements such as the crowning of an emperor, designation of the Jesus stories as 'Gospel' underlined that for Christians, this message had more than the future of an empire as its concern.

Honest acknowledgement that each Gospel exhibits a deliberate theological patterning of the life of Jesus should not lead their central figure to be dismissed as purely imaginary. To be sure, external evidence for the Gospels is limited but this should be no surprise given that Palestine was hardly the central concern for most Roman historians who first begin to remark on the activities of Jesus' followers around 60 CE. The main corroboration of the life of Jesus available from what might be called a contemporary and neutral point of view comes from a short paragraph in the account by Josephus on the Jewish War of 70 CE:

> At this time there was a wise man who was called Jesus, and his conduct was good, and he was known to be virtuous. And many people from among the Jews and the other nations became his disciples. Pilate condemned him to be crucified and to die. And those who had become his disciples did not abandon their loyalty to him. They reported that he had appeared to them three days after his crucifixion, and that he was alive. Accordingly they believed that he was the Messiah, concerning whom the Prophets have recounted wonders. (Pines, 1971, p. 69)

While versions of this manuscript differ in detail, they do offer confirmation of the basic historicity of Jesus as a prophetic figure who gathered followers that believed in his messianic claims. To get much beyond this on a purely historical basis is difficult. Just as there is an entire biblical industry dedicated to the 'Quest for the Historical Israel', there is an even more extended debate generated by the 'Quest for the Historical Jesus' (cf. Keith and Hurtado, 2011). In short, both quests attempt to get behind the biblical text to identify the core facts of the events recounted, and some of the detective work can be fascinating. That said, those beginning theological study should be aware that tides of opinion do rather ebb and flow in these matters. For example, although the event of the Exodus is much more contested nowadays (Davies, 2004, pp. 23–40), more store is set by the 'eyewitness' nature of the Gospel claims than would have been considered a generation ago (cf. Bauckham, 2006 with Bultmann, 1951).

e) One Gospel, four flavours

To some extent, the doubt, debate and drama of the historical questions act as a tasty 'starter' for the flavours of the main dish – the Gospels themselves. The accounts of Matthew, Mark, Luke and John which eventually became the standard versions of the life of Jesus were primarily written in order to be heard in gatherings of the Christian assembly. Set directly beside each other as a modern critic is minded to do, their lives of Jesus do yield inconsistencies of detail and content, such as *The Sermon on the Mount* in Matthew seems to be *The Sermon on the Plain* in Luke and is definitely not as long. Theologically it might have been easier to have had a single approved official biography. In the early Church, there was an attempt to write such a composite Gospel – Tatian's *Diatessaron,* but it never really caught on precisely because it inevitably diluted the different theological colours of the four evangelists and the particular ways they interpreted and identified Jesus. The ancient Church clearly preferred the idea of having more than one flavour.

Matthew is strong on scriptural references, which fits with the tradition that he was writing for a mainly Jewish audience who would be familiar with the quotations used in his argument. Coherent with this, early tradition suggests the original language of the Gospel was Aramaic, the Hebrew-derived language of the people at the time of Jesus. Although this theory is generally doubted today, the 'five-fold' structure of the work does lead to a general consensus that Matthew is offering an alternative to the Torah and that its *Sitz im Leben* – its 'life context' – is a Jewish community. The question of Jesus' identity is at the centre of his work (16:13-20) where it is linked with Peter and the leadership of twelve new tribes, a new chosen people, the *Church* which will baptize all nations.

By contrast, Mark is a high-speed Gospel tumbling from one incident to another, big on miracles rather than speeches. Early tradition attributed this Gospel to the preaching of Peter in Rome which would perhaps explain its 'live-performance/highlights programme' style. Unlike Matthew with its studied precision, the text is in such a hurry it appears to attribute a quote from Malachi to Isaiah right at the start (Mark 1:2) and the incidents of the first chapters are action packed, full of *immediatelys* and *amazements.* A strong theme running through Mark is the slow-wittedness of the disciples who fail to understand the mission of Jesus and ultimately desert him. By highlighting 'discipleship failure', the purpose may have been to encourage those listening to do the opposite – to believe and to have courage. Understood in this way, it may well be that the 'lived context' was a time of persecution whether in the early years of the Jesus movement or later when it had attracted the disapproval of Imperial Rome.

Luke's version on the other hand is in two parts, the Gospel events surrounding Jesus including his identification as the Messiah (9:18-21) and the experience of the early Christian Church in the Acts of the Apostles. He avowedly sets out to compose an 'orderly account' and addresses his work to Theophilus. This could be an individual, but since it literally means 'God-friend', it may well mean that it is deliberately open-ended and addressed to anyone seeking God. In support of this view, Luke's writings vividly depict the spread of the Good News beyond the ethnic, religious and geographical boundaries of the chosen people to include Jew and Gentile alike. The Acts of the Apostles recounts the theological disputes caused by the messianic understanding of Jesus between Paul and his co-religionists across the synagogues of Asia Minor.

The fourth, more intimate and symbolic account attributed to John is very different to the other three, which are called 'syn-optic' – 'same view' – Gospels. After a spectacularly cosmic prologue rich in scriptural and philosophical allusions, the writer shapes the account of Jesus' ministry around seven distinct miracles or 'signs'. Traditionally thought to have been written late in life by John at Ephesus, the presentation of Jesus' inner life is far more developed and his use of 'I AM' sayings make an explicit connection between his identity and the revelation of God to Moses in Ex 3:14. John's Gospel is also sensitive to the consequences of identifying Jesus as Messiah and from the outset the tensions between traditional Jewish belief and the followers of Jesus are highlighted (1:11; 41). Taken together, these considerations suggest a *Sitz im Leben/*'life context' of a later period when those calling themselves Christians had developed clearly distinct theological views and were no longer welcome in the traditional worship of the Jewish synagogue.

While I have lived long enough to enjoy reading scholarly claims that Matthew, Luke and even parts of John constitute the first Gospel, the more widely held view at the moment is that Mark was written first and was woven together by Matthew and Luke with a 'sayings' document called 'Q' along with material proper to themselves. The main strength of this argument is that it helps explain many of the commonalities between these 'synoptic'– 'same view' Gospels and conforms to a natural intuition that the simpler Gospel of Mark (it lacks infancy and extended apparition accounts) was developed by the more structured syntheses of Matthew and Luke. The main weakness is that 'Q' remains a hypothetical document of which there is no manuscript evidence. Moreover, commonalities and discrepancies between the Gospels can be just as easily explained if Matthew used Mark and both were subsequently consulted by Luke, or even that Mark was written as an abridged version.

Although I'd prefer to call it 'puzzle' or 'conundrum', this dilemma is called the *Synoptic problem* which gives off a needlessly negative vibe. It remains a fascinating question for biblical scholars and so too does the exact dating of the finished Gospel texts. The argument for a dating late in the first century and as far as 120 CE essentially picks up on the notion that a developed sense of Jesus as Christ and Son of God must have taken a long time to evolve and that the Gospels make allusions to the Fall of Jerusalem in 70 CE. Equally articulate are those who point out that since St Paul's letters (c.50–60 CE) demonstrate a highly developed sense of Jesus as Christ and Son of God, there is no need to presume a late date for the Gospels. Moreover, the destruction of Jerusalem is rather poorly pre-figured in the texts – unthinkable if the Jesus movement was engaged in a propaganda battle with more traditional Judaism. Like many scriptural debates, both have prompted much classic but as yet inconclusive detective work. However, there is some consolation for certainty seekers since no one disputes the 'finished product' is a fourfold identification of Jesus as Messiah – and that is the theological question at the centre of this enquiry.

f) Messiah as title

Without being trite, it is yet another paradox that while the proclamation of Jesus as the Messiah is at the root of the 'Good News', it is clear that for the bearer of that title, messiahship was *bad* news and little short of a death sentence. This perhaps explains the tension which can be detected within the Gospel testimony. On the one hand, all four evangelists articulate their understanding of the Jesus event precisely in order to demonstrate the truth of his messiahship. On the other, they also record Jesus' reluctance to acknowledge his identity as the Christ (the 'Messianic Secret'), not surprisingly both in the general context of the time and in particular following the execution of John the Baptist, his friend, kinsman and mentor.

The traditional prophetic, priestly and kingly attributes of messiahship suffuse even what many think is the earliest Gospel. In Mark, Jesus is a prophetic figure preaching conversion (1:15), gathering disciples (1:16-20), working signs (1:28) and prophetic actions (11:15-19). Jesus is identified as a prophet by Herod (6:16), and again in the trial accounts (14:65). Priestly actions are typified in Jesus' forgiveness of sins, which causes scandal (2:1-12), his modifying of cherished religious teachings and practices (7:1ff) and most shockingly in his identification with the Temple during the trial (14:58). To be Temple was to be the interface between God and humanity rendering the traditional sacrifices and actions of the Levitical priesthood irrelevant. Last but not least, the heart of Jesus' message was the proclamation of a 'Kingdom of God' (1:14-15). As a slogan it could not fail to attract attention among an oppressed people with a tradition of insurgency. As a rallying call it could not fail to cause concern among politically vested interests. Ultimately, Mark has the kingship of Jesus as a key facet of the trial in the minds of the soldiers and Pilate himself (15:2, 16-20; 26). To repeat – messiahship was a threat to vested interests. 'Christ' was not the comfortable surname of a Nazarene carpenter, it was the title that threatened *metanoia* – a word that in current Christianity means 'Repent!' (add your own gloom), but would probably be more accurately translated in context as 'Think Differently!' (add your own dazzle).

Whatever Jesus was accused of and whatever he was called by others, the title he would appear to have applied to himself was *ho huios tou anthrōpou* – 'the Son of Man'. This enigmatic term resonates in several different ways. At base, it refers to the clod-like condition of any 'human one', 'ordinary guy', 'man like me', 'someone in my situation'. On the other hand, it appears that Jesus may have connected this title with very specific aspects of his ministry. For example, it seems to be explicitly linked with his 'earthly' work (Mark 2:10 and Luke 9:43-5) and his imminent suffering (Mark 8:31). There are also hints that 'Son of Man' may have been part of Jesus' and/or the disciples' understanding of the resurrection and the second coming (cf. Mark 8:38; 9:9), which in turn resonates with the famous messianic passage from Daniel:

> As I watched in the night visions, I saw one like a son of man coming with the clouds of heaven. And he came to the Ancient One and was presented before him. To him was given dominion and glory and kingship that all peoples, nations, and languages should serve him. His dominion is an everlasting dominion that shall not pass away, and his kingship is one that shall never be destroyed. (Dan 7:13-14)

Since Acts 7:55-6, Rev 1:13 and 14:14 explicitly make this connection, there is little doubt that *ho huios tou anthrōpou* could be understood in this majestic cosmic sense. So which do we choose – the humble sense or the cosmic sense? Once more we are faced with a classic Christian paradox since it is perhaps 'both/and' not 'either/or'. Jesus may have deliberately chosen this name as a *double entendre* identifying himself with everyman, but also with the heavenly man and leaving his listeners to work it out for themselves.

Meanwhile, the fact that the one whom Christianity prefers to call Son of God preferred to call himself Son of Man is just another sweet paradox of biblical study. Although there are arguments that the title 'Son of God' emerged only after the events depicted in the Gospels, the received text of Mark 1:1 announces itself with 'The beginning of the good news of Jesus Christ, the Son of God' and is content at later points to confirm this appellation (5:7, 8:29, 14:61). At one level, the *huiou theou* of Mark 1:1 can simply mean 'divinely originated male' and not directly imply physical procreation. After all, cross-breed heavenly/earthly heroes were part of ancient Hebrew as well as Greek and Roman mythologies (Gen 6:4). That said, Matthew and Lukes' infancy narratives explicitly make the claim of sacred procreation by the action of the Holy Spirit (Matt 1:18-2.12 and Luke 1:35) and John's Gospel if anything takes matters further with the pre-existent only Son of God becoming flesh (1:14-18) and being identified as such by John the Baptist (1:34).

If we recall that the rallying cry of Judaism unto this day begins 'Hear O Israel, the Lord our God is One' (Deut 6:4), it is unsurprising that identifying a human as the physical Son of God would prove divisive. In some ways this is the fork in the road which sends Judaism (and later, Islam) in a different direction to the Christian theological path. Yet in a further twist, the Christian picture of messiahship which began rooted in power archetypes becomes transformed almost beyond recognition – even disfigured – by the powerlessness of the 'Suffering Servant'.

g) Messiah as servant

Written around the time of the Exile in Babylon, the Songs of the '*Ebed YHWH* (Servant of YHWH) formed part of a series of oracles from 'Deutero' or 'Second Phase' Isaiah. Traditionally they were interpreted as representative either of a heroic prophetic individual in the mould of Jeremiah, or more usually as representative of the collective people – Israel, called to endure hardship with steadfast fidelity in the hope of vindication. The depiction of the so-called Fourth Song is particularly vivid and worth quoting at length:

> See, my servant shall prosper; he shall be exalted and lifted up, and shall be very high. Just as there were many who were astonished at him – so marred was his appearance, beyond human semblance, and his form beyond that of mortals – so he shall startle many nations; kings shall shut their mouths because of him; for that which had not been told them they shall see, and that which they had not heard they shall contemplate. Who has believed what we have heard? And to whom has the arm of the Lord been revealed?

> For he grew up before Him like a young plant, and like a root out of dry ground; he had no form or majesty that we should look at him, nothing in his appearance that we should desire him. He was despised and rejected by others; a man of suffering and acquainted with infirmity; and as one from whom others hide their faces he was despised, and we held him of no account.

> Surely he has borne our infirmities and carried our diseases; yet we accounted him stricken, struck down by God, and afflicted. But he was wounded for our transgressions, crushed for our iniquities; upon him was the punishment that made us whole and by his bruises we are healed. All we like sheep have gone astray; we have all turned to our own way, and the Lord has laid on him the iniquity of us all.

> He was oppressed, and he was afflicted yet he did not open his mouth; like a lamb that is led to the slaughter, and like a sheep that before its shearers is silent, so he

did not open his mouth. By a perversion of justice he was taken away. Who could have imagined his future? For he was cut off from the land of the living, stricken for the transgression of my people. They made his grave with the wicked and his tomb with the rich, although he had done no violence, and there was no deceit in his mouth.

Yet it was the will of the Lord to crush him with pain. When you make his life an offering for sin, he shall see his offspring, and shall prolong his days; through him the will of the Lord shall prosper. Out of his anguish he shall see light; he shall find satisfaction through his knowledge. The righteous one, my servant, shall make many righteous, and he shall bear their iniquities. Therefore I will allot him a portion with the great, and he shall divide the spoil with the strong, because he poured out himself to death, and was numbered with the transgressors; yet he bore the sin of many, and made intercession for the transgressors.

(Isa 52:13-53:12)

In the context of the Jesus-event, early Christians applied these moving passages to the events of Good Friday with the theological result that a Messiah was proclaimed 'who was destined to suffer' (Luke 24:26). Clean contrary to the classic messianic expectations where humiliating defeat was not part of the picture, Christianity found itself preaching the foolishness of a crucified Christ (cf. Acts 8:26-40). As Paul notes, this was a stumbling block for Jews and folly for non-Jews, in other words, not particularly attractive to anyone (1 Cor 1:22-25). Despite this awkwardness, the power of the servant motif not only enabled the disciples to make theological sense of a suffering Messiah, it also helped them to make sense of the central message of Jesus' preaching – the paradox of an upside-down Kingdom.

Summary

At the risk of simplifying the theological landscape of Judea at the time of Jesus, there is ample evidence from apocalyptic and 'inter-testamental' literature that there was a confused but convinced expectation that God would interrupt history and liberate the chosen people through the agency of a Messiah. This is exemplified in the religious lifestyle and literature of the Essene community at Qumran and by the activity of John the Baptizer which seems to act as a trigger for the public ministry of Jesus. The four accounts of Jesus' life or 'Gospels' of Jesus, though differing both in style and detail, all concur and identify him as the Messiah, the Christ, the Anointed One of God. As stylized, theological biographies, they present Jesus in vocabulary drawn from scriptural messianic heritage to provide evidence that Jesus fulfils the prophetic, priestly and kingly expectations which the composite understanding of 'anointing' had come to express. Though 'The Anointed One' or 'Christ' is the core title accorded Jesus, paradox abounds in his self-presentation as 'Son of Man', his Gospel identification as 'Son of God' and the understanding of power expressed in the passion narratives which clearly connect his suffering with the 'Ebed YHWH of Isa 52:13-53:12.

7

The Theology of the Kingdom

The previous chapter has demonstrated that the titles ascribed to Jesus are already theologically rich, pointing to his messiahship, uniqueness and divine origin even in the theo-logic of Mark, commonly regarded as the earliest of the Gospel writers. In that light, we might reasonably ask what on earth did he say and do to merit this acclaim? Obviously the few chapters available to us do not permit the pursuit of every aspect of his life or teaching. Instead the following will attempt to examine the 'Kingdom of God' as the central motif of his preaching in the synoptic Gospel accounts before turning to the next chapter on the controversial events of his last days.

a) The preaching of the Kingdom

In a decision that might not have impacted too greatly on the rest of the Christian Church, the late Pope John Paul II revolutionized centuries of practice and modified the mysteries of the Rosary, one of the most familiar prayers in the Catholic tradition. The Rosary hitherto had been a fifteen-part meditation on the infancy, the passion and the post-resurrection events in the drama of Jesus. To these, John Paul II added five more key meditations from the life of Christ, at the heart of which he placed 'The Proclamation of the Kingdom'. In biblical terms, this could not be a better theme to emphasize since 'The Kingdom' is used over ninety times by Jesus in the Synoptics and is at the centre of his preaching.

Yet this is the beginning of the intrigue. While a convincing argument can be made that the *basilea tou theou* (the Kingdom of God) *is* the *eu-angelion*, 'the Good News', its nature is far more difficult to determine. Indeed, the 'What?' 'Where?' 'When?' and 'How come?' questions of the disciples still puzzle biblical scholars and the Christian faithful of today.

As a first distinction it might be noted that Matthew tends to use 'Kingdom of Heaven' rather than the 'Kingdom of God' favoured by Mark and Luke. With heaven being the 'place of the presence of God', the meaning can be understood as the same and it may be just linguistic preference to avoid over-use of the divine name on the part of Matthew. Kingdom preaching on the part of Jesus follows on directly from John the Baptist, who likewise preached the coming of a new reality. John's reported words in Matt 3:1 mirror those of Mark's depiction of Jesus, who came to Galilee proclaiming the Good News of God and saying: 'The time is fulfilled and the Kingdom of God has come near. Repent and believe the good news' (Mark 1:15). Without labouring the Qumran connection noted in the previous chapter, the expectation of an imminent 'inbreaking' of God into history – an 'appointed time' – was part of the theological context of this announcement and would have excited attention, especially given the earlier use of the phrase in the second chapter of Daniel. In this apocalyptic oracle, a succession of empires are destined to be destroyed by an everlasting Kingdom of God:

> And in the days of those kings the God of heaven will set up a kingdom that shall never be destroyed, nor shall this kingdom be left to another people. It shall crush all these kingdoms and bring them to an end, and it shall stand for ever. (Dan 2:44)

b) Good news or bad news?

Crushing kingdoms is hardly what most people associate with the classic beard, sandals and kindly image of Jesus. At the risk of over-simplification, one can identify this 'Kingdom conundrum' as the major theological tension running through the synoptic accounts. Jesus appears somewhat troubled by the expectations of the crowds and is not keen on even the disciples using the name 'Messiah' (Mark 8:30). His followers seem more gung-ho and seem to have found it difficult to let go of the idea that God's Kingdom necessitated violence through the direct action of God or of themselves (cf. Luke 9:54 and Mark 13:47). Viewed in this way, the Gospels become the story of Jesus' re-education programme for the disciples of what the 'Kingdom of God' really is.

The evangelists are fairly honest about the problem. Part of the difficulty that the disciples faced was that so much of what was happening around Jesus had the hallmarks of the divine. In Mark's Gospel, the miraculous dimension of the 'works' of Jesus are greeted with shock and awe – the *mysterium fascinans et tremendum* of the encounter with the Holy that is alluring and frightening at the same time (Mark 1:22-27, 2:12, 4:41, 5:15, 5:20, 5:33, 5:42; 6:2, 6:50-51, 7:37). This was akin to the 'tearing open of the heavens' spoken of in Isa 64:1 and reminiscent too of the oracle of Isaiah 61 directly alluded to in the 'Nazareth Manifesto' of Luke 4:18-20:

> The Spirit of the Lord is upon me,
> because he has anointed me
> to bring good news to the poor.
> He has sent me to proclaim release to the captives
> and recovery of sight to the blind,
> to let the oppressed go free,
> to proclaim the year of the Lord's favour.'
> And he rolled up the scroll, gave it back to the attendant, and sat down.
> The eyes of all in the synagogue were fixed on him.

While neither Mark nor Matthew repeats the detail of this, they both note the astonishment Jesus caused in his home town synagogue (cf. Matt 13:53-58 and Mark 6:1-6). To proclaim a messianic Kingdom and a 'year of God's favour' was to proclaim divine and social revolution (Prior, 1999). The 'jubilee year' tradition outlined in Leviticus 25 was that after every fifty years, whatever the bagatelle of commerce, harvests, warfare and misfortunes might have befallen a family, there would be a redistribution of land in favour of the poor and dispossessed. This was not, therefore, a purely apocalyptic 'heavenly kingdom' allusion which in itself was problematic. 'Good News' for the poor usually means 'Bad News' for the rich, and Luke implies that this apparently presumptuous announcement made Jesus unpopular among his own community and they try to end him and his ministry there and then (4:28-30).

Like John the Baptist before him, Jesus was causing reactions that he was not entirely in control of, and it may well be that Jesus' own conception of the manner in which his mission would be fulfilled developed accordingly. The disciples seem caught between conviction and confusion. For example, though Mark seems at pains to demonstrate that the disciples were in awe of this man who like God at the dawn of creation could calm the storms of the deep, he goes on to show how slow they were to understand what all this might mean (6:51-2; 9:32). Ultimately, they are depicted as misunderstanding Jesus and deserting him such that Mark's Gospel *may* be conceived as a story of 'discipleship failure' written for early Christians undergoing persecution and designed to encourage them not to make the same mistake (cf. Horsley, 2001, pp. 81–6 and Section 6e above).

c) Parables and a paradigm shift

To be fair, the disciples were caught in the middle of what the modern parlance would call a 'paradigm shift' – a sudden move to a very different way of thinking. It probably didn't help that Jesus was continually calling for new eyes to see and ears to hear so as to understand this Kingdom (Mark 8:18). As if to irritate them still further, the method he used to get them to 'think differently' was the story-puzzle teaching form of *parable*.

Parables were Jesus' preferred method of teaching. This Greek term means literally 'to throw alongside' corresponding to *mashal*, a form familiar in the Hebrew wisdom tradition. In some ways these 'stories with intent' fit into the genre of fable. They are an indirect form of communicating which is so often more effective than simple instruction or simple argument. One way of conceiving parables is as examples of 'right-brain thinking' which is imaginative, pictorial and paradoxical rather than that more typical of learned argument – rational, logical and consistent. Anyone who has tried to repair a relationship with a brother, a sister, a friend or spouse knows that a full frontal step-by-step rehearsal of all the things that were done and said rarely works as well as an appropriate gesture, a kindness or a well-timed humorous comment. It stands to reason that if the Kingdom of God meant a restoration of right relationship and lived covenant, Jesus would use indirect teaching methods which, as Kierkegaard famously remarked, could 'deceive the hearer into truth' (Oden, 1978, xiii).

Prompting a new way of thinking through the stories, metaphors and similes of the parables appears to be something Jesus used throughout his public ministry. The fact that he so often rooted them in domestic and rural realities familiar to the people of his time and place served to 'earth' the teachings and directly connect them with daily life (Snodgrass, 2004, pp. 177–90). That said, the twists and turns in some of the plots seem to have confused a number of his listeners and left the disciples eager for *nimshal* or 'explanation' of the imagery (e.g. cf. Matt 13:10-23 and Mark 4:10-20).

d) On originals, allegories and context

Much ink has been spilled trying to excavate the parables to get back to the 'originals' so that they may be more readily understood. While attempts to take the puzzle out of the conundrum might seem to be a contradiction in terms, such historical reconstructions can be partly understood because later theologizing of the parables did take the search for allegories and hidden meaning in the text to new heights. Using the Good Samaritan as an example, we can usefully contrast the symbolic reading of St Augustine with a modern interpretation more sensitive to the historical context. The original reads as follows:

> Just then a lawyer stood up to test Jesus. "Teacher," he said, "what must I do to inherit eternal life?" He said to him, "What is written in the law? What do you read there?" He answered, "You shall love the Lord your God with all your heart, and with all your soul, and with all your strength, and with all your mind; and your neighbour as yourself." And he said to him, "You have given the right answer; do this, and you will live."
>
> But wanting to justify himself, he asked Jesus, "And who is my neighbour?" Jesus replied, "A man was going down from Jerusalem to Jericho, and fell into the hands of robbers, who stripped him, beat him, and went away, leaving him half dead. Now by chance a priest was going down that road; and when he saw him, he passed by on the other side. So likewise a Levite, when he came to the place and saw him, passed by on the other side. But a Samaritan while travelling came near him; and when he saw him, he was moved with pity. He went to him and bandaged his wounds, having poured oil and wine on them. Then he put him on his own animal, brought him to an inn, and took care of him. The next day he took out two denarii, gave them to the innkeeper, and said, "Take care of him; and when I come back, I will repay you whatever more you spend." Which of these three, do you think, was a neighbour to the man who fell into the hands of the robbers?" He said, "The one who showed him mercy." Jesus said to him, "Go and do likewise." (Luke 10:25-37)

In Augustine's symbolism, the man is Adam and the journey is taking him away from Jerusalem – representing heaven – towards Jericho – representing our mortality. The robbers are the devil and his demons that lead us into sin and the priest and the Levite who pass by are the now ineffective ministers of the Old Covenant that can no longer mediate the restoration of relationship with God that Adam craves. Christ is the Good Samaritan whose bandages restrain our sin. The donkey is the Incarnation which brings Adam into the Church (the Inn), and the awakening next day becomes a type of the resurrection. The two denarii left behind are either understood as the two great commands to love God and our neighbour or the promise of this life and the world to come. By the time the Innkeeper is identified as St Paul, even the most pious reader can surely concur that this was hardly the *original* meaning of the parable whatever echoes or images might be heard or conjured up by later meditations (see Dunn and McKnight, 2005, pp. 248–9).

A reading of the parable sensitive to its historical context would in the first instance identify the exchange to be patterned on legal debate. A lawyer is clarifying not just a point of law, but *the point* of the Law and Jesus agrees with his summary of the heart of the Torah – 'You shall love the Lord your God and your neighbour as yourself'. However, in the familiar manner of strutting attorneys, he is testing Jesus to see if he is as good as his reputation would imply and asks for clarification on the definition of 'neighbour'. This is a clever question about exclusion, about whom the Law applies to and it is testing where Jesus would 'draw the line'. The response of Jesus is to offer a test-case for comment.

A man is attacked, stripped, abandoned and left for dead by the side of the road. A priest passes by. If the man's nakedness reveals him to be uncircumcised, the neighbour rule does not apply and if he is dead (as he seems to be), he cannot be touched without rendering the priest unclean (Lev 21:1-4). The Levite is less trammelled by the Law than the priest but may still have misgivings which excuse him from helping (Num 19:11-13). At this point, the expectation would be that a simple Israelite is presented as part of the test case, but instead, Jesus introduces a Samaritan. As noted above, they were considered to be mixed race, mixed up religious odd bods (2 Kings 17:24-41). The time and financial generosity of the Samaritan unexpectedly turn the question away from whether the priest and the Levite are correct in their actions according to the Law. Instead, the Law itself and its legalistic definition of neighbour are in the spotlight. The lawyer is left disconcerted – the Law has been best upheld by the hated Samaritan, but he cannot say as much, instead referring to him only as '*The One* who showed mercy to him'. In context, Jesus' invitation to 'Go and do likewise' becomes much more than a simple invitation to do good deeds, instead voicing a much broader universal call for a reduction in inter-group, religio-ethnic conflict (Esler, 2000, pp. 325–57).

e) Jesus and the new mind

The presentation of Jesus as a brilliant master of exchange has led to debates as to whether his ministry should be better characterized in the 'wisdom' rather than 'prophetic' traditions of Israel. To my mind, this sets up a false opposition – it is another case of 'both/and' being more accurate than 'either/ or' since Jesus does seem to self-identify with both traditions (cf. Luke 7:35; 13.33). Jesus is fundamentally difficult to categorize and in terms of 'thinking differently', it is significant that in the same section as the Good Samaritan, Luke's text has Jesus clearly preferring the mind of the child to that of the so-called learned and the clever:

> At that same hour Jesus rejoiced in the Holy Spirit and said, 'I thank you, Father, Lord of heaven and earth, because you have hidden these things from the wise and the intelligent and have revealed them to infants; yes, Father, for such was your gracious will. (Luke 10:21)

This is troubling indeed for anyone writing a book about Jesus or still worse making a living out of talking about him! Is this because the younger mind is clearer, less cluttered, more trusting and less proud? While the implication from the above text seems to be that the scholarly may be less open to the gift of revelation, it does not necessarily mean that Jesus is 'anti-mind' – rather that the mind should be put at the service of God (cf. Paul in 2 Cor 10:5). This might explain why along with Matthew, Luke has Jesus *inserting* a specific reference to 'the mind' into Moses' famous 'Hear O Israel' invitation 'to love God with all your heart, soul and strength' (cf. Luke 10:27 and Deut 6:5).

Since this prayer, *The Shema*, was and remains a daily recitation in the Judaic tradition, it can hardly have been a simple typographical error on the part of the evangelists. On the one hand, this may convey an ambitious theological corrective to the Tree of Knowledge catastrophe in Eden. On the other, it may be more simply that the evangelists have altered the tradition, to reflect the Greek rather than Hebrew understanding of what made up a human being. After all, to only mention heart, soul and strength to a Greek would be to miss out the part of themselves of which they were most proud.

Suffice to say, it seems to be that there is a spoken and unspoken need for a new mind in the engagement with Jesus' Kingdom-thinking in general and the parables in particular. Hence, while all scholars will agree that the parables do capture authentic and key components of Jesus' teaching of the Kingdom, consensus as to the exact nature of the Kingdom is more difficult to find (Voorvinde, 2010, pp. 329–53). The parables are a collection of puzzles and images which Jesus seems to have left as permanent discussion starters destined to tease us forever. The truth can't be seen directly and has to be viewed with new eyes. It is as if 'Kingdom spectacles' are needed – new varifocals, lensed as dragnet, lamp, lost coin, lost sheep, lost son, fig trees, mustard seeds, salt, yeast, darnel, corn and barns – all of which form the Kingdom's kaleidoscope of truth. Unjust stewards, grumpy elder brothers, bad debtors, murderers, victims, rich, poor, the foolish and the wise all mirror the profile of humanity in its ancient and modern context. Such caricatures were bound to provoke uneasy reactions as listeners wondered exactly who Jesus was referring to and whether he was getting at *them*.

As well as being 'discussion starters', some tales were also 'action starters' and it is likely that the disciples had the same problem with certain parables as the contemporary reader. It can be captured with the lovely phrase *Take up your parable and walk!* The task might vary from the simple practicality of 'Go and do likewise' from the Good Samaritan (Luke 10:37) to the more ambitious challenge to forgive and forego jealousy recalled by the Parable of the Lost Son (Luke 15:11-32). Similarly, the difficulty in the Parable of the Vineyard Labourers, where people who work for one hour get the same as those who work for twelve, is not that some imaginary future Kingdom of God would have such wage agreements. Rather the challenge for the reader is to avoid the sin of begrudgery (Matt 20:1-16). The parables comfort the afflicted but afflict the comfortable, with images to accompany the listener for a lifetime.

f) Marvels and miracles

By using parables, Jesus both 'earths' Kingdom imagery and renders it elusive at the same time. He states more than once that the Kingdom is by definition difficult to grasp and is not at all likely to be understood via the portal of the plausible, but by the wonderful – hence the use of Jesus' other teaching method – miracles.

For centuries, miracles have been a controversial topic in biblical scholarship. To some, the miracles constitute compelling evidence of Jesus' divine power and vouchsafe his status as the God-man. For others, they are a later addition to the tradition designed to impress gentile hearers of the Good News by casting Christ in the same mould as heroes of the Greek myths. Yet as noted above, even those who did not believe in Jesus as Messiah, such as Josephus, seem to have been quite ready to acknowledge him as a *thaumaturge* – a 'wonder worker'. Indeed, within the context of the Near East, prayer, healings, miracles and magic were all part of a religious-medical continuum that formed the background to the way people lived in the every day. In that sense, the wonders of Jesus were within a healing tradition associated not only with the priestly and prophetic power archetypes of Messiah but one within the purview of Hebrew and Hellenistic-Roman culture. These 'works' as Jesus called them are so clearly at the heart of the synoptic tradition that it is both unnecessary and constitutes theological double-think to try and eliminate them from the Gospel (Ashley, 2010, pp. 395–416).

Theologically, the miracles may be generically understood as 'Kingdom signs' since the Synoptic Gospels all have Jesus beginning his ministry after a confrontation with Satan in the wilderness. As noted above, the dualistic 'Good v Evil' picture of the cosmos had gathered momentum in Jewish Theology since the Exile and was certainly part of the dramatic imaginings of the Qumran community. In the Gospel accounts, after refusing to misuse power for evil, Jesus immediately begins his public ministry with a string of exorcisms to demonstrate that the Kingdom of God is replacing the rule of the forces of darkness. Demons are silenced because they know far better than the disciples the nature of Jesus' true identity (e.g. Mark 1:24-25).

As a sign of the tearing-down of heaven and the in-breaking of the Kingdom, the miracles repeatedly include those on the margins of the community such as lepers, foreigners and the variously unclean. Moreover, these signs of the Kingdom are often carried out on the Sabbath to the consternation of the Torah-observant Pharisees (e.g. Mark 3:1-6). They clearly find it difficult to identify the actions of Jesus within their religious sphere and are inclined to ascribe them to the power of Beelzebub (e.g. Mark 3:22-30). For them, since there was a rabbinic tradition that miracles could constitute confirmation of authentic teaching, it was a particular scandal that Jesus' miracles did not conform to an expected pattern.

It is inevitable that surprising, unexpected things should yield very different interpretations. In basic terms, one might agree with Schleiermacher that miracles are the religious interpretation of an unusual event but there is no shortage of Christian theologians who are uneasy with the unusual. Many regard miracles as counter to nature, evidence of a primitive unscientific mindset and something of an 'elephant in the room', calling into question the historical accuracy of the Gospel accounts. Yet there has long been a counter claim that miracles may be understood not as contrary to nature but as an unleashing of the inner potential of creation. On this argument, through his divinized humanity, Jesus was uniquely, but not exclusively, in a position to understand the wonder of the created order and make things happen that appeared unusual and which could be described as miraculous or 'super-natural'.

This might explain why Jesus seems quite at ease with the idea that others can do similar things, while insisting that the 'works' he performs are ultimately connected with faith and the rule of the Kingdom (Matt 11:20). At what one might call the 'human' level, they evidence his compassion and care for the sick – he is moved from the pit of his stomach by suffering (Mark 1:41). At the cosmic level they evidence his power, his ability to still storms, walk on water, to transcend normal human limitations and to astonish. Insofar as the Synoptic Gospels considered Jesus an embodiment of the Kingdom of God, the promised Messiah, then the miracles act as portals of wonder of the appointed time, which invite a different mindset, a different way of thinking, a revolution of life.

g) The new Moses

The proposal outlined so far is that in the Gospel picture of the Kingdom, Jesus was clustering earthly and cosmic expectations in theological shorthand. The main vocabulary available to the Gospel writers as they recalled his teachings and tried to express them was the imagery of their own religious tradition which recognized power, but was not quite ready for demonstrations of the power of powerlessness. Yet this seemed to be exactly what was being proposed by Jesus in his new version of the Law, presented in Matthew as 'The Sermon on the Mount'. With echoes of the Moses tradition, Matthew has Jesus on the mountain proclaiming a new standard higher than the old and an understanding of the Kingdom which was equally challenging:

> When Jesus saw the crowds, he went up the mountain; and after he sat down, his disciples came to him. Then he began to speak, and taught them, saying: "Blessed are the poor in spirit, for theirs is the kingdom of heaven. Blessed are those who mourn, for they will be comforted. Blessed are the meek, for they will inherit the earth. Blessed are those who hunger and thirst for righteousness, for they will be filled. Blessed are the merciful, for they will receive mercy. Blessed are the pure in heart, for they will see God. Blessed are the peacemakers, for they will be called children of God. Blessed are those who are persecuted for righteousness' sake, for theirs is the kingdom of heaven. Blessed are you when people revile you and persecute you and utter all kinds of evil against you falsely on my account. Rejoice and be glad, for your reward is great in heaven, for in the same way they persecuted the prophets who were before you. (Matt 5:1-12)

These words are both paradoxical and subversive. Ironically, a friend of mine once entered the public gallery of Congress during a debate on military policy and declaimed this extract from Matthew. On trial after his arrest, he was acquitted on the grounds that the Gospel could not be regarded as subversive. And yet the notion that the Kingdom of Heaven should belong to the humble, or that the meek should inherit the earth, is exactly the kind of cosmic and earthly contradiction that was puzzling enough for the disciples who heard it first, never mind congressmen voting on standing armies and nuclear warheads twenty centuries later.

'The poor in spirit' call to mind the *Anawim* – the little ones of YHWH – whose only hope is in God. This alludes to the 'Nazareth Manifesto' of Luke 4 noted above, which in turn has Isaiah's comfort promises at its root (Isa 40:1; 61:2). Indeed, Isaiah's vision of God (Isa 6:5-7) and his invitation to the table of the Lord (Isa 55:1-3) offer a theological background for the beatitudes complementary to the more obvious Exodus and Sinai traditions of Moses. The translation of the Hebrew *ashre* – or Greek *makarios* – is usually phrased as 'blessed' but is sometimes rendered as 'happy'. In either case, the one word translation is attempting to capture the sense of 'grateful contentment in God's providence' that is the opposite of smug self-reliance.

If the commandments of the Decalogue offered a matrix for behaviour that would capture the essence of the covenant between Israel and YHWH, the Beatitudes are more like invitations into a second, more authentic life. In a re-patterning of thinking that will be taken up by Paul, the rules and regulations of the Law which had ultimately become a series of indicators for pleasing God are 'fulfilled' and recast rather than replaced. Instead, the challenge is to alter disposition so rather than merely reiterating the injunctions on murder and adultery, Jesus challenges the anger or lust of the heart that leads to such wrongdoing (Matt 5:21-30). In similar fashion, frivolous divorce, needless oath-taking and vengeance are subsumed in a challenge to concentrate instead on a disposition of love, even for one's enemies (Matt 5:31-48). The Sermon goes on to recommend religious practice that is neither showy nor gloomy and has a conscious reliance on the providence of God (Matt 6:1-34). The famous 'do not judge, so that you may not be judged' saying (Matt 7:1ff) precedes a series of exhortations to seek integrity of life in which, ultimately, the 'Golden Rule' should take centre stage: 'In everything do to others as you would have them do to you - this is the Law and the prophets' (Matt 7:12).

h) Abba father – the Lord's Prayer

One final illustration of the conundrum and clarity of Kingdom offered by Matthew in the context of the Sermon on the Mount is the 'Lord's Prayer' which is found in a shorter form in Luke (cf. Matt 6:9-15; Luke 11:2-4). In both versions, a yearning for the Kingdom is at the heart of the prayer (see O'Collins, 2006). Seen as a resumé of covenant, it calls to mind an intimate belonging to God as 'Abba' – 'Dada' – 'Papa' (Our Father) and a prayer not for self-glorification but for God's honour (Hallowed be thy name). Praying this petition does not mean God's name is not holy – of course it is. Praying this petition expresses a desire that what is already true becomes more obvious. In similar fashion, the prayer that the Kingdom should come can be understood in a strongly apocalyptic sense ('O God, tear down the heavens quick and transform this hell hole!') or in a more patient but steadfast sense familiar to other strands of the Jewish 'Qaddish' prayer tradition ('Your Kingdom is already present – may it become more evident!') This paradox of the 'already present but not yet fulfilled' understanding of Kingdom is a key concept of Christian thinking and will be discussed more fully in considering the theological viewpoint of St Paul (see below Section 10d).

The petition for 'daily bread' can be read as a calling to radical permanent dependence on the providence of God as exemplified by the story of the manna in the desert which was only edible for one day and could not be stored (Ex 16:1-36). 'Daily bread' may also be indicative of the audience that Jesus was addressing, Galilean peasants who led simple, unlardered lives and for whom this petition would be a prayer from the heart. A third, more 'eschatological' – 'last things' – reading would connect it with the messianic apocalyptic tradition. Perhaps more accurately translated as 'give us today the bread of tomorrow', the tone of the prayer may well have been understood with a more futuristic sense indicating the idea of nourishment at the end-time banquet inaugurated by the Messiah (Rev 2:17).

In similar 'dual' fashion, the forgiveness of 'debts' can be understood as the forgiveness of wrongs or 'sins' but it would in all likelihood have resonated with the Jubilee promises of the restoration of God's rule Jesus alludes to (cf. Luke 4:18 and Lev 25:13). This would be especially so among the poor who would most likely be in debt rather than in a position to lend. That this is a community rather than solo prayer is underlined in that forgiveness as received from God should be extended to one another. This mirroring of God's mercy in mutual relationships seems to be a theme of the Kingdom and is echoed in Mark 11:25-26.

Last but not least, there is a plea for protection in 'temptation' which might be more usefully understood as 'testing' or in 'time of trial'. Again, an earthly and a cosmic picture of this Kingdom concern can be painted. In the context of the early Christian communities, it might be seen as a petition to be spared persecution from Jewish or Roman Imperial authorities. Equally, though, it can be understood in the messianic tradition as a reference to the time of tribulation that would accompany the Day of YHWH (cf. Joel 3:14-16).

i) Kingdom: Vocation not location

This chapter began with a Pope but ends in a paradox. While no one can seriously deny that the 'Kingdom of God' is shorthand for Jesus' proclamation in the synoptic Gospel tradition, the pattern of paradox mapped by Jesus' self-identification as the Son of Man is repeated. On the one hand, the 'Kingdom of God' is a concept clearly understandable as a cosmic, apocalyptic rallying call, marked by signs and wonders which identify Jesus as the Messiah inaugurating a new period of Israel's history by the power of YHWH. On the other, Jesus teaches the Kingdom with parables and metaphors drawn from the kitchen, the farm yard and the untidy lives of his contemporaries. The Kingdom is intimately earthed in a deeper law. The Kingdom is not pie in the sky, it involves a transformation of the dispositions that cause human heartache into compassion for family, friend, neighbour and enemy alike.

The Kingdom of God as preached by Jesus seems at once cosmic and earthly, here and not here, now and not yet, fulfilled and not fulfilled. It seems more of a vocation than a location, and certainly more about right recognition than being recognized. The Kingdom of God is at the heart of Jesus' preaching and his call for *metanoia* – 'conversion' or 'repentance'. This literal 'turn-around' is an invitation to a revolution in thinking which involves seeing with different eyes, hearing with different ears and speaking without judgement. Ultimately, it seems that the Kingdom is the covenant experienced – mutual love and responsibility actively uniting humanity to God and to each other. In this sense, the Kingdom is restoring the lost communion of Eden and even healing the divided cosmos by conjoining heaven with earth once more.

Summary

The preaching of the Kingdom is the central message of Jesus in the synoptic tradition. Not an advisable thing to do in an Empire that already has legitimated authority, Jesus seems to have combined his preaching with connotations of Jubilee, a time of restoration of land in favour of the poor. Parables are one of the favoured methods by which Jesus teaches, and their quizzical counter-intuitive nature seems to be designed to encourage his listeners to 'think differently'. Miracles and authoritative pronouncements are also part of the picture which could not fail to produce excitement and expectation. At the heart of the message, however, was the cry 'Abba – Father' – a call to tender, child-like dependence on God. The deliberately elusive concept of Kingdom appears to be as much a calling as a country, a vocation rather than a location, but one which would lead Jesus himself to a very specific rendezvous in Jerusalem.

Death and Resurrection

The sequence of events during the last week of Jesus' life remain the controversial heart of the Gospel accounts. Although the entry into Jerusalem seems joyful enough, the dark clouds that gather point to an inevitable confrontation. Symbolism is very evident in the cleansing of the Temple, the Last Supper and the events of Good Friday. The resurrection accounts remain the most controversial element in the Gospels, but their differences and similarities only add to the intrigue.

a) The entry into Jerusalem

The events of the last week of Jesus' life dominate the Gospels. This is a deliberate theological choice on the part of the Evangelists and demonstrates what the culmination of his life meant for them. Although John implies Jesus made three visits to Jerusalem, the Synoptics recount only one if we exclude Luke's infancy narrative and the temptation accounts. For the Gospel writers, all the parables, miracles and incidents that lead up to the passion can be seen as an extended preamble to the fateful arrival in Jerusalem which is the climax of Jesus' public ministry. The journey is marked by foreboding as Jesus anticipates what will happen when he reaches Jerusalem. This seems fairly natural and should not be piously taken as evidence that Jesus was all-knowingly 'omniscient'. From the death of John the Baptist onwards, the Gospel is proclaimed in an atmosphere of danger, the uneasiness of Jesus regarding the use of the title 'Messiah' is consistent and Jerusalem as both destiny and destination casts a haunting shadow (cf. Matt 16:21, 20:18; Mark 3:22, 7:1, 10:33; Luke 9:51, 13:33, 18:31; John 7:25).

All the Gospels recount that Jesus arrived in Jerusalem riding a donkey, taking the acclaim of a crowd who waved palm branches and shouted blessings:

> Then those who went ahead and those who followed were shouting "Hosanna! Blessed is the one who comes in the name of the Lord! Blessed is the coming kingdom of our ancestor David! Hosanna in the highest heaven!" (Mark 11:9-10, cf. Matt 21:7-9; Luke 19:33-38; John 12:13-15)

There may be a deliberate stylization here since it clusters a series of messianic images. As well as being a suitable form of transport, the donkey recalls a prophecy of Zechariah concerning a kingly and possibly messianic figure entering the city (Zech 9:9). The cry 'Hosanna' is the imperative form of *ysh'* – the verb 'to save' which is also the root of the name Joshua and of Jesus. Since names bore significance in Semitic culture as designations of identity, the crowd can be understood here as calling Jesus to act out his true nature, act out who he was on their behalf – 'Save us O Saviour!'. By connecting this cry with the titles 'King' or 'Son of David', the Gospels in turn highlight the messianic tone of this moment – an inauguration of the Kingdom, a decisive moment of God's intervention. Palm branches – celebration – welcome – this is presented as a regal procession and needless to say, the authorities are none too keen on the acclaim received by Jesus (Matt 21:10, Luke 19:39, John 12:19).

b) The cleansing of the Temple

Things do not improve with Jesus' next symbolic action. As if to drive home the expectant intensity, the Synoptics juxtapose these cries of 'Hosanna!' with Jesus' cleansing of the Temple. As noted above, the merchants and money changers were part of the economics of the holy place (cf. Hanson and

Oakman, 2009, pp. 144–5). This involved the slaughter of vast numbers of animals and a great deal of money changing hands as the people bought *clean* animals with *clean money* from the Temple franchises in reparation for their *unclean* lives. The passionate and very physical intervention of Jesus is evident from the Markan text:

> Then they came to Jerusalem. And he entered the temple and began to drive out those who were selling and those who were buying in the temple, and he overturned the tables of the money-changers and the seats of those who sold doves; and he would not allow anyone to carry anything through the temple. He was teaching and saying, "Is it not written, 'My house shall be called a house of prayer for all the nations?' But you have made it a den of robbers." (Mark 11:15-17)

On the one hand, the turning over of the tables of the money changers can be seen as yet another example of an inspired action on behalf of the poor in the classic tradition of prophets such as Amos and Jeremiah. Since pigeons were the typical sacrifice of the poor who could not afford anything better, this may be underlined by the text. On the other hand, Jesus' coming into the Temple also echoes the prophecy of Malachi that the judgement of a covenant messenger would presage a cataclysmic Day of YHWH and restore proper offerings pleasing to God:

> See, I am sending my messenger to prepare the way before me, and the Lord whom you seek will suddenly come to his temple. The messenger of the covenant in whom you delight—indeed, he is coming, says the LORD of hosts. But who can endure the day of his coming, and who can stand when he appears?
> For he is like a refiner's fire and like fullers' soap; he will sit as a refiner and purifier of silver, and he will purify the descendants of Levi and refine them like gold and silver, until they present offerings to the LORD in righteousness. Then the offering of Judah and Jerusalem will be pleasing to the LORD as in the days of old and as in former years.
> Then I will draw near to you for judgment; I will be swift to bear witness against the sorcerers, against the adulterers, against those who swear falsely, against those who oppress the hired workers in their wages, the widow, and the orphan, against those who thrust aside the alien, and do not fear me, says the LORD of hosts. (Mal 3:1-5)

Whether understood as a prophetic action or as a preparation for cataclysm, the authorities felt that this disturbance was unjustified and it is identified by Mark as the final straw for the chief priests and scribes (cf. Mark 11:18, Matt 11:15 and Luke 19:47). In the heated exchanges that follow, Jesus appears to have made some threat about the destruction of the sanctuary. Although it is only in John's account that he makes the extraordinary step of identifying himself *with* the Temple, the authors all retain echoes of this controversial exchange (cf. John 2:18-22; Mark 13:2, 14:58, 15:29; Matt 26:60; Acts 6:13-14). Like Jeremiah before him, Jesus was to find that criticizing the Temple was tantamount to blasphemy, central as it was to the identity of Israel as the chosen people of YHWH (Jer 26:8).

c) Revolutionary Messiah?

The cleansing of the Temple is thought in certain quarters to be a deliberate attempt to foment a revolution which proved a disastrous gamble on the part of Jesus. Alongside the increasingly caustic, critical denunciations he makes of the Pharisees and scribes, the Jerusalem ministry can be read literally as a 'death or glory' moment for the Jesus movement (Matt 23:1-36; Mark 12:37-40; Luke 20:45-7). On this reading, Jesus unsuccessfully tries to spark an insurgency but the 'Kingdom' revolution does not take place. Jesus is put to death as a failure and the disciples reinterpret the whole ministry in a non-earthly way which is theologically rather than politically successful. These ideas have been around for several centuries now, being generally first associated with Herman Reimarus (1694–1768). Although I would contend that the picture is a lot more complex than the 'failed revolutionary' thesis allows, it does at least have the merit of being more realistic than the twee imagery of the sandals, beardy, placid Jesus beloved of art and popular culture. The Markan picture of him even preventing people carrying things through the Temple is physical, decisive and strong.

Moreover, as if to rub in the messianism, a further symbolic gesture recounted by all the Gospels is placed here by Matthew, Mark and John. After the cleansing of the Temple, there seems to be a resilient tradition that Jesus spent time in Bethany, a short distance from Jerusalem. While there, Jesus was anointed by a woman who is nameless in the early tradition but is identified by John as Mary, sister of Lazarus (cf. Matt 26:6-13; Mark 14:3-9; John 12:1-8). It cannot be emphasized enough that 'anointed' = 'christed' = 'messiahed' and it is more than feasible that an increasingly disgruntled Judas may have reported this action to the chief priests as part of the evidence against Jesus (John 12:4).

d) The Last Supper

The scenes outlined in the Gospels inexorably move towards the gathering known to history as the *Last Supper* which the Synoptics present as a celebration of Passover between Jesus and his disciples (cf. Stuhlmacher, 2005, pp. 392–412). As much as parables and miracles, Jesus had used meals as a teaching and mission tool throughout the public ministry, becoming notorious for eating with disreputable types (cf. Matt 9:9-13, Mark 2:13-17, Luke 5:27-32). Although it is impossible at this distance to know exactly who was in the 'Upper Room' for the occasion, it is not surprising that there is an emphasis on the actions and conversations of the Twelve since this meal serves theologically to emphasize that Jesus is trying to found a new Israel of twelve new tribes. It is representative of a new Passover, a new Exodus. Again, whether the disciples or Jesus himself saw this as a necessary preamble to a dramatic intervention by God reminiscent of the time of Moses, one can only speculate. Clearly, by the time the Gospel accounts were set down, the legacy of this night had become the commemoration of Jesus through the sharing of bread and wine as the signs of the 'new' covenant. The bread and wine as body and blood symbolize the replacement of the Passover lamb with Jesus, the Lamb of God. The Passover lamb which delivered the Hebrews from death and led them to freedom is now understood as the cipher for understanding Jesus' death on the Cross as the sacrifice which delivers the new Israel to freedom. That these were early theological features of the Jesus movement can be attested not just in the immediate accounts of the Last Supper but also elsewhere in the New Testament (cf. 1 Cor 11:23-26; Luke 24:30; Acts 2:46 and Heb 10:11-18).

The different accounts of the Last Supper all evidence a Jesus troubled by the betrayal of Judas and the prospect of desertion by his friends including Peter (cf. Matt 26:21-35; Mark 14:18-31; Luke 22:21-34; John 13:21-38). The poor showing of the disciples, their misunderstandings, their petty rivalries, their failure to understand and their cowardice is almost too familiar to readers to be shocking. To repeat, since one can reasonably propose that by the time the Gospels were being set down, the *Sitz im Leben* or 'lived context' of Christians was as a persecuted minority in mortal danger for their faith, then this emphasis begins to make sense as an example to the early Church of how *not* to behave. The drama of the two key betrayers, Judas and Peter, plays out with both letting Jesus down badly, one in the face of financial temptation, the other in the face of fear. The tradition of big macho fisherman Peter being scared even of servant girls seems to be deliberately preserved and given remarkable prominence (Matt 27:69, Mark 14:66, Luke 22:56 and John 18:17). In the contemporary era where spin-doctors and media advisors enable leaders of religions and nations to maintain their 'image', it is counter-intuitive that the Gospels embarrass perhaps the most significant figure of the early Church with these recollections. The fact that both these friends of Jesus end up distraught is also recorded with tragic consequences in Matthew's account. Peter weeping at cock-crow is bad enough, but a remorseful Judas commits suicide (cf. Matt. 26:69-75; 27:3-10). Despair can have different outcomes and the Gospels seem to suggest that big boys should learn how to cry (Mark 14:72; Luke 19:41, 22:62; John 11:35).

A final point to note is the consistent tradition at the Last Supper that Jesus makes an allusion to not drinking from the final cup until the Kingdom is fully come. The fourth or final cup in the Passover ritual follows the singing of the celebratory psalms and ends the meal. It is noticeable that in all three Synoptics this does not happen, and it can reasonably be concluded that this may be a deliberate framing of the events of Good Friday as the completion of the New Passover. As will be noted below, in this argument, the last act of Jesus before he dies is to taste the final 'cup' on the cross (cf. Matt 26:29, Mark 14:25, Luke 22:18 with John 19:29-30 [see Pitre, 2011, pp. 149-170]).

e) Gethsemane

The events that follow in Gethsemane tend to support the 'cup' theme where Matthew, Mark and Luke all have Jesus referring to a 'cup' of suffering (cf. Matt 26:39, Mark 14:36, Luke 22:42). The juxtaposition of 'cup', 'suffering' and 'Kingdom' is also found in the disputes about who should be considered the greatest among the disciples (cf. Matt 20:22-8; Mark 10:35-45; Luke 22:24-7). The uncertainty of Jesus at this point is one of the key texts for later thinking about his divine-human nature. The simplistic proposal that if he was God he wouldn't be agonizing about what to do convinces some that the Gospels *do not* present a divine picture of Jesus. There does seem to be a genuine struggle of the will presented by the Gospel writers which somewhat torpedoes any notions that he was a holy robot with no doubts and automatic 'will-of-the-Father' programming. Indeed one can argue that Gethsemane, contrasted with the desert of temptation, deliberately frames the synoptic picture of Jesus' public ministry. They each depict a Jesus engaged in a human struggle to find the courage and self-discipline to fulfil a destiny, or more mundanely, 'to get the job done'. By contrast, in another episode of discipleship failure, the Twelve, who have heard Jesus speak parables of watchfulness, still fail to 'stay awake' (cf. Mark 13:34-7; 14:41).

The arrest is a scuffled affair in the Gospel accounts. There seems to be a futile attempt at resistance with all the Gospels noting that the ear of one of the servants was cut off. John identifies the victim as Malchus and the perpetrator as a hot-headed Peter, with the incident being calmed by a Jesus reconciled to his fate (Matt 26:47-56, Mark 14:43-52, Luke 22:47-53 and John 18:2-12). Recent attempts to rehabilitate Judas as the fall-guy merely carrying out the strict orders of Jesus are based on the neutrality of the verb *paradidomai* which can mean 'betray' or more simply 'hand over'. Although it does contradict the force of the narrative there is a certain charm to the idea that *someone* had to do it and it happened to be poor old Judas (e.g. Archer and Moloney, 2007). Such thinking is hardly new; it is many years since Bob Dylan famously questioned: 'Well I can't think for yer, you'll have to decide, whether Judas Iscariot, had God on his side' (Dylan, 1963).

That said, the thesis that Jesus organized the Gethsemane arrest himself has little scholarly pedigree and flies in the face of the tradition which presents Judas' kiss as dramatic, intimate infidelity. Moreover, while betrayal is a common feature in hero-literature, biblical precedent from Adam onwards places broken relationship at the heart of the drama – it's as if the collected texts are an extended meditation on how *not* to behave. In this light, there is no particular reason to assume the Twelve or Jesus would be exempt from the kind of heartache that is faced by so many through broken friendships, divided families and fractured faith communities in all cultures at all times.

f) Trial

Following the arrest, the trial of Jesus is likewise an untidy, hurried affair. It would have been helpful if proper records had been kept with which to compare the Gospels as they agree in general but differ in detail. Mark's account mentions the aforementioned 'Temple threat' but crystallizes with the exchange:

> But he was silent and did not answer. Again the high priest asked him, "Are you the Messiah, the Son of the Blessed One?" Jesus said, "I am; and you will see the Son of Man seated at the right hand of the Power, and coming with the clouds of heaven." (Mark 14:61-62)

'Son of Man' imagery is part of the foreground of these events (cf. Matt 24:29-31, Mark 13:24-27, Luke 21:25-28). In the trial accounts, Matthew and Luke also imply that Jesus allows those gathered to come to this fateful conclusion, which is enough for the high priest to tear his robes in protest at the blasphemy. As we have noted already, it is ironic that this title, which can be understood as 'an ordinary guy' becomes the fateful turning point. Here it is taken to mean the extraordinary apocalyptic figure of Daniel discussed above, 'someone like God' who is at the right hand of the Power who will come on the clouds of heaven (cf. Matt 26:64, Mark 14:62, Luke 22:69).

Abruptly, the company march Jesus off to Pilate. Here the charge turns from religious to political sedition as Pilate questions Jesus on the accusation that he is claiming to be King of the Jews (Matt 27:11, Mark 15:2, Luke 23:3 and John 18:33). Jesus retorts 'You have said so' – an answer which intensifies the drama in several ways:

- First, in terms of personality, it seems typical of the elusiveness with which Jesus is exasperatingly 'coy and clear' about his identity throughout the Gospel accounts.
- Secondly, this section of the Gospel is in effect a 'courtroom drama', a genre familiar from TV and literature. To admit to an enforcer of Imperial Roman power that you are a self-declared king would probably end the conversation there and then. A retelling of the account would struggle to propose that Pilate (who had a tough reputation) would have wasted any more breath beyond the order for execution – 'King, you say? Crucify!'
- Instead, the reply of Jesus puts Pilate in a quandary which allows the Gospel writers once more to point out an irony to the reader. Namely, that it is the pagan Roman procurator who is inadvertently confessing the true identity of Jesus. He is the Messiah and King of the Jews and his own people do not recognize it.
- If this were not enough, the charge sheet of Pilate which reads 'King of the Jews' puts it all in writing. It might arguably have acted as the shock-trigger for the disciples to re-think their understanding of messiahship (see John 19:19-22). The crucified one is a king after all, a king whose kingdom is no longer a place or location but a calling, a way, a vocation.

Meanwhile, there are further dramatic and stylistic issues at play in Pilate's offer to release Jesus. The life-giving *Bar-Abba* –'Son of the Father' is given the chance to live. Agonizingly, he is spurned by the crowd in favour of the life-taking murderer 'Barabbas' (cf. Matt 27:16; Mark 15:11; Luke 23:18). Once more there is something of a warning here. It can be noted that Jesus wasn't always at ease with crowds (cf. Matt 8:18, 11:7, 13:34, 13:57, 14:22, Mark 6:4 and Luke 4:29). Mobs can easily turn nasty and again the dramatic irony is that having entered Jerusalem to the cheers of a crowd welcoming him as a King, a Son of David, he will exit Jerusalem with the jeers of the mob, a failed rejected fool from Nazareth. The Gospels don't miss the literary power of this failure to recognize who Jesus is, and since Pilate's conviction turns on kingship, the soldiers become the villains who act out all the mockery of failed messianism, with insults, jibes, purple robes and a crown of thorns (cf. Matt 27:27-31; Mark 15:16-20; Luke 23:11; John 19:1-15).

g) Crucifixion – Good Friday

Crucifixion was a standard form of capital punishment in Roman times. In this sense, Jesus was not being singled out for special treatment. Crucifixion was deemed especially useful as a public deterrent because of the prolonged exposure of the victim during and after the process. The swifter, less painful execution of beheading by the sword was a right of Roman citizens and partly explains why in subsequent decades St Paul would understandably keep reminding his prosecutors of his dual nationality (Acts 22:26-29). Comparing the accounts of the crucifixion, they are essentially similar. Simon of Cyrene is identified in the synoptic accounts as being of physical assistance to Jesus, but all the Gospels make mention of the macabre location – 'Golgotha' – 'the skull strewn place'. The tradition is strong that he was crucified with two thieves and all remark that he was mocked by passers-by. Furthermore, each of the Gospels say lots were cast for Jesus' clothes, and this may form part of the 'priestly' imagery of messiahship since the garment of the High Priest was traditionally a seamless linen robe that could not be easily divided (cf. Matt 27:34-56, Mark 15:15-41, Luke 23:24-49, John 19:16-27).

The pitiful scene of broken humanity begins to develop more cosmic dimensions as the moment of death approaches. Suddenly there is darkness at the height of the day, from noon until 3 o'clock in the afternoon. Mark and Matthew have Jesus crying out the opening verse of Psalm 22, 'My God, My God - Why have you forsaken me?' Although seeming to imply despair and 'kingdom failure' on the lips of the crucified, this particular psalm begins in abject desolation and ends in a proclamation of triumph. Hence, it is equally likely that Mark and Matthew are hinting at the ultimate vindication of resurrection. The bystanders understandably mistake the cry *Eloi Eloi* ('My God, My God') as a call for *Elijah* ('My God is YHWH'). All the Gospels then note that Jesus accepts the sponge soaked in wine and vinegar offered on a hyssop stick. In the first Exodus, the hyssop stick was used to smear the doorposts of the Hebrews such that their firstborn should escape death and live (Ex 12:22). The possible imagery here is of Jesus accepting the 'fourth cup' as a completion of the New Passover. This 'cup' is the deliverance promise of the Kingdom, namely, that in the death of Jesus as the Lamb of God, this cruel sign of death will become the promise of life for all (John 3:14).

With profound symbolism, as Jesus breathes his last, the Synoptics mention that the veil of the Temple is torn in two (Matt 27:51, Mark 15:38, Luke 23:45). It can be claimed that this image was perhaps formed in the minds of the Gospel writers by events which occurred in 70 CE when the Second Temple was destroyed. Here, the theological function denotes that the separation of God from humanity is removed by Jesus who is the true mediator, the true High Priest, the true Anointed One. The Holy of Holies is now accessible to all in the New Covenant and a new 'at-one-ment' between God and God's people is effected. No more sacrifices, no more genocides, no more sin offerings, no more money changers, no more lambs and pigeons are necessary. Later, the idea that there is no more need for a Temple – since Jesus has become the Temple – is fully developed in the writings of John (John 2:21, 4:21-24). James McCaffrey has summed up this argument as follows: 'The journey of Jesus is a priestly activity. Jesus enters through his passion-resurrection into the heavenly temple of the Father's House by the sacrificial transformation of his body into the new Temple of his risen body in which believers have permanent and abiding at-one-ment with God' (McCaffrey, 1988, p. 256).

This collision of images enriches the triple understanding of the Messiah as 'prophet, priest and king'. Crucified as a *king*, the true *priest* is stripped of his sacred garment and dies rejected like a *prophet*, as naked as the poorest of the poor. If the core understanding of covenant is relationship, then all barriers are now removed for true intimacy between God and humanity. Through a renewed Israel, a new pathway to God has been opened up – the Jesus Way – which Jew and Gentile alike can tread. As if to offer a foretaste of what this might mean, three of the Gospels propose that a centurion – presumably a Roman pagan – is the first to configure the disfigured face of the Son of Man, as the face of the Son of God (Matt 27:54, Mark 15:39, Luke 23:47).

h) Death – Holy Saturday

The lead actors in the next phase of the Passion narratives are Joseph of Arimathea and a group of women close to Jesus. The tradition here is very resilient and there is no especial reason to doubt that a humanitarian request for the body took place and that with linen cloths, Jesus was cleansed and prepared for entombment. The burial procedure outlined is typical of first century Judea and took place outside the city walls. Graveyards, like execution areas, were considered unclean both for ritual and hygienic reasons. Hence it is plausible that a garden-graveyard with a tomb, belonging to Joseph, could be situated near to Golgotha. Likewise, the tradition is unanimous that it was a new tomb that was sealed with a large stone (cf. Matt 27:57-61; Mark 15:42-47; Luke 23:50-56, 24:2; John 19:38-42, 20:1).

Theologically, the fact that Jesus 'rests' in death may have a possible significance since the mortal inaction of Jesus has him (almost for once in the

Synoptics) obeying the commandment of the Sabbath. The reality and importance of Jesus 'tasting death' (see Heb 2:7) will prove a fertile ground for later thinking, and will include Jesus preaching among the dead and taking possession of the keys to the gates of the Underworld (cf. 1 Pet 3:19 and Rev 1:18). On this point, it is perhaps worth mentioning that Jewish post-mortem expectations varied. Although 'pit', 'stillness' and 'deep darkness' were all part of the metaphors, 'Sheol' was the most popular description of the dead zone. Probably derived from the verb 'to inquire' in the way that oracle seekers and necromancers sought information from the dead (see 1 Sam 28:15), Sheol was likened to either the watery chaos described in Gen 1:2 (cf. Job 26:5 and 2 Sam 22:5) or an insatiable devouring beast perhaps connected with Mot, the Canaanite God of the Underworld (Isa 5:14, Prov 30:15).

In the traditional Jewish thinking represented by the Sadducees, those descending to Sheol did not expect much of themselves or of their surroundings (Wright, 2003, pp. 85–128). Pallid empty 'shades' in a land of nothingness, King Hezekiah's prayer during his illness sums things up quite well: 'Sheol cannot thank you. Death cannot praise you; those who go down to the Pit cannot hope for your faithfulness' (Isa 38:18 [cf. 14:10, Ps 88:12, Ecc 9:10]). In contrast, other groups such as the Pharisees were influenced by later Jewish apocalyptic literature which did begin to conceive of a judgment, resurrection and eternal reward: 'Many of those who sleep in the dust of the earth shall awake, some to everlasting life, and some to shame and everlasting contempt' (Dan 12:2). The kind of dispute that arose between these two influential groups is recorded in the Synoptics but perhaps appropriately, the Gospels are silent about this day (cf. Matt 22:22, Mark 12:18, Luke 20:27). All that seems intended is that like any other body, the expectation is that Jesus would rot and stink (cf. John 11:39) – hence the need for aromatic spices to be brought by the women.

i) The empty tomb

But rot he did not. Apparently, he rose. For many religious thinkers of every stripe, this point is where the Gospels irrevocably part company with history and stretch the credulity of the reader. It must immediately be said that nothing is proved here, but from the Gospel accounts a fairly consistent chain of events is articulated:

- Early the next day, a group of women, which included Mary Magdalene, go to the tomb.
- The stone portal has been moved.
- They discover that the tomb is empty.

- In John, the risen Jesus himself speaks to Mary, in the Synoptics, angels announce that Jesus is risen and that they are to tell the disciples.
- The Gospels *do not* describe the resurrection – Matthew comes closest but his 'earthquake plus angels' account only serves to reveal that the tomb is empty anyway.
- Consistent with their slow-witted depiction by the Evangelists, the guys who deserted Jesus during the passion, on hearing the account, are unsurprisingly somewhat reluctant to believe the story (cf. Matt 28:1-10, 17; Mark 16:1-11; Luke 24:1-11; John 20:1-18).

In fairness to the hapless disciples, the empty tomb clearly proves nothing at either an historical or theological level. The Gospels acknowledge this. Theft is the obvious answer – even Mary Magdalene thinks this is the case (John 20:2). Despite narrating the deployment of guards in the graveyard, Matthew acknowledges that theft is 'the story that has been spread among the Jews until this day' and in his account the soldiers are paid off and become 'counter-witnesses' to the resurrection (28:11-15). It is somewhat intriguing that imperial edicts which forbid grave robbing do exist from Pilate's protectorate around this time, though it is unlikely they were precipitated by resurrection stories among Jews about Jesus. Rather, the tendency to bury several people in one tomb with personal artefacts such as jewellery meant that tomb raiding has long been a lucrative business – as countless archaeologists and *Indiana Jones* types will testify.

If the tomb proves nothing in itself, the witness of women was also somewhat compromised. Though the tradition that women were the first heralds of the resurrection is robust, their absence from Paul's list in 1 Cor 15:3-5 may be because the preferred gender of witnesses was masculine. By and large, the witness of women was invalid as testimony in the first-century Judea, partly due to menstrual regulations which still perdure in some Near Eastern cultures. Perhaps in a negative way, this proves the metal in the mix since a completely fabricated tradition would have been unlikely to accord a key role to 'unreliable' witnesses. Celsus claimed that since it was a little early and the women were mildly hysterical with grief, they simply went to the wrong grave, but contemporary exegesis rightly challenges such prejudice, emphasizing instead the subversive power of the women's testimony (Setzer, 1997, p. 271).

j) Apparitions

In short, though the empty tomb was proof enough for the disciples that *something* had happened, it wasn't enough to explain exactly *what* had happened. The empty tomb clearly forms an essential part of the testimony but it was not fully explanatory. The convincing moments for the disciples seem to turn on the apparitions of Jesus which are recalled by all the Gospel writers. It is here that a cursory reading of the texts seems to be a little confusing, but taking an overview of the passages they evidence two key themes: a strong Galilee/commission tradition (cf. Matt 28:16ff; Mark 16:7, 15; Luke 5:1-11, 24:47-48; John 20:21, 21:1-14) and a strong gathered meal tradition (Mark 16:14, Luke 24:36-43, John 20:19-23).

Arguments rage about the provenance of these accounts and why they differ. Their united testimony is of physical apparitions which, though stretching the imagination of the disciples, give impetus to their proclamation that 'Jesus is risen!' This picture is perhaps strengthened with an appeal to Paul, who in the Letter to the Corinthians seems to have an 'official line' that was being 'handed on' during the immediate apostolic period. Paul confirms the death, burial, resurrection and apparition to Peter and the Twelve (so far so good), but then adds the equivalent of a stadium apparition (to 500 brethren) as well as specific mention of an apparition to James and ultimately Paul himself (1 Cor 15:3-8).

Whatever the conviction of the reader, the upshot is that a first-century community is spawned which has a most unusual take on a crucified Nazarene. He proclaimed a kingdom, was condemned as a king and has risen from the dead. This is clearly not your average yarn and the incredulity of disciples and hearers alike is amusingly depicted by Luke. On the road to Emmaus, he has two disciples confessing to being baffled by it all in the very presence of the risen Jesus and much later he has Athenian philosophers dismissing Paul as a parrot for talking such nonsense (cf. Luke 24:22 and Acts 17:18). In other words, it is clear that this group were forced into a serious 're-think' of their understanding of their own religious tradition. This is acknowledged by the evangelists, such that by the time Paul hears the Good News, the message is already deliberately presented as being in 'accordance with the scriptures' (cf. Matt 26:31-32; Mark 16:14; Luke 24:27, 44; John 16:13; 1 Cor 15:3-8). The problem they faced was that a crucified, dying and rising individual was simply not a typical pattern to be expected of a Hebrew Messiah and the difficulty in persuading others of the truth of this account would ultimately lead to violent, fatal estrangement from their own religious tradition (e.g. Acts 6:1-60, 12:2).

The scandal of the cross and the awkward incredulity of the resurrection stem from these passages and remain theological inconveniences at the heart of Christian Theology. While the drama of this distinctiveness is vividly articulated in the pages of Acts and the letters of Paul, for some the 'interruption' is too marked and inevitably alternative theories have been advanced to explain these events in a different way. Some explanations are more challenging than the Gospel accounts and combine 'physical' and 'psychological' components. In one retelling, Jesus never makes it to the tomb, he is eaten by dogs on Golgotha and this disappearance is construed as a resurrection. In another, a bloodied Jesus staggers out of the tomb revived by special opiates and lives happily ever after in Galilee with Mary Magdalene. In another, a 'group rethink' in denial at the tragedy of the death of Jesus imagines through a charismatically charged group ecstasy that he is somehow alive. In another, the key is liturgical, the practice of revisiting the tomb of Jesus leads to a sense that he never died.

In my view, none of these explanations can be argued at all convincingly from *within* the accounts. The Gospels are at pains to underline that the women and apostles found that the designated tomb of Joseph of Arimathea was empty and that subsequently Jesus appeared to them. Furthermore, there is no implication that the apparitions are dream sequences, ghost moments, group hysteria or holograms. If one wishes to say that the apostles were mistaken, duped by a third-party tomb raider or that they deluded themselves then it is no more or no less than was said at the time by others. Whether anyone else believes it or not, *they* did, and their Gospels were written in order to involve their contemporaries and subsequent generations in the resurrection debate and what it might mean about Jesus (Luke 1:1-4 and John 20:31).

Having said that, the resurrection claims do act as a watershed for what scholars sometimes characterize as a distinction between the 'Jesus of history' and the 'Christ of faith' which will be a core concern of the next three chapters and much of the rest of the book. This distinction can be argued from the nature of the resurrection appearances which mark a rupture with normality beyond the category of miracle and involve the interaction with a Jesus who is outside the space-time limitations which confine us. As such, Jesus is 'outside history' and despite the distinct claims of the Gospels that he ate and was physically present to the disciples, he will in future be identified with the radar of faith rather than with physical senses (John 20:29). He will be heard through the preaching of the apostles rather than through his own voice (Matt 28:20). He will be understood indirectly through the deeds of his followers rather than his own actions (Mark 16:14-18).

This era of *kerygma* – 'the apostolic preaching' of the Christ event in the power of the Spirit – begins a new phase in the unfolding of God's revelation as understood by the followers of Jesus. It is a phase marked by the roller coaster emergence of the Church, a topic to which this survey now turns.

Summary

The events leading up to the death of Jesus and the happenings during and after his execution are at the centre of Christian Theology. The reasons for his arrest and conviction are easily discernible from the Gospel tradition. The entry into Jerusalem and the cleansing of the Temple are effectively understood to be confrontations with religious authorities. This leads eventually to conviction by the secular power in the form of Pontius Pilate. The Last Supper and the Crucifixion are presented in heavily symbolic terms. The tearing of the veil of the Temple means that the old order has passed and is a prelude to the events of Easter Day where women become the unlikely heralds of an unlikely claim, but one which would define the eventual Christian movement.

9

The Jesus Movement in the Acts of the Apostles

The Acts of the Apostles is the sequel to the Gospel of Luke and is even livelier, if that were possible, than the main event. There is an attractive verve to the dizzying series of happenings which Luke uses to describe the growth of the Jesus movement. The account deliberately charts the proclamation of the Gospel from Jerusalem to Rome. The main protagonists are Peter, Stephen (the first martyr), and increasingly Paul, whose trials and tribulations meeting mobs, witches, officials and companions dominate the second half of the work.

a) Good news – the sequel

Like a popular film franchise, at least one of the Gospels, Luke, offers a sequel to his 'Good News'. The plot of the *Acts of the Apostles* is simple enough, the story of how, through a mystifying series of events, the bewildered disciples manage to carry the good news of Jesus from Jerusalem all the way to Rome –

the centre of the Empire. Marked by episodes of miracle, daring, persecution and bravery, the *Acts of the Apostles* is probably the most entertaining section of the New Testament. There is plenty of argument as to whether the author was a witness to at least some of the later events in the narrative (see Acts 16:10ff), and similar debates as to precisely when this account reached its final form. Those who would date it before 70 CE note the absence of explicit reference to the destruction of the Temple or to the deaths of the two main protagonists, Peter and Paul, both of whom are thought to have been martyred in Rome during the Neronian persecution c.64 CE. Others who argue for a later date are in part persuaded by the need for Luke to be subsequent to Mark, by implicit references to the temple calamity (Acts 6:14) and by the sophistication of its literary style. Whatever the date, the theological 'macro-theme' which follows through the whole of Luke-Acts is maintained, namely that the Good News is for everyone, Judean and Gentile alike (cf. Witherington, 1998, p. 72).

b) Ascension as essential

Luke's 'sequel' begins with the Ascension of Jesus into heaven:

> In the first book, Theophilus, I wrote about all that Jesus did and taught from the beginning until the day when he was taken up to heaven, after giving instructions through the Holy Spirit to the apostles whom he had chosen. After his suffering he presented himself alive to them by many convincing proofs, appearing to them over the course of forty days and speaking about the kingdom of God. While staying with them, he ordered them not to leave Jerusalem, but to wait there for the promise of the Father. "This," he said, "is what you have heard from me; for John baptized with water, but you will be baptized with the Holy Spirit not many days from now."
>
> So when they had come together, they asked him, "Lord, is this the time when you will restore the kingdom to Israel?" He replied, "It is not for you to know the times or periods that the Father has set by his own authority. But you will receive power when the Holy Spirit has come upon you; and you will be my witnesses in Jerusalem, in all Judea and Samaria, and to the ends of the earth." When he had said this, as they were watching, he was lifted up, and a cloud took him out of their sight. While he was going and they were gazing up towards heaven, suddenly two men in white robes stood by them. They said, "Men of Galilee, why do you stand looking up towards heaven? This Jesus, who has been taken up from you into heaven, will come in the same way as you saw him go into heaven." Then they returned to Jerusalem from the mount called Olivet, which is near Jerusalem, a sabbath day's journey away. (Acts 1:1-12)

Thus the apparitions of Jesus are ended in Acts after the elapse of forty days, which once again designates a period of transformation. Although the Ascension in Acts 1 is not recounted in such detail elsewhere, there are similarities with the description in Matthew where Jesus entrusts the Twelve with a commission to proclaim the good news to the ends of the earth (Matt 28:16-20). A later ending of Mark also has an ascension type scene (Mark 16:15-20) and one can likewise link the tenor of the event with the witness commission of John's Gospel (John 15:26-7). Jesus insists in John's account that it is better that he should go so that the fullness of the Spirit might be bestowed (John 16:7). Theologically, the Ascension clearly has cosmic overtones – the receiving of Jesus, Son of Man, into heaven which allows the earthly Jesus to give way to the Christ of faith (cf. Dan 7:13–14). Perhaps more importantly the narrative has an ecclesiological – 'church-logic' – basis. It allows the believers, moved by the Spirit, to take centre stage and ultimately take on the 'corporate identity' of the risen Jesus (Acts 9:5).

While it would be wrong to identify this 'church-logic' too readily with the shape of ecclesiastical institutions we are now familiar with, we can note that in the passage that follows, Luke is at pains to point out that the Twelve apostles have to be restored to full number – so that the symbolism of the Twelve tribes is maintained (Acts 1:15-26). The fact that the short-listing process to replace Judas culminates in what was effectively a toss of the coin may surprise some people familiar with current employment legislation. It did, however, have good biblical precedent since the tradition of the *urim and thummin* – 'the sacred lots' – is prevalent throughout the Torah and beyond (cf. Ex 28:30, Lev 8:8, Num 27:21, Deut 33:8 1, Sam 14:41, Neh 7:65, Sir 45:10). This text cements Luke's emphasis on the continuity of the message back through the preaching of John the Baptist to the ancient traditions of the Hebrews. This is the true Israel with a true message (cf. Seccombe, 1998, pp. 350–71).

c) Pentecost

Pentecost constituted one of many religious festivals in the Jewish calendar. Originally a wheat harvest thanksgiving, it had by now become synonymous with the celebration of the giving of the Law. As such, Luke's text builds up the reader's anticipation that a new proclamation is at hand and the subsequent *theophany* – 'God-manifestation' – is charged with symbolism. The disciples have returned to the semi-secretive upper room and are gathered in prayer as community with a number of women including Mary the mother of Jesus, who is specifically named. The presence of women in the upper room has led to much speculation regarding respective roles in the Jesus community. With

Mary, however, Luke may be deliberately sketching parallels with the infancy narrative and the birth of Jesus, hence here it is possible that the birth of the body of Christ *as the Church* is in view.

If the scene begins with a closeted group of believers gathered in fearful faith, the theophany of the Spirit soon changes all that. The Hebrew tradition understood the Spirit's activity to be cosmic, creative, prophetic and empowering but here, the howling wind and bonfires on the heads of the believers are not only a health and safety nightmare, they clearly make it more dangerous to be inside than out (Acts 2:1-3). Hang the consequences, out they go 'filled with the Holy Spirit' and begin praising God through *glossolalia* – 'speaking in tongues' (Acts 2:4). Such ecstatic – 'being beside yourself' – behaviour was not uncommon in the prophetic traditions of Israel (e.g. 1 Sam 19:20), and in contemporary Christian churches lively praise of God is a common phenomenon in Pentecostal or charismatic worship (cf. Pilch, 2004, pp. 25–37 and Johnson, 1998, pp. 105–36). The emphasis in the text is that all peoples can understand this good news of Jesus and it will not be restricted to one nation. This theme at the heart of Luke's Theology has the side effect of 'healing' the confusion which began at the Tower of Babel where humanity tried to access heaven by a feat of engineering (Gen 11:1-9). In that tale God confused the languages so that no one could understand each other, while in this episode all can understand *despite* the differences in language, which perfectly serves Luke's 'internationalizing' of the Good News (Acts 2:6-11). All nations can come together as one under the one God. There is no need to build a tower to heaven as God's presence is bestowed upon earth through the Spirit.

d) The *kerygma*

At this point, the *kerygma* – 'the apostolic preaching' – begins. Much time has been spent analysing, itemizing, categorizing and distilling the essence of the original preaching of the original disciples concerning the original Jesus. While there may be merit in trying to get behind Luke's version of that original proclamation, some of the humour present in the actual text can be missed. Let's face it, most people would expect the *kerygma*, or original apostolic preaching, to begin with something like 'Hear O Israel, Jesus the Nazarene is the One Risen Messiah sent by the One Living God'. In fact, Luke has Peter beginning the *kerygma* with:

> Men of Judea and all who live in Jerusalem, let this be known to you, and listen to what I say. Indeed, these men are not drunk, as you suppose, since it is only nine o'clock in the morning. (Acts 2:14-15)

Although Christian Theology can be a very serious subject, I do love the fact that the biblical record of its first public proclamation begins with Peter denying that his gang of friends have been on the hooch. From the off, the proclamation of faith is met with derision and in this case it meets with the accusation that the disciples are out of their heads. Maybe the boys had a reputation – after all, Jesus was accused of being a drunkard and the Twelve may have had something to do with why the wine ran dry at the marriage feast of Cana (cf. Matt 11:19 and John 2:1-11). Intriguingly we can note that Peter doesn't deny the charge because they are abstemious teetotallers. No, Peter issues his denial based on the fact that it is only nine in the morning. Too early even for Galileans to quaff a skinful? Who knows? But it is worth noting that identifying joyfulness as a sign of God's spirit is also biblical (cf. Ps 4:7, Ps 51:12, Luke 10:21). In this regard, a comment by Friedrich Nietzsche from *Thus Spoke Zarathustra* might be apposite. Often regarded as the father of modern atheism, he once remarked of Christians: 'They would have to sing better songs for me to believe in their Redeemer: his disciples would have to look more redeemed!' (Nietzsche, [1885] 1969, p. 116).

In fairness, Luke does go on to depict Peter explaining what has happened in categories that the religiously minded would understand, recalling a prophecy from Joel that includes the bestowal of the Spirit upon all (Acts 2:17-21 cf. Joel 2:28-32). This dream that the Spirit – the very life and power of God – could be freely available to all was not only present in the older traditions of Moses (Num 11:29), but was a feature of the aspirations regarding the Messiah. Indeed, it can be argued that the designation of the Messiah as the 'One who will Baptize with the Holy Spirit and Fire' is perhaps the earliest messianic 'title' evidenced in the Synoptics (cf. Matt 3:11, Mark 1:8, Luke 3:16). No one can deny the significance of the early preaching of John the Baptist as formative in the consciousness of the disciples – it is a criterion of authentic apostleship in Luke's view which has been called to mind only a few verses prior to the choosing of Matthias as successor to Judas (Acts 1:22-26). What makes Luke's use of the Spirit and fire imagery intriguing is that Jesus referred to the same connection at various points in his ministry. This may form part of the 'background template' of Luke which patterns Jesus on Elijah since the latter was a man of God, fire and spirit (cf. 2 Kings 1:9-14). But then Luke has Jesus rejecting the misuse of Elijan-style 'fire-power' in the face of unbelieving Samaritans (Luke 9:54) and in what may be an allusion to Pentecost, Jesus cries out 'I came to bring fire to the earth, and how I wish it were already kindled!' (Luke 12:49).

If Jesus did indeed come to 'cast fire upon the earth', then the preaching of Peter proved suitably inflammatory according to Luke's account. Referring to the 'latter days' and taking David's psalms as the theological template to explain both the resurrection and the heavenly authority of Jesus, Peter proclaims him as Lord and Holy One, seated at the right hand of God (Acts 2:22-40). The picture is of fervent, effective preaching and with the promise of forgiveness and the Holy Spirit, no fewer than three thousand believe and are baptized (Acts 2:41). Without getting too concerned about the head count, contemporary cynics might say that story could be contrasted with current preaching skills, which would need more like three thousand sermons to convince one unbeliever.

e) Life in common

The discipleship band that had followed Jesus during his ministry seems always to have had some sense of a common life (cf. Matt 27:55, Luke 8:1-3, John 13:29). This tradition appears to have carried on after Pentecost where it at first appeared idyllic, with the text implying it formed part of the power and attraction of the baptized. Compare the following passages:

> And they devoted themselves to the apostles' teaching and fellowship, to the breaking of bread and the prayers. Awe came upon everyone, because many wonders and signs were being done by the apostles. All who believed were together and had all things in common. (Acts 2:42-44)

> Now the whole group of those who believed were of one heart and soul, and no one claimed private ownership of any possessions, but everything they owned was held in common. With great power the apostles gave their testimony to the resurrection of the Lord Jesus, and great grace was upon them all. There was not a needy person among them, for as many as owned lands or houses sold them and brought the proceeds of what was sold. They laid it at the apostles' feet, and it was distributed to each as any had need. (Acts 4:32-35)

In line with liberation and kingdom themes that mark his Gospel from the 'Nazareth Manifesto' onwards, it seems that for Luke the miracles and mutuality go hand in hand (cf. Luke 4:16-21). The two passages cited above act as bookends to the healing story of the lame man cured by Peter in Jesus' name at the Beautiful Gate of the Temple precinct. It would seem that the power of the witnesses to work wonders is being deliberately linked to the radical, communal lifestyle being proposed. Hence while the miracles drew attention to the *kerygmatic* preaching in a dramatic fashion, there does seem a strong indication that the growth of the early community is attributable to a *kerygmatic programme* which includes radical generosity, group belonging and mutual help. Here, theological and sociological themes intersect. Social analysts reviewing this period suggest that the *koinonia* – or 'communality' – of the Pentecost community was perhaps more important than preaching or miracles in the success of the young movement in its early days and decades (see Finger, 2007, pp. 53–67 and below Section 15g).

Notwithstanding these ideals, Luke is candid enough to retell increasing tensions with regard to this shared life. Not only is the dramatic deceit of one couple exposed (Acts 5:1-10), a fissure along linguistic if not racial grounds comes to the fore in the disagreements between Jewish and Greek-speaking widows (Acts 6:1). Characteristically poor and unprotected, the distribution of food to widows was central and sensitive. To ease the tensions, in what might be seen as the beginnings of organizational hierarchy, the apostles appoint seven deacons to help manage matters (Acts 6:2-7). Unfortunately, if the deacons brought a semblance of serenity to the community within, that did not guarantee tranquillity without.

f) Persecution – the death of Stephen

One of the most vexed questions of modern biblical exegesis concerns the manner in which the original followers of Jesus emerged as a group distinct, separate, and ultimately opposed to the Judaism from whence they came. Sometimes called the 'parting of the ways', it has considerable impact on how one reads the writings of Paul, John and Luke-Acts since the distinctions between Jews and Christians so familiar to us were not necessarily so evident at the time. This is worth bearing in mind as one reads the conflict that led to the death of Stephen. In the text, tensions between the Pentecostal group and the authorities were growing. Mirroring Gospel disputes, a healing by Peter on the Sabbath led to unease among the Jerusalem authorities (Acts 3:1-4:31, 5:15-42). There follow rebukes, arrests, miraculous deliverance and the defiance of authority of which Stephen becomes an exemplar (Acts 6:8-15).

One can glean from the description of the argument between Stephen and the Synagogue of Freedmen that both sides are claiming the scriptural traditions as their own – each claiming to be authentic exponents of Judaism. It is noteworthy that Stephen is accused of sedition for making reference to the destruction of the Temple since the very same charge formed part of the trial scene of Jesus (cf. Acts 6:14). In response, all seems well in Stephen's lengthy summary of Israel's salvific past since it culminates with Solomon's building of the Temple. However, he then abruptly presses three red buttons, any one of which would cause fatal alarm in a rabbinical context:

- He dismisses the construction of the Temple as unnecessary to God who is Lord of heaven and earth (Acts 7:48).
- He dismisses his listeners as 'stiff-necked people' who have never listened to the prophets and who by crucifying Jesus acted according to type (Acts 7:51).
- He claims a vision which reveals Jesus as the cosmic Son of Man at God's right hand (Acts 7:56).

The result is that Stephen is stoned to death (Acts 7:60). As Stephen becomes the first *martyr* ('witness') of the now frightened *ekklesia* ('assembly' or 'church'), another young man, Saul of Tarsus, begins a systematic persecution of the group (Acts 8:1-4). As a result, while many remain in Jerusalem, other believers are scattered, including Philip. The story of Philip's witness to the Ethiopian eunuch has rich theological resonance, not least since it emphasizes the global reach of the good news to Africa. It also underlines the importance of the oracles of the *'ebed* YHWH – the Servant of God from Isa 52-53 as the key to understanding the notion of Jesus as a suffering Messiah (Acts 8:29-38). Luke's Gospel has alluded to this already in the post-resurrection story of the Emmaus road: 'Was it not necessary that the Messiah should suffer these things and then enter into his glory?' (Luke 24:26). In the story of Philip, the narration makes plain that the systematic identification of Jesus as Lamb of God and *'ebed* YHWH was complete.

Another neat irony worth noting here is that the Synagogue of Freedmen would have been Hellenist, and the seven deacons, from their Greek names, were Hellenist, including Philip who has to flee. Hence we have the first mission conducted not by the Judean apostles, but by the Greeks, to the Africans. Note also that Saul/Paul is presented as a Hellenist (being from Tarsus), and the Twelve – Hebrews – seem unaffected by the persecution.

g) Paul, Peter, James and the Council of Jerusalem

The narrative of Acts then continues with the story of Paul's life-changing experience on the Damascus road. This famous incident is discussed at some length in the next chapter but the well-known consequence is from being a persecutor of the Church, Paul becomes its most fervent missionary. That said, although the activities of Paul will become synonymous with the proclamation of the Gospel to the Gentiles, Acts first highlights the miracles and preaching of Peter in Lydda and Joppa before taking great lengths to explain the change in dietary laws which seems to have been authorized early on in the evolution of the movement. The episode is sparked by a Roman centurion who is a typical 'Lukan' hero – the God-fearing foreigner who becomes a witness (Acts 10:1-2). His vision coincides with Peter's dream that declared all animals clean and the ensuing meeting between the two is sealed by another 'descent of the Spirit' which confirms the bond of unity (Acts 10:44). It can be argued that this revolution, which was undoing sacred traditions at the heart of Jewish religious expression, was as important as 'communality' in enabling the rapid expansion of the movement. Along with the later relaxation of the rules on circumcision, the dietary changes meant that 'God-fearers' on the edges of monotheistic belief could embrace the tenets of this 'new' version of Judaism without the kind of radical change in lifestyle that more traditional rabbinical observance demanded. Though modern scholars neither agree on how numerous such 'God-fearers' were, nor the extent of their familiarity with Jewish scriptures and practices, the theory goes that a kind of 'Judaism-lite' could have been attractive to religious-minded folk unimpressed with polytheism in either its Greek or Roman forms.

More generally, however, religious people are notorious for being sticklers for traditions and it is no surprise that hostility to Peter's innovation can be found in the pages of Acts. Linked with the disagreements occasioned by the activities of Paul and Barnabas among the Gentiles, it is clear there was some crisis among the 'Followers of the Way' about which direction to take. Ironically, Luke describes matters reaching crisis point in Antioch – where believers were first called Christians (Acts 11:26). A deputation is sent southwards and a resolution of these vexed questions is sought in the context of what has become known as the 'Council of Jerusalem' recounted in Acts 15:1-29. Luke's scene is perhaps stylized. Set like a courtroom drama, it has 'the circumcision faction' denouncing Peter, who is pleading that the Gentiles be excused the obligation to keep the Law of Moses. With Paul and Barnabas as convincing witnesses, the liberalizing faction appears to win the day and it is James who pronounces the judgement:

> But we should write to them to abstain only from things polluted by idols and from fornication and from whatever has been strangled and from blood. For in every city, for generations past, Moses has had those who proclaim him, for he has been read aloud every sabbath in the synagogues. (Acts 15:20-21)

Much is made of the role that James plays here. Was this a one-off brilliant insight on his part or did this intervention mean that he was ultimately in charge of the movement rather than Peter? Was it that James, as leader of the movement in Jerusalem, had the role of 'chair' and was arbitrating in a situation where Peter was partisan? Such questions are intriguing but need not detain us just now since it is the secondary argument of James which has left a more problematic legacy. Meant to allay the fears of the more traditionally-minded believers, James asserts that 'Moses has had those who proclaim him, for he has been read aloud every sabbath in the synagogues' (Acts 15:21). In other words, James is not particularly worried by this new direction, as the Moses tradition is resilient and has lasted centuries. It need not be imposed on the new believers.

To unpack this a little, let us note what remains intact from the extensive Law of Moses. Food offered to idols remains forbidden. These offerings were part and parcel of Roman culture and were made at the various temples dedicated to the various deities of their polytheistic ('many gods') system. Since this was the equivalent of worshipping a false God, this remained unacceptable. Unchastity and sexual licentiousness, a facet largely tolerated in the broader culture also remains here as a religious marker for the movement. Meanwhile, since the blood of a living creature was understood to bear its life and nature, it remained important that animals should be properly slaughtered. To partake of blood or of an animal merely strangled (thus leaving their blood within them) was not acceptable (Lev 7:26-27) – it would be tantamount to taking on their nature.

With these minimum requirements in place, there remained plenty of other food for thought. While the text claims one accord (Acts 15:25, 28), ultimately, this solution did not please everybody since it is astonishingly radical at one level, yet a classic compromise at another.

- On the one hand, it is radical by letting go of the hallowed traditions of generations. The movement was making a more radical decision than if the Pope and other Christian leaders of today were to suddenly declare that Christmas was cancelled, hymns were banned or that Wednesday was to become the new Sunday.
- On the other, it is a compromise. Luke's account clearly leaves the *classical* position intact whereby faithful Hebrews in traditional circumstances continue to observe the customs handed down since Moses.
- God then affirms both. In a pattern that will be echoed down the centuries, the mandate from this Council is issued with divine authority: 'For it has seemed good to the Holy Spirit and to us to impose on you no further burden than these essentials: that you abstain from what has been sacrificed to idols and from blood and from what is strangled and from fornication. If you keep yourselves from these, you will do well'. (Acts 15:28-29)

So what's not to like? Well, wherever there are two official ways of doing things, there's bound to be trouble, and the rest of the Acts of the Apostles is basically a description of how Paul found that trouble wherever he went (cf. Shillington, 2007, pp. 53–67). In terms of following The Way, it is as if Paul ends up trying to conduct traffic going in both directions down both sides of the road. To be sure, the conflicts and scrapes that he got into are not all to do with the Law of Moses in the light of the Gospel, but it was a topic that did pre-occupy him throughout the rest of his journeyings and the rest of his life.

h) The *kerygma* reaches Rome

Following the Council of Jerusalem, the narrative of Acts is almost entirely taken up with the activities of Paul. The easiest explanation for this is that Luke actually joins Paul's circle (see 16:10ff) and becomes a companion on a number of the journeys by which Paul criss-crosses the Mediterranean proclaiming Jesus as Messiah. Another view suggests these 'we' passages are written a bit like a *Star Trek* 'captain's log' because that was the stylized way of narrating adventure journeys at that time. In any event, while Peter disappears from the account there is enough excitement in Paul's adventures to keep the narrative alive. Some are hilarious such as his exorcizing of a possessed girl to get some peace and inadvertently causing a riot (16:16ff). Some are theological banter at its best where he makes headway with Athenians via their concept of the unknown God, but is dismissed as laughable on account of the resurrection (17:16-34). Others are dramatic, such as his shipwreck, deliverance and miraculous deeds on arrival in Malta (27:1-28:10).

Withal, the theme that connects these episodes remains the tension between Paul's preaching and the traditional synagogue beliefs. In Luke's account, the tensions are in two directions: the proclamation of Jesus as the Christ, and the freedom from the Law of Moses that Paul grants to Gentiles. Paul was no fool and at times seems to have taken trouble not to offend, such as when he has his Greek companion Timothy circumcised (16:3) and when on James' advice he makes the effort to fulfil ritual requirements in the Temple (21:18ff). The following, however, is more typical of the pattern of Paul's activity and the reaction to it repeated throughout the rest of the Acts:

> After Paul and Silas had passed through Amphipolis and Apollonia, they came to Thessalonica, where there was a synagogue of the Jews. And Paul went in, as was his custom, and on three sabbath days argued with them from the scriptures, explaining and proving that it was necessary for the Messiah to suffer and to rise from the dead, and saying, "This is the Messiah, Jesus whom I am proclaiming to

you." Some of them were persuaded and joined Paul and Silas, as did a great many of the devout Greeks and not a few of the leading women. But the Jews became jealous, and with the help of some ruffians in the market-places they formed a mob and set the city in an uproar. While they were searching for Paul and Silas to bring them out to the assembly, they attacked Jason's house. When they could not find them, they dragged Jason and some believers before the city authorities, shouting, "These people who have been turning the world upside down have come here also, and Jason has entertained them as guests. They are all acting contrary to the decrees of the emperor, saying that there is another king named Jesus."(Acts 17:1-7)

Basically, theological dispute in the synagogue is followed by charges of disturbing the peace and the involvement of civil authorities. Ultimately, after numerous narrow escapes, and against the advice of prophets in every town, Paul returns to Jerusalem where he is arrested, survives a plot against his life and goes on to defend his views before a series of imperial tribunals (cf. Acts 23:1-35 and 25:1-26). His last years were a combination of trial, travel, prison, house arrest and bail conditions, eventually being transferred to Rome itself (Acts 27:1). The final scenes in Acts depict him free to proclaim his beliefs among his fellow Hebrews in Rome who thankfully don't know of his personal reputation but are aware of the controversies of his sect (Acts 28:21-22). He remains as feisty as ever:

After they had fixed a day to meet him, they came to him at his lodgings in great numbers. From morning until evening he explained the matter to them, testifying to the kingdom of God and trying to convince them about Jesus both from the law of Moses and from the prophets. Some were convinced by what he had said, while others refused to believe. So they disagreed with each other; and as they were leaving, Paul made one further statement: "The Holy Spirit was right in saying to your ancestors through the prophet Isaiah, "Go to this people and say, You will indeed listen, but never understand, and you will indeed look, but never perceive. For this people's heart has grown dull, and their ears are hard of hearing, and they have shut their eyes; so that they might not look with their eyes, and listen with their ears, and understand with their heart and turn - and I would heal them." Let it be known to you then that this salvation of God has been sent to the Gentiles; they will listen." He lived there for two whole years at his own expense and welcomed all who came to him, proclaiming the kingdom of God and teaching about the Lord Jesus Christ with all boldness and without hindrance. (Acts 28:23-31)

So what *is* Paul at this stage and what is this *sect* and its relationship to more traditional Judaism? To these questions this study now turns by looking in more detail at the thinking of this unique Christian theologian.

Summary

The Book of Acts is a highly theologized but nonetheless entertaining account of the Jesus movement's early days. The promise of the Spirit is fulfilled in the events of Pentecost day which unleashes the Kerygma, the 'apostolic preaching' of the Good News of Jesus as Lord and Messiah. Peter's leadership is key in the early chapters but conflict with authority is also a feature and the death of Stephen is described in some detail. The side effects of this tragedy include the first missionary exploits of Philip, but also the 'conversion' of Paul. The gradual unfolding of the story has the Council of Jerusalem at its theological heart. There, decisions are made which effectively make the break with observance of Torah practice. Thereafter, Paul, the most earnest proponent of the changes and erstwhile persecutor of the Church then becomes its main protagonist in a series of episodes which see the Good News being brought all the way to Rome, to the heart of Empire.

3. The Mediterranean in the New Testament Era

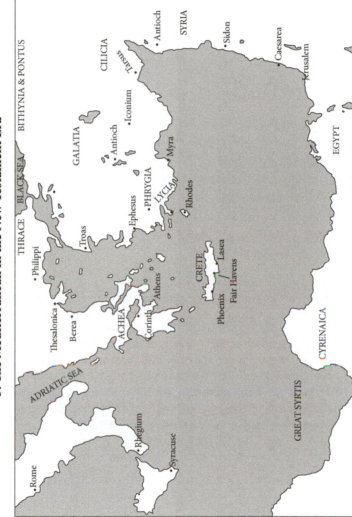

10

Paul

Paul is the single most controversial figure in the New Testament. He is popularly understood as the one who turned the peaceful, loving message of Jesus into an aggressive missionary religion with reactionary tendencies. A fairer reading of his writings reveals, yes, a passionate man, but one who lived his Christian faith backwards. Paul is the apostle who begins with resurrection and only later begins to understand what crucifixion, love and weakness means.

a) Paul: Global citizen and religious revolutionary

Of all the theologians whose words grace the New Testament, Paul is undoubtedly the most controversial. Not only do Paul's character and tone divide opinion, his writings uniquely carry a biblical health warning lest they be misunderstood (2 Pet 3:16). On the one hand, there is no voice so lucid and poetic in describing the nature of love yet on the other, none so strident in wishing graphic misfortune on his enemies (cf. 1 Cor 13:1-13 and Gal 5:12). Despite his daring and admirable deeds as the greatest missionary of the early Church, he is accused of being anti-women, anti-Semitic and even anti-Christian. Indeed it has become a commonplace to claim that the simple liberating Gospel of Jesus was transformed by Paul into the controlling rule-bound religion of Christianity by means of his cosmic theological exaggerations which proclaimed the humble carpenter as Lord of the Universe (cf. Maccoby, 1986, pp. 184–5 and Horrell, 2000, pp. 1–3). Unfortunately such views will not be supported in the summary of Paul's Theology here – if anything they just aren't radical enough!

Paul was born to a Jewish family, around the same time as Jesus, in a trading port called Tarsus on the southern coast of present-day Turkey which was then part of the Roman Empire. Paul was naturally cosmopolitan. Growing up as a Roman citizen in a busy Greek-speaking port and learning a trade as a tent-maker, Paul was well-equipped for social and geographical mobility – factors which would prove excellent training for his life's work. At a certain point, Paul ('Saul' was the Hebrew equivalent – he never changed his name) set out to train as a Pharisee in Jerusalem under Gamaliel (Acts 5:33-39, 22:3). Zealous for the Law, Paul knew his Hebrew scriptures and lets us know that he was top of the class (Gal 1:14). This passion for his faith led him into conflict with the early Jesus movement and in what would prove a fateful turn of events, Luke depicts him assisting at the first execution of a follower of Jesus – Stephen (Acts 8:1). Then, emboldened by a mandate from Ananias the High Priest, Paul sets out for Damascus to carry on a persecution of the sect (Acts 5:17-18, 9:1-12).

It is said that travel is good for us because it can help us to change and to see things from a different perspective. Paul's planned journey from Jerusalem was only around 135 miles, but he would arrive in Damascus with a radically different mind-set which not only changed him, but the entire Jesus movement.

From then until his death some thirty years later in Rome during the reign of Nero (62–64 CE), Paul lived a life of travel and trouble, traversing the Mediterranean and leaving behind a series of communiqués which have bedazzled and befuddled theologians ever since. Since thirteen letters or 'epistles' are attributed to him, it is obviously impossible in just one chapter to do justice to the breadth of his thinking and his many theological concerns. It may also be worth pointing out that scholars disagree regarding which of the letters are indisputably from his hand and which are writings merely bearing hallmarks of his thinking. Romans, 1 and 2 Corinthians, Galatians, 1 Thessalonians and Philemon are rarely questioned while 1 and 2 Timothy and Titus are much less well supported. Colossians, Philippians, Ephesians and II

Thessalonians over the years tend to be tugged one way or the other (cf. Morton & McLeman, 1966 and Johnson, 2010). To keep things simple, this text will:

• Limit any detailed argumentation to evidence from the 'undisputed' letters.
• Focus on selected aspects of his thinking that can be traced to his transforming encounter on the road to Damascus.
• Shamelessly contrive to offset some of the bad press Paul receives by ending with a section on love.

b) Damascus: Conversion, call or conundrum?

So what happened on the way to Damascus? It is easy to go along with the popular image of Paul falling from his horse, 'seeing the light' and being immediately transformed into a firebrand apostle. This image is firmly entrenched in works of art and in the common Christian consciousness. The 'Road to Damascus' remains a paradigm of conversion familiar even in secular culture. But while Churches still celebrate the moment with a designated feast, there is some controversy about the event in terms of its nature and its narrative (see Longnecker, 1997).

In terms of its nature, there are feisty exchanges among scholars about whether this event is better described as a 'call' rather than a 'conversion', since Paul remains true to his faith and ethnic identity until his death. There is no time here to rehearse all the arguments, but there are obvious sensitivities regarding Jewish-Christian relations which impinge on the debate. Whether the event be considered a conversion or a radical rethinking, the exact description need not delay us. It is enough to assert that 'Damascus' denotes a life-changing experience for Paul which determined his Theology.

In terms of the biblical text, with all due respect to Murillo, Caravaggio and other famous painters, the most familiar account in Acts 9 makes no mention of a horse, but provides a vivid picture of Paul, knocked to the ground by a flash of light and hearing a voice calling his name in Hebrew or Aramaic:

> Now as he was going along and approaching Damascus, suddenly a light from heaven flashed around him. He fell to the ground and heard a voice saying to him, "Saul, Saul, why do you persecute me?" He asked, "Who are you, Lord?" The reply came, "I am Jesus, whom you are persecuting. But get up and enter the city, and you will be told what you are to do." The men who were travelling with him stood speechless because they heard the voice but saw no one. Saul got up from the ground, and though his eyes were open, he could see nothing; so they led him by the hand and brought him into Damascus. For three days he was without sight, and neither ate nor drank. (Acts 9:3-9)

The account continues with the symbolic restoration of Paul's sight at the hand of a Damascus Christian named Ananias, who understandably takes some persuading to go and visit the sworn enemy of the faith. At this point, although the account in Acts has Paul entering synagogues almost immediately to proclaim Jesus as the Son of God (Acts 9:20), his own version of the incident in the Letter to the Galatians proposes a time lapse between this transformative moment and his new ministry.

> You have heard, no doubt, of my earlier life in Judaism. I was violently persecuting the church of God and was trying to destroy it. I advanced in Judaism beyond many among my people of the same age, for I was far more zealous for the traditions of my ancestors. But when God, who had set me apart before I was born and called me through his grace, was pleased to reveal his Son to me, so that I might proclaim him among the Gentiles, I did not confer with any human being, nor did I go up to Jerusalem to those who were already apostles before me, but I went away at once into Arabia, and afterwards I returned to Damascus. (Gal 1:13-17)

This leaves the reader with a bit of a conundrum. Here there is no mention of voices or lights. No mention of blindness, Straight Street, companions, Ananias or anyone else for that matter – he confers with no one. There is no mention even of a journey to Damascus. Inevitably, differences between the accounts have vexed scholars for generations, but the peopled drama of Acts has lived longer in the imagination than the individualistic picture of Galatians. After all, the poignant image of Paul approving Stephen's death for the sake of the Word, only to find himself becoming the most famous servant of the Word, is just one of the many elegant juxtapositions that structure the Luke-Acts narrative.

In terms of core theological themes, however, the similarities far outweigh the different details of the storyline. If we concede that we will never know exactly what happened at Damascus and take only Paul's avowed statement as our main evidence (Gal 1:20), we still find at least three key components echoed in Acts as well as 1 Cor.

- Paul persecuted the Church of God. (Acts 9:1, Gal 1:13, 1 Cor 15:9)
- Paul believes he has encountered the risen Jesus (Acts 9:5, Gal 1:16, 1 Cor 9:1)
- Paul's life is now a mission to outsiders (Acts 9:15, Gal 1:16, 1 Cor 15:10)

In each of these matters there is a humiliation and consolation for Paul. They each demand a transformative acceptance that he has been wrong yet paradoxically they will be the locus of his greatest insights. Indeed, I would suggest that this single experience provides the key for understanding

Paul's principle missionary concerns and why he is best understood not as an advocate of stringent religious control but instead as a theological revolutionary.

c) The Church as Body of Christ

Like all of us, Paul has to live with his past and he is excruciatingly aware that his first encounter with the Christian Way was as an enemy, a stance which has earned him notoriety (Gal 1:23). Yet Paul could not have been more wrong about this Galilean sect, whom he believed to be followers of another mistaken Messiah. Far from being vermin to be exterminated, this rabble actually bear the sacred presence of the God Paul adores. Unimaginably difficult to take on board, this searing experience underpins the developed ecclesiology – 'church thinking' – of Paul. For him, the Church is the Body of Christ, its members are the very instruments and presence of the Lord alive in the world through the Spirit (Rom 12:5, 1 Cor 12:27, Eph 4:11-12).

This awareness of God's presence in the guise of the ordinary is one of the strongest theological messages of the New Testament and Paul is not alone in accentuating this insight. The Parable of the Sheep and the Goats of Matt 25:31-46 takes up this theme of recognizing Jesus in the least of the brethren. 1 John 4:20 also emphasizes the same point – 'Those who do not love a brother or sister whom they have seen, cannot love God whom they have not seen'. This developed sense of the Spirit of Jesus making the collected believers the body of Christ was clearly part of the early consciousness of the movement and Paul's most vivid expression of it comes in First Corinthians where he explicitly uses the analogy of the body:

> For just as the body is one and has many members, and all the members of the body, though many, are one body, so it is with Christ. For in the one Spirit we were all baptized into one body - Jews or Greeks, slaves or free - and we were all made to drink of one Spirit. Indeed, the body does not consist of one member but of many. If the foot were to say, "Because I am not a hand, I do not belong to the body," that would not make it any less a part of the body. And if the ear were to say, "Because I am not an eye, I do not belong to the body," that would not make it any less a part of the body. If the whole body were an eye, where would the hearing be? If the whole body were hearing, where would the sense of smell be? But as it is, God arranged the members in the body, each one of them, as he chose. If all were a single member, where would the body be? (1 Cor 12:12-19)

It is easy to forget that Paul sees himself firstly as an apostle rather than a theologian. Paul's letters abound with concern for the Body of Christ that is the Church. Almost amusingly, when forced to speak about all the trials he has suffered which include imprisonment, starvation, shipwreck and the lash, he concludes that his worst hardship is his anxiety about the Church (2 Cor 11:21-29). Why? Because it is the presence of Christ on earth. He believes this in his bones – he was so wrong about the Church before, he will not make the same mistake again and despite arguments and factions, he will not allow others to do so either.

As we will see below, Paul's passion for the unity of the believers is precisely what gives some of his writing an intensity which from a distance seems inappropriate (Gal 4:6). It also explains why the recognition of the risen Lord in the context of Eucharist is so important to him. The idea that Jesus was especially present in the breaking of the bread is evident also from Luke's account of the apparition of Jesus to the disciples on the road to Emmaus (Luke 24:13-35). For Paul this becomes a double recognition – the community members as the Body of Christ recognizing themselves as the Body of Christ through the ritual of remembrance commanded by Jesus (1 Cor 11:17-13:13).

d) Paul as a resurrection theologian

Another aspect of Paul's own personal testimony helps explain why he comes to faith in Jesus from a very different angle to the Gospel writers. The Evangelists are at pains to explain how the disciples only gradually realized who Jesus truly was. By contrast, Paul is often criticized for not mentioning any of Jesus' miracles or parables and almost ignoring his biography altogether. This leaves him open to the charge noted above that he invented his own version of the Gospels which had little connection with the historical Jesus. Theologically, however, this is entirely understandable since he approaches the mystery of Jesus following what he believes to be an encounter with the risen 'Lord'.

The term 'Lord' (Greek *Kyrios* and Aramaic *Mar*) when used in Jewish religious circles was reserved as a designation for God. The use of this term as a title for Jesus by Paul and other early members of the movement was controversial – indeed it seems to have been one of the first markers of belonging in Christianity (1 Cor 12:3). To defend this use, early Christians used Psalm 110 – commonly understood to be a messianic psalm – which begins 'The Lord says to my lord, "Sit at my right hand until I make your enemies your footstool"' (cf. Mark 12:35, 1 Cor 15:25, Eph 1:20). Since this elusive phrase could imply a sharing of cosmic sovereignty in the heavens, it neatly authenticates the post-resurrection designation of *Jesus* as Lord without compromising the authority of *Ho Theos* – God/YHWH. Likewise, it is consistent with the key pre-resurrection title used of Jesus in the Gospels – the Son of Man. As noted above, this elusive name can be understood in an 'ordinary Joe' sense or in an extraordinary cosmic sense as in the prophecies of Dan 7:13-14.

Paul revels in the theological consequences of this mystery. He does the height and the depth. He goes cosmic. He sinks to the bottom and stays there. It is this glorious power which for him guarantees the ultimate righting of all wrongs and the reconciliation of all things.

> No, in all these things we are more than conquerors through him who loved us. For I am convinced that neither death, nor life, nor angels, nor rulers, nor things present, nor things to come, nor powers, nor height, nor depth, nor anything else in all creation, will be able to separate us from the love of God in Christ Jesus our Lord. (Rom 8:37-39)

In a sense, Paul is understanding Jesus' life in a reverse perspective. He was probably very familiar with key aspects of the traditions of Jesus and in all likelihood sought to be more informed through his contact with pillars of the Church such as Peter (cf. Gal 1:18). Unlike the Twelve, however, his first encounter was with the risen, glorious Lord. Hence he views the cross through the prism of victory without having personally faced the shattering trial of Good Friday. The Damascus encounter has this personal revelation as its fulcrum such that he classes his own experience among Jesus' resurrection appearances and likens it to a new birth (1 Cor 15:8). With alluring linguistic ambiguity, the experience can be translated as a revelation *to him* but also *in him* (Gal 1:16). So, while an enduring talking point among biblical scholars is how few details there are about Jesus' life in the writings of Paul, one could argue that there don't need to be – he carries the Good News of resurrection triumph in his very being (cf. Smith, 2010, pp. 27–45 and Towey, 2009, pp. 26–9).

Paul does not believe he had an epileptic fit, nor does he refer to it in the same manner as a vision, trance or ecstasy which he is familiar with (e.g. cf. 2 Cor 12: 1-10 and Acts 16:9). His blunt statement, 'Have I not seen Jesus our Lord?' (1 Cor 9:1) infuses all his God-logic with hope and a conviction in the promise of the deathless one. Paul's theological understanding is that humanity is remade in Christ's rising with immortal material. It is as if we have been reborn with Christ's deathless chromosomes, not Adam's mortal genes (1 Cor 15:20-24). To be sure, this was not the easiest of messages to put across – it brought him a fair share of derision and argument with friend and foe alike (cf. 1 Thess 4:13-18 and Acts 17:32). Nevertheless, Paul is no longer to be intimidated by the fears that beset those who have not heard this Good News, echoing with lighter tone Hosea's phrases: 'Where, O death, is your victory? Where, O death, is your sting?' (1 Cor 15:55).

Ultimately, Paul's vivid sense of resurrection reality leaves his ministry and theologizing on the edge in a liminal space between the challenges and delights of this world and the promise of the next. He expresses indifference to life or death, such is his vivid sense of the glory to come, because ultimately 'our citizenship is in heaven' (cf. Philip 1:23, 3:20). His preaching clearly generated expectation of a further definitive divine intervention, a cosmic manifestation of the power of Jesus such that some followers of the movement gave up work (cf. 1 Thess 4:11 and 2 Thess 3:11).

The cosmic cry of these early Christians was *Maranatha* – 'Our Lord, Come!' This 'millenarian' or 'apocalyptic' dimension to Paul's preaching cannot and should not be erased from the theological record since it explains some of the urgencies present in his mission and writing. He seems to have expected to live to hear the Last Trumpet and experience *Parousia* – a useful word denoting the reconciliation of all things in Christ, the judgement of all, the restoration of God's rule on earth and the dotting of all theological 'i's and crossing of 't's. His understanding of this unfolds directly from his meditation on what the resurrection of Christ means (cf. 1 Cor 15:1-58 and 1 Thess 4:13-5:28). Since this did not happen, it might be tempting to dismiss Paul's ideas out of hand, but again, to do so would be to underestimate the legacy of his resurrection-thinking which actually mapped out the terrain which Christian Theology has inhabited ever since.

For Paul, the outpouring of the Spirit was both a blessing and a warning that the End Times were approaching. As noted above, the gift of the Spirit and an age of miracles were part of the apocalyptic expectations in Jewish thought, (see Section 6b). Mindful of this background, Paul's theological legacy includes his explanation of the revelation of Jesus as only partially fulfilled, with its culmination near at hand. This notion that the mystery of Jesus' messiahship and the Kingdom of God was 'already revealed but not yet complete' is not only another typical biblical paradox, it almost defines the space within which Christian Theology understands itself. 'Already/Not yet' explains the manner in which Paul is led to defend the Christian claims that in Jesus there has *already* been definitive revelation, *not yet* fulfilled – a cosmos *already* redeemed in principle, *not yet* redeemed in time – an end *already* to the power of death, but *not yet* to earthly mortality.

Lastly, the resurrection paradox of 'already/not yet' serves to contextualize not just the immediate preaching of Paul and the Kingdom of God proclamation so vivid in the Gospels, it usefully allows the key concept of Christ's abiding presence among believers to be both hidden to outsiders, yet revealed to those privy to the mysteries. One of the most fascinating of those hidden mysteries for Paul was the insight for which he is perhaps most famous for, namely:

God Saves, Religion Doesn't

e) Paul and justification by faith

From the get go, from the 'b' of the bang, Paul's moment at Damascus left him with a stunning realization that marked his thinking forever. By the time the literal or figurative scales fell from Paul's eyes, it had become clear to him that religious self-righteousness was not only impossible, it was downright dangerous, if not damnable. Why? The logic of his life told him so. After all, Paul was pretty good at his religion – he was better than most and had letters to prove it. In contemporary terms, he would be looking forward to a good clerical career – he would maybe make Chief Rabbi or Cardinal, or at least hold an influential Chair of Theology. But at Damascus he realized that all this piety, all his theologic and all his religious conviction had only served to make him become a murderer of believers and an enemy of God. Paul had made a life-error which had led him to be the opposite of what he set out to be, a friend of God. What on earth could redeem such a situation?

Only the mercy of God revealed in Jesus.

This led Paul to a series of startling conclusions.

- Keeping the Law is not a guarantee of being at rights with God – he himself was living proof of that.
- The Law, ironically, does not reduce sin, it makes sin more obvious. Just like lumps left in the bottom of a sieve, the Law doesn't remove sin, it puts it on display.
- Sin is what separates us from God. It is not our following of rules that will reunite us with God, it is our connection with the God-one, Jesus.
- Death is the reward for human sin. The resurrection of Jesus is proof that he is the sinless one, the one who does not suffer the mortal curse of Adam. Christ is the deathless one who has taken the curse of sin away, something the Law could never do.
- The faith of Jesus, believing utterly in the promises of God, takes the faith of Abraham to a different level. It is this faith that reconciles humanity to God and conquers death.

- What makes us reconciled ('justified'/'declared innocent'/'righteous') is the faith of Jesus, not our own worthiness.
- Our task is to accept this gift in Jesus' name, that is, to identify ourselves with him.
- Identified with Jesus we are made one as children and co-heirs in the same Spirit – so intimate that we are no longer separated from God, but can call Him 'Abba/Dada/Papa'.

f) Paul on the futility of works and the Law

The genuinely liberating message that Paul brings with these insights is that the Good News is for everyone, no matter what they have or have not done. Far from being in contrast to the simple message of Jesus, it is theologically consistent with the teaching and action of Jesus as depicted by the Gospel accounts. Controversially, however, it would appear that Paul's emphasis on faith downplays, downgrades and ultimately damns human deeds and the works of the Law as useless in relation to redemption. It led him to fierce contestation with his co-religionists and has been a matter of theological controversy ever since. So what was he getting at?

In my view, the simplest explanation is that Paul realizes that religion tends to come down to a series of key performance indicators which human beings think will please God. All faiths, all religions have these markers of piety and identity – sacred days, food rules, dress codes, moral expectations. The religious observances of the Judaism of Paul's time included numerous injunctions regarding diet, circumcision and cleanliness as well as ritual and moral obligations. Paul was not against good deeds in themselves and at times he is at pains to emphasize that (cf. Rom 2:13 and 3:31). However, what he seems to have realized *from his own experience* was that any series of religious obligations can all too easily obscure or even *replace* the relationship with God that such observances are supposed to signify. Even worse, because human beings are so susceptible to appearances, the religious mind is constantly tempted to do things for the sake of what other people will think rather than for motives of God-friendship. Bizarre competitiveness can creep in. As evidenced by the New Testament, through controversies of how exactly the Sabbath should be kept, religious people can even get into arguments about how to do nothing (cf. Matt 12:1-14 and Col 2:16-17).

It is for these reasons that we find Paul writing to the Galatians and referring to the Law as accursed and wishing that those who were telling the locals to be circumcised should cut their own testicles off (cf. Gal 3:10, 5:12). Paul is ready to challenge Peter and indeed anyone indulging in 'appearance piety' on these matters (Gal 2:11-14). He knows that this type of religion doesn't work, but rather it is God's grace that works, and that's what makes it Good News. Anything else is performance religion which he was an expert in and came to realize was futile (Phil 3:8). Paul emphasizes that the good works associated with true religion come from within and *are the fruit of the Spirit* working in the believer – an expression of joy and life in God rather than a source of pride and arrogance in oneself:

> Live by the Spirit, I say, and do not gratify the desires of the flesh. For what the flesh desires is opposed to the Spirit, and what the Spirit desires is opposed to the flesh; for these are opposed to each other, to prevent you from doing what you want. But if you are led by the Spirit, you are not subject to the law. Now the works of the flesh are obvious: fornication, impurity, licentiousness, idolatry, sorcery, enmities, strife, jealousy, anger, quarrels, dissensions, factions, envy, drunkenness, carousing, and things like these. I am warning you, as I warned you before: those who do such things will not inherit the kingdom of God. By contrast, the fruit of the Spirit is love, joy, peace, patience, kindness, generosity, faithfulness, gentleness, and self-control. There is no law against such things. And those who belong to Christ Jesus have crucified the flesh with its passions and desires. If we live by the Spirit, let us also be guided by the Spirit. Let us not become conceited, competing against one another, envying one another. (Gal 5:16-26)

Paul's challenge to followers on 'observance religion' is only matched in the New Testament by Jesus' challenge to the Pharisees in Matthew. It makes sobering reading for anyone who belongs to a church, synagogue, mosque or temple and explains why Paul's preaching and writing is inflammatory. As noted above, some Thessalonians seem to have thought they needn't bother working or doing anything as they waited for the Lord's return. Others, such as some Corinthians, seem to have taken his advice to consider themselves free from the Law as an excuse for indulgent behaviour (1 Cor 5:1). In this light, it is perhaps not surprising that the Second Letter of Peter warns believers to be careful not to misunderstand Paul (2 Pet 3:15-16). Nevertheless, although his downgrading of the requirements of the Law led him to a lifetime of controversy, it crucially enabled him to respond creatively to the third challenge which emerged from his Damascus experience – the Mission to the Gentiles.

g) Paul's life is a mission to outsiders

From Paul's own understanding of his calling at Damascus, he received a vocation to proclaim the Good News among the *ethne*. While this term can mean nations, peoples, pagans, foreigners and non-Jews, there is some claim that here it includes the 'Diaspora' – the Jewish faithful living outside the Promised Land. Certainly Paul's missions as described include visits to synagogues as well as preaching to those with no obvious connection with Judaism. However we classify the term, Paul's mission is a mission which de-emphasizes the Law (Gal 2:1-10). In the light of the inadequacy of the Law, true religion for Paul must begin not with belonging to the Hebrew bloodline, but with a belonging to Christ. This comes through acceptance of God's love in Jesus, not from personal worthiness. It is a grace – a free gift of God – from which nothing can separate believers (Rom 8:35-39).

Hence the call became to share this Good News not just with the tribes of Jacob but with the whole world. The personal consequences for Paul were a lifetime of travel and trouble. His first missionary journey took him from Antioch to Cyprus, and then to Pisidia and Pamphylia in what is present-day south-central Turkey. His second, more extensive journey traversed North from Antioch through the provinces of Cilicia and Galatia in present-day Central Turkey, across to Macedonia and down through Greece, then seawards back to Antioch via Jerusalem. His third journey loosely revisited these earlier missions before his final journey to Rome which included a shipwreck off Malta. In the course all this journeying, Paul is continually harassed by those who suggest his de-emphasis of the Law is a betrayal of his religious identity rather than its fulfilment. He is never far away from trouble and although the famous description of his woes in Second Corinthians is not key to understanding his theological *approach*, it does go some way to explaining its *intensity*:

> Are they Hebrews? So am I. Are they Israelites? So am I. Are they descendants of Abraham? So am I. Are they ministers of Christ? I am talking like a madman—I am a better one: with far greater labours, far more imprisonments, with countless floggings, and often near death. Five times I have received from the Jews the forty lashes minus one. Three times I was beaten with rods. Once I received a stoning. Three times I was shipwrecked; for a night and a day I was adrift at sea; on frequent journeys, in danger from rivers, danger from bandits, danger from my own people, danger from Gentiles, danger in the city, danger in the wilderness, danger at sea, danger from false brothers and sisters; in toil and hardship, through many a sleepless night, hungry and thirsty, often without food, cold and naked. And, besides other things, I am under daily pressure because of my anxiety for all the churches. (2 Cor 11:22-28)

Given this violent background, it is no surprise that the missionary theological drive of Paul has been perceived as somewhat aggressive and intolerant. At turns, his de-emphasis of the Law may appear to be anti-Semitic, his counsel regarding the organization of Churches anti-women and his tolerance of slavery unenlightened (cf. Ehrensperger, 2009, pp. 179–200 and Campbell, 2008, pp. 33–52). However, such accusations can be challenged by awareness of the social context of his time. For example, the injunction that women should wear a head covering may have been a simple assertion of gender distinctions, but may also connote protection from lustful demons or concern that an uncovered head was a symbol of sexual availability linked to prostitution and slavery (1 Cor 11:3-16).

Meanwhile, the core theme of Paul's Theology runs contrary to accusations of small-mindedness:

> As many of you as were baptized into Christ have clothed yourselves with Christ. There is no longer Jew or Greek, there is no longer slave or free, there is no longer male and female; for all of you are one in Christ Jesus.(Gal 3:27-28)

For Paul, identity with Christ is the key. Racial, religious, gender and class differences are obliterated in Jesus, who through the gift of the Spirit unites all in one body. For the Jesus movement, the identification with Christ occurs in baptism. The death of the plunge represents the crucifixion, and the resurrection is symbolized by the re-surfacing from the waters into the new, shared life of the risen Jesus where divisive human distinctions are a thing of the past.

h) Paul and the Theology of Love

Since this short survey of Paul's work has been happy to emphasize the controversial dimensions of his mission and theologizing, it is perhaps appropriate to conclude by looking at the 'softer' side of Paul's personality and thinking. No matter how feisty his character was, he seems to have been held in great affection by those who knew him (see Acts 20:36-38). His ability to found churches and travel so extensively is indicative of an outgoing, engaging character. Far from being misogynistic, he seems to have relied upon women to co-ordinate much of his missionary work (see Rom 16:1-16), and despite his occasional demonstrations of self-importance, he is also aware of his limitations and reliance upon God. The personal nature of his letters lends them an autobiographical, intimate tone unique in the New Testament and nowhere is he more lucid than in this magnificent hymn to love:

> If I speak in the tongues of mortals and of angels, but do not have love, I am a noisy gong or a clanging cymbal. And if I have prophetic powers, and understand all mysteries and all knowledge, and if I have all faith, so as to remove mountains,

but do not have love, I am nothing. If I give away all my possessions, and if I hand over my body so that I may boast, but do not have love, I gain nothing.

Love is patient; love is kind; love is not envious or boastful or arrogant or rude. It does not insist on its own way; it is not irritable or resentful; it does not rejoice in wrongdoing, but rejoices in the truth. It bears all things, believes all things, hopes all things, endures all things . . . . And now faith, hope, and love abide, these three; and the greatest of these is love. (1 Cor 13:1-7, 13)

Here again, Paul is offering an implicit corrective to mistaken religiosity. His view in this text conforms to the Golden Rule of the Gospel – 'to love one's neighbour as oneself' – and undermines claims that he represents a rupture with the message of Jesus. Paul did not need the Beatles to tell him 'All you need is Love' – he knew that already. Moreover, Paul was not the only New Testament writer to propose the sovereignty of love as the heart of the Jesus message. His views are mirrored by another great poet of love and Christian Theology, John, to whom this study will now turn.

Summary

Paul is a religious revolutionary. Like most reformers, he made enemies as well as friends, but at the heart of his message was a radical call to freedom – from religion. His understanding of the Church as the Body of Christ and his insistence on the gratuitous saving power of Jesus led him to a profound concern for the communities under his care which was reciprocated with much affection. Well-equipped to bring the message of Jesus to the Gentiles, his theological interpretation was unequivocal – the followers of the Way were now the authentic heirs to the promises of Abraham. The life of the Spirit rather than the works of the Law was the mark of the true believer in the lordship of Jesus.

11

John as Theologian

'This is my commandment, that you love one another as I have loved you.' (John 15:12)

The Fourth Gospel represents the theological heights of Christian New Testament thinking. By the time this Gospel was completed in its present form, Jesus is not only the Messiah, he is unambiguously a manifestation of God who self-identifies himself as such (8:58). If Jesus predominantly preaches the Kingdom in the Synoptics, he actually becomes the preaching in the Fourth Gospel and the text can be understood as a cosmic trial of this truth. The narrative style is different. Instead of parables Jesus teaches through a combination of intimate lucid dialogues with friends and 'courtroom drama' arguments with enemies. Painful religious division and later theological controversy may well explain the tone and thought present in the writing which also hints at both Jewish apocalyptic and Greek wisdom traditions. These theological connections serve to confirm that the Presence and Wisdom of God has been revealed enfleshed in Jesus the Christ. The intimate life of Father, Son and Spirit finds articulation in the Farewell discourse. The Lamb who takes away the sins of the world rises as the New Adam, breathing forth the Spirit upon a new humanity remade in the image of the God of love.

a) The writings of John

For better or for worse, the Fourth Gospel along with the other 'Johannine' writings – the three Epistles of John and the Book of Revelation – have long been regarded as 'a bit different'. These writings, which have the command of love at their heart, also have more than their fair share of conflict. There is a cosmic, mysterious 'sacred and spooky' quality to these writings which gives them a tone quite distinct from other New Testament literature. While the controversies regarding this Gospel and its many themes are intriguing, they are never quite as wild as the symbolism in the Book of Revelation or *Apocalypse* which attracts the attention of scriptural nerd and internet conspiracy theorist alike. To be sure, the dualistic, 'two-world' style of Revelation is present in the Gospel and letters, but since it is usually considered to be crafted by a different hand, it will be considered separately.

Meanwhile, if ever Christians needed to acknowledge that Gospel gears are not set in neutral, they should look no further than John. Towards the end of his account, in a wonderfully disarming statement, the writer declares:

> 'Now Jesus did many other signs in the presence of his disciples, which are not written in this book. But these are written so that you may come to believe that Jesus is the Messiah, the Son of God, and that through believing you may have life in his name.' (John 20: 29-31)

To make his point and invite belief, this theologian evangelist elegantly constructs this Gospel in a 'double seven' pattern which serves to emphasize the perfection of the signs given by Jesus and his identification with the unutterable, unfathomable I AM God of Ex 3:14.

7 Signs:

1 Turning water into wine (2:1-12)
2 Healing the Official's son (4:46-54)
3 Healing the man at Bethesda (5:1-47)
4 Feeding the 5000 (6:1-4)
5 Walking on Water (6:15-21)
6 Healing the Blind Man (9:1-41)
7 Raising of Lazarus (11:1-57)

7 'I AM' Statements:

1 I AM the Bread of Life (6:35)
2 I AM the Light of the World (8:12)
3 Before Abraham was, I AM (8:58)
4 I AM the Good Shepherd (10:11)
5 I AM the Resurrection and the Life (11:25)
6 I AM the Way, the Truth, and the Life (14:6)
7 I AM the True Vine (15:1)

Around this central core, the Gospel has a sweeping prologue coupled with the preaching of the Baptist as preamble to the Public Ministry. The events of his final days include an extended 'Farewell Discourse' during the Last Supper, and similar but more detailed accounts of the death and resurrection than are found in the synoptic tradition. Jesus uses allusions rather than parables and teaches by extended argumentation and reflection. Vivid contrasts such as light-dark and night-day are typical and conjure mystique. Most striking is that whereas the preaching of the Kingdom may be considered the central message in the Synoptic tradition, here the focus is much more explicitly on who Jesus *is*. Besides explaining the designation of the miracles as 'signs' pointing to his identity, the sayings also become part of the revelation of Jesus' divine nature. The sacred 'I AM' is the glaring clue. At the risk of oversimplifying its richly symbolic imagery, the whole Gospel may be understood as a 'cosmic trial of truth'. This reaches a peak of intensity when the representative of earthly power, Pilate, asks Jesus: 'What is truth?' (18:38). Once more the destiny of humankind is represented in the drama of one individual. Understood in this way, it is easy to see how the Gospel is designed to draw the reader or listener into this other worldly courtroom drama, to listen to the *witnesses* such as John the Baptist, the Samaritan woman, the Man born blind and the 'Beloved disciple' and make a judgement on whether the case presented is true.

b) Overview and undertones

Whizzing through the narrative and highlighting some key themes, the Prologue (1:1-16) alerts the reader that nothing less than a new creation is taking place. The witness of John the Baptist follows, and the text yields perhaps the clearest evidence of all the Gospels that the Jesus group was connected to that of John, and thereby to the kind of messianic thinking prevalent at Qumran among the Essenes (cf. 1:19-51, 3:22-4:3 and Chapter 6 of this book). The identification of Jesus as the 'Lamb of God' by the Baptizer drenches this Gospel in sacrificial symbolism (1:29), a point emphasized by a displaced timeline which locates the crucifixion of Jesus on preparation day, at the time when the Passover lamb is slain for the purpose of the saving meal (19:14, 19:28-37). The replacement of central motifs of the Jewish religion by the person of Jesus himself is continued by the Gospel writer with the cleansing of the Temple, which will soon be replaced by the sanctuary of his own body (2:21).

The Fourth Gospel also has the famous 'born again' line in a conversation with Nicodemus which is necessary for him to have *zōē* – 'life'. This 'life' is of a different quality to *bios* – it is not of this world. This does not mean that the believer will inhabit a parallel universe, rather the believer's life is lived deeper, in an enduring experience of transcendent truth. Note also that this meeting begins 'by night' but ends with the invitation to 'come to the light' (3:1-21). Such dark-light, night-day motifs are strong throughout, most chillingly evidenced when Judas leaves to betray Jesus: 'And it was night' (13:30). By contrast, the encounter with the Samaritan woman in the heat of the day is all about light and insight (4:4-42). The fact that they meet beside a well (with biblical connotations of romance) and she is a foreigner with a dodgy track record of relationships (five husbands and now living with someone else) causes consternation among the disciples (4:27). However, in a Luke-style role reversal, she unexpectedly believes and becomes a *witness* – exemplifying another key theme of this Gospel (4:39).

The subsequent healing of the official's son, the healing of a paralytic and the feeding of the 5000 are all reminiscent of traditions in the other Gospels (cf. Matt 8:5, 9:6, 14:13-21). For much of the last century, John's symbolic presentation of the 'signs' led to a dismissal of the author's connection with events. More recently, archaeological discoveries in Jerusalem such as the Pool of Bethesda (House of Mercy), which confirmed its five portico description in John (5:2), have led to a consensus that however late this Gospel was finally put together, it retains details of settings and scenes from Jesus' ministry which point to a knowledgeable, early source quite distinct from the Synoptics.

c) Timelines and differences

Only in John is there a hint that the ministry of Jesus lasted for more than a year since it includes separate visits to Jerusalem prior to the Passion (2:13, 5:1, 7:10, 10:22). The sequencing of events is one of the most obvious among a number of differences from the synoptic tradition. Times and festivals are important and Jesus' 'hour' of destiny is a key concern (e.g. 2:4, 4:23, 12:27).

Like the other Gospels, the danger inherent in going to Jerusalem is never far away (7:1), but as the narrative progresses, Jesus somewhat reluctantly attends the Feast of Tabernacles or 'Booths'. This traditional harvest celebration included the balancing memory of tough times represented by the construction of temporary shelters or *Sukkoth* (7:2-52) which the Hebrews had inhabited in Egypt. It is during this visit that the received text of the Gospel includes the famous incident of the woman caught in adultery (7:53-8:11). Although it is absent from the earliest manuscripts of John and may have instead been written by Luke or another early writer, the classic challenge – 'Let anyone among you who is without sin cast the first stone' (8:7) is among the most famous lines in the Bible.

The meditation on Jesus as the Light of the World which is present in the Gospel from the beginning deliberately prefaces the cure of a blind man (cf. 1:4-5, 8:12, 9:1-41). The Good Shepherd passages (10:1-42) and the raising of Lazarus (11:1-44) close out the ministry of Jesus which culminates in the deadly plot to kill him and sets the scene for the Passion (11:45-55). The depiction of his final days in John lays emphasis on his *messianizing* in the *anointing* at Bethany (12:1-8) prior to the triumphal entry into Jerusalem with all its messianic symbolism (Zech 9:9-10).

That this Gospel frames the Passion in prophetic light is further confirmed by the specific reference both to Daniel's 'Son of Man' being lifted up (cf. 12:32-35, 3:13-16) and Isaiah's 'Servant of YHWH' being unrecognized by hardened hearts and blinded eyes (12:37-41). This 'summing up' concludes the evidence represented by the words and deeds of Jesus' public ministry, and acts as a preface to the trial of truth which will take place during his last days (see Bauckham, 2006, p. 383).

d) Themes of the end

The Last Supper includes the extended 'Farewell Discourse' where Jesus is presented in a mood of foreboding (14:1-17:26). Yet it is from this section of the Gospel that some of the most enduringly encouraging lines of the New Testament are drawn: 'Do not let your hearts be troubled' (14:1), 'In my Father's house there are many rooms' (14:2), 'I will do whatever you ask in my name' (14:13), 'This is my commandment, that you love one another as I have loved you' (15:12), 'No one has greater love than this, to lay down one's life for one's friends' (15:13). The subsequent farewell prayer is full of reflection upon the divine intimacy between Father, Son and Spirit from which later Christian 'Trinitarian' theologizing draws much of its evidence.

The arrest, trial, death and resurrection are similar to the synoptic pattern, though the apparitions sequence and epilogue are notably extended. There are stylistic ironies, he is arrested in darkness and lamps are needed to arraign the light of the world (18:3). As noted above, the trial before a reluctant Pilate becomes a trial of truth and yields the official recognition of his messiahship by dint of the famous INRI charge sheet *Iesus Nazarenus Rex Iudaeorum* — 'Jesus of Nazareth, King of the Jews' (19:19). The pathos of the cross scene includes the entrusting of Jesus' mother to the beloved disciple. Significantly, Mary appears right at the beginning and right at the end of Jesus' public ministry in John and the 'transfer of kinship' indicates that from now on, true belonging is through faith rather than the blood ties of family (19:26-27). The piercing of the side is another example of detail and symbol dovetailing in John where blood and water flow forth. Although this is a conceivable medical consequence of crucifixion, it is symbolically understood here as Life conquering Death. The centurion who attempts to confirm *death* by piercing his side does precisely the opposite and instead unleashes a tidal wave of *life*. Through the 'saving blood' of the Eucharist, the New Passover, the deliverance from the power of death is completed (6:53-4). Through the 'living water' of the Spirit, the messianic promise of God-filled life is assured (7:38).

More developed than the synoptic tradition, the resurrection and apparition accounts in John continue to combine theological symbolism with specific details. This alluring style is seen in the appearance to Mary Magdalene and the disciples (20:1-23) and the brilliant encounter with Thomas the Twin. Thomas has missed out on an apparition of Jesus and demands proof. Despite artistic impressions of this, it is very doubtful that he needed to dig fingers in nail holes and stick his hand into a gaping wound (20:24-29). However, driving home the point to the very end, the Gospel is involving the audience in the drama of belief. While Thomas is consoled through meeting the risen Jesus, the one who comes to faith through testimony is greater:

Blessed are those who have not seen and yet have come to believe. (20:29)

Further apparitions entrust an overall shepherd role to *Kephas* (Peter) which is confirmed differently by the other Gospels (cf. John 21:15-19 with Matt 16:13-20). Intriguingly, the last scene seems to hint at a rivalry between Peter and the 'Beloved Disciple' – or at least some tension. After all, Jesus' comments seem to promise Peter both an onerous life task and a death sentence while his companion seems to be half-promised immortal tranquillity (21:20-23). At one level this should not be surprising, given the strong tradition of 'who's the greatest' behaviour among the Twelve, but it does provoke the question which has drained plenty of ink from the printing presses of this world, namely, who was this favourite of Jesus, this 'Beloved Disciple?'

e) The beloved disciple: Man, woman or committee?

Given the two-world, dualistic nature of the writing, it is understandable that scholars have sought clues to authorship, and thereby the identity of the Beloved Disciple from the Jewish apocalyptic tradition. As remarked in Chapter 6, it is reasonable to suggest that John the Baptist was either an Essene or at least familiar with the messianic thinking and two-world categories of the community at Qumran. The Fourth Gospel strongly emphasizes that the first disciples of Jesus came from among the Baptist's followers and it is a short step from this to conclude that the 'Beloved Disciple' was perhaps one of these early companions of Jesus. It would help explain the intensity of the messianic-judgement themes in the writings and explain the familiarity with Judean geography and customs which the Gospel displays.

That said, the identification of 'Beloved Disciple' with John, brother of James and son of Zebedee, who is clearly one of Jesus' inner circle according to the other Gospels, is less easily ascertained. The early Church historian Eusebius notes the confusions possible, but he hands on the tradition that the Fourth Gospel was deliberately written by John to fill in the gaps left by the others and repeats Irenaeus' view that John was the beloved who leant on the Lord's breast (Eusebius [325] 1989, III:24 and VII:8, John 13:23). The extreme emphasis on both the divinity and fleshly nature of Jesus in this Gospel would indicate a community troubled by groups like the Ebionites who claimed Jesus was not divine on the one hand and Docetists who claimed he was really an angel and not human on the other. The Gospel arrows firmly down the middle with a conscious depiction of Jesus as vividly divine and vividly human. After all, it is in this Gospel that we have hints of an all-knowing Messiah who identifies with Godself, yet it is also in this Gospel where Jesus is most shudderingly human, as when he weeps at the death of his friend Lazarus (11:35).

On this reading, the apostle John is identified as the figure known in the Gospel as the 'Beloved Disciple' who passes on this privileged intimate writing which is deliberately distinct from the way in which the other Gospels have been written (13:23, 19:26, 20:2, 21:7, 21:20). However, counter claims must be acknowledged that the 'Beloved Disciple' was a different Gospel figure such as

Lazarus whom Jesus loved, or Mary Magdalene who loved Jesus (cf. 11:5, 20:11-18). In theory, both would have been 'close to the action' and have been able to furnish some of the detail that sets this Gospel apart.

Another popular claim submits that the Fourth Gospel is more helpfully considered as the product of a distinctive 'Beloved Disciple' group within the Jesus movement. Edited over time by one or two hands, its final composition reflects the situation of Christians who, as we shall see below, may have had very definite reasons for presenting Gospel events in such a distinctive manner. Lastly, it can be argued that 'Beloved Disciple' serves like 'Theophilus' or 'God-friend' does in Luke 1:1, as a catch-all name which draws the listener or reader deeper into the text. The motif then acts as a literary device such that the reader identifies themselves with the author and comes to see themselves as a 'Beloved Disciple' who will be a 'witness to the truth'.

f) *Sitz im Leben* – Expulsion from the synagogue?

For simplicity, this text will refer to this wonderful writer and theologian as John and although one might despair at the lack of consensus on authorship, there is generally more agreement on context because of the particular conflict pattern between Jesus and the Jewish authorities which characterizes this Gospel. This may come as a surprise to some readers because traditionally, John is often depicted as the most 'spiritual' of the New Testament theologians. His symbol in many churches is the eagle – the creature that soars to the heavens and is blest with the 'view from above'. As a younger and more eager man, I once avowed to read the Gospel of John line by line as a study-prayer exercise during Lent. I was shocked at the extent to which every good act recounted occasioned bitter dispute. Far from making me feel all spiritual, woozy and holy, my reading made me cross and ready for an argument with myself. I happened to mention this to my local parish priest who said – 'that's not John's fault – you must have read it in a bad mood'. I wasn't persuaded; even I would have struggled to be grumpy for forty days and forty nights! And it is some comfort that following the work of J. L. Martyn, contemporary studies of John often begin by identifying the fractious context of these fascinating writings (Martyn, 1968 and 2003).

There are three times in the Gospel of John that the phrase *aposynagôgos* 'put out of the synagogue' is used (9:22, 12:42, 16:2). Now if the *Sitz im Leben* – 'the lived context' – of the writer of this Gospel coincided with the split between traditional Jewish belief and Christianity, then it is possible to explain numerous features of the writings. First, it explains why the Gospel has an explicit intent to persuade the reader or listener to believe. It is unashamed to declare the reasons for its design and argument (20:31) and in the context of disputes between brothers, sisters and co-religionists, this is understandable. Other features, namely the depiction of traditional Jewish believers as perversely unjust and the superiority of the new belief over the old, are also exemplified:

> The Jews took up stones again to stone him. Jesus answered them, "I have shown you many good works from the Father; for which of these are you going to stone me?" (10:31-32)
>
> "Your ancestor Abraham rejoiced that he was to see my day; he saw it and was glad." Then the Jews said to him, "You are not yet fifty years old and have you seen Abraham?" Jesus said to them, "Very truly I tell you, before Abraham was, I am." (John 8:56-8)

The Fourth Gospel even has the Jews plotting to kill the recently dead Lazarus (12:9-11), and while the modern reader might wince at the intensity of such exchanges, one has to acknowledge that if the lived-context is one of painful division, it would be odd not to hear some of that mutual hurt in the writings. There were dearly held convictions on either side, and as noted in the life of Jesus and the life of Paul, the New Testament writings are shadowed from start to finish by violence. Indeed, the fact that strife accompanied early Christianity from the start makes it difficult to isolate a precise date for the composition of the Gospel of John on the basis of a troubled background, but the majority of scholars tend to place its final composition sometime after the destruction of the Temple in 70 CE following Roman military action to quell a Jewish revolt.

This shattering event irrevocably changed the pattern of Jewish worship. With the Temple destroyed and the local synagogues acting as the natural focus for religious expression, it is not hard to theorize that the kind of synagogue controversies courted by Jesus' followers would eventually lead to a 'parting of the ways'. As further evidence, some scholars point to the emergence of the *Birkat ha Minim* around this time. Literally a 'Blessing upon heretics', it unfortunately reads more like a curse and is indicative of intense feelings:

> Let there be no hope for the apostates
> and quickly root up the kingdom of arrogance.
> Let the *Nazarenes* and sectarians [minim] vanish in a moment.

Blot them out of the book of life
and do not record them among the righteous.
Blessed are you LORD, who humble the arrogant!

Although it remains unclear as to where this came from and how this explicit denunciation of 'Nazarenes' was circulated and actioned in synagogue circles, it is hardly surprising that the existence of such prayer-curses have been used to explain some of the negativity that can be found amid the otherwise poetic imagery of John's Gospel (Marcus, 2009, p. 551).

g) The man born blind

A classic example of this kind of conflict is the story of the 'Man born blind'. All the Gospels include healings of the blind, which was one of the criteria for the coming of the messianic age. John makes it explicit here that the man was blind from birth, which in the context of the strong 'darkness-light' duality of the text means that he has always been in the shadows of the dead zone. Straight away, despite the insights of the Book of Job, the classic understanding that someone must have sinned for this situation to arise is offered by his disciples. The answer to this conundrum is not found by looking for faults but for glory, not through focus on the darkness of blindness, but through focus on the light of the world (9:1-5).

Jesus then conducts a *theandric* act – a 'God-human' action – whereby saliva, mud, water, as well as the divinely voiced command, are all constituent parts of the miracle. Christian sacramental ritual rests on the notion of 'theandric acts' but for now it is suffice to note that just as Jesus was 'sent' by the Father, the blind man too is 'sent'. And in what can be identified as an allusion to Baptism, the one who was 'sent' returns healed to the general consternation of those who knew him. Now one of the features of John's Gospel is that he explicitly includes the argument of the 'opposition' – it is an extended courtroom drama in which the audience (you) are expected to give the (correct) verdict! There is a genuine dilemma here for the Pharisees who would be naturally suspicious because the miracle was so spectacular. Moreover, that a holy person would 'work' on the Sabbath and 'make clay' in the manner that might recall of the Hebrew slaves in Pharaoh's Egypt is even more unsettling (9:6-12).

Keeping up the legal tone, the Pharisees look for reliable testimony and his parents are sought out. At this point, we see classic evidence of the *Sitz im Leben* 'lived context' of John (9:13-17). The parents are afraid of 'the Jews' lest they be 'put out of the synagogue' (9:18-23). By this stage, the hostilities are more marked. The blind man is now becoming a *witness* to Jesus even though he doesn't know who Jesus is. He becomes a bit 'sassy' with the religious authorities who cite Moses in support. He refuses to back down and inevitably he is cast out (9:24-34). In an unusual turn but one entirely consonant with a 'Good Shepherd', Jesus is the one who goes in search of the one who has been 'cast out'. The man can see, but he still does not know who Jesus is. This gradual 'coming to true sight' is made complete as he believes and then worships him. The recognition phases of the man born blind are contrasted with the perspectives of the Pharisees who are portrayed as not only blind, but becoming more obstinate and more guilty. A story that begins with the blind man being accused of having sinned ends with the supposedly sighted and holy religious experts being the blind and guilty ones (9:35-41).

Withal, it does not take too imaginative a leap to understand the power of this story for people likewise cast out of synagogues, also accused of being irreligious on the authority of Moses, punished for believing in the uniqueness of Jesus. Religious convictions, religious divisions and religious guilt all run deep. By presenting the strong tradition of Jesus' healing of a blind man in the context of this religious disagreement, John can use the story to encourage community members to identify with someone who comes to see clearly, who is braver than his parents, who is unafraid of rejection. Favourite Gospel themes collide here, light versus dark, witness versus rejection, healing versus resentment, solace versus sabbath – all oppositions which yield the new reality, a man born again, who recognizes in Jesus the face of God and worships him.

h) Jewish themes in John

Now while the degree of negativity towards Judaism is troubling, it must also be emphasized that the Gospel of John at times excels the Synoptics in its weaving of themes and symbolism from the Hebrew scriptures throughout the narrative. This is nowhere more true than in the Johannine understanding of Jesus. As the famous German scholar Martin Hengel remarks:

> One could point out that no New Testament writing has such a wealth of titles and designations provided from (the Old Testament) and Judaism: the Anointed, Messiah, King, Rabbi, Rabbouni, Son of God and Son of Man, the Lord, the Holy One of God, the Elect, the Only-Begotten, the Prophet, the Lamb of God, the Light of the World, the True Vine, the Good Shepherd, and – not least – the absolute I AM or even God himself. (Hengel, 2008, p. 271)

Appropriately, this starts at the very beginning of John's Gospel with the resonant tones of the Prologue. Anyone looking for stars, donkeys, angels and shepherds as an entry point would be disappointed with John's version of the Christmas story. If Mark starts with the preaching of John the Baptist and Luke and Matthew begin with the Infancy narratives, John takes matters even further back by presenting Jesus as pre-existent in a timeless past. Deliberately calling to mind the first words of Genesis, John's Prologue starts with 'In the Beginning . . .' and by means of a magnificent poem centred on *logos* and on 'light' the Gospel presents Jesus as the key to life, the key to light, the origin and destiny of all creation:

> In the beginning was the Word,
> and the Word was with God,
> and the Word was God.
> He was in the beginning with God.
> All things came into being through him,
> and without him not one thing came into being.
> What has come into being in him was life,
> and the life was the light of all people.
> The light shines in the darkness,
> and the darkness did not overcome it.
> (John 1:1-5)

While there are intriguing connections with Greek thinking, this prologue most directly calls to mind the opening lines of Genesis – a chaotic darkness put to flight by the word-command 'Let there be Light'. John's Gospel thus echoes and underlines the importance of God's word by emphasizing that all things are created by it – not one thing existed without God's word – God's word IS reality. But John's thinking does not stop there, it becomes even more radical with the assertion that this *logos* not only underpins reality, but has in fact become *enfleshed* in the being of Jesus.

i) Incarnation

Theologically, the core idea at work here is that whatever the wisdom of other traditions, Israel was privileged with the deepest insight through its chosen, intimate relationship with the Creator God. The Prologue captures this conviction by deliberately paralleling Jewish writings which personified Wisdom as a divine being, seeking a suitable place to *pitch tent*:

> Then the Creator of all things gave me a command, and my Creator chose the place for my tent. He said, "Make your dwelling in Jacob, and in Israel receive your inheritance." (Sir 24:8)

The tent imagery is important. The *Shekinah* of 'God's holy presence' among the chosen people was originally identified with the sacred *mishkan*, the 'tent' or 'tabernacle' which accompanied the people in their wanderings (Ex 40:35). Ultimately, this presence was 'earthed' when the building of a permanent Temple with its Holy of Holies began under King Solomon (1 Kings 5:3-5). John's Gospel takes all this one step further. John proposes that Wisdom-Reason-Insight has not only *pitched its tent*, but God's presence has become *incarnate*.

> And the word *became flesh* and *pitched tent* among us.
> (A literal translation of John 1:14)

Most translations render *kai eskēnōsen en hēmin* as 'lived among us' but this misses some of the symbolism. Theologically, the 'enfleshment' and the 'ententing' of the Word are radical and problematic for the traditional Jewish view which could accept *logos/wisdom* as an attribute humans might *share* with God, but not that a human would *be* God's wisdom. There is no more need to look for illumination anywhere other than in the life that is the light of humankind. You want wisdom? Listen to Jesus. You want insight? See like Jesus. You want to know how to live? Imitate Jesus. The patterning of John's Gospel then becomes a series of 'signs' which help point to this truth, which if believed, will lead the listener to 'live life to the full' (John 10:10).

In this fashion, the Prologue typifies the Gospel in that it is both cosmic and intimate. The majestic secret of the whole universe is described on the one hand while being rendered humble, human and intimate by 'incarnation'/enfleshment on the other. It is sometimes argued that the Prologue may have either pre-dated or have been a later addition to the main Gospel narrative, since the theological themes mirror each other so closely. Whatever the case, a simple comparison with the beginning of the First Letter of John demonstrates that this key theological proposal – divine enfleshment – is core to the understanding of the community to which this author belonged:

> We declare to you what was from the beginning, what we have heard, what we have seen with our eyes, what we have looked at and touched with our hands, concerning the word of life – this life was revealed, and we have seen it and testify to it, and declare to you the eternal life that was with the Father and was revealed to us – we declare to you what we have seen and heard so that you also may have fellowship with us; and truly our fellowship is with the Father and with his Son Jesus Christ. We are writing these things so that our joy may be complete.
> (1 John 1:1-4)

And later:

> Beloved, do not believe every spirit, but test the spirits to see whether they are from God; for many false prophets have gone out into the world. By this you know the Spirit of God: every spirit that confesses that Jesus Christ has come in the flesh is from God, and every spirit that does not confess Jesus is not from God. And this is the spirit of the antichrist, of which you have heard that it is coming; and now it is already in the world. (1 John 4:1-3)

In other words, it can be seen that 'incarnation' is key to whether people 'belong' or 'don't belong' to this community. The enfleshment issue is a touchstone for membership and once more, the in-crowd/out-crowd dividing lines of the Johannine writings are strikingly vivid. John's writing is never free of the dramatic division between belief and unbelief, between light and darkness – between the drama of the man born blind and the challenge to be born again (John 3:1-21).

j) The image of God: Adam remade

If the Incarnation of God in Jesus is a key concern of John's writings, perhaps a last word might make allusion to another striking parallel which is achieved in his resurrection account. In common with the other Gospels, John accords women the primary role but with a particular focus on Mary Magdalene. Here there are also intriguing allusions to Genesis which serve to conclude the drama started by the 'In the Beginning' of the Prologue.

Jesus is arrested and driven from a garden. He is tried and crucified on a *Tree of Death* – the polar opposite of the *Tree of Life*. And yet he is then brought to a new garden, 'in this garden there was a new tomb in which no one had ever been laid . . . they laid Jesus there' (John 19:41-2). In John's version of the Passion, the slain Jesus then participates in the Sabbath rest (the sacred seventh day), and Mary Magdalene is the first to arrive on the scene on 'the first day of the week'. This is highly significant for Christian thinking as it will become not only the 'Lord's Day' but also the 'Eighth Day' since it will be the first day of the New Creation. Why? Well in this new Garden of Eden, the roles are reversed. The woman is the one seeking the man. She alerts the Twelve, and even though Peter and John visit the tomb, they return to their companions while she remains (John 20:2-11). Weeping, she turns to see someone she thinks is the gardener – but it isn't – it is the risen Jesus. Just as the Old Adam was a gardener (Gen 2:5) – so the New Adam appears as such, and she does not recognize him until he calls her name (John 20:16).

We see the issue of recognition at the heart of the theological question. The resurrection accounts in John's Gospel all retain ambiguity in relation to the recognition of the risen Jesus. While later Christian Theology will speculate about the notion of Jesus having a glorified body, the simpler implication is that as the New Adam, the risen Jesus could be *anyone*. This recognition challenge is well attested in the accounts of Paul, Matthew and Luke, and the mystery of how humanity bears the image of God is a concluding paradox of John's Gospel. The New Gardener, the New Adam makes this possible – he restores dignity to *Clod Man*. The first Adam inhales and receives divine breath from God (Gen 2:7). The new Adam exhales – breathes out upon the disciples the new life of the Spirit (20:19-22). Undoing the curse of Cain, Lamech and the violence which brought about the destruction of the earth (cf. Gen 4:1-6:6), the empowerment is instead for forgiveness – fulfilling covenant through reconciliation with God and with one another (20:23).

Ultimately, the radical theological proposals which emerge in these scenes are taken to their logical conclusion in John's letter. No one can truly say they love God unless they love their neighbour who bears the image of God. In no uncertain terms the author challenges those who claim that they can love the God they do not see while hating the brother that they do see (1 John 4:20). In the end, like Paul, John falls back on the heart of the matter: 'God is love' (1 John 4:16).

Summary

The Gospel of John is written 'so that you might believe'. Deliberately theological, it is elegantly styled in a 'double seven' arrangement which points to the magnificent signs of Jesus' power and divine identity. The text itself does bear the signs of deep tension between the followers of Jesus and those who reject his messiahship. The drama of this is perhaps best illustrated by the story of the Man born Blind in John 9. The sustained reflection on Jesus' divinity evident in the text begins with the very first words of this Gospel and the cosmic philosophical and theological richness of the Prologue (John 1:1-18) is perhaps unsurpassed in all Christian writing. That said, the more mundane challenge to recognize the image of God in a brother and to 'love one another' abide as the core commands to be followed by the followers of the Nazarene (John 15:17).

Part 4
Theology in the Classical Period

12

Canon: Scriptural Basis of Theology

Theological methodology in Christianity demands close attention to the Canon, Creeds and Councils of the Church. The next four chapters will explore their development since together they provide the co-ordinates for any mapping of Christian Theology. The 'canon' - 'rules' or 'lists' - of the various scriptures which became known as the Bible were those texts which over many decades became hallowed by their use in the gatherings of Christians and together captured the breadth and depth of the mystery of the Jesus event. To the fundamental heritage of the Torah, Prophets and Writings, the varied letters and exhortations which would come to complete the collection known as the New Testament were circulated. The works ascribed to Paul, along with those ascribed to John, Luke, Mark and Matthew, would be increased with Hebrews and the letters of James, Peter, Jude and the Book of Revelation. Although in large part these writings were extended enquiries deliberately mining the fundamental theological images present in the TaNaK, this connection did not go unchallenged. The arguments of

Marcion (c.160 CE) proposed a deliberate separation of Christian thinking from the YHWH texts, but his view was ultimately rejected yielding the recognizable biblical collection of the present day.

a) Canon – a collection of unity and diversity

There is no doubt that the great theologians of the Jesus event – Mark, Matthew, Luke, Paul, John – all saw the messianic revelation of the Nazarene as a 'game-changer', but it is equally clear that their attempts to articulate a precise understanding thereof ran up against the limitations of explanation and stretched the symbols and techniques of their own Judean heritage. Likewise, the Letters of Peter, James and Jude which emerged from Jesus' followers in the decades of the first century of proclamation combined traditional moral thinking with changed theological categories. Traditionally, interpretation of the *TaNaK* followed three lines of *DRŠ* – 'enquiry'. From *HLK* – 'to walk' the *Halakah* took legal instruction as its focus, seeking guidance on what to do and how to act. From *NGD* – 'to narrate' the *Haggadah* was more allegorical, allowing a more discursive, 'learning from the story' approach. From *PŠR* – 'to interpret' the *Pesher* was much more sensitive to the symbolic, and the notion of hidden meanings now revealed. At its most vivid in apocalyptic literature, it covered the broad genre of the prophetic writings and their interpretation. In particular, *Pesher* framed understanding in terms of fulfilment, allowing for two ages to collide, the word of the past with its realization in the present. Hence, though all three methods are used by the New Testament theologians, the whole caboodle can be understood as one great big Jesus based *Pesher* on the *TaNaK*. The anonymous Epistle to the Hebrews sums up the radically altered landscape:

> Long ago God spoke to our ancestors in many and various ways by the prophets, but in these last days he has spoken to us by a Son, whom he appointed heir of all things, through whom he also created the worlds. He is the reflection of God's glory and the exact imprint of God's very being, and he sustains all things by his powerful word. When he had made purification for sins, he sat down at the right hand of the Majesty on high, having become as much superior to angels as the name he has inherited is more excellent than theirs. (Heb 1:1-4)

Even these few lines combine massive themes of creation, covenant, redemption, messiahship and angel theologies. In fairness, whether they be considered major or minor theologians, the various New Testament authors were struggling to plait a whirlwind. Perhaps John's Gospel provides the paradoxical clue. Although Jesus promises that the Spirit will guide 'into all the truth' (16:13), he has already warned them that the Spirit will blow those born from above in directions unknown to them (3:7-8). Carried on the God-storm of Jesus, followers of the Way were not immune to the odd theological collision or moral misunderstanding (Acts 9:2, 18:26, 19:9, 19:23, 22:4, 24:14, 24:22). Indeed it can be argued that most of the letters which comprise the rest of the New Testament are attempts to re-theologize those who seem to have grasped the wrong end of the stick.

As an example, James' letter is wonderfully down to earth and 'anti-smug' – a challenge to complacent, self-satisfied, arrogant believers. In the classic prophetic tradition, James insists on getting the basics right – love of neighbour, impartiality, help for the poor, avoidance of litigation (2:1-13). It is as direct as Paul's letter to the Corinthians and like Matthew's Jesus, James is not particularly impressed by belief. After all, even demons believe:

> What good is it, my brothers and sisters, if you say you have faith but do not have works? Can faith save you? If a brother or sister is naked and lacks daily food, and one of you says to them, "Go in peace; keep warm and eat your fill," and yet you do not supply their bodily needs, what is the good of that? So faith by itself, if it has no works, is dead. But someone will say, "You have faith and I have works." Show me your faith without works, and I by my works will show you my faith. You believe that God is one; you do well. Even the demons believe – and shudder. (Jas 2:14-19 cf. Matt 7:21-23)

This text can be read as a classic contrast to the approach of Paul, especially since James illustrates his point using the example of Abraham which Paul makes much of in Rom 4:1-25. Understood in a certain way, Paul's emphasis on the importance of faith in Christ rather than 'works of the Law' could seem to de-emphasize the importance of moral behaviour and clearly did lead to abuses in his churches – hence his need to write so many letters! As noted before, the Acts of the Apostles as well as Paul himself testify to tensions with James, Peter and John – the leading 'pillars of the Church' (cf. Acts 15:1-5 and Gal 2:1ff).

> But when Cephas (Peter) came to Antioch, I opposed him to his face, because he stood self-condemned; for until certain people came from James, he used to eat with the Gentiles. But after they came, he drew back and kept himself separate for fear of the circumcision faction. And the other Jews joined him in this hypocrisy,

> so that even Barnabas was led astray by their hypocrisy. But when I saw that they were not acting consistently with the truth of the gospel, I said to Cephas before them all, "If you, though a Jew, live like a Gentile and not like a Jew, how can you compel the Gentiles to live like Jews?" We ourselves are Jews by birth and not Gentile sinners; yet we know that a person is justified not by the works of the law but through faith in Jesus Christ. (Gal 2:11-16)

This impassioned disagreement is far from the 'Happy Families' picture of Acts 4:32 which describes the followers of Jesus as being of 'one heart and soul'. The different situations and challenges presented by encounters with other cultures and precipitous events inevitably forced communities to reflect along different lines. A pattern of unity *and* diversity emerged among the early followers of the Way. Indeed the fact that there was disagreement and passionate argument about core issues even among the central figures of the original movement is almost a historical constant. Just as the sacred foundational YHWH writings of Law, Prophets and Writings were varied in emphasis and tone, the diverse emphases of the various Gospels and the different letters *together* became the Jesus picture.

b) Canon – patterning an explosion

Alerting the reader to theological tensions in the New Testament is important. Trying to force a theoretical construct to ensure consistency or a fixed pattern of development is tempting but doomed to fail. As an example, take the diagram below which was a popular if flawed way of understanding the New Testament theologians and their relationship to one another. The construct supposed that layer on layer of thinking was carefully built one stratum on top of another to construct an ever higher tower of faith in Jesus as Christ and Lord. Thus the New Testament is supposed to move from a basic understanding of Jesus as a prophet – 'low' Christology – to a 'high' view of Jesus as identical with the great I AM creator and redeemer God of Israel. This thinking accompanies an ever-growing sophistication in the organization of the Jesus movement. Year on year, as it becomes more consciously Church, so it more consciously exalts Jesus. The more marvellous the message, the bigger the gap between the original recollections – the historical Jesus, and the 'Christ of faith'. All very neat, but not very likely.

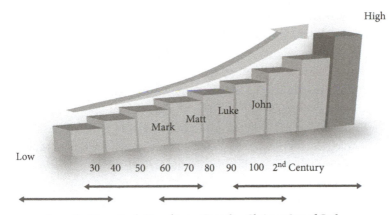

Jesus the Man – Early Preaching – Gospels – Christ as Son of God
Jesus becomes more exalted as Church authority becomes more important

As noted above in Section 6e, unfortunately the life and writings of Paul scupper this picture since his letters (which date from around 50 CE onwards) demonstrate a very developed understanding of Jesus and the Church. A standard argument then follows that it was the rather over-excited Paul who must therefore have invented Christianity – but there really is no need for such contrivance. Everyone was excited. But the inauguration of the messianic age through the death and resurrection of Jesus did not lend itself to baking the theological equivalent of a layer cake. Reality was less tidy than this diagram suggests – it was far more exciting. Life is never as neat as such systems purport and every generation demonstrates anticipations, retrojections, inconsistencies and commonalities. It is probably better depicted more like this:

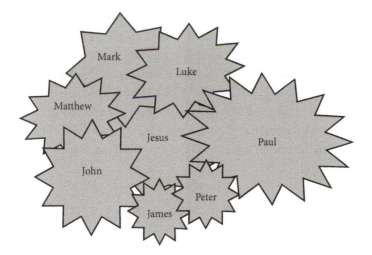

In other words, whatever dates, life situations, redactions, religious influences and parallels are ascribed to the New Testament authors, there isn't any need to impose a step-by-step intensification of theological density regarding Jesus. There is little merit in such views, and as a mental picture, I submit that the second diagram above is much more apt than the 'layer cake' model. It was an explosive time and the best food analogy I can think of is popcorn. Same colour but different shapes. Same core beliefs but taking on different theological expressions. Vibrant with some particular end time flavours, so imagine the arrow of time coming straight at you!

The related question which concerns the dating of the Gospels is, again, one where scholarly tides ebb and flow. Of late, there seems to be a moving towards earlier assignation, and persuasive arguments have been made for a widespread 'Early High Christology' (Hurtado, 2003), the 'eyewitness' nature of the Gospel accounts (Bauckham, 2006) and a date of c.40 CE for Mark's Gospel (Crossley, 2004). That said, such discussions can slightly distract from the core theological questions being posed by all the New Testament writers. I'm sure if the authors could speak they'd be less worried about when anybody thought the ink dried on their work, they'd probably be more concerned that humanity should 'get with the programme'.

This is not to say that any old rubbish could be written down and taken as Gospel. There was an anxiety within the early movement for writings to be seen as authentic. Especially if the authors were not recounting eye-witness events, then connection to an apostle in theological terms was very important since fidelity to the tradition of the Twelve was key to the self-understanding of the group (Acts 2:42). Though Mark and Luke never purported to be part of the early circle of Jesus, their traditional respective connections with Peter and Paul secured their legitimacy. The need for a link probably explains how Hebrews became belatedly appended to Paul's letters, while other anonymous writings were less successful. What is undeniable is that the circulation of written recollections of Jesus and apostolic exhortations became much more important as a twin horror distended and disorientated the co-ordinates of the movement: The irruption of Imperial violence against the Jesus movement and the destruction of Jerusalem in 70 CE, following the First Jewish War (66–73 CE).

c) The fall of Jerusalem and the Canon

The destruction of Jerusalem and the First Temple in 587 BCE by Nebuchadnezzar vies with the story of Moses and the Exodus as the theological epicentre of the Hebrew or Old Testament scriptures. It has been noted above (Chapter 4) that many modern scholars see the experience of Exile as the defining moment when all the traditions of the people were reviewed and the thematic imagery of the *TaNaK* as we know it was cast. Read in such a fashion, Creation, Abraham, Jacob and Moses all become metaphors for the rebuilding of a shattered identity that had been crushed by the trauma suffered by the people of YHWH. In a similar manner, the Jewish revolt of 66 CE which led to the Roman military annihilating the rebellion, besieging Jerusalem and destroying the Second Temple accelerated the process by which YHWH faith would become defined separately in terms of Rabbinic Judaism and Apostolic Christianity.

Initially, a series of religious and taxation grievances led to skirmishes and attacks on Roman citizens of sufficient violence to persuade Imperial forces to intervene first under Gallus and then, more successfully, under Vespasian and his son Titus. According to Josephus, the Jewish commander who changed sides to assist the Roman military, the conquest of the country was mostly completed by 68 CE as siege was laid to Jerusalem. Weakened by bloody infighting, the defenders eventually succumbed despite ferocious resistance. It was a human and religious tragedy, hundreds of thousands may have perished in the war and tens of thousands were enslaved or exiled. Without Zion and its Temple, the heart of Jewish identity and religious expression was excised. Subsequently, its theological centre of gravity and its religious emphasis would come to be focused even more upon the sacred scriptures as the unifying bond of faith. Family homes, which had always been significant in Jewish ritual, buffered the loss of the Temple as the centre of the cult. Likewise, the synagogues of the Mediterranean Diaspora communities became more important.

In the decades that followed, a theory that in response to the crisis Jewish rabbis eventually gathered in some sort of council to decide key matters once held considerable sway. The location identified was Jamnia on the Mediterranean coast just south of present-day Tel Aviv, perhaps between 90–95 CE. The matters discussed included which scrolls should be regarded as sacred Hebrew scriptures and the regulation of other issues pertinent to Jewish worship such as who should be able to participate in synagogue meetings. The attractiveness of this theory is that it allows for a neat 'parting of the ways' between eventual 'Jews' and eventual 'Christians' as well as the appearance of a definitive collection of Hebrew writings being established by the end of the first century. In turn, this was neatly complemented by the collection of texts written by members of the Jesus movement and Hey Presto! – there's Christianity, there's Judaism and there's the Bible.

Unfortunately, things were probably not that simple and though there is evidence of a notable rabbinical school at Jamnia, it is perhaps best to tolerate the *emergence* of the Canon as a process rather than a project completed at one time by rabbis and apostles. It can't be stressed enough that in this period eventual Judaism and eventual Christianity were pluriform as were their scriptures. If the collection or library of the Essenes at Qumran is anything to go by, scrolls that later generations would regard as Holy Writ were kept alongside writings that were not ultimately accorded sacred status in either Rabbinical Judaism or Apostolic Christianity. Ironically, it would appear that the Samaritans came to their conclusions first, restricting the sacred collection to the five scrolls of the Torah. Since we have evidence of Rabbi Aqiba having to argue in support of the theological validity of the Song of Songs as late as 130 CE, it might have to be enough for us to say that the 'process' of identifying the *TaNaK* began after the destruction of the Second Temple in 70 CE and may only have been completed during the middle part of the following century, maybe around the time of the Bar-Kochba Rebellion of 134 CE. Simon *Bar Kochba* – 'Son of a Star' was identified as the liberating Messiah of the Book of Numbers: 'A star shall come forth from Jacob' (Num 24:17). His rebellion made temporary gains but was ultimately crushed by the Emperor Hadrian in a conflict every bit as bloody as that of the First Jewish War (Ulrich, 1999, p. 31).

d) Canon and Christian persecution

The reaction of early Christians to the destruction of the Temple is a matter of scholarly debate. Some New Testament writings such as Paul's letters seem oblivious to it which fits with the notion that he was martyred around the time of Nero's persecution c.64 CE. As noted above, while the Synoptic Gospels all recall the action of Jesus in the 'Cleansing of the Temple', the allusions to troubled prospects for the sanctuary in the trial accounts, as well as the prophecies of its demise, are less easy to identify as reflections on the event. They manage to be fierce but vague, which leads to mixed views on whether Mark, Matthew and Luke were composed before or after its destruction. Apart from the prophecy of Temple calamity placed on the lips of Stephen (Acts 6:14), the picture of the early church outlined in Acts does not make explicit reference to a civil rebellion in Judea against the Romans and still less its catastrophic consequences.

By contrast, in keeping with the presumption of a later date, John's Gospel seems to have absorbed/theologized Temple absence – Jesus is clearly identified as the replacement God location (John 2:19-22). Likewise, in Jesus' exchange with the Samaritan woman, the implication is that the entire region has suffered a religious desolation:

> The woman said to him, "Sir, I perceive you are a prophet. Our fathers worshipped on this mountain; and you say that in Jerusalem is the place where men ought to worship." Jesus said to her, "Woman, believe me, the hour is coming when neither on this mountain nor in Jerusalem will you worship the Father." (John 4:20-21)

Meanwhile, paralleling the wars and destructions in the religious homeland, the experience of the Jesus movement was not without specific experience of bloodshed. Imperial persecutions mark the decades during which the writings of the New Testament were being circulated. The first, under the madcap psychopath Nero (37–68 CE), seems to have taken place in 64 CE following the Great Fire of Rome which he himself is thought to have started in order to clear land to build the *Domus Aurea* – the Palace of Gold. The Roman historian Tacitus (56–117 CE) takes up the story:

> And so, to get rid of this rumour, Nero set up as the culprits and punished with the utmost refined of cruelty a class hated for their abominations, who are commonly called Christians. Christus, from whom their name is derived, was executed at the hands of the procurator Pontius Pilate in the reign of Tiberius. Checked for the moment, this pernicious superstition again broke out, not only in Judea, the source of the evil, but even in Rome, that receptacle for everything that is sordid and degrading from every quarter of the globe, which there finds a following. Accordingly, arrest was first made of those who confessed [to being Christians]; then, on their evidence, an immense multitude was convicted, not so much on the charge of arson as because of hatred of the human race. Besides being put to death they were made to serve as objects of amusement; they were clad in the hides of beasts and torn to death by dogs; others were crucified, others set on fire to serve to illuminate the night when daylight failed. Nero had thrown open his grounds for the display and was putting on a show in the circus where he mingled with the people in the dress of a charioteer or drove about in his chariot. All this gave a feeling of pity, even towards men whose guilt merited the most exemplary punishment; for it was felt that they were being destroyed not for the public good but to gratify the cruelty of an individual. (Bettenson & Maunder, 2011, p.2)

Part of the problem for the 'Christians' was that their sect was considered novel, whacky and therefore able to be eliminated. In fairness, a semi-secret group who refused to offer sacrifices to the Emperor or to other gods for the public good was not a promising start. Since Christians preferred instead to gather for an *agape* – a 'Love Feast' to celebrate the eating of the flesh and blood of their leader, it is hardly surprising that they were considered to be a treasonous crowd of orgiastic cannibals.

It is not clear how frequent, how systematic, how widespread or how localized the persecutions of the movement were by the Roman authorities in the early decades. The likelihood is that the period between Nero's attacks in 64 CE recounted by Tacitus and the considered reflections by his friend Pliny the Younger on his own localized tortures of Christians in Bithynia around 112 CE, bracket an unpredictable, erratically violent time for the early followers which may have peaked under the Emperor Domitian towards the end of the first century. Withal, the combination of violence in Judea and violence in Rome provides an understandable context for the religious literary reaction articulated in the Christian *Apocalypse* or *Book of Revelation*, which tradition has placed as the closing scroll of the biblical collection.

e) Apocalypse – summing up the Canon

The double instability caused by horrific warfare in the homeland and vicious persecution at the heart of the Empire provide classic background for the cosmic contemplations of the *Book of Revelation* or *Apocalypse*. Though the latter term has become a word meaning 'cataclysmic doom' in modern vocabulary, as noted above, both words mean 'unveil'. To repeat, apocalyptic literature seems to have emerged as one of Israel's literary-theological responses to disorientating violence or identity instability from the time of Ezekiel (during the Babylonian Exile) to the writings of Daniel (during the Greek oppression). Similar themes are prevalent in the numerous writings collectively called 'inter-testamental literature' and dichotomies of dark-light, good-evil and cosmic battle were characteristic of numerous writings found among the Dead Sea Scrolls, such as 1 Enoch. Sharing this theological and literary tradition, it is no surprise that Christian apocalyptic emerged and there are traces dispersed among the Gospels and in Paul's letters. None, however, quite reach the level of symbolism or intensity of the Book of Revelation which was written during the early years of persecution by an exiled Christian named John on the island of Patmos in the Eastern Mediterranean (Rev 1:9). From the outset, this was assumed to be a different John to the one associated with the Fourth Gospel, though that distinction was blurred over time. This scroll demands particular theological attention since as Luke Timothy Johnson remarks:

> Few writings in all of literature have been so obsessively read with such generally disastrous results as the Book of Revelation. Its history of interpretation is largely a story of tragic misinterpretation, resulting from a fundamental misapprehension of the work's literary form and purpose. Insofar as its arcane symbols have fed the treasury of prayer and poetry, its influence has been benign. More often, these same symbols have nurtured delusionary systems, both private and public, to the destruction of their fashioners and to the discredit of the writing. (Johnson, 2010, p. 507)

With irritating frequency, I tease my students that 'If you don't understand the Book of Revelation – not to worry – it's not the end of the world' (feel free to groan). In a strange way the disease which plagues naïve readers of the Apocalypse is a severe case of anachronistic – 'time slip/time error' thinking. Blindly preferring a present context without reference to the past sufferings and insights of the communities that are the original subjects of the drama, the various symbolic images are applied to anything global that seems to be happening at the time. The upshot is that the European Union becomes identified either with the Twelve stars around the head of the celestial Woman (12:1) or alternatively the Ten horned beast out to devour the faithful (13:1). Instead of Nero Caesar, a name which in traditional numerology and historical context fits the bill perfectly, the notorious 666 character of 13:18 is identified as Ronald Reagan, Bill Clinton or Saddam Hussein depending on your politics. It might have been fair enough for medieval commentators to liken the two witnesses of Revelation 11 (probably Peter and Paul) to the sack-clothed St Francis and St Dominic, but when you get multiple murderer Charles Manson acting on a hunch that John, Paul, George and Ringo of the Beatles were the four horsemen of the apocalypse (Rev 6:1-8) you know you're in trouble. Not for nothing did Chesterton once remark that of the many strange beasts John saw in his visions 'none were as strange as his commentators' – and as usual, he has a point (Chesterton, [1908] 1996, p. 17).

In fairness to some of the controversy that surrounds Revelation and its interpretation, it is a perfectly human thing to want to be in on a secret, to be an insider, to know what is *really* happening. And since part of the subject matter is the end of the world as we know it, it seems reasonable to be a little *curious*. This is classic *Pesher* interpretation instinct and is more than manifest in the Gospels which themselves seem to indicate tensions and speculations among the disciples regarding a glorious future intervention by God (cf. Mark

10:37, 13:1-37, Acts 1:6, John 21:23). Even though Jesus' recommendation is *not* to know (Mark 13:32), obsession with the 'end of the world' has proved a feature of every generation of Christian believers and is often called 'millenarianism' after the thousand year reign depicted in Rev 20:1-6. One reaction to such speculations would be to leave Revelation well alone, but that would risk ignoring enduring theological features of Christian thinking vividly expressed in this intriguing book. In somewhat stylized fashion, they may be clustered around the three famous 'theological powers' identified by Paul as 'Faith, Hope and Love'.

First, the basic conceptual matrix of apocalyptic literature was, and remains, significant for Christian Theology. No matter what tragedies might be happening to individuals or groups, the challenge to be faithful and courageous is the key to eventual vindication and reward. There will be a judgement, there will be consolation – every tear will be wiped away (Rev 7:17, 21:4). If the watery chaos of Genesis is necessarily mastered by the power of the word of God, the spiritual chaos of the battle between good and evil will eventually be mastered by the one whose voice is 'like the sound of many waters' (Rev 1:15). Understood in this fashion, the garish and gory details of ten horned beasts, lakes of fire and bowls of wrath – even the disappearance of a third of the earth and a third of the stars paradoxically express the final overwhelming power of God (Rev 8:7-13). The 'revelation', the 'unveiling' that must take place is that the two ages – the eternal and the earthly – are actually connected, and God's favourable judgement on the faithful believer is the sacred consequence of secular life. There is nothing new in this. It is rooted in the classic heritage of the Jewish prophetic and wisdom traditions. A guiding vision for life based on a guiding vision of cosmic possibility. It is a Theology of Faith.

Secondly, it is all too easy to miss the vivid insights into liturgical and community life that bejewel the poetic imagery of Revelation. Indeed it can be argued that *the* key to understanding the text is liturgical. The vision is received on the Lord's Day (1:10). The sanctuary of God is at the heart of the drama where the angels utter the threefold 'Holy, Holy, Holy' witnessed by Isaiah (Rev 4:8 cf. Isa 6:3). The seven lamp stands and the seven branched 'menorah' are symbolic of Temple liturgy and religious perfection (2:1). The seven churches under the warning are invited to listen to the Word just as they would during their gatherings and the scroll with seven seals awaits to be opened (Rev 5:1). Believers who remain faithful will form the white robed array who may at once be representative of the priesthood of Israel and the baptized of the Christian movement (5:10, 7:13-14). The numerous songs that break forth in the text are likely to be among the most ancient hymns known to Christianity (e.g. 4:11, 5:9-10, 15:3-4, 19:1-9). Their Theology is clear – the Lamb of God who has won the victory is worthy of glory, honour and power, so blessed are those who are called to the wedding feast/love feast/Eucharist of the Lamb (19:9). It is a Theology of Hope.

Thirdly, Revelation deliberately provides something of a last word on symbolic identities whereby the 'unveiling' or 'opening of heaven' serves to 'close the book' on the whole biblical narrative. Eden is refounded and Genesis imagery restored around the sanctuary as God 'makes all things new' (21:5). A tree of life is there with healing for the nations and living waters flowing forth for the peoples (22:1-2). Capturing the Torah tradition, the Ark of the Covenant is seen enthroned in heaven replete with its shattering theophany-earthquake power as Holy Word (11:19). The famous 144,000, the new multiplied and perfected Israel of twelve thousand times twelve tribes become the new global chosen people called to glorious fellowship with God (7:1-17, 14:1-4). Ultimately, the destruction of Judah, the desecration of the Temple and the persecutions of the present are forgotten as a New Jerusalem, where God dwells with humanity once again comes down from heaven (21:10). With intimate nuptial imagery reminiscent of the Song of Songs, the Church as bride prepares herself in the Spirit for a second glorious coming of the exalted Christ (19:7-9). At the beginning and end of the book (1:8, 22:13) this linen clad, risen, cosmic Son of Man is identified as the Alpha and the Omega – the beginning and the end – the first word and the last word in the revelation of God whose will is expressed most perfectly in a cosmic marriage celebration (22:17). It is a Theology of Love.

Sociologically, it is easy to see the 'identity confirming' power of this writing. Against a background of persecution, where the pressures to conform are immense, the motives to be different reach cosmic levels. Theologically, the paradox emphasized by this scroll is that Christian thinking ultimately inhabits a 'liminal space' between the 'unveiling' of the mystery of God in Jesus and the glorious renewal of all things that he promised. Appeal to 'the already glimpsed but not yet fully realized' can be seen as a cop-out for the non-return of Christ or equally badly, a sort of no-man's land of religious knowledge where partial sight rules OK. While this criticism is understandable, the 'already-not yet' paradox also seems to be key to the explanation of Jesus offered by the various New Testament theologians. As later chapters will demonstrate, the moment that paradox is removed, Christian Theology either crashes to the ground in mundanity or floats off into the sky as a wispy irrelevance.

f) Authorship and the Canon

Despite the fact that of all the New Testament writings, the Book of Revelation made the most allusions, citations and connections with the *TaNaK/LXX*, it was not well received in all parts of the nascent Christian Church. As the various scrolls were circulated among the followers of the Jesus movement, some were deemed worthy of inclusion and solemn reading in the celebrations of the community and others were not. It would seem that only gradually was Revelation accepted as one of the inspired contributions and it may have been helped by the confusion surrounding its origins, as even accidental connection with John would have been viewed as a positive.

Since the authorship of some of the later writings was disputed even in those days, it can be perplexing for the modern mind to rest easy with the thought that there are possible examples of *pseudepigraphia* or 'falsely ascribed writings' in the sacred collection. Without wanting to pass on cheap tranquillizers to allay legitimate concerns for truth, I would first want to point out that this practice, this style of appropriation, was already common in Jewish and other literary traditions – there was nothing out of the ordinary for early Jesus followers to imitate the practice. Hence, just as there seem to have been prophetic 'schools' at work in the production over time of the Isaiah oracles which demonstrably span several centuries, this same factor is possibly at play in the idea of communities founded by apostles continuing to produce literature in a given tradition – be that of Paul, Peter, or John.

This notion of style or 'school' is reminiscent in our own time of 'franchise names' and 'trademark styles' in commerce or fashion. As an even clearer example, anyone who has followed popular music will know there are a number of bands out there singing songs written by original members who are no longer in the line-up, whether claimed by the ravages of lifestyle, the acrimony of bad contracts or simply the passage of time. Some bands have none of their original members and yet we still buy the downloads, we still go to the concerts. There is the strange phenomenon that Tupac Shakur has produced more records since his death than when he was alive and some of us will even confess to having enjoyed an Elvis tribute night in Las Vegas. This whole thing can be quite confusing. Ask yourself, if you went to see your favourite band and they only played songs from *Thriller* and *Bad*, would you have 'heard' your band or Michael Jackson? Fundamentally, the fan is looking for continuity with the original authors or at least the musical tradition that they represent.

While none of the foregoing excuses deliberate forgeries, it may perhaps help explain why there was a naturally grey area in literary convention and authorial authenticity as the New Testament emerged. For example, a letter written down by someone who visited Paul in prison might be accepted as authentic since the 'song' would have some of the recognizable harmonies, even if some of the phrasing might be different. That said, it would be naïve to think that the early community of the Church was gullible. The ultimate test was not *just* the message and nor was the simple arrogation of authorship to an apostle the only criterion. Some writings simply did not 'ring true' with Christian thinking and dramatic episodes guaranteed little, as epitomized by this episode from *The Acts of John*:

> Now on the first day we arrived at a deserted inn, and when we were at a loss for a bed for John, we saw a droll matter. There was one bedstead lying somewhere there without coverings, whereon we spread the cloaks which we were wearing, and we prayed him to lie down upon it and rest, while the rest of us all slept upon the floor. But he when he lay down was troubled by the bugs, and as they continued to become yet more troublesome to him, when it was now about the middle of the night, in the hearing of us all he said to them: I say unto you, O bugs, behave yourselves, one and all, and leave your abode for this night and remain quiet in one place, and keep your distance from the servants of God. And as we laughed, and went on talking for some time, John addressed himself to sleep; and we, talking low, gave him no disturbance (or, thanks to him we were not disturbed).
>
> But when the day was now dawning I arose first, and with me Verus and Andronicus, and we saw at the door of the house which we had taken a great number of bugs standing, and while we wondered at the great sight of them, and all the brethren were roused up because of them, John continued sleeping. And when he was awaked we declared to him what we had seen. And he sat up on the bed and looked at them and said: Since ye have well behaved yourselves in hearkening to my rebuke, come unto your place. And when he had said this, and risen from the bed, the bugs running from the door hasted to the bed and climbed up by the legs thereof and disappeared into the joints. And John said again: This creature hearkened unto the voice of a man, and abode by itself and was quiet and trespassed not; but we which hear the voice and commandments of God disobey and are light-minded: and for how long? (James, 1924, pp. 242–43).

While Jesus seems to have had some concerns about sleeping and wakefulness and used equally basic images to illustrate aspects of the Kingdom, bedbug stories from the *Acts of John*, supernatural carpentry alterations in the *Gospel of Thomas* and the wilder shores of the *Acts of Peter* did not quite fit. Moreover, most of these writings emerged well over a century after the writings of Paul. During an epoch which thought little of novelty but revered the pedigree of the past, the early Christian communities simply did not accord them widespread acceptance. In other words, to be part of the *canon*, writings had to be recognizably coherent with the core message of Jesus, the community traditions and apostolic teaching. While there was an acceptance of diversity, some things were just too 'far out' and therefore not deemed authentic.

g) Marcion blasts the Canon

But where did this leave the foundational scriptures which had provided the raw material and vocabulary of the Christian writings? The relevance of these earlier traditions was challenged in particular by Marcion, a native of Pontus who made his way to Rome around 140 CE where he began to form his own separate Christian community. For Marcion, the God revealed by Jesus was completely different to the Creator God depicted in the ancient scriptures who was demonstrably fickle, conniving and cruel. For this reason, he rejected the foundational heritage and even the usefulness of the Gospels of Matthew, Mark and John on the grounds that they were still tinged with the old traditions. For Marcion, only Paul understood properly that Jesus had radically changed the script. Among the Gospels, he thought only Luke understood the essence of the universal grace that was on offer.

Modern readers might have some sympathy with this approach. Randolph Churchill (1911–68), son of Winston, was challenged to read the Old Testament by the novelist Evelyn Waugh and is reputed to have summed up his findings saying 'Isn't God a Sh*t?' Indeed, if the Marcionites had concentrated on some of the more dubious passages of the *TaNaK*, their position might have found more favour. Instead, the force of Marcion's argument rested on a fundamental assumption that creation was evil. Based partly on the dualism of Plato, the premise was that the physical world was corrupt while the spiritual world was infinitely more perfect. In turn, this led the Marcionites to propose a form of 'Docetism' clean contrary to the explicit affirmations of John's Gospel. Docetists believed that Jesus was a kind of spiritual avatar and had not really come in the flesh.

Ironically, in proposing a God of love that had little to do with the world, Marcion was successfully opposed by Tertullian and particularly Irenaeus who saw Jesus as precisely the medication needed by created order. God had created the world and it was good – humanity had corrupted the earth, not God. For these theologians, the continuity between Jesus and the Creator God was clear from the testimony that 'all things were made through him – the first born of all creation' (John 1:1, Col 1:15). It was these connections and the notion of Jesus as the new Adam rather than rootedness in Moses and the Law that elicited the defence of the ancient collection as part of the religious heritage of the Jesus movement. This may well have been due to the increasing estrangement from rabbinical Torah traditions which accompanied the 'parting of the ways' of the second century. Yet while a *canon* inclusive of the *TaNaK* was finally defined within the Christian community by 382 CE, the problem that Marcion had highlighted remained, *viz.* the connection between Jesus in the New Testament and the Creator God of the Old. This dilemma was destined to pre-occupy the best Christian thinkers of those early centuries and will be the central concern of the next two chapters.

h) Epilogue – the Bibles of the Christian tradition

One by-product of the dispute with Marcion was that it seems to have pointed up the need to articulate what were thought to be authentic writings to be held sacred by all. One of the earliest appears to be the Muratorian fragment, commonly dated around 200 CE, which constitutes something of an annotated bibliography. The common core was generally affirmed by a series of authoritative voices and the connection with the ancient writings never again put in doubt. It would appear that the practice of reading out the foundational texts of the *TaNaK* in Christian gatherings continued uninterrupted.

To be clear, however, the majority of those who were by now participating in such meetings were not conversant with Hebrew and had been hearing a Greek translation of the *TaNaK* for some time which originated in Alexandria around 160 BCE. Legend has it that after the task was commissioned, the seventy scribes employed finished their work independently only to find that they had all translated the words in exactly the same way. While one might doubt the story, the resulting collection of writings became known over time as 'The Seventy' or in Latin *The Septuagint* – usually shortened to *LXX* – in Roman numerals. This collection included a number of writings that have only been handed on in Greek and not in Hebrew. What gradually happened in the years following the Jesus event was that the emerging 'Christians' became identified linguistically with the Greek language and the *LXX* collection. As noted above, jolted into reflection by the trauma of the Jewish wars, a process of defining the limits of the Hebrew language collection probably only began following the destruction of the Temple but ultimately yielded a *TaNaK* that was less extensive than the *LXX*.

Formal identification of the sacred collection of Christianity was not made until the declaration of Pope Damasus in 382 CE which rubber stamped the

Septuagint as the official Church version of the Old Testament. Damasus then commissioned St. Jerome to translate this into a *Latin* version of Scripture which became called the 'Vulgate' – because Latin was the 'vulgar' or 'common' language of his day. Not a man short of opinions, Jerome did as he was asked, but cast some doubt on whether one section of the collection, Esdras, should be considered properly biblical. As the Vulgate gradually became the main text for the Western Church, the Greek-speaking Eastern Christians, less influenced by Jerome, continued to use the *LXX* and for a thousand years, despite other differences, Greeks and Latins still had the same collection. This all exploded at the Reformation when, in trying to get at the heart of the biblical message, Martin Luther (1483–1546) placed greater focus on the Hebrew scriptures rather than the Vulgate or the *LXX*. This meant that Protestantism effectively 'de-commissioned' Tobit, Judith, parts of Esther, Wisdom, Sirach, Baruch, parts of Daniel, Maccabees and Esdras. These became known in Protestant Churches as 'The Apocrypha' – 'The Hidden Collection' – which could be read for edification, but were not to be considered Holy Writ. Though the Latin Catholic Church defended the validity of these books, the Council of Trent on 5 April 1546 acted on Jerome's thousand-year-old doubts and excluded Esdras which the Greek-speaking churches have retained.

Summary

The biblical collection, or 'Canon' of scriptures, contains Christianity's foundational documents and as such constitutes the 'Soul of Theology'. The writings of the New Testament, though varying in style and emphasis, may be understood as an extended Pesher interpretation of the ancient scriptures in the light of the Jesus revelation. Written recollections of the Jesus event became even more important in the light of tribulations in Judea which loosened the connection of YHWH faith with Temple ritual. As rabbinical reaction to this disaster took place, so persecution of the apostolic communities prompted identity forging literature among believers which took measured form in the Epistle to the Hebrews and spectacular apocalyptic form in the Book of Revelation. As the newer writings were circulated among the communities, a common collection began to emerge but which remained undefined for centuries. The main theological crisis precipitated by Marcion concerned the acceptability or otherwise of the Old Testament. Since early Christian theologians understood themselves as the true heirs of YHWH faith, they denied as false any separation of the Creator God from the Redeeming Messiah. But that left the problem of how Jesus and the Creator were connected. . . .

Kerygma to Creeds

Chapter Outline

This chapter takes as its conundrum the way in which the simple liturgical acclamations of the Lordship of Jesus eventually gave rise to the complexities of 'consubstantiality' and Trinity that are a feature of the most classic summary of Christian belief, the Nicene Creed. It is a commonplace to suppose that the sub-clause constructs of later creedal formulas mark a watershed in the Hellenization ('Greek-ifying') of the original 'kerygma' or proclamation of Peter and the Galilean crew that followed Jesus. While there is some truth in this apprehension, the theological novelty in the later creeds should not be exaggerated. The creeds are better understood as determinedly rooted in the theological tradition of the Jesus movement which, by being Judean, was necessarily interpenetrated with Torah and Wisdom themes.

a) *Kerygma* to creed

The previous chapters have described how the raw preaching of the first followers of Jesus eventually led to an agreed list of the writings essential for an understanding of the Christ event. The process by which zesty, succinct and brief proclamation culminated in a fairly extensive collection of over seventy scrolls of Theology involved some pretty sharp exchanges and took place over decades and centuries. The eventual list included the New Testament, the fourfold Gospel and the letters of the apostolic era with their theological reflections and advice on the practical ramifications of the Jesus revelation for Christian communities. Marcion's attempt to sever the Jesus movement from its ancient Old Testament scriptural tradition of the Torah, the Prophets and the Writings was also noted, but ultimately not accepted by the majority view, well articulated by Irenaeus.

In a similar fashion, this chapter will examine how the simple acclamations found in the earliest Christian writings of the Canon developed into the multi-clause proposals of the Christian creeds. Likewise, just as the Canon took decades and even centuries to consolidate, so a comparable period was required for the classic conciliar creeds to be agreed. There were many bitter disputes involved as the eventual summaries of Christian faith ran the risk of separation from their Judean origins. For some, the emergence of the creeds plot a transition whereby the intimate, historical nature of the biblical revelation of a personal, proximate God is eventually articulated in the philosophical terms of a Greek culture wedded to the notion of a transcendent, far out, impersonal God. While this view is commonplace and is seen as part of the 'Hellenization' of the Jesus movement, it risks making the same mistake as Marcion, since the creeds actually emphasize the theological rootedness of Christianity in Judean thinking.

b) Creeds in the Canon

If we take the majority view and surmise that our earliest insights into the central 'confessions' or creedal statements of the Jesus movements appear in Paul's letters, then we can identify short exclamations such as *Kyrios Iesous* ('Jesus is Lord!') or *Maranatha!* ('Our Lord! Come!') as indicative of early Christian belief formulas. As noted above (§10d) *Mar – Kyrios* – 'Lord' was a term identifiable with God from common usage in the *LXX* – the Septuagint Greek translation of the *TaNaK*. Whether Paul actually understood such exclamations to be equating Jesus with God at this stage is a moot point and remains one of the more contested areas in biblical–theological studies. Perhaps 'Lord' is to be understood more modestly as a term of veneration rather than worship, but in any event, these statements in this context function powerfully as indicators of belonging. Their proclamation indicates the presence of the Spirit, the guarantee of filial/family belonging to the eternal Father. A similar giveaway is the follower who cries out 'Abba! Father!' By referring to God in the same intimate infant-trusting fashion as Jesus – 'Dada' – the believer belongs and is heir to all the promises of the risen Christ (Gal 4:6). To be sure, these exclamatory shouts may be short, but they are sweet with theological flavour. *Maranatha* unraveled reads: *This Jesus to whom we belong is the Messiah whom God has made Lord by raising him from the dead and he will come again to inaugurate the Kingdom of God on earth in the deathless glory of which I am destined to be fulfilled*'. Not bad for four syllables!

Since Paul's writings are addressed to young communities finding their way in sometimes hostile environments, it is perhaps unsurprising that 'belief as belonging' is a theme which is also present in his Roman correspondence:

> "The word is near you, on your lips and in your heart" (that is, the word of faith that we proclaim); because if you confess with your lips that Jesus is Lord and believe in your heart that God raised him from the dead, you will be saved. For one believes with the heart and so is justified, and one confesses with the mouth and so is saved. The Scripture says, 'No one who believes in him will be put to shame.' For there is no distinction between Jew and Greek; the same Lord is Lord of all and is generous to all who call on him. For, 'Everyone who calls on the name of the Lord shall be saved." (Rom 10:8-13)

In identifying vocal confession as a mark of belonging, Paul was not doing anything new but rather confirming a practice common to religions in general and to his own particular tradition:

> Hear, O Israel: The LORD is our God, the LORD alone. You shall love the LORD your God with all your heart, and with all your soul, and with all your might. (Deut 6:4-5)

To repeat, this treasured *Shema* of Deut 6:4 was not only a daily recitation of those faithful to YHWH, they were words of identity-belonging. Tiny written versions of it came to be worn by the pious in phylacteries – leather pouches worn on the forehead and arm. The same treasured words were embedded in the *Mezuzah*, a niche in the doorpost of an observant household.

> Keep these words that I am commanding you today in your heart. Recite them to your children and talk about them when you are at home and when you are away, when you lie down and when you rise. Bind them as a sign on your hand, fix them as an emblem on your forehead, and write them on the doorposts of your house and on your gates. (Deut 6:6-9)

Throughout the *TaNaK* other traditions evidence similar summary portions of proclamation and belonging (Deut 26:5-9, 1 Kings 18:39, Ps 24:1-6).

Hence it is no surprise that the development of the tradition among the Jesus movement theologians embraced prayer/confession formulas which crystallized identity and belonging through worship tropes. Though Paul is the richest source of these, the classic confessions of Peter present in all the Synoptics and excerpts from speeches attributed to him in Acts are likewise of interest. The Synoptic tradition juxtaposes Peter's miraculous insight into the truth of the 'Messiah-Jesus' claim with the promise of a belonging through suffering which is understandably off-putting to the disciples (Matt 16: 13-28, Mark 8:27-38, Luke 9:18-27). By contrast, Acts has the erstwhile denial junkie Peter proclaiming with certainty that God has made the crucified Jesus both 'Lord and Messiah', and despite laying the guilt upon his hearers, they sign up to belong in their thousands (Acts 2:36).

c) Creeds and Baptism

Striking though some of these 'Creeds from the Canon' might be, the clearest belonging formula appears right at the end of Matthew's Gospel:

> Now the eleven disciples went to Galilee, to the mountain to which Jesus had directed them. When they saw him, they worshipped him; but some doubted. And Jesus came and said to them, "All authority in heaven and on earth has been given to me. Go therefore and make disciples of all nations, baptizing them in the name of the Father and of the Son and of the Holy Spirit, and teaching them to obey everything that I have commanded you. And remember, I am with you always, to the end of the age." (Matt 28:16-20)

There are many fascinating aspects of this text, not least its connection with the transfiguration traditions as well as doubt motifs in John and ascension motifs in Luke. The key feature in the present discussion is the central imperative, namely *to make disciples of all nations, baptizing them in the name of the Father and of the Son and of the Holy Spirit*. This clearly links the ritual of belonging – Baptism, with the confession of the mystery – Father, Son and Spirit. There is little need to gather evidence relating to the importance of this ritual for the Jesus theologians. Familiarity with the genesis of the movement from the ministry of John the Baptist seems to have been a key criterion when the group looked to replace Judas (Acts 1:22). From the writings of Paul through to Revelation it is clearly presented as *the* initiation ritual, the sacred portal of mercy and belonging (Rom 6:4, Rev 7:14). Although collated in stylized fashion, the accounts in Acts explicitly link the connection between confession of belief and belonging in baptism. They also acknowledge a certain early confusion regarding the practice (cf. Acts 2:41, 19:4-6).

It is against this background that the particularity of the confession present in Matthew is to be considered since the explicit avowal of what comes to be known as a Trinitarian formula is weighty evidence that the threefold blessing was a feature of the apostolic Church. Antecedents for it in the prior theological tradition *might* be discernible in Dan 7:14, which is clearly where the granting of all authority to the Son of Man is prefigured. In that passage one might also discern an 'apocalyptic triad' of God/Ancient One, Son of Man/Elect and Angel/Presence which *may* likewise be a feature of Ezekiel 1:26-28. What is probably easier to explain is that the formula was based on the shared experience of early Christian worship whereby honour was given to *ho theos* – God (the Father), for his *kyrios christos* – Lord Christ, in the power of the *pneuma hagion* – Holy Spirit. Thus we have Paul's famous farewell blessing to the Corinthians 'The grace of our Lord Jesus Christ, the love of God and the fellowship of the Holy Spirit be with you all' (2 Cor 13:14).

The proposal that creeds might emerge from the worship of believers is an example of what theologians call *lex orandi – lex credendi*. Literally translatable as 'law of prayer/law of belief', it is best understood as the notion that 'prayer patterns belief' and in the case of Matt 28:19, it seems obvious that this 'belonging formula' had a prayer context, namely, the baptismal liturgy. Moreover, when going beyond the biblical writings in search of early creedal formula, it is highly likely that the questions asked of the candidate during the ritual are likely to have generated the kind of faith summary that would eventually take on more developed forms. The following are two of the earliest cited in J. N. D Kelly's classic *Early Christian Creeds* from a manuscript entitled *The Epistle of the Apostles*.

> (I believe) in (the Father) ruler of the universe
> And in Jesus Christ (our Redeemer)
> And in the Holy Spirit (the Paraclete)
> And in the Holy Church
> And in the forgiveness of sins.
> (Kelly, 1972, p. 82)

Note that the words in brackets are not present in all the manuscripts we have of this text. Note also that this is set in a 'five-fold' set of propositions which the *Epistle of the Apostles* explains as being modelled on the five loaves by which the multitude were miraculously fed by Jesus. Kelly has argued that this text, along with the *Der Balyzeh Papyrus* below, originated in baptismal contexts

> I believe in God the Father Almighty,
> And his only begotten Son our Lord Jesus Christ

And in the Holy Spirit
And in the resurrection of the flesh
And the Holy Catholic Church.
(Kelly, 1972, p. 88)

The statements are still short, simple, straightforward. Congruent with the Judean heritage, not much longer than the *Shema* from Deut 6:4-5. Neither are they philosophical. The first is a proclamation of threefold belief and belonging through mercy, the second a threefold belief in belonging and resurrection. For good or for ill, however, as time went on things all got a little more complicated.

d) The rule of faith: Creeds in the community

Although the context of baptism was a typical place where creeds or 'belief statements of belonging' were voiced, a rarer but significant arena was that of theological disputation. Taking Irenaeus as an example, his defence of the validity of the ancient scriptures against the claims of Marcion in large part rested on his appeal to something consistently referred to as the 'Rule of Faith'. The term 'Rule of Faith' is not peculiar to Irenaeus, it is used by Tertullian, Eusebius and other early writers. It seems to have consisted of a series of key propositions which outlined the core elements of lived Christian faith which were in circulation during the period following the death of the Twelve. It served to guide scriptural interpretation and delineate the path of 'proper glorification' – *orthodoxy* from 'choosiness' or separatist thinking – *heresy*.

In his various battles with dissenters, Ireneaus' basic method is clear. He refers them to that tradition which originates from the Twelve, which is preserved by means of the succession of elders in the churches (cf. Jenson, 2011, p. 34). In so doing, Ireneaus was only imitating the practice which had begun very early on in the Jesus movement. Paul is conscious 'to hand on what I received' (cf. 1 Cor 11:2, 15). Paul is also at pains in his letters to distinguish what he has received from the Lord and what he hasn't, what he does in contrast to the other apostles and where he is in harmony. In later correspondence connected with Paul's communities, the same themes are emphasized. 'Stand fast and hold to the traditions which you have been taught, whether by word or by our letter' (2 Thess 2:15). 'The things which you have heard of me among many witnesses, commit those to faithful men who will be able to teach others also' (2 Tim 2:2). Such concerns were not unique to Paul. The Letter of Jude, one of the less familiar texts of the New Testament, emphasizes in similar fashion that believers should 'Contend earnestly for the faith once for all delivered to the saints' (Jude 1:3).

The desire of believers to remain faithful to the 'Teachings of the Apostles, the Fellowship and the Prayers' stood to reason in the culture of that time. In the contemporary West, the attraction to novelty and the new can blind us to the fact that for the sake of its own credibility, the Jesus movement was more concerned to demonstrate its continuity with the past. Although the 'Rule of Faith' seems to have varied somewhat from place to place, Irenaeus' version exemplifies a summary which is beginning to take on the shape of later creeds.

> This faith: in one God, the Father Almighty, who made the heaven and the earth and the seas and all the things that are in them; and in one Christ Jesus, the Son of God, who was made flesh for our salvation; and in the Holy Spirit, who made known through the prophets the plan of salvation, and the coming, and the birth from a virgin, and the passion, and the resurrection from the dead, and the bodily ascension into heaven of the beloved Christ Jesus, our Lord, and his future appearing from heaven in the glory of the Father to sum up all things and to raise anew all flesh of the whole human race. (Stevenson, 1987, pp. 111–12)

Part of the fascination in reading such summaries is to speculate why what was put in was put in, and why what was not was left out. For example, there is nothing in the outline above that says anything about what Jesus actually did during his life. It calls to my mind a *Peanuts* cartoon where Lucy, the grumpy elder sister, is asked to read a story and curtly declaims: 'A man was born, he lived, he died. The End'. Still full of wonder, her brother replies: 'Wow! Makes you wish you knew the guy!' That said, while there were no birth stories, miracles or speeches, this 'Rule of Faith' is very much rooted in the original *kerygma* which sought to explain the messianic claims of Jesus. Confirming the general sense that such summary statements contained the core tradition, we find a later author, Rufinus, referring to the 'Rule of Faith of the Apostles' in the following fashion:

> I believe in God almighty [Rufinus has 'the Father almighty']
> And in Christ Jesus, his only Son, our Lord
> Who was born of the Holy Spirit and the Virgin Mary
> Who was crucified under Pontius Pilate and was buried
> And the third day rose from the dead
> Who ascended into heaven

> And sitteth on the right hand of the Father
> Whence he cometh to judge the living and the dead.
> And in the Holy Spirit
> The holy church
> The remission of sins
> The resurrection of the flesh
> The life everlasting [Rufinus omits this clause]
> (Bettenson & Maunder, 2011, p. 25)

It is impossible at this distance to vouchsafe Rufinus' claim that these exact phrases were framed originally by the Twelve for the Church in Jerusalem. That said, prayers are the kind of thing handed on from one generation to the next and form neural pathways of memory that run deep. (It is a slightly different argument, but after my mother had been rushed to hospital following a stroke, I hurried to her bedside to find her having lost her power of speech. Half mischievously I asked her if she could try saying a prayer, and I began the 'Our Father' which she then continued both at top speed and at top volume. Nurses came running and one clutched my arm as if a miracle had happened. It hadn't – it was just a well established speech line of the frontal lobe.)

Withal, there is nothing in this set of propositions that sits uneasily with the biblical testimony and therefore the writings more immediately associated with apostolic theologizing. Ultimately, as the basis of what became known to tradition as *The Apostles' Creed*, it has been recited in Christian gatherings for centuries and has *formed* thinking-belonging ever since.

e) Hellenization of the Gospel?

So where did all the complicated stuff come from? A common view of the development of Christian Theology runs as follows: The evidence for Jesus being the promised Messiah of Israel was not convincing enough for all Judeans to swallow since the people had not been liberated from Imperial oppression. Instead, the Jesus movement re-launched their Messiah as a Redeemer/Saviour of the Gentiles – the Universal Christ.

- The bright side of this thinking was that it 'de-nationalized' Jesus and paved the way for the belonging of all peoples. A good thing.
- The dark side was that it 'de-Judaized' him, cutting him and the movement from their properly Judaic roots. This not only led to Marcion-like thinning out of the theological heritage of the Jesus movement, it also had centuries-long consequences for Christian anti-Semitism. A bad thing.

- The foggy side was that it 'hellenized' the Gospel Theology such that the intimately human picture of the 'Abba-God' revealed by Jesus became obscured by the need to accommodate the mystery to the distant, not-bothered God of Greek thought. A dubious thing.

The problem with the theory as set out above is that it does not accurately depict early Christian thinking. The 'Greek-ification' of Judean Theology and life experience occurred before, during and after the emergence of the Jesus movement. Centuries of being part of the Greek Empire had left its mark on the people, many of whom would have been bilingual. As noted above in Section 12h, activity among 'Diaspora' Judeans in Alexandria had given rise to a Greek collection of biblical scrolls – the *LXX*/Septuagint – perhaps as early as 162BCE. Furthermore, as Chapter 11 demonstrated, John's Gospel makes free and full use of imagery drawn from this *LXX* tradition. Building on Prov 8:22, which depicted a pre-existent Wisdom of God, the *Logos*/Word of YHWH became understood as a pre-existing Torah by which the whole world was ordered. The Law was given by God to Moses on the mountain top. Since it came from heaven, it predated the earth.

In a similar way, Christian belief proposed that Jesus predated the earth to which he came. The powerful synthesis of Hebrew and Greek thinking evident in the Prologue to John's Gospel fed the hunger of theologian and philosopher alike. On the one hand, the theologian attempting to understand the nature of God and the meaning of life, on the other, the philosopher looking for the proper patterning of knowledge in order to understand reality. It should be stressed that such an enterprise among YHWH believers was not novel. The Diaspora community of Alexandria which gave rise to the *LXX* also boasted in Philo (20 BCE–50 CE) one of the pre-eminent Judean thinkers of the period. Both a believer and a philosopher, he actively sought to synthesize the two loves of his life, Plato and the Torah. The extent to which Philo influenced theologians of the Jesus movement is difficult to assess, but the same reconciling enterprise can be seen in John's Prologue with the person of Jesus replacing the Torah as the supreme expression of wisdom.

The idea that the whole of the world was patterned and *intelligible* ('understandable') because of a Creator God was not at all foreign in Greek thinking. In the very first sentence of this book, it was noted that the Greek *logos*, which translates into English as 'word', also connotes 'logic', 'reason' and 'meaning'. The idea that humanity can only understand reality through the principle of reason or *logos* is at the heart of Plato's system of thinking. For Plato, the physical world is temporary and shabby and can be contrasted with the non-physical dimension of the mind which is permanent and clear. As an example, think of a cat – in your mind you picture it there with whiskers, ears and everything in place. But experience is more confusing. Not only are there lots of cats, but the next cat you see might have a paw missing, or no tail, and still worse, if you watch it for long enough it will get old, die and start to rot – yet in your head, you will still have the idea of a cat. Now (pause for thought), if you can accept that the *idea of a cat* is more permanent than *a physical cat* you are half-way to understanding Plato's main point namely:

> The dimension or 'world' of ideas is more real than the physical.

And this is where it gets interesting:

- In Plato's system, 'logos' is the interface between the world of ideas and the physical world.
- By identifying 'logos' with Jesus, early Christian thinking could connect the divided realms of reality – the seen and the unseen, the temporal and eternal – in one person.
- Jesus thus becomes the cosmic mediator of truth whom any sincere philosopher, any sincere 'lover of wisdom,' should seek in order to be enlightened.

If that argument didn't grab you, you can go at this from another angle. In Book VII of his most famous work, *The Republic*, Plato depicts the true philosopher as one who realizes that because humanity is so dominated by the five senses, it becomes fooled and trapped in the temporary pleasures of life. Beer, football, music, kissing, chocolate – even mum's home cooking – are just a dance of shadows because all these things pass – your team gets beaten and too much food and drink make you sick. He uses his own parable *The Allegory of the Cave* to demonstrate the strength of character the wise person must have to break the chains of sensory illusion. To realize instead that ideas such as truth, justice and beauty are the enduring realities to strive for and which are at the core of human life. In his story, the philosopher leaves the darkness of the sensory but senseless cave to seek the light of absolute Goodness. Yet having seen this light, he feels compelled to return to the darkness to liberate his former companions. Instead, they refuse to believe his account of reality and they kill him – preferring their own ignorant ideas to the truth and freedom that lies beyond their dark and shackled world.

While the parallels being drawn by Plato are connected with the trial and death of his mentor Socrates, the connotations are also glaringly reminiscent of the 'trial of truth' that John and later Christian theologians depict for Jesus. Jesus has broken the chains and smashed the cave. Prisoners no more, the light of the Absolute Good shines clear and Wisdom is available to all. Jesus is the *logos*, the interface, the access to right thinking as well as the personal model of right action. Jesus is the truth which will set you free (John 8:32).

f) Light from light: Justin as the first theologian

This way of understanding the revelation of Jesus became known as 'Logos Christology' and it is worth juggling a little with the concept to get the force of its proposal. By identifying Jesus as the 'Logos', the connecting principle of the cosmos is revealed. It is a bit like the recent search for the Higgs-Boson particle and the scientific desire to articulate a 'Theory of Everything'. Scientifically, the Higgs-Boson particle is understood to enable matter/mass to hold together. Theologically, identifying Jesus as Torah – Logos, early Christians were able to proclaim not only a Messiah who 'is the first born of all creation' but that 'in him the fullness of God was pleased to dwell' and that 'in him all things hold together' (Col 1:15-20). The planet, the stars, the whole caboodle would fall apart without him. In other words, if reality is relationship, then the centrifugal force, the gravity of life, is the love of God revealed in Jesus. Love not only makes the world go round, it brought it into being in the first place and it will bring it to an end in the last place since Jesus is the Alpha and the Omega. No wonder they shouted *Maranatha* – 'Our Lord, Come!'

Cosmic though the argument seemed, the rationale wasn't a million miles from traditional Judean thinking. Indeed discussions around the identification of 'Messiah Jesus' with Wisdom, with the eternal Torah and the eternal patterning of creation form part of the theological heritage of Justin Martyr (165 CE). Justin has often been identified as 'the first Christian theologian' since he is one of the most prominent writers of the generation following the death of the Twelve. Though I strongly disagree with this title (it obscures the fact that the Apostles and the other New Testament writers were themselves theologians), the faith journey Justin describes is a perfect illustration of how thinkers in the Jesus movement confluenced with the prevailing currents of the Greek philosophical tradition.

Justin was born around 100 CE in what is modern-day Nablus, the ancient Shechem of biblical Samaria. Although his autobiographical writings may be a little stylized, he describes himself as something of a 'seeker'. Having been born uncircumcised, he sought out a series of different guides in an attempt to understand the world in its material and spiritual dimensions. The wisdom of the Stoics was one part of the journey, an influential movement which saw each individual as possessed of a divine spark of God-like *logos*. It commended a serene acceptance, the *amor fati* – 'love of fate' – as a principle for coping with the vicissitudes or unexpected ups and downs of life. He claims to have dallied also with Pythagorean ideas which gave pre-eminence to mathematical, geometric and musical insights before finding in Plato's theories a more satisfying explanation of the matrix of reality. This delighted him until he met a mysterious old stranger walking along the sea shore who told him that the soul could not truly arrive at the knowledge of God without being illuminated by the insights of the Hebrew prophets and the Holy Spirit.

These details form part of Justin Martyr's *Dialogue with Trypho* which are likely to have taken place in Ephesus sometime before the Bar-Kochba rebellion of 135 CE. Trypho is a more traditional Judean who is not at all convinced that Jesus is the awaited Messiah and questions Justin's judgement on numerous things. In the *Dialogue*, he evidences a thorough knowledge of the common scriptures they share, and attempts to prove to Trypho that Jesus is the promised Messiah – the *Kyrios Christos* – the Lord Christ promised by the prophets. It is clear that for Trypho a key difficulty is how Jesus can be accorded the exalted God-like status that Christians seem to be affording him since it implies a separation from the Creator YHWH. Justin acknowledges some of the difficulty here and that God's activity in the scriptures might be ascribed to angels. However, he is adamant that there is biblical evidence and by alluding to light from light imagery (the sun and its rays) as well as the revelation of the I AM God of the burning bush in Ex 3:14, he invites Trypho to recognize 'same but different' imagery from the common tradition. He gives the example of kindling one fire from another – the new fire is not exactly the same as the original, but it has not reduced the original in any way either.

This use of metaphor and analogy are part of the method he employs in giving 'reasoned explanation for his position' (cf. 1 Pet 3:14). This form of writing is usually termed *apologia* and even today, as a form of theologizing, it is referred to as *apologetics*. Far from being some kind of guilt-ridden reasoning as a modern reading of the name might imply, for Justin it is convicted articulation of his belief (the man eventually died for this stuff!). To be noted is the way in which Justin at turns roots his argument in the liturgical and the scriptural/historic Jesus tradition, but is equally happy to commandeer Plato's philosophical and cosmic analogies to explain why, in his opinion, it is possible to give credence to the notion of an incarnate *logos* who remains one with the transcendent Creator.

Liturgy and History:

> What sober-minded man, then, will not acknowledge that we are not atheists, worshipping as we do the Maker of this universe, and declaring, as we have been taught, that He has no need of streams of blood and libations and incense . . . Our teacher of these things is Jesus Christ, who also was born for this purpose, and was crucified under Pontius Pilate, procurator of Judæa, in the times of Tiberius Caesar; and that we reasonably worship Him, having learned that He is the Son of the true God Himself, and holding Him in the second place, and the prophetic Spirit in the third, we will prove. For they proclaim our madness to consist in this, that we give to a crucified man a place second to the unchangeable and eternal God, the Creator of all; for they do not discern the mystery that is herein, to which, as we make it plain to you, we pray you to give heed. (First Apology, 13, in Roberts & Donaldson, 2007, pp. 166–7)

Contemporary Philosophy

> Plato's teachings are not contrary to Christ's but they are not in all respects identical with them: as is the case with the doctrines of others, the Stoics, the poets and the prose authors. For each through his share in the divine generative Logos, spoke well, seeing what was suited to his capacity . . . whatever has been spoken of aright by anyone belongs to us Christians; for we worship and love, next to God, the Logos who is from the unbegotten and ineffable God . . . . All those writers were able, through the seed of the Logos implanted in them, to see reality darkly. For it is one thing to have the seed of a thing and to imitate it up to one's capacity; far different is the thing itself, shared and imitated in virtue of its own grace. (Second Apology, 13 in O'Collins, 1999, p. 92)

Reading from a different cultural perspective which wants to respect 'each to his or her own', it does seem a little cheeky on Justin's part to claim every right thinking thought really belongs to the Jesus movement, but again, he is only following in a classic biblical tradition, which, as we shall see, becomes a touchstone for Christian Theology throughout the centuries (cf. 2 Cor 10:6). Indeed it is arguably Justin's *method* that marks him out as the 'First Christian Theologian' since his extant writings show classic theological technique – thorough knowledge of the *biblical* text, firsthand acquaintance with the liturgical, ethical and belief *tradition* of community belonging and lively engagement with the issues of his day *in dialogue* with other faith/belief systems of his era. His *thoughtful conversations about God* are counted among the earliest writings of the *Patristic* era – the 'Fathers of Christian Theology' whose ruminations on the mysteries of their faith in the generations following the death of the Twelve have been revered ever since as a particularly significant source for scholars of Jesus thinking.

g) The Nicene Creed

The lives of Justin and other early theologians are celebrated by Eusebius of Caesarea (d.325) in his *History of the Church*. This much quoted source serves as a bridge between the reflections of the early theologians and the formal articulation of the *regula fidei*, the 'rule of faith' that became known as the Nicaea or Nicene Creed. Oskar Skarsaune points out that Eusebius would have been baptized as an infant or in his youth in what was once the province of Judea around 260 or 270 CE. Taking the second article which has Jesus as its focus, Skarsaune annotates the biblical roots of the 'rule of faith' into which Eusebius was baptized as follows:

> And [we believe] in one Lord, Jesus
> Christ, (1 Cor 8:6)
> the Logos of God, (John 1:1f)
> God from God, (John 1:1)
> light from light, (Wis 7:26)
> life from life, (John 5:21, 26)
> Son only begotten, (John 1:14, 18, 3:16, 18)
> first-begotten before all creation, (Col 1:15; Prov 8:22)
> begotten before all ages from the Father, (Prov 8:23 Septuagint)
> through whom [i.e. the Son] all things came into being,
> (1 Cor 8:6; John 1:3; Col 1:16;
> Heb 1:2; Gen 1:1;
> Prov 8:22.30; Wis 7:22)
> who because of our salvation was incarnate, (John 1:14, Sir 24:8)
> and dwelt among men, (Bar 3:38)
> and suffered,
> and rose again on the third day,
> and ascended to the Father,
> and will come again in glory to judge
> the living and the dead. (Skarsuane, 2008, p. 232)

Caesarea is only seventy miles from Jerusalem, and the argument here is that the varied background of thinking provided by the *Maranatha* acclamations, the liturgies of baptism and the theological metaphors already rich in wisdom imagery have together already yielded a rule of faith/early creed which is rooted in ancient Judean-Jesus tradition. Unravelling the Greek-sounding images already woven into the thinking, and separating out the hymn singing of the early Jesus movement, does violence to its internal tradition and is in any case unnecessary. The only incentive to do so is to retrospectively purify along falsely identified ethnic grounds some imaginary original religious faith which never existed. Since the rallying cry of the *kerygma* includes the shattering of such ethnic distinctions, this enterprise so beloved of the nineteenth- and twentieth-century theologians seems all the more bizarre and misconceived.

It is highly likely that the creed eventually agreed at Nicaea was based on a local rule of faith similar to that of Eusebius. Taking on the dualistic mindset of the epoch, the first part of the confession clearly makes sure that the Creator God of the Jesus movement is understood not *only* as creator of material things (which might impress people in our era but not in theirs) nor *only* as creator of spiritual things (which would have impressed people in their era but not in ours). Like the original confessions which marked out faith and belonging, the prayer here goes global and embraces all peoples and all things. Everything belongs to the 'Is God' – the one 'in whom we live and move and have our being' (Acts 17.28). This translation is from *The Christian Faith* (Neuner & Dupuis, 1983, p. 6):

> We believe in one God,
> the Father almighty
> maker of all things visible and invisible

The second article is very similar to the creed of Eusebius, noted above, but there is one insertion which I have italicized and there'll be more on that in a minute (at least half a chapter!).

> And in one Lord, Jesus Christ,
> the Son of God, the only-begotten,
> generated from the Father,
> that is, from the being *(ousia)* of the Father,
> God from God, Light from Light,
> true God from true God,
> begotten, not made,
> *one in Being with the Father*.
> through whom all things were made
> those in heaven and those on earth.

The next section of the creed is the biblical-Gospel testimony in brief:

> For us men and for our salvation
> he came down, and became flesh,
> was made man, suffered,
> and rose again on the third day.
> He ascended to the heavens
> And shall come again to judge the living and the dead

The last section of the creed at Nicaea concerning the Holy Spirit runs as follows:

> And in the Holy Spirit

Full stop. OK – so it is one thing to be elusive and exclusive, and blow in ways no one knows, but not for nothing is the Holy Spirit sometimes called the 'forgotten member of the Trinity!' It was not until the subsequent council of Constantinople in 381 CE that the following was added completing the familiar creed used in Christian worship today:

> (56 year pause) . . . the Lord, *(to Kurion)* and Giver of life,
> who proceeds *(ekporeuomenon)* from the Father,
> Who together with the Father and Son
> is worshipped and glorified,
> who has spoken through the prophets.
> (And) in one Holy Catholic and apostolic Church
> We acknowledge one baptism for the forgiveness of sins.
> We expect the resurrection of the dead
> and the life of the world to come. Amen.
> (Neuner & Dupuis, 1983, p. 9)

So why was there a gathering at Nicaea anyway and why was there a 56-year pause between the start of the creed and the end of it? For an explanation, one need to look no further than the short phrase highlighted above:

> *One in Being with the Father*

Wrestling with these words was to embroil theologians, emperors and bishops alike into one of the most celebrated contestations in Christian Theology. If this chapter has given some insight into how original acclamations of Jesus were eventually expressed in cosmos-inclusive creeds of belonging, then the next examines the mechanism by which these formulae were derived. The focus becomes the historic, definitive Councils of the Church whose deliberations are part of the core heritage and method of Christian Theology. But be warned, the story of these gatherings is not for the faint-hearted.

Summary

If the original Jesus proclamation was the Kingdom, then the kerygma of the apostles proclaimed the Kingdom in terms of a new belonging to the Father in the Spirit of the risen Jesus. The first summaries of this proclamation, like the Shema *of Israel, were short prayers or creedal formulas that signified belonging. From the very basic threefold formulas for baptism, these 'rules of faith' became broader, embracing both cosmic and historical aspects of Jesus Theology. Greek influences on Hebrew wisdom thinking had already identified the Torah as a pre-existent divine template for creation and for life lived well. By identifying Jesus as the incarnate Torah, the Logos made flesh, Christianity was making divinity intimate, the heavenly earthly, the eternal temporal, the unapproachable personal.* Imago dei imago hominis *– The image of God [is] in the image of man. But how could this be . . . .?*

4. The Roman Empire and the Early Church

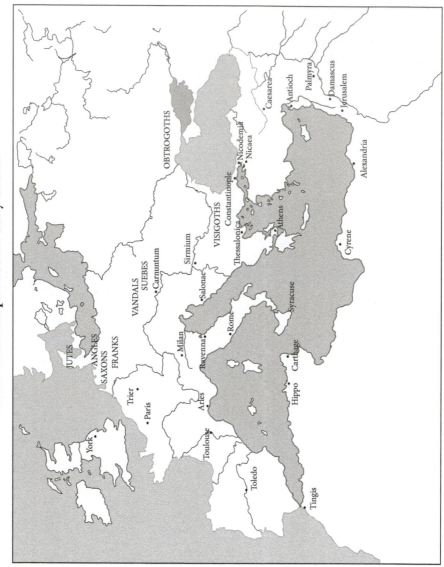

14

Councils and Controversy

Chapter Outline

In Christian Theology the deliberations of the 'Ecumenical Councils' of the Church have a particular role. Especially in the early centuries, these gatherings left an enduring theological legacy in terms of creeds and doctrinal formula which have remained reference points for Christian reflection ever since. Because many of the matters considered by these councils were dear to the heads as well as the hearts of the delegates, it is fair to say that such occasions were not always characterized by Christian charity. However, due consideration of the conciliar history profiles the way in which Christian theologians have struggled to find language to express the God conundrum posed by the Jesus revelation. The mysterious paradox of Trinity and conceptual criss-cross of the God-man stretched the best minds of the Patristic period to the limits of theological expression. But it was a rocky path, which even now requires theological alertness to retrace.

a) Councils, controversy and Christianity

The ecumenical councils of the Church during the Patristic period have remained definitive events in the theological life of Christianity. Nicaea (325) and Constantinople (381) were very much concerned with the issues linked to the doctrine of Trinity, whereas Ephesus (431) and Chalcedon (451) were more linked to the nature of Christ's Incarnation. Along with the Second and Third councils of Constantinople (553 and 680) and the Second council of Nicaea (787), these gatherings understood their decisions to be binding on all Christians. Insofar as their membership was predominantly made up of Christian bishops, it might be thought that *ecumenical* – 'whole world' – councils would have been serene affairs. Unfortunately, as some of the words and deeds of such gatherings indicate, the contrary has often been the case and the difficulty in convening a fully recognized council since 787 only serves to emphasize the point.

Once more, however, this need not surprise us. Part of the reason the Councils of the Church proved so fraught is that they were often convened in times of theological crisis. Acts 15 is commonly taken as the prototype ecumenical council and it is clear from those discussions that even gatherings among the disciples in the first flush of the Jesus mission were somewhat intense and sincerely felt disagreements persisted (see Chapter 12). Indeed, it is perhaps false piety and dubious theologizing to assume Christians should always agree, since there is no evidence that Jesus was a false irenicist/'peacemaker', still less a woolly minded wimp. If anything, the evidence is to the contrary, with Jesus almost specializing in challenging cherished traditions which provoked predictable and ultimately violent consequences.

Rulings or changes in cherished traditions whether of religious, political, national or local provenance can cause immense anxiety since they can be *felt* as identity interference. And nobody likes being messed with. Recently, for example, the England national football team fell foul of the international ruling body because they wanted to wear a poppy, an emblem of war remembrance, on their team shirts. England had never worn it before, and the European governing body (understandably) didn't particularly want to profile a period of history they would reasonably prefer to forget. The uproar in England was immense, and could only be understood by people sensitive to all the nationalistic, heroic and mournful feelings that the simple red poppy symbolizes in the United Kingdom. To ban the poppy was to mess with British identity.

In the context of Christian faith, especially in consideration of the belonging prayers of the creeds, sensitivities were, and remain, intense. 'Creeds' were referred to as 'symbols' in earlier times which served to emphasize the dimension of togetherness expressed by such confessions of faith. The opposite of *dia-bolic* – 'to throw apart', *sym-bolic* meant 'together-put'. Just as two parts of a broken seal when matched together identify the sender of the message, so the 'symbol' of faith, when matched together, identified the believers united in Christ the word. Yet it is important to note that the most celebrated summary of Christian Theology, the Nicene-Constantinople creed, was as much 'put together' by the political endeavours of emperors as by the religious resolution of bishops. And even a script writer couldn't have bettered the brilliant historical and theological irony, that this first worldwide gathering of a group who had suffered three centuries of persecution would witness Santa Claus beating someone up for not understanding the importance of Christmas.

b) Begotten not made

Well sort of. It might be more accurate to say that a Christian guy called Nicholas, who became Bishop of Myra, who was eventually canonized and became associated with gift-giving, and whose name 'Saint Niclaus' became mixed up/morphed into Santa Claus, took exception to a theologian who was arguing at Nicaea that Jesus was not 'of one being with the Father', and slapped him in the face.

This book placed a warning on 'of one being with the Father' at the end of the last chapter, and in a way, it dominates the theological discussions of the first two ecumenical councils at Nicaea (325) and Constantinople (381) as well as most of the years in between. The immediate background to the Council of Nicaea was the heated disputes regarding the specific equivalence (or otherwise) of the Father, Son and Spirit in the understanding of the Church. These had reached such a pitch that the Emperor Constantine became involved and he convened a council which gathered in Nicaea in the Western part of modern-day Turkey in May 325. There is little evidence that the Emperor was taking sides and it is likely his motives were probably more to secure a united response to what was becoming a vexed question. As we have seen, references to Father, Son and Spirit were present in some of the earliest confessions of faith in the New Testament writings. Theological problems arose, however, in attempting to describe how God could be both One and Three. Justin had addressed the issue with some intellectual dexterity and Irenaeus would probably be considered his theological successor in terms of enduring influence.

With regard to how and in what way the Son came to be, Irenaeus is a little scornful of the opinions of his opponents:

> If anyone asks us how the Son was 'produced' from the Father, we reply that no one understands that 'production' or 'generation' . . . or whatever term anyone applies to his begetting, which in truth is indescribable. Valentinus does not understand it, nor Marcion, nor Saturninus, nor Basilides, nor angels, nor archangels, nor principalities, nor powers. Only the Father who begat him knows and the Son who was begotten. Thus, since his generation cannot be described, sensible persons do not exert themselves to talk of begettings and 'productions' or undertake to explain what is indefinable . . . And it is not our duty to indulge in conjectures and make guesses about infinite matters which concern God. The knowledge of such things is to be left to God. (*Adversus Haereses 2.28.6* in O'Collins, 1999, p. 98)

The recommendation to tiptoe around the mystery by saying what God is not (e.g. not describable, not finite, not definable) is sometimes called the *via negativa* or 'negative path'. Another technical word for it is *apophatic* Theology – literally 'away saying' or 'denial' Theology. Unsurprisingly, however, even its protagonists find it difficult to keep up the discipline and Irenaeus found himself tinkering with the notion of begetting and emitting as 'production as in matter'. That sort of take would be flattened at Nicaea by the phrase 'begotten not made' – so maybe he should have taken his own advice and tiptoed a bit further in his 'away saying'!

c) Tertullian: One God, three persons, Trinity

A different reaction to the 'unsayability' of God is evidenced by Tertullian 165–220 CE. Brought up as a pagan in Carthage, Tertullian was a well-educated man who became a Christian in midlife. Driven to apologetics – 'faith defence' – by hostile circumstances, Tertullian took great pains to argue that Christians were not disloyal citizens, their beliefs were superior to pagan superstitions and their moral life was of the highest order. In relation to his theological approach, he is most noted for battles with various forms of 'Modalism'. Associated at that time with thinkers such as Noetus and Praxeus, the modalist proposal was that in God there was but One Principle, *Monos-Archē*. The different ways that God had been manifest in the biblical revelation meant nothing in terms of what God was really like within Godself, they were just 'modes of expression'. Thinking along these lines also led to a *Patripassian* or 'Father-passion' understanding of God – the idea that really it was the Father and not a distinct son who was born in human history and suffered on the cross. Sabellius would later continue this argument and simply propose that the Father of the Old Testament, the Son in the New and the Spirit manifest at Pentecost were just three dimensions of the same God present as creating, redeeming and sanctifying.

To counter this teaching, Tertullian follows Justin in pursuing analogies that might serve the contention he wants to make that God's substance is the same, while preserving a sense of proper threefold distinctions:

> The Son was 'produced' from the Father, but not separated from him. For God (The Father) produced the Word . . . as a root produces the shoot, a spring the river, the sun a ray . . . . The Spirit makes the third from God and the Son, as the fruit from the shoot is the third from the tree, the canal from the river the third from the source, the point of focus of a ray third from the sun. But none of these is divorced from the origin of which it derives its own properties. Thus the Trinity derives from the Father by continuous and connected steps. (*Adversus Praxean 8*, in O'Collins, 1999, p. 106)

Like Justin, Tertullian was able to see the extension of reason to all things as the basis of an 'all inclusive' possibility of salvation.

> God is rational and Reason *(ratio)* existed first with him, and from him extended to all things. That Reason is his own consciousness of himself. The Greeks call it Logos, which is the term we use for discourse or speech *(sermo)* . . . . Speech is something within you that is *distinct* from yourself; by speech you talk in thinking and think in talking. (*Adversus Praexean 5*, in O'Collins 1999, p. 107)

Straining the language, Tertullian's contention was that God must be understood as One in *substantia* – 'essence'/'nature', yet Three in *persona* – 'persons'. He is the first to coin the term *Trinitas* and apply it theologically in *De pudicitia* 21.16 and *Adversus Praxean* 8. The formula that is derived from this and has come into Western language is 'One substance in three persons' which riskily sloganized into 'three whos and one what' has become a base line of orthodox expression. Regarded as the 'Father of Latin Theology', Tertullian was wrestling not just with the mystery of the Trinity, but with the question of how best to translate fuzzy Greek concepts. Tertullian used '*substantia*' in the first instance to translate *ousia* which in common parlance could mean something as banal as 'basic stuff' or 'things' but in philosophical and theological terminology identified 'thingy-ness', 'fundamental reality' or 'essence'.

To get across the idea of the uniqueness of Father, Son and Spirit, Tertullian chose *persona*. This term most nearly corresponded to the Greek *prosopon* which meant 'mask' (perhaps a bit superficial) but also carried with it a sense of 'relationality' (theologically much more promising). For us, *persona* suffers from a classic anachronistic 'time-slip' problem because our contemporary Western concept of 'person' is radically individualized. We think of person as a skull bound, rib cage unbreachable fortress of 'I think therefore I am' conscious selfhood. This sense of individuality would have been more permeable in a Mediterranean culture where communal self-identity and belonging meant a stronger emphasis on 'I am who I am part of'. A Gospel example of this would be the way Jesus changes the names of the disciples, He consciously acknowledges their original roots but changes their identity formulas as their new belonging, their new identity, is linked to the gang of Twelve. Simon *son of* Jonah becomes *Kephas* the Rock, James and John, *Sons of Zebedee* become *Boanerges* – the Sons of Thunder. In the context of Trinity then, it is not possible to conceive *the persons* without conceiving *what they are part of*. In other words, this unique being is constituted as three-one – as Trinity. God cannot be divided into three nor blancmanged into one. The *Is* God *is* Trinity.

d) Arius

Though Tertullian's use of *substantia, persona* and *trinitas* was novel, it did begin to gain ground as a formula in the Latin West, not least because it maintained oneness and distinctiveness which is the core paradox at the heart of Trinitarian Theology. Despite this, in the broad territories around the Mediterranean, disputations regarding the nature of God continued to break out within Christianity and found two legendary protagonists in Arius and Athanasius within the same livewire city of Alexandria. Arius was probably born in Libya sometime after 260 CE and was ordained deacon and then priest in Alexandria. Tensions in the Church there led to him being temporarily excommunicated for association with the Melitan sect which thought the mainstream Christian community too lax in relation to those who had repudiated their faith during the all-too-frequent persecutions of the period.

A noted preacher and revered for his way of life, Arius was, like many Alexandrians, influenced by the legacy of Origen (185–254 CE) in his Trinitarian thinking. While Origen vehemently argued against all those who implied that the Son and Spirit were born in time like other aspects of Creation, he did tend to emphasize the pre-eminence of the Father as the absolutely ungenerated principle of being. In turn, this meant the Son tended to be viewed as 'subordinate' to the Father and with the Spirit proceeding thereafter. In Olympic terms, the Son and Spirit seemed to occupy the silver and bronze medal positions. Arius took this notion of a three-level hierarchy as orthodox, 'right thinking' tradition. In effect, Arius distinguished this hierarchy in real terms such that the 'persons' of the Trinity were not really of the same *ousia* – the same *stuff.* Jesus had said 'The Father is greater than me' (John 14:28) and Arius, while agreeing that the Son was created before time, deemed that since the Father must have preceded him in terms of *causality,* he must be *greater.* Not only is the Son unequal, the demonstrable suffering of Jesus witnessed in the passion did not sit well with a less involved vision of true Divinity as *impassible* – 'unchangeable' – beyond the vagaries and emotions of human life.

In his letter of explanation to the appropriately named Bishop Alexander of Alexandria, Arius takes pains to praise his bishop and affirm the constancy of their mutual teaching in the face of classic modalist heretical positions. It is to be noted that Arius is content to identify three divine *hypostases* ('ways of being') but is very sensitive to any suggestion that God – *The Monad* – 'The One' – can be divided. Instead, he attests that Christ *cannot be of the same stuff as* God:

> For he is not eternal or co-eternal or co-originate with the Father, nor has he his being together with the Father, as some speak of relations introducing two ingenerate beginnings, but God (the Father) is before all things as the Monad and Beginning of all. (Stevenson, 1987, p. 327)

Arius sums things up:

> The Unbegun appointed the Son to be the Beginning of things begotten. And bore him as his own Son, in this case giving birth. He has nothing proper to God in his essential property, for neither is he equal nor yet consubstantial with him. (Stevenson, 1987, p. 331)

e) The Council of Nicaea

Theological opposition to Arius came from Bishop Alexander (d.328) and his young deacon secretary Athanasius (c.296–373). Alexander complained that the errors of the 'Arians' were manifold and detracted from the dignity of Jesus as Lord, Christ and God:

> They deny his divinity and declare him to be on a level with all mankind. They pick out every saying relative to his saving dispensation, and to his humiliation for us (Phil 2:14) and try to compound from the proclamation of their own impiety, by abandoning the words showing his divinity from the beginning and his ineffable glory with the Father. They make their own the impious view of Greeks and Jews about Christ, and endeavour as far as they possibly can, to get praised among them. (Stevenson, 1987, p. 328)

We can notice that Alexander's critique includes a complaint that too much effort is being made to take on board the views both of Greek philosophers who stressed the 'impassibility' of God and the Jewish belief that God could not be other than One. The uniqueness of the Christian revelation is not being preserved. With core identity at stake, it is therefore not too surprising that the disagreements became violent as Arius was excommunicated by Alexander and clashes occurred between supporters of both parties. The matter drew the attention of Emperor Constantine whose coming to faith had fundamentally altered relations between the Jesus movement and the Empire. At first he seems to have thought that the matter was a trivial detail based on a question Alexander was ill-advised to ask and Arius ill-advised to answer:

> Let therefore both the unguarded question and the inconsiderate answer receive your mutual forgiveness. For the cause of your difference has not been any of the leading doctrines or precepts of the law, nor has any new heresy respecting the worship of God arisen among you. You are in truth of one and the same judgement: you may therefore well join in communion and fellowship. (Stevenson, 1987, p. 333)

Unfortunately, things weren't so simple, and Constantine felt eventually compelled to call the bishops to gather in Nicaea, because it would be 'easier for the bishops of Italy to come and because of the excellent temperature of the air, and in order that I may be present as a spectator and participator in those things that will be done' (Stevenson, 1987, p. 338). According to Eusebius' account of the proceedings, Constantine was no mere spectator. The 'most pious emperor' is reported to have spoken approvingly of Eusebius' own Ceaserean creed suggesting only the addition of a single word – the storied *homoousios* – 'of the same being' – 'consubstantial'. It has been suggested that this word was deliberately brought forth at Nicaea to force the issue with the supporters of Arius. In so doing, Constantine was coming down firmly on the side of the Alexander and Athanasian party. From Eusebius' account, however, it would appear that there remained much debate concerning the sense in which this was meant to be understood:

> On their suggesting this formula, we did not let it pass without inquiry in what sense they used the expressions 'of the substance of the Father' and 'Consubstantial with the Father'. Accordingly, questions and explanations took place, and the discussion tested the meaning of these phrases. And they professed that the phrase 'of the substance' was indicative of the Son's being indeed from the Father, yet without being as if part of him. And with this understanding, we thought good to assent to the pious teaching suggesting the Son was from the Father, not, however, a part of his substance. On this account we assented to the meaning ourselves without declining even the term 'consubstantial,' peace being the aim which we set before us, and fear of deviating from the correct meaning. (Stevenson, 1987, pp. 345–6)

Although the tones of Eusebius are those familiar to any of us who have sat in a long meeting and had to come to a compromise, it is clear from other testimony that reaching agreement was not a smooth journey for the Council fathers. In the hagiography ('holyfying-writing') of Nicholas of Myra (the model for the eventual Santa Claus), the sight and hearing of Arius 'spewing forth' was all too much and he slapped him in full sight of everyone. Suspended from the assembly by the Emperor, the legend has him restored to the proceedings the next day following dreams and holy confirmations among the delegates that Nicholas had acted rightly (Velimorovich, 2008). Perhaps some of the passion is audible in the culmination of proceedings on the creed which included a coda of banned phrases which would earn *anathema* – 'condemned separation' from the community:

> As for those who say: 'There was a time when he was not' and 'Before being begotten he was not' or who declare that 'He was made from nothing,' or that 'the Son of God is from a different substance or being,' that is, created or subject to change and alteration – (such persons) the Catholic and apostolic Church condemns. (Neuner and Dupuis, 1983, p. 6)

Constantine thought that the affair was settled. A letter was sent to the Alexandrian Church for it to submit to the ruling and in the Emperor's view, 'all points which seemed to produce doubt or excuse for discord have been discussed and accurately examined'. Demonstrating a developing 'Theology of Councils' – the conviction that the Holy Spirit was especially present just as it had been at the apostolic Council of Jerusalem – Constantine concluded:

> For that which has commended itself to the judgement of three hundred bishops cannot be other than the judgement of God; seeing that the Holy Spirit dwelling in the minds of persons of such character and dignity has effectually enlightened them respecting the Divine Will. 'Wherefore let no one vacillate or linger, but let all with alacrity return to the undoubted path of truth. (Stevenson, 1987, p. 350)

Unfortunately, his hopes of tranquillity were not to be. With *homoousios* – 'of one being' there was still substantial trouble ahead.

f) The Council of Constantinople

Difficulty with finding a common understanding of technical words is not a problem unique to theologians but it is probably fair to say that down the years, some words and phrases have been more trouble than others. Those who had issues with *homoousios* left Nicaea not wholly convinced of the validity of the term primarily since it *could* be understood as a return to conceiving God as 'one being sequentially manifesting as three' – *modalism*. There followed a period of ebb and flow as either side tried to persuade the Emperor to vouchsafe their position. Alexandria remained unsettled long after Athanasius became its bishop and even the death of Arius in 336 did little to calm things. Athanasius steadfastly refused a compromise proposal that *homoiousios* – 'of like being' would suffice to preserve the dignity of the Son and the integrity of the Father. In a confusing outworking of the controversy, depositions, representations by rival factions to various Emperors and a multiplicity of confrontations meant Athanasius was condemned to exile five separate times. The addition of 'i' (the Greek vowel *iota*) to make 'of one being' less absolute was not accepted by Arians either. Indeed, later protagonists of the cause such as Aetius and Eunomius hardened their position and in what became known as the 'dissimilar' or *anomean* view countered that the Father and Son were 'of unlike being'.

Intriguingly, the theological impasse was broken by *hypostasis* – another word with a troubled history. *Hypostasis* – 'way of being' was a Greek composite of 'beneath be' or (and behold the irony here) 'stand under' or 'under stand!' A sort of bifocal word, it could be taken two ways:

- The first more generalized – similar to *ousia* 'thingy-ness' – corresponding to Tertullian's *substantia* or 'substance'.
- The other meaning was more specific – 'particular being' – or 'particular *way* of being' similar to Tertullian's 'persona'.

Although Origen's early use of the term to identify distinctions within God had aroused suspicion, as the fourth century wore on, theologians increasingly began to use it to mean 'particular being'. By the time a second great council was called in Constantinople in 381, the influential 'Cappadocian Fathers' – Basil, Gregory Nazianzus and Gregory of Nyssa had persuasively begun to speak of one God in terms of *ousia* 'essence' and three distinct *hypostases* in terms of relation.

Withal, when Emperor Theodosius I convened the council fathers, although the attendees were predominantly from the Eastern Church, its deliberations and pronouncements were accepted as universally binding. With the avowed aim of ending the Arian controversy regarding the equality of Father and Son, it also ended speculation regarding the dignity of the Holy Spirit. Hence the Council expanded the one line of affirmation at Nicaea into a more fitting articulation of its mystery. The Spirit too is to be worshipped and glorified as life giver and inspirer of the prophetic word. As a result, the council fathers also 'anathematized' the marvellously named *Pneumatomachi.* Although this group sent representatives to the Council, they did not believe in the equal dignity of the Spirit and it may be speculated that their lobbying helped prevent the Spirit being defined as 'consubstantial' in the final draft of the approved symbol of faith. As it was, the 'Pneumatomacheans' were soon on their way home as yet another tense gathering of the leadership pronounced on behalf of the many. The differences between the proclamation at Constantinople and Nicaea are noted by italics for additions and square brackets for omissions.

> We believe in one God,
> the Father all powerful,
> maker *of heaven and of earth, and*
> of all things both seen and unseen.
> And in one Lord Jesus Christ,
> the only begotten Son of God,
> begotten from the Father,
> [before all the ages],
> light from light, true God from true God,
> begotten not made,

consubstantial with the Father,
through whom all things came to be;
For us humans and for our salvation
he came down from the heavens
and became incarnate *from the Holy Spirit and the Virgin Mary,*
became human, *and was crucifed on our behalf under Pontius Pilate;*
He suffered *and was buried* and rose up on the third day *in accordance with the scriptures;*
he went up into the heavens *and is seated at the Father's right hand;*
He is coming *again with glory* to judge the living and the dead;
his kingdom will have no end.
And in the Spirit, the holy,
the lordly, and life giving one, proceeding forth from the father,
co-worshipped and co-glorified with the father and the son,
the one who spoke through the prophets.
In one holy, catholic and apostolic church.
We confess one baptism for the forgiveness of sins.
We look forward to a resurrection of the dead
and life in the age to come. Amen
(Tanner, 2011, p. 33)

Apart from one controversial addition (see Chapter 18), it was this 'symbol' – this putting together of faith and belonging – that became and has remained *the* normative creed of Christians ever since. Even if it is normally known as the Nicaea or Nicene Creed, the legacy of the Council of Constantinople mapped the outline of the Christian understanding of God as God: Creator, One, Father, Son and Spirit. What it did not resolve, however, was God as man. How the mystery of Jesus as Son of God and Son of Man could be reasonably understood would be the challenge for the next generation of bishops and theologians who gathered at Ephesus in 431 and Chalcedon in 451.

g) Ephesus 431

It bears repeating that from the moment Jesus began to preach in Nazareth of the Galilee, the conundrum of his identity seems to have been a problem. By the beginning of the fifth century, there was no doubt about his significance but the perennial problem of theologizing exactly how Jesus could be both one being with the transcendent Creator yet perspire with self-doubt in Gethsemane reasserted itself once more. This time, however, the storm clouds gathered not so much over a title of Jesus, but over a title commonly attributed to one of the family, Mary – Jesus' mother. Once more it would take a Council to resolve the issue.

Nestorius (c.381–452) was a Syrian who entered monastic life and began his scholarly career at Antioch. The third most important city in the Roman Empire after Constantinople and Rome itself, Antioch had developed a theological tradition to rival that of Alexandria. A number of scholars such as Diodore of Tarsus, Theodore of Mopsuestia and John Chrysostom were to be associated with the Antiochene School which by and large emphasized a Theology 'from below' – very much at ease with Christ's humanity and the reality of his moral choices. In contrast, Alexandria tended to emphasize a Theology 'from above'. Stressing the pre-existence of Jesus as the eternal Logos, a title long revered there, Alexandria preferred allegory in scriptural interpretation, while Antioch was more literal. In time, Nestorius won fame for his learned preaching and the Emperor Theodosius II, ignoring the claims of local candidates, made him Patriarch of Constantinople in 428.

As Patriarch, Nestorius soon became embroiled in disagreements regarding *Theotokos* – a popular devotional title of Mary which means 'The One who gave birth to God'. Although *Theotokos* seems to have been an early acclamation for Mary, it is also easy to see why there might be problems should the title be misunderstood. After all, no Christian believed that *Theotokos* meant that the maidservant of Nazareth was now even more important than the eternal Creator God, but such a misunderstanding was not impossible. What Nestorius and his chaplain Anastasius were more concerned about was that this sort of language obscured the distinction of the two natures in Jesus, the divine and the human. In no sense could it be said that Mary was the mother of the divine nature, hence *Theotokos* was inaccurate. He was troubled by popular Christmas hymns that sang of 'God in swaddling bands' and called them 'barbaric impiety'. According to Nestorius, the title *Theotokos* implies that the Word changes when he becomes man and he undergoes what is incompatible with the impassibility of God: he is not only born but he hungers and thirsts, suffers and dies. Crazy. Nestorius could tolerate *Christotokos* 'Birthgiver of Christ' – but not *Theotokos*.

Here it would be perhaps fair to say that Nestorius lacked something of a sense of history, poetry and paradox. One of the earliest post-apostolic reflections on Jesus' nature was by another famous son of Antioch. Ignatius (c.35–107) had remarked in his *Letter to the Ephesians* that:

> There is one Physician, who is
> both flesh and spirit,
> begotten and unbegotten,
> in man God

in death, true life,
both from Mary and from God,
first able to suffer and
then unable to suffer,
Jesus Christ our Lord.
(cf. Sparks, 1978, p. 80)

This 'double exchange' of humanity and divinity which had occurred in Jesus became known as the *communicatio idiomatum*. Another classic shorthand phrase ('interchange of the properties'), it meant that what was said humanly of Jesus could be said of God and likewise what was said divinely about Jesus could be attributed to his humanity. This was nothing new insofar as Paul and John had explored similar if not identical themes (cf. Phil 2:1ff and John 1:1-14, 1 John 1:1-4) Hence it could be said that God as the man Jesus is born, is able to suffer and to die. And on this basis, it was no great leap of the imagination to call Mary *Theotokos*, Mother of God.

It was perhaps inevitable that Nestorius' opponents would turn to Alexandria for help where Cyril (c.378–444) was Patriarch. For Cyril it was a case of *lex orandi lex credendi* – the preaching, liturgy, worship and practice of the faithful all pointed to the fact that the divine Word came to exist as a human being while remaining who he was, the Second Person of the Trinity. Cyril thought that, by rejecting the title of *Theotokos*, Nestorius was jeopardizing the *kerygma*. Nestorius' overuse of the word 'person' perhaps made Cyril reluctant to adopt the same language, so he eventually settled on *hypostasis* – the 'particular way of being' that would become the equivalent of a magic bullet fired at the bullseye of the Christian mystery.

Instead of conceiving the Incarnation as a union of natures, Cyril followed his own tradition closely by focusing on the single subjectivity of the divine *Logos* personally present in Jesus Christ. So whatever Jesus did, whether it was performing miracles or suffering hunger, it was the work of God-logic embodied and living in the first-century Palestine. For Cyril there is no change in the eternal 'Second Person' though there is a change in his condition: he becomes man. Where Nestorius, by emphasizing the binary non-mixed up nature of the mystery saw a contradiction, Cyril was content with Christ bearing the strange and rare paradox of Lordship in servant's form and divine glory in human abasement. Importantly, Cyril is then able to deliver the *coup de grace* by emphasizing as Ignatius, Irenaeus, Athanasius *et al* had done before him, that the Word becomes human so that we might become divine. By the Incarnation, God-logic re-forms human nature. The Word made flesh is, says Cyril, both the 'wound and medicine' the 'sickness and physician', he descends so that we can rise with him. In the classic formulation 'what hasn't been assumed has not been redeemed' – if the divine in Jesus had not fully become human, then our creaturely mortal state remains exactly that – dead.

What came next was as much political and personal chicanery as anything else. Following a futile exchange of letters, both Nestorius and Cyril appealed to Pope Celestine in Rome. Celestine held a synod in 430 where he confirmed the title *Theotokos* and condemned Nestorius, untactfully asking Cyril to convey his decision. The dispute escalated as Cyril added twelve anathemas to Celestine's message. A series of charges and counter-charges against Cyril followed. Once more the Emperor was brought in to help sort out the Church and Theodosius II summoned what became known as the Third Ecumenical Council at Ephesus in 431. The deputation from Rome was delayed by storms at sea, which were tranquil compared to the scenes that would await them.

First, Cyril took it upon himself to preside which hardly made for a fair theological fight. Nestorius refused to attend and proceedings began before many of Nestorius' Syrian supporters, including John of Antioch, had arrived. Nestorius was duly denounced and deposed but when the Syrians arrived they did likewise to Cyril. To make the circle complete, when the representatives from Rome arrived John was deposed and the Emperor put both Cyril and Nestorius under house arrest! When the music finally stopped, Theodosius decided in favour of Cyril and Nestorius was exiled. Agreement with the Syrians was eventually reached when Cyril and John of Antioch signed the *Formula of Reunion*. Calling to mind the compromise at Nicaea and Constantinople, this document accepted that Christ's humanity was *consubstantial* to our own. Cyril clarified that there were two natures after the union and the Syrians accepted both the 'communication of idioms' and the title *Theotokos*.

h) Chalcedon 451

All seemed settled then, but there was one more classic twist. If there is one thing in life worse than a bad loser it is a bad winner, and since the Alexandrians had won, it was all too easy for their tradition to topple over too far in one direction. Almost inevitably, extreme Alexandrians like Eutyches (c.378–454) decided to reject the *Formula of Reunion*. Thinking that he was following Cyril, Eutyches argued that after the union the divine nature absorbs the human nature. Christ was 'from' two natures rather than 'in' two natures ultimately producing precisely what Nestorius charged Cyril with – a hybrid or divinized man.

Since Eutyches was the Abbot of a monastery near Constantinople, Flavian, the Patriarch of Constantinople, held a local synod in 448 to discuss the case. Flavian condemned Eutyches charging him with a form of Apollinarianism. This view proposed that the God-principle in Jesus was such that he had neither a human mind nor a human soul and hence could not be considered fully man. Once more Theodosius called a Council at Ephesus in 449 but things did not go well. There was no time for the Western bishops, except for the deacon Hilarus, to attend. It seems that the accusations against Eutyches were not allowed to be heard and not only was Flavian not given the opportunity to defend himself he was not allowed to read a letter from Leo, the formidable successor of Peter in Rome. Amid scenes of violence it seems that Eutyches was absolved but Flavian deposed and exiled, dying shortly afterwards. With some difficulty the dissenting Hilarus managed to leave. Reports of the disgraceful events earned it the nickname the 'Robber Council' and prevented it being received as a truly 'whole world' ecumenical event. Then, whether due to luck or providence, Emperor Theodosius died suddenly in a horse riding accident and the new emperor, Marcian, agreed to review the affair calling a new council at Chalcedon in 451.

The Council of Chalcedon was intended to be a council of reconciliation. Given that Leo's letter or Tome had not even been read at the 'Robber Council', it took central place at Chalcedon alongside the Creed, Cyril's Second Letter to Nestorius and the Formula of Reunion. The Tome is a classic rendition of *communicatio idiomatum* or 'interchange of natures' reasoning:

> Without detriment therefore to the properties of either nature and substance which then came together in one person, majesty took on humility, strength weakness, eternity mortality: and for the paying off of the debt belonging to our condition inviolable nature was united with possible nature, so that, as suited the needs of our case, one and the same Mediator between God and men, the Man Christ Jesus, could both die with the one and not die with the other. Thus in the whole and perfect nature of true man was true God born, complete in what was His own, complete in what was ours. And by ours we mean what the Creator formed in us from the beginning and what He undertook to repair. For what the Deceiver brought in and man deceived committed, had no trace in the Saviour. Nor, because He partook of man's weaknesses, did He therefore share our faults. He took the form of a slave without stain of sin, increasing the human and not diminishing the divine: because that emptying of Himself whereby the Invisible made Himself visible and, Creator and Lord of all things though He be, wished to be a mortal, was the bending down of pity, not the failing of power.

Accordingly He who while remaining in the form of God made man, was also made man in the form of a slave. For both natures retain their own proper character without loss: and as the form of God did not do away with the form of a slave, so the form of a slave did not impair the form of God. (Bettenson, 1982, p. 279)

In the definition promulgated by the Emperor and bishops, it stressed that:

- There is only one unique *hypostasis*, the Son and Word who is perfect in Godhead and perfect in manhood.
- In this 'becoming' the natures are 'without confusion, without change, without division, without separation'.
- The one and the same Son and Word is consubstantial with the Father (against Arius).
- Consubstantial with us, he has a human soul, body and mind (against Apollinarius).
- Since Jesus is the Son existing as man, Mary is truly the *Theotokos*, Mother of God (against Nestorius).
- He is 'one person' 'made known in two natures' (against Eutyches).

Certainly, Chalcedon left many issues open. In a reaction to the 'unmixability' of the natures, the 'One nature' – 'Monophysite' theologians held out for a strict understanding of Cyril's formula, 'one incarnate nature (physis) of the divine Word'. Today, the Egyptian and Ethiopian Coptic Church and Armenian Christianity remain monophysite and indeed there are still Nestorians among Iraqi Christians. The broader consensus meanwhile took Chalcedon as its basis:

- That Jesus Christ is the eternal Son and Word, so fully God.
- That Jesus Christ has a human body, soul, intellect and will since he is fully man.
- That the one subject of the union is Jesus who is the Son of God existing as man.

Summary

The period under review, which witnessed the gathering of the first four 'ecumenical councils', was a period of discovery and definition in doctrine. The theologians of the era, whether from Alexandria or from Antioch, had the daunting task of finding ways to express the inexpressible. Insofar as they were helped to do so by the very pragmatic interventions of the Emperor, the conciliar heritage is a classic locus of the interplay of sacred and secular. The exchanges at the Councils were often heated, since no one likes admitting they were wrong, especially about something to which they've given their lives. That said, robust exchange was a constant part of the Jesus heritage from the first proclamation of the Kingdom; it is yet another example where the Christian paradox of the divine-human dynamic assists in understanding these occasions. Hence, in the broad understanding of Christian thinking, these Councils and their proclamations, no matter how conspired politically are also considered inspired theologically. In particular, their conclusions regarding Trinity and the double nature of the one Christ have remained normative expressions of Christian faith for theologians and believers of all the main Christian traditions.

15

Ecclesiology: New Israel, New Jesus, New Empire?

Although the word 'Church' can immediately call to mind images of spires, bell towers, arched windows and uncomfortable seating, such thoughts would have made no sense to the earliest members of the Jesus movement. From apostolic roots, however, if they were initially short on buildings they were not short on motifs for self-understanding, two of the most potent being the New Israel and the Body of Christ. The 'success' of the Church despite the persecution of the Empire has attracted the attention of theologian and historian alike. Drawing on the insights of both, the analysis below points to the role of good networking and good motherhood as well as godly witness in the face of torture and death. Christianity was to change forever with the conversion of Constantine, and the working out of its new identity in its new relationship with the Empire provided a profound challenge to the self-understanding of both Church and State.

a) New Israel, New Kingdom

On a hill outside Jerusalem, sometime around the year 33, a naked criminal deserted by his followers was crucified. In 312, imperial armies engaged in battle emboldened by the sign of his cross, and another thousand years later his official representatives were able to announce on embossed notepaper that the whole world belonged to him. Impressive! For good or for ill, the last had become first. Yet because the claim for planetary power by the Church was theologically justified, this status transformation demands some analysis. And the roots of it were set deep in the consciousness of Jesus' first followers, the troublesome Twelve.

In Luke's gospel, it says that Jesus stayed up all night praying and the following day he announced his inner council of twelve followers. Given the unreliability of the men he chose, it is likely that the good Lord occasionally wished he'd stayed in bed (Luke 6:12). After all, these were not the kind of guys to stay awake for him (Luke 22:45). Known generally as disciples (*mathētai* – pupil/s), but specifically as apostles (*apostoloi* – 'sent ones'), the key significance of the group was their number – Twelve, clearly a scriptural connection with the number of Jacob's sons, the tribes of Israel who were in covenant with YHWH, the inheritors of the promises made to Abraham that their descendents would number as the stars of heaven.

Israel, or 'Good's struggler', was the name given to Jacob after he wrestled with an angel and his sons were hardly the epitome of harmonious fraternity (Gen 32:28, 37:5). In similar fashion, the New Israel of the Twelve were every bit as wrestly, struggly and competitive as their symbolic forebears. The most cosmic aspirations of the Twelve were just that – cosmic – to participate at the eternal judgement of the nations, and win the competition to sit at the right and left of the Son (Matt 20:20-28). The communal notion of Israel as 'light to the nations' and harbinger of the new Kingdom of God endured among the immediate disciples, and to some extent the Twelve had the dilemma which faces any 'in group' – knowing that they were 'special' but trying to relate to others. Like the chosen Israel before them, the New Testament shows the Twelve struggling to work this out. Whether to be friendly to Samaritans or call down fire upon them (Luke 9:51-56). Whether to approve of miracles being worked in Jesus' name by those outside the inner circle or not (Mark 9:38). Such sentiments remain theologically problematic for some Christian churches even today.

Furthermore, the problem of hierarchy within the group clearly caused tension. Despite the tradition in the Fourth Gospel that has Andrew as an original follower, Peter, James and John seem to have been the acknowledged inner circle of Jesus in the synoptic view and among them, Peter had especial pre-eminence (cf. John 1:40 and Mark 9:2-5). Originally called Simon bar Jonah, he is renamed *Kephas*, and as 'Rock' his name is to symbolize his pivotal role. With the caveat that James seems to have had a decisive voice at the Council of Jerusalem, the otherwise unanimous Synoptic/Acts tradition is that Peter has a clear mandate to exercise divine authority on behalf of the group (cf. Acts 15:13 with Matt 16:18, Luke 22:32, Mark 16:7). That said, since hierarchy and power within the Christian Church has always been a hot topic, it is worth recalling that the unanimous tradition is also at pains to demonstrate the very human frailty of the man. It would appear that the early Christian communities were emphasizing some kind of paradox. Peter's famous denial *may* have been a deliberate desire to avoid a false sanctification of the leadership, or it *may* have been the desire noted above to encourage persecuted Christians to *do better* than the founders of the faith.

Withal, the apostolic communities which themselves generated the writings known as the New Testament eventually germinated in different soils through their diverse geographic, ethnic or religious contexts. Just as this determined the way they presented their shared Jesus memory, their life context inevitably left its mark on their understanding of themselves as communities. To some extent the motif of the New Israel/New People of God/New Kingdom is most clearly seen in Galatians, First Peter, Hebrews and Matthew since in its various forms, the theological argument presented by these authors takes care to depict the Jesus movement as the *true* Israel and authentic inheritors of the promise of Abraham. Such theological arguments had sociological impact. By cohering the identity of the group in the deepest roots of its religious traditions, these theologians were providing a 'meta-narrative' which embraced the past, explained the disastrous present and the loss of the land, while painting a glorious future for an Israel which would be a light to the nations.

b) New Jesus: The body of Christ

Yet while self-identification as the New Israel was remarkable enough, such views were perhaps not as radical as another strong New Testament image identifiable in Acts, Paul and discernible too in John. The second enduring image of the Church was that symbolized by the Last Supper, namely the identification of the believers with the risen Body of Christ. The importance of this understanding in the life and theological understanding of Paul has been noted (see Section 10b), but the strength of this tradition common also in John and Luke is theologically vital. Above all it helps to explain the importance of the breaking of bread as the sign of being one body, a sign of being a 'member', a sign of co-union with Christ. For Paul, it is the motif of radical equality, the ability of believers to recognize in one another the face of Christ which is the key to understanding the mystery of the sharing of one bread and one cup (1 Cor 11:27-29). For John, it was linked to command to 'love one another' and the sign of foot-washing – the symbol of mutual service without which the disciple could have 'no part' of Jesus (John 13:8).

Added to the vivid symbolism of this ritual union, it is important to acknowledge the enthusiastic (literally 'in God-ism') of communities on fire with the Holy Spirit. Throughout the ancient tradition, the *ruah haqodeš* (Ps 51:11) was intimately connected with prophetic, life-giving traditions and had become the expected grace-filled sign of messianic end times. There is clear evidence among the early Pauline communities and beyond that ecstatic activity and *charisms* were part of community experience. These special gifts of grace included *glossolalia* (speaking in tongues) and prophetic activity alongside acknowledged leadership roles. The Spirit was understood as the life-giving power that had raised Jesus from the dead (Rom 1:11). That same Spirit was now animating ('soul-ing') the many believers into the one body of the risen Christ.

Thus by conceptualizing individual members of the 'called out' – the *ekklesia*, as divinized parts of the cosmic deathless Lord, the cries of belonging which evolved into the creeds of the Jesus movement inevitably expressed faith in this *ekklesia* or 'Church' as Holy. Indeed the earliest extant creedal formulas outside the New Testament precisely include faith in this truth and without too much contrivance, can be seen as designed precisely to emphasize this 'all inclusive eternal belonging' (cf. Arnold, 1972, p. 329)

I believe in:

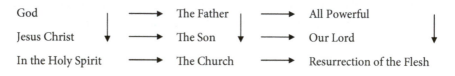

God	→	The Father	→	All Powerful	
Jesus Christ	→	The Son	→	Our Lord	
In the Holy Spirit	→	The Church	→	Resurrection of the Flesh	

In short, to participate in the life of the Triune God involved belonging and belief in the 'mystical body' – the Church of *Kyrios Christos*.

c) New Order

Whether New Israel, Body of Christ or Temple of the Lord, the 'body of believers' inevitably developed 'corporeal'/'corporate' structure. While the Twelve were around, there doesn't seem to have been much concern for what would happen next. The implied explanation of the appointment of *diakonoi* 'servants' in Acts 6 is that essential tasks such as community food distribution had become a bit distracting to the *apostoloi* – the 'sent' who had the more urgent task to preach the word. Happily but puzzlingly, far from being quasi-muted slaves as the term *diakonoi* would imply, Stephen and Philip, the two 'deacons' that Acts goes on to narrate, have star quality. Both are graced with theological eloquence, the one becoming the first martyr and (arguably) the second the first itinerant missionary (cf. Acts 7:60, 8:4 ff). The fluidity evidenced within the organization at this stage is normally explained by a sense of the imminence of the Lord's return which fuelled the fire of the *kerygma*. In Paul's churches, there seem to be a variety of tasks to be done and a number of titles accorded (1 Cor 12:1-31). Only belatedly, in what are assumed to be later New Testament writings, does a well-structured organization need to be put in place to handle the inexplicable delay.

It is difficult not to allow this view to set up a 'charism v committee' view of the evolution of Church structure. Instead of a 'forming – norming – storming' organizational picture, the result is more a 'storming – norming – boring' pattern whereby all that is ordered is bad and all that is maverick is deemed good. Generally, however, scholars do suggest that the 'handing on of the torch' language which comes in the letters of Paul to Timothy and Titus is evidence of a change in perspective. These 'pastoral' epistles are markedly different from the early Pauline letters which are sparky and urgent in style. While the concerns of the pastorals mirror issues relevant also to the lively letters (especially Church order and truth), the style is more inward looking – more concerned with the well-being of the flock rather than the missionary spreading of the word. In the letter of Titus, there is expressed need to appoint a structure of leadership in every town. Hitherto the key thing has been to be an 'apostle' – certainly Paul cared for no other title. Now the emphasis is more on *presbyteroi* – 'elders' and *episkopoi* – 'overseers'.

'Presbyter' generically meant 'elder' and in common with cultural norms and the pattern of synagogue governance, it would seem that the early Christian community developed a similar structure. The second term, *episkopos* meant 'overseer, supervisor, bishop' which seems to have been present among the sectarian Essene community whose overseers were figuratively described as 'shepherds' – imagery which is likewise taken up in the Christian tradition (Acts 20:28-29; 1 Pet 5:1-3, John 21:15-19). As Raymond Brown points out, there is some irony to find Paul's churches forbidding recent converts no matter how talented from having a leading role in the communities (1970, p. 63). With their emphasis on stability, anger management and a demonstrable commitment to marriage and household practicalities (1 Tim 3:1-7), it is small wonder that many think these epistles were written long after Paul's time.

Since there are examples of specific commissions given by the apostles in entrusting local leadership roles, and likewise ample evidence that connectedness with authoritative figures is a marked concern in the early Church, there is no need to presume that internal patterns and structure took too long to emerge. Although it is unlikely that the organization was entirely homogenous – it never has been – by the time that Ignatius of Antioch is writing early in the first century there seems to be a clear threefold structure that he can presume to refer to in all his letters – bishop, presbyter and deacon. Simplifying what doubtless had nuanced expression on the ground, 'Bishop' had become the designation for the local overseer governing in conjunction with a 'Presbyterate' of elders with 'Deacons' as his assistants. Though this 'norming' of arrangements did indicate a transition, it is important not to assume that ordered witness was necessarily less passionate than charismatic community. Indeed, as the life of Bishop Ignatius and countless other fellow believers of the period would attest, being members of the *risen* Body of Christ did not bring an exemption certificate from Calvary.

d) New Calvary

Among the non-biblical Christian literature associated with the period between the Jewish rebellions of 66 and 132 CE, a special honour belongs to the series of letters sent by Ignatius as he travelled to Rome to die. As Bishop of Antioch, the first place where Jesus' followers were called Christians (Acts 11:26), Ignatius was clearly sensitive to the need to set an example and he had fallen foul of the authorities who demanded he offer public worship to the Emperor. This crime was punishable by death, a fate which Ignatius accepted as a further opportunity to witness. His letters are marked by key passions – to plead for respect for the threefold Church order, for the unity of the Church in Eucharist and to plead for blessing on his desire for martyrdom – all of which he expresses with strong imagery and colourful language:

> All are to respect the deacons as Jesus Christ and the Bishop as a copy of the Father and the presbyters as the Council of God and the band of the apostles. For apart from these no group can be called Church. *Trallians 3* (Sparks, 1978, p. 93)
> Be eager, therefore to use one Eucharist – for there is one flesh of our Lord Jesus Christ and one cup for union with his blood, one sanctuary, as there is one bishop, together with the presbytery and the deacons my fellow slaves – so that, whatever you do, you do it in relation to God. *Philadelphians 4* (Sparks, 1978, p. 105)

> Indulge me; I know what is to my advantage. Now I am beginning to be a disciple. May nothing visible or invisible be jealous of my attaining to Jesus Christ. Fire and cross, packs of wild beasts, cuttings, rendings, crushing of bones, mangling of limbs, grinding of my whole body, wicked torture of the devil – let them come upon me if only I may attain to Jesus Christ. *Romans 5* (Sparks, 1978, p. 100)

To some extent, Ignatius' writing jars with prevailing contemporary thinking which (for good reason) sits light on authority, is less drawn to the intensities of community expression and is inclined to question the motives of anyone over-enthused by the prospect of death. In his own epoch, however, Ignatius was striving to imitate his own heroes of the faith, Peter and Paul and the many other martyrs who were suffering under the sporadic outbreaks of institutionalized violence unleashed against the infant Church. Let it immediately be noted that the Church was not being treated unusually – the Roman Empire was violent towards anything that it regarded as a threat as the multiple massacres associated with the Judean rebellions of 66 and 134 amply evidence. That said, the systematic nature of Christian persecution is vividly attested not just in its earliest form under Nero, but by Pliny the Younger and the Emperor Trajan during a much later persecution in Bithynia, North Africa. Pliny is asking advice on how to handle members of this obstinate sect. He is not, however, clarifying whether they deserve to die or not and makes no apology for executing Christians if they persevered in their confession. He is, however, a little perplexed by his findings concerning the abomination. Even under torture, they are a moving insight into the heroism of ordinary folk caught up in religious repression:

Pliny's Epistle to Trajan (c.112)

> I have taken this course about those who have been brought before me as Christians. I asked them whether they were Christians or not? If they confessed that they were Christians, I asked them again, and a third time, intermixing threatenings with the questions. If they persevered in their confession, I ordered them to be executed.
>
> However, they assured me that the main of their fault, or of their mistake was this:– That they were wont, on a stated day, to meet together before it was light, and to sing a hymn to Christ, as to a god, alternately; and to oblige themselves by a sacrament [or oath], not to do anything that was ill: but that they would commit no theft, or pilfering, or adultery; that they would not break their promises, or deny what was deposited with them, when it was required back again; after which it was their custom to depart, and to meet again at a common but innocent meal.
>
> These examinations made me think it necessary to inquire by torture what the truth was; which I did of two servant maids, who were called Deaconesses: but

> still I discovered no more than that they were addicted to a bad and to an extravagant superstition. . . . To be sure, the temples, which were almost forsaken, begin already to be frequented; and the holy solemnities, which were long intermitted, begin to be revived. (Bettenson, [1963] 2011, pp. 3–4)

Trajan's Reply:

> My Pliny, You have taken the method which you ought in examining the causes of those that had been accused as Christians . . . These people are not to be sought for; but if they be accused and convicted, they are to be punished; but with this caution, that he who denies himself to be a Christian, and makes it plain that he is not so by supplicating to our gods, although he had been so formerly, may be allowed pardon, upon his repentance. As for libels sent without an author, they ought to have no place in any accusation whatsoever, for that would be a thing of very ill example, and not agreeable to my reign. (Arnold, 1972, pp. 63–5)

Their exchange of letters on the matter is chillingly polite, and probably typifies totalitarian violence of every age. It is clear from the correspondence that the practice of betrayal and denouncing neighbours, friends and erstwhile co-religionists is part of the disorientating picture which the Emperor at least insists should not be done anonymously. As noted above, it is impossible at this distance to establish the extent to which official Empire-wide persecutions affected individual communities but that of Domitian in 95 CE, and the more sporadic North African and Asian persecutions were bloody affairs. Christianity was a new-fangled superstition which increasingly did not *appear* to have the ancient pedigree of the more recognizable Torah – Judean tradition. As far as the Empire was concerned, the persecutions were theologically justified. Those who did not honour official gods with sacrifices were undermining the fate of Rome, an argument for persecution that Augustine finds himself still contesting a century *after* Christianity has become officially tolerated. Paul had written enigmatically 'I make up in my body what is lacking in the sufferings of Christ' (Col 1:24), but the vivid accounts of martyrdom which 'empurple' this period effectively sealed in sacrifice the theological understanding of Church as the crucified mystical body of the Lord.

e) The Diaspora, Greeks and God fearers

But if faith and belonging to the messianic community of the Church were a life-and-death decision for most individuals, why did they join? A traditional theological answer to this question asserts that it was a divine/human 'one-two' whereby the power of the Spirit working through the miraculous deeds and words of the Twelve coupled with the heroic witness of the martyrs bedazzled unbelievers into affiliation. 'The blood of the martyrs' being 'the seed of the Church' was a theme prevalent in Eusebius' *History of the Church*. Written in the wake of the conversion of the Emperor, there is an air of inevitability that the sustained heroism of the martyrs and storied Christian figures would eventually triumph over the pagan unbelieving hordes. Without wishing to quibble with someone like Eusebius who was much closer to the events than myself, there was probably more to it than that. Indeed contemporary historians and theorists have nuanced the debate in interesting ways. In particular, social scientific thinking regarding the nature of 'identity' and 'group belonging' offer intriguing explanations as to why, despite increasing intense levels of persecution, the years between the death of Ignatius and the accession of Constantine saw the nascent Church grow to number as many as six million Christians.

From Paul's letters and the Acts of the Apostles, it is reasonable to assume that one of the advantages of the Jesus movement was they were able to use a network that was already in place due to the Mediterranean *diaspora* of 'scattered' Judean faithful. Since minority ethno-religious groups are characterized by close knit contact, and since Moses had his 'advocates in every town' (Acts 15:21), the proclaimers of Jesus as Lord Messiah were able to immediately engage with strong local networks. For observant YHWH faithful well versed in the ancient scriptural tradition, the theological argumentation based on a messianic interpretation of the *TaNaK* would have had some persuasive force. An obvious place to look is the Epistle to the Hebrews where the arguments take the identity territory of the listeners (Esler, 2011). The rhetoric seeks to convince the hearer that true Hebrew ethnic identity is *not* secured by continuing the ways of the ancient tradition, but by understanding the symbols of the new. In other words, to be true to Torah, to be true to your forefathers, to be true to *yourselves* you must be true to Christ. As if to underline the point, the very same style of argumentation is used by Justin in his *Dialogue with Trypho* which makes little appeal to the Gospels but constitutes an exhaustive tour of the ancient scriptures of YHWH understood from a *Kyrios Christos* perspective.

Beyond Judean ethnic identity, the New Testament's first point of call tends to be 'Hellenists' or 'Greeks'. The standard history of the Church would have it that the early Greek-speaking members of the Jesus movement were the bridge between the Torah observant Palestinian proclamation of James and the Gentile friendly 'Torah-lite' proclamation of Paul. It would be fair to say that modern writers, more sensitive to the interpenetration of culture evidenced by the biblical texts themselves, have softened some of the presumed distinctions between the two constituencies. After all, the 'Greeks' are in the mix from the beginning according to Acts 6:1. Part of the confusion is that 'Greek' acted as a generic term for *goyim* 'Gentiles'. When Paul speaks of Jews and Greeks, he is using the ethnic equivalent of A–Z and implying that God's promises are for 'everyone'. None of this is to make light of the self-conscious appeal made to Greeks or to Greek culture, perhaps stylized in Acts 20:15-34, but certainly present in parts of Paul's letters and the theological exposition of Logos Christology found in John. While ostensibly at ease with the polytheistic civic system of specialized gods found in Athens and Rome, 'One God Philosophers' were typical of sophisticated Greek thinking. Though there are no stories of serried ranks of converts from schools of Stoicism or Sophistry, examples such as Justin or returnees such as Augustine are at least partial examples of 'intellectual conversion'.

Meanwhile, there may have been another attraction for less observant members of the Diaspora, referred to sometimes as 'God Fearers' who might be 'adherents' rather than full members of the synagogue. Being a 'God fearer' seems to have connoted religious mindedness in the context of Empire (Lieu, 2002, p. 67). Acts presents a positive view of 'God fearers/God reverers' who were long supposed to constitute a group on the fringes of the synagogue who might be ripe for conversion (cf. Acts 10:2, 13:26, 43). It seems reasonable to accept that the convulsions suffered in biblical Israel-Judea between the revolt of 66 CE and the end of the Bar-Kochba rebellion in 136 CE effectively produced two new religious options – Rabbinic Judaism and Christian Judaism. With the Temple now gone and the Promised Land wrenched away, Torah strong scripture-based synagogue life was one option of identity-belonging, Christian enthusiastic church life another. It has been reasonably surmised that the somewhat 'de-Torahfied' proclamation of the Jesus movement would have suited generic 'God Fearers' or indeed YHWH believers less able or eager to follow the dietary, ritual washing and circumcision rules of the Moses tradition. For these believers, the Church may have given them a *way* to be faithful to their heritage in their contemporary context.

f) Monasticism

So, still one, but what about holy? The development of monasticism constitutes one of the most enduring glories of the Christian tradition. As the era of persecution ended and the Church increasingly accommodated itself to the ways of the world, a movement sometimes called the 'white martyrdom' developed. Characterized by a flight from 'normality' to a life of sexual renunciation, fasting and prayer, radical Christians sought to witness in divers ways. Since the tradition of celibacy and community living did exist at the time of Jesus among the Essenes, it might be considered to have been a natural development among a movement conscious of its end-time context. In formal organized pattern, however, it was not until the third and fourth centuries that it began to flourish. Though it is rightly claimed that Christian rejection of the world was influenced by Gnostic or Manichean tendencies, there is no need to look too far beyond the core tradition of the Gospels. Some such as Simon Stylites (390–459) chose to sit atop a pole as a visible sign of 'between world' living, but while his idea of a ladder to heaven did attract some followers, his method was not as successful as Pachomius (290–346) and Anthony (251–356) along the Nile and in the Egyptian desert, respectively. The call of Antony is perhaps a good way into the spirituality of those who, in imitation of Jesus' example, went into the wilderness to beat the devil and to praise God. Athanasius' *Life of Antony* recounts:

> He was left alone, after his parents' death, with one quite young sister. He was about eighteen or even twenty years old, and he was responsible both for the home and his sister. Six months had not passed since the death of his parents when, going to the Lord's house as usual and gathering his thoughts, he considered while he walked how the apostles forsaking everything, followed the Savior, and how in Acts some sold what they possessed and took the proceeds and placed them at the feet of the apostles for distribution among those in need, and what great hope is stored up for such people in heaven. He went into the church pondering these things, and just then it happened that the Gospel was being read, and he heard the Lord saying to the rich man, *If you would be perfect, go, sell what you possess and give to the poor, and you will have treasure in heaven* (Mt. 19:21). It was as if by God's design he held the saints in his recollection, and as if the passage were read on his account. Immediately Antony went out from the Lord's house and gave to the townspeople the possessions he had from his forebears (three hundred fertile and very beautiful *arourae* [measures of land], so that they would not disturb him or his sister in the least. And selling all the rest that was portable, when he collected sufficient money, he donated it to the poor, keeping a few things for his sister. (Athanasius, [c.360], 1980, p. 31)

These characters were something else. Their devotion and their asceticism became the stuff of legend and like the theological rivalry of Alexandria and Antioch, there was a certain amount of competition between these 'hermits' (from *eremos* – desert). Having fled to seek solitude, Antony ended up with something of an organizing role among the hermits. The pattern was to mentor novices into the life of contemplation by discipline and prayer tasks that would stretch their abilities and test their obedience. The spiritual wisdom generated by the 'sayings of the desert fathers' is one of the treasures of the Church and inspired a variety of forms of 'religious life' which were to have enduring influence. Pachomius meanwhile was more deliberately organizational, founding communities in villages but patterned with a shared life that inevitably had local impact. As time went on, St Basil in the East (c.330–379) and Augustine (354–430) in the West wrote rules for communities living shared lives under their jurisdiction. Across Europe, the classic expression of common life was expressed in the Rule of St Benedict (c. 480–550). A healthy combination of aspirational piety and common sense, it framed a way of life that turned on *orare, laborare, contemplare* – prayer, work and contemplation. Benedictines would probably say that this has been much imitated but never bettered by other Christian orders and since it has proved enduringly attractive for a millennium and a half, they may have a point.

A significant aspect of the monastic development was that it provided an alternative source of religious authority. Keeping paradox in mind, it is perhaps no surprise that such flights from the world changed the society that they had left behind. In particular, the creative independence of radical young Christian believers almost always helped to raise the profile of spirituality and challenge the functional everyday *modus operandi* of the 'Church organizational'. The various flowerings of religious life whether among the Celtic monks that swept across Europe in the sixth and seventh centuries or in the Frankish Cistercian movement of the twelfth century, all changed the ecology of the Church. Monasteries were not just centres of prayer and sacraments. They functioned as prototype pharmacies and infirmaries. They pioneered agricultural techniques, food production and brewing. (Next time you raise a glass of champagne, offer a toast to Dom Perignon.) The sheer size of some of the monasteries and the lands that they were responsible for meant that they could anchor the entire economy of a region. Though numerical man/woman power varied, throughout both East and West, the contribution of the various orders to the preservation of the Greco-Roman cultural heritage as well as the development of Christian Theology and devotion is hard to underestimate.

g) Church growth: Stark realities

Meanwhile, just as J. L. Martyn identified a context of tension which offered a theological key to the Fourth Gospel, so Rodney Stark has identified a cluster of social realities which go some way to explaining the 'miraculous' growth of the Church. In his 1996, *The Rise of Christianity*, Stark identified in the first instance the ritualized generosity which characterized early Christianity and formed part of its attraction to marginalized groups such as widows, orphans and the elderly. Nothing special there. The notion of 'Rice Christianity' associated with the early Oriental missions whereby if you went to Church you got some food is a no-brainer for Church growth. Since both Satan and the 5000 tried this one on Jesus, I'm not sure how much approval it gets as a method, but there is the corollary that the earliest communities were noted for their generosity and this proved attractive (Acts 2:47). Where Stark changed the script, however, was to theorize that this welfare network may have been particularly effective in changing medical conditions during times of plague, changing life expectancy among younger women and changing fertility patterns among sections of society.

Terrible epidemics were a feature of the period which saw the expansion of Christianity. The plague during the reign of Marcus Aurelius around 165 accounted for a third of the population of the Empire and a subsequent epidemic in 251 wreaked similar devastation. For Stark, not only did such depopulation weaken the civil structures of the Empire, they also sounded the death knell to official religion since Christianity afforded theological and practical advantage over the traditional pagan matrix. As this text has emphasized from the outset, Theology articulates narratives of meaning. In such a bewildering context of sorrow, Christianity made suffering meaningful since though its founder had endured agony and death, Calvary proved to be a portal for resurrection and eternal life. With the Cross as a Christian symbol, suffering was the very mark of an authentic member of the body of Christ (the Church). Furthermore, the radical altruism of Christian self-giving connected with medical care in such situations is corroborated by imperial exhortations for pagan doctors to imitate their Christian counterparts. Basic washing, hygiene, and a reluctance of Christian doctors to flee the dangers of pestilence may also have been a factor which even at the margins would have made a difference to population profiles. In the aftermath of a depopulating plague, the resilient tightly supportive networks associated with the early Church may have been the only community option left for decimated remnants of towns and villages. For Stark, these plagues were part of paganism's fatal illness that caused it almost to 'topple over dead' in the face of the Christian Church.

Women, too, are seen to be a sociological key to Christianity's success. Despite contemporary tensions regarding women and ministry, no one disputes that from the earliest days of the Church women had played a conspicuous role. While there are pros and cons to the arguments as to whether Jesus or Paul revolutionized treatment of women, it is probably safe to agree with Stark's view that within the Christian subculture, women were afforded more protection within the Church than in wider society. In Christian Theology, women were children of God, shared the destiny of the saved and were recognized as equal to their male counterparts. Such dignity found practical expression in the discouraging of divorce, the forbidding of polygamy and the delaying of marriage and reproductive activity. Christian morality precluded birth control as well as abortion and was strongly against the practice of 'exposing' unwanted babies (usually female). The cumulative outcome was not just healthier, more fertile, more socially secure Christian women – there were simply more of them. A surplus of Christian women was both a demographic and religious time bomb. In the event of inter-marriage, Christian woman plus pagan man would normally have meant Christian children and further explain the 'explosion' of Christianity. Stark confirms this by comparing spousal behaviour in sociological studies of groups such as the Mormons and Moonies. He suggests that the *practical* advantages of belonging to a group generally outweigh *ideological* misgivings held by one partner or the other. And since the historically observed expansion of these splinter Christian groups is of the same numerical order as the astonishing 'rise' of Christianity, it may owe more to mothers than to martyrs.

Hence, while acknowledging the witness value of those who were executed for the faith, Stark's view is that its main advantage to Christianity was that it reduced the numbers of 'free-riders' and kept the Church a vital, intense community. The upshot was an increasingly successful movement with effective support structures and a socially liberalizing meta-narrative of equality and ultimate destiny.

h) Eastern Emperor, Western Pope

They say that the darkest hour comes before the dawn. If Constantine's accession would ultimately herald the emergence of the Church from the shadows, the two-decade rule of his predecessor Diocletian (286–305 CE) and his rescripts against Christianity ensured that many would not see that daytime. Particularly directed against clergy, a persecution commenced in 303 which continued on and off for almost a decade. Son of Constantius Chlorus and Helena, Constantine's exact birth date is disputed but he was sent to the court of Diocletian in the East in 293 CE. In a confusing chain of events all too characteristic of imperial power struggles, he was proclaimed Emperor at York on the death of his father in 306 CE, but it was not until 312 CE when he defeated his rival Maxentius that he could claim unrivalled authority. This decisive battle, fought at the Milvian Bridge outside Rome, would prove doubly significant. According to the account of Lactantius, Constantine had seen a vision of the cross in a dream on the eve of the battle and received the instruction *In hoc signo vinces* – 'By this sign shall you conquer'. Overnight – in the course of one battle – the religious and political history of the West became inextricably intertwined. For good or for ill, for better or for worse? A popular current view is that it proved a triumph for the Church but was a disaster for Christianity, since the body of Christ now wore the imperial crown and wielded the imperial sword, never again wearing the humble apron of service, or the single undivided garment of priesthood. Back then? Well, back then, Constantine was readily understood as the Thirteenth apostle who in theological and practical terms helped to reform the Empire and unify the Church.

A man of power, familiar with power, before Constantine or his family had even professed their faith in Christianity, he immediately became involved in changing the religious landscape. At Milan in 313, he agreed with Licinius, his Eastern imperial counterpart, an Edict of Toleration, which confirmed Empire-wide ending of the persecutions of Christians and restoration of Church property. With ostensibly good intentions, he busied himself alongside local bishops to put an end to disagreements and as seen above (Section 14e), directly concerned himself with the Council of Nicaea which he convened to end the Arian crisis. Constantine modified or remodelled legislation in favour of debtors, clergy, children and slaves while criminalizing 'exposure' or infanticide. He made Sunday a public holiday and funded church building far and wide. While it may seem odd to the modern reader, Constantine did all this not as a Christian but as a *catechumen*, someone preparing to be baptized. In the context, this was quite theo-logical. Baptism was *the* pre-eminent symbol of forgiveness, and the ritual of Penance for past sins was only permitted once in a lifetime. Like others in civil and military life, Constantine would have been keenly aware that his duties compromised his Christian purity and his being numbered among the saints. Meanwhile his mother Helena embraced the new faith with enthusiasm. As a prototype pilgrim, she journeyed throughout the Holy Land and with Constantine's approval, was instrumental in the founding of Churches and memorials on the sacred sites of Christianity that have remained to this day.

So far so good, but whatever the intentions of the Emperor-Churchman, there were historical and theological consequences. Historically, Constantine consolidated the Empire around a new city built on the fortress isthmus of the Black Sea at the junction of Europe and Asia. Geographically and politically this made sense, but for the Church it led to the beginnings of an organizational tension that would eventually polarize East from West. Architecturally and theologically, the brand new Christian city compared favourably with decaying pagan Rome where sacrifices were still offered to a variety of deities in the many temples still frequented by the locals. Built on the site of the mainly Christian town of Byzantium, 'Constantinople' was completed in 330 CE and inevitably its Bishop became an influential figure in the imperial court.

So what's not to like? Hitherto, the Catholic or Universal Church had accorded greatest honour to the Bishops of the founding or 'patriarchal' churches of Jerusalem, Antioch, Alexandria and Rome. Of these, Rome had acquired a pre-eminent position which at the political level could be naturally explained by its importance as the founding centre of the Empire. More importantly, however, the theological reasoning was due to Rome's association with Peter, *Kephas*, the leader of the Twelve, the rock on whom Christ promised to build the Church (Matt 16:18). Although Peter was martyred there during the Neronian persecution in 64 CE, it was acknowledged that because of this *petrine* (Peter) connection, his successors should enjoy special honour. This is evidenced from an early successor, Clement I (c.96 CE) in his correspondence to the Corinthians and from the various disputes of the first centuries when Rome was often called upon to arbitrate disagreements that had broken out within or between other local Churches.

The verbal formulation of Rome's pre-eminence oscillated around – *primus inter pares* – 'first among equals' and it was significant that at the ecumenical Council at Nicaea, the Bishop of Rome led the clergy procession followed by the leaders of the other great ancient churches. But after 330 CE, there was a new bishop on the block – the Patriarch of the New Rome. While Alexandria had formerly considered itself the leader of the Eastern congregations, already, by the time of the next universal gathering of the Church which took place in 381 CE, the Patriarch of Constantinople was accorded pre-eminence, ahead of the others and *right behind* Rome.

Now in some ways, attention to processional line-ups among successors to the apostles only mirrors the kind of 'seating position' competitions that the original Twelve had among themselves (cf. Matt 20:23 and Luke 9:46). Unfortunately, rivalries among bishops and patriarchs would eventually lead to divisions between these two great Churches, with centuries of painful consequences. Meanwhile, if the Emperor in the East was finding himself increasingly involved in Church affairs, the Pope or Bishop of Rome was finding himself increasingly involved in affairs of state. The migration of the Imperial court to the East left a power vacuum in the West which the Pope began to fill. In the century that followed the conversion of Constantine, Rome was increasingly vulnerable to incursions from German tribes. By 452, when Attila the Hun arrived at its gates, only the direct intervention of Pope Leo I saved the city. As the infrastructure of Empire crumbled, bishops in general and the Pope in particular were becoming embroiled in civic affairs whether they liked it or not. Gregory the Great (540–604) didn't like it and ponders the dilemma in his Homilies on Ezekiel:

> I am forced to consider questions concerning churches and monasteries and often I must judge the lives and actions of individuals; at one moment I am forced to take part in civil affairs, next I must worry about the incursions of barbarians and fear the wolves who menace the flock entrusted to my care; now I must accept political responsibility in order to support those who preserve the rule of law; now I must bear patiently the villanies of brigands, and then I must confront them in all charity. My mind is sundered and torn to pieces by the many and serious things I have to think about . . . And yet the creator and redeemer of mankind can give me, unworthy though I be, the grace to see life whole and power to speak effectively of it. (*Hom. Ezek.* Bk. I, II, 5)

Unfortunately, other successors of Peter were less reticent about exercising 'temporal' power and in the West, Emperor Constantine's infamous *Donation* did not help. This document, which claimed to originate from the time of Constantine's profession of faith, included a number of stipulations that were destined to rankle for centuries. The document asserted the primacy of Rome above the claims of the other four patriarchal sees (Jerusalem, Antioch, Alexandria and Constantinople) and the Pope was made supreme judge over all clergy, thereby excluding them from the control of emperors, kings or anyone else. The document attests that while turning down the offer of the Imperial Crown, the Pope did nevertheless accept political domination over Rome, the cities of Italy and all the Western regions. Though the *Donation* was proved to be a fake by Nicholas of Cusa in the fifteenth century, it had by then caused enough mischief. It certainly contributed to the thinking of Pope Boniface VIII, who in 1302 pronounced in the Bull *Unam Sanctam* that everything was under the authority of the one apostolic church. Possessed of two swords representing spiritual and temporal power, the Church had ultimate sanction over all human affairs. Those fishermen had come a long way. A cosmic Kingdom of God. The Body of Christ, undisputedly in charge:

> We are taught by the words of the Gospel that in this Church and under its control there are two swords, the spiritual and the temporal . . . Both of these, that is, the spiritual and the temporal swords, are under the control of the Church.

> The first is wielded by the Church; the second is wielded on behalf of the Church. the first is wielded by the hand of the priest, the second by the hand of kings and soldiers but at the wish and by the permission of the priests. Sword must be subordinated to sword, and it is only fitting that the temporal authority should be subject to the spiritual . . . We must be all the more explicit in declaring that the spiritual power is as far superior to any earthly power both in dignity and nobility as spiritual things are superior to temporal . . . For, as Truth witnesses, the spiritual power can both establish the earthly power and judge it, if it proves to be no good . . . Therefore, if the earthly power goes astray, it will be judged by the spiritual power; and if the lesser spiritual power goes astray, it will be judged by its superior; but if the supreme power goes astray, it will not be judged by men, but only by God, as the Apostle says, "The spiritual man judges all things, and he himself is judged by no man." (1 Cor 2:15) (Clarkson, 1960, pp. 74–5)

Is this problematic? Surely no one would object to the Body of Christ being in charge of the world? Yet of all the pronouncements of the successors of Peter, *Unam Sanctam* ranks among the most controversial because of its privileging of the role of the Church in general and of Rome in particular. In fairness, Boniface was a man of his time who was actually wrestling (though not very humbly) with the theological and practical dilemma presented centuries before by the conversion of Constantine. How on earth (literally) should the Church act?

While this question was at the heart of numerous meditations from the New Testament onwards, it was rendered particularly acute by the circumstances that followed the events of 312. Previously, when it was hidden and persecuted, the Church could choose to stay out of civic affairs and concern itself instead with charity and liturgy. But this was a changed landscape. If the Christian's true commonwealth was in heaven (Phil 3:20), what was the relationship between the New Israel, the New Kingdom and the Old World? Thankfully, it was to this question that one of the greatest figures of the post-Constantinian generation had turned his mind. His motif was the *City of God*. His name was Augustine.

Summary

The old canard that Jesus preached the Kingdom but got the Church instead makes a neat headline but does not cohere with the early awareness of a symbolic Twelve with a designated leader (1 Cor 15:5). Although there are numerous motifs to describe the self-understanding of the Jesus movement in the New Testament, two of the clearest are that of the New Israel and the Body of Christ. The evolution of Church order through the leadership of Bishop, Priest and Deacon is clearly attested at the turn of the first century by Ignatius of Antioch, whose journey to martyrdom was just one example from a heroic age. The already present network of the ethnic Diaspora and the support systems available through Church communities meant that the movement could spread rapidly, especially in the face of a literally less healthy pagan culture. The conversion of Constantine brought with it a different challenge. For the first time, the Church could be directly engaged in the conduct of the state and judging the proper extent of that involvement became and remains a key conundrum for Christian Theology.

16

Augustine, Anselm, Aquinas

From Justin Martyr onwards, the succession of thinkers whose names entered the annals as the 'Fathers' of Christian Theology was impressive and the 'Patristic' era (100–600CE) is often studied with a particular reverence. As the Empire increasingly looked to the East, the Church became a key custodian of the Greco-Roman cultural heritage of the West. For a thousand years the philosophical, artistic and literary traditions of the Mediterranean civilizations were woven into a tapestry of thought that included the intricate braid of Christian revelation. Of the many theologians who contributed distinctive threads to the weave, Augustine, Anselm and Aquinas have a measure of pre-eminence in the West. Augustine's famous 'Confessions' anticipated the contemporary 'turn to the self' of modern psychology while his 'City of God' proved a definitive meditation on Empire and Christianity. Anselm's fame endures through his lyrical views on redemption and his infuriatingly simple 'proof' of the existence of God. Meanwhile, despite being a natural born rebel, Aquinas has enjoyed long standing ecclesiastical approval as the supreme example of 'scholastic' Theology. All three exemplify the classical Christian theological approach, believers using their intellectual powers to articulate the Jesus revelation in dialogue with their age.

a) Augustine of Hippo: Restless heart

Augustine was born in 354 at Thagaste in present-day Algeria of a pagan father and a devoutly Christian mother. Though his mother Monica ensured Augustine had a Christian education, he was neither baptized by the waters of faith nor convinced by the arguments of Theology as he embarked instead on an intellectual career teaching Logic, Philosophy and Rhetoric in Rome and Milan. A precocious soul, Augustine kept a mistress from the age of 17. Though she bore him a child, named *Adeodatus* meaning 'given by God', he left her behind when he moved to Milan, possibly because of her low social status. So far, so bad – an intellectual snob with no sense of spousal responsibility. Almost wish you didn't know the guy!

Trialling a series of different belief systems in the fashion of Justin before him, it was his meetings with Ambrose, the Bishop of Milan, that changed his life. Augustine recounts that his conversion to Christianity took place in a garden in July 386 where he heard a child's voice telling him to pick up the Bible where he read the call to 'put on Christ'. With his son and some friends he withdrew to prepare for Baptism and within four years Augustine was ordained a priest. In 391, the people of Hippo near Carthage almost kidnapped him that he might become their Bishop. Between then and his death in 430, Augustine became renowned for his eloquence and stunning fecundity of thought which yielded a scarcely believable number of writings. He is without doubt the single most influential figure on Western Christian Theology and an enduring reference point for serious students of the discipline.

Part of the reason Augustine has retained his fascination is that his *Confessions* (written c.398) are one of the earliest examples of what we would recognize as autobiography. His candid recollections, whether of stealing apples, of childhood friendships, of family loves or intellectual quests, actually *do* allow us 'to know the guy'. Reduced to a summary, the understanding of humanity that shines through his life story is that 'our hearts are restless' until they rest in God. His framework for this conclusion is not a million miles from Plato's thinking with which he was familiar. The idea of the true philosopher seeking the light as if in a darkened cave can be 'heard' in Augustine's writing and his dalliance with the dualistic material hating sect of the Manicheans seems to have left its mark on his distrust of sensory pleasures in a fallen world.

Still, *Confessions* rehearses perfectly the drama of the gifted individual learning to choose good which dominates the meta-narrative of Christianity from Genesis onwards. What makes Augustine's writing 'feel' so modern is that he conveys this drama well. Peril never seems far away under the threat of

Original Sin with *concupiscence* as its active agent of destruction. This 'turn to the self' means that everything, every action, every moment takes on theological import, all part of the adventure of salvation and the promise of eternal friendship with God.

As a Neo-Platonist ('new Plato-type thinker'), Augustine's understanding of humanity is that we are uniquely amphibious, connected both to the material and heavenly realms. Since our physical reality cannot image God as readily as our rational soul, Augustine privileged the 'inner' rather than the 'outer' self. Despite the best efforts of thinkers as diverse as Aquinas and Wittgenstein, this has led to a bias against bodiliness that has proved almost impossible for earthy, blood-red incarnational Christian Theology to rebalance. In fairness, Augustine's fidelity to Christian belief in the resurrection of the body does mitigate his dualistic reputation since he does not regard the body as a set of clothes that can be merely discarded. Nevertheless, the human drama remains the avoidance of sin, because its fruit is death, which wrenches body and soul apart in the tragedy of mortality.

b) The City of God

Though Augustine could paint intimate, almost psychoanalytical pictures of the human heart, he could also work on a broader canvas, and none of his masterpieces was quite as big as his reflections on Church and Empire in *The City of God*. The trigger for this work was the sack of Rome by the Visigoths in 410. Indubitably violent, it was the symbolism of the incursion that seems to have disturbed Augustine. Theologically, many of those who fled the city pointed the finger at the evil of Christianity which had led to the calamity. Although the Christian basilicas of the city had provided refuge for those fleeing the carnage, they perhaps had a point, since Alaric's Visigoths were by this stage nominally Christian. Symbolically, the catastrophic collapse of the mother city of imperial civilization before barbarian hordes marked a pivotal moment – a sense that the world would never be the same again. If the destruction of Jerusalem by the Romans had accelerated the metamorphosis of Judean religion into Rabbinic Judaism and Christianity, so the sack of Rome and the power vacuum that followed accelerated the process whereby the Christian Church took on political as well as spiritual guardianship of the West.

As survivors and refugees found their way to North Africa, a lingering controversy attended the event. What did a Christianity of 'turn the other cheek' pacifism have to say about such calamities and organization of the *res publica* – civil affairs? Augustine's reaction was to write the longest single work of Greco-Roman antiquity. It can be viewed either as a grand design or a polemic that he got carried away with and like Jack and the Beanstalk it 'just grew and grew and grew'. True, it is discursive at times and not as succinct, for example, as Plato's *Republic*. However, given that Augustine had already conceived of the motif of two loves building two cities from his commentaries on Genesis, it coheres with his lifelong theological task to contextualize the drama of Christian life in an often alien world.

The first half of his great work is an historical *tour de force*, reviewing the great stories of Rome's origins and demolishing the view that Christianity was responsible for its weakness which was actually due to the poverty of the pagan mindset. For Augustine, even great thinkers such as Plato could not wholly break free from the self-referential nature of human knowledge. Having swung his wrecking ball at attempts to reach true wisdom without God, Augustine then reorientates the mindset/heartset of humanity:

> Accordingly, two cities have been formed by two loves: the earthly by the love of self, even to the contempt of God; the heavenly by the love of God, even to the contempt of self. The former, in a word, glories in itself, the latter in the Lord. For the one seeks glory from men; but the greatest glory of the other is God, the witness of conscience. The one lifts up its head in its own glory; the other says to its God, "Thou art my glory, and the lifter up of mine head." In the one, the princes and the nations it subdues are ruled by the love of ruling; in the other, the princes and the subjects serve one another in love, the latter obeying, while the former take thought for all. The one delights in its own strength, represented in the persons of its rulers; the other says to its God, "I will love Thee, O Lord, my strength." . . . there is no human wisdom, but only godliness, which offers due worship to the true God, and looks for its reward in the society of the saints, of holy angels as well as holy men, "that God may be all in all." (*City of God*, Bk. 14:28)

Though this sort of dualism is reminiscent of the Platonism and Manicheism of Augustine's early adulthood, it is also well supported within the Christian tradition. Moreover, the detail of his approach is nuanced – that Christians should live *in* the world but not be *of* it. The blessings of the world are to be enjoyed, but they are not forever. Following St Paul, whose writings were influential in his conversion, for Augustine heaven is the true homeland of the Christian and to this end should actions be orientated (Phil 3:20). Although there may be polemic in his stylistic turns (teasing the pagan refugees who looked longingly back to Rome), Augustine's message is that the wise should transfer their longing to something less tangible but more enduring – the City of God.

Consonant with his view of the individual human condition, it can be argued that the theological master key here is Original Sin. For Augustine, the root problem for humanity is that reason has been contaminated through the bewilderment of misdirected love. This calamity began with the angelic fall and it is a schism within which makes true self-knowledge difficult. By extension, human society, left to its own devices, selects misguided priorities and tends to self-destruction (cf. *City of God*, Bk 12.7). While the city of this world, barred from communion with God, is destined to perish, from Abel onwards, favoured heroes have raised the banners, the rallying standards of the heavenly city. In whichever epoch, *ante legem, sub lege et sub gratia,* 'before the Law, under the Law and under Grace' the stretch of human history between Adam and Armageddon is destined to be confusing and marked by disasters and war. Underneath, however, the true architecture of the heavenly city is dimly visible yet bright with hope. Ultimately, the demolition, the destruction of even the greatest of earthly cities cannot faze the one whose life is mapped according to the grand plan of the City of God.

The incredible sweep of this work meant that in one summary, the kings, the clergy and the educators of Christendom had a theological understanding of history and a narrative key to open the doors of the future. This future would put a premium on ecclesial organization. Sharp distinctions within the work fostered an already strong sense of the Church as a community of the elect, the chosen, those predestined for glory in contrast to the *massa damnata* – the multitude of the damned. The inextricable intermingling of the two cities set a premium on the importance of Christian sovereignty and vouchsafed the notion of ruling authorities being ministers of God (Rom 13:1ff.). Augustine's *City of God* became the reference text for a millennium and its fundamental understanding of ordered governance as an essential for Christian society would indelibly influence Political Theology. Excess – whether in the secular power of the Church or in the divine rights of kings – can hardly be blamed on the *City of God*. However, by affirming the possibility of *theocracy* – 'God rule', Augustine helped to shape the dream of 'Christendom' which contextualized the political, ecclesiastical and theological evolution of the West for a thousand years and more.

c) Augustine and Pelagius

Two other significant legacies of Augustine arose from theological contestations with the Donatists and the Pelagians. In both cases, there is merit in the arguments of his opponents, but the consistency of Augustine's position wins through. In the decade before Constantine's conversion, the Diocletian persecution launched in 303 had terrorized Christian communities. Some Church members, not unlike St Peter himself, had wilted under interrogation and renounced their faith. One of these was Felix of Aptunga who in 311, by now back in the bosom of the Church, consecrated Caecilian as Bishop of Carthage. This did not go down well in some quarters and the Numidian bishops (modern-day Algeria) supported the objectors. Caecilian's authority was rejected and eventually Donatus, from whom the movement took its name, was consecrated instead.

While the strength of feelings can be imagined, the position taken by Augustine was that the consecration by Felix was valid – the properly observed ritual in good faith conducted according to the mind of the Church made the action effective. It was not dependent upon the particular holiness of the clergyman which couldn't ever be guaranteed, but rather on the holiness of the Church which was guaranteed by Christ. As will be seen below, the principle that the sacraments function *ex opere operato* – 'from the doing of the action' rather than 'from the doing of the minister' remains a somewhat controversial aspect of Christian Theology.

A further series of theological ramifications arose from the intriguing disputation with a British monk named Pelagius (c.354–420). An ascetic, Pelagius taught in Rome towards the end of the fourth century and seems to have inspired a holiness movement among lay-people aspiring to live for God. For Pelagius, God had equipped humanity with potential (*posse*), volition (*velle*) and realization (*esse*) which together gave the tools for saintly, even sinless life. Hence, though the roots of a good action are ultimately in the benevolence of God who has given human beings the potential to act, the choice and realization of good deeds enacted by someone can also be counted to their individual credit, since:

> In his willing, therefore, and doing a good work consists man's praise . . . Whenever we say a man can live without sin, we also give praise to God by our acknowledgement of the power we have received from him, who has bestowed such power on us. (Stevenson and Frend, 1989, pp. 232–3)

To some extent, this is perfectly reasonable and is the way judgements are commonly made regarding the praiseworthiness or otherwise of people's actions. So and so is judged a 'good guy' or a 'great woman' by his or her actions. Unfortunately, however, Pelagius and his followers were falling into the classic trap of performance indicator religion which Augustine, like St Paul, was so wary of. If Pelagius and his followers were taking the credit for their good actions, what was their need of God beyond being part of the created order? If they could be so holy as to be sinless, did that mean they did not partake in the Fall of Adam? And if they were not in need of redemption, what was their need for Christ? Again, like Paul, the personal experience of Augustine might be significant here since he was touched by the grace of God while still 'a sinner'.

Augustine's response centred on the absolute necessity of the grace of God for the achievement of anything good. All is gift. Humanity can claim no credit, it can only give thanks. The whole swirl of Augustine's conversion was wrapped up in passion and desire. Sexual continence had been a big issue – he had famously prayed, 'Grant me chastity O Lord, but not yet!' (*Conf.* Bk. 8.7) Reconciled that only in God's power could such things be achieved, his keen awareness was summed up in a slogan which apparently irritated Pelagius: 'Give what thou commandest and command what thou wilt'. (*Conf.* Bk. 10.29) Augustine's position not only retained a sense that God was the beginning, the course and the end of good deeds, it retained a sense that everyone, even infants, need the healing of the cosmic physician who is Christ:

> Truly the nature of man was originally created blameless and without any vice; but that nature of man, with which each is born of Adam, now needs a physician because it is not healthy. Every good thing, indeed, which it possesses in its constitution, life, senses, intellect, it has taken from the most high God, its Creator and Maker. But the vice which darkens and weakens those good gifts of nature, so that it needs illumination and healing, was not derived from its blameless nature but from original sin which was committed through free choice; and on this account a penal nature is a part of a most righteous punishment. For if we are now in Christ a new creature, still we were by nature children of wrath, even as the rest also; but God who is rich in mercy, for his great love wherewith he loved us, even when we were dead in sins, quickened us together with Christ, by whose grace we have been made whole. (Stevenson and Frend, 1989, p. 238)

Though the controversy drew genuine and thoughtful contributions from either side, the African bishops pronounced decisively in favour of Augustine's views at the Council of Carthage in 418, a stance ratified by the Church Universal at Ephesus in 431. While this settled the matter for the best part of a millennium, these kind of questions – the relationship between nature and grace, the drama of choice and destiny, the relationship of faith and good works – all would re-emerge as theological conundra at the heart of the Reformation controversies.

There are compelling reasons why Augustine should be thought of as an optimistic rather than pessimistic theologian. He was so taken with the blest, guiding power of grace that he famously said '*Ama et fac quod vis*' – 'Love - then do what you want!' (See below, p.398). He clearly was a passionate pastor and charismatic leader – he was no dry old stick, he even liked hymns – since singing involved loving as well as believing. He proposed that those outside the Church may, by inner 'desire' be counted as baptized and therefore among the saved (see below, Section 17b). However, the awareness of sin that he carried with him from his own life story left Augustine with a pessimistic understanding of the unredeemed human condition and the shadow this cast on later theologizing was a long one.

d) Anselm on the God thought (the ontological argument)

Anselm (c.1033–1109) was born into a noble family in Aosta, Italy, spent most of his formative years in France at the famous monastery of Bec and ended his days as Archbishop of Canterbury in England. Famous for his definition of Theology, famous for his definition of God and famous for his understanding of Redemption, any one of these would have won him the Nobel Prize for Theology, if such a thing had ever existed. He didn't have life all his own way, he did not get on with William II of England and fared little better with Henry I, but his theological legacy is such that his work not only inaugurated a golden age of Western Christian thinking but also remains relevant in academic discourse today.

Within Christianity, Anselm's definition of Theology as *fides quaerens intellectum* – 'Faith seeking understanding' has become axiomatic. It is important not to confuse this pithy phrase as the cry of a bewildered believer groping in the dark. Anselm would be more likely to complain about the abundance of revealed light. In a fashion reminiscent of Augustine, what marked him out was the passionate way he set out to explore the faith with all the power of his intellect. In so doing, he set the tone for what became known to history as 'scholasticism', a theological method which flourished in Europe over the next three centuries.

Even more deliberately than in the Patristic era, scholastic theologians aimed to integrate biblical revelation and the doctrines and traditions of the Church with tools of reason and logic. This did not mean that deductive syllogisms took precedence over eternal truths, but it did suppose a positive, optimistic view of the power of human reasoning. So, while Anselm was not convinced that reasoned arguments will necessarily lead an unbeliever to faith and nor did he subscribe to the view that mere mortals could know the sum of all truth, he was convinced that there should be dialogue between faith and reason. Faith can use reason as a tool both to confirm the believer in faith and to explain that faith to others.

Perhaps it is best to use his famous argument for the existence of God as an example. An imaginary dialogue might proceed as follows:

- ANSELM: 'The fool has said in his heart there is no God'
- NOVICE: What do we mean by 'God?'
- ANSELM: God is 'that than which nothing greater can be thought'
  - Even the simplest soul and even the unbeliever can imagine such.
- NOVICE: But does that mean God exists? I can imagine unicorns, but they aren't real.
- ANSELM: Yes it does. Because anything that exists both in the mind and in reality is better than just a purely imaginary thing.
- Hence to say 'God does not exist' becomes a contradiction.
- NOVICE: So you're saying a supreme, eternal, creating, life-giving, loving, personal, omniscient, omnipotent, omnibenevolent entity must have Is-ness?
- ANSELM: Exactly. Checkmate. *Touché!*
- NOVICE: Good grief! How did that happen?

Conjuring trick? Charming joke? Stroke of genius? My first Philosophy teacher, Bob Moloney, liked to imagine that Anselm thought this argument up one day in a distracted moment in the monastery chapel. It probably caused havoc among the monks and it continues to occupy philosophers and theologians today. Not everyone likes it. His contemporary, Gaunilo, disputed with him and Aquinas was not impressed. The most well-known critique comes from Kant, who questioned whether 'it exists' adds anything to a description of a thing. After all, although we usually say 'Ooo – there *is* a Castle' or 'Hey, there *is* a horse' we could just say 'Castle!' 'Horse!' This led Kant to reflect whether existence is a property or whether it actually opens up a completely different question. After all, it seems that if we say 'a unicorn is an animal with the shape of a horse and with a horn – *and it exists*,' the '*it exists*' seems to be of a different order to its general description (see below, Section 19c). Nevertheless the very fact that Descartes, Kant and moderns such as Plantinga have become involved in the debate demonstrates the infuriating power of God defined as 'that than which nothing greater can be thought'.

e) Anselm on redemption: Why did God become man?

Meanwhile, however much modern theologians might want to drain the biblical and ancient tradition of spooky stuff, the battle between good and evil was a significant part of the Jesus movement thinking and experience. Whether personalized as Satan, Beelzebul, the Devil or as ancillary demons, evil and evil activity have some prominence in Christian revelation. The Synoptics describe numerous exorcisms of Jesus whose power over the diabolic is seen to be both a messianic manifestation of the Kingdom of God and a witness to his divine nature. John's Gospel also offered plenty of scriptural evidence that the 'Ruler of this World' held formidable sway (cf. Matt 9:34, Mark 3:22, Luke 11:15 and John 12:31). As a result, theological luminaries of the ancient Church such as Irenaeus, Origen and Gregory of Nyssa had suggested that as a consequence of sin, the Devil had acquired rights over fallen man that only the cross could satisfy. For centuries, the idea that the cross was the necessary *ransom* had currency among Christian theologians, even being imaged as fish bait or even a cosmic mouse trap that fooled the devil. In his treatise *Cur Deus Homo* – 'Why did God become Man?' Anselm took a different view.

For Anselm, drawing on Genesis, Paul and Augustinian traditions, the problem with sin was that it had disordered not just the mind of humanity but the entire order of creation. Honour, which is due to God rightfully as Creator, has not been paid. If you like, 'cosmic karma' needs to be restored since for the scales of justice to balance, something must be done that outweighs the misdemeanour of human sin. The only thing that can restore harmony is the God-man, allowing restoration through the perfect obedience of a human being, but who as God, owes nothing to God. This free super-abundance of grace surpasses all the sin of the world. Taking Paul's view of restoration in Christ, this becomes the reason for the Incarnation of the Son (Rom 5:20). The death on the cross, yes, is a conquest of sin but is not *per se* some kind of pay off for the devil. It is much more the restoration of the image of God in the sacred artwork that is humankind through the free self-giving of the Human One (*Cur Deus Homo*, Bk X).

While this might be seen as a step in the right direction for theological consciousness since it moved away from a cosmic squabble between Satan and YHWH, the nagging doubt left by Anselm's approach was that there was a need for God, or at least God's sense of justice to be wholly satisfied. At the very least this left some toxicity in the system since anyone wishing to imitate Christ could be left with the fearful premise of a displeased God whom only total sacrifice would appease. It is worth noting that there was disagreement on this even within the classical era. Other theologians, such as Rupert of Deutz (c. 1075–1130) and Robert Grosseteste (1168–1253) offered an alternative view of which that of Duns Scotus (1265–1308) is perhaps the most celebrated. In this tradition, for God to be God, God's plans could not be dependent on human action. The Incarnation was not 'caused' by sin, its root purpose was God's forever desire to share divine life and divine love with humanity. Christ as Alpha and Omega is the beginning and the end of a creation which is charged with the goodness of God and is a sacred arena of love. God revealed Godself in Jesus who loved us but whom humanity crucified. There is no deal here, it is just how love happened. In other words, the fulfilment of the beauty and wonder of creation *is* the revelation of God's love in Jesus (cf. Cross, 1999 and Horan, 2011). Very much part of the Franciscan tradition to which Duns Scotus belonged, recent thinking on 'theological ecology' has also made appeal to this part of the classical heritage which resists the separation of Christian concern for holiness from Christian concern for the earth (Mulholland, 2011).

f) Aquinas: Rebel with a cause

Following the death of Anselm and on into the late Middle Ages, cathedral schools and monastic *studia* were evolving into the great universities of the West – Paris, Bologna, Cologne, Oxford. United through Latin by a common language of learning, academic discourse took place across Europe unfettered by what would much later become more restrictive national boundaries. Theologically, the period reached its peak in the thirteenth century with the creative contributions of new religious orders, particularly the Franciscans and the Dominicans. The Franciscans were originally discouraged from being too involved in learning, but soon developed an enviable tradition of scholarship represented by Alexander of Hales (1185–1245), Bonaventure (1221–1274) and Scotus (1265–1308). Founded about the same time, the Dominicans were more directly committed to the intellectual life and were ably represented by Albert the Great (c.1206–1280) who doubled as a scientist, and the towering figure of Thomas Aquinas.

Thomas was born at Roccasecca, a hill town between Rome and Naples c.1225. A legend from his childhood has his parents wresting a scrunched piece of paper from his infant hand on which was written *Quid est Deus* – What is God? In what would be considered a deliberate career move by minor nobility of the time, Thomas was sent to the great Benedictine foundation at Monte Cassino where his prospects would have included becoming Abbot and effective ruler of its extensive and lucrative monastic lands. Instead, while attending Naples University, Thomas encountered members of the newly formed Dominican order. The Dominicans and the Franciscans were *mendicant* - 'begging' friars regarded with some suspicion as fanatical fundamentalists by parish clergy and the more established religious orders. To the consternation of his family Thomas determined to join the Dominicans and a storied battle of wills ensued. Teenage rebel Thomas was kidnapped and imprisoned but a clumsy attempt to deflower the young monk with the help of a local prostitute proved unsuccessful. Steadfast in his resolve, Thomas proved intransigent. His family relented and he was eventually permitted to study with the Dominicans who sent him first to Paris and then to the famous *studium* of Albert the Great in Cologne. A youth of few words, Thomas was nicknamed 'The Dumb Ox' by his fellow students. Already impressed by the young Italian's intellect, Albert is reputed to have remarked: 'We call him the Dumb Ox, but the bellowing of that ox will resound throughout the whole world' (Weisheipl, 1983, p. 45).

Returning to Paris in 1251, Thomas began to write. The common text-book of the era was the *Sentences* by Peter Lombard, which set out a series of doctrinal assertions followed by short theological explanations. Like many of the great thinkers of this 'scholastic' period, Thomas was soon composing a commentary on the *Sentences* in which many of the arguments of his master work *Summa Theologiae* were rehearsed. The *Summa* was undertaken some time after his return to Italy in 1258 during sojourns in Rome, Orvieto and Naples and uses the philosophical device of 'a going out and a returning' (*exitus-reditus*), on the grand scale. In the *prima pars* – the first part – he begins with God and the nature of man, in the *secunda* he deals with humanity in its personal, social and moral context, and details the return to God through Christ and his Church in the *tertia pars*. The novelty in Thomas' approach was that from his earliest time in Naples and from studying under Albert in Cologne he had been exposed to the newly arrived translations of Aristotle into Latin. Hitherto, not least through the enormous influence of Augustine, the somewhat dualistic views of Plato had provided the philosophical framework for Christian thinking in the West. Instead, the Aristotelian tradition was associated particularly with the works of Islamic scholars such as Avicinna (980–1037) and Averroes (1126–1198) with whom Thomas also engaged.

g) Summa Theologiae: The five ways

Thomas begins the *Summa* scrutinizing the proper subject of Theology, God. Other things are brought into the discussion as they relate to God and by the end of the *Summa* this will be seen to include the whole of human life and many things beyond it. While Thomas respects the power of reasoning and therefore the possibility of 'Natural Theology', God has illuminated the path to truth in the biblical revelation. Deliberately juxtaposing the reasonings of

Aristotle whom he affectionately calls 'The Philosopher' with biblical insight and words of wisdom from the patristic and conciliar tradition, Thomas patterns his study in a series of questions which are reviewed from both sides before a considered conclusion is drawn.

In contrast to Plato, Aristotle trusted and privileged the five senses as the origin of our knowing. For example, the 'idea of a cat' does not originate from some non-physical realm accessible only through our minds, it is a mental abstraction from our *experience*, our seeing of cats. This allows Aristotle to retain much of the vocabulary of Plato's system – forms, matter, etc. without some of the dualism associated with it. Bertrand Russell famously put forward that Aristotle is 'Plato diluted by common sense' ([1946] 1984, p. 159) but his approach enabled Thomas not only to propose a less dualistic matrix for Christian thinking, it also gave him a method grounded in observation. An example would be his famous 'Five Ways' which are pointers rather than 'proofs' for the existence of God that all begin with a common experience. In terms of importance to Thomas it is worth noting that they only occupy one section of one question in the *prima pars* and in my copy of the *Summa* that amounts to almost one page out of over 2,750. Anyway, here goes:

- The 'first way' considers our experience of things changing. Thomas uses the word 'in motion' – things are always on the way to being something else. Hence fire which is hot causes wood which is *potentially* hot to become *actually* hot. Heraclitus had once famously said that 'the only thing that is permanent is change' but for Thomas, since there cannot be infinite regress, the only permanent thing is God – the unchanged changer, the unmoved mover. How can this be? Well how about these for unmoved movers. Note how the saucer of milk effortlessly attracts the cat, how the glamorous VIP is surrounded by admirers or how a smelly person can create space even in an elevator.

- The 'second way' focuses not on change but on our experience of basic cause and effect. Thomas regards this as so obvious he doesn't give an example, but if I said that the statue is made by the sculptor, you are made by your parents, the valley by the river etc. you'd get the idea. Again, to prevent infinite regress there must be an uncaused cause. And as with the first way, the first cause that is uncaused is 'what everybody understands by God'.

- The 'third way' is similar to these but the focus is on our experience of existence. However much we think of ourselves, we can imagine the planet or indeed the universe getting on just fine without us. We know we aren't entirely *necessary* – we are dependent *contingent* beings. But there must be something that is essential. If at one time nothing was in existence, it would have been impossible for anything to have begun to exist, and so even now nothing would be in existence – which is absurd. The necessary being? God.

- The 'fourth way' is related to our experience of perfection. If there's good, then there's better and best. Although Thomas says he doesn't like Anselm's ontological argument he tiptoes near it here. He suggests there must be something that is best at 'is-ing' or 'be-ing' and hence is at the root of all perfection. As noted above, YHWH perhaps did mention this to Moses (Ex 3:14), and extended reflection leads to the idea of God in scholastic thought being one, good, true and beautiful.
- The 'fifth way' is based on our experience of nature and would commonly be called the 'design argument'. Thomas observes that all things obey natural laws, even when they lack awareness, so that all things tend towards a goal. Just as an arrow needs an archer, everything in nature is directed towards its goal by someone with understanding and 'this we call God'. (cf. *Summa Theologiae* Ia, q.2. art.3)

Now this kind of argumentation either grabs you or it doesn't. God on this account is now the Unmoved Mover, the Unchanged Changer, the Necessary Being, the Perfect Perfector and the Intelligent Designer. Aquinas and the theologians of this 'scholastic' period are often accused of going too far in their application of philosophical matrices to God, and the impersonal nature of these titles seems far away from the intimacy of the Father-Son-Spirit indwelling God of the Christian revelation. So how did this happen and what does Thomas do to 'intimize' things?

h) Baptizing Aristotle and drowning YHWH?

In following Aristotle, Thomas was having to grapple with the whole notion of the *impassability* or *unchangeablity* of God which had been part of the conciliar controversies of the Patristic period. The idea of a 'bigger picture' God had become established in Greek philosophical-religious thought centuries before Christ. If polytheism involved a certain amount of busyness on the part of specialist gods who guarded the seas or love or inebriation etc., activity was not the trademark of the God of the philosophers. Always ready to work from basic principles, Aristotle reasoned that a feature of created things was that they were ordered/designed to fulfil or *actualize* their potential. As an example, a truly fulfilled acorn would grow into a mighty oak tree and ping out acorns of its own. For human beings, while there are basic needs to be fulfilled, the highest human activity could not involve eating or sexual pleasure since excess in one leads to inevitable indigestion, while excess in the other leads to exhaustion. Instead, as rational animals, humans *actualize* their greatest potential when they *reason*, when they contemplate truth – an activity that can be continued almost indefinitely. Now this is where it gets clever and two neat conclusions tumble out of his reasoning:

- For God to be God, God must have reached God's full potential. There is nothing left to *actualise* in God – otherwise the humblest acorn would have done better. God is pure actualisation. *God is pure act.*
- On that basis, if God is understood to be doing anything, God must be thinking and if God is thinking about the best/most fascinating thing then God must be thinking about . . . Godself! *God is thought thinking itself.* (Cf. Aristotle, *Metaphysics*, 1074b 34)

Now you may object to these conclusions. While theologically the word used to describe God's unperturbable state is *impassible*, on this reading the word that comes to mind is 'smug'. I don't know about you, but this picture of a self-absorbed deity not troubled by any doings or deeds of mortals conjures up all sorts of images in my mind, most of which involve sunglasses, cocktails and languid lounging beside a swimming pool. At one level, the notion of a chilled out distant God could be deduced from some elements of the ancient tradition, notably the compulsory downtime of Sabbath. Otherwise, the Torah God is intimately part of the covenant life and drama of the chosen people, YHWH is a God who acts and gets involved. 'His nose burned' is a common phrase which signals raw emotion in the biblical text – and YHWH's nose burns far more than everyone else's. Part of the problem here is commandment #1 – the making of images of God. You will notice in this reading that Aristotle's God 'thinking deep thoughts' is very much in the image of a Greek philosopher. Indeed the tendency of humans to create God in their own image will become one of the main planks of the Enlightenment critique of theological discourse (see below, Section 21c).

So how does Thomas soften this desiccated presentation? In the *secunda pars* dealing with the movement of the rational creature to God, Thomas identifies that the ultimate goal of human life is *caritas* – 'holy love' – which he defines as *'a certain type of friendship with God'* (II-IIa q.23. art.1). Friendship *amicitia* is at the heart of his understanding and Thomas uses this same philosophical motif to explore social and political organization which he regards as part of the natural order. Furthermore, by drawing on Aristotle, biblical creation and the revelation of YHWH as the God who Is, Thomas asserts the fundamental goodness of all things. The maxim *omnia bona sunt* – 'All things are good' is the basic Christian mainstay against theological dualism and the denigration of the material world. This fundamentally positive view of the cosmos draws on a saying of Boethius that, *Some are just, some are not, but everything is good* (cf. ST Ia q.6 arts 3 & 4). Shockingly to some, this means that classic Christian Theology holds that even Satan is essentially a good, if misdirected creature, held in existence by the wholly good God in whom everything 'lives and breathes and has its being' (Acts 17:28).

By recognizing that human beings seek the good, Thomas then explores the way in which freedom and its limits help or hinder. He discusses the place of habits, fundamental dispositions, the dynamic nature of the virtues as well as the gifts of the Holy Spirit: Faith, hope and charity, prudence, justice, fortitude and temperance. Life is understood as a journey whose *telos* – 'final purpose', lies in a share in God's own life, 'the beatific vision'. This is made possible by God's kindness at work through Christ and his body the Church. Hence the *tertia pars* deals with the Jesus event before turning to the sacraments as ministries of Christ, and then . . . he stops. In December 1273, while celebrating Mass, Thomas seems to have had some kind of mystical experience and turning to his friend Reginald of Piperno, he remarked 'all I have written is so much straw'. There is speculation as to whether Thomas endured a stroke or was suffering from exhaustion. At any rate, though not yet fifty, he abandoned his great labour and wrote no more. Not long afterwards, summoned to attend a council at Arles in 1274, Thomas died on the journey, at the monastery of Santa Maria, Fossanova, south of Rome.

Although Aquinas has since become synonymous with orthodox Catholic thinking, in the years that immediately followed, his writings had a rocky road and at one stage they were condemned as heretical. Ultimately, his works were not only vindicated, but the *Summa* itself has since been declared by more than one Pope to be the official textbook of the Catholic Church. From any perspective, his achievements were remarkable, but they also represented a high-water mark for scholastic thinking which through its tenacious desire to reconcile faith and reason had helped to define an entire spectrum of doctrine. And as the next chapter will demonstrate, nowhere was this more apparent than in the way that the scholastic tradition classified, analysed and theologized the core activity of the Church: the Seven Sacraments.

Summary

A key component of Christian Theology is the contribution made in every epoch by significant thinkers. Through brief summaries of these three giants of the discipline, the reader can get a taste of how these theologians practised their craft. By any measure, Augustine stands as a defining figure in the Western tradition. His sense of the self, his sense of the drama of the human condition and his continual insistence on the need for God's grace were reminiscent of

Paul and anticipated the theologies of the Protestant Reform. The broad sweep of his thinking embraced everything from individual sin to the fall of the Empire. As Europe emerged from the 'Dark Ages' which followed, Anselm helped to define the purpose of Theology and advanced its method. Whatever the merits of his curious 'ontological' argument for God's existence, his views on how redemption had been achieved through the cross of Christ were theologically more influential. Finally, Thomas Aquinas, in his hugely ambitious masterwork the Summa Theologiae, *endeavoured to reconcile the philosophical approach of Aristotle with the great doctrines and biblical insights of the Christian tradition. Ruggedly incarnational, his work came to an abrupt end just as he was finishing his reflections on sacraments, to which we now turn.*

17

Sacraments

Theologically, sacraments are rituals which continue the sanctifying work of Christ through his mystical body, the Church. Pithily described as 'outward signs of an inward grace' the classical framework of scholastics like Thomas Aquinas offered seven: Baptism, Confirmation, Eucharist, Penance, Marriage, Holy Orders, Anointing of the Sick. This sevenfold system only became standardized at the turn of the first millennium with the different emphases of the different rituals reflecting different aspects of the work of Christ. If the Creeds were verbal expressions of faith belonging, the sacraments, particularly Baptism and Communion, became the ritual signs of Christian identity. Theologies of the sacraments ultimately would come to vary greatly between denominations, but in the classical period, they were at the heart of Christian self-understanding.

a) Signs of love

One of the great legacies of the scholastic period was its schematization of ... well ... everything. At its heart, however, was a 'sacramental economy' which through the ministry of the Church was nothing less than a prolongation of the Incarnation. Understood as the Body of Christ, understood as One, Holy, Universal and Apostolic, it was a pretty short theological step for the Church to conceive its own ministry as the mediation of God's grace, and its sacred rituals as the means of salvation. Though by origin the Latin word *sacramentum* was associated with the swearing of an oath, in the ecclesial context it was the Latin attempt to translate *mysterion* – 'mystery'. For the first millennium of Christianity, it is worth saying that the primary mystery or sacrament was Jesus as the revelation of God. Throughout that time, 'sacrament', understood in the widest sense, could extend to include almost any of the numerous ceremonies, prayers and pieties experienced in lived Christian life. Somewhere in between, the term was occasionally used to identify a restricted number of rituals, but this only reached its classic sevenfold form in Book IV of the *Sentences* (written 1155–8) of Peter Lombard. In this classic medieval textbook, Peter identified Baptism, Confirmation, Eucharist, Penance, Marriage, Holy Orders and Extreme Unction as rituals of salvific grace derived from the work of Christ in the New Testament (Rosemann, 2004, p.146).

Though ritual actions performed with ritual words and sacred intent are characteristic of innumerable religious traditions, a key to understanding classical Christian sacramental theory is to recognize its roots deep within the Torah heritage. Two particular aspects, *zkr* – *anamnesis* or 'remembrance' and *'oth* –'prophetic sign' fitted very well into the 'already-not yet' time matrix of the Jesus group. The celebration of commemorative festivals was a way of re-entering, re-*present*-ing the great events of the past such as the Passover with its recollection of the Exodus from Egypt. In the prophetic tradition, particular acts were performed to depict future events that would come to pass. Jeremiah specialized in these, wearing chains to foretell the exile and buying a field to foretell the return (Jer 27:1-8 and 32:1-42). The *TaNaK* heritage explains the 'time-warp' feature of sacraments which captures the religious power of the past, in the present, for fulfilment in the future. In the internet age, one might say sacraments are a permanent interface of grace. From prayers specially written for the inaugural feast of *Corpus Christi* – 'The Body of Christ' in 1264, Thomas Aquinas expressed this more poetically (my italics):

> O sacred banquet, in which Christ *is* received, the *memory* of his Passion is renewed, the mind is filled with grace, and a pledge of *future* glory is given to us.
> (cf. Fatula, 1993, p. 251)

As ritual language, sacramental prayer was rooted in a theological understanding of God's word as the transformative creating power of the Universe (see Section 2b). Sacramental enunciations are thus 'performative words' – they effect what they say. 'I baptize you . . .' 'I absolve you' etc. were not understood as suggestions, but rather the prayer of Christ, voiced through his mystical body the Church. Unlike the magic spells of primitive religion, Christian Theology insisted that there must be sacred intent on the part of the minister and both freedom and the desire to receive on the part of the recipient. The disposition of the believer was understood to be key to the effectiveness of the *gratia* – the 'love gift' on offer. Hence even the Eucharist, understood as a presence *par excellence* of the love of Christ, may be physically received but the grace not 'tasted' if the recipient were improperly disposed. In the technical language of Thomas and other scholastics, this was explained by distinguishing the *sacramentum* – the physical signs (e.g. bread and wine), the *sacramentum et res* (the body and blood of Christ) and the inner *res* or essential effective power of the ritual (to unite believers in the Body of Christ). And since the fundamental pre-requisite for receiving grace and belonging was to have been 'born again', the essential sacrament that made all the others possible was the symbol of new birth, Baptism.

b) Baptism

From the Greek *baptizein* – 'immerse', Baptism formed the rugged ritual link between the practice of the Jesus movement and its precursor in the ministry of John the Baptist. The most basic reflection on the baptismal mystery for the early Christian was that the initiation rite was a straightforward imitation of the humble action of Jesus, earning for the recipient adoption into the Trinitarian family as beloved (Mark 1:11). While the immersion in water could be linked to the burial in the tomb and the re-emergence to resurrection, the imagery of Exodus was also a favoured motif. In the Exodus, the children of Israel had passed through waters of the Red Sea from slavery to freedom, from death to life. Enduring forty years of transformative desolation they were nonetheless given the Law and reached the Promised Land once more through water by way of the River Jordan. The Gospel parallels with Exodus also appear to be deliberate. Jesus is baptized in the Jordan, the gateway to the Promised Land, he immediately endures the wilderness, confronts evil and the temptation to infidelity (Matt 3:13-4:25). As the New Moses, Jesus is the one who will bring the living water and the true manna for a people who hunger and thirst (John 4:10, 6:31). Paul had no hesitation in linking the imagery:

> I do not want you to be unaware, brothers and sisters, that our ancestors were all under the cloud, and all passed through the sea, and all were baptized into Moses

in the cloud and in the sea, and all ate the same spiritual food, and all drank the same spiritual drink. For they drank from the spiritual rock that followed them, and the rock was Christ. (1 Cor 10:1-4)

The fecundity of the symbolism inherent in baptismal ritual meant that it lent itself to a rich vision of the Church not just as the New Israel, but also as the Ark of Salvation by which humanity would be saved, the Well of wisdom and knowledge, the new Temple and the new Eden (1 Pet 3:21). As noted, the great commission of Matt 28:16-20 explicitly linked the ritual to Triune creedal proclamation and, with the passage of time, this was emphasized by the use of a triple immersion attested by the *Didache*. By the era of Justin Martyr, the ritual was preceded by a period of instruction for the *catechumens* – those preparing for Baptism.

In these early years, the liturgy included fasting, vigil, confession of sins as well as renunciation of the Devil and anointing. The discarding of old clothes and putting on white garments alongside the partaking of milk and honey as foretaste of the Promised Land constituted a theatrical enactment of spiritual transformation. Generally administered only at Easter and by a Bishop, it is clear that as the community spread, necessity began to loosen these restrictions. Since the responsibilities of being a Christian were manifold, it was not unusual for believers to postpone reception of the sacrament until nearer death. The most famous of the *clinici* – 'bed Christians' was Constantine himself, but the practice of hedging one's bets for as long as possible eventually fell out of use as infant initiation became the norm.

Since the practice of entire households coming to faith was attested in the New Testament (e.g. Acts 16:33), broadly speaking, infant initiation was not the main concern of the Fathers who were more vexed as to whether a Christian baptized by a heretic truly belonged. Pope Stephen I (d.257) and Cyprian of Carthage (d.258) took opposite sides with Cyprian arguing that rebaptism would be necessary. On this matter, Augustine would ultimately have the last word since the principle which emerged from the Donatist crisis was that the sacraments function *ex opere operato* – 'from the doing of the action' rather than 'from the doing of the minister'. Though Augustine's view that even infants are stained with Original Sin, has tended to mark him out as a pessimist, he did allow fuzzy edges that are worth noting. He recognized that someone yet to be received might be 'baptized in blood' by giving their life in martyrdom and like the 'Good Thief' (Luke 23:43) that there could be recognized in some a 'Baptism of desire' as an unexpressed equivalent of the sacrament, both views echoed by Aquinas (ST III q.66 art. 11).

Such speculations were alive in the scholastic tradition, as was the idea that Baptism conferred a special royal 'character' marking the soul as forever belonging. Indeed throughout patristic and scholastic literature, the mystery of Baptism proved a central consideration. As if to emphasize the fact, a thousand years of Church architecture saw the construction of increasingly elaborate baptisteries as affirmation of the foundational nature of the sacrament. The cosmic scope of these striking mini-basilicas would eventually include imagery such as the signs of the zodiac, which far from being theologically dubious meant that through belonging to the Lord of the heavens, the born-again Christian would never be 'dis-astered' – 'separated from their guiding star'. Instead of the buffetings of fate, through the grace of Baptism, life would instead be guided by providence and ennobled by other sacraments of initiation, healing and calling.

c) Confirmation

In classical understanding, Confirmation formed part of the initiation of the Christian and was essentially the *anamnesis* – 'ritual memorial' of the bestowal of the Holy Spirit upon the disciples. Though the gift of the Spirit was very much part of the messianic promise, ministry and resurrection gift of Jesus (Mark 1:8, Luke 10:21, John 20:22), it is most vivid in the accounts of Acts and in the Pauline tradition. There it would appear from the earliest times that Baptism was not identical with the experience/reception of the fullness of the Spirit (Acts 10:47-48). In the tumbling sequence of events associated with the early missions, it seems to be connected with the laying on of hands, though in Paul a distinct ritual may also be behind the 'sealing with the Spirit' (cf. Acts 8:14-17 and 2 Cor 1:22).

Through the early centuries, while Tertullian and the *Apostolic Tradition* of Hippolytus connected the 'laying on of hands' with Baptism, Cyprian identified a ritual of the Spirit distinct from Baptism and it was the latter practice which became most common. This may well have been a side effect of success. As time went on it became impossible for bishops to conduct *every* initiation. Hence while Baptism was devolved to local priests, the Western Church saw the 'sealing' with the Spirit reserved for the bishop which would be performed during his periodic visitations. This was fine in the good times, but it did mean that in periods of history or parts of the country where travel was dangerous or difficult, Confirmation/Chrismation was only sporadically administered. The East developed somewhat differently and priests began to 'seal' the newly baptized and give them communion immediately, thus completing the

'Sacraments of Initiation' in one go. Though episcopal connection was symbolized by using oil consecrated by the local bishop, it meant a divergent practice between East and West emerged.

Theologically, there were differences of opinion regarding its significance. Linkage to the manifestation of *charisms*, 'Spirit power gifts' described by St Paul in 1 Cor 12:4-11 had, by the scholastic period, been replaced by connection with *virtues* or 'Spirit wisdom gifts' associated with Isa 11:1-3. The general scholastic opinion was that the sacrament conferred a particular gift, marking the soul with an especial character and strengthening (*firmare*) the candidate in their Christian calling in contestation with evil. This was perhaps most vivid in Bonaventure's understanding of it as 'a sacrament of warriors'. The impact of such thinking helps explain why, in the Western Catholic tradition, the original sign of peace given by the bishop evolved into a slap on the cheek, designed to ready the recipient for future difficulties. The reader will be pleased to know that this practice has since been reversed, which fits better with modern health and safety regulations but also with the idea that the 'seal' prepared the candidate to receive love, in the *caritas* of communion.

d) Eucharist

Christian celebration of Eucharist is present in the earliest accounts of Church activity. Attested in the writings of Paul, it is connected to the celebration of the Last Supper in the synoptic traditions (cf. 1 Cor 11:23-26 and Mark 11:22-25). The symbolism present in the use by Jesus of bread and wine for body and blood is shot through with *anamnesis* – recollected memory. Food and faith are intimately connected in covenant theologies and it is possible to explain the whole biblical trajectory from Genesis to Revelation in terms of symbolic meals. The food that tempts man (Gen 3:3), the food that tempts God (Gen 8:21), the food of hospitality (Gen 18:6), the food of liberation (Ex 12:8), the food of survival (Ex 16:31), the food for the journey (1 Kings 19:8), the food of judgement (Ps 75:8), the food of prophetic fulfilment (Isa 7:21-23), the food of the proclamation (Luke 9:13), the food shared with outcasts (Luke 19:7), the food of suffering (Mark 10:38), the food of celebration (Luke 15:23), the food of eternal life (John 6:51).

So powerful are the New Testament identifications of the bread and wine with the bodily life of the risen Jesus that it is possible to argue there was early belief that the Eucharist literally had the power of preventing death (cf. John 6:51 and 1 Cor 11:30). As noted above, there was confusion aplenty among outsiders who with half-heard stories supposed that this secret sect was gathering to have some kind of strange love meal during which the God they worshipped was eaten (Section 15d). But was this religious confusion or theological genius? The eucharistic 'mysteries' involve a multiple miracle of symbolic belonging which is worth rehearsing step by step:

- The Church, in the Spirit, is the Body of Christ.
- It invites its disciples to the Last Supper.
- To partake in an intimate promise-meal of belonging.
- The mystery is pronounced. This is my body, this is my blood.
- The mystery is eaten. The bread of resurrection, blood of eternal life.
- Through word and meal the covenant is sealed.
- The believer is now one with Christ.
- The *imago dei* – the image of God is restored anew in the believer.
- The believer becomes the believed in.
- As the many grains make one loaf and as the many share one cup.
- The many church members become one body.
- So the mystery of Eucharist re-makes the Church.

Following this logic of sacrament, it is easy to see how quickly it came to be understood that separation from this communion or indeed unworthy reception of it was to be separated from Christ. Hence the drama and the tragedy of ex-communication. To be excluded from this mystery was to be sundered from the Lord and to have no part in the promise of eternal belonging.

For centuries, theological understanding of the Eucharist was relatively uncontroversial apart from the divergent tradition of East and West to use leavened and unleavened bread, respectively. It was not until the early Middle Ages when two monks from the same congregation enjoyed a famous exchange that eucharistic thinking took on a theological edge. A monk of Corbie in France, Paschasius Radbertus (786–860) wrote a short treatise *De Corpore et Sanguine Christi* – 'On the Body and Blood of Christ' which began to consider the way in which Christ was present in the Eucharist. Paschasius was anxious to emphasize that the 'real presence' meant that the eucharistic body of Christ could be identified with the natural or historical body of the incarnate Lord: *non alia plane caro, quam quae nata est de Maria et passa in cruce et resurrexit de sepulchro* – 'It is none other than the flesh which was born of Mary, died on the cross and has risen from the tomb'. Theologically, his reasoning was straightforward, since the Lord's words 'This is my body' must be true (*veritas*), then Jesus could not have been talking figuratively (*figura*).

Paschasius, by now Abbot of Corbie, presented the treatise to the wonderfully named Emperor Charles the Bald, on the occasion of his coronation. Seeking clarification on the matter, Charles engaged Ratramnus (d.870) who was part of the *same* monastic community as Paschasius. Awkward. A definite Platonist, Ratramnus was of the view that 'forms'/'ideas' were more real than material things, hence he was not so keen on the very physicalist views of his Abbot. Ratramnus redressed the balance by insisting on the distinct nature of *sacramental* presence. That is to say, though there is a proper identity between the eucharistic presence and that of the historical Christ, the *way* in which Jesus is present is by a deliberately imperceptible grace-based reality – in 'form' rather than in a garish physical and bloody manner. For him, the Eucharist could be both figurative and true.

Though commonly termed a controversy, neither of the opinions was condemned and everyone seems to have lived 'happily ever after' until the matter flared up again in a more celebrated crisis associated with Berengar of Tours (d.1088) and his nemesis, Lanfranc of Bec (d.1089). To some extent it was as simple an exchange as 'figurative v realist' again, except more extreme. The weakness of the figurative position was that it seemed to de-emphasize the salvific power of the bread of life and the saving cup, since if they were 'not real' then they couldn't be effective. Worse still, any expression of piety or veneration of the sacrament would be tantamount to idolatry. The problem faced by the 'realists' related to *how* Christ could be physically present in the sacrament without contradicting his present state of eternal glory, and without suffering the indignity of the human digestion system with all its, shall we say, 'hygienic' consequences (see Macy, 1993, pp. 67–101).

It was to this classic dilemma that Thomas Aquinas turned his mind in the last completed treatise of the *Summa Theologiae*. The High Middle Ages had seen a flowering of eucharistic devotion of which the institution of the Feast of Corpus Christi in 1264 was but one example. Thomas had been commissioned by the Pope to contribute hymns and prayers to the liturgy of the celebration – poetry that is still used in Churches even today. If anything the stakes had been raised on 'real presence' by reports of eucharistic miracles whereby hosts had bled on the altar during Mass. In the course of his discussions, as a possible way of understanding the process of 'real presence', Thomas outlines how one option, the theory of *transubstantiation* might pan out. This word was already in use long before Thomas was born, even making it into Canon 1 of Lateran Council IV in 1215. It is a curiosity of history that generations of Christians have pinned it to Thomas' lapel, but perhaps it is all Aristotle's fault. Thomas was a big fan of 'The Philosopher' and to get behind this magic word we need to do a bit of Aristotle. So deep breaths. . . .

Take a cat. I hope you won't be annoyed if I were to say that for a cat to be a cat, it must have 'catness'. For Aristotle, this is the 'substance', the essential nature of the little creature. Now cats can be different colours – one cat may be ginger, one cat might be grey, one big, one little. These particular attributes govern *what they look like*, but are not as fundamental to the furry felines as their being cats – such things just 'happen' to be so. The reason we call something an 'accident' is because it needn't have happened. In similar fashion, the non-essential features of cats, or the non-essentials of anything, Aristotle calls 'accidents'.

Now suppose in a sacramental context that the *appearances* of bread and wine remain, but their *substance* or *inner reality* is transformed into the presence of Christ. Transubstantiation is both as simple and as miraculous as that. But philosophically it is risky, since (technically) it requires dimension rather than substance to be the cohering 'reality' principle. If it is any consolation, no one was more aware than Thomas that this stretched the limits of his beloved Aristotle's system (see ST III q.77 arts. 1-2). However, it did provide an interesting theory as to how his even more beloved Lord could be present in the Eucharist without being multiplied, ludicrously dispersed or totally massive as Berengar had jibed. This *kind* of transformation meant that Thomas could respect the realist tradition – Jesus was truly present as the essential constituent of the eucharistic elements, but not in a repulsive fleshly way that would be intolerable to the faithful. The communicant would not be in some non-physical Platonic relationship, but truly, consummately and bodily joined to the Lord, present in distinctive, timeless, sacramental manner. In the poetry of *Adoro te devote* rather than in his analysis, Thomas summed up the mystery:

> Seeing, touching, tasting, are in thee deceived, what says trusty hearing, that may be believed, what my Lord has said to me, take for truth I do, truth itself speaks truly, or there's nothing true ([1264] 2003).

Through the remaining questions of the eucharistic treatise of the *Summa*, Thomas covers a range of topics. Since the appearance and sensory experience of bread and wine remained, it really didn't matter to Thomas if a mouse chewed its way into the tabernacle since the physical elements would be all it would experience. A mouse couldn't possibly 'receive' the presence of Christ anyway – only those made in the image of God can receive and thereby be received into the Body of Christ (ST III q.80 art.3). As for those who might receive unworthily or even mistreat Christ in his eucharistic guise, Thomas acknowledges the gravity of the sin but balances any hyper-sensitivity, since, although it might be upsetting to the faithful, humanity did not treat Jesus particularly well when he walked among us in the flesh ST III q.80 art.5. In fact, even when it came to discussions on whether people should be publically refused the sacrament because of their perceived sinfulness, Thomas was inclined for the sake of decency and charity to avoid any upsetting scenes. After all, he wrote, Jesus gave the bread to Judas, knowing full well what he was about to do (cf. ST III q.81 art.2 and Towey, 1995, pp. 78–92).

Withal, though Thomas and transubstantiation marked a moment in the classic presentation of 'real presence', there was another aspect of eucharistic thinking that was destined to be even more controversial: sacrifice. As commemoration of the Passover and the Passion, the eucharistic liturgy had an implicit sacrificial context in the New Testament and from at least the first century, this motif is strongly evidenced, not least in the writings of Ignatius of Antioch. The matter was discussed extensively at the synod convened in Constantinople in 1157 where the teaching that the celebration of Eucharist makes present the eternal saving sacrifice of Jesus was affirmed. In the West, the notion was so enthusiastically embraced that the celebration of Mass became in part linked to theologies of 'ransom' whereby the more 're-presentations' of Calvary made on your behalf (i.e. Masses said for your soul), the better chance you had of making it to heaven. Rich folk in general and kings in particular founded Chantry Chapels and left huge legacies in their wills to fund 'Massing Priests' who could keep churning out this most powerful intercession for years after their death. Thus, while theologically this idea had begun as an extension of God's mercy, by the time of the High Middle Ages it had become a key part of the Church's financial as well as sacramental economy. Since tying mercy to money was part of the reason Jesus had turned over the Temple tables, it is not surprising that such practices would come under the scrutiny of later generations. In fairness to the scholastic theologians, they never conceived the sacrifice of mercy and communion which was Eucharist as something to be accessed by money, but they were conscious that it should be accessed worthily. Eucharistic reception was only recommended in a 'state of grace' and to be sure of that, it was necessary for the believer to have received absolution from sin in the sacrament of Penance.

e) Penance

The drama of disobedience with covenant as its remedy is at the heart of the biblical tradition of Israel. As a consequence, much of the ritual expression of YHWH worship had forgiveness, mercy and sacrifice entwined in a variety of ways. During the desert wanderings, the infamous 'scapegoat' served such a purpose. Burdened by the sins of the people, it was driven into the wilderness symbolically removing the iniquity far away from a people called to be close to one another and to God (Lev 16:10). Holiness and cleanliness codes also formed part of the priestly traditions with purity laws and ritual washings key elements of their expression. Ultimately, the vortex of the covenant became synonymous with the rituals of the Temple. It literally became an economy of salvation where individual and communal sacrifices purchased by the people and offered by priests may have accounted for as much as a third of commercial activity in the first-century Judea. As noted above, Section 6c, one consequence of this was that anyone offering alternative access to the mercy of God was a financial as well as religious threat. If the actions of John the Baptist were threatening enough, those of Jesus were even more disturbing to the status quo.

By the time of Jesus, the solemnities of *yom kippur* – 'The Day of Atonement' were the most vivid expression of reconciliation and covenant renewal with YHWH. Uniquely on that day, the High Priest entered in behind the veil of the Temple to the Holy of Holies – the place of YHWH's presence on earth. There he renewed the covenant with the blood of an animal offered in sacrifice for the sins of the people. It is clear that the Jesus movement took this imagery on and explicitly applied it to what had been accomplished by the crucified Messiah. The theologizing of reconciliation is well expressed in Ephesians:

> But now in Christ Jesus you who once were far off have been brought near by the blood of Christ. For he is our peace; in his flesh he has made both groups into one and has broken down the dividing wall, that is, the hostility between us. He has abolished the law with its commandments and ordinances, so that he might create in himself one new humanity in place of the two, thus making peace, and might reconcile both groups to God in one body through the cross, thus putting to death that hostility through it. So he came and proclaimed peace to you who were far off and peace to those who were near; for through him both of us have access in one Spirit to the Father. So then you are no longer strangers and aliens, but you are citizens with the saints and also members of the household of God, built upon the foundation of the apostles and prophets, with Christ Jesus himself as the cornerstone. In him the whole structure is joined together and grows into a holy temple in the Lord; in whom you also are built together spiritually into a dwelling-place for God. (Eph 2:13-22)

If the first strand of thinking emphasises Jesus replacing the Temple, replacing the sacrifices, being the new and eternal High Priest, the second strand theologizes the Church as the embodiment of his continuing presence, with the parallel commission to be and do the same. Once again the Church became understood as the primary expression of the theological reality of reconciliation, the community of the Elect whose robes had been washed white in the blood of the Lamb. As time elapsed, however, the problem of misdemeanour and unholy living among the baptized white robed army of the Jesus movement presented itself. This may have generally been dealt with by admonition, commitment to fraternal harmony and the prayers of elders in the community. Within two hundred years, however, a very public and arduous sacramental system of Penance had developed. The sinner, either at the request of the community or by their own desire was enrolled in the order of Penitents and excluded from Eucharist while enduring a period of classic spiritual discipline – that is, prayer, fasting and almsgiving. The period of exclusion seems, logically, to have depended on the severity of the sin. More shocking to the modern mind were the restrictions, namely, that the sacrament could only be received once in a lifetime and that besides being banned from military service, the reconciled sinner might be asked to remain celibate for the rest of their life.

While modern sport has copied this ancient idea of a 'sin bin' for misdemeanours, it is unlikely that compulsory celibacy will form part of its punishments anytime soon. Meanwhile, back in the day it was from the edges of Christendom that a different, more pastoral solution was proposed. As Celtic and Anglo-Saxon monks flooded Europe through the sixth and seventh centuries, they brought with them a new system of reconciliation in their famous 'Penitential Books' which had the tariffs for iniquities outlined in some detail. Although this still included public fasting, abstinence and almsgiving, the confession of the actual sins was done in secret. Perhaps more significantly, the absolution from the sin migrated from the end of the penance to the beginning. In the West, by the time of the Lateran Council IV of 1215, individual private confession to a priest with individual private penance was not only the norm but was the recommended pattern to be undergone by all the faithful at least once a year. For many centuries in the East, the confession of sins was more associated with what might be called spiritual direction and associated with the strong monastic tradition but eventually took on something of a similar shape.

Like any ancient model of 'satisfaction' or 'punishment', the problem of balancing mercy and justice was a key theological conundrum. In order to shorten the time spent in penitential mode, intense prayer, pilgrimage or remittance through charitable donation became theologically acceptable options. Through the power of the Church to grant pardon, it was a short step for the notion of special occasions, 'indulgent moments of grace' to become attached to pilgrimages, shrines and special feasts or celebrations. Unfortunately, these 'indulgences' which started out as a lovely idea of gratuitous blessing and reconciliation with God were destined to become a vexatious and divisive issue among believers during the Reformation (see Section 18d below).

f) Extreme unction

Linked to the notion of reconciliation but with a distinct aspect was 'Extreme Unction'. Recently, this sacrament has had something of a makeover and been renamed 'Anointing of the Sick'. This is good news pastorally and theologically since for centuries these 'last rites' were as much a signal that the Grim Reaper was in town as that there was hope of healing for an ailing Christian. Whatever the 'death-prep' emphasis that had crept into scholastic thinking, the roots of 'unction' in the ministry of Jesus were clear. Miracles are a major feature of the Gospel and apostolic traditions. As noted above, Section 6d, even extra-biblical literature refers to Jesus as a *thaumaturg* – 'wonder worker' – and the practice of anointing has clear New Testament roots where James advises:

> Are any among you suffering? They should pray. Are any cheerful? They should sing songs of praise. Are any among you sick? They should call for the elders of the church and have them pray over them, anointing them with oil in the name of the Lord. The prayer of faith will save the sick, and the Lord will raise them up; and anyone who has committed sins will be forgiven. Therefore confess your sins to one another, and pray for one another, so that you may be healed. (Jas 5:13-16, cf. Mark 6:13)

Present in the *Apostolic Tradition* of Hippolytus (d.236), the practice of the sacrament seems to have been accompanied by expectation of recovery for several centuries. Already by Augustine's time there was debate over what had happened to the healing ministry of the Church which had done 'even greater things' than Christ in its early days (John 14:12). The general line was that the Church had needed spectacular powers in order to attract the attention of a sceptical world which were now unnecessary due to its success in spreading the Gospel. As time went on, not least because of the connection with absolution, the sacrament was increasingly postponed until death was near and recovery unlikely – hence the emergence of the term 'extreme unction'. For centuries in the West, absolution, anointing and communion constituted the perfect sacramental preparation for death – the Last Rites:

- Freed from sin by sacramental absolution (Last Confession).
- Anointed, like Jesus, in preparation for death (Extreme Unction).
- Receiving the bread of life as *viaticum* food for the final journey (Final Communion).

In the East, the sacrament of euchelaion – 'prayer oil' had more readily remained associated with physical well-being though it also could be received as a preparation for communion, particularly during Holy Week. Meanwhile, although it was theologically unintentional, the practice whereby Unction was gradually pushed towards the end of life and Baptism to its beginning meant that the sacraments, as set out by the scholastics, began to look increasingly like the classic rites of passage so common across a variety of religious cultures, especially since the sacred seven included Matrimony and Holy Orders at life's decision junction.

g) Marriage

From the earliest times, the exclusive and permanent nature of marriage within the Jesus movement seems to have been problematic against a Hebrew background which privileged the status of the husband (Matt 19:4-6). The ancient tradition tolerated polygamy and concubinage among the Patriarchs (Gen 16:1-15, 29:15-35). The Torah of Moses, while resistant to the buying and selling of wives, emphasized the power of the husband insofar as he was the only one who could issue writs of divorce (cf. Ex 21:7 and Deut 24:1). Inheritance rights were withheld and the vulnerable state of widows and rejected women provides the backdrop to some of the most troubling passages in the ancient texts (cf. Gen 38 and Ruth 1). That said, beautiful spousal imagery is present in Genesis where male and female are said to image God (Gen 1:28, 2:18) and poetic peaks are likewise reached in Hos 2:14-23 and throughout the Song of Songs.

In fairness, by the time of Jesus, monogamy was much the most common practice in Judean tradition but it is also worth noting that it was also a period which manifested a fascination with asceticism and celibacy, especially among the Essenes. This perhaps explains why, in the Gospels, there seems to be evidence that Jesus, like Paul, gives off mixed messages regarding the importance of marriage and family life.

a) As a messianic/ end time movement, marriage is seen as a temporary, earth-bound arrangement (cf. Mark 12:25 and Matt 22:30).

b) As a holiness/exemplary movement, both the Jesus tradition and the writings of Paul emphasize the exclusivity and permanence of matrimony (Matt 19:1-12 and 1 Cor 7:1-16).

While the New Testament does seem to allow certain reasons why separation might take place, testimony regarding the early communities does seem to profile exclusive, monogamous, permanent Christian marriage as one of its distinctive features. As noted above (Section 15g), Rodney Stark includes the social side effects of health and fecundity of the Christian family unit as part of his explanation for its success. Although the ready availability of divorce and the restrictions of marriage between social classes did not sit so well with Christian thinking, other Roman imperial traditions were amenable. The legal framework of Roman marital law subscribed to the ideal of its lifelong, exclusive nature while 'consent and consummation' have remained factors in its governance within the Church.

Despite Cana being the first 'sign' in John's Gospel (2:1-11), the notion that marriage was in itself *sacramental* appears to have been a little late in developing. Augustine is sometimes criticized for regarding it in a negative light as a necessary cure for avoiding sexual sin (following 1 Cor 7:9), though this is a somewhat thin reading of his views. Hincmar of Rheims (d.882) is credited with affirming the dignity of the sacrament and by the time Peter Lombard was writing his *Sentences*, we find it included and thoroughly discussed in his famous sevenfold system, cf. Rosemann, 2004, pp.172-178. The Lombard also engagingly defends the notion of equality between the sexes from the Genesis account.

> Woman was made from man, not from any part of the man's body, but she was formed from his side, so that there might be shown, that she was created in a partnership of love, lest perchance, if she had been made from his head, she might seem to be preferred to man for his domination, or if from his feet, to be subjected to him for his service. (*Sentences* Bk. II Dist. XVIII c.2)

The sacrament of marriage was unusual since it was conferred by the Christian spouses through the priesthood of their own Baptism. By entering into their covenant of mutual self-giving, the minister acted only as witness. Theoretically, the triple purpose of marriage – 'fidelity, children, union' could be understood as mimetic of the Trinitarian mystery which is eternal, generative and unifying. It was less successfully understood, however, as an 'imitation of Christ' which was perceived as the most immediate path to holiness. And by the scholastic period, to imitate Jesus most readily was to reject marriage, choose celibacy and to receive the sacrament of Holy Orders.

h) Holy Orders

The formal ministerial roles in the Church seem to have evolved relatively swiftly from the core group of Twelve apostles to embrace categories of servant leadership of *diakonoi* – deacons, *presbyteroi* – elders and *episkopoi* – bishops.

The commissioning of these various roles is attested at different points in the New Testament (cf. Acts 6:6, 14:23, 20:28). It is clear from the anxieties of Paul that the link to Christ and the Twelve was already identified as a feature of authentic leadership, a point confirmed by the letter of Clement who was Peter's third successor as fourth overseer of the Roman community (1 Clement 42-44) While there are indications of prophetic and charismatic forms of leadership (cf. 1 Cor 12:10), the basic threefold pattern of order is passionately advocated by Ignatius of Antioch (c.100 CE) as a protection against heretical thinking and community division, (see above, Section 15d).

Given the significance attached to apostolic succession, it is somewhat appropriate that one of the earliest examples of ordination rites comes from *The Apostolic Tradition* of Hippolytus (c.215). While it includes an element of democracy long lost to the Church in the form of episcopal election, it exemplifies already a threefold consecration which articulates the specific roles of bishops, presbyters and deacons. That said, it is important to note that the increasing consciousness of order neither restricted other forms of ministry developing, nor did it imply supine quiescence on the part of the 'normal' believer. The increasing responsibilities of the Bishop or 'overseer' demanded multiple forms of assistance (e.g. sub-deacon, acolyte, exorcist, reader and doorkeeper). Moreover, in the age of martyrdom and fervent witness, all believers were conceived as 'saints', a royal priesthood, offering a lifelong sacrifice of praise to God (1 Pet 2:9).

As time went on, however, while a re-emphasis of the 'priesthood of all believers' would be something of a rallying cry of the sixteenth-century reformers, the intervening centuries were characterized by an increasing distinction between clergy and laypeople. The association of celibacy with the clerical state probably did not help in this regard. Though sometimes imagined to be a medieval invention, the tradition of celibacy is easily connected to the Gospel tradition. There is no credible evidence that Jesus was married and his itinerant lifestyle with 'nowhere to lay his head' connects his ministry more immediately with figures from the prophetic tradition (Matt 8:20). As noted *ad nauseum,* both Essene influence and 'end time' thinking associated with the proclamation of the Kingdom mitigated against family commitment. Moreover, Jesus seems to deliberately challenge the overriding power of the family-clan system with its implicit honour-shame structures. When Peter remarks 'It is better not to marry', Jesus does not contradict him but enigmatically replies that 'Some men are born eunuchs, some are made eunuchs and some are eunuchs for the sake of the Kingdom of God' (Matt 19:12). While Paul specifically says that celibacy was not handed on as a command of the Lord, his own personal example and preferences are clear, despite the choices made by other leaders (1 Cor 7:7, 9:3).

If anything, the development of monasticism, the esteem held for virginity and the lifestyle choices of influential figures such as Basil, Augustine and others, cemented the ideal of celibacy as the preferred clerical state. Given that there was a theological suspicion that even marital intercourse was sinful, and a practical suspicion that Church property might be dissipated by the inheritance claims of clergy children, married clerics were very much in the minority in the West when Pope Gregory VII (1073–1085) took canonical measures to enforce celibacy in 1074. By the time high scholasticism was in its pomp, vows of poverty, chastity and obedience (rejecting greed, lust and power) were a well-trodden path for the numerous men and women entering religious communities. Though diocesan bishops and priests were allowed to own property and land, celibacy had become a condition for entering Holy Orders. Hence while forms of devotion among lay-movements such as the guilds of medieval Europe were an aspect of common piety, the scholastic theologians emphasized that since ministers of the sacraments were the graced life-source of the community, they were to all intents and purposes ordained custodians of human destiny.

If that were true on the local level, then it was all the more vivid on the universal scale where in the authority of Peter, the sacrament of orders found its most complete expression. On the one hand, the office of the successor of Peter was understood as the symbol of the unity of the Church, the rock on which it was built, the original recipient and conveyor of the apostolic tradition which guaranteed all ministry as deriving from the Lord (Matt 16:16-19). On the other, the all encompassing power which divine authority seemed to have endowed to the Church meant that there were inevitable tensions with the emerging political entities which would become the future nations of Europe. Through the deliberations of synods and the judgements of Councils, the Church had its own legislative regulations – 'Canon Law'. This included the power to declare the cessation of the celebration of sacraments or 'interdict' not just on churches of a single city but on entire regions. Carrying economic as well as religious consequences, by the High Middle Ages 'interdict' had been variously imposed as a penalty on whole populations, including Scotland, France and England. Yet while this was problematic, it was not schismatic. Instead the threat to the unity of the Church would come from papal-patriarchal conflict East and West and the later crisis of authority caused by the European Reform. Ultimately, the sacred cohering power of Holy Orders yielded to ecclesiastical disorder.

Understood institutionally, it would signify organizational incompetence – a human failure. Understood sacramentally, it would signify dismemberment of the Body of Christ – a sacred tragedy.

Summary

And Jesus came and said to them, "All authority in heaven and on earth has been given to me. Go therefore and make disciples of all nations, baptizing them in the name of the Father and of the Son and of the Holy Spirit, and teaching them to obey everything that I have commanded you. And remember, I am with you always, to the end of the age." (Matt 28:18)

Sacraments simply understood were ritual moments of caritas – *Jesus love. Though governed from their apostolic beginnings by the authority of designated ministers, they were understood theologically to be actions instituted and effected by Christ for the permanent sanctification of the Church. 'Grace in action', the sacraments patterned a liturgy of life but were not identical with rites of passage since Baptism and Unction only gradually became associated with the beginning and the end of life. In the Middle Ages, Peter Lombard's formulation of seven sacraments became the traditional template for Western practice and theological reflection. This period saw 'faith seeking understanding' most vividly in the exploration of the eucharistic mystery which yielded new doctrinal terminology including 'transubstantiation'. Ultimately, the governance of the whole 'sacramental economy' was conducted under Petrine authority working through the agency of local bishops and their clergy. It was the exercise of this 'holy order' that would come under increasing strain as tensions between East and West and, subsequently North and South, took their toll.*

18

Ecclesiology in Three Dimensions

The great creedal formula of Nicaea-Constantinople summarized Christian ecclesiology ('Church logic') as 'One, Holy, Catholic and Apostolic.' Entered into through Baptism, reaching its most intense expression in Eucharist it was structured by the sacrament of Holy Orders. Though the Petrine office constituted the foundation and apex of ecclesiastical authority for a thousand years, it was complemented by the spiritual power of the great monastic and religious traditions. The united nature of 'Christendom' of this time owed much to its underlying substructure of theological and political cohesion guaranteed by Church and Empire. As the centuries passed, a series of challenges began to fracture this coherence such that Eastern and Western Christianity was sundered by disagreements over creed and communion, the very symbols of unity. The nations and monarchs of Europe became increasingly independent of papal power just as humanism and the new learning of the Renaissance cultivated independent thinking. These new conditions permitted the irruption that was the Protestant Reformation which left a radically changed map of Christianity and a divided Church more three than one.

a) One, Holy, Catholic, Apostolic?

In the creed of Constantinople 381, the self-understanding of the Church was articulated as '*one, holy, catholic* and *apostolic*' These theological characteristics were based on *one-ness* in faith as the Body of Christ, *holy-ness* through the presence of the life-giving Spirit of God, *universal-ness (catholic)* because it was a worldwide community and *apostolicity* because it held the very same divine authority entrusted by Jesus to the Twelve. However this might be understood in prayer or in theory, the visible structure which safeguarded this identity was the network of diocesan bishops with jurisdiction over cities and their hinterlands. Through regional gatherings (synods) and the Ecumenical Councils, Church governance transcended local boundaries. Theologians such as Cyprian (d.258) with a highly developed ecclesiology could propose that *extram ecclesiam nulla salus* – 'outside the Church there is no salvation' and that 'he who has not the Church as his mother cannot have God as his Father' (Johnson, 2005, p. 76). At the apex of this hierarchy of authority was the Pope, successor of Peter, Bishop of Rome, such that for a thousand years the Church could, with some caveats, claim to have maintained the verity of this creedal formula. There had been some knotty problems and difficult moments along the way, but there was still visible communion between the great traditions of East and West, even if by the end of the first millennium, they *looked* very different.

The classic distinction made between the theological traditions of the West and the East is that while the Roman – Latin regions of the Church sought to express the truths of God explicitly or *kataphatically* – 'according to the revelation', the Byzantine – Greek zones were more mystical and emphasized the *apophatic* – 'inexpressibility' of God. It is an over-simplification, but perhaps due to the influence of Roman law, the precision theologies of the West tended to focus on juridical understandings of the faith with one eye on the final judgement. Hence the arguments between Augustine and Pelagius on sin and its damning effects, hence the development of salvific satisfaction in Anselm, hence the tightly argued sacramental thinking of Thomas' *Summa Theologiae*. Holding all this together was a theological matrix focused on the Cross – *crux Christi probat omnia* – 'The Cross of Christ is the test of all things', a motif which emphasized the re-presentation of Calvary.

The East, by contrast, was more focused on birth and resurrection. It wasn't that they missed out the Cross, they just (quite reasonably) didn't stay there. The task of life was *apotheosis* – divinization by the Holy Spirit. Sin understood as *hamartia* was 'missing the mark', a sense of falling short of what is possible rather than acquiring penalty points on a driving licence. The great father of Eastern thinking was Origen, master of allegory and an imaginative theologian. Although even his own tradition rejected Origen's idea of *apokatastasis* – the ultimate reconciliation of ALL things cosmically collapsing into God – it was indicative of a line of thought which increasingly used iconography of Jesus as *Christos Pantokrator* – Christ the All-Creator, complete with symbols of imperial and universal power. It was in the Eastern Church that the idea of the *perichoresis* – 'the eternal dance' of love became a favoured theological conceptualization of Trinity while eucharistic tradition generated elaborate liturgies, rich in symbolism of the heavenly places.

b) The Great Schism

Meanwhile, although there were some Eastern criticisms of the West such as the eating of dairy products during Lent and the insistence on priestly celibacy, two crises that occurred towards the end of the first millennium concerning art and belief proved much more serious. In the Eastern tradition, the depiction of Christ and the saints by means of 'icons' (heavily symbolized oil paintings on wood) had become one of its most striking features. Conveying truths to the illiterate as a book to the literate, they were venerated widely in churches, monasteries and homes. Unfortunately, partly based on the kinds of injunctions found in the Torah, and partly due to growing Islamic influence in some provinces of the Empire, antipathy towards imagery developed. In Byzantium, theological disquiet had often led to political action and in 726, Emperor Leo III banned the use of icons and ordered their destruction. A century of turmoil was to follow. Monks and laypeople protested vehemently against the *iconoclasts* – 'image breakers'. A persecution was unleashed and the Patriarch was deposed. A succession of Emperors tried to enforce the ban and Constantine V called a Synod at Hieria in 753 to rubber stamp the policy and though neither the Pope, nor the Patriarchs of Jerusalem, Alexandria or Antioch attended, the gathering went ahead. Theologically, the justification given by the iconoclasts was that in depicting the human face of Christ those who venerated icons were heretical because by only honouring one aspect of the mystery (the human) they were guilty of dividing the Lord's nature. The other images of saints and the Virgin Mary were simply idolatrous and were to be destroyed.

Rome was supportive of traditional veneration and the iconoclasts had already been condemned there as early as 731, but the action had little effect. The impotence of the papacy in the matter was evident even when Pope

Hadrian sent delegates to the Second Council of Nicaea in 787. Again the gathering of bishops found against the imperial policies, but still to no avail. Ultimately, the crisis did not end until the death of Emperor Theophilus in 842, and the subsequent restoration of their icons on the First Sunday of Lent by the Patriarch Methodius in 843 has since become a great feast of Orthodoxy. Unfortunately, a quirk of history meant the papal support for the Eastern iconography tradition led to a deterioration in the relationship between Rome and the Emperors of Byzantium which in turn rebounded on the relationship between the papacy and the patriarchs. Estranged from its historical support in the East, papal power and authority became dependent upon the burgeoning strength of the Carolingian dynasty of the Franks in the West. In this regard, Pepin the Short's defeat of the Lombards at Rome's request in 755 cast a long shadow, leading directly to the papacy becoming a provincial political power. The formation of the 'Papal States' embroiled the successors of Peter directly in civic governance for over a thousand years until Italian reunification was completed by Garibaldi in 1870. Henceforth, a succession of Popes needed to be sensitive to political alliances and since the French were the new power in the European playground, there was only one way to look. By crowning Charlemagne 'Holy Roman Emperor' in 800, the die was cast. Since the time of Constantine, there had been an East – West political underpinning to Church unity. By severing that foundational link, the gesture made the two traditions more vulnerable to theological tremors which reached seismic levels during the *filioque* crisis.

Though the Nicene-Constantinople creed had stated that the Holy Spirit proceeded 'from the Father', a tradition began in the West whereby *filioque* 'and the Son' was added to the clause. Though it was first formally set down at the Council of Toledo in 589, it was only at the beginning of the ninth century that a storm began to brew. By now this addition had found its way into songs, and as any Church goer knows, you can tolerate the odd dodgy sermon, but you can't mess around with the congregation's favourite hymns. The introduction of the practice by French monks in Jerusalem was protested by the Eastern rite monastery of St Sabas in 807. Appeal was made to Pope Leo III, who tried to steer a middle course by approving the doctrine of *filioque* while endorsing the original language of the creed and to that end, he deposited engraved silver tablets of the original Nicene-Constantinople creed at the tomb of St Peter. But the years passed and the singers did not fall silent. By 1000, *filioque* had become a standard clause in the creed as prayed in the Western Church.

Though a theological case could be made that the Spirit be understood as love proceeding from love in the mutuality of the Father and the Son, it did provide Eastern theologians and Eastern patriarchs with a doctrinal bazooka to fire. Tetchy interference in local Eastern rite Churches in Sicily brought tit-for-tat retaliations in oriental Mediterranean provinces. Fingers on the trigger, the final schism came when the strong minded Pope Leo IX (1048–1054) clashed with the equally formidable Michael Keroularius (Patriarch of Constantinople, 1043–1058). Theologically, the immediate pretext concerned whether leavened or unleavened bread should be used at communion. Equally biblical, the unleavened bread had the advantage of not dropping so many crumbs at the distribution, a matter which had become more sensitive in the West due to the developing theologies of eucharistic realism noted above (Section 17d). Unfortunately, the outcome left more than scattered crumbs. In 1054, a delegation led by Cardinal Humbert was sent to Constantinople, which took the drastic step of excommunicating Michael in his own cathedral, the famous basilica of *Hagia Sophia* – Holy Wisdom. Although the excommunication was personal to Michael and his associates, it effectively fractured the communion of the Church and the anathemas of Rome were returned in kind by Constantinople. The 'Great Schism' of 1054 effectively sundered the Church in two and sullied relations for a thousand years. And if there wasn't sadness enough already, any chance of reconciliation in the centuries that followed was effectively derailed by the heroic, misguided and bloody tragedy of the Crusades.

c) Crusades

There is a shadow side to youthful enthusiasm. The same energetic idealistic dynamism which can change the world can also destroy what it seeks to change. This propensity is illustrated graphically and tragically by the Crusades and the emergence of the Knights Templar. By the turn of the millennium, a militant and missionary Islam had swept through many of the ancient territories of the Southern Mediterranean which had once been predominantly Christian. Part of the theological attraction of the Islamic synthesis was that it emphasized the One God of Judaism while still venerating the prophetic work of Jesus and the role of Mary as maternal archetype. In addition to the attractiveness of the theological package, there was also survival to consider. Though the extent to which local populations of Jews or Christians were coerced by the invading armies probably varied from place to place, one of the side effects of the expansion of Islam was that the sacred places of Jerusalem and the Holy Land were no longer under Jewish or Christian suzerainty. Although theologically, Christianity's early success was due precisely to it not being wedded to a particular sacred place such as the Temple in Jerusalem, a tribal desire to regain what had once belonged began to simmer. Pilgrimages to the Holy Land had been a feature of devotional life since the journeys of Constantine's mother, Helena, in the fourth century. But by 1071, the military aggression of Seljuk Turks on the frontiers of Eastern Christendom was not only menacing the political and religious stability of the region, safe passage to Jerusalem was becoming impossible.

In 1095, the first crusade was preached by Pope Urban II. Linking the high-minded ideals of religious sacrifice with more basic warrior instincts proved an attractive combination to young knights in need of a cause to live and die for. While heavenly promises of indulgences and the martyr's crown were one side of the coin, the prospect of more earthly rewards in the form of lands and estates in the sun-kissed East also helped to mint the idea. In the confusion of the following centuries, Jerusalem changed hands several times and for a short period the 'Frankish East' was a geographical and political reality. In truth, two centuries of invasions, sieges, sacks and sacrileges left almost nothing changed except levels of mutual resentment and bitterness. By the time the last Latin outpost fell in 1291, the Western Church and Islam had drawn battle lines that some would claim exist even today. Moreover, turns of treachery such as the destruction of Constantinople (1204) left the Eastern Church as well as Diaspora Judaism in the confused state of not knowing whether the Papal tiara or the Sultan's turban was the most trustworthy symbol of allegiance.

In the midst of all this were the 'Poor Knights of Christ and of the Temple of Solomon' – the Knights Templar. Founded in Jerusalem, c.1120, they undertook protection for pilgrims against bandits. Quickly gaining ecclesiastical approval and much encouraged by the legendarily influential St Bernard of Clairvaux (1090–1153), they flourished in numbers, wealth and military strength. Central figures in the enterprise of the Crusades, their huge castle-monasteries were the last outposts of the ill-fated Frankish East to fall. Despite their storied bravery, their end came not quite at the hand of the Turk, but at the hand of the French king Philip the Fair, who was both threatened and tempted by their wealth and influence. A quiescent Pope Clement V did not protect them from capital charges of heresy and immorality, and the Order was violently suppressed in 1312. It is likely that on the substantive charges brought against them, the Templars were fundamentally innocent. (Dan Brown's *Da Vinci Code* was not the first wild fantasy conceived in their regard!) They did, however, become a motif for military Christianity which historians have at turns praised and pilloried. In the current pillory phase, it is perhaps important to recall that the theologically dubious symbolism of cross and conquest had its first outing at Constantine's victory at the Milvian Bridge.

Though contemporary Christian Theology is increasingly proposing non-violence as the essential Gospel stance, the notion of Holy War has proved to be as much a part of Church history as it has in the Jewish traditions of Joshua and the military heritage of Islam.

d) The European reform: Martin Luther

Although losing control of biblical lands was a blow to the self-confidence of the Western military tradition, it did nothing to curtail the ecclesiological self-confidence of the Papacy nor the intellectual advance of Latin Theology, by now generating ever broader interests through the universities that it helped to create. The scintillating effects of both the pastoral and academic traditions of the Franciscans and Dominicans in the High Middle Ages mark this as something of a high water-mark for the Western Church. Throughout Europe, festivals and fasts of the liturgical year marked the very pattern of life. In England, for example, colourful devotions like the Corpus Christi processions and theatrical events such as the Lenten mystery plays were entertaining ways of conveying theological truths. In literature Chaucer's *Canterbury Tales* and Dante's *Divina Commedia* both wrestled brilliantly with the drama of sin and redemption, marking turning points in the linguistic evolution of English and Italian, respectively.

As the years turned and Europe's population grew again following the Black Death, a swirl of artistic activity left behind the stilted lines of the medieval past as sculpture and painting rediscovered the realism of classical Greece and Rome. Despite a troubled sojourn in Avignon (1309–1376), the Papal court became one of the great sponsors of this *renaissance* – 'rebirth' of the classical art. Given brilliant expression in Florence and Rome through the genius of Lippi, Botticelli, Titian, Raphael, Cellini and Michelangelo, the creativity of the moment was symbolized by the rebuilding of St Peter's on the Vatican Hill where the leader of the apostles had been martyred fifteen centuries earlier. All rather wonderful. But 1517 would change all that. A priest theologian, Martin Luther, invited another priest theologian, Johann Tetzel, to a public university disputation. No big deal? Well, within a hundred years the sequence of events triggered not only tore apart the Western Church but, with much bloodshed, had done much the same to Europe itself. And ironically the argument was about God's mercy.

The spark that lit the fires of the Reformation was the sale of indulgences by Johan Tetzel, an itinerant Dominican sent on tour to raise funds for the rebuilding of St Peter's. As noted above, Section 17e, though indulgences were a generally positive idea, the minute they became 'grace for sale' was the minute they risked the charge (*sic*) of simony. In an era when life was fairly short and death fairly near, anxiety about eternal destiny was theologically logical so to speak. Indulgences were sold as remittance of 'time' spent in Purgatory. Although nowhere mentioned in the biblical tradition, the theological idea of Purgatory arose quite naturally from the constant tradition of praying for the dead attested in both the East and the West. If there were only two doors at death, one granting the immediate beatific vision of God and the other being eternal damnation, praying for the departed soul made no sense since there was no traffic between the two. Hence the theological proposal of an interim state evolved, a place where one could undergo a final preparatory purification or 'purgation' from sin. Purgatory also fitted well with the vivid sense of solidarity between the living and those beyond the curtain of death, still united in the 'communion of saints'. Prayers of consolation and mitigation from the earthly side of the veil for souls awaiting final bliss were acts of charity of which those left behind were very mindful. Attested to in the works of Augustine among others (cf. *City of God,* 21:13), by 1500, Purgatory was theologically well established and by all accounts, pretty busy.

As an Augustinian himself, Martin Luther was well aware of the teachings of his founding master. He was familiar, too, with some of the newer ideas emerging from the Renaissance that were breaking free from the theological matrix of Aristotelian and Scholastic thinking which governed the 'sacramental economy' of the Church. As professor of biblical exegesis, Luther seems to have been increasingly caught up in the drama of 'what makes us acceptable to God', so vivid in the ruminations of Paul in Galatians and Romans. As noted above, Paul seems to have broadly rejected the notion of 'performance religion', which ran the risk of fallen human nature turning in on itself. If a believer can stand before God on his own two holy feet, then the sacrifice of Christ has been in vain. No. All are in need of 'salvation' accessible only through faith in Christ. This, it may be recalled, is the basis of the argument that Augustine had used against Pelagius. Its strength is that it guarantees eternal gratitude for God's free gift of love in Christ rather than having heaven full of smug, self-satisfied religious types. The error of the smug is that they think they can earn God's love. The truth of the sinner is that he or she at least knows that they have come up short. Understood as the last moments of a courtroom drama, it works as follows:

- Death brings judgement, all have sinned.
- The only logical conclusion of the court is 'Guilty!'
- Yet at that very moment, the condemned soul is declared innocent!

- Why? Because faith in Christ has 'righteoused' or 'justified' them.
- How? Because just like on Mt. Moriah when Isaac was spared by the ram (Gen 22:13), so Jesus, the Lamb of God has taken away the sin (John 1:29).
- The guilty one is now set free!
- The only response is gratitude in worship and the living of a thankful holy life.

Akin to the conversion of Paul, the sudden liberating realization of this approach was bequeathed to history in Luther's description of the *Turmerlebnis* – his 'Tower Experience' – which occurred during a severe depression in his life, while on the loo. Compelling arguments have been made that suggest this may have been a later, stylized recollection designed to help a confrère struggling with his faith (see MacCulloch, 2009, pp. 604–14). Whatever the location, Luther experienced an overwhelming sense that grace, gratuitous kindness on the part of God had broken down the barrier separating believers from their maker. In this light, indulgences – indeed the whole sacramental system – began to look a little contrived. As a symbolic gesture, Luther pinned 95 objections to indulgences on a church door in Wittenberg on 31 October 1517 (LW 31:193-195). His 'theses' were also sent to his local bishop, who had approved the collection for St Peter's and stood to gain from the fund-raising. A storm gathered. Through 1518, the 'protest' began to gain notoriety throughout Saxony. Although attempts at theological resolution were made, whatever agreement there was between, say, Luther and the somewhat sympathetic Roman delegate Cajetan, unconditional demands to submit to Church authority made Luther increasingly uncomfortable. By now his challenge included the validity of any doctrines not vouchsafed by God's word, whether voiced by Popes or even the General Councils. '*Sola Scriptura*' – 'By Scripture Alone!' – was becoming something of a slogan. His re-thinking of the situation gathered apace and his ideas were disseminated in a trilogy of pamphlets easily reproduced by the new technology of printing presses. As revolutionary as the internet today, the presses enabled Luther's movement to spread like wildfire, drawing sympathizers to his cause as not just authority, but the Church's entire 'economy of salvation' was challenged.

In *An Address to the Christian Nobility of the German People* (LW 44:41-85), Luther challenged the spiritual and temporal authority of the Pope. He questioned whether the Pope should have the last word on the interpretation of the Bible and whether princes should pay tribute to Rome. This rebalancing of power away from hierarchical clericalism towards the laity was further emphasized by the call for a general council of the people, the abolition of celibacy and Masses for the dead. For centuries, probably for very obvious hygienic and practical reasons, the Eucharist in the West was shared with the congregation by means of the bread only. In his *Babylonian Captivity of the Church* (LW 36:3-126) Luther saw this as another false distinction between clergy and laity which led him to review the whole sacramental system, denying its importance apart from Baptism and Eucharist. The latter was not to be understood as sacrificial and the real presence was not to be understood as transubstantial, which as far as Luther was concerned was bad Philosophy as well as bad Theology. Finally, *On Christian Liberty* (LW 31:327-77) turned attention to the classic 'grace v works' dilemma already contrasted in the New Testament views of James and Paul, but in this extract answered using his knowledge of Peter and John:

> Wherefore it ought to be the first concern of every Christian to lay aside all confidence in works and increasingly to strengthen faith alone and through faith to grow in the knowledge, not of works, but of Christ Jesus, who suffered and rose for him, as Peter teaches in the last chapter of his first Epistle (I Pet. 5:10). No other work makes a Christian. Thus when the Jews asked Christ, as related in [John 6:28], what they must do "to be doing the work of God," he brushed aside the multitude of works which he saw they did in great profusion and suggested one work, saying, "This is the work of God, that you believe in him whom he has sent" [John 6:29]; "for on him has God the Father set his seal" [John 6:27] (LW 31:337).

With some inevitability, a Roman censure arrived in 1520 and Luther promptly set fire to *Exsurge Domini* – a papal bull which likened him to a wild boar. Excommunication was thus inevitable and followed on 3 January 1521.

Dark though the clouds gathered, a major hope for reconciliation at the time was the accession of Charles V. As occupant of the thrones of Spain and of the Holy Roman Empire, Charles had jurisdiction over a huge swathe of Europe, which included the Netherlands, parts of Italy and the federal, semi-independent provinces of Germany and the Balkans. In 1521, reminiscent of Constantine's attempts to reconcile the Arian crisis, the young Emperor called Luther to the Diet of Worms, which, despite its name, had reconciliation not punishment on the menu. The Diet was a council of the 'Electors' who ruled the German provinces and on this occasion included representatives both from the Church and the 'protesting' side. This was a nervous moment for Luther. Inquisitions, witch-hunts and trials for heresy did not normally end well. A century earlier, the Bohemian John Hus (1369–1415) had challenged authority with grave consequences. Promised safety, Hus had entered such a disputation and had 'lost' the argument. Not only was he executed, his long dead English mentor, John Wycliffe (1330–84) was later disinterred, tried and burnt as well! In the event, Charles' guarantee of safety held good in the face of

Luther's refusal to recant. Although it cannot be entirely confirmed that Luther actually uttered the famous words *Hier stehe ich. Ich kann nicht anders* – 'Here I stand. I can do no other' he soon (wisely) was on the move.

Failure to resolve matters at Worms meant Luther was put under the ban of the Empire which, true to post-Constantinian theological tradition, linked arms with the Church. In hiding and with a false I.D. of 'Farmer George', Luther commenced his translation of the Bible, an enduring contribution to Christian Theology and a defining moment for the German language. He published the New Testament as early as September 1522, followed later by a liturgical translation of the Eucharist in 1526. Such works enabled the movement to spread despite the tumult of the situation. There were inevitably tensions and estrangements from early sympathizers such as Erasmus of Rotterdam, who had looked for a more humanist, reason-driven reform of the Church rather than one fuelled by an Augustinian-Pauline fervour. Erasmus was a talented writer whose *In Praise of Folly* (1509) had cleverly pointed the finger at ecclesiastical corruption, but to him the movement was too pessimistic with regard to human potential, since it regarded reason as fatally fallen. Others worked more closely with Luther, especially Philip Melancthon. By 1530, at the Diet of Augsburg, partly designed to appease a furious Emperor, the outlines of a recognizably distinctive doctrinal church were presented by Philip. Well before Luther's death in 1546 with the agreement and protection of local rulers, a new ecclesial entity had arisen in Europe, and by then it was only one of many.

e) The Swiss reform: Zwingli and Calvin

It may seem odd, but in the midst of Luther's revolution, this miner's son at Wittenburg had condemned the so-called Peasants' Revolt (1524–1526), which had mistakenly envisaged the change in the old order as one which would inaugurate a new jubilee, free of tithes, bondage and serfdom. The key theological justification for suppression of the movement was the text from Rom 13:1ff which would prove to be as important as any in the self-understanding of the Reformation:

> Let every person be subject to the governing authorities; for there is no authority except from God, and those authorities that exist have been instituted by God. Therefore whoever resists authority resists what God has appointed, and those who resist will incur judgement. For rulers are not a terror to good conduct, but to bad. Do you wish to have no fear of the authority? Then do what is good, and you will receive its approval; for it is God's servant for your good. But if you do what is wrong, you should be afraid, for the authority does not bear the sword

in vain! It is the servant of God to execute wrath on the wrongdoer. Therefore one must be subject, not only because of wrath but also because of conscience. For the same reason you also pay taxes, for the authorities are God's servants, busy with this very thing. Pay to all what is due to them - taxes to whom taxes are due, revenue to whom revenue is due, respect to whom respect is due, honour to whom honour is due. (Rom 13:1-7)

Like early Christianity, Lutheranism first began to take hold in more populous towns and cities which had no shortage of magistrates, councillors and 'authorities' who, in the face of a disempowered hierarchical Church, were ready to take its place. Nowhere was this more vivid than in Zurich, already a notable city within the Swiss federation which had enjoyed independence from imperial authority since 1499. There, a local pastor, Huldrych Zwingli (1484–1531), began to preach 'salvation by faith' and drew support for his views among the local council. The extent to which Zwingli was influenced by Luther's thinking is unclear, but he could match him for dramatic gestures. By ostentatiously breaking the Lenten fast with a sausage and the discipline of celibacy with a wife, Zwingli's charismatic preaching catalysed the formation of an urban church community governed by the city magistrates. And the idea of such a group of ersatz elders deciding doctrine unhindered by theologians, priests, monks or popes would make Luther's organizational model look normal.

The first decision following debate was the removal of all sacred images from churches and waysides. Iconoclasm had returned and the even more radical step of banning Mass followed. If sacrament meant 'oath' – the swearing of covenant – then rituals could be dispensed with since the true pledge of covenant belonging constituted the essential sacrament of the believing Church. Baptism became community-welcome, not an act of God, Eucharist a symbolic commemoration but essentially a human gesture. Luther could scarcely believe what he was hearing from Switzerland and disputed vociferously with Zwingli, whom he regarded as more in error than the Pope.

Undeterred by excommunication in 1525, Zwingli's reform was under way, though like many a revolution, it wasn't very tolerant. Let loose to think and consider biblical texts anew, some concluded that since infant baptism was not commanded in the New Testament, they should be re-baptized in acknowledgement of their adult faith commitment. The practice was not approved in Zurich, and after the execution of four *Anabaptists* ('again baptized ones'), groups of believers were soon taking refuge in rural enclaves and experimenting with communitarian living based on Acts 2:42. The period saw a whole series of minority holiness groups develop which proved forerunners of Church communities still present today such as the Mennonite and Moravian traditions. But it was also a violent time, a period when even popes and Zwingli himself felt free to don the armour of battle. Killed in 1530, contesting with princes from the Catholic cantons at Keppel, Zwingli's flame was extinguished. Phase One of the Swiss reform was over, but in Geneva an equally significant figure was about to carry on the torch.

Having trained for both the priesthood and the law, John Calvin (1509–1564) was perhaps uniquely equipped to find a synthesis of new thinking and new organization necessary to harness the enthusiasm of early reform. He himself had experienced a conversion in 1533 and feeling called to purify the Church, he spent time in Basel, Geneva and Strasbourg, where he came under the influence of the reformist Martin Bucer (1491–1551). Leading a Zurich-style civic-church experiment, Bucer had a definite leadership structure in place which included pastors, elders and deacons, a pattern Calvin would later copy. When the reform at Strasbourg was suppressed, Calvin returned to Geneva where he was soon in a leadership role. From the age of 26 he had begun to compose the *Institutes of the Christian Religion* which he continued to revise until 1559 and proved to be one of the most important theological treatises of the Western Church. With Romans 13 firmly in mind, Geneva's civil governance could be theologically understood as divinely ordained. In the years 1541–1555, Calvin was thus able with clear conscience to experiment with *theocracy* – 'governance by God'. With the master matrix modelled on the very nature of Christ himself (the divine and human natures united in one person), Calvin went about his life's work.

In Geneva, all citizens were understood to be members of the Elect, but leadership was entrusted to pastors, theologians, elders and deacons. Calvin had not been at all impressed by the chaotic reform happenings such as the crazed New Jerusalem inaugurated in Munster by John of Leyden (1509–1536), which, after becoming dubiously sexualized and violent, had been suppressed by surrounding nobles. Since the administration of matters civic and religious was integrated, 'church' power was immediate and as able to regulate the private lives of citizens as it was to regulate the public squares. In Geneva, religious conformity could be immediately imposed and during the theocracy, well over a hundred citizens paid the price for dissent in either execution or exile. The most infamous example was the case of Michael Servetus from Navarre, on the borders of France and Spain. A reform-minded thinker, Michael had read the *Institutes* but returned it with critical comments to Calvin. Forced to flee the Inquisition in Spain, he arrived in Geneva only to be immediately tried as a heretic and burned at the stake in 1555.

Such incidents confirmed, were it necessary, that Calvin's reform movement was of serious purpose. Calvin saw the Geneva reform as recapturing the purity of early Catholicism before it succumbed to the gradual contamination of Constantine's imperial influence. Like Zwingli's Zurich, worship was stripped of any trace of idolatry as stained glass, iconography and statues were all summarily removed from places of worship. God's Godness was the key and the pattern of prayer and sermon took a form more reminiscent of Judaism rather than the elaborate rituals of Western Catholicism and Eastern Orthodoxy. Theologically, Calvin took the classic Pauline-Augustinian line regarding faith and works. Humanity is fallen and doomed to damnation. Only those chosen by Christ and justified by him through their Spirit-given faith are saved. Everyone else is damned. This doctrine of 'Double Pre-destination' did not absent Christians from good works, indeed they are saved precisely *to do* good works, develop honest character and live moral lives. On sacraments he was similarly direct. There is no confusion in Eucharist, the bread remains bread. Against Luther and the Catholics he insists there is no 'real presence', no multiplying of Jesus across the globe. Against Zwingli, however, he insists that the sign is nonetheless effective through the grace of Christ, who draws partaking believers into divine union at the right hand of the Father.

The lucid clarity of Calvin's thinking and the unfussy simplicity of a Church governance led by elders (presbyters), was quick to catch on. Reformed communities took root in the Netherlands. John Knox in Scotland and the Italian, Peter Vermigli also spread a version of the Reform based on Calvin's model which eventually impacted on his beloved France through the Huguenots. Luther's model remained restricted to Northern Europe and Scandinavia. In broadly geographical terms, Southern Europe remained untouched by either. As for England – well – it proved quite another story.

f) English reform

The shape the Reformation took in England was unique across Europe insofar as the monarchy deliberately set the pace at every turn. Yet at Henry VIII's accession in 1509, this would not have seemed likely. Every bit as Catholic as his Spanish wife, Henry was a renaissance prince, a man of many talents, sporting, literary and theological. When the storm of reform caught fire in Germany, there were absolutely no hints that England would be affected. There was lively devotion to the old faith, England was the 'Dowry of Mary' with well-frequented pilgrimage shrines such as Walsingham. Clerical and monastic life was by no means perfect but appeared fairly healthy and generally well regarded. To confirm the loyalty of England, Henry himself wrote a rebuttal of Luther's opinions on the seven sacraments in 1521 for which Pope Leo X awarded him the title 'Defender of the Faith', an honour still recorded on the coinage of the crown to this day.

Unfortunately, Henry also had a problem. He had a daughter, Mary, but his ageing wife had not yet borne him a son and looked increasingly unlikely to. Widow of his own brother, Catherine of Aragon had been somewhat foisted on Henry for dynastic reasons since, as a Spanish princess, she linked the two maritime powers in royal alliance. The story is well known. Henry became impatient and in 1527 began to lobby Rome to allow him to divorce on grounds that the marriage was invalid. Henry became convinced that Lev 18:16 'You shall not uncover the nakedness of your brother's wife' had been transgressed and his lack of a male heir was proof of God's displeasure. Despite a series of sabre rattling gestures designed to intimidate local clergy and make Rome more compliant, majority theological opinion did not agree with an increasingly frustrated Henry, by now in love with Anne Boleyn. Pope Clement found himself caught between pleasing a faraway King (Henry) or a nearby Emperor (Charles V) who happened to be Catherine's nephew. No contest. The marriage bond was upheld. Henry concluded that the only way he could secure the dynasty was to declare himself to be in charge of state *and* church. Assisted by a new, more amenable Archbishop of Canterbury, Thomas Cranmer, and a notable political 'fixer', Thomas Cromwell, Henry embarked on ecclesiastical transformation.

The first phase of the changes involved getting rid of Catherine, breaking with Rome and a general coercion of the nobility and the clergy. There were some stand-out rebels such as the Cardinal, John Fisher (1469–1535) and the Lord Chancellor, Thomas More (1478–1535), but by and large things went smoothly. The next decision, the 'Dissolution of the Monasteries', caused unrest since the monks were generally popular in rural England and the motivation seemed rapaciously financial rather than theological. Eyewitness accounts attest to the violence of the campaign but also the dilemma of locals caught between loyalty to the monks and the fear of missing out on the general looting of the estates. Theologically, there wasn't really a plan. Although his second wife Anne Boleyn had provided Henry with some reformist inclinations and another child, Elizabeth, he soon had her beheaded on dubious charges of treason and married Jane Seymour. With her, the desired son arrived, Edward, but Jane herself did not survive post-natality. A short fourth marriage to Anne of Cleves in 1540 was so unsuccessful that Henry broke with tradition and chopped off Cromwell's head instead for his poor dating agency skills. Catherine Howard met the same fate in 1542 but Catherine Parr did survive as a bloody, bloated, syphilitic Henry finally died in 1547, leaving England in the hands of his fourteen-year-old son.

Edward's reign (1547–1553) offered a chance for reformist advisors in the English court to exert an influence. Liturgical changes began under Cranmer, whose elegant Book of Common Prayer became a template not just for national worship but reconfigured the expressions and cadences of the English language. The young monarch seems to have genuinely approved of the direction things were going but died in 1553 before anything like the Swiss reform could be achieved. Faced with the threat of public disorder, the reformists were immediately on the defensive as the accession of Edward's half-sister Mary signalled religious reversal. Restoring the hierarchy and demanding that the reformers recant, Mary inaugurated an era of Protestant martyrs. Cranmer, having first signed a renunciation of his views, later committed his hand to the flames before being burned at the stake. Like her father before her, Mary's marriage to Philip II was clouded by her concern to provide an heir but she was to die childless in 1559.

When Elizabeth Tudor took the throne, the religious fate of England still hung in the balance. By the time of her death in 1601, an almost biblical 40-year period of transformation had shaped the defining characteristics of the English Church. With traditional trappings but an independence of mind, the peculiar, semi-reformed 'Anglican' experiment began. From the records, it is not clear that Elizabeth deliberately sought a *Via Media* or 'Middle Way', but she seems to have been fond of the ceremonial ritual of the sacraments in general and Mass in particular. She saw neither rhyme nor reason in getting rid of a network of bishops that pledged loyalty to her and allowed a relaxation in the requirement for celibacy. The Thirty Nine Articles of 1563 identify the prevailing theological tone as broadly anti-Catholic, but pilot a course which, while sympathetic to different aspects of the German and Swiss reforms, remains unwedded to either. The result was 'a broad Church' and while protagonists continued to lobby for a more thoroughgoing reform, they were classified disparagingly as 'Puritans' due to their serious demeanour, and were marginalized by the merry, adventurous court of Elizabeth.

The main strain came from Spain. The fear of Spanish-sponsored rebellion meant that Elizabeth's spies kept a tight and often cruel grip on those who remained loyal to the old faith. The Jesuit Edmund Campion was a notable victim of her policing as were Ralph Sherwin and ultimately over 40 others from the newly founded missionary seminary based at the English hospice in Rome, sufferings shared by its sister college at Douai. The decisive turn of events was the defeat of the Spanish Armada in 1588, which put an end to invasion fears but also put an end to the dreams of a re-Catholicized England. Henceforth, not only would England be the leading Protestant power in Europe, it would, through its colonies, become a major global exporter of religion with profound consequences for the New World, Africa and Oceania.

g) Nationalized theology and Catholic reform

Although the English experiment in Church reform may have seemed to be the most patchwork of the sixteenth-century movements, Henry's model of rulers declaring independence from the Papacy and deciding the faith and fate of their citizens became the norm across Europe. A century of confusion and rising tension between powers now divided by nationality and religion culminated in the tragic Thirty Years War which raged across Central Europe until the Treaty of Westphalia in 1648. The exhausted parties ratified the Augsburg Settlement of 1555, that the religious affiliation of the nations and provinces of Europe would be decided *cuius regio eius religio* – 'In a ruler's country, the ruler's religion'. Some protection was afforded to minorities already present, but it wasn't the best of times to be out of theological step with the neighbours and disaffected Christians of every stripe sought asylum from persecution in the colonies of the New World. Nationalism and religious self-determination in the West were partly imitated by similar developments in the East, where the communion became increasingly *auto-kephalous* – 'self-headed'. Less affiliated to a by now Turk-dominated Constantinople, Eastern churches were more sensitive and more shaped by local ethnic boundaries. The emergence of Muscovy (Russia), and the ennobling of Moscow with a patriarchate, was further evidence that ecclesiastical power followed national power rather than the other way round.

Though the unity and universality of the Church had taken a blow, the period did see Rome initiating Catholic Reform. Reacting somewhat tardily to events in Northern Europe, a Council was convened at Trent on the borders of present-day Italy and Croatia. The three sessions which took place between 1545 and 1563 were doctrinally conservative insofar as they restated the coherence of the scholastic tradition. The efficacy of the sacraments was underlined and the significance of 'grace prompted good deeds' in the drama of human destiny and salvation was affirmed. More radical were the changes to Canon Law which led to much better training of clergy and the eradication of many problematic practices such as absentee bishops and multiple benefices. Spanish Catholicism was particularly influential on numerous levels. For a century or more, the Inquisition had conjoined ecclesiastical and monarchical powers to such effect that a country once boasting substantial populations of Muslims and Jews was pretty much homogenously Catholic. And life wasn't too easy for them either. Wonderfully gifted writers on the spiritual life such as John of the Cross (1542–1591) and Theresa of Avila (1515–1582) suffered travails at the hands of an intolerant regime which was busily exporting its strong arm version of Christianity to the New World.

All the more ironic, then, that these same missions would be softened by the influence of an ex-soldier who wanted to look good in tights (Caraman, 1990, p. 26). Ignatius of Loyola (1491–1556) had been injured in a siege at Pamplona, and while recovering he noticed that his shattered leg had not set right. Not wanting to have a bony protrusion ruining the line of his calf and thus being an unattractive dancing partner to the many ladies he wanted to impress, he requested it be broken again so that he would look the part at the party. Bored to distraction during his convalescence from the second operation, he was driven to read stories of the saints and noted that his yearning to be a military hero was not as satisfying as when he daydreamed about imitating the likes of Francis or Dominic. Aha! Our truest desire is that which brings the deepest joy. Back on his feet and armed with this disarmingly simple method of *spiritual discernment,* he dedicated himself to God's service, eventually forming the *Society of Jesus* among his university companions in Paris. Better known as 'Jesuits', the Society became a dynamic theological, educational and pastoral force at the heart of the Catholic Reform. Breaking new missionary ground in both East and West, Jesuits also broke moulds across Europe as religious sisters such as England's Mary Ward deliberately copied their model and formed active congregations no longer confined to the cloister. In time, such sisters became the vanguard of education and service to both rich and poor throughout Catholic Europe and its colonies.

Summary

Although 'all authority in heaven and on earth' had effectively been granted to the Apostles (cf. Matt 28:16-20), maintaining the visible unity of the ekklesia – 'the called out' had never been easy. Under the aegis of the successors of Peter in

Rome and the Patriarchs of Constantinople, Alexandria, Jerusalem and Antioch, communion between East and West was sustained for a thousand years. As much destabilized by changes in the substructure of political power in Eurasia as by the theological and military impact of Islam, the great traditions of Rome and Constantinople became estranged, a schism further exacerbated by the ill-judged tragedy of the Crusades. Despite the Western theological tradition and Church life reaching new heights in the Middle Ages, the end of the Scholastic era gave way to new ways of thinking associated with Renaissance humanism. In a wave of theological, pastoral and political critique, the authority of the Pope was swept aside by the various reform leaders who emerged and the sacramental system was radically reconfigured. By 1555, not only was the Church divided East and West by the Great Schism, it was now divided North and South by the Protestant Reformation. 'Going forward', the dialogue that Christian Theology came to conduct with 'Modernity' was no longer articulated in one voice or witnessed to by one body.

Part 5
Theology in Modern and Contemporary Dialogue

19

Theology 'versus' Philosophy?

Since the time of the first Christian apologist, Justin Martyr, faith thinkers had worked with philosophical tools to engage in their 'thoughtful conversations about God.' The extent to which this reached its peak in the Neo-Platonism of Augustine and the Aristotelianism of Aquinas has been noted. If Theology was the 'Queen of the Sciences,' then Philosophy was understood as its 'Handmaid.' Following the Renaissance and the Reformation, all this changed. Renewed hunger for learning and access to classical literature unfiltered by the control of ecclesiastical authority led to new ways of thinking which coalesced around a quest for philosophical and scientific certainty. This somewhat self-styled 'Enlightenment' ushered in 'Modernity' which was to prevail as the dominant style of Western thinking until the recent past. It is perhaps a little naughty to put 'versus' in the title of the three chapters below which scrutinize Christian Theology in this epoch. However, since Modernity was characterized by marked distinctions between the views of theologians on the one hand and philosophers, scientists and anthropologists on the other, it may sharpen the drama of the time and excuse the very specific choice of protagonists who will be examined. In this first episode, the plot is nothing less than the story of a palace coup and the outline of a royal recovery.

a) Descartes and the Enlightenment

Although the Jesuits' first major theologian, Francisco Suarez (1548–1617), was very much of the 'Big System' scholastic school, their own educational programme was helping to draw a line under the past. By the time the ink was dry on the Treaty of Westphalia, the Jesuit-educated mathematician and philosophical genius, René Descartes (1596–1650), had already undermined the very foundations of such huge syntheses. Indeed his *Discourse on Method* (1637) and *Meditations on First Philosophy* (1641) were so revolutionary, they inaugurated an entire epoch because he *changed the way we think*.

Descartes was a mathematician and enamoured of the clean lines and logical certainties of that discipline, he looked for a first principle which would guarantee clarity of thought in . . . thought! In readable, dramatic style, Descartes describe his growing panic as he realized that all the things around him could be an illusion, he could be dreaming or even were he not, a malicious demon could be fooling his senses and confounding his mind. Woe! In the midst of this conundrum, Descartes found his first principle, namely, that even if he was being fooled by someone or something, he was thinking about it – hence his famous first principle, *cogito ergo sum* – for centuries translated as 'I think therefore I am' but more popularly now as 'I think therefore I exist'.

From this certain start point, Descartes, whether he is being fooled or not, *knows for certain* he is having conscious experiences. At this juncture, his reflections take an Anselm-like God turn. He is conscious that he is limited and cannot sustain himself – he is a mortal, finite *contingent* being. Yet despite his limitations, he can also imagine an immortal, infinite *necessary* being. He concludes that this thought must have been put into his head by whatever brought him into being, like the signature of the craftsman. He concludes, therefore, that there is a God who is benevolent and wouldn't spend all day fooling him maliciously and that the supreme gift he has given to humanity is reason and the use thereof.

Now it should perhaps be said that some scholars think that Descartes added the God bit to keep the Inquisition off his back, but if we are to assume some sincerity on his part, then in terms of Christian Theology, what's not to like?

Indeed *why is* this almost universally regarded as a turning point in the history of Western thought marking a liberation from the superstitions of Theology and the great leap forward of reason? Well, I suppose the problem wasn't so much the conclusion as the method. A philosophical Luther, he wittingly or unwittingly posted theses on the foreheads of Western intellectuals:

- Certainty is possible and therefore universally applicable truth.
- It is discovered through systematic doubt which eliminates error.
- It is constructed through rational thinking.
- 'Epistemology' – the logic of knowing – is the basis of Philosophy.
- I am a dualistic reality – mind and body.
- But I am most truly myself in my self-conscious mental state.
- Therefore I am mainly a mind that can use its body as it wishes.

The seismic results of this methodology were soon felt in his native France where the so-called Enlightenment or 'Age of Reason' flowered in a wealth of scholarship, literature and revolutionary ideas epitomized by thinkers such as Diderot (1713–1784), Voltaire (1694–1778) and Rousseau (1712–1778). These figures deliberately set out to change the way people thought. Diderot through his *Encyclopaedia,* Voltaire through his coruscating satires of state and religious authority. Rousseau anticipating the revolutionary call for 'Liberty, Equality and Fraternity' called citizens 'born free, yet everywhere in chains' to throw off the last shackles of medieval suzerainty represented by Catholicism. Theologically, the problem was that Descartes' method left little room for a personal God, had no need for revelation, excised Jesus from the drama of faith and absolutely wiped out blanket acceptance of magisterial 'teaching authority' on the part of any Church, Catholic, Reformed or Orthodox. The details of Christianity disappeared down the plughole of systematic doubt. What remained was the absentee Greek God who had set up the possibility of life and reasoned reflection upon it, but wasn't too bothered about what was happening on the planet. The options were obvious. The first was a Deist position which acknowledged God as Craftsman of a world whose work was to be continued by like-minded intelligent men who should lead society. While such thinking had a benign influence through the founding fathers of the American Revolution, it accelerated the development of the Masonic movement in Europe which was more deliberately anti-Christian. The other option was to dispense with God altogether. And by symbolically enthroning the Goddess of Reason on the High Altar at Notre Dame Cathedral in 1793, the French revolutionaries did exactly that. The 'Handmaid' had usurped the throne, and the 'Queen of the Sciences' was on the run.

b) Hume and empiricism

If the almost religious exaltation of reason was a rallying cry through the streets and universities of Europe, a very different but equally radical review of *epistemology* – 'knowledge logic' was happening in Britain. John Locke (1632–1704) and George Berkeley (1685–1753) had pursued the path of sense experience in search for certainty in knowledge. While Locke's theorizing had the sound ring of common sense to it, he himself was aware that his *empirical* or 'experiential' focus demanded a certain modesty. Since we operate according to working probabilities rather than absolute certainties, this was good news for religious tolerance, but less helpful for dogmatic convictions.

Berkeley was more taken with Locke's insight that although we have the experience of objects, we cannot know them *in themselves*. What Berkeley observed was that when we see a red flower, a furry cat etc. we are somehow experiencing these objects through representations in our mind – a completely different experience to the way the pretty pansy *is* or the cute kitten *is*. A bit like Descartes, rather than get trapped in his head, Berkeley suggested that God makes the connection between our senses and the objects we are sensing such that they correspond and so that we can say that our experiences are accurate and our knowledge can be certain. But God would not stay the guarantor of the 'empirical school' for long, David Hume would see to that.

Sometime soldier, diplomat and man of letters, David Hume (1711–1776) is variously regarded as the greatest English-speaking philosopher ever, or as a mischievous cynic, with more wit than wisdom. He was committed to the empiricist manifesto and emphasized the importance of the senses. He was therefore particularly unimpressed by the speculations of metaphysics such as Plato's 'matter and form' or Aristotle's 'substance and accident'. As far as Hume was concerned, if any writings go too far beyond the natural ken, they should be committed to the flames. In a brilliantly consistent fashion, he shook the substructure of Greco-Christian thinking by questioning cause, effect and the supernatural.

Hume is at his most lucid and disturbing in *An Enquiry Concerning Human Understanding* (1748), where he describes and dismantles our knowledge in equal measure. In Section IV he points out that 'All the objects of human reason or enquiry may naturally be divided into two kinds, to wit, relations of ideas, and matters of fact'. The first kind are exemplified by geometry, algebra, and arithmetic 'discoverable by mere operation of thought, without dependence on what is anywhere existent in the universe' (Hume, [1748] 2007, p. 28).

Matters of fact, however, can only be gained through experience, and our experience is dominated by our assumptions regarding cause and effect. Hume points out that everything else we know, we conclude through a conjunction of experience and expectation. In other words, what we call 'natural' is actually a shorthand term for our experience; since we never see 'cause' what we do is observe *sequences*. Using the most basic example of a collision between two billiard balls Hume notes that: 'Motion in the second billiard ball is a quite distinct event from the motion in the first. nor is there anything in the one to suggest the smallest hint of the other' (Hume, [1748] 2007, pp. 31–2). In other words, we presume 'cause and effect' but being brutally honest, what we see is a familiar sequence. This critique demands modesty and has repercussions for how we know what we know and what we consider to be natural, unnatural and supernatural. The balls may react the same way a million times, but does that make it certain? You may see a million white swans and think a black one is miraculous, but in fact it is merely Australian.

Kant would later say that by such acute observations on epistemology, Hume woke him from his 'dogmatic slumber'. No presumption and certainly no dogmas were safe around our David. Not at all sympathetic to the 'Design Argument' supporting the existence of a Creator, Hume was typically forthright in his *Dialogues Concerning Natural Religion* (1779). The genius implicit in any facet of nature could have been the result of a committee, or a discussion among several gods. But, since there are a few unpleasant things associated with creation like earthquakes and disease, maybe this world was the result of an apprentice God or a deity not quite up to the mark.

You get the drift. Razor sharp, witty, infectious. His friends persuaded him not to publish some of his writings during his lifetime but to keep quiet for fear there would be problems for him at home in Edinburgh. But the message for theologians was loud and clear. Sharpen up or ship out. Hume's arguments may appear quixotic and somewhat two-dimensional in terms of reasoning, but they left an indelible mark on Western philosophies of religion. It is with grudging respect that I have to say I largely agree with aspects of Hume's critique, especially with regard to miracles. While fully respecting the wonder working traditions of the Gospel, and having lived long enough to have been astonished by several things that have happened before my own eyes, there is no way that they can suffice as irrefutable 'proof' of God's action. They may be understood as signs of the Kingdom, moments of grace and wonder, events to rejoice in, but they are never sufficient in themselves to determine the proposals of faith, which always involve the dimension of meaning.

The problem is that a striking event can occur, but it is always possible to attribute something to cosmic coincidence, spontaneous regeneration, psycho-somatic reactions or whatever. Put it this way, even if the armed guards at the resurrection tomb had videoed everything, it still could not be proved from what might be seen that Jesus was the Son of God, Logos Incarnate, 'through whom all things were made' each of which are *theological* conclusions drawn from the Jesus event. A modern example? There is real-time footage of President Kennedy being shot in 1963. He received fatal wounds – everyone agrees up to this point. But if someone asks 'by whom?' it gets more difficult and when they ask 'why' you've got even greater difficulties. Finding *meaning* is not so straightforward, and it is unsurprising that Hume, wedded to the quest for certainty, wanted to avoid treading such a necessarily speculative path.

c) Kant and the unknowable God

The challenging nature of Hume's views quickened the quest for rationalist certainty which arguably reached its peak in the work of Immanuel Kant (1724–1804). Though he hardly left his home town, his writings managed to make the whole world come to him . . . and to you. His work has been likened to a reversed Copernican revolution, whereby the understanding of the whole cosmos is discovered to revolve not around the sun or another celestial being, but around us. As his philosophical project, Kant crystallized three profound questions, *What can I know? What must I do? What can I hope for?* ([1781] 1952, p.236) Taking seriously the 'doubt leading to certainty' tradition of Descartes, but seeking an explanation for the paradoxical observations of experience made by Berkeley and Hume, Kant set about answering the first question, the conundrum of our knowing. The theory he eventually proposed in his *Critique of Pure Reason* was that our minds are hardwired to process the multiple sensations (phenomena) that we experience. It is our intelligence that makes things 'intelligible' or understandable. It imposes order upon the confusion of the sense data we are constantly receiving by processing them in terms of 'cause and effect', 'reality', 'existence' and other such *categories*. Knowledge is thus a synthesis of the action of the mind and what is presented to it by sense-experience. We can't hope to know material objects 'in themselves' – everything is mediated through *us*. Nor can reason prove the existence of the soul (yourself), divinity (God) or ultimate reality (the Cosmos), all three of which he classes as 'transcendental ideas'. They are operative as a backdrop to our understanding but are not its proper object.

The upshot of his theory was that it placed human consciousness back at the centre of knowing even more radically than Descartes had. The world, as we know it, is how we know it. It has no objectivity beyond us. A very different character to Hume, Kant did not particularly want to go picking fights with either theologians at university nor officialdom from the government-sponsored Lutheran Church. He didn't have to. By marginalizing God from being a proper object of rational discourse in his *Critique of Pure Reason*, he had done enough. Not only is Anselm's ontological argument flawed since 'exists' is something we ourselves impute; God is not a concept that submits to pure rational enquiry.

True, in his subsequent writings, Kant did propose the necessity of a deity in his *Critique of Practical Reason*. In the second and third parts of his brilliant triple question he makes an argument based on *doing* one's duty and a *hoping* for cosmic justice. Since it is demonstrable that injustice is suffered by good people who have acted dutifully, there must be some redress beyond death and therefore an immortal guarantor, 'God'. Otherwise the 'moral law within,' which in a rare poetic moment he described as being as 'marvellous as the starry heavens', ([1788] 1952, p.360) would be fundamentally mistaken. This would contradict the logic of his *Practical* reason and he wasn't having any of that. Nietzsche would later describe this as a disappointing development, as if Kant had 'strayed back' into the cage of religious belief having freed himself. That said, it *could* be read as exactly the kind of reduced Deist conclusion that the intelligentsia of Europe were increasingly subscribing to, and hardly designed to enamour theologians in the Lutheran heartland of Prussia. The Reform theologians who privileged the absolute centrality of Christ crucified could marvel all they wanted at Kant's critiques, but Jesus was predominantly part of the picture as a good example, way short of being the Word through whom all things were made. Kant had led philosophers in a Copernican revolution and man was at the centre of the Universe, not God.

d) The unknowable Jesus?

If it wasn't bad enough that Philosophy and Christian Theology were becoming fundamentally estranged in the universities of Europe, yet another project associated with the Enlightenment 'quest for certainty' brought Descartes' method right into the sacred precincts of the pulpit and the sanctuary. In an era addicted to literal certainty, an unsubtle approach to the literature of the Bible which may roughly be caricatured as 'historical good, allegorical bad' led to increasing scepticism regarding the factuality of Holy Writ. Not only did a series of thinkers openly begin to question the veracity of various episodes in the Old Testament, scrutiny also focused on writings at the very centre of Christian revelation. Hitherto, 'Gospel Truth' was accepted, anchored as it was in the vivid figure of Jesus represented by the various evangelists in their accounts. With the Enlightenment, however, there began what came to be known as the 'Quest for the Historical Jesus', a laudable attempt to access the truth of the original Nazarene which ended by making him almost disappear altogether.

Hermann Samuel Reimarus (1694–1768) was cognizant of Philosophy, Theology and Oriental languages and therefore well equipped to pursue the Enlightenment project with some conviction. Between 1744 and 1767, he composed a treatise too dangerous to release prior to his death. It came to light in the form of the 'Wolfenbüttel Fragments' (scary name, scary writings) published in 1774–1778. Accusing the biblical writers of conscious fraud and impossible contradictions, the fragments denied the biblical miracles at the heart of the revelation. The genie out of the bottle, the Bible was not only now subjected to the systematic doubt of Enlightenment methodology, it was subjected to it with more severity both because of the importance of the text and the truth claims that it made.

Hitherto, the scholarly activity most associated with biblical endeavour was the 'lower criticism' analysis which addressed issues related to variant readings of texts and the development of more subtle translations through familiarity with Hebrew, Greek and other Near Eastern languages. Henceforth, the analysis of the text would more consciously involve a quest for historical certainty and theological accuracy. The key motivation in this task of 'Higher Biblical Criticism' was the attempt to strip away all the accretions and barnacles of later dogma, to uncover the earliest possible unsullied picture of Jesus. The problem was, the more Jesus was investigated, the more uncertain he became. A prime example was David Strauss' *Life of Jesus, Critically Examined*. It was published in 1835 and translated into English by Marian Evans (aka. George Eliot) in 1846. The relatively straightforward thesis of the book was that the Gospels had been deliberately framed to depict Jesus fulfilling the messianic prophecies of the Old Testament so they couldn't really be trusted as historical documents. Instead, they belong to the category of *myth*. As noted above, a subtle understanding of this word points to a genre which is designed to disclose perennial truths. An unsubtle understanding is that such writings are fabricated, fabulous and untrue, which Strauss was aware would wither all the consolations of the Gospel for ordinary folk. A storm of protest led to him resigning his post at Tübingen and Strauss' attitude began to harden such that by the end of his life he had concluded that Jesus was a deceiver and imposter whom he ultimately repudiated in *The Old and New Faith* of 1872.

Since one of the boasts of Judeo-Christian theologizing was its rootedness in real events brought about through the supernatural intervention of a personal God, the Enlightenment challenge to the historical certainties of Christian thinking was more than an impolite inconvenience. Christianity was not like the cyclical, timeless reincarnation religion of the Orient nor a mystery religion of the ancient Mediterranean. It was actualized in a race, a story, a God-man. For sure, there had always been an acknowledgement of the difficulties in finding the words to express the revelation, but not the essential facts of the faith. No matter, Strauss and the other 'Higher Biblical Critics' had set something of an iconoclastic tone in their quest for biblical certainty which shook the foundations of Western Christian Theology.

e) The unspeakable science?

As a last example of how the Enlightenment quest for certainty led to a 'Philosophy versus Theology' stand-off, it is necessary to return to the project begun by the British empiricist tradition. The Locke – Hume refusal to go too far from plain evidence had given English-speaking philosophies a 'common-sense', grounded complexion which would find expression in the British 'utilitarian' tradition of Jeremy Bentham and John Stuart Mill and the American 'pragmatic' tradition of Charles Sanders Pierce, William James and John Dewey. Digging deeper into the ground of common knowledge, Bertrand Russell and Alfred North Whitehead took the practical step of exploring what principles governed that most logical of human endeavours, mathematics. Their momentous work *Principia Mathematica* (1910–1913) proved a prelude to life as the public face of Philosophy for Russell. Wedded to the quest for certainty, he then turned his attention to grounding other things according to solid first principles.

It was only a matter of time before he was turning his attention to language and applying all the logical force of his mind to some of the very obvious things we say. Troubling to his experience/evidence-based mind, he noticed that we can make statements that may seem fairly straightforward, but which we are unable to test in terms of truth. His famous example is that while you can say 'The heir to the British throne is bald' and check out whether it is true (because there is a monarchy), you can't check out 'The heir to the French throne is bald' because there is no monarchy there. This second statement is neither true, nor false, in fact it is meaningless. Rather than remaining a parlour game for witty intellectuals, Russell's puzzles helped to launch an entire school of 'Analytical Philosophy' whose aim was to clarify language such that our knowledge would be more certain.

The standard task was 'What are we *really* saying when we say so and so'. The trouble was that while that sounded fun, it led to unexpected tangles in the quest to determine what could and couldn't be said, what was and what wasn't meaningless. The movement began to acquire its own 'inquisitorial' tone and almost suffocated a generation of British philosophers in stilted conversations reminiscent of an Orwellian nightmare. One of the victims of the linguistic revolution was any form of religious language. A noted movement within the analytical tradition was 'Logical Positivism', which assessed the validity of statements according to its famous 'verification principle'. This asked the question: 'What would we have to do to establish the truth or falsehood of this statement?' A bit like the bald French heir, if there is no test, the statement must be meaningless. Popularized by A. J. Ayer's *Language, Truth and Logic* in 1936, it launched a slash-and-burn campaign against the credibility of all sorts of things, but since so many religious tenets of Christianity such as the Trinity, the Incarnation, miracles etc. are pretty much unprovable, there wasn't much that *could* be said. If the debunking of a miracle, the finding of a non-risen body in a Jerusalem tomb, personal grief, international disaster or the suffering of millions cannot disavow someone of their faith in an omnipotent, benevolent God, then that belief is meaningless. If Christian Theology is 'thoughtful conversation about God', then it would not be a very long discussion with any self-respecting practitioner of the analytical tradition.

In summary, the quest for certainty of the Enlightenment which launched the Modern period dealt severe blows to the philosophical foundations of traditional Christian beliefs. For some 1600 years, Christian theologians had readily employed the definitive insights of Plato and Aristotle in service of their understanding of God, Trinity, Creation, Humanity – the whole revelation of the thinking Church. Theology had been known as the Queen of the Sciences, and in a series of turns, Philosophy had launched a palace revolution:

- If doubt was the path to knowledge (Descartes) where did that leave faith?
- If metaphysics and all its speculations should be committed to the flames (Hume), where did that leave Theology?
- If God was on the margins of absolute reason, discernible only through a sense of cosmic justice (Kant) where did that leave Jesus?
- If Jesus was only a accessible through a foundation *myth* constructed by duplicitous fraudsters (Strauss), where did that leave Gospel truth?
- If religious language was meaningless (Russell/Ayer) where did that leave doctrine?

Essentially, the Enlightenment project had left Christian Theology doubting a disappearing irrational God represented by a duplicitous Jesus with words that made no sense. Time for a rethink? Time to pray?

f) Enlightenment in the spirit

In one way, it is perhaps unsurprising that part of the response to the cerebral assault on the credibility and even possibility of Christian Theology would be fuelled by 'spiritual experience'. After all, the apostolic *kerygma* had only begun following such an event. And since the fine mess of modernity had partly been caused by a French Catholic mathematical genius, it was only fitting that one of the first and most famous antidotes to the rationalist draught was provided by another one. Blaise Pascal was born in 1623, he was a precociously talented youth contributing original advances to Science and Mathematics. For most of his life he was attracted to the Jansenist movement within French Catholicism which emphasized strict personal discipline and to which his sister belonged. This probably owed something to his classically Augustinian sense of the wretchedness of the human state, but also to an anxiety that the Church should return to its early pre-Constantinian purity. Highly intelligent, his Enlightenment compromise position was effectively: 'If we submit everything to reason, our religion will be left with nothing mysterious or supernatural. If we offend the principles of reason, our religion will be absurd or ridiculous' ([1662] 1966, p.83). However, while still frequenting polite society, his life was fundamentally changed, not by arguments with the Jesuits or his considerations of the intricate scholastic metaphysical proofs, but by a clean contrast with all such mental gymnastics which he memorably described as his 'Night of Fire':

> The year of grace 1654
> Monday, 23 November, feast of Saint Clement, Pope and Martyr, and of others
> in the Martyrology.
> Eve of Saint Chrysogonus, Martyr and others.
> From about half past ten in the evening until half past midnight.
> Fire
> 'God of Abraham, God of Isaac, God of Jacob,' not of philosophers and scholars.
> Certainty, certainty, heartfelt, joy, peace.
> God of Jesus Christ.
> God of Jesus Christ.
> *My God and your God.*
> ' Thy God shall be my God.'
> The world forgotten, and everything except God.

He can only be found by the ways taught in the Gospels.
Greatness of the human soul.
'O righteous Father, the world had not known thee, but I have known thee.'
Joy, joy, joy, tears of joy.
I have cut myself off from him.
They have forsaken me, the fountain of living waters.
'My God wilt thou forsake me?'
Let me not be cut off from him for ever!
And this is life eternal, that they might know thee, the only true God, and Jesus Christ
whom thou hast sent.'
Jesus Christ.
Jesus Christ.
I have cut myself off from him, shunned him, denied him, crucified him.
Let me never be cut off from him!
He can only be kept by the ways taught in the Gospel.
Sweet and total renunciation.
Total submission to Jesus Christ and my director.
Everlasting joy in return for one day's effort on earth.
I will not forget thy word. Amen. (Pascal, [1662] 1966, p. 309)

Pascal carried this memorial on his person for the rest of his life and it is the description of a classic conversion experience familiar to the Christian tradition. Note that Pascal finds a certainty not available to him from learning, nor an encounter at all similar to the 'God of philosophers and scholars'. Very much like Augustine's heart, restless until it rested in God, Pascal had found a Christ-centred comfort which was 'everlasting joy' never to be forgotten. While Pascal's high profile and standing as a leading European intellectual was a particular factor, in more broad theological, terms, the significance of this occurrence was that it reminded the academy of the brute fact of religious experience as an argument for the existence of God. Man wasn't the first principle, God was. Doubt wasn't the vehicle for truth, but faith.

g) Enlightenment through intuition

If the testimony of Pascal and the likes of John Wesley (1703–1791) provided a 'back to basics' reminder to the Christian tradition that its original heritage was not in an argument but in transformative experience, a second level of response was provided by a minister from the Moravian tradition. Friedrich Schleiermacher (1768–1834), 'the Father of modern Theology', was born in Breslau, Germany. Already familiar with the Enlightenment project through his university studies at Halle, his first important work betrays, by its very title, the thoroughgoing challenge that was facing Christian apologetics. In his *Religion: Speeches to its Cultured Despisers* (1893), Schleiermacher attempts to persuade the educated classes to reconsider their attitude to matters of faith. He does so by first conceding ground to Philosophy, Science and Morals so that the proper domain of religious thinking can be more clearly defined:

> In order to take possession of its own domain, religion renounces herewith all claims to whatever belongs to those others and gives back everything that has been forced upon it. It does not wish to determine and explain the universe . . . and perfect it by the power of freedom and the divine free choice of a human being . . . Religion's essence is neither thinking nor acting, but intuition and feeling. (Schleiermacher, [1893], 1996, p. 22)

By rebuilding the credibility of religion upon *Anschauung und Gefühl*, 'intuition and feeling' – Schleiermacher was using an everyday experience which even David Hume would have recognized. By beginning from a 'dogma free' point of departure, he was also able to respect the fundamental freedom so prized by Modernity while holding out as the ultimate goal of *intuition and feeling* the sensation of 'union with the infinite' which the great Christian mystics had experienced. Interrupted by the small matter of the Napoleonic invasions, his later and most famous theological work was *The Christian Faith* (1821–1822) in which he developed his core thesis. True religious feeling reveals our absolute dependence on God. Taking this feeling as the centre of the faith question leads to a focus on personal issues such as the drama of sin and grace rather than doctrinal issues which in turn allowed him to acknowledge a validity in other non-Christian religions. It also allowed him to propose that in biblical interpretation, the intention of the author (*sensus auctoris*) was the reader's true quest, which again, through the intuitions of 'universal reason' and 'congeniality' we can come to understand (cf. Acts 8:34).

There is clearly a certain *romantic* dimension to Schleiermacher's line of thinking, yet despite some negative reactions both within and outside the household of the Church, his appeal was broad and influential because his critique struck a chord. Is there not more to a human being than reason? Is there not more to life than moral action?

Schleiermacher was challenging a touchstone of the Enlightenment by reminding European intellectuals of every stripe that humanity is *homo religiosus* 'a religious being' as well as *homo sapiens* 'a knowing being'. Hume may have wanted to commit doctrinal speculations to the flames, but he wouldn't have wanted to incinerate feelings or experiences. Schleiermacher reopened the parlours of the academy to 'thoughtful conversations about God' and enabled numerous thinkers such as Dilthey (1833–1911) – 'nature we *explain*, man we *understand*' and Bergson (1859–1941) '*intuition* is the way we access reality' to pursue his insight in properly philosophical directions.

h) Enlightenment of the word

Not everyone within the broad Protestant tradition was enamoured of Schleiermacher's 'turn to feeling'. The crisis posed by the philosophical and biblical critiques of the Enlightenment had not only marginalized the importance of Jesus but called into question the entire compendium of Holy Writ. Schleiermacher's hermenutics – his search for the *sense of the author* – had not solved that problem since quests for the 'original source', (to 'get behind' the biblical text rather than engage with what was on the page), led to more and more dissection of the testimony. For Reformed Churches still largely united under the banner of *Sola Scriptura*, 'By Scripture alone', the situation was particularly acute. There was a need for a new Luther, a new Zwingli or Calvin to restate the primacy of the Word of God. That man was Karl Barth.

Barth was born in Berne in 1886 and in the course of a long academic career spent in German and Swiss universities which could have been a bit boring, he instead managed to become internationally famous, fight Hitler and turn the biblical and theological world upside down. Like many revolutions, the seeds of his project had already been sown. There had been inklings both in Kant and Schleiermacher that religion occupied its own proper epistemological space. Barth got out the map, drew thick lines around the territory proper to Christian Theology and put 'Keep Out' signs up to prevent the trespass of philosophical intruders. He regarded the attempts to synthesize Christian Theology and the culture of Modernity as mistaken. The Enlightenment and its methods were clean contrary to 'Evangelical Theology' which he called the 'Happy Science', a delightful endeavour because it begins and ends with the sacred Word. Present in, but not to be entirely identified with the biblical text, the sense of Barth's revolution was that far from humanity having the temerity to judge the Bible, the Word judges us. 'As proclaimed, as revealed and as written' the Christian stands under this Word, as does the world, even though it does not necessarily acknowledge it. Theology thus stands over against any human thinking or Philosophy, it is not anxious to woo, wed or even have it as a 'handmaid'. The master principle of Theology is Christ – he is not a moral guide and an optional extra tacked on to woozy religious feeling. In Barth's view, understanding the religious nature of man does not begin either by studying primitive tribes in the jungle or by analysing the working of the human mind, it begins with the Word of God. Christ defines *us*, not the other way round.

As an example of how brilliant his Christological insights could be, Barth managed to take a core judgemental tenet of reform Theology, 'election' or 'predestination', and turn it into a Theology of God's 'yes' rather than God's 'no' to humankind:

> Rejection cannot again become the portion or affair of man. The exchange which took place on Golgotha, when God chose as His throne the malefactor's cross, when the Son of God bore what the son of man ought to have borne, took place once and for all in the fulfillment of God's eternal will, and it can never be reversed. There is no condemnation – literally none – for those that are in Christ Jesus. For this reason, faith in the divine election as such, as *per se* means faith in the non-rejection of man, or disbelief in his rejection. Man is not rejected. In God's eternal purpose, it is God himself who is rejected in his Son. The self-giving of God consists, the giving and sending of his son is fulfilled, in the fact that he is rejected in order that we might not be rejected. Predestination means that from all eternity God has determined on man's acquittal at his own cost. (Barth, 1957, p. 167)

Barth's project was enormous, his immense multi-volume *Church Dogmatics* has often been likened (with due irony) as the reformed equivalent of Aquinas' *Summa Theologiae*. As one of its immediate consequences, it somewhat immunized evangelical exegesis from liberal biblical criticism. Barth opposed Rudolf Bultmann, whose 'demythologization' of the New Testament and preference for the preached word diminished the relevance of the traditional Gospel picture of Jesus. For Barth, the Word interprets *us*, not the other way round. His contrary nature made him a formidable opponent and his writings were sometimes distracted as he took sideswipes at theological positions with which he disagreed. Neither was he known for his humility, as Diesslin wittily summarizes:

> As to Luther, we are saved by God not by faith. As to Calvin, Jesus was predestined, not us: As to Kant, Jesus achieved his maxim, not us: As to Schleiermacher, God reveals so we can feel, not vice versa; As to Bultmann, God demythologises man, not vice versa; As to Tillich, it is God that is ultimately concerned about man, not otherwise. (Anderson, 2010, p. 338)

The upside to this kind of 'prophetic' temperament, however, was that it enabled him to stand up to Hitler, and not many people did that and got away with it! Although it meant he had to leave Germany and end his days at Basle, his displacement was merely geographical as his reputation went global. Easily the best known twentieth-century theologian, he had done his bit to restore a Jesus displaced by the Enlightenment back, once more, to the centre of Christian Theology.

i) Enlightenment made reasonable

If Protestant Theology had found in Barth its own Aquinas, the Catholic Church had belatedly given up the search by the end of the nineteenth century and decided to go back to the original! In 1893, Pope Leo XIII decided to restore Aquinas as the core syllabus of Catholic Theology in its many seminaries, training colleges and universities. It is probably fair to say that something of a 'fortress mentality' had prevailed in Rome against the waves of Enlightenment critique. Intense anti-clericalism in France may have found witty expression in Voltaire's writings but it was lethal in the aftermath of Revolution where many priests and religious met their deaths as 'liberty, equality and fraternity' morphed into the Great Terror. The shocking events fostered suspicion of novelty, and even ostensibly positive developments as diverse as democracy and train travel were viewed with suspicion. The Church Universal had always understood itself to be guaranteed and guided in truth by the Holy Spirit, and it is perhaps not surprising that against unremitting rationalist critique, the First Vatican Council in 1870 formalized the doctrine of 'Infallibility'. Much misunderstood, it did not mean that if the Pope declares it to be raining, all loyal Catholics must agree. Rather, that the Pope, as successor of Peter, could, in consultation with the worldwide body of bishops, in harmony with the *sensus fidelium* – 'the body of believers', make infallible declarations regarding faith and morals. Though the sheer number of commas in that sentence indicate the technical, conditional nature of 'infallibility', it was nonetheless seen as a clear signal to any Enlightenment 'Modernists' inside the Church to fall into line, and to any outside, to stay away from the flock.

Despite this generally defensive stance, the ancient, dogged Christian belief that 'truth cannot be divided' remained a touchstone of Catholic thinking. The hotly debated compatibility of 'Faith and Reason' was affirmed at Vatican I and Pope Leo XIII's project began to bear fruit in surprising ways. By sending Catholic scholars back to a period of thinking *before* the entrenched controversies of the Reformation, a fertile ground was opened up. A new generation of scholars already breathing the exhilarating air of European idealism, imagination and phenomenology were suddenly reading Aquinas in new ways and finding original syntheses. As good philosophers of the

Enlightenment they wanted epistemology – 'What can I know?' to be at the centre of their enquiry. As good theologians of the Church they believed there must be coherence between the insights of the Enlightenment and Divine Revelation. Jacques Maritain, Joseph Marechal, Marie Dominque Chenu, Henri de Lubac, Yves Congar, Bernard Lonergan and pre-eminently Karl Rahner, began to apply the insights of Thomas to all sorts of things, including the ideas that Kant had classified as 'transcendental' – Self-Divinity-Reality (Soul-God-World).

Karl Rahner was born in 1904 and followed his brother, Hugo, into the Jesuit order. Though his writings are mostly occasional papers and run to many volumes, The *Foundations of Christian Faith* (1982) summarizes Rahner's thinking. Like other scholars coming fresh to Thomas, Rahner was struck by the dynamism in Aquinas' theory of knowledge which depended on the 'agent intellect' – the interaction of the mind with the world through the mediation of the senses. Thomas had defined truth as *adequatio mentis ad rem* which might be loosely translated as 'getting your head around something'. Rahner was excited by this, because he noticed in a Kantian way, that when we have the *experience* of knowing, we *always* think, observe, contemplate, wonder against an *infinite* background. Even if something *really* exciting happens like your football team actually wins a game or you are reading a gripping book, one nanosecond of reflection will alert you to the fact you are experiencing those events against an infinite background hum, an 'ultimate horizon of being'. Rahner called this our experience of the 'supernatural existential'. We are finite creatures who (literally) only make sense against an infinite background (Rahner, 1982, pp. 24–43).

Rahner's theory is that this basic experience of 'me against a background' is in fact the fundamental 'holy mystery' wherein all creatures 'live and move and have their being'. God is not some scary, hairy, weirdy, beardy, cloud-dweller, but the reality that our lives are naturally reaching for rather than reacting to. This optimistic theological view proposes that as human beings we all live in a sacred or 'graced arena'. Our knowing of ourselves and each other – our being persons – is therefore what is made possible by Holy Mystery. We live by the grace of God. Any decision we might make that affirms personhood is thus an act affirming the Godness of God. And by synthesizing action and worship, Rahner is thus melting some of the 'faith v works' dilemmas of the past (Rahner, 1982, 44–89).

Now the weakness you might spot is that like Schleiermacher, Rahner seems to be offering access to the Holy One without going via the narrow gate of faith in Jesus. And Rahner seems basically happy about that. The term 'anonymous Christians' became famously associated with him, and was largely endorsed by the Second Vatican Council which refers to people who:

> Through no fault of their own, do not know the Gospel of Christ or His Church, but who nevertheless seek God with a sincere heart, and moved by grace, try in their actions to do His will as they know it through the dictates of their conscience - those too may achieve eternal salvation. (*Lumen Gentium* II.16)

Far from being some new fangled trendy thought, the coherence in his system is rooted in the Gospel verity which demands a recognition of the image of God in the least of the brothers and sisters of the earth (Matt 25:31-46). He further protects his thinking from the charge of vague religiosity by insisting that the historical revelation of God as Father, Son and Spirit *must* correspond to God as Godself. Why? Because if revelation is the self-communication of God, we can be sure that God is not going to falsely self-represent. The distinctions which have been experienced in history (the 'economic' Trinity) must be the same as the hidden or 'immanent' Trinity. Hence, because the centre point of this revelation is the God-man, the Incarnation, Rahner can confidently insist that Jesus is crucial, literally the axial point of history, who through the gift of the Spirit within enables us to become 'Hearers of the Word'.

Rahner's influence on Catholicism is perhaps best assessed by comparing the documents of Vatican I (1869–1870) with those of Vatican II (1962–1965). In the course of a century, the Church went from understandable anxiety about the relationship between faith and reason to confident expressions of their complementarity. If Thomas had baptized Aristotle in service of the medieval Church, Rahner had baptized Kant for the sake of the modern one. In so doing, he baptized people of good will everywhere as 'anonymous Christians' – whether they liked it or not! The Enlightenment quest for knowing how we know had found itself on the path to God. Trust a Jesuit to work that out.

j) Enlightenment through language

Meanwhile, back in the parlour, the arguments between philosophers about what they could or couldn't say was hotting up. Nobody likes being told to shut up and some people were falling out. In a legendary estrangement, Russell's protégé, Ludwig Wittgenstein (1889–1951) broke ranks with his mentor. Wittgenstein's life remains at once fascinating and tragic. Born to a very wealthy family and raised in the cultural ferment of Vienna, he studied engineering in Berlin and Manchester before becoming obsessed with mathematics, which in turn led him to Cambridge, where he joined Russell in 1912. He then returned to Austria to serve in World War I. It seems remarkable that in the midst of the mayhem (he experienced both the Russian and Italian fronts and was a prisoner of war), Wittgenstein completed his *Tractatus Logico-Philosophicus* in August 1918. A masterpiece of analytical thinking, it is a classic example of 'Philosophy as an Activity' clarifying the issues, identifying what can and cannot be said. Although Wittgenstein appears to have thought, somewhat immodestly, that that he had solved the problems of Philosophy, his essentially humble nature was typified as he subsequently trained as a teacher working in village schools and building a house for his sister. Drawn back into philosophical debate by the 'Logical Positivists' of the 'Vienna Circle' who were using the *Tractatus* in a manner he had not quite intended, Wittgenstein returned to Cambridge in 1929. He eventually became Professor of Philosophy in 1939, just in time to take up duties during World War II as a hospital porter and laboratory technician! Never the most predictable tutor, he gave up teaching in 1947 to focus on writings later collated by Elizabeth Anscombe and others, a selection of which appeared posthumously entitled *Philosophical Investigations* in 1953.

The publication of this later work led to some controversy, since, rather than seeking to reduce language to a mechanical syllabification of certainty, as he had been inclined to do in his earlier *Tractatus Logico Philosophicus*, this 'later Wittgenstein' instead accentuated the 'bewitching' nature of our communication. Far from being an instrument that we use like a tool, language was always and everywhere a medium which trapped, tripped and troubled our quest for certainty. Wittgenstein began to identify the different types of 'language games' which appeared to have their own rules, whether religious, scientific, poetic, personal or epistemological. The side effects of this approach were multiple. The 'Verification Principle' was just another example, a game people play, and one which, when applied to itself ('What test could disprove it?'), was by its own logic rendered meaningless. Descartes' 'mind-body' dualism was also deconstructed. 'I think therefore I am' is a glaring indication that human beings are interactive social entities, since, if you affirm the statement, you are mediating yourself to yourself, in a language which you have, ironically, learnt from another. You might be better off saying: 'I can think because we are'.

Wittgenstein's demonstrations of the inherent paradox of our discourse could be enigmatic and infuriatingly puzzling, but that was partly his point. His project was precisely to puncture the pomposity of the Enlightenment presumption that man *could* know everything when the real challenge was to rediscover wonder, which is all too often derailed by our desire to seek solutions. Regarding God, while his early writing in the *Tractatus* famously ends with his comment 'whereof we cannot speak, thereof we must remain silent', his later thinking more obviously contradicted the analytical tradition, and affirmed the meaningful nature of religious discourse. Drawn ultimately to the New Testament 'as an insect buzzes to the light' he opined:

> The religious question is a 'life question' or (empty) chatter.
> This language game, we could say, only deals with 'life questions.'
> (Tyler, 2011, pp. 225 & 236)

And since the 'life questions' had always been the very web and weave of theological discourse from the Garden of Eden onwards, what was not to like? Theologians could start talking again, the 'thoughtful conversation about God' could continue. The 'handmaid' had rescued the 'Queen'.

Summary

The Western intellectual movement which became known as the Enlightenment had a quest for certainty as its inner force. This had a necessarily critical dimension since epistemology – 'the theory of knowing' was at the heart of philosophical discourse. Variously attempting to find the foundation of certainty through doubt, experience, mental synthesis, historical analysis and language, great figures of the era such as Descartes, Hume, Kant, Strauss and Russell made proposals which shook the foundations of traditional Christian Theology. It didn't quite topple over, however. Though the 'response' outlined above is highly selective, the contributions of thinkers from a variety of traditions such as Pascal, Schleiermacher, Barth, Rahner and Wittgenstein opened up ways for theologians to engage fruitfully with these philosophical critiques. The success or otherwise of their endeavours is moot and is reserved, dear reader, to your own judgement. In the meantime, philosophical certainty was not the only challenge to be faced by Theology in the Modern era. Scientific discoveries, scientific method and scientific certainty were also on the agenda of the Enlightenment and their relationship to Theology forms the subject matter of the next chapter.

20

Theology 'versus' Science

Despite their mutual origin in the sense of wonder and the quest to understand reality, the related disciplines of Theology, Science and Philosophy became increasingly estranged through the Modern Period. This was not self-evident among the pre-Socratic Greeks, nor from the biblical understanding, which allowed for 'Natural Theology' – the possibility of anyone coming to recognize the truth of God by reflection upon the goodness and order of Creation. Over the early centuries, Christian Theology increasingly understood the creative act of God to have been 'ex nihilo' – out of nothing, and the Medieval period, endowed with figures such as Albert the Great, understood the entire enterprise of knowledge to be seamless. The controversies of Copernicus, Galileo and later Darwin would change all that whereby Christian Theology was increasingly seen as a hindrance to the truth of reality, accessible only through scientific method. Despite the theistic perspectives of Newton and Leibniz, it wasn't until the Twentieth Century with its counter-intuitive discoveries concerning relativity, atomic physics and cosmology that some of the complementary concerns of theological and scientific method would come to the fore.

a) Origin of the thesis

If it took a while for theologians to grapple fruitfully with the philosophical challenges of Modernity, it proved a similar story in relation to Science. The presumption that Theology and Science are at loggerheads is so deeply ingrained in popular Western consciousness that it is almost shorthand for contestations of belief or unbelief. One of the fastest ways to shut down a theological conversation is to declare instead 'I don't believe in God, I believe in Science' as if the two were incompatible. Although this presumption is itself 'unscientific', it demands explanation. Once more the roots of the 'versus' in the title of this chapter lie in the quest for certainty so characteristic of the Modernity which can be said to have begun with the Enlightenment.

But 'twas not always thus. In the past, the now distinct disciplines of Theology, Philosophy and Science were pursued as one coherent search for understanding. Since each owe their origins to reflection upon the common human experience of wonder, this should not be surprising. Thales (c.600 BCE), the famed philosopher of Greek antiquity was the first thinker to offer a 'Theory of Everything' namely, that water was the 'primal womb and origin of all things'. No less an authority than Nietzsche acclaims the philosophical genius of Thales as the Father of Philosophy because in embryo we first find here the thought 'all things are one'. In *Philosophy in the Tragic Age of the Greeks* ([1872] 1962), Nietzsche is (unsurprisingly) less impressed that Thales gets caught up in the banal question of 'water' (a scientific question), and (really unsurprisingly) not impressed that he discusses 'origins' (a theological question). In due course, the successors of Thales such as Anaximander (c.610-546 BCE) and Heraclitus (c.535-475 BCE) offered similarly fascinating options for the Theory of Everything. Anaximander, by observing the fact that all things were coming to be and passing away, agreed that the source of all things must be from the 'eternal womb of the indefinite'. The notion of permanence and change fascinated the Greeks because it was wonderfully unsettling. We cannot be entirely sure of what we know – reality is a sort of moving target – we need something permanent as a reference point. Hence the famous intervention of Heraclitus with his evocative idea that 'the only permanence is change'. Theorizing that the dynamism of reality came from 'a game fire plays with itself', Heraclitus was tapping into the religio-scientific nature of fire. In Greek myth, the hero Prometheus stole the secret of fire from the Gods and was punished for doing so. Fire, alongside earth, air and water was one of the four elements constitutive of physical things. The mysterious, seemingly permanent stars of the heavens were made of a 'quintessence', a 'fifth element'.

Now before you start chuckling about all of creation being made of fire, just think on modern ideas that the whole cosmic caboodle might be made of energy and light. Before you start chuckling at permanence and change, just try working out what time is without it. Even more importantly, before you start chuckling at everything being made out of water, take note of the fact that it accounts for over 90 per cent of your physique. Worrying. As the American comedian Steven Wright says, 'We're all within an inch of drowning'. It is also worth noting that from around the same time, the notion 'all is one' was hardly a foreign thought in Oriental or even Semitic Near Eastern culture. Moreover, the idea of water being the elemental physical reality was clearly acceptable to the biblical thinking of Genesis 1 which was busy connecting all things through a Creator God launching clarity and clocks with light (Gen 1:1-3). Likewise, the passing and coming to be from the eternal womb of the indefinite had obvious parallels with 'Is-God' revealed in fire to Moses, whose name, I AM can also read I WILL BE (Ex 3:14).

Of all the Greek progenitors, however, it was Aristotle (384-322 BCE) who would provide the Christian West with its master scientific thinker. Keenly observant, keen to analyse and keen to systematize in a matrix of meaning, (see Section 16g), Aristotle's emphasis on the priority of empirical evidence identified him as more 'scientific' than his famous tutor Plato, who mistrusted the senses. Aristotle's painstaking classifications of animate and inanimate objects marked him out as a brilliant observational scholar. There were four causes of things in his system, and a chair may serve to exemplify them. The causes that together make a chair may be identified as 'material' (e.g. wood), 'formal' (e.g. desk-chair design), 'efficient' (the carpenter) and 'final' (its purpose – to be sat upon). Of these, it is the 'final' cause that attracts most attention since that is why it came to be in the first place – 'its end is its beginning'. This pattern matches his general theory of a dynamic cosmos, evolving and 'in motion' through the attraction of the divine 'Unmoved Mover' who can thus be understood as both the 'First' and 'Final Cause'. Although his speculation covered what would now be distinguished as Science – Philosophy – Theology, the almost incidental ordering of his writings helped sunder their relationship. A section treating of more general theories on how reality is structured (substance, accidents, etc.) was placed *after* his chapter on *physics* – the examination of experience. This juxtaposition of *physics* and *metaphysics* would in due course become more of a chasm than a continuity, a fissure which would become particularly deep following the Enlightenment.

b) Biblical science, natural theology?

As Christian theologians began to enter such debates, they were confronted with an original biblical reflection upon creation which mirrored the broad understanding of the Greeks. Philo of Alexandria (20 BCE–50 CE) had already wrestled with this prior to the New Testament writers cutting their teeth on the mystery, namely, that the material cosmos was an ever-present reality – the primordial type watery *chaos* to which God had brought order (Gen 1:1). Hooking this Thales-type theory with the threat of Heraclitus-type judgement, the Second Letter of Peter couldn't be clearer:

> By the word of God heavens existed long ago and an earth was formed out of water and by means of water, through which the world of that time was deluged with water and perished. But by the same word the present heavens and earth have been reserved for fire, being kept until the day of judgement and destruction of the godless. (2 Pet 3:5-7)

It should hastily be said that any fear of judgement did not mean that biblical theologians had a negative view of material reality. God had pronounced Creation 'good' (Gen 1:31), and this fundamental truth was the bulwark against the negative view of matter evidenced in the dualistic tendencies of Greek, Jewish apocalyptic and Mediterranean Gnostic thought. Indeed, the wonder of creation was not only a stimulus for prayer (e.g. Ps 8, 104, 139, 148), it seems to have been God's conclusive argument that caused Job to fall silent, to 'lay his hand on [his] mouth' (38:1-40:5). Furthermore, the possibility of human beings coming to belief in God through the wonder of nature seems to have been allowed by the biblical tradition in a variety of ways.

The Book of Wisdom seems to ponder the issue thoughtfully:

> For all people who were ignorant of God were foolish by nature;
> and they were unable from the good things that are seen to know the one who exists,
> nor did they recognize the artisan while paying heed to his works;
> For from the greatness and beauty of created things
> comes a corresponding perception of their Creator.
> Yet these people are little to be blamed,
> for perhaps they go astray
> while seeking God and desiring to find him.
> For while they live among his works, they keep searching,

and they trust in what they see, because the things that are seen are beautiful.
Yet again, not even they are to be excused;
for if they had the power to know so much
that they could investigate the world,
how did they fail to find sooner the Lord of these things? (Wis 13:1, 5-9)

Jesus in the Gospel teases his listeners:

And why do you worry about clothing? Consider the lilies of the field, how they grow; they neither toil nor spin, yet I tell you, even Solomon in all his glory was not clothed like one of these. But if God so clothes the grass of the field, which is alive today and tomorrow is thrown into the oven, will he not much more clothe you - you of little faith? (Matt 6:28-30)

And Paul in Romans puts the scaries on everyone:

For the wrath of God is revealed from heaven against all ungodliness and wickedness of those who by their wickedness suppress the truth. For what can be known about God is plain to them, because God has shown it to them. Ever since the creation of the world his eternal power and divine nature, invisible though they are, have been understood and seen through the things he has made. So they are without excuse; for though they knew God, they did not honour him as God or give thanks to him, but they became futile in their thinking, and their senseless minds were darkened. Claiming to be wise, they became fools; and they exchanged the glory of the immortal God for images resembling a mortal human being or birds or four-footed animals or reptiles. (Rom 1:18-23)

This notion that human beings can attain some knowledge of God through the witness of creation became a recurrent theme in the Christian Theology of the West. Nature was not God, but rather pointed to its Creator. On this reading, to explore Natural Science could be understood as a quest to explore what Augustine had called the *vestigia dei* – the 'footprints of God'. The highest creation of God was humanity, whose particular glory was its power of reasoning, which, though compromised through the disobedience of Eden, had God as its natural orientation. Added to the mix was the growing conviction among Christian theologians that God had created *ex nihilo* – 'out of nothing'. While this was by no means the common biblical tradition, it can be read implicitly by the translation of Gen 1:1 in the *LXX* and is made explicit in Second Maccabees:

I beg you, my child, to look at the heaven and the earth and see everything that is in them, and recognize that God did not make them out of things that existed. And in the same way, the human race came into being (2 Macc 7:28).

It is difficult to doubt that the assembled theologians and bishops had this in mind by the Council of Nicaea (325 CE) in declaring that God 'created all things visible and invisible'. After all, the notion of *ex nihilo*:

- Kept God separate from Creation which avoided the confusions of *pantheism* (God is not just everywhere, God is identical with everything)
- Uniquely allowed God to have a monopoly on anything infinite or eternal allowing invisible realities not mentioned in Genesis such as angels and even time to be part of that creation
- Made everything dependent or *contingent* upon the providence of God

Though the doctrine *ex nihilo* was not made explicit until Lateran IV in 1215, the need to make the declaration at that time was precisely to contradict the notion that the world was eternal, as could be construed from the earlier Greek and by now problematic biblical tradition. As noted above, Section 16g, this period saw the 'rediscovery' of Aristotle's writings, mediated to the West through Jewish and Islamic scholars, which if anything aroused further suspicion. It is a tribute to the qualities of theologian – philosopher – scientists such as Albert the Great and his more famous protégé, Thomas Aquinas, that they were able to present such novel ideas in theologically acceptable ways. The tenacious priority Thomas accorded to sense experience throughout his writings is likely to have been rooted in those formative years at Albert's *Studium* in Cologne. The seasoning of Aristotle's theories with Christian thought which is clearly evidenced from the opening lines of the *Summa Theologiae* even-handedly offers the possibility of *Natural Theology*, while defending the need for Christian revelation (ST I q.1 art.1).

Aristotle's understanding of everything having a *telos* – 'final cause' or 'purpose' enabled Aquinas and other scholastics to underpin Genesis with this newly rediscovered 'Natural Science' which affirmed the biblical picture that all things are ordered from, by and towards God. Medieval Christianity was 'pro-Science' – creation is good, God created the cosmos rationally therefore humanity can seek to understand it, master it and exercise dominion over it (Gen 1:28). The scholastics rejected 'Occasionalism' – the notion that God is the only guarantor of the correspondence between experience and the mind, a refusal that has long been seen as the reason why subsequent Christian and Islamic scientific thinking took different paths. It was ironically the theological distinction between the natural order and the realm of grace which *enabled* Western experimentation to develop so successfully, but unfortunately the seeds of an estrangement between the 'Queen' and 'Science' were already in the mix.

The Medieval heritage not only included intriguing speculations of early atomic theory, it also included speculations about the heavens which, with the help of Ptolemy of Alexandria (c.90–168 CE) construed that the world was surrounded by concentric star-studded glassy spheres, beyond the furthest of which, was God's domain. Since this seemed to confirm the 'earth centric' view of Genesis, speculations in Science, Theology and Philosophy all became a little entangled. Let's face it, even Thomas regarded 'Natural Theology' as part of 'Philosophy' and since 'Science' was pursued under the heading of 'Natural Philosophy', it is easy to see how doctrinal, philosophical and scientific convictions were part of one big matrix of knowledge. Dante's famous *Divina Commedia* exemplifies the synthesis of all three (see below, Section 24f). Human reasoning, whether you would want to call it theological, philosophical or scientific had, among other things, successfully put God in his heaven, man on the earth and angels somewhere in between. And everything was nicely settled until a priest decided to serve God with an eviction order.

c) Copernicus and Galileo

It wasn't a problem so much of not seeing the wood for the trees, it was more a problem of not seeing the sun for its brightness. Nicholas Copernicus (1473–1543) was a Polish priest who had spent time in three of the most prestigious universities of Europe – Cracow, Padua and Bologna. Copernicus determined from his observations that the traditional understanding of the movements of the sun and stars was unsustainable. Far from everything orbiting round the earth in perfect circular movement to give us night and day, it was the earth that revolved every 24 hours and was itself in a yearly orbit around the sun. He also correctly deduced that the stars were much further away than the sun. Already, by 1514, he had outlined his revolutionary (*sic*) ideas on the movements of the heavens which were eventually articulated more fully in *On the Revolutions of the Heavenly Spheres* in 1543. This was originally not too controversial, possibly because in its early published form, a disclaimer that the work was theoretical rather than factual was added by a Lutheran, Andreas Osiander (1496–1552). There is a double irony since this seems to have been added unbeknownst to Copernicus, who had dedicated his original manuscript to the Pope.

Inspired by the work of Copernicus, Giordano Bruno (1548–1600) decided that the distinction between heavenly and earthly had finally been undone and opting for a pantheistic cosmic view of God as beginning, middle and end of everything, soon found himself facing serious charges of heresy as life on other planets and reincarnation appeared in his thinking. Working as a spy for Elizabeth I did nothing to endear him to Church authorities sensitive to the betrayal of priests returning to England. After capture in Venice, he was burned at the stake in Rome's Campo dei Fiori where his brooding, hooded figure stands to this day. Meanwhile, Francis Bacon (1561–1626) was echoing the views of his namesake Roger (1220–1292) in advocating the merits of what became known as the 'scientific' or 'inductive' method. Conclusions should only be drawn from evidence and not from predetermined systems of thought which can blind us to actuality – and there was definitely one great big cosmic blind spot that was about to be cured.

Galileo Galilei (1564–1642) was the man who shattered the glassy spheres once and for all. Professor of Mathematics at Pisa from 1589, he moved to Padua in 1592 and thence to Florence from 1610 as Chief Mathematician and Philosopher to the Grand Duke of Tuscany. Already contributing recognizably Newtonian speculations regarding unhindered motion, he famously tested gravitational acceleration from the top of the already leaning Tower at Pisa. Life was good, but a letter to the Grand Duchess earned him notoriety, since his advice to the good lady was that biblical passages inconsistent with the actual motion of the earth should not be treated literally. This came to the attention of the Inquisition which banned Copernicus' writings in 1616 and Galileo had to tread more carefully. Later, emboldened by the accession of his friend, Matteo Barberini, as Pope Urban VIII in 1623, he began to write again. Though he had been advised to keep everything hypothetical and non-biblical, his *Dialogue of the Two Chief World Systems* in 1632 was pretty convicted, basically Copernican, and definitely controversial. The infamous trial then took place of a professor who had a scientific understanding of how the world *actually* worked being asked to recant by clerics wedded to theological views of how they thought the world *should* work. The one informed by accurate observation, the others informed by simplistic acceptance of Holy Writ. Inevitably, this became a PR disaster for the Church. Although Galileo did go through the motions of recanting, his famous comment – *Eppure si muove* – 'But it still moves' was what actually echoed around Europe. Despite the fact that he would have been more correct to say 'they both move', by spending the rest of his days under house arrest, he became something of a martyr for academic freedom. It is no coincidence that it took a pope from Poland, where Copernicus is a hero, to finally rescind the judgements made against Galileo. But it did take over three and a half centuries to do so, years which saw the relationship between Theology and Science endure further difficult, and perhaps even trickier times.

d) Newton, Leibniz and Theodicy

Galileo was active at the start of what would become a fantastic century of progress in scientific knowledge. Isaac Newton (1642–1727) was fascinated by many things, and though his numerous religious writings were of equal interest to him as were his scientific insights, it is the latter for which he is rightly more famous. Briefly put, the genius of Newton connected motion with mass, force, gravity and friction. By doing so, he appeared to explain the dynamics of the entire universe, which could and would stay 'in motion' with the regularity of a cosmic clock. His *Mathematical Principles of Natural Philosophy* (1687) demonstrated that the logical language of the universe was algebraic, not Hebraic, or Latin or Greek or any of the other tongues of Theology. The 'natural' conclusion that many educated people drew from this was that since God did not have to sustain seasonal cycles, meteorological or any other natural phenomena, it didn't make a great deal of sense to have him interfering in any kind of biblical, personal way. Newton's regularized cosmos fitted perfectly with the reasoned certainty of the Enlightenment:

- Predictably, it provided substantial impetus to the Deist movement, which as noted above, understood the craftsman God to have set the world in motion and left it to tick on like a well sprung clock.
- It also sowed the seeds for scientific determinism which had implications for the understanding and limits of human freedom. If everything was the result of a reaction to a previous cause, then human actions, conceivably, were purely the function of past impacts. Freedom, in this frame, becomes an illusion.
- It brought into even sharper focus the 'Design Argument' – if God had put the whole thing together, did that provide evidence for, or against, the existence of a supernatural Creator?

In an improbable synchronicity, wrestling with all these questions was an equally brilliant mathematician, Gottfried Leibniz (1646–1716). Leibniz was a prodigious intellect; being offered a professorship at 21, he invented calculus independently of Newton and since he hit the printing presses first, it is his notation that became standard. In a contribution to philosophical reasoning that would become key to Logic, Mathematics and experimental Science, he distinguished between 'analytic' statements (true or false in themselves) and 'synthetic' statements (things which must be investigated) His insights into kinetic energy and his tentative steps towards atomic theory were similarly perspicacious. Though he struggled to explain how his system of atoms, which he called 'monads', functioned, he was ahead of his time in proposing that matter had energy within itself – this would only become clear in the twentieth century. Because his terminology of monads seems quirky, and his use of 'soul' as an approximation of energy was somewhat odd, his writings on such matters may appear strangely quaint. That said, because 'monadology' meant that the universe operated according to 'pre-existent harmony', it would eventually find strong echoes in later theoretical approaches to Physics, Biology and Ecology.

Since Leibniz' scientific system was 'by nature' a little less mechanical than Newton's, it is no surprise that his two main contributions to the God – Science – Philosophy debates were equally potent.

- With regard to the question of Creation, Leibniz took the view that the proposal that God had brought the cosmos into being was reasonable on the grounds of his 'principle of sufficient reason'. The core cosmological question is 'Why is there something rather than nothing?' So far as Leibniz was concerned, there was enough evidence to point to a Creator, just as in a court of law, everyone accepts there can be 'sufficient reason' to make a sound judgement.

- Taking this a stage further, and anticipating the objections that Hume and others would make, Leibniz took seriously the problem of suffering and the question mark that placed over the idea of there being an omnipotent and still benevolent Creator. Leibniz pondered and concluded that there must be a reason why the world is as it is. Why, for example, do we have five fingers and not six? Why is nature like this and not that? His proposal was that this world is the 'best of all possible worlds'. The way the world *is*, must be as God has fundamentally intended it, and a possible reason for its arrangement may be that it is the only world wherein humanity can experience freedom, self-determination and providence at the same time.

It was perhaps fitting that a master of algebra should have a go at solving the equation of Omnipotent God + Innocent Suffering + Benevolent God = Wisdom or Absurdity? Sometimes called the 'Irreconcilable Triangle', Leibniz's attempt to solve it became known as *Theodicy* – a Greek amalgam of 'God' and 'Justice' which he coined as a term in his *Essays on the Goodness of God* (1710). He saw evil as a necessary feature, the shade that contrasts with the light necessary for moral life in this, the 'Best of all possible Worlds'. Though the above may appear as much of a 'conjuring trick' as Anselm's Ontological Argument, it is once again indicative of Leibniz' genius that 'Possible World' arguments not only resonate with classical theologians such as Irenaeus and Augustine, they are also quite fashionable in contemporary perspective.

e) Nineteenth century: Darwin and design

Voltaire (1694-1778) took it upon himself to parody Leibniz in *Candide*, where the dizzy Dr Pangloss is the relevant caricature. Whether Leibniz was too far ahead of his contemporaries or not is a moot point, but the Newtonian picture of a mechanical, predictable universe could not have been a more perfect fit with the *zeitgeist* – the 'spirit of the time'. Mathematics and the aspects of 'Natural Philosophy' we might refer to as Physics were not the only disciplines to progress. Geology was another, and the discoveries of weird and wonderful fossil remains were posing a problem. Part of the picture painted by Genesis was that all earth's species were created by God, named by Man and saved by Noah on his Ark. Furthermore, a literal reading of the text offered the possibility of a calculation of when God actually created the world and the first earthlings on it; 4004 BCE to be precise, making the world 6000 years old. Rather marvellously, one of the first geologists to send this theory down the tubes was a drainage engineer named William Smith (1769–1839). His study of rock strata and discovery of different fossils, many stranger than he could imagine, led him to propose a series of creations – possibly corresponding to six ages rather than six days of Creation. Basic, but brilliant, his proposal still resonates with various 'catastrophe theories' of evolution and human origins, since extinction seems to be as much a feature of life on the planet as germination and generation of ever more specialized species.

Smith was not alone in exploring the debate emanating from geological discoveries and what we might call nascent theories of evolution. Charles Lyell (1797-1875), Hugh Miller (1802-1856) and Philip Gosse (1810-1888) all pondered how to reconcile the biblical testimony with that of the rocks and the fossils. Gosse speculated about Adam's belly button and whether the rocks of Eden may themselves have had duplicitous designer fossils in them, put there by God, along with tree rings to give the place some 'mature garden' credibility. On the other hand, Robert Chambers (1802-1871) and Herbert Spencer (1820-1903) were more critical, the latter arguing that the sheer number of different species implied a preposterously large number of acts of creation by God (cf. Knight, 2003).

The stage was set for the insights of Charles Darwin (1809–1882) published as *The Origin of Species* in (1859) and *The Descent of Man* (1871). Darwin had come to his own conclusions while travelling as a naturalist aboard *HMS Beagle* in its journey to the Galapagos Islands off the Western coast of South

America. His five years of travelling were not in vain. He surmised that the process by which creatures are modified must be connected with reproduction. In simple form, his theory is straightforward. In any given environment, conditions are suitable to a given creature with certain characteristics. This creature is more likely than others of its species to reach maturity and reproduce. This means both that there are more creatures of this type than less suitable types, it also means that the particular features of this well-adapted animal will begin to prevail. The idea was summed up (not by Darwin but by Herbert Spencer) as 'survival of the fittest' and it neatly explained seemingly redundant features of creatures such as male nipples that don't produce milk and ostrich feathers that can't flap enough to fly. It also allowed Darwin to explain why species might die out. Using the population studies of Thomas Malthus (1766–1834), extinction occurred where creatures simply could not compete with better adapted species more able to be sustained by the environment. There was no need for catastrophe, since atrophy and competition provided a sufficient explanation.

Theologically, Darwin had dropped bombshells on two of the most cherished concepts of Christian doctrine. The first was that far from creation being a process guided by the benevolent hand of the Creator God, it put chance, competition, violence, even mutation and *error*, at the heart of evolution. Worse still, the notion of humanity being made in the *imago dei*, 'the image of God', upon which so much of theological anthropology rested, had to be radically rethought. After all, the post-Beagle Design Argument looked a bit tatty. God created life, and the more competitive and mutated it got, the upshot just happened to include us, but we are nowhere near as successful as flies or plankton.

At this distance, it is quite difficult to assess the shockwave caused by Darwin's theories in religious circles. On the one hand, the spotlight tends to fall upon the famous debate that took place in Oxford at the British Association in 1860 which was discussing *The Origin of Species* in the absence of Darwin, who was unwell. According to legend, there was a classic 'Galileo' moment as the forces of progress met the follies of ecclesiastical dogma. Darwin's friend Thomas Huxley was in the intellectually robust Science corner while Bishop Wilberforce was guided by the whimsical wonder of the Faery dell. Alister McGrath's summary of the account is worth repeating:

> The classic statement of this legend dates from 1898, and takes the form of an autobiographical memory from Mrs Isabella Sidgewick, published in *Macmillan's Magazine*:

I was happy enough to be present on the memorable occasion at Oxford when Mr Huxley bearded Bishop Wilberforce . . . The Bishop rose, and in a light and scoffing tone, florid and fluent, he assured us that there was nothing in the idea of evolution; rock pigeons were what rock pigeons always had been. Then, turning to his antagonist with a smiling insolence, he begged to know, was it through his grandfather or his grandmother that he claimed descent from a monkey?

This account, which dates from 1898, contradicts accounts published or in circulation closer to the meeting itself. The truth of the matter was that Wilberforce had written an extensive review of the *Origin of Species,* pointing out some serious weaknesses. Darwin regarded this review as significant, and modified his discussion at several points in response to Wilberforce's criticisms. (McGrath, 1999, pp. 24–5)

To be honest, I almost prefer to believe the legend, since it appeals to my sense of drama. That said, I do think it important to heed the broader point made by McGrath which is that there was a mixed reaction among believers to what Darwin was proposing. The theological problems varied for different Christian traditions. Although by now fairly rare, *Sola Scriptura* communities in the Reformed tradition where no nuancing of the biblical testimony had occurred were left in a dilemma. The fork in the road that many felt they faced was either to consider Genesis and the Creation accounts as part of the non-negotiable 'fundamentals' of the faith, or to reject the whole scriptural testimony. It is fanciful to suggest that Fundamentalism, which gathered momentum at the turn of the twentieth century was entirely triggered by Darwin, but the persistence of Creationism as a theologico-scientific proposal did lead to the famous 'monkey trial' of John Scopes who was effectively found guilty of evolutionary theory in Tennessee in 1925. The Catholic Church displayed something of a mixed response. On the one hand, it remained somewhat sensitive to the question of origins well into the pontificate of Pius XII, whose *Humani Generis* (1950) raised some eyebrows. On the other, most twentieth-century theologians embraced evolutionary thinking with gusto. Very much a factor in Rahner's system, it was most explicit in the work of Pierre Teilhard de Chardin (1881–1955). Theologian, scientist and paleontologist, he saw evolutionary theory as an insight into the cosmic 'Christification' of creation which, through the raising of human consciousness, would collaborate in drawing the whole universe towards the 'Omega Point' of reconciliation in God.

Meanwhile, back in the day, Darwin himself, probably to his credit, stayed somewhat aloof from the intensities of the furore. He is 'claimed' as a hero by both 'sides' – a fearless seeker of scientific truth, but one buried with full religious honours in Westminster Abbey. Perhaps he should have the last (ambiguous) word:

> There is grandeur in this view of life, with its several powers having been originally breathed by the Creator into a few forms or into one; and that while this planet has gone cycling on according to the forced law of gravity, from so simple a beginning, endless forms most beautiful have been and are being evolved. (Darwin, 1872, p. 490)

f) Twentieth century: Einstein and particle physics

Darwin's insight, while less disturbing to the educated theological élite, certainly accelerated the common perception that the Bible was 'not true' and that it had 'been proved wrong by Science'. Despite the longstanding idea that there were 'Two Books' – one of nature and one of revelation proper to the different disciplines of scientific and theological discourse, the scientists in the white coats of the laboratory seemed to be more incisive and honest than the black garbed ministers equivocating on what were and weren't essential truths of biblical Christianity. To be sure, religiously minded scientists such as Michael Faraday (Electromagnetics) and Gregor Mendel (Genetics) were still operating at the forefront of discovery. That said, if the nineteenth century had proved turbulent, the collective earthlings, believers or otherwise were in for an even more disorientating set of discoveries in the twentieth century. By the time that Einstein, Rutherford, Bohr, Heisenberg, Hubble, Hoyle *et al.* had finished mapping the outer reaches of the cosmos and the inner depths of the atom, it would be fair to say that theologians were only as dizzy as their scientific and philosophical counterparts.

'Let there be light' may have been the first words of God in Genesis, but light, among other things, was about to get a makeover. Having failed to secure a university post, Albert Einstein (1879–1955) was working at a patent office in Berne, Switzerland. Since this involved assessment of innovative ideas, it may have been fortuitous both for him and for Physics. In a series of papers from 1905 to 1916, he blew away the hitherto all encompassing Newtonian understanding of the universe. There were a number of magical moments of insight; in his famous formula, $e = mc^2$, he identified that Leibniz was basically correct, energy, matter and light were connected, atomic reality was relational, intense and potentially explosive. Light – well, where do we start? Light velocity appears to be one of the few universal constants, but if that is so, then all other perceptions of speed are just that, perceptions that are based on our confusion of distance, time and relative motion. Instead of operating in three dimensions, Einstein starts with four. The upshot is that since time, space, movement, location are all relative concepts, you can 'prove' that at the speed of light, time stops 'because' distance disappears.

Now although this is not the secret of eternal youth, it does perhaps explain why mid-life crisis males buy sports cars since every little bit of acceleration keeps you slightly younger *relative* to other people. Einstein was happy to use very simple examples to get people to think differently – the tick and tock of a clock – what is it anyway? Anyone who sits on an oven will experience 30 seconds very differently to someone gazing into the eyes of their beloved. Science had been defined by the ancients as 'the study of objects in motion'. Einstein was just saying that time is also one of the variables.

Since theologians were generally pretty happy to work beyond three dimensions, the fact that Einstein seemed to be making an 'eternal present' reasonable and 'omnipresence' not inconceivable, there was much speculation regarding Einstein's own religious convictions. The balance of evidence is that Einstein was an agnostic, with an admiration for Spinoza (1632–1677), who had proposed an intrinsic, pantheistic view of God-in-nature. Yet despite being equally critical of both the idea of a personal God and the unfounded conviction of atheists, his occasional religious comments were dragged in all directions to serve or subvert belief. For him, theological approaches rooted in cosmic awe were in harmony, but distinct from, scientific endeavours, a position made clear with his famous sentiment: 'Science without religion is lame, religion without science is blind' (Einstein, [1941] 2010, p. 46).

To have one scientific revolution is normally enough for any self-respecting century to cope with, but as Einstein's speculations were increasingly confirmed by experiments on the cosmic scale, Max Planck (1858–1947), Nils Bohr (1885–1962) and Werner Heisenberg (1901–1976) were busy plumbing the nature of the atom. Radiation, it transpired, was not emitted in a constant pattern but in little bursts or 'quanta'. As 'Quantum' or 'Particle' Physics developed, not even Einstein was ready for some of the conclusions – as if God was playing dice with the cosmos. It *appears* that entities can be in two places at once and it *seems* some things such as light can be either particles or waves and it has been *observed* that *observation* seems to change things. Every atom is a whirl of relational realities whose operations are so bewildering that Bohr remarked that anyone not shocked by quantum theory cannot possibly have understood it.

Theologically, the side effects of quantum theory were almost as quirky as the quanta. The apparent unpredictability of atomic reality could be understood as a sub-atomic support for the idea of free will. Quantum theory only works by means of probabilities because the behaviour of individual particles cannot be ascertained. This 'indeterminacy within a larger context of predictability' offers a possible solution to the theological conundrum of free will and determinism, always a problem with the Design Argument in its strongest mechanistic form. After all, if God has set things going, mapped out the laws of nature and knows what's going to happen, human beings are not free. The experience of choice and the notion of moral responsibility are both illusions.

Heisenberg's quantum 'Uncertainty Principle' likewise triggered theological reflection. Since it notes the impact of observation on subatomic realities, it implies a more 'holistic' view of reality, an interconnectedness that involves rather than excludes. No less a figure than Joseph Ratzinger (Pope Benedict XVI) considered this insight to be relevant to the authentic interpretation of the Bible. It validates different possibilities and different meanings through the interaction of believers with the text in their own time and place. The validation of this *sensus plenior* – 'fuller meaning' is in contrast to the quest for univocal exegetical certainty which the harder edge of Higher Criticism had been attempting since the Enlightenment. While other religious scientists such as Stanley Jaki (1924–2009) would be more cautious about the instant application of theoretical scientific models to theological constructs (they might change tomorrow, and then what will you say?), it is *so* tempting. I recently heard a sermon where the preacher remarked with cool understatement 'It is a lot easier to imagine the Risen Lord entering a locked room when we realize the porous nature of sub-atomic reality'. And he is sort of right. Among the disturbing and shocking consequences of quantum analysis is the rather upsetting proposal that 95 per cent of each of us is a waste of space. Far from being solid citizens, we are nature's finest string vests – our infinitesimal self, trellised more like the rhythms of a jazz band than a cluster of impermeable glued marbles.

g) Big Bang and the Anthropic principle

Impressive though the achievements of atomic physicists had proven to be, there was a dark side to their discoveries, namely, the development of nuclear weaponry. Suddenly, humanity had gained an unwanted possibility, the ability to completely destroy itself. In the meantime, the more traditional battleground of cosmology was drawing attention in the Theology 'versus' Science debate. The observation that the Cosmos was expanding led to the 'Big Bang' theory of the origin of the Universe. There is a good claim made that a priest-scientist, George Lamaître (1894–1966) was the first to work on this theory, yet ironically, the secular astronomer who coined the phrase and made it famous, Fred Hoyle (1915–2001), was not keen on the theory at all. He rightly suspected that it would attract the attention of theists with their notions of a Creator God calling all things into being. He also reasoned (again rightly) that Creator thinking would be further encouraged because he reckoned the infinitesimally small chances of a cosmic explosion producing the observable ordered universe were about the same as a whirlwind sweeping through an aircraft factory and assembling a jumbo jet. Hoyle himself preferred the 'steady-state' notion of a permanently expanding and contracting picture of the universe which was solidly in the ancient Greek tradition of matter being permanently present and also allowed the infinite possibilities necessary for the emergence of life (cf. Hoyle, 2000).

By and large, whether origins were imagined as 'Steady State' or 'Big Bang', neither theory affected the fundamental disagreement between the theistic and atheistic accounts of Cosmology, namely, 'Why is there something rather than nothing?' In a famous 1948 BBC radio debate between Bertrand Russell and the Jesuit philosopher Frederick Copleston (1907–1994), the protagonists managed to agree on a definition of God (*A supreme personal being – distinct from the world and creator of the world*), but fell out over questions regarding cosmic origins. Russell opined that the Universe is a 'brute fact' and speculations regarding its origin were intellectually out of bounds, while Copleston expressed astonishment that scientists, philosophers and theologians were condemned to accept such an arbitrary limit to their enquiry. Yet such debates were indicative that 'Big Questions' remained on the intellectual agenda and as Hoyle anticipated, the 'Big Bang' theory certainly breathed life back into the Design Argument. This had been under sustained critique in post-war Britain and America, not least from Anthony Flew (1923–2010). Combining John Wisdom's *Parable of the Absent Gardener* with a hint of Logical Positivism, he reasoned along the following lines.

Two sojourners happen upon a garden in a dense wood. The two travellers begin to argue, one that there must be a gardener that has arranged things since there are flowers and signs of order, the other that this is not the case since there are weeds and other unattractive elements. They decide to keep watch to see if the gardener will come, but to no avail. They use bloodhounds and set traps to see if he has come at night or when they have not been looking – but still no sound or alarm is raised. Since one of the travellers remains convinced there must be someone responsible, the question turns as to whether the absent gardener might have extraordinary powers and might be invisible and so forth, but the consequence is that no agreement can be found. How can an intangible, invisible, undemonstrable gardener differ from no gardener at all? The 'believer' in this case suffers 'death by a thousand qualifications', which led Flew to think that since there is no test that can be devised to falsify the claim that there is a gardener, then that claim, like the notion that there is a God, must be of dubious validity (cf. Flew, 2007, pp. 42–5, Towey, 2007).

To some extent, the theo-cosmological response to all this got a bit personal – well sort of. Far from looking to the stars or earthly perfection for the clue to the design, why not look once more at the *imago dei*, humanity itself. To be sure, the vast 1.3-billion-year timescale from the Big Bang to the arrival of human beings had somewhat dwarfed the 6000-odd-year-old option calculated from a dubious exegesis of Genesis. It also implied (in an oft cited analogy) that if creation was a day, then life appeared within the last hour and human beings on the stroke of midnight. However, while viewed one way this might imply humans to be insignificant, viewed another it's because we were worth waiting for! This theory, that the entire organization of the Cosmos was geared to produce humanity became known as the *Anthropic Principle*. Moreover, it was not only theologians such as Pierre Teilhard de Chardin who were proposing this sort of an understanding of Creation. Since an alteration by the merest fraction of the atomic structure of the cosmos would have rendered life impossible, and such a series of numerical accidents seems inexplicable, thinkers such as Nobel prize-winning mathematician Freeman Dyson were led to conclude that the more the details of the universe were explored, the more it seemed that human life on earth was all part of a plan – 'the universe in some sense knew we were coming' (1978, p. 250).

Hope you feel special. But the Anthropic Principle was not new, it was really Aristotle's 'Final Cause' writ large. Always the slightly spooky side of Aristotle, 'Final Cause' can only be recognized *looking back*, whereas classic scientific method was more geared to accurate observation of the present in order to furnish accurate prediction *of the future*. This, surely, was what marked out its methodology from the dubious constructs of Theology and Philosophy which had circumscribed human advancement in the past?

But by now even the basics of scientific method itself were coming under scrutiny. When thumbing back through the history books, it could be observed that Science had progressed by means of brilliant experiments, often allied to acute mathematical analysis, which changed the way things were understood. In good Enlightenment fashion, Science actually progressed by *doubting* contemporary ways of thinking, demonstrating that the prevailing perception of reality was mistaken. After all, you don't see too many fans of the flat earth or of *phlogiston* around these days. The trouble is that by necessity this makes scientists cannibals of their own knowledge. The open-minded scientist is thus committed *not* to regard scientific knowledge as certain after all. Counter to popular perception, Science was thus seen to proceed by *theory* not by *fact*, a matter famously discussed by Karl Popper in *The Logic of Scientific Discovery* (1959). Shortly after, in *The Structure of Scientific Revolutions* (1962), Thomas Kuhn identified significant moments of progression in Science as 'paradigm shifts' whereby a whole way of thinking about the world has to change. At such pivotal points, Kuhn observed that it is more likely to be other scientists rather than theologians or philosophers who most directly resist new ways of thinking, because they have perhaps wedded their whole careers to mistaken assumptions. *Scientific theory is merely the best explanation available at the present time.* It is a working hypothesis, which makes it much more like Philosophy and Theology than modern perceptions had presumed.

h) Epilogue

Back to a harmonious square one? Not quite. The latter part of the twentieth century saw the gloves coming off as the mutual relationships between Science, Philosophy and Theology continued to come under strain. From the point of view of Cosmology at least, Scientists found themselves unavoidably on the threshold of what are in essence philosophical and theological questions. Stephen Hawking wrote critically in his bestseller *Brief History of Time*:

> Up to now, most scientists have been too occupied with the development of new theories that describe *what* the universe is to ask the question *why*. On the other hand, the people whose business it is to ask *why*, the philosophers, have not been able to keep up (1988, p. 174).

He then ended with the comment that the quest for a unifying theory of the universe would be the ultimate triumph of human reason – 'for then we would know the mind of God' (p. 175). This was clearly a case of Science becoming theological via cosmology, an inevitability caustically anticipated by Robert Jastrow decades earlier in his book *God and the Astronomers*. He concluded:

> At this moment it seems as though science will never be able to raise the curtain on the mystery of creation. For the scientist who has lived by his faith in the power of reason, the story ends like a bad dream. He has scaled the mountains of ignorance; he is about to conquer the highest peak; as he pulls himself over the final rock, he is greeted by a band of theologians who have been sitting there for centuries. (Jastrow, 1978, p. 116)

Because such spiky points of view have continued to characterize some of the dialogue between Theology Philosophy and Science, the future significance of the debate (and some possible peace initiatives) will be discussed further in the concluding chapter of this book. While the history of thought did not force a conclusion that Science and Theology should be at loggerheads, as the chapter has outlined, there were understandable reasons why the *impression* of a fundamental opposition became ingrained in the consciousness of Modernity. In the meantime, if Theology had experienced some tongue-tied moments in relation to the Natural Sciences, it had also struggled to articulate its own insights in relation to the Human Sciences, an intellectual, political and psychological drama which forms the subject of the next chapter.

Summary

The wonder and goodness of Creation are constitutive for Christian thinking and enabled the discipline of 'Natural Philosophy' to develop into 'Natural Science'. Unfortunately, the medieval continuities of Theology, Philosophy and Science appeared to be ruptured in the Modern period by a series of crises whereby solemnly held positions in Theology seemed to be contradicted by the findings of scientists. Copernicus, Galileo, Newton and Darwin reversed centuries of presumption and the collective conclusion drawn from their work supported the notion of an impersonal distant deity or none at all. The twentieth century saw the picture becoming altogether more curious through the advances of Einstein and the Quantum theorists. Their findings, along with cosmological hypotheses such as the 'Big Bang', seemed to open up dialogue once more. Theologians, by and large, were more comfortable with the notion that reality began in a 'singularity' and is paradoxical to its core. This not only opened up parallels with the idea of a Creator God, it also meant that discussion of theological conundra such as free will and determinism seemed somehow more at home in the riddle of nature. Ultimately, despite any lingering suspicions, the mutual quest for a 'Theory of Everything' has meant that on the summits of human knowledge and speculation, the three discourses of Theology, Philosophy and Science have inevitably continued to meet.

21

Theology 'versus' Anthropology?

Chapter Outline

Part of the dynamism of Western Modernity with its quest to ground all things in reason was a desire to emancipate society from the perceived shackles of religion. Enlightenment reflections on the social, political and psychological dimensions of human beings vehemently argued that God had inadvertently been made in the image of man rather than the other way round. Theology was not just founded on fairy tales, it was part of the wider phenomenon of religiosity which urgently needed to be either eradicated or cured for people to reach the full expression of their humanity. Whilst the theoretical 'battleground' took place in the traditional arenas of the academy, the contest for the hearts and minds of humanity spilled over into global political action, therapeutic techniques and sociologies of the 'holy.'

a) Human beings, socio-political animals

Although the favoured Medieval and indeed Enlightenment motif for understanding human beings was as rational animals – or *homo sapiens* – 'knowing man', the social dimension of life was also thoroughly reviewed in the Modern period. This was not exactly novel, and certainly not 'un-theological'. It was noted above (see Section 2d), that until Adam met Eve he was mute, unknown, unknowable – the drama of the individual life being somewhat unspectacular without companionship. The unfolding saga of the storied individuals in the Bible had a plural, societal dimension as a 'chosen people', a 'covenant community' struggling with the challenge of how to live together rightly. Whether clan-based (Genesis), tribal (Joshua – Judges), kingly (1 Sam – 2 Kings), priest-ruled (Ezra), colonial (Maccabees), communal-millenarian (Gospel/Acts), the Bible presented a whole range of ways of living together, each with their different challenges, blights and blessings. Adding to this mix, the Christian Church had lived experience ranging from being a persecuted minority to becoming an imperial majority, while dipping its toe into alternative monastic and religious lifestyles.

As the Modern period dawned, however, it was the old feudal arrangement of king, nobles, freemen and peasants that seemed to be sanctioned by Christian theologians. Even though the schism of 1054 and the upheavals of the sixteenth century had left Christendom divided, the link between political authority and religious authority first forged by Constantine was not broken, indeed it was strangely reinforced. As noted above (Section 18g), the Treaty of Westphalia in 1648 sanctioned the idea that national and religious identities were synonymous with the ruler. Among other things, this made it very difficult to discern the extent to which the many conflicts which peppered Europe and the globe from the Reformation to the French Revolution were for reasons of faith or of flag. The symbiosis of Church and State – their shared life – was of such mutual benefit that it made it nigh impossible for theologians to 'think differently', despite the potential for critique readily available in the Gospels. This made the Church ill-equipped for the revolutionary forms of social thought that would emerge with Modernity.

Ironically, alternative socio-political thinking was long part of the Greco-Latin-Christian heritage. According to Cicero, Socrates had 'first called Philosophy down from the sky, set it in cities and even introduced it into homes, and compelled it to consider life and morals, good and evil' (Guthrie, 1971, pp. 98–9). The thought experiments of his pupil Plato in *The Republic* were an attempt to apply philosophical principles to governance: 'What would life be like in a state ruled by reason?' The aspiration to live in an ideal society was not limited to philosophers – think 'Messianic Kingdom' in occupied first century Judea or Augustine's 'City of God' in post-imperial context. On the cusp of the Modern period, it was given intriguing expression by none other than the soon-to-be-decapitated friend of Henry VIII, Thomas More, in his famous *Utopia* (1516). The title is a play on the Greek which can be read as either 'good place' or 'nowhere'. In the text, Thomas More imagines a place where among other things, gold is readily available (he was Lord Chancellor . . .) and for this and other reasons, life takes on an idyllic harmonious pattern.

Back on the planet, meanwhile, his near contemporary, Macchiavelli (1469–1527), had come to very different conclusions regarding the ideal state. He saw it as one in which *Il Principe* – 'The Prince' should rule with decisive authority and to that end, a leader is better seeking to be feared than to be loved. If political visionaries such as Plato and More give impetus to change, political pragmatists get on with the job at hand. The somewhat cynical view of Macchiavelli was echoed in *Leviathan* (1651) by Thomas Hobbes (1588–1679), who, without any need for recourse to the doctrine of Original Sin, saw human beings as inescapably competitive and mutually dangerous. As far as Hobbes was concerned, without the sovereign rule of a monarchy enforcing law and order, life would be 'nasty, brutish and short'. For Hobbes, our very equality was dangerous – it made us vulnerable to each other. It was a rational maxim of prudence to give up our personal rights to a national sovereign such that we could enjoy the basic peace necessary for existence.

Taking Hobbes' notion of 'social contract' in a different direction, John Locke (1632–1704) laid the Enlightenment groundwork for democracy. Locke was much more inclined, like Aquinas, to see the nation state as a natural human entity. Starting from a quasi-theological distinction between Adam being entrusted with authority, but not *royal* authority, he saw government *emerging* from the common intention of humanity, the government being *entrusted* to secure the untransferred rights of the community. In Locke's contract only one right is given up, whereas in Hobbes' only one right is retained. Hobbes used the ideas of contract and natural law to put forward a defence of absolute sovereignty, Locke, on the other hand, used these same concepts to limit government.

You know the rest. Locke has some claim to be the most influential political thinker ever, providing an inspiring but *rational* basis for the French and American Revolutions. Yet in order to be authentically of the people, for the people and by the people, the 1648 post-Reformation 'nationalized religion' settlement of *cuius regio eius religio* had to be defenestrated ('thrown out of the window'). But whereas the ejection of Church from government in the newly formed United States allowed both religious and theological freedom to flourish, Europe proved a different matter. Removal of theological and ecclesiological considerations from political discourse became, well, an almost religious pursuit. Nowhere was this more evident than in the thinking of the (second?) most influential political thinker ever.

b) Marx and the eradication of religion

Karl Marx (1818–1883) was born in Germany to Jewish parents and studied Philosophy at a time when Hegel's thought was dominating the universities. He became a radical journalist advocating insurgency and after a series of difficulties, he eventually sought political asylum in England in 1849 where he lived until his death. His paradoxical life saw him almost exclusively supported by Friedrich Engels (1820–1895), whose vast industrial riches didn't prevent them both co-authoring the *Communist Manifesto* in 1848 which called for a radical redistribution of wealth. *Das Kapital* (1867) did a similar demolition job on the fundaments of the Industrial Revolution. His legacy was incredible, providing a template for socio-political experimentation which at one point involved half the population of the earth. Not only was this experiment based on reason, it was an experiment which deliberately excluded theological and religious considerations, while manifesting classic characteristics of 'Kingdom-eschatological' motifs.

To understand the power of the Marxist moment, it is necessary to enter into the *zeitgeist* – the very 'spirit of the time.' G. W. F. Hegel (1770–1831) bestrode European thought in the early nineteenth century with his philosophical analysis of the evolution of global civilizations. Though Bertrand Russell would later deride Hegel's version of History as 'jellied thought', it is not difficult to see why it captured the imagination of young European intellectuals and why it still has influence today. Hegel classified History into 'epochs' – a technique which this book is employing right now. He saw great dynamic phases of human achievement evolving in stages to ever greater sophistication of the socio-political system. Hence:

- I Childhood – Oriental World
  - Society is run by despots – Only one person is free
- II Adolescence – Greek World
  - Immature Democracy – Love of argument (think 'teenage') to the detriment of progress.
- III Manhood – Nation State – Rome
  - Vivid recognition of the greater good – bravery and sacrifice – but violent, hard and bitter – proved by disappearance of democracy and re-emergence of Caesars.
- IV Maturity: Christian West/Prussia
  - Reconciliation of individual with communal. Balance between authority and freedom.

Now one might cynically point out that by identifying Prussia as the ideal state, Hegel was being as philosophically flirtatious as any compromised ecclesiastic in imperial Christendom. Nevertheless, the exciting thing for Marx was that he reckoned to know what the *next* epoch would be – Communism. In Hegel's system, human development happens through a struggle of opposites, 'thesis and antithesis', a process he called *dialectic*. Hegel identified the inner dynamic of this development as the *weltgeist*, which literally means 'world spirit'. Despite the religious connotations, this notoriously elusive concept has tended to be understood as 'the evolutionary power of consciousness'. Certainly the way Marx bought into this idea of progress involved ditching any notion that *geist* might have a religious dimension. Famously 'standing Hegel on his head', Marx's system was instead based on *dialectical materialism* which effectively identified as 'thesis and antithesis' the two great social opposites of Capital and Labour. The inevitable struggle between them would yield the new synthesis of Communism. Hence his passionate advocacy of revolutionary action – it was necessary to trigger the emergence of the next stage of human development.

The motive for the revolution was pretty simple and reminiscent of Eden and Kingdom themes. Increasing industrialization was *alienating* men and women from their simple connection whereby what they laboured for, they ate. Workers were increasingly cogs in the machines of factories, which were owned by the few, but served by the many. Capital is like a vampire, preying on workers 'so long as there is a muscle, a nerve, a drop of blood to be exploited'. (Marx, [1867] 1988, p. 475). This alienation was wrong. The next stage of world history, the next epoch of maturity, must mean that the factories served by the many should be owned by the many. If workers unite, they can bring about the redistribution of wealth to those who are creating it. Like a prophecy of the Kingdom, in this new world, the era of rivalry between neighbours will end, since the economy will be organized on a radical basis according to mutual abilities and mutual needs. This will be resisted, so workers must be prepared to fight.

While it might appear that his thinking would be conducive to Christian egalitarianism, Marx saw, with some justification, that upheaval in the social order would be met with theological and ecclesiastical opposition. Church denominations would be *reactionary* – inherently counter-revolutionary organizations. Worse, religions in general, and Christian Theology in particular, traded on promises of an after-life which would make up for the sorrows of this world. Religion was thus the 'opium of the people', sedating them into acceptance of the *status quo* rather than activating them in the cause of revolution. For the next epoch to emerge, religion must be eradicated – it is nothing less than a holy cause and an act of justice which is the duty of the revolution:

> Religion is, indeed, the self-consciousness and self-awareness of man who either has not yet attained to himself, or has already lost himself again. But man is no abstract being squatting outside the world. Man is the world of man, the state, society. This state, this society, produces religion's inverted attitude to the world, because they are an inverted world themselves . . .
>
> Religious suffering is at the same time an expression of real suffering and a protest against real suffering. Religion is the sigh of the oppressed creature, the feeling of a heartless world, and the soul of soulless circumstances. It is the opium of the people.
>
> The abolition of religion as the illusory happiness of the people is the demand for their real happiness. The demand to give up their illusions about their condition is the demand to give up a condition that requires illusion. The criticism of religion is, therefore, the germ of the criticism of the valley of tears whose halo is religion. (Marx, [1843] 1988, pp. 63–4)

Marx had famously said in his *Theses on Feuerbach* that 'The philosophers have only interpreted the world, in various ways; the point is to change it.' (Marx [1845] 1988, p. 158). For a century, he was the epitome of a world-changing thinker whereby at one point, particularly through the domino effects of the Russian and Chinese revolutions of 1917 and 1949, communist régimes were responsible for half the human race. Characterized by an all-encompassing provision of the necessities of life, they were also coupled with an all-excluding attitude to religious and theological expression. Reason's brief sojourn on top of the altar in Notre Dame in 1789 proved shorter and far less bloody than its enthronement beside St Basil's Cathedral in Moscow. In a sense, theologians of the Church could not complain too much, it was Westphalia once more – the ruler(s) deciding the (non) religion on behalf of the people.

And this was part of its downfall. Marx and his successors had inadequately taken into account the fact that *homo sapiens* is also both *homo economicus* and *homo religiosus* – individuals keen to look after their own affairs and express their own sense of transcendence. In Europe, a combination of the inevitable and the unexpected led to the hugely symbolic destruction of the Berlin Wall in 1989, a fairly unique barrier that had been built primarily to keep people *in* rather than *out* of a citadel. Economic stagnation, a crippling arms race and the unsettling election of a Polish Pope did not help. Ironically, the imposition of the communist ideal, like attempts to impose theocracies in Geneva or to impose inquisitions in Spain, had fateful consequences for individual freedom. Whether political or religious, the minute anyone tries to impose an ideal, it becomes a slavery. The communist experiment may have been rational, but it wasn't human. Was this because it wasn't sufficiently theological?

c) God in man's image? Feuerbach and Newman

Well maybe. Although they were later to fall out, one of the early influences on Marx was his fellow 'Young Hegelian', Ludwig Feuerbach (1804–1872). Besides spawning political revolutionary consciousness, Hegel's conception of human history as an inexorable series of stages through the ages was taken up by Feuerbach and applied to *theological anthropology* – 'the nature of humanity understood in the context of divinity'. In reflecting on the way that human beings come to self-awareness, he concluded that religious sensibility was a fruit of early stage maturation. Far from human beings bearing the *imago dei*, the upshot was that God was effectively *imago hominis* – the Image of Man. He published *The Essence of Christianity* in 1841, contrasting the way humans experience exterior physical things from God thoughts. He points out:

> In the perceptions of the senses consciousness of the object is distinguishable from consciousness of the self; but in religion, consciousness of the object and self-consciousness coincide. The object of the senses is outside man, but the religious object is within him . . . it is the intimate, the closest object. 'God' says Augustine, for example, is nearer, more related to us and therefore more easily known by us than sensible corporeal things . . .

He then makes his main point with poetic and polemical force:

> Consciousness of God is self-consciousness, knowledge of God is self-knowledge. By his God thou knowest the man and by the man his God. The two are identical. Whatever is God to a man, that is his heart and soul; and conversely, God is the manifested inward nature, the expressed self of a man – religion is the solemn unveiling of a man's hidden treasures, the revelation of his intimate thoughts, the confession of his love secrets.

The upshot is:

> The divine being is nothing else than the human being, or, rather, the human nature purified, freed from the limits of the individual man, made objective – i.e., contemplated and revered as another, a distinct being. All the attributes of the

divine nature are, therefore, attributes of the human nature. (Feuerbach, [1854]
1959, pp. 12–14)

This is a sort of polar opposite of Anselm's ontological argument. Thinking outwards, Anselm had proposed the necessary existence of God who in turn sustains humanity. Thinking inwards, Feuerbach was proposing the non-existence of God who is only an idea sustained by the projected aspirations of humanity. Worse still, this led to a disempowering of humanity, a point which both Marx and particularly Nietzsche would echo.

In any event, his 'turn to the self' was an early critique in what might be classified as 'psychological' explanations for religious belief. His method did have drawbacks, among which the most obvious was that 'introspection leading to God thoughts' was hardly new, Anselm and Descartes had both spoken of it. It would make complete sense that a Creator of *theomorphic* ('God-shaped') human beings, might have mapped this reflective interior path as the royal road to faith, universally open to all. Traditionally, the locus for this encounter in Christian Theology was 'conscience', and a celebrated contemporary of Feuerbach, John Henry Newman (1901–1890) drew very different conclusions from the 'turn to self'.

Newman was the most famous English theologian of the nineteenth century and has continued to win admirers ever since. His life as an Anglican and Roman Catholic meant that he had great impact on two denominational traditions, each of which he enriched with his acute mind and gifted eloquence. Newman was too astute and essentially too evangelical to try and offer proofs of God's existence to the Victorian intelligentsia, but he had no doubt where he would look – inwardly, to conscience. In so doing, Newman took a different line on conscience to the tradition of Aquinas or Joseph Butler (1692–1752), both of whom saw it as an essentially rational faculty rooted in *synderesis,* an inner compass of volition pointing humanity in the direction of moral good. Standing in the more romantic tradition, Newman understood conscience to be an intuition. And more than that, he strongly identified the witness of the well-formed conscience as the 'voice of God'.

Rightness and wrongness seem to be concepts which transcend individuals and societies. In the *Grammar of Assent* (1870), he wrote that if humans feel responsible, it implies that there is a being that we are responsible to. An important aspect of this argument is that it implies a personal God and clearly opens up the possibility of relationship in a way that the Design Argument, for example, does not. Moreover, the moral law involves us in the question of God in a way that other arguments do not – there is pressure for us to respond.

In arguing thus he had solid backing – the common perception of believers in a whole range of Christian denominations, and even the doctrinal pronouncement of Lateran IV, Canon 23 which had stated that 'whatever is contrary to conscience, prepares one for Hell'. In a celebrated letter to the Duke of Norfolk, he considered the question as to whether someone's conscience can come 'into collision' with the word of the Pope. The nineteenth century move towards papal infallibility was very much part of the background and there was considerable debate as to whether this would lead to a crisis in Catholic intellectual life. Far from being a simplistic treatment, Newman is well aware of the possibility that conscience could be an artefact of upbringing, but he insists on going beyond that – it is a first principle:

> This view of conscience, I know, is very different from that ordinarily taken of it, both by the science and literature, and by the public opinion of this day. It is founded on the doctrine that conscience is the voice of God, whereas it is fashionable on all hands now to consider it in one way or another, a creation of man . . . I am using the word 'conscience,' in the high sense in which I have already explained it, not as a fancy or an opinion, but as a dutiful obedience to what claims to be a divine voice, speaking within us; and that is the view properly to be taken of it, I shall not attempt to prove here, but shall assume it as a first principle. (Newman, 1875, p. 80)

It is with this conviction that he sees 'conscience' as a moral guide and more, a safeguard and security against bad faith, whatever its provenance. He closes the letter with a famous quotation:

> 'If I am obliged to bring religion into after-dinner toasts (which indeed does not seem quite the thing) I shall drink - to the Pope, if you please, - still, to Conscience first, and to the Pope afterwards.' (Newman, 1875, p. 86)

This remark, though significant for Catholicism in terms of balancing individual moral judgement with Church authority, is of still wider relevance because it emphasizes the extent to which someone of Newman's standing accorded authority to the 'inner' experience of *homo religiosus*. While his views would find much favour within ecclesiastical circles, the validity of his reasoning would be seriously questioned by a new breed of scholars, even more intrigued by the 'turn to the self'.

d) Psychoanalysis: Freud, Jung, Frankl

It is rare for a scientist, such as Einstein, to bring about what Kuhn called a 'paradigm shift'. It is even rarer for a theorist to successfully invent an entire discipline, attempt to put an end to another one, identify an uncharted territory of the human mind and with semi-falsified case studies dressed in classical mythology provoke controversies that still rage. Sigmund Freud did all that. Born in Freiburg, 1856, and educated in Vienna, having passed through medical school and further studies in Paris, he turned his attention to hypnosis. This proved a momentous step, since as part of his experimentation, he had patients re-live stressful experiences in order to regain mental health. Freud made this the core of his therapeutic technique and sought, through his medical practice, to confront and disarm repressed emotions.

Part of Freud's genius was to provide tools for what would become the modern discipline of *psuchē* – *logic*, 'Psychology'. Although it literally means 'Science of the Soul', Freud's emphasis was very much on mental health. His approach was based on a division of the *psyche* or mind into three sections: *das Es*, *das Ich* and *das Über-Ich*. Literally, these mean 'the I', 'the It' and 'the Over I', though most people will have heard them identified by his early translators Jones and Strachey as the deliberately more scientific sounding *Id*, *Ego* and *Superego*:

> The ID is the basic elemental life force – uncivilized and natural
>
> The EGO is the 'person(a)' that we present to others – it is what we recognize as our identity. This is the "mask" of our everyday existence.
>
> The SUPEREGO is basically the internalized voice of our parents, forebears and society. We commonly call this conscience.

At root, Freud believed that sexual urge (libido) was the key factor operating in psychological development and that religion and the moral life are side effects of its *repression*. He explained why in *Totem* and *Taboo* (1913) where Freud claimed that religion is ultimately based on sons repenting of having killed their fathers to have sex with their mothers (the Oedipus complex). They create a *taboo* (forbidden topic) surrounding incest and a *totem* (object of worship) which represents the lost father. This latter 'totemic ancestor' gradually develops into the more impersonal God of the great religions, reinforced by the concept of the *Primal Horde*, groups of people who gather around a single, dominant, authoritative male. In turn, such leaders may likewise become a focus for envy, hostility, death and divinization. Hence for Freud, belief in divinities is ultimately divinized worship of lamented human ancestors.

In Freud's understanding, morality comes from an attempt to civilize and tame our basic instincts. What we commonly call 'conscience' is not evidence for a voice of God, but rather the working of the Superego which often overrides the Id and the Ego to help us act in a manner which is considered moral. This explains why there is a sense of morality in all cultures, but that the specific details of these moral codes can vary greatly. None of this points to Newman's inner voice of God, rather to the inner anguish of the human creature.

For Freud, then, we are basically animals with attitudes. We are not souls and bodies or anything like that, just complicated creatures. Inevitably, this made him sceptical of spirituality which he classed as pathological. When patients presented themselves to him with particular obsessions or neuroses, he likened them to individual religious systems and a form of mental illness. To Freud, religious systems represented the obsessional neuroses of mankind on the grand scale.

You wouldn't have to be an archbishop to be a little fazed by all this. Freud's view was that religion and theological discourse were based on the regretted memory of incestual sex gone vengefully and violently wrong. Faith systems were a form of control designed to repress the deepest *You*. No question, the only way to be free is to reject religion as false, silence the parental voice control of the superego and allow the repressed libido to express itself. Goodbye God – Hello Sexual Revolution. Freud's theorizing launched what has since been called the 'Century of the Self'. The implicit project of psychoanalysis in the Freudian tradition was to 'get behind' the individual's Ego mask, separate the individual from the external controls of the Superego and reveal the primitive Id. On this view, organized belonging systems such as the Church are definitely to be avoided, since they are a second mechanism preventing individuality from being expressed.

In later writings such as *Civilization and its Discontents* (1930), Freud did acknowledge a less violent root to religion which he identified as 'Oceanic feeling' – the sense of indissoluble oneness with the universe which he noted that mystics in particular have celebrated as the fundamental religious experience. He regarded this as nostalgia for the intimate sense of union that every individual has with their mother in the womb and during early stages of post-natal development. He considered this longing to be stronger in some than the desire for an omnipotent father, and speculated whether this might explain some of the tension in religious traditions between the 'active life' as compared to the 'contemplative life' of the faithful. What he was in no doubt about was the potential for social upheaval that might follow should his project lead to an unravelling of religion in society. In what would now be termed 'politically incorrect' language, he concluded civilization had nothing to worry about from educated people, but that the uneducated and oppressed – those who believed in religion – would be its enemies.

Yet almost as soon as the Freudian revolution got under way, there were disagreements among the revolutionaries. Carl Gustav Jung (1875–1961) was Freud's most famous disciple, but came to disagree with Freud on his method of analysis. He felt Freud built his theories almost exclusively on people who were mentally defective, hence he was bound to come to some dubious conclusions. In particular, Jung disagreed with Freud's focus on sexuality, which he saw as only one aspect of human psychological development. Far from being a disease, Jung regarded spirituality as a fact of humanity every bit as obvious as sex. He regarded religion as something which brought psychological balance to humanity, opining that the children of God, rather than the children of the flesh, are the ones who know freedom.

With this drastic step taken, Jung set about reworking the major Freudian insight, namely, the influence of the subconscious on the thinking and acting individual. Jung suggested that the psychology of the mind is rooted in the *personal* unconscious and the *collective* unconscious. He situates the origin of religion in a collective unconscious which is common to all humanity. This finds expression in the symbolic language of the great myths that so vividly reflect our nature back to us in narrative form. In the collective unconscious there are archetypal images – a central one being that of God – the Supreme Being. With a nod to Feuerbach, he acknowledged this image may be modified by our *personal* experiences which govern the picture we form of God, but the process is common to everyone. Jung goes on to say that we experience life as a journey of self-discovery in which we *increasingly* become our true selves. This is a process of individuation like a second birth or awakening – that as we become our own selves we increasingly recognize the nature of the 'archetypal self' or God. Jung thus identified religion as the outward expression of this inner truth, and its importance is to give psychological integration and balance to humanity.

> For thousands of years rites of initiation have been teaching spiritual rebirth . . . yet the penalty of misunderstanding is heavy, for it is nothing less than neurotic decay, embitterment, atrophy and sterility. It is easy enough to drive the Spirit out of the door, but when we have done so, the salt of life grows flat - it loses its flavour. Fortunately, we have proof that the Spirit always renews itself in the fact that the central teaching of the ancient initiations is handed on from generation to generation. Ever and again human beings arise who understand what is meant by

the fact that God is our father. The equal balance of the flesh and the spirit is not
lost to the world. (Jung, [1936] 2001, p. 126)

Now you wouldn't have to be an archbishop to be a little reassured by this.
God is allowed to make a comeback and religions are a good thing. Even
better, the notion of life as a journey of rebirth into both self-discovery and
God-discovery was one already identified by Jesus and Paul (cf. John 3:7
and 1 Cor 13:13). That is not to say that the Jungian synthesis was entirely
amenable to classic theological standpoints. The 'self-help' aspect of personal
realization appeared to some as the worst possible combination of Pelagian
perfectionism accessed through Gnostic secrets – no need for Bible or Jesus
in this approach, just the right jargon and a good therapist. Nevertheless,
since the practice of 'spiritual direction/guidance' and the possibility of 'ways
of perfection' were very much part of the monastic and holiness movements
of both East and West, the acknowledgement of the need for personal
reflection in the light of transcendent realities resonated well with traditional
Christian thinking.

If anything, theological synergies with psychoanalysis were to grow stronger
as the decades passed, and a luminous example emerged during one of
humanity's darkest hours. As part of the ethnic cleansing of Austria under the
Nazis, Viktor Frankl, the third of our Viennese Jewish physicians, found
himself in the unimaginable horror of Auschwitz. Frankl could not help
noticing that the inmates of the camp who sustained better levels of health
were those who sustained reasons to hope. The reasons could be fairly
mundane, one man survived until his birthday, for example, and then passed
away. More generally, however, it was the prisoners who had reasons to live
and retained a sense of meaning to their lives, who were most likely to survive.
His recollections were eventually published in *Man's Search for Meaning*
in 1962. In this small book, Frankl outlined his own psychotherapeutic
methodology which he called 'Logotherapy'. Taking the basic premise of the
'talking cure' pioneered by the early Viennese psychoanalysts, his particular
version of the therapy involved the identification of meaning and significance
for patients who, through various forms of depression, were to a greater or
lesser extent, losing the will to live. Logotherapy in itself was not necessarily
connected to religious revelation, but inevitably, by invoking the search for
meaning as part of its cure for humanity, it had obvious parallels with
therapeutic dimensions of theological discourse.

e) Sociology of religion: James and Durkheim

Meanwhile, the Hegelian heritage which through Marx and Feuerbach had triggered a turn to society and a turn to the self, still had further twists. Besides the revolutionary direction of Marx, 'human scientists' were following up the Enlightenment consensus that Christianity was just another religion, that all faith systems had a basic equivalence, and that the spiritual dimension of mankind could be explained. To that end, James Frazer (1854–1941) in *The Golden Bough* surveyed the manifestations of religious experience in various epochs and cultures, in order to find commonalities and features which might explain the phenomenon of religion and allow its scientific classification. Even more famously, William James (1842–1910), a philosopher of the American pragmatic school, also attempted to chart religious territory. In his *Varieties of religious/ mystical experience* (1902), he identified four characteristics thereof:

- **Ineffable** – it is beyond words. Perhaps the most easily recognizable aspect of religious experience. Its sensations are beyond verbal description.
- **Noetic** – they impart 'divine knowledge'. Religious experience seems to communicate *unobtainable truths*. The Knowledge is like a revelation – grasped through some kind of intuition and perception (e.g. Peter's food revelation in Acts 10).
- **Transient** – they are temporary but permanent. Religious experience may only last a few minutes, but has effects which last for a long time (e.g. Paul, Acts 9). Momentary timelessness, like in dreams, is also a feature.
- **Passive** – During a religious experience one loses control to a more powerful being. People are temporarily passive and in this state sometimes endowed with abilities which in 'normal' life they are incapable of. Again, Acts 2 – speaking in tongues is a classic example.

Genuine religious experience cannot be 'conjured up', but James does recognize that 'induced experience' through drugs or alcohol may mimic aspects of the mystical consciousness. James concluded that although it is difficult to examine every detail of religious experience or explain the differing expressions which religious people give to their 'encounters', religion itself seems to serve an important purpose in the human psyche and contributes to the cohesion of society. As a pragmatist, like the founding fathers of his nation and the entrepreneurs who made it great, James believed in practicality. Since religion 'works' it is fine as far as James is concerned, whether or not its truth claims are correct.

But how did it work? Emile Durkheim (1858–1917), arguably the 'Father of Sociology', purported to know. A pioneer of the discipline, working with statistical data and field enquiries which have become core to its methodology, Durkheim was interested to find out what forces held society together. In *The Elementary Forms of Religious Life* (1912), Durkheim considered religion a unified system of beliefs and practices relative to sacred things. There is no need in this definition for reference to a God, since for Durkheim, the separation of the natural and the supernatural was something that the relatively recent rationalizing tendencies of mankind had imposed. For primitive man, everything is supernatural – hence the all-encompassing nature of divinity and deities characteristic of primal tribes.

Three things are core to religion, the sacred, the collective effervescence and the moral, the middle term referring to the way in which beliefs and practices become invested with symbolic significance, cohering and identifying the group. The resultant 'collective consciousness' is one of Durkheim's key ideas, since, although he saw a limited future for religion, he nevertheless anticipated that rationalism and the 'turn to the self' would exacerbate tendencies to individualism and moral mediocrity. It left him in the odd position of affirming that although most societal institutions and even scientific achievements were all traceable to the cohering power of religion, faith systems were in fact a by-product of the collective consciousness and hence have no intrinsic truth in themselves. (see pp. 487–8 below).

f) The Holy: Otto and Tillich

Once more challenged to articulate the objective uniqueness of religious claims, both agreement and disagreement with James and Durkheim could be traced in the work of Rudolf Otto (1868–1937). Standing firmly in the theological tradition of Schleiermacher, Otto had embarked on his own fact-finding travels, and in searching for the right vocabulary to describe the 'ineffable', he ventured where William James and even Moses himself had feared to tread. Otto's conclusion was that all religious experience involves a sense of the 'holy'. Otto realized something increasingly apparent to theologians of the Protestant tradition: inadvertently, the conceptualization of God, the prized achievement of classical thinking, had reduced God to the status of an empty hypothesis. Reason unfettered makes God an intellectual and rationalistic concept which fails to see value in the non-rational core of religious experience.

The escape route is provided by the constant tradition, the idea of the 'holy'. In this context, holy does not mean pious, devout or virtuous. It refers to something far more powerful – the awesome, the unspeakable *numinous*, the utterly different, which is felt as both dangerous and attractive at the same time. A '*mysterium fascinans et tremendum*' which can leave a person simultaneously daunted, desirous and dizzy:

> The 'mystery' is for him not something to be wondered at but something that entrances him, and beside that and in it, which bewilders and confounds, he feels a something that captivates and transports him with a strange ravishment, rising often enough to the pitch of dizzy intoxication; it is the Dionysiac-element in the numen. (Otto, 1923, p. 31)

As far as Otto was concerned, people and cultures throughout history have borne witness to this sense of the Holy. Moreover, as the immensely influential work *I and Thou*, by the Jewish theologian Martin Buber (1878–1965) would later assert, God is most intimately encountered not as an abstract 'It' but as a 'Thou', a sacred and inviolable *someone*. Though this personalization of the Universe echoes the 'graced arena' described by Karl Rahner, it is easy to see how more immediately this conclusion is reached in the romantic, rather than rational tradition.

The very fact that Otto had been forced to stretch vocabulary to articulate the core theological idea at the heart of religious experience pushed other Christian thinkers in a different direction. The psychoanalytical school of Freud and Jung had drawn attention to the importance of symbol rather than straightforward language as the means by which the subconscious processed the experiences of life. More subtle, nuanced and involving than signs, a symbol tends to have a surplus of meanings, it can signify many things to many people. The most obvious example is a cloth with colours on as a National Flag which can have all sorts of responses. To a citizen it may be reassuring, to an enemy, fearful. While a sign might simply point you in a given direction, symbols tend to embroil the observer in their own reality – they are not neutral, they are much more interactive.

The potential of the 'symbolic' in the rethinking of Christianity was a creative strand in twentieth century theological method touching on key areas such as Christology and sacraments. Particularly in the work of Paul Tillich (1886–1965), use of the 'symbolic' enabled him to re-present the God question in an involving fashion which attempted some sort of synthesis between the rationalism of Modernity and the romanticism advocated by Schleiermacher and Otto. Tillich had served as a chaplain during World War I and his approach to Theology was governed henceforth by a sensitivity to the fragility of life. We are contingent beings, always under threat, the threat of non-being. What stops us falling apart? Tillich argued that every human anchors themselves in their basic or 'ultimate' concern – whether that be family, friends, faith, fame, fun, follies or whatever. To all intents and purposes, according to Tillich, this is a person's God. But the sting in this woozy 'everybody is really religious' scene is that if you reflect on what your 'God' is, you will see the limitations of your life.

He then points out that the genius of religious language consists in its symbolic imagery which grounds us without confining us:

- For example, 'God is Creator' does not explain exactly how the universe was made, it responds to our experience of being contingent fragile beings.
- For example, to combat the non-sense of the world, he points out that from Plato to John's Gospel, the symbol of 'Logos' or 'Reason' gives all of humanity the potential to agree and to pursue the good. As a symbol it calls us to be reasonable whilst at the same time transcending reason. This is the 'involving' 'engaging' dimension of symbols and how they work.
- For example, the threat of despair at death – 'non-being' – is answered by the symbol of the resurrected Jesus as conqueror of death. Resurrection is both mystery and certainty, it is not a bald statement, it escapes definition because it transcends meaning. (cf. Tillich, 1951, pp. 49–50)

It is important to recognize that Tillich understood symbols as *mediating* truth, rather than being the truth itself. An entire cathedral full of symbols does not equal God. Symbols draw you *in* and *through* to the reality of God. Nevertheless, Tillich's work was indicative of an endeavour on the part of Western theologians to respond to the critiques of modernity in an attempt to find a language that would speak to their 'cultured contemporaries'. Certainly the notion that 'symbol' rather than 'logic' was the essence of religious language was a way round the reductionist critiques of both linguistic philosophers and scientific positivists which silenced the voice of a revelation tradition steeped in paradox. Indeed the entire rationalistic endeavour associated with the Enlightenment, whether expressed in Philosophy, Science or Anthropology, can be characterized as a refusal to accept paradox as the core reality of human and indeed cosmic existence. There was one prophetic figure who saw this all too well, and saw it ahead of his time. And by becoming the father of Postmodernism, Soren Kierkegaard proved to be a quizzical brooding undertaker of the whole Enlightenment project.

Summary

From a secular anthropological perspective, the Christian view of human nature could be construed as an entrapment at the social, political and individual level which Marx and Freud profoundly challenged in the nineteenth and twentieth centuries. The phenomenon of religion was scrutinized by scholars not from the perspective of God's revelation, but rather as a by-product of the social need for meaning in life. Though each of these critiques drew intriguing and creative responses from theologians, it was perhaps the non-negotiable idea of the 'Holy' in religious experience that proved the most irreducible concept. The need for life to be lived with meaning was partly intuited from the mud of World War I trenches and the concentration camps of World War II. 'The drama of the gifted individual learning to choose good' was being rewritten in symbolic form, but from now on it would do so without the sub-structure of certainty that the Modern period had promised. Post-modernity had arrived.

22

Dialogues in Different Voices

Insofar as it has been given a popular label, the current epoch has been designated as 'Postmodern' as Western thinking has largely abandoned the quest for objective certainty desired by the Enlightenment in favour of subjectivity and the lived experience of the individual. Owing much to Kierkegaard, Nietzsche and the outworking of 'Existentialism,' the search for 'authenticity' in lives defined by actions rather than grand meta-narratives has loosened some of the nuts and bolts of traditional theological method. Postmodernity has had particular impact on Christian Theology through biblical interpretation since it legitimates particular readings of the sacred text. The upshot is a series of dialogues with different voices. Under the broad umbrella of 'Liberation' readings, attention will be paid to Post-Colonial and Feminist analysis as well as Mariology as examples of how the search for meaning from different places can be creative.

a) Kierkegaard and Nietzsche

If the Modern period can be characterized as an epoch wherein Western thinkers sought objective philosophical certainty emboldened by complete confidence in scientific progress, then the Postmodern period marks an era where these aims and expectations no longer apply. Characteristics can risk being caricatures, but in place of the Enlightenment enthronement of Reason, the altar is now occupied by a deity of your own choice, and no one has the authority to question its exalted status. Objective truth, apart from the founding principle of Postmodernism itself, is a thing of the past. Meaning for me has superseded meaning for all. The demise of 'meta-narratives', the all embracing explanatory frameworks within which groups of people find personal significance, is a natural consequence of the death of God. Quite how this happened is a matter of some debate. Though the consequent turbulence in contemporary theological discourse was partly anticipated by Barth and Tillich (especially with the latter's theory of 'ultimate concern'), the original agitation might reasonably be traced to two whirlpools of nineteenth century thinking, Søren Kierkegaard and Friedrich Nietzsche. Among the most quotable writers ever to have wielded pens, they appear as prophetic twins, one in dramatic affirmation of God's sovereignty, the other heralding God's death and the coming *Übermensch* – the Superman.

Søren Kierkegaard was an unusual 'game-changer' for Western thought. Born in Denmark, 1813, his name means 'churchyard' or 'graveyard' and his was a life shadowed by death. He was the youngest of seven children, but three of his sisters, two brothers and his mother had all died before he was 21. Though heir to the family fortune, he was convinced that he too would die before the age of 33. As a consequence, he forsook happiness with his betrothed and resolved at 22, to find a truth for which he was willing to live and die. A millionaire in need of purpose, he appeared to find it in the paradox of faith and the deep waters of the Absolute. In *Fear and Trembling*, he wrote: 'Faith is the highest passion in a human being, I'm by no means standing still in my love, for I have my life in it' ([1843] 1986, p. 147). With literary intensity, he completed numerous works, composing them in his particular ironic style or 'dialectical lyric', usually in the persona of characters he invented. He died in 1855, at just 42 years of age.

As well as emphasizing passion over reason (as would be expected from the romantic tradition), a key contribution to subsequent thought was his argument for the primacy of the individual over the communal:

> We shall not be so arrogant as to do anything on a grand scale. Rather, let us speak of the individual human life and of the way that it can be lived out here on earth. If one can see God in history, one can see him also in the life of the individual; to suppose otherwise is to yield to the brutish imbecility which sees

God only in the observations of nature; being taught, say that Sirius is 180,000 miles away from the earth. The materialistic man is astounded by such large data. If every single man is not an individual, simply by being human, then everything is lost and it is not worth hearing about world-shaking historical events. (Kierkegaard, [1845] 1967, pp. 20–1)

This option for the particular rather than the universal was a direct critique of the great Hegelian view of inevitable human progress, so vividly taken up by Marx in the idea of Communism. The privileging of the fragmentary over the systemic is a key concept in Postmodernism, but it is not the only factor traceable here. Equally pertinent is the passionate way the individual lives out the drama of his or her existence by way of choice, the authentic becoming of a person through freedom. Kierkegaard noticed that our moral behaviour can be guided by customs or 'ethics' – (commanded from outside) or by immediate stimulus – 'aesthetics' – (urges or reactions from within). Neither of these properly involve personal choice. It is only when you freely *choose* that you are entering into authentic moral life and in so doing you are gaining access to something Absolute, something not mediated by others, but which is instead the sacred drama of the life that is *you*. The ethic that should direct our life is based not on reward, not on selfish desires, not on smug piety, not on the approval of others, but a conscious acceptance of the fragile absurdity of life and a breaking through to relationship with Absolute being. The biblical example he uses to illustrate this in *Fear and Trembling* is Abraham's sacrifice of Isaac from Genesis 22. In this story, he sees a radical acceptance of absurdity, betrayal of trust by a father, the possible cruel death of a son, yet the very breakthrough moment of utter relationship with God through faith.

The allusion to absurdity in his approach is not accidental. Not only was Kierkegaard himself a bit of an oddity and figure of fun, he was adamant that Jesus was not presentable as anything other than Absolute Paradox, the paradox of the God-man. Though he concedes that the theologian can acknowledge this, there is always a tendency to smooth things over, not *staying* with the disturbing reality. Ultimately, the speculative thinker misses the passion and absolute nature of religion. Kierkegaard is not one for half measures, you can't half believe or suggest Christianity is partly true. The question of Christianity is not primarily about you pondering this or that doctrine, but about *you being in it*. Faith therefore becomes a matter of your true existence in the presence of the Absolute. It is not something you can imitate by the example of others, it is *you*. The only difference between the believer and the unbeliever is their awareness of being loved. In one testimonial he wrote:

> Were someone to ask me if I in any way think that I have some special relationship with God, I would answer No, oh no, oh no! Far from it! There has never lived anyone in Christendom, there is no one, unconditionally no one, who is not unconditionally equally close to God, loved by him. But on the other hand I really do not believe that there are many who have been so occupied as I have been day after day with the blessed undertaking of contemplating that God loves them – and I cannot help it if others disdain the love God lavishes upon them just as richly as on me. (Kierkegaard, [1848] 1997, p. 389)

The potent themes of the individual outranking the universal, the fragmentary being more authentic than the systemic, the relative over the absolute, plurality over conformity, revelation over speculation, the discovery of self through the other, and the acceptance of lived absurdity over insistence on speculative coherence which all tumble forth from his writings, anticipate by a clear century and more the central concerns of postmodernist culture and epistemology. His only prophetic rival in such a melting of the matrices of certainty was a similarly unusual figure, but one who was instead keen to reject faith and declare total independence from 'God'.

Friedrich Nietzsche (1844–1900) was the son of a Lutheran minister. A brilliant student, he gave up on the option to pursue a university career and instead became a wandering, solitary, philosopher publishing a series of stirring part narrative, part *aphoristic* ('sayings based') writings. By the time his works became successful, Nietzsche was oblivious, having become insane, perhaps triggered by the trauma of seeing a horse flogged, more likely due to the side effects of syphilis. Even more than Kierkegaard, Nietzsche had been influenced by Schopenhauer (1788–1860), whose atheism and somewhat bleak descriptions of the human condition were so vivid. Against this, Nietzsche was to react. As passionate as Kierkegaard, his project was to rid the world of religion and any illusory systems based on past mythologies or customs no longer applicable to modern man. Once it is realized that humanity itself creates its notions of good and evil, it can be free to create its own set of rules that will not be fettered by the twin shackles of Church and State. The iconoclastic tone of his writing is unmistakable. In *The Gay Science*, he writes:

> 'Whither is God?' he cried; 'I will tell you. We have killed him—you and I. All of us are his murderers. But how did we do this? How could we drink up the sea? Who gave us the sponge to wipe away the entire horizon? What were we doing when

we unchained this earth from its sun? Whither is it moving now? Whither are we moving? Away from all suns? Are we not plunging continually? Backward, sideward, forward, in all directions? Is there still any up or down? Are we not straying, as through an infinite nothing? Do we not feel the breath of empty space? Has it not become colder? Is not night continually closing in on us? Do we not need to light lanterns in the morning? Do we hear nothing as yet of the noise of the gravediggers who are burying God? Do we smell nothing as yet of the divine decomposition? Gods, too, decompose. God is dead. God remains dead. And we have killed him. (Nietzsche, [1882] 1974, p. 181)

With classic literary device, in this 'Parable of the Madman', the prophetic figure realizes he has come too soon, his word cannot be heard yet. Like the Gospels, the involving appeal to the reader is obvious: 'If you want to be ahead of the game, hear the message *now*'. It is also worth noting that like many European intellectuals (such as Freud), Nietzsche has a concern that removing the classical co-ordinates of life provided by religion and state may well cause social upheaval. There is also a death of man here in the deliberate undoing of the meta-narrative, the context of meaning and significance provided by Christianity.

It can be argued that Nietzsche's concept of the *übermensch* – 'superman' – was itself a replacement meta-narrative. His exaltation of the kind of human who will stand strong and unsupported by such mythic constructs, his exhortations to 'dare to become what you are' form part of a stirring call to arms, to put away weakness and celebrate strength. In this model, good becomes 'life-assertion' and if this brings conflict then so be it, since strength will overcome weakness to the betterment of the world. While it is not difficult to hear echoes of such thinking in the rise of Nazism with its pathologies of ethnic and cultural superiority, it is in his anticipation of the removal of common social constructs that Nietzsche saw beyond the Modern period. Moreover, in offering an atheistic version of Kierkegaard's drama of self-actualization through personal choice, he was to have immense influence on twentieth-century 'Existentialism'.

b) Existentialism and the birth of postmodernism

What eventually became known in Europe as 'Existentialism', happily inherited Nietzsche's positive emphasis on the passionate self-actualization of the individual, combined with the iconoclastic destruction of the matrix of meaning provided by theological narratives. In France, thinkers such as Albert

Camus (1913–1960) and Jean Paul Sartre (1905–1980) took the conclusions of Nietzsche to a more logical conclusion than the Nazis. They understood all too well that feelings of *angst* – 'anxiety' – are the side effect of the dreadful truth that we are mortal, finite, dependent, vulnerable creatures. Using the medium of literature and the personalization of attitudes through fictional characters, they were able to express vividly the absurdity and pointlessness of the human condition. In Germany, however, the movement took a different turn due to the influence of Martin Heidegger (1889–1976). Couched in more difficult philosophical terminology, Heidegger emphasized the foundational nature of our 'being in the world'. Our 'there-ness' *(dasein)* is the key component for authentic living and knowing, which, easily interpreted as a rallying call to self-awareness, impacts on theological discourse. Life understood *as* interpretation nudged debate back towards the quest for meaning, at least at an individual level.

Withal, the shattering experiences of World War II and the discrediting of idealistic regimes of the political left and right meant that intellectual allegiance to systems of thinking was becoming a thing of the past. Since Western Philosophy was exploring either the existential drama of the individual or the puzzles inherent in the linguistic nature of humanity, it was perhaps inevitable that a movement would combine both and emerge more self-consciously distinct from the previous mindset. After all, if the most cultured nation in Europe could invent the gas chambers and the most brilliant scientists could create the atomic bomb, then there must have been some nightmare seeds in the Enlightenment dream of human progress through reason alone. The scene was set for 'Postmodernity'.

The name itself is a little polemical, signifying that the intelligentsia have 'moved on' and implying a put-down of the past. It was associated with a cadre of French thinkers such as Emmanuel Levinas (1906–1995), Michel Foucault (1926–1984), Jean François Lyotard (1924–1998) and Jacques Derrida (1930–2004). The various ways in which Postmodernism distinguishes itself have already been telegraphed:

- Subjectivity is more important than objectivity, the existential concerns and lived actions of the individual are where significance lies, not in systems of meaning.
- Relativism and difference are preferable to absolutes and conformity – the absence of fixed co-ordinates predicted by Nietzsche is something that has to be lived with.
- Language is unstable, meaning is never fully articulated. Knowledge is finally recognized as a social construct, greatly influenced by family, ethnic and gendered environments hence no one group (except perhaps Postmodernists) should dominate reflective discourse.

- Moreover, our knowledge and the conduits of its appropriation must include more than the rational mind. Clarity isn't all that we should seek, ambiguity is human.
- And as for truth, well, it is personal to you. It sizzles, resonates, is uncovered and revealed rather than found in the banality of a formula. The experiences of body, senses, taste, sight, music – these often include the passionate dimensions of our knowing - and must be deliberately cultivated and recognized as such.

The reader is asked to ignore for a moment (or perhaps the next twenty years), some of the grave inconsistencies in this movement. For example, the mere articulation of these proposals presumes that postmodernists believe they are objectively correct, and therefore not so wedded to subjectivity after all. But the supreme advantage of the postmodernist approach is very attractive, namely that the litmus test for relevance is what is important to *you*. This inevitably unleashes imaginative discourse in all directions. From micro personal concerns regarding your own reaction to an advertisement to macro-themes such as gender issues affecting half the human race, the postmodernist turn allows thoughtful investigation without prior permission having to be granted by a state, a church, or some philosophical system of control whether Kantian, Hegelian or Scholastic. The floor is yours.

c) Postmodern hermeneutics

In theological circles, this inevitably meant that there were consequences for the interpretation of biblical texts. The classic method of analysis in the 'modern' period as exemplified by Ernesti and Schleiermacher involved serious engagement with the text in terms of variant readings, translation and contextual information, but with the ultimate aim of understanding the *sensus auctoris* – the mind of the author. This concern placed a premium on identifying the original sources and assiduous attempts to remove what appeared to be later literary and theological features. Though David Strauss was a classic example of this kind of analysis in the nineteenth century, the works of innumerable later exegetes were driven by the same quest for certainty and manifested the same methodology, namely strip away accretions to find the 'authentic' message. Unfortunately, by the last third of the twentieth century, concerns with such 'Historico-critical' methods began to emerge and coalesced around a growing sense of its sterility. Systematic line by line atomizing of narrative documents did not really work as a fruitful way of engaging with the purpose of the text. Moreover, the obsession with what might be 'behind' the writing did not respect the finished composition that was staring the reader in the face. It was as if appreciation of Leonardo's *Mona Lisa* would depend upon knowing which was his first brush stroke.

Frustration with the Historico-critical method had already led to a series of alternative methods of approaching textual criticism. Analysing the narrative structure of passages in order to identify more clearly the way in which a plot might be presented, thicken and resolve was one method. Other aspects such as the style, use of irony, rhetoric and other literary devices attracted attention. In a narrative such as the story of Jacob's sons, the *drama* took centre stage rather than the exact location of the hole Joseph's brothers might have thrown him into (Gen 37:24). Canonical criticism, associated with Harvard's Brevard Childs, was another proposal which suggested that rather than isolating texts, the proper horizon of interpretation includes the contextualization of the accounts *within* the collection. Childs countered the increasing tendency to separate Old and New Testament studies since such divisions make no *canonical* sense. After all, the placing of the Prophets immediately before the New Testament is deliberate and essential to its Christian interpretation.

To some extent, the emergence of 'Social-scientific' criticism as a subset of the Historico-critical method proved fruitful. Deeper awareness of the lived social constructs such as honour-shame in a tribal context or notions of class, ethnicity, identity and gender in the urban missions of Paul proved thought-provoking. But in the course of the late twentieth century, not only did the quest for historical certainty and a univocal 'correct' reading of biblical texts begin to look increasingly quaint, it began to look philosophically unsound:

- On the one hand, Heidegger's existentialist turn was centring the focus of interpretation on the reader – did your reading or hearing of the text make a difference? Your life is an interpretation of what is important – either the text makes a difference to you or not. If it doesn't – it has no meaning for you.
- On the other, the postmodern twist added by Derrida was that the quest for a single meaning was folly anyway. A text has a life of its own and the ultimate cumulative meaning of a passage is deferred. This is not being controversial, it is merely stating what is always the case. So long as there are new readers, there will be new interpretations.

d) Liberation theologies

In fact Derrida and Co. were only offering an intellectual framework for what was happening already. Associated in the first instance with *Basic Ecclesial Communities* in South America, the privileging of the interpretation by readers through their lived experience reversed the tendency for the biblical word and therefore theological discourse to take place 'from above'. The early protagonists of Liberation Theology were theologians and catechists working with the poor in the slums of South America. Gustavo Gutiérrez, arguably its founder, identified its origin in the 'premature and unjust death of many people'. Its point of departure for interpretation was a lived Theology of the Cross, rather than a Christian apologetic addressed to a Western intelligentsia who weren't listening anyway.

> The question in Latin America will not be how to speak of God in a world come of age, but rather how to proclaim God as Father in a world that is inhumane. What can it mean to tell a non-person that he or she is God's child? (Gutiérrez, 1983, p. 57)

Gutiérrez was not alone. Jon Sobrino's critique of European thinking was well made. Too concerned to reflect upon truth and 'explain' faith, it risked irrelevance in comparison to a liberational approach to the saving message of the Gospel, rooted in lived commitment to the poor and enabling faith and doctrine to be illuminated by practical discipleship. After all, understanding the Bible must entail more than use of the mind (cf. Rowland, 2007, p. 3).

There were concerns. First, Western theologians and Church authorities were troubled by its sometime ideological connection with Marxist models of social progress rather than the traditional call to charity constitutive of the Christian 'Kingdom of God'. This was perfectly summed up in the famous poster of Dom Helder Camara bearing the legend: 'When I give food to the poor they call me a saint. When I ask why the poor have no food, they call me a communist'. In defence of its theological integrity, protagonists pointed to the radical biblical prophetic tradition, whether of Amos, Jeremiah, John the Baptist or Jesus himself. Underpinning the conviction of Liberation Theology was that Christianity should be configured around a 'preferential option for the poor'. As such, Liberation Theology burst forth in a new voice, practical, generous and 'Kingdom-building', in a manner distinct from the often detached cerebral commentaries of academics and religious authorities.

Besides this ideological critique, the inevitable hermeneutical concern arose that 'anything might go' in such a context. This is a problem with any 'bottom up' rebalancing within a social organization. For the Basic Ecclesial Communities, the argument was that since the interpretation of the biblical text generally takes place in a community context, Church discernment is readily to hand. This entails biblical engagement with tradition and doctrine as well as action and worship. Gutiérrez writes:

> Without prophecy, the language of contemplation risks not involving itself in the history in which God acts and where we find him. Without the mystical dimension, the language of prophecy can narrow the vision and weaken the understanding, of Him who makes all things new. 'Sing to YHWH, praise YHWH, for he has liberated the poor from the hands of evil men' (Jer 20:13). Sing and liberate, the act of thanksgiving and the demand for justice. (Rowland, 2007, p. 36)

Ultimately, for Gutiérrez, there is no opposition between the prophetic reading of the text and the mystical contemplation of God's wonder. The Word of God alive and active is part of the recognition of Church as Body of Christ in the celebration of the Eucharist. The language of the prophet and the contemplative are two languages that need each other.

If the vantage point of the South American poor was arguably the first of the theologies of liberation, geographically specific theologies, whether African, Asian or Oceanic, subsequently emerged. Even regions as tiny as Mayo, a county in Ireland, identified their own particular interpretative matrix (McDonagh, 1990). Some of these approaches might appear exclusivist, insofar as anybody who is, for example, western, white, educated and able-bodied may feel uncatered for by the concerns of Black or Disabled theologies and their interpretations of the scriptures. *Voila!* That is exactly how so many for so long have felt about the dominant desiccated academic exegesis practised within theological faculties, the doctrinal obsessions of ecclesial bodies and the often inane pomposities of the pulpit. The quest for meaning in theological discourse has taken a turn towards human life in all its diversity, and the interrogatives of minority groups comprise a broader set of questions than has previously been asked.

As an example of a hitherto disenfranchised group aiming to reverse the direction of theological travel, it might be helpful briefly to consider some salient aspects of 'Post-colonial' biblical criticism. The reader may recall that the invasion of Canaan as recorded in the Book of Joshua, which, although hardly easy reading for the squeamish, is positively lethal from the point of view of the Canaanites. The successful conquest of the Promised Land has been used as theological justification for heinous behaviour on the part of colonizers. In *The Bible and Colonialism* (1997), Michael Prior pointed out the troubling connections between oppressive régimes in Europe, Africa, America and finally, in the Holy Land itself. In every case, the position of the local was one of humiliation and disenfranchisement. Prior's view was that some parts of the Bible, if they are to remain within the Canon, should at least carry some kind of hermeneutical health warning. Colonialism and racism have never received the same condemnation in Anglo-Saxon history books as Fascism and Communism for the simple reason that the British and American 'empires' were instrumental in conquering the latter while perhaps forgetting the fate of slaves and Indians, West, East and Native.

Post-colonial critiques take this matter seriously. As Rasiah Sugirtharajah says, 'The Bible, for all its sophisticated theological ideals like tolerance and compassion, contains equally repressive and predatory elements which provide textual ammunition for spiritual and physical conquest' (Sugirtharajah, 2012, pp. 31–2). The awkward truth concomitant with global Christianity is that the spread of the Gospel has been in part a function of territorial as well as 'spiritual' conquest. French and British colonizers have tended to hide behind the excesses of the Portuguese and Spanish, but that is a little disingenuous. As Archbishop Desmond Tutu memorably commented:

> When the first white men came to Africa we had the land and they had the Bible. They said, 'Close your eyes and pray.' When we opened them, we had the Bible and the white man had the land.' (Mullin, 2011, p. 73)

The global reach of nineteenth century Europe was also the extension of the arms of 'Christendom', even if the concept thereof was weakening already. As a tiny example of 'spiritual' conquest, the original name for God in the Bemba language was an intimate non-gendered term, *Lesa* 'One who nurtures' (cf. Hinfelaar, 1994, 53). The colonizers unhelpfully invented a more suitable name which was definitely masculine, and might have seemed a good idea at the time, but was hardly the finest hour for Christian inculturation. Such examples are regarded in Post-colonial biblical critique as the exercise of hegemony – overbearing rule. The theological position of the colonized is one of the 'sub-altern', permanently in the lowest place.

e) Feminist biblical criticism

And speaking of the lowest place, what about the situation of women? While something of a case has been made in favour of the view that Jesus and Paul were revolutionary in their treatment of women, as Christianity evolved, it eventually settled into the somewhat dissatisfactory patriarchal pattern predicted but not approved of in Gen 3:16 'Your desire shall be for your husband and he shall rule over you'. Though there are ambiguous, hotly contested biblical texts regarding female ministry in the New Testament and early Church (e.g. was Junia an apostle? [Rom 16:7] What kind of duties did Lydia have as deaconess [Acts 16:14]?), the formal ordination of women into the threefold ministry was not a feature of Christianity for most of its history. That there were amazing, outstanding women across the centuries is not in doubt. A roll call from A to Z of those officially raised to sainthood such as Agnes of Rome, Bridget of Sweden, Claire of Assisi, St Dymphna, Edith Stein, St Felicity, could be matched by an A–Z of unofficial saints such as Anne Hutchinson, Beatrice of Nazareth, Corrie Ten Boom, Dorothy Day, Elizabeth Fry, Florence Nightingale and so on. Traditionally, while the contribution of women such as St Monica (mother of Augustine), St Hilda (Abbess at Whitby), Hildegard (Abbess at Bingen) and Catherine of Siena has never been in doubt, it is perhaps fair to say that just like the Bible, most of the starring roles in the history of the Church have belonged to men. But why wouldn't that be the case, since men were the authors?

In the late nineteenth century an American feminist writer, Elizabeth Cady Stanton looked to rectify this imbalance. She concluded that the Bible degraded women from Genesis to Revelation and set about remedying the wrong. With the help of her revising committee, she completed the '*Women's Bible*' in 1898. Refreshingly direct, the commentary effectively sanctions some parts of the Bible and excises others. As an example, the creation account of Genesis 1 meets the approval of the committee since it broadly agrees with Science and explicitly acknowledges that women as well as men are made in the image of God. By contrast, the second account in Genesis 2 has little to commend it. It is an allegory present in other cultures and in it women are created as an afterthought, a cure for man's solitude. Cady Stanton is in no doubt as to what has happened:

> It is evident that some wily writer, seeing the perfect equality of man and woman in the first chapter, felt it important for the dignity and dominion of man to effect woman's subordination in some way. To do this a spirit of evil must be introduced, which at once proved itself stronger than the spirit of good, and man's supremacy was based on the downfall of all that had just been pronounced very good. This spirit of evil evidently existed before the supposed fall of man, hence woman was not the origin of sin as so often asserted (Stanton, [1898] 1999, p. 21).

While this 'scissors and paste' method may not be ideal, there is a directness about the approach of the Committee. Key texts such as Paul's famous line in Gal 3:28 – 'There is neither Jew nor Greek, nor slave nor free, nor woman nor man' are already at the centre of this revolutionary hermeneutic which towards the end of the twentieth century, found abundant expression. As the movement developed, numerous 'schools' within feminist theologies of liberation emerged, not all of which have continued to engage with either the biblical text or male analytical traditions on account of them being irredeemably distorted by patriarchy. Others have preferred to see the task as one of correcting the mistaken male interpretation of the revealed literature. Woman understood as an 'afterthought' in Cady Stanton's view of Genesis 2 became part of a literary *inclusion* and the culmination of creation in Phyllis Trible's much reprinted analysis. The apparently demeaning notion of 'spare rib' is similarly recast:

> The rib means solidarity and equality. *Adham* recognizes this meaning in a poem: 'This at last is bone of my bone and flesh of my flesh. She will be called *ishshah* [woman] because she was taken out of *ish* [man] (Gen 2:23). The pun proclaims both the differentiation and the similarity of female and male. Before this episode the Yahwist has used only the generic term *adham*. No exclusively male reference has appeared. Only with the specific creation of woman (*ishshah)* occurs the first specific terms for man as male *(ish)*. In other words, sexuality is simultaneous for woman and man. The sexes are interrelated and interdependent. Man as male does not precede woman as female but happens concurrently (2:7) and the last is the creation of sexuality (2:23). Male embodies female, and female embodies male. The two are neither dichotomies or duplicates. The birth of woman corresponds to the birth of man but does not copy it. Only in responding to the female does the man discover himself as male. No longer a passive creature, *ish* comes alive in meeting *ishshah*. (Trible, 1973, p. 254)

Elizabeth Schüssler-Fiorenza's classic work, *In Memory of Her*, first published in 1983, also marked a significant moment in the development of feminist hermeneutics. Like the woman in Luke 15:8-10, Schüssler-Fiorenza is in 'search of the lost coins', the forgotten stories of the women in the Bible which have become hidden behind layers of *androcentric* ('male-centred') tradition. By sharpening the attention upon the numerous women whose characters manage to break through the male monotony, it becomes possible to recover important theological insights and the deleterious effects of patriarchy from half-hidden depictions of Eve, Hagar, Miriam, Deborah, Huldah, Mary Magdalene, Martha and Mary. The choice of title for the book is highly significant, taken as it is from an exchange between Jesus and his disapproving (male) disciples disturbed by a nameless woman intimately ministering to their Master. The reply of Jesus, 'Truly I tell you, wherever the Good News is proclaimed, what she has done will be told in memory of her' (Mark 14:9, Matt 26:13) becomes a liberation statement for Schüssler-Fiorenza. The forgotten and nameless *are* the story, and a reading strategy for biblical texts must endeavour to critique and create in equal measure. Social and historical knowledge of the situation of women and the marginalized in ancient times becomes a key factor in a restoration of women to history and history to women. Schüssler-Fiorenza's 'Critical Rhetorical Model' is particularly attentive to symbolic worlds and the way biblical discourses further the struggle for liberation or in the way they sustain oppressive values.

A corollary of the search for the lost voices is the controversial 'inter-textual' approach to biblical narratives. These include imaginative reconstruction of scriptural passages which are designed to enable the disenfranchised to see themselves in the texts and hear their concerns articulated. Though this may strike some readers as a highly dubious novelty, it has long existed in the *haggadic* tradition of interpretation and is analogous to the way preachers or spiritual writers ask their audiences to imagine themselves as 'part of the scene'. An example of this approach from Mary Grey's *Sacred Longings* is included in the further reading. It is of significance that the inter-textual method can serve to broaden the appeal of biblical passages beyond the immediate audience of committed Christians, facilitating dialogues between women of other faiths and none (cf. Fry, 2005).

The accentuation of the prophetic 'game changing' dimension of new interpretations of biblical literature has been part of the reformist strand of feminism associated with Rosemary Radford Reuther, Ruth Carter Heyward and Elizabeth Moltmann. These approaches see changes in gender relations as part of a greater work for justice and 'this world' redemption characteristic of all Liberation theologies. Alienation, oppressive power structures – any death giving aspects of human activity must be challenged by the life-changing possibilities of the prophetic word. In this context, the question arises as to whether Christianity is a necessary agent of change if its inner dynamic can be replaced by an ethic of justice. Clearly acknowledging the problematic nature of both the maleness of Incarnation as well as reductionist views of the historical Jesus, Radford Reuther can still justify the continuing importance of the Gospel as a paradigm and ecclesial belonging as significant:

> A Jesus whose life message and praxis were redemption from patriarchy pulls the rug out from under Christian patriarchy and grounds a feminist Christianity as the 'true' gospel of Jesus. This is a powerful claim, powerful in a different way from telling our own individual stories in small communities. However paradigmatic for us in those small communities our stories may be, they do not have the historical weight of being claimed as the root story for two thousand years and by two

billion people in the world today. To ground our liberative stories in the Jesus story
is to lay claim to that whole people in prophetic judgement and call to repentence.
(Radford Reuther, 2011, p. 254)

f) Mariology as liberation?

At first glance, the somewhat limited profile that Mary the Mother of Jesus
enjoys in the Gospel accounts does not seem to justify the extent to which
she figures as a focus of veneration in the broad Christian tradition. The
many explanations offered for this phenomenon, whether theological, artistic,
sociological or psychological, only serve to complicate the puzzle or enrich
the mystery, depending on your point of view. Traditional stories of Mary's
background are derived from the non-canonical Infancy Gospel of James,
which tells the story of her parents, Joachim and Anna (see Barnstone, 2005,
pp. 385–92). Otherwise, the first encounter with the 'Marian' tradition is
through the infancy narratives of Matthew 1-2 and particularly Luke 1-2. The
angel, the donkey, the shepherds, the star – these are some of the best known
images of the Bible and for many people are associated with the good feelings
of Christmas time as experienced from childhood.

Looked at in liberation and feminist light, however, the infancy narratives
are anything but a gentle story of sweet contentment. In the first instance, it is
a classic moment of the anonymous *particular* – an encounter between a
young girl and an angel, which is the pre-requisite for the *universal* dimension
of its consequences. Their exchange mixes absurdity, transgression and faith,
as the promise is made that contradicts reason and risks an implied breaking
of Torah expectations. The message of the Angel Gabriel is reminiscent of the
miraculous child promise made to Abraham (cf. Gen 18:10, Judg 13:6). Unlike
old, cynical Sarah, Mary, the youthful virginal handmaid, does not laugh, and
it is easy to see how her *fiat* – 'let it be' would become a paradigm of faith in
God's promises and for Christian self-giving. She is betrothed, between the
patriarchy of her father's house and that of her fiancée. In this fluid, in-between
space she is free to act. The drama unfolds in the pregnancy outside wedlock
of a young, vulnerable woman. The sanctions for the presumed infidelity
include the possibility of execution – Mary is already a victim of a patriarchal
system geared in favour of male domination. She is a woman, in the lowest
place. Her fate is in the hand of her betrothed. Styled on the Old Testament
technicolour coated dreamer, Joseph is more inclined to believe his own
dreams of angels than the word of his beloved. She is a lowly handmaid. She is
incredible. She has no voice in Matthew's account.

By contrast, Luke inserts the drama of the Visitation, a sisterly act of solidarity, whereby the pregnancy of the barren, marginalized Elizabeth provides Mary with the confirmation that the message she has received is true. Motherhoods meet, and even unborn infants recognize and communicate with each other. In Luke's account, it is the male priest who is struck dumb. There then follows what can only be described as a proto-Gospel, an original proclamation of the Kingdom 'from below' as Mary says:

> 'My soul magnifies the Lord,
> and my spirit rejoices in God my Saviour,
> for he has looked with favour on the lowliness of his servant.
> Surely, from now on all generations will call me blessed;
> for the Mighty One has done great things for me,
> and holy is his name.
> His mercy is for those who fear him
> from generation to generation.
> He has shown strength with his arm;
> he has scattered the proud in the thoughts of their hearts.
> He has brought down the powerful from their thrones,
> and lifted up the lowly;
> he has filled the hungry with good things,
> and sent the rich away empty.
> He has helped his servant Israel,
> in remembrance of his mercy,
> according to the promise he made to our ancestors,
> to Abraham and to his descendants for ever.'
> (Luke 1:46-55)

Mary's soul *megalunei* – 'mega-praises' the Lord, her liberator and cause for her rejoicing because it is in her lowliness she has found favour with the Holy One. In terms of Gospel and blessing, the disregarded status of the poor is Position A. Her portion is the Lord, her status is assured. The song drives this point home by the prophecy that the proud will be scattered as if a scorpion had been thrown among them *(dieskorpisen)*. The rich will be sent away empty, while the poor will be exalted in a typically biblical role reversal. It is not the system *status quo*, it is the undoing of the system, the inversion of the status. This is not an idle one-off notion, it is the essence of the covenant with Abraham. Mary is reclaiming it for the poor, the lowly, the woman, the marginalized, the silenced. It is the Nazareth Manifesto of Jesus announced before Bethlehem has even happened (cf. Luke 4:18-19 and 1 Sam 2:1-10).

The birth story in Luke continues with the census and the dislocation of the vulnerable at the behest of the powerful. Bethlehem ('House of Bread') serves not only to secure the royal Davidic line necessary to authenticate the messiahship of Jesus, it also evokes the daily bread, the manna in the desert, the eucharist of life, the sustenance of the poor. The marginalized shepherds rather than the townsfolk are the ones that recognize the new David, the new shepherd King, in the swaddled disguise of the poor. Only the mystics, Simeon and Anna are given the insight among the religious folk and Mary ponders these things in her heart, her interiority another witness to the individual nature and significance of this global drama (Luke 2:1-39, 52). Where Luke has the shadows cast by prophesies of suffering, Matthew has threat close to hand throughout. The wicked King Herod is representative of earthly power, violently insecure, persecuting the defenceless, deceiving the wise and killing the innocent. The Star is the sign of heavenly destiny, the Magi the wise who track the paths of God, the gifts the signs of glory and sorrow. The anointed family become refugees, asylum seekers in a foreign land – Egypt itself is safer than the land of covenant. The narrative concludes with edgy, economic migrancy, as the family settle in Nazareth (Matt 2:1-23).

Ellen Clark-King concludes that the biblical truth of these passages confirms that:

> Patriarchy is not part of God's plan, since Mary stood outside it.
> The birth of Jesus ushers in a new order of justice and radical change
> Nothing is impossible to God . . .

Using poetry, a prevalent technique in postmodern theological discourse, she goes on to illustrate the liberation-feminist themes of the narratives quoting Mary Hanrahan on the Virgin as 'beautiful rebel mother', a different voice from the lowest place. The poem concludes:

> Lady of Liberation,
> Foster in us
> > The spirit of revolution
> > That mirrors God's justice
> So that our souls too may glorify the Lord.
> (Clark-King, 2006, p. 86)

g) Epilogue: Marian veneration

Although such a reading of Marian texts may appear non-traditional to some, they reflect not only classic conclusions of liberation-feminist reflection, but exemplify a postmodernist approach, which mixes intuitive, poetic and exegetical methods in response to the creativity of life-contextualized analysis. Yet such readings of the Marian traditions in the Gospels seem a step removed from traditional imagery – far away from the ultra-holy, almost untouchable representations of Mary, so visible in Orthodox and Catholic iconography. How come?

The Gospel tradition is obviously important. John and Luke accord Mary key significance. In John 2:1-11, she is instrumental at Cana in the outpouring of the New Wine. Inaugurating the messianic signs, she is also present on Calvary as Jesus is 'lifted up', his last gift being to bequeath her belonging and her motherhood to the beloved disciple (John 19:26). The potent double presence of Mary at Annunciation and Pentecost is Luke's theological guarantee that the birth of the Church is seen as the new birth of the Body of Christ. In the modern context, it not only serves as a reminder that the apostolic community was not exclusively male, but more importantly associates Mary with charism, life and the *natality* ('birth giving') of the Spirit.

Though Paul hardly dwells on her at all, Mary already features in the piety of Ignatius of Antioch at the turn of the first century CE (see p. 219). Fascination with the role of Mary seems to have developed particularly in the fourth and fifth centuries. The combination of an argument from silence (there is no tomb, nor record of hallowed burial place), along with non-canonical accounts of Mary's last days (recounting her *transitus* or 'Assumption'), augmented devotion. Liturgically, Mary became symbolized as the Ark of the New Covenant – Word made in her flesh. Just as the Ark was made from the finest material (Ex 25:10-22), so Mary was created free from sin (the Immaculate Conception). Just as the Ark could not be contained when held hostage in the land of Philistia (1 Sam 5:1-7:1), so Mary could not be held by the janitors of shadowland. Just as the great statue of Dagon crashed down before the Ark (1 Sam 5:4), so Death is powerless before the New Ark that is Mary, taken up to heaven (Rev 11:19-12:6).

Although this kind of patristic typology does not always meet with universal approval, it was certainly a mode of meditation which by the fifth century, as noted above (Section 14g), led to Mary being accorded the title of *Theotokos* – 'God bearer'. Through iconography, sculpture and popular devotion, the symbolic depiction of Mary and the dedication of churches and holy places to her intercession flowered enormously, especially in Medieval times. By now she represented a perfect womanhood and perfect motherhood, virginal yet fecund. Her veneration was ubiquitous in Christianity until the Reformation. Subsequently, the sweeping away of images and the sweeping away of non-canonical literature took out much of the Marian heritage. Suspicions that Marian devotion was actually idolatrous had been around since Nestorian times. Looking into historical and biblical parallels, Mariology was suspected of being merely Mariolotry, a Christian version of the perennial idolatry of Ashtarte, the Heavenly Goddess, so often the target of Israel's prophetic tradition (2 Kings 23:13). Where Israel's prophets were jealous on behalf of YHWH, there has been similar sensitivity to the possibility of Mary complicating, rivalling or even replacing the relationship with Jesus in the life of a believer.

To some extent, this is a question closely linked with the mediation of grace in ecclesiological understanding. For the Catholic and Orthodox Church, the multiple mediations of grace through the sacraments make this experience of faith a common one and the notion of the deathless communion of saints is a key component of intercessory prayer. Mary is the most 'blessed among all women' and has a good track record of persuading Jesus to do things (John 2:1-12). For the Reformed tradition, though there is a strong custom of fervent personal prayer on behalf of fellow church members, the emphasis is on the immediate intimacy with God accessible through Jesus in the grace of the Holy Spirit which makes such intermediary agency unnecessary.

In recent times, from being an object of intense suspicion between Christian denominations, Mariology seems to be occupying its own particular space. As noted above, her story has been appropriated as an exemplar for Liberation and Feminist theologies, while retaining its traditional attraction in popular piety. It is perhaps significant that during an epoch which defined the doctrinal verity of the Immaculate Conception (1854) and the Assumption of the Virgin (1950), Vatican Council II (1962–1965) would emphasize the importance of Mary as the model disciple in *Lumen Gentium* VIII, an avenue of biblical interpretation which is more easily appropriated by the Reformed tradition. Moreover, the growth of Pentecostal and Evangelical Churches among the Hispanic population of the Americas promises interesting developments. By origin a local Mexican apparition, devotion to Our Lady of Guadaloupe is now strong throughout Latin America. Hispanic Evangelical and Pentecostal Church members often retain a lively sense of Marian piety which has attracted curiosity among scholars and beyond. It is one of the more recent ironies of Christian Theology that with all the Catholics there are in New York, it was Protestant devotion that made Mary appear on 23 March, 2005 . . . on the cover of *Time* (Van Biema, 2005).

Summary

Different and divergent voices in Theology have always been around, but for centuries, the platform was either clerical or academic. Whether Kierkegaard was pushing for passion over reason and the primacy of the individual over the community, or Nietzsche was arguing the need to rid the world of religion so as to allow humanity to create its own rules, the effect of these surging voices was to recast the question of truth and meaning. Taken on by the Existentialists in the twentieth century, this mindset sought knowledge as lived experience in its drama and banality. Privileging of the individual and the particular was at odds with the traditional 'theoretical' patterning of Christian Theology and in the irruption of post-modernity, the whole notion of objectivity and the value of all-embracing religious meta-narrative was questioned. Meanwhile, experiential Theology that laid down its roots in impoverished South America was giving a language to the voiceless. Liberation and Post-colonial Theology sounded very different to that commonly espoused by the Western intelligentsia. Feminist Theology also emerged, speaking in a different register. Those that had been traditionally silent had begun to speak up to reclaim positive and empowering aspects of Theology, re-interpreting where possible, and re-writing where necessary. Even Marian devotion became more 'earthy' – the radical praise on the lips of the handmaid a reminder of YHWH's enduring option for the poor. In sum, Liberation Theology is a quest to narrow the distance between theological 'thought' and 'action', a challenge which is further explored in the next chapter.

23

Dialogues in Ethics

Whatever criticisms might be levelled at the Existential/Postmodern turn and the proliferation of specific readings of the Bible, a characteristic of many theologies that have emerged is their rootedness in action. Though the central revelation of Christianity was a lived life, not a set of propositions, the instinct to formulate general guidelines for personal and social behaviour is as old as humanity itself. For centuries in the West, the broad lines of moral behaviour were sanctioned by Church on the one hand and underpinned by the laws of the State on the other. This consensus has broken down in the face of a pluralist world view where tolerance and autonomy are contemporary watchwords. As a result, Christian theological approaches to moral issues as diverse as nuclear war and sexual intimacy are part of a broader dialogue involving secular viewpoints and other models of ethical behaviour.

a) What must I do?

One of the touchstones of recent developments in Christian thinking has been the emphasis on lived experience as the starting point for theological reflection. This approach has good biblical pedigree, since the New Testament revelation has at its heart an example of living, rather than a set of rules or a speculative system. In a very real sense, the 'Ten Words' or Commandments of the Torah written on stone are theologically replaced by the One Word, spoken by a life, written on a heart. The self-understanding of the Christian is that he or she is part of the Body of Christ, bearing a responsibility for right action in accordance with the divine command to love God and neighbour. Unfortunately, there is a double difficulty in this challenge. The first is sheer reluctance to do the right thing, the instincts of selfishness which Augustine gathered under the umbrella term of *concupiscence* and in traditional terms can be understood as a consequence of Original Sin. The second problem is not knowing what might be the right thing to do. And while discerning the right course of action has always caused dilemmas, there are good reasons to argue that it has never been more difficult.

Why? Well at the risk of over-simplification, from the time of Constantine until about 1950, there was a congruence of state legislation and Church teaching which served both the secular and sacred authorities well. As noted above, Constantine revised Roman laws in accordance with Christian teaching and from then on, although various emperors, popes, kings and governments down the ages had the odd falling out, the broad patterning of life along lines guided by biblical teaching and Christian tradition was pretty constant. Though there were obvious exceptions, such as the totalitarian regimes of Nazi Germany and Soviet Russia which deliberately adopted other ideological matrices, by and large, being a good Christian meant obeying the Church in matters of personal discipline (Matt 16:16) and the law of the State in matters of public behaviour (Rom 13:1ff.). In both cases, you were told what to do, and the task was to get on with it.

This is not to say that the Modern period did not offer secular alternatives to Christian moral principles, Kant and the Utilitarians being the obvious examples. But as Nietzsche foresaw, the radical individualistic turn, self-actualization and the proclamation of the 'Death of God' – all themes which developed apace during the twentieth century – have left a world 'away from all suns', without agreed co-ordinates for behaviour. This changed landscape has been most clearly in evidence since the end of World War II, from which time there has been a general tendency of governments to liberalize all legislation relating to personal morality and issues relating to the beginning of life. Contemporaneously, Churches acquired a tendency to take increasingly critical standpoints on matters relating to war and economic injustice. Inasmuch as ecclesial communities are urged to be prophetic, seeking to change or ameliorate national policies according to a biblical agenda, so governments are increasingly challenging the independence of churches to maintain practices or regulations that run counter to legal obligations, many of which are based on master principles of tolerance, autonomy and equality. Though this unravelling of the vestiges of the Constantinian settlement is somewhat destabilizing, it does at least allow clearer demarcation between the moral thinking proposed by Christianity and that proposed by other, more secular viewpoints.

At the heart of moral discourse is an understanding of the human person. In Christian Theology, this is rooted in the notion that the human being is *imago dei* – an image of God, a sacred entity with an eternal destiny over which humanity itself is not sovereign. In secular approaches, human beings are contextualized in the realm of nature, with social obligations based on the common good, but whose destiny is primarily determined by the wishes and desires of the autonomous individual. It stands to reason that ethical theory follows on from this understanding, since it hardly makes sense to discuss the morality of right or wrong actions without reflection on what a human being is in the first place. That said, since both Christian and secular approaches to ethical theory coalesce around notions of authenticity and the common good, it is an area where dialogue is possible and potentially fruitful. After all, Western values of tolerance, self-realization and equality are at least in part derived from the Gospels, and hence dialogue with secularity can at times be a mirroring of the biblical revelation back to theologians from a non-confessional standpoint. To that end, this chapter will discuss some of the most common constructs of ethical decision-making, sacred and secular, before assaying key moral dilemmas that impact on humanity, whether at global, ecclesial or personal levels.

b) Ethical theory in Christianity

Recklessly trying to summarize 6000 years of biblical and ecclesial reflection, several currents feed into Christian ethical thinking. The first and most obvious is the notion of 'Divine Command' – God says it, so it must be right. Get on and do it! In Christian tradition, the goodness of God's commands flow from the goodness of Godself. There is no external standard of goodness outside God which might apply. God is not good according to our judgement. We only know goodness because it flows from God. This is the key attraction of Divine Command thinking and in its classic 'Ten Commandment' type form, it endows a permanently applicable moral guide not based on the whims of humanity in its many and varied cultural forms. As such, it can be construed very much as a 'duty based' or *deontological* ethic based around proper action, deeds that are good in themselves. It contributes absolute guidance to our fuzzy foggy minds in whatever era, whatever culture, whatever circumstance.

If Divine Command is the equivalent of a bolt from the blue, Natural Law is a bolt from within. While the Christian ethic of the 'sanctity of life' can be derived from a command such as 'Thou shalt not murder', it is also derived from the notion of life being a *gift* from God from the beginning of Creation. The principle established is that humanity is not sovereign over life, God is. In the Christian understanding, creation is good and has been ordered by God's wisdom (cf. Gen 1:31, Prov 8:22ff and Psalm 8). God's *purpose* can be seen in nature, some things are meant to be and other things can be seen to be disordered. Though the classic example of this is in sexual ethics (the *nature* of the male seed entails its purpose to fertilize the female ovum, if it isn't on its way to doing that, it shouldn't be on its way anywhere), the concept is broader than biology. Owing much to Aristotle's observations on *teleology* or 'final purpose', the idea is that Nature can assist in the discernment of what is the right way to act, and the advantage is that 'just as fire burns' in Greece and in Persia, principles so derived are applicable everywhere, all the time.

As a Christian Aristotelian, the Natural Law approach is most often linked with Thomas Aquinas, who identifies our basic moral instinct to do good and avoid evil as an endowment of nature. This pivotal primal orientation he calls *synderesis.* Through observation, Aquinas highlighted primary precepts of Natural Law such as self-preservation and the protection of the innocent, reproduction and the nurture/education of children. Sociability is a primary precept and by our seeking to do good, he identifies a natural inclination to know the truth about God. From these, further secondary precepts are derived, for example: Do not murder, defend the defenceless, don't commit suicide. In this perspective, 'grace builds on nature' allowing a commonplace holiness within the created order. Led by reason, all men have the Law written on their hearts – it can't be blotted out (ST I-II, q. 94, art. 1-6, cf. Rom 2:15). Though there is a tendency to associate Divine Command with the Reformed tradition and Natural Law with Catholic ethics, they are clearly not mutually exclusive and both have the characteristic of proposing moral absolutes. In fact, common cause between Catholics and Evangelicals has been a feature of ethical discourse and Church relations in recent decades.

Things become a bit more nuanced as approaches tied more closely to the New Testament are blended with the strong reference points of Natural Law and Divine Command. Jesus regularly operated at the edges of legal regulation, and seems to have had a hierarchy of moral priorities whereby, for example, the healing of a blind man was more important than the observance of the Sabbath (John 9:16). This led Joseph Fletcher (1905–1991) to base his *Situation Ethics* (1966) on the core dynamic of *āgape* – 'selfless love'. In his reading, Jesus' teaching deliberately undermines an absolutist, legalistic approach and is characteristically personal and non-prescriptive. Against the charge that it is an 'anything goes' morality, Situation Ethics would claim to imitate the wisdom of Jesus' 'agapeic' love – 'it relativizes the absolute, it does not absolutize the relative!' (Fletcher, 1966, p. 45) In its favour, it recognizes the way we so often make ethical decisions, but adds a universalizing criterion: 'What is the loving thing to do in this situation?' Hence although we may be committed to telling the truth, it may be simply inappropriate to tell someone short on confidence and just about to go to a party that they look awful. In a sense, Situation Ethics in its simplest form can also claim to have something of a Divine Command pedigree too, since it is a re-presentation of the so-called *Golden Rule*: 'In everything, do unto others as you would have them do unto you, for this is the Law and the Prophets' (Matt 7:12).

Also discernible from the biblical testimony is an invitation to 'character formation' or the development of 'virtue'. Linked to the cultivation of heroic qualities, virtue is understood to be a character trait which is admirable or praiseworthy. Qualities such as courage, generosity, friendliness – these are the kind of things which we aspire to and are at the heart of ethical behaviour. Although clearly present in the New Testament (cf. Gal 5:22 and 1 Cor 13:13) as well as in the work of Augustine and Aquinas, the rediscovery of 'Virtue Ethics' in recent times has been assisted by a revival of interest in Aristotle's *Nichomachean Ethics*. His list of virtues, while obviously connected to cultural norms of his own day, extol the quality of prudence, which judges the right course of action between two extremes; for example, stewardship is a disposition that stands between being completely foolish with money and being a miser; proper friendliness is half-way between being cantankerous and being slimy (*Ethics* 2, vii). The exercise of judgement is an ancient and perennial notion (cf. Psalm 1), which demands that everyone enter the drama of choosing the right thing to do. It also recognizes that imitation is more powerful than regulation and explains the importance of 'moral narratives'. The natural retelling of the stories of Jesus, the martyrs and the saints *is* the way that ethics are learnt. An entire culture can be transformed by rising to imitate the heroic, or conversely sinking to the lowest common denominator and giving up on virtue. In that sense, Virtue Ethics demands a certain amount of maturity, it is a skill of moral judgement which we can develop. Viewed in this light, Virtue

Ethics effectively plots your personal moral narrative. After all, the question at the end of life is rarely 'Did you do this or that wrong?' but more likely 'Were you a good person?' As Jesus' own epitaph might read: 'A man can have no greater love than to lay down his life for his friends' (John 15:13).

c) Secular ethical theory

At the risk of committing a 'secular sin', a hurried summary of three influential ethical approaches based on non-Christian principles might run as follows. In terms of an attempt at a universalist ethic, Kant's discernment of 'absolute musts' for behaviour, his famous 'categorical imperative' began with reflection on the fact that the only thing that is always good, is good will. Now many people will have heard of the saying, 'The Road to Hell is paved with good intentions', but Kant himself had no intention of ending up there. He was merely safeguarding the fundamental integrity of moral actions since they cannot be deemed 'good' on the basis of what might or might not happen. Why? Well take the Situation Ethics example used above (Section 23b). You tell someone they look good because you feel sorry for them and it has a good effect in the short term. However, they then go out to a party and are humiliated by the comments of a careless crowd because of their bad hairstyle or whatever. They drink excessively to cope with their discombobulation and fall into the canal and drown on the way home. Feeling guilty? Kant preferred to focus on what you are in control of, thus distinguishing between his own *deontological* ethic and *consequentialism* which demands that you know the future, but you don't.

For him, the answer to his question 'What must I do?' involved a discernment of those moral duties which could be universally applied, would not take advantage of others and which should be actively pursued as though everyone was so minded. As an example, 'telling the truth' is one of the most fundamental. It is a 'categorical must', since a society of lies would be madness. Like Natural Law, critics of Kant's views point to the unbending nature of such absolutist ethics, but it is important to recognize in both of these approaches that they are drawing attention to the kind of 'self-evident' concerns of humanity. It is impossible to even talk about 'common good' and human rights unless you have some universal sense of what they might mean.

That said, the Utilitarian approach would claim to serve the common good even more directly and practically than the absolutist principles of Kant. Associated with the names of Jeremy Bentham (1748–1832), and John Stuart Mill (1806–1873), the original Utilitarian insight was to observe that human beings had been placed under 'two sovereign masters', pain and pleasure. The aim of moral choice becomes to minimize pain and maximize pleasure. Utility or 'usefulness' refers to the amount of pleasure caused by a deed, hence for Bentham *an action is right if it produces the greatest good for the greatest number* ([1789] 1962, p. 33). Taking this original model, Mill modified its trajectory somewhat, since it allowed nasty things to be judged as morally good; for example, several sadistic guards torturing a prisoner could be construed as a right action according to the 'Hedonic Calculus' (Bentham's pleasure measure). Mill's solution was to suggest that a sense of society was implied in the Utilitarian slogan – 'the greatest happiness for the greatest number' which in turn means that there are some general rules which protect the Common Good. For example, I drive on the correct side of the road, not because it brings me pleasure, but because it is for the good of society. For similar reasons, I shouldn't lie. Mill also moved the aim from a maximization of *pleasure* to maximization of *happiness* and made the focus on *quality* rather *quantity*. 'It is better to be a human being dissatisfied than a pig satisfied; better to be Socrates dissatisfied than a fool satisfied' (Mill, [1861] 1962, p. 260).

The direct, democratic, and pragmatic appeal of Utilitarianism made it a transformative force for change in the nineteenth century. Great public projects, health, housing, parks, libraries and infrastructure were part of its outworking. As it has evolved through the twentieth and into the twenty-first century, however, a curious twist has occurred. Increasingly sophisticated presentations of the theory which acknowledge that perceptions of happiness can vary, have quite logically reformulated the calculus to endorse as morally good those actions which *maximize the amount of choice for the greatest number*. This has moved it somewhat ironically from its socialist-style roots, to a modelling which puts an emphasis on individualism compatible with the political right. By placing a premium value on individual choice, Utilitarianism has intensified the already well-developed sense of *autonomy* or 'self-lawism' characteristic of the times.

While the British analytical tradition and the Postmodernist revision have sincerely held linguistic aversions to discussion of concepts of right and wrong, a more persistent stream of discussion germane to the twenty-first century is emerging from *Social Darwinism* or 'Evolutionary Ethics'. Traceable to Darwin's contemporaries, Herbert Spencer and Thomas Huxley, it has been further developed through the evolutionary psychology theories of Edward Wilson and more recently through the writings of Richard Dawkins. The principles of the theory are that ethical action is a by-product of successful evolution on the part of humanity. Altruism and notions of good and bad are part of the picture. The hard-headed side of Dawkins' model suggests that the dynamism for our behaviour is provided by the 'Selfish Gene'. You, dear reader, are merely a vehicle for the successful transmission of your DNA. Your romance and your love for your children are of no intrinsic moral value, they are merely a way of guaranteeing another generation of genes. The softer side of Dawkins' model is that he insists we can rebel against this biology of what theologians would be tempted to classify as Original Sin:

> We can even discuss ways of cultivating and nurturing pure, disinterested altruism, something that has no place in nature, something that has never existed before in the whole history of the world. . . . We have the power to turn against our creators. We, alone on earth, can rebel against the tyranny of the selfish replicators. (Dawkins, 1976, p. 215)

Ignoring the philosophical contradictions (predication of moral agency on functional chemicals, omniscient historical knowledge, hard determinism possibly reversed by the need for a happy ending), this very different version of Natural Law does have the attraction of integrating humanity into the drama of cosmic creation. Mixing nature sentiments with utilitarian themes, Peter Singer and others are pushing for an ethic which no longer regards human life as a privileged category separate from the sentience of higher primates in the animal kingdom. Singer's *Animal Liberation* published in 1975 set out the agenda – to challenge the tyranny of human over non-human animals. In strict 'pain and pleasure' terms, there is a consistency in this approach which ultimately 'rates' quality of life independent of species. This has obvious implications in dialogues with Christian views, particularly in relation to the beginning and end of life, to which we now turn.

d) Beginning and end of life

Nowhere has the ethical 'parting of the ways' of Church and State since World War II been more obvious than in pre-natal ethics and the legalization of abortion on demand. For centuries, the practices of abortion and infanticide, not uncommon in Greco-Roman culture, had been condemned. State, Church and the medical profession, were all united in condemnation of the practice which was also explicitly forbidden in the Hippocratic Oath, the medical vow taken by doctors since time immemorial:

> I will give no deadly medicine to any one if asked, nor suggest any such counsel; and in like manner I will not give to a woman a pessary to produce abortion. With purity and with holiness I will pass my life and practice my Art. (cf. Cameron, 2001)

Unfortunately, the ethical dilemma this entailed was that it created the dark art of the 'back street' abortionist, operating outside the law, outside medical control, outside of regard for the often tragic consequences for frightened women. Though post-war breakthroughs in contraceptive technology allowed women increasing control of their fertility, a series of Western governments took the step to legalize abortion, normally with the proviso that there had to be sound medical or psychological reasons. While the direct consequence of these legislative decisions has been an unexpected exponential rise in the number of abortions, it has also called into question the moral status of both the foetal embryo and the infant.

- As a non-person, the developing embryo is now legally subject to experimentation. Taking the United Kingdom as an example, this is limited to the first fourteen days of existence since until that time, twinning is still possible and therefore (the logic goes), such procedures cannot be affecting an individual and are therefore morally acceptable. Embryo production in service of fertility treatments and medical 'stem cell' research is also permitted and the production of human-animal 'cybrids'.
- The moral status of the infant is increasingly questioned. In medical terms, the difference between an unborn human at nine months' gestation and a one week old infant in a cot is purely one of location. Since neither can be said to be rational, as Singer and others have argued, they are less self-aware than higher primates to which we do not accord moral rights. They are 'potential persons' and are not, therefore, to be accorded the same rights as *actual* persons.

These challenges to Christian ethical thinking are new. The biblical testimony is full of the drama of fertility and storied births, but the clearest point of reference for the beginning of human life in the drama of the Incarnation is conception (Luke 1:31). It is a weird situation. A virgin birth is now possible, as is the overcoming of the biblical tragedy of being barren, but since such procedures may involve the creation and destruction of numerous other embryos, Christian theologians cannot celebrate such events with any kind of unanimous voice. The earliest testimony to the messiahship of Jesus was that of the unborn John the Baptist (Luke 1:41), and the womb, which in the biblical sense was the safest place, has become a dangerous place (Isa 49:15). Moreover, on the grounds that an infant is not fully a person, even the cot may become problematic. This goes beyond the desire to avoid reproduction of handicapped or less-abled humans, but its logic leads to the recent suggestion made in the Journal of Medical Ethics.

> Abortion is largely accepted even for reasons that do not have anything to do with the fetus' health. By showing that (1) both fetuses and newborns do not

have the same moral status as actual persons, (2) the fact that both are potential persons is morally irrelevant and (3) adoption is not always in the best interest of actual people, the authors argue that what we call 'after-birth abortion' (killing a newborn) should be permissible in all the cases where abortion is, including cases where the newborn is not disabled. (Giubilini & Minerva, 2011)

It is unlikely that such views will find sympathetic hearing within mainstream Christian Theology anytime soon, but opinions like this do serve to highlight the key component in moral discourse, namely the nature and meaning of human life. If natal and pre-natal life is not truly human, belonging not to itself, but to the mother and/or the medical practitioner who have produced it, then it is not protected by the same rights enjoyed by mature citizens.

Similar dilemmas present themselves at the other end of the spectrum where once more, medical advancement and questions regarding autonomy and 'quality of life' have impinged on ethical decision-making. Among other things, autonomy *tends* to identify the human being with the conscious mind and instrumentalize the body. One of the consequences of this is the increasing phenomenon of self-rejection with concomitant requests to die prematurely by assisted suicide or through euthanasia. Furthermore, because the desire *to measure* the effects of actions is integral to the rationality of its system, utilitarian techniques such as 'cost-benefit analysis' end up assessing even the *value* of human life in monetary terms and its *usefulness* in new conceptual currency units such as the *qualy* – a 'quality adjusted life year'. It is easy to see how the accent on 'quality of life' and therefore 'life worth' come into equations which govern, say, resourcing of healthcare and therefore decisions on patient treatment. No one can say that the legislatures have an easy job in making such decisions, but from the point of view of Christian ethics, an alarm bell might ring. As Oscar Wilde acutely observed, it is possible to know the *price* of everything and the *value* of nothing. Since the fundamental consideration in Christianity is safeguarding of the 'human being' rather than 'human person', the value of the individual is not dependent upon the perfect functioning of either mind or body. Moreover, autonomy has limits in Christian ethics. As noted above, since life is a gift from God, its symbolic value is not at the disposal of the individual.

Withal, utilitarian views which seek to maximize individual choice easily lead to the conclusion that the practice of euthanasia ('happy death') should be permitted. Holland, Switzerland and individual states within both Australia and the United States are among the legislatures which permit or have permitted the termination of life when an individual no longer regards it as being worth living. In parallel, the manifold ways in which seriously ill people can be kept alive through modern medical techniques not only presents the dilemma of whether or not to 'turn off the machine', it also raises the thorny question of organ harvesting. From a utilitarian perspective, this makes complete sense. Why waste a good heart on a brain dead person kept alive on a ventilator when, through a medical clause in a 'living will', this may be effected in the most direct manner possible? Again, the Christian theologian is given a dilemma which has not been faced by previous generations. Life is sacred, surely this is morally wrong? Yet Christianity values self-sacrifice in its master principle: 'Greater love hath no one than to lay down their life for their friends' (John 15:13). Might a Virtue Ethics/biblical approach lead me to want to help others, even as my life is ending?

e) War and peace

If dilemmas regarding life and death can occur within the controlled environment of the hospital, it is hardly surprising that discerning right and wrong has proved problematic in the mayhem of the battlefield. Theatres of war, muddy and bloody, constitute the gross spectaculars which mark eras of human history (note the reference in this very chapter to 'post-war' morality). With some justification, however, Christian ethics has been criticized for being very clear about the sanctity of life in the medical arena, and yet untroubled by the long tradition of violent military action conducted in the name of Christ. As noted above (Section 18e), Renaissance popes and Reform leaders were not averse to taking to the battlefield. Flags bedeck cathedrals, blessing is called down upon weaponry and the tradition of Christian chaplains accompanying front line troops is one of the most established roles outside the normal pattern of pastoral ministry. National anthems in Britain and America stress the connection:

> 'Send her victorious, happy and glorious,
> Long to reign over us, God save our Queen.' (UK)

> 'Then conquer we must when our cause it is just,
> and this be our motto, "In God is our trust."' (USA)

Yet all this is against a background of Jesus' fundamentally non-violent revelation of God. The pattern of YHWH getting his point across by means of military intervention had become what Robert Farrar Capon has called a 'rhapsody of indirection' by the time of the Jesus event where it is God who becomes the violenced (2002, p. 17). Only a choosy reading can avoid the predominantly non-violent message of the Gospels and the aversion of early Christians to military service confirms this as a component of the Jesus tradition. The problematic passages usually cited are the Cleansing of the Temple (Mark 11:15-19, Matt 21:12-17, Luke 19:45-48), the defence of the household by the strong man (Mark 3:27), and particularly Jesus' allusion to violence on the eve of his arrest (Luke 22:35-38). The action in the Temple is clearly in the tradition of a prophetic sign, and the household image is easily understood as a metaphor/parable, but when Jesus says: 'The one who has no sword must sell his cloak and buy one' (Luke 22:35), he appears to be suggesting that weaponry is more important than clothing. Without wanting to whitewash the evidence, however, since the injurious use of the sword in Luke is immediately healed by Jesus, his final word on violence 'No more of this!' can probably be taken as a categorical imperative (Luke 22:51).

The problem for most of Christian history is that when nationality and religion become competing identity markers, the former normally wins out as the trump card in the game of belonging. The charge of disloyalty, betrayal or treasonable insurgency has been a common accusation against Christianity since Calvary: 'It is better for one man to die for the people' (John 11:50). As noted above, Augustine was very sensitive to this accusation and on the gallows of the English Reformation, Catholic and Protestant martyrs alike were anxious to profess their national loyalty notwithstanding the fateful consequences of their religious conviction. Despite the theological identification of being the Body of Christ on earth, following the Constantine settlement it has almost always been felt to be in the interests of official Churches to stand alongside national governments in times of war. As a consequence and as an example, it was smaller Christian groups such as Quakers and Christadelphians registering as conscientious objectors who raised the profile of Christian non-violence in England during World War I rather than Anglicans and Catholics. It also probably explains why, despite clear Church opposition to the Nazi rise to power, baptized German Christians during wartime were able to follow orders which amounted to the systematic elimination of former friends and neighbours in their millions.

The unfathomable horror of the Holocaust for the Jewish people *must* be a cause for sustained sorrow and reflection within Christianity. Critics inside and outside the Christian ethical tradition point out that in a century which at turns witnessed clarion calls for abstinence from pre-marital sex, pre-mature alcohol and pre-natal terminations, the apparent official tolerance of total war culminating in the dropping of atomic bombs by Christian nations on innocent civilians borders on a blasphemy against humanity. True, Christians can, and do, point to Maximilian Kolbe, Edith Stein and Sophie Scholl as heroes of that time and the writings of Dietrich Bonhoeffer in particular have left an enduring theological testimony of one man's faith wrestling with the call to make a difference in harrowing circumstances. That said, it has effectively only been since World War II that 'non-violence' has actually entered the vocabulary of Christian theological discourse. Yet though exemplified by the American activist Dorothy Day and so effectively put into practice by Martin Luther King Jr. in the 1960s, non-violent protest was anticipated many decades previously by a *non-Christian,* Mohandas Gandhi, in his liberation of Hindu India from Christian British rule. Could it be true that 'the only people who can't see that Christianity teaches non-violence are Christians?'

Well perhaps. Theologically, the 'Just War' theory is often cited as the reason for Christian accommodation of military violence. Associated with Augustine, Aquinas, Suarez and Grotius, the theological framework tends to consider *jus ad bellum* – 'rules for going to war' and *jus in bello* – 'rules during war'. In generic form, it runs as follows:

- There must be just cause (e.g. self-defence)
- It must be a last resort (after avenues of negotiation etc. have been exhausted)
- It must declared by a competent authority (the mandate is on behalf of the common good)
- There must be right intention for the stated cause (not waged by deceit or for economic gain)
- The long term aim must be peace and reconciliation (humiliating peace terms must not be imposed)
- There must be some probability of success (hopeless cause means waste of life)

During war, consideration must be given to matters such as:

- Comparative justice: the rights of both sides need to be considered
- Proportionality: Minimum force necessary should be used and the injustice that led to war must not be exceeded by the damage done during the war.
- Legitimate means: Weapons of mass destruction and indiscriminate killing not approved
- Rules of engagement: Treatment of injured combatants, proper treatment of prisoners etc. to be honoured.
- Innocents: Injury to non-combatants must be avoided

It is for the reader to think back to consider whether the numerous past and present worldwide conflicts have come close to meeting any or all of these criteria. Christian pacifism would remain unhappy about such a codification of action which seems to 'baptize the sin' involved in the taking of life. They point out that widespread abolition of Capital Punishment on the national scale should be imitated on the international scale. To take the life of another is to disfigure the face of Christ in the *imago dei* of the human being. More moderate positions would accept that the fallen nature of humanity means that war is inevitable. For Christians in this category, it is by strengthening institutions such as the United Nations that the dream of peace when 'swords may be beaten into ploughshares' (Isa 2:4) is most likely to be fulfilled.

f) Environment

Although despoliation of the earth had always been one of the side effects of war, the advancement in weaponry such as defoliation agents developed for combat in South-East Asia and the enduring, life-mutating effects of nuclear weaponry have inadvertently helped to raise consciousness regarding the fate of the world itself. After all, it is one thing to have strong opinions about someone's personal moral behaviour or sinfulness, but all that would seem a bit irrelevant if there was no, er . . . planet. In Christian thinking, the traditional view is that the earth belongs to God and the task of humanity is to be good, kind stewards of creation. Or is it? The word used in Gen 1:28 is 'to fill the earth and *subdue* it' a command which the industrialized children of Eve have done to a disturbing extent. As a result, ecological ethics has been given major impetus in recent times by awareness of several factors which are of global concern:

- Dominion over creatures is not the same as causing their extinction. The reduction in biodiversity is seen by some to be the most heinous of human actions, removing entire species from the habitat of the planet forever.
- General pollution of the earth's atmosphere has increased to the extent that both macro- and micro-climates are being altered by global warming which has the potential for immense human and species suffering.
- Concomitantly, specific changes in the earth's atmosphere such as the diminution of the ozone layer have led to photosynthesis problems for plants and skin cancers and blindness in humans.
- Over-farming, deforestation and intrusive irrigation have led to the phenomenon of soil erosion which now threatens the fertility of large swathes of the earth. Instead of making the desert bloom, humankind is well on the way to making the pastures barren.

In fairness to the broad biblical tradition, 'subduing the earth' and the curse of Adam being at enmity with his nature is not the whole picture. Awareness of creation has inspired some of the most beautiful poetry and prayer of the biblical Canon. All of creation, from the angelic heights to creepy crawlies, is caught up in the liturgy of life that is a chorus of praise to God.

> Praise the LORD!
> Praise the LORD from the heavens;
> praise him in the heights!
> Praise him, all his angels;
> praise him, all his host!
> Praise him, sun and moon;
> praise him, all you shining stars!
>
> Praise the LORD from the earth,
> you sea monsters and all deeps,
> fire and hail, snow and frost,
> stormy wind fulfilling his command!
> Mountains and all hills,
> fruit trees and all cedars!
> Wild animals and all cattle,
> creeping things and flying birds!
> Kings of the earth and all peoples,
> princes and all rulers of the earth!
> Young men and women alike,
> old and young together!
> Let them praise the name of the LORD.
> (Ps 148:1-3, 7-13)

Although there is a rather troubling episode between Jesus and a fig tree (Matt 21:18-22), the very fact that so many of his illustrations of the Kingdom involve nature, imply that the New Adam was very much at home, even in the fallen, post-paradise surroundings of the first century Galilee. In the biblical tradition, both the enfleshment and the resurrection of Christ are signals of a radical acceptance of the created order and are at the heart of the transformative, evangelical Gospel which includes *everything* in reconciliation with the One in whom the fullness of God was pleased to dwell.

> With all wisdom and insight [9]he has made known to us the mystery of his will, according to his good pleasure that he set forth in Christ, as a plan for the fullness of time, to gather up all things in him, things in heaven and things on earth. (Eph 1:9-10)

Against any kind of Platonic, Gnostic, Manichean negativity, Creation in the Christian conspectus is understood not just as a positive, but as a thoroughly Trinitarian event. Father, Word and Spirit in Genesis 1 are mirrored in the baptismal accounts of Jesus. With Easter understood as the Father raising the Son in the Spirit, the result is a new, sanctified reality, made holy by the participation in the natural order of the Godhead, which through the action of the Holy Spirit charges the world with *life*. Small wonder that storied figures such as St. Francis (1182–1226) and Hildegard of Bingen (1098–1179) were swept up in the wonder of Creation as God's proto-sacrament.

Theology is one thing, though, praxis is another. The shadow cast by theories of domination did not initially put Christians in the forefront of what might be termed 'Green Issues'. That role more readily fell to evolutionary ethicists somewhat critical of the Christian position, hence the redoubling of the 'human-centric' critique of theological approaches made by Singer:

> According to the Dominant Western tradition, the natural world exists for the benefit of human beings. God gave human beings dominion over the natural world, and God does not care how we treat it. Human beings are the only morally important members of this world. Nature itself is of no intrinsic value, and the destruction of plants and animals cannot be sinful, unless by this destruction we harm human beings. (1979, pp. 267–8)

While Singer's critique is a simplification, and has perhaps never been true, it is no accident that many of the protagonists of feminist and liberation readings of the Bible are also involved in 'speaking up' on behalf of the voiceless earth. In *A New Climate for Theology*, Sally McFague writes:

> We have been given permission to love the world by the incarnation of God in the world. Thus our assignment becomes figuring out what loving the world means. We have been given some hints in the contemporary, evolutionary, ecological worldview of our time that has replaced the three-storey universe of heaven, earth and hell. This new worldview says that all human beings and other life-forms are interrelated and interdependent. (2008, p. 34)

Once more it may 'feel' like a revolution to some, but stating the obvious to others. The corollary can be observed, in that organizations committed to the alleviation of poverty are increasingly involving themselves in environmental issues of sustainability. Christian Aid, a British development organization, has the catchy slogan 'We believe in life before death' and its Catholic counterpart Cafod uses 'Live simply, that others may simply live'. In so doing, such organizations are enacting a practical theological approach which refuses to accept that the predominant 'meta-narrative' of Capitalism is the last word on the distribution of the world's resources. In an era when 2 per cent of the world's population own half of its wealth, and 50 per cent of the population own 1 per cent of its resources, you don't have to be a Marxist, Jesus or even his

Mother to have issues with Capitalism. The point being that if the unthinking actions of affluent Christians in the West are gradually destroying the lives not just of their poorer brothers and sisters around the world, but also the animals, plants and the earth itself, then traditional examinations of conscience used in Christian prayer might need to be reviewed.

g) Sex, family and relationships

And talking of which, what about human relationships, intimacy and the everyday common life? Obviously at one level, the classic examination of Christian conscience based on the Ten Commandments and given extra fizz by the Sermon on the Mount may appear to be a series of negatives, but as noted above, read within their context of liberation, they are counsels of freedom. After all, it is a lot quicker to list things you shouldn't do than to list the many things you *can* do. So how come Christian ethics is so often perceived to be a raft of negative instructions designed to take all the fun out of life? Part of the reason is probably a function of the active search for norms that seems to be a feature of human beings in general and religious groups in particular. Possibilities easily become prohibitions and the religious mind is often attracted to 'Key Performance Indicator' faith (see Section 10f). The result is that the motive for good behaviour becomes external rather than internal, and discernment of right and wrong can be pulled in seemingly opposite directions.

For the Christian tradition, sex is often held up as a prime example. The 'original blessing' of the Garden and the passionate biblical exploration of the erotic witnessed in the Song of Songs are surrounded by more restrained, even repressed approaches to such matters. Exposure of genitalia or nakedness was closely linked to notions of shame (Gen 9:20-23, Lev 18:6-19). In the teaching of Jesus, with the focus on the coming of the Kingdom, the importance of family relationships and therefore sexuality was, if anything, de-emphasized (cf. Matt 19:19:1-12, Mark 3:31-35, Luke 12:49-53). Strong celibate traditions in imitation of Christ and Paul, as well as the development of monastic life, were a feature of Early Christianity. Sober views on sexuality were maintained by the Reformed and Orthodox tradition with the result that in a hugely ironic turn, a Christianity which boasted an incarnate Lord, seemed 'anti-flesh'. Hence, while throughout Christian Europe, the phenomenon of prostitution was accepted as a disapproved of but inevitable feature of society, the expectation of female virginity before marriage and fidelity during it was a constant. Fear of pregnancy outside of wedlock was very real for both men and women, and divorce was generally granted only on grounds of adultery. The State agreed with the Church, that's how sex and family life worked.

As a result, Christian leaders were caught a little unawares by the social revolution of the late twentieth century. Apart from the radical new trends in thought which proposed a more permissive society, contraceptive advances meant women and men were much more in control of their fertility. With the fear of pregnancy diminished and role models from film, music and media advocating lifestyles in which marriage and exclusive relationships were undesirable, the Churches were faced with a stark truth: for centuries, entire populations had been conforming to the moral norms of society, rather than the moral norms of Christianity.

The response of theologians was many and varied. Situation ethicists were more at ease with matters than absolutist theologians. In a famous decision, arrived at following much deliberation, Pope Paul VI chose to maintain the strong link between Catholic sexual ethics and Natural Law in *Humanae Vitae*, 1968. By reaffirming that procreation was the proper context for sexual activity, which should always be open to the possibility of life, it was unexpectedly out of step with the *zeitgeist*. Its legacy is much debated, many regarding it as unnecessarily intrusive and unsustainable as an ethic in the modern world. Others see it as prophetic, not least because by clarifying the context and purpose of sexual behaviour, it provides a much needed Christian reference point in the confusion of relatively recent phenomena such as widespread cohabitation, homosexual liberation and contraceptive mentalities. The wider Christian family, which had tended to be less concerned with contraceptive practice, was more immediately concerned to work out ways to justify the tradition of pre-marital virginity in the face of a liberal presentation of sex as a harmless form of self-discovery and mutual pleasure. If, in the 1950s, Elvis had hit the top of the charts with *Love me tender, love me true*, by the 1980s, Tina Turner was expressing different sentiments with *What's Love Got to do with It?* A cynic might say that sexual union had gone from being associated with the romantic expression of everlasting companionship, to the addictive exploration of advanced tickling skills, in the space of three increasingly hedonistic decades. I recall with some amusement from around the same time, a low key meditation by Pope John Paul II on Matt 22:25-35, leading to a classic newspaper headline: 'No sex in heaven - Official!'

That said, the apparent mayhem in personal morality was revealing deep-seated truths that had become somewhat obscured in the Christian tradition, especially desire and authenticity. Desire, the characteristic inner passion of the erotic drive, which had been such a feature of many of the mystical writers and the kind of fire that enabled the early martyrs to witness, made something of a return to theological discourse. Likewise, while self-indulgence is always a danger, the implicit ideal of personal authenticity at the core of Postmodern morality has served as something of an antidote to the besetting sin of Church and State, namely hypocrisy – wanting to *look* good, while not *being* good. Moreover, since the question of authentic self-realization is a problem common to all, it has provided an accessible point of consideration and exploration across the 'sacred and secular' ethical discourse.

A couple of examples may suffice. For Karol Wojtyla (John Paul II), the dignity of the human being dominated his philosophical ethics, forged as it was against the background of a Poland torn between the two dehumanizing regimes of Soviet Russia and Nazi Germany. Theatre was part of the resistance to occupation, and in his play, *The Jeweller's Shop,* a series of tableaux are enacted whereby the characters explore *what they really want.* From a contrasting background of American Methodism, Stanley Hauerwas has persuasively argued that the moral narratives which inform virtuous behaviour in Christianity *must* be separated from the prevailing narratives of both the secular state and liberal culture. In his *Communities of Character* (1981), he suggests that a return to authentic Christian practice is essential.

> The kind of character the Christian seeks to develop is a correlative of a narrative that trains the self to be sufficient to negotiate existence, without illusion or deception (Hauerwas, 1981, p. 132).

In other words, the somewhat wild quest for personal authenticity in contemporary moral choice calls for a renewed sincerity in the choices of Christian communities. If the moral narrative of Christianity is more *human* than the so-called humanist approach, then Christians will evidence greater happiness due to the wisdom of lives well lived. It is as simple as that. The proposals of Christian sexual morality are perfectly coherent with the personalist view of actualized self-giving through relationship. Likewise, the customary Christian profile of the nuclear family is something to be enjoyed rather than imposed. After all, there is little to suggest that liberalized sexual mores have resolved the problem of human happiness. There are costs involved in human moral choices. Just as a bad marriage can be damaging, the effects of multiple mirroring by serial partners can be problematic in terms of psychological health, and children can find it difficult to thrive in the less stable domestic environments of separated families.

One issue which remains a conundrum however is the integration of homosexuality into the Christian framework. In the search for personal authenticity, matters of gender identity and sexual orientation are pretty central and the 'coming out' of the Gay community after centuries of fearful oppression may be viewed as another example of a late twentieth century liberation movement. In the mainstream Churches, when the focus of attention is the homosexual person, there is clear consensus. There is no difference before God. Respect and dignity must be accorded and discrimination at whatever level against homosexuals is wrong. When the focus falls on sexual expression, however, there is a different picture because traditional approaches are pretty unequivocal – Divine Command judging such acts sinful and Natural Law judging them disordered. The famous incident at Sodom and Gomorrah (Gen 19:1-29) can partly be understood as a crime against hospitality, though other injunctions such as Lev 18:22 and 1 Cor 6:9 are much less ambiguous. Though there is clear affectivity within same-sex friendships in the Bible (Jonathan and David [1 Sam 18:1-4], Naomi and Ruth [Ruth 1:14-18], Jesus and the Beloved Disciple [John 13:23]), it constitutes an ambitious argument from silence to construe them as homoerotic. Early Judean and Christian traditions consistently distanced themselves from the varied expressions of sexuality in Canaanite religion and in the Greco-Roman world. As things stand, these are probably still early days in such matters and the ramifications of this movement for the mainstream Churches are still in process. Some, such as the Episcopalian/Anglican communion, have wrestled with the matter more publicly than others, but the long-term outcomes remain to be seen.

Withal, the personalist turn in ethical analysis does bring back to centre stage older templates for behaviour such as the paradigms extolled by Thomas Aquinas and Augustine. While fully aware of traditional ethical matrices, both were able to look within for the source and impetus to moral action. In the *Summa Theologiae*, Thomas regarded the reciprocal mutuality of friendship as the best motif for understanding God's love for humanity and as a paradigm for our relationship with others. Augustine was typically more aflame, and he may as well have the last word on the drama of how to live:

> Love, and do what you will. If you keep silence, keep silence in love; if you speak, speak in love; if you correct, correct in love; if you forbear, forbear in love. Let love's root be within you, for from that root nothing but good can spring. *(Epist. Ioannis 7.8 in McCoy 2004, p.142)*

Summary

Christian ethical theory forms a major part of modern theological discourse and one of the most contentious. A key part of the self-understanding of Christianity is the desire to pursue a life well-lived in accordance with the will of God and imitation of Christ. Moral theories are designed to help decision-making, and Christianity is not short of such matrices. Divine Command and Natural Law provide 'absolutist' principles, Situation Ethics and Virtue Ethics are more 'relativist'. The changed situation for Christian theologians is that after over 1500 years of dictating morality, they are having to enter into dialogue with a dominant secular culture which is mapping the social landscape with a different ethical compass. Moreover, technological advances have fundamentally altered how issues at the beginning and end of life are framed. Likewise, war, peace and poverty. Although there may be some lament for the increasing dissonance between secular culture and traditional Christian Theology of the life lived well, it has at least forced the discourse to re-emphasize the fundamental inner directedness of moral choice rather than outward conformity.

24

Dialogues in Prayer

It can be argued that all the speculations, theorizing and theological conversations so far alluded to are ultimately derived from prayer – the essential dialogue which Christianity proposes takes place between human beings and God. Since twenty centuries of devotion, discipleship and spirituality have yielded an almost infinite variety of Christian prayer forms, this brief survey will be necessarily restricted. In the first instance, the overview of liturgical prayer will focus on Christian communal worship patterns broadly characteristic of the main denominations. Secondly, in considering Christian spirituality as a whole, the survey restricts itself to showing how classic themes such as mission, martyrdom, monasticism and the pilgrim way continue to shape the prayer-lives of believers today. Deliberately illustrating these paradigms with insights from writers associated with different Christian traditions, the reader is led to consider why dialogues in prayer appear both to reinforce and to undermine notions of denominational division.

a) The liturgical paradigm

Although the core thesis of this book affirms that anyone can engage with theology, understanding the way that Christian 'conversation *about* God' has developed demands some familiarity with the way Christian 'conversation *with* God' has been practised by believers themselves. In discussing the mutuality of baptismal practice and early creeds, Section 13c has already shown the importance of the axiomatic principle of *lex orandi, lex credendi* ('doctrine follows on from prayer'). Yet it can be argued that even these most basic and ancient prayers and liturgies were themselves derivatives of an essential ritual hunger on the part of early Christians, namely to have the *same encounter,* the *same relationship* with God as their founder.

So if that is the aim, why does Christian worship vary so much? For example, in keeping with its strong eucharistic tradition, the Roman Rite of Catholicism is firmly rooted in Jewish Passover symbolism. Understood through the prism of the Last Supper and the sacrifice of Jesus on Calvary, the Mass begins by consciously entering into the presence (the name) of the Triune God, acknowledging a need for reconciliation by a rite of penance and then listening to the saving work of God in the Scriptures. The offering of the gifts and their transformative consecration in the Spirit is at the heart of the Eucharistic prayer, which voices the 'words of institution' attributed to Jesus and variously evidenced in the Gospels and by St. Paul. The classical spirituality of Communion in the Catholic tradition goes beyond a symbol of sharing, is denser than Platonic categories of friendship and is arguably only captured by nuptial imagery. The *outworking* of the prayer experience is likewise 'incarnate' in the final command – *Ite missa est*. This is the phrase from which the Mass takes its name and can be understood both to conclude the ritual and to continue it, as if to say: 'Go – be the Mass'.

If anything, the symbolic actions of the Eastern Rite take these motifs even further. Although the Greek word *leitourgia* ('liturgy') originally referred to the public duties of civic officials, it is the private and indeed intimate nature of Eucharist which is emphasized in the Eastern tradition. While sharing the same overall pattern of the Roman/Catholic Rite, the focal liturgical actions of the Eastern tradition are performed by the clergy behind the closed doors of the *iconastasis* – a wooden screen which represents the Veil of the Temple:

> The call to close the doors reveals that Christian worship is essentially a closed, family affair, the private meeting of the heavenly Bridegroom with His earthly Bride, far from the eyes of the world. This closing of the doors reveals the separation of the Church from the world, for we Christians no longer belong to this age. (Farley, 2007, p. 64)

The deliberate connotations with Temple worship precisely evoke the central purpose of the liturgy which is *divinization* of the believer through sacramental experience of the presence of God. Indeed, the fact that Russia follows a Byzantine rather than Roman tradition is attributed to the experience of Prince Vladimir's emissaries in 988, who, when visiting *Hagia Sophia* in Constantinople, famously reported back that they 'didn't know whether they were on earth or in heaven'.

Engaging all senses with artistic imagery, aroma and careful clerical choreography, worship in the Eastern tradition is very distinct from the normal prayer experience of Protestant gatherings which themselves fall into two broad categories. At the risk of simplification, Lutheran and Anglican traditions largely retain a sacramental style of liturgy, whereas more Reformed/Evangelical congregations have simpler 'prayer, praise and preaching' patterns. The latter emphasize the proclamation of the word – the call to repentance which convicts the hearer of the need to turn from sin, to believe and to receive life. Arguably, this is the archetypal Gospel 'liturgy' at the heart of the transformative work of 'disciple-ing' (see Mark 1:14-15). It is the reason not just for the gathering but also for the existence of the Christian Church in the first place, namely, to evangelize. Meetings can take place almost anywhere and the praise of prayer and song that honours God effects the edification of the believer readying the heart to receive the Word through scriptural reading and sermon. Across the broad spectrum of Protestant denominations it is often the case that Eucharist is celebrated only periodically and would be understood primarily as a graced moment of symbolic recollection. The more constant feature is the call to holiness, the golden thread which connects the believers to the Lord through the graced power of the Word.

All three of these great traditions manifest roots in biblical paradigms of prayer, but it is worth noting that the Anglican/Episcopalian Church manages to host both very Catholic looking liturgies (High Church) and more Reformed/Evangelical congregational worship (Low Church), depending on the tradition of the local parish. It is also to be noted that although Pentecostal traditions follow a broadly Protestant pattern and purpose in liturgy, a more definite emphasis on the immediate experiential nature of prayer is emphasized. Since Pentecostal groups form the fastest growing branch of the Christian movement, a short review of their origin is outlined in the next section. Suffice to say, by linking ritual rationale to the defining experience of the early believers on Pentecost Day (Acts 2), worshippers believe that God's Spirit is actively present among the faithful, speaking to them not just through biblical recitation but also through the exercise of charisms, such as prophetic words and healing prayer (1 Cor 12:1-31).

Yet Christian dialogue with God entails more than liturgy on Sunday, it is a liturgy of life. It is a dialogue which involves a response of 'mind, body and soul', a calling to follow Christ in thought, word and deed '24/7' in which prayer is the relational essential. Christian prayer may be defined as 'the raising of the heart and mind to God' but there seems to be more to it than that. If 'what you believe is what your life is', then the idea that the whole of life is a prayer means this particular dialogue is sometimes framed in broader terms such as 'discipleship' or more commonly 'spirituality'.

Briefly put, *Spirituality* is an umbrella term describing 'how, individually and collectively, we personally appropriate the traditional Christian beliefs about God, humanity, and the world, and express them in terms of our basic attitudes, life-style and activity'. (Sheldrake, 1987, p. 2). Strictly speaking, since each individual Christian is therefore engaged in their own dialogue with God, it might be considered somewhat implausible to make generalizations. What permits us to do so, however, is that Christian history from its origin to the present has not only made manifest different *prayer* styles through the collective worship of denominations, but it has also framed certain classic *life styles* or paradigms of spirituality which characterize the relationship of believer and beloved. Among these it may suffice to identify *mission, martyrdom, monasticism* and *journey* in the main text while profiling other examples such as *creation* and *poverty* in the corresponding supplementary section of the book. Then, in order to help the reader explore this very intimate dimension of Theology, the study proceeds by choosing a selection of influential denominational 'witnesses' to demonstrate how these classic paradigms of spirituality have remained relevant to contemporary Christianity.

b) The mission paradigm

Some time ago, I was present when a well-known evangelist opined that at the so-called 'Pearly Gates', the only question asked of a Christian wishing to enter heaven would be 'have you brought anyone else?' While this doesn't *entirely* accord with Mathew 25:31-46, it would hardly have troubled Peter and his fellow apostles whose giddy inebriation at Pentecost eventually led them out of their closed room, beyond the walls of Jerusalem, on mission to the ends of the known world. The Great Commission of Jesus *was* mission (Matt 28:16-20) – they were sent and they went. To be sure, while the Book of Acts witnesses almost immediately to the different ways in which early followers of Jesus lived out their devotion (Acts 6:1-6), there is no doubt that emboldened by 'the teaching of the Apostles, the Breaking of the Bread and the Prayers'

(Acts 2:42), the *spirituality* of the first Christians was conceived within the matrix of what we might call a 'Mission Paradigm'.

Without fear of contradiction, the fact that Christianity is a global religion is evidence enough that the mission model has remained a feature of Christian life and identity. Moreover, it has, if anything, taken on new impetus in the past century due not only to a broad-based interdenominational *evangelical* movement, but also by what many regard as a 'New Pentecost'. At Topeka in Kansas, on 1 January 1901, members of Charles F. Parham's Bethel Bible School who had been praying to receive the biblical promise of the Baptism in the Holy Spirit began to speak in other tongues (cf. Mark 1:8 and 16:17). To be clear, the phenomenon of *glossolalia* had not been unknown down the centuries but at least two aspects of this particular event proved to be enormously influential.

- First, by Parham identifying speaking in tongues as *the* authentic sign of Baptism in the Holy Spirit, he provided the distinctive marker of the holiness movement which coalesced into the World Assemblies of God Fellowship – the largest of the global Pentecostal Church federations. Although Parham insisted that the more specific event of *xenoglossy* (speaking a specific foreign language) had taken place in his Church, the movement would later accept utterances unknown to human speech as 'tongues of angels' and therefore authentic manifestation of the Baptism in the Spirit (1 Cor 13:1 & 14:4).
- Secondly, by actively working with African-American members, he helped foster the work of William J. Seymour (1870–1922) who presided over the even more storied Asuza Street revival of 1906 in Los Angeles. For many it was redolent of the biblical Pentecost in the ethnic inclusivity of its congregation of 'blacks, whites and hispanics', which was almost unheard of on the American scene at that time. The three-year revival also broke new ground in other ways as 'men and women shared leadership responsibilities together' and 'the barrier between clergy and laity vanished' (Burgess and Van der Maas, 2002, p. 3).

The rest, as they say, is history. The widespread revival of worship in a manner reminiscent of the Acts of the Apostles and the active seeking of the kind of charisms associated with the Early Church spread like wildfire (cf. Acts 5:12-16 & 1 Cor 12). Despite the inevitable growing pains common to new movements (e.g. Seymour and Parham soon fell out – cf. Acts 15:36-41, Gal 2:11-21), similar congregations sprang up in a whole variety of places, especially among poorer social groupings of all types. In particular, African American communities characterized by strong musical traditions, interactive call and response homiletics and a lively sense of spiritual warfare were at ease in the more expressive Pentecostal prayer milieu. Healing ministries formed part of the attraction of the movement with astonishing characters such as the Yorkshire 'plumber-evangelist' Smith Wigglesworth (1859–1947) achieving worldwide renown. Subsequently the movement has continued to expand apace. Besides having especial missionary traction in Latin America, Africa and the Far East, it also evidences an ability to foster 'mega-churches' such as that founded in Seoul by David Yonggi Cho in 1958 which coordinates almost half a million members.

Characterized by effusive praise, effervescent hymnody and miraculous claims, the demonstrative and audacious aspects of Pentecostal spirituality aroused suspicion in the more traditional churches prior to World War II. Thereafter, Pentecostal-style spirituality gradually began to emerge *within* the historic churches which were helped in their understanding of the phenomenon by impressive mainstream Pentecostal figures such as the South African, David du Plessis (1905–87). Under the umbrella term 'charismatic', participants largely flourished in settings outside the 'normal' Sunday worship, groups of families often forming 'covenant communities', which experimented with varying degrees of shared life in imitation of models found in Acts. More generally, the 'Charismatic turn' typified by a hunger for biblical nourishment and a passion for praise are part of what might be called a 'democratization' of spirituality which has raised lay-people into significant leadership roles. In the historic churches, since such devotional expression has normally run parallel rather than as a replacement to parochial life, Pentecostal-style spirituality has been broadly welcomed. With some 130 million Catholics involved, a series of Popes have given backing to what has become known as 'Charismatic Renewal' and the current Archbishop of Canterbury, Justin Welby seems equally at home with the movement.

Yet while the historic churches seem to have *managed* the charismatic irruption, the movement presents a more fundamental conundrum for traditional Evangelical congregations which are also committed to a prayer life based on the Mission paradigm. On the whole, conservative Evangelicals subscribe to various forms of 'dispensationalism' – the idea that God deals with humanity in different ways during different epochs. A common feature of this view is that the miraculous activities of the Apostles and the first generations of Christians were a time of specific grace, which soon passed. Thereafter, the supreme gift of the biblical Word of God, with its clarion call to make a choice for Jesus, becomes the only thing necessary for the Christian missionary.

Although Pentecostals may regard this as unnecessarily restrictive, one benefit of this view is that traditional Evangelicals can stay closer to the sober *sola scriptura* traditions of the Reformers, confess Jesus as 'Lord and Saviour' and simply get on with winning the world for Christ. The American Billy Graham (1919–) stands out as a colossus of such mission spirituality. A disarmingly straightforward preacher, biblical teacher, model pastor and family man, it is commonly acknowledged he has proclaimed the Gospel in person to more people than anyone in the history of Christianity without ever adverting to the gift of tongues. From the same Southern Baptist tradition, Rick Warren is another remarkable American leader, who, through publications and clear-minded church organization, has become a worldwide witness for the *Mission paradigm*. With no obvious charismatic influence, his book, *The Purpose Driven Life* has sold an estimated 40 million copies since publication in 2002. A manual of discipleship, he begins in a wonderfully direct manner, based on the biblical idea that 'forty' is connected to transformation:

> Today the average life span is 25,550 days. That's how long you will live if you are typical. Don't you think it would be a wise use of time to set aside 40 of those days to figure out what God wants you to do with the rest of them? (Warren, 2002, p. 9)

Though Evangelicals have sometimes been criticized for a tendency to foster spirituality so heavenly orientated it has risked being insensitive to more earthly social concerns, Warren typifies a more holistic theological approach which demands regard for the disadvantaged as a key to the Mission paradigm. While dealing a sideswipe to celebrity evangelicalism he writes:

> Unfortunately, many leaders today start off as servants but end up as celebrities. They become addicted to attention, unaware that always being in the spotlight blinds you. ... In heaven God is going to openly reward some of his most obscure and unknown servants – people we have never heard of on earth, who taught emotionally disturbed children, cleaned up after incontinent elderly, nursed AIDS patients, and served in thousands of other unnoticed ways.' (Warren, 2002, p. 263)

With chapter headings such as *Planned for God's Pleasure, Formed for God's Family, To become like Christ* and, and *Shaped for Service*, the book culminates in *Made for Mission*. There, in just a few sentences, Warren describes what it means to be a 'world class Christian':

The Great Commission is your commission.

> You have a choice to make. You will be either a *world-class* Christian or a *worldly* Christian. Worldly Christians look to God primarily for personal fulfilment. They

are saved but self-centred. They love to attend concerts and enrichment seminars, but you would never find them at a mission conference because they aren't interested. Their prayers focus on their own needs, blessings and happiness.

In contrast World class Christians know they are saved to serve and made for mission. They are eager to receive a personal assignment and excited about the privilege of being used by God. (Warren, 2002, p. 297)

In such a fashion, this modern iteration of the Mission paradigm, which often involves groups of families choosing to move house in order to 'plant Churches' at home and abroad, not only avoids accusations of insularity, but also manifests the 'vertical and horizontal' dimensions at the heart of Christian spirituality whereby authentic prayer always leads to love (1 John 4:20).

c) The martyr paradigm

Meanwhile, if a sense of mission marked an initial phase of Christian self-understanding, the paradigm of martyrdom was a close companion. The Book of Acts confirms this in recalling the deaths of Stephen and James (cf. Acts 7:54-60 & 12:2). Just as Jesus was willing to die, as the Apostles were willing to die, so the Christian disciple must be willing to die as witness. Though it has been noted that the spread of Christianity was not due only to the heroism of the martyrs, (see section 15g), it is a haunting truth that what was true for the first century was more than exemplified by the most recent which can be said to have begun with a new Pentecostal outpouring and ended with a new phase of persecution.

While the New Testament witnesses to the tensions between the emerging Christian movement and more traditional Judaism in the Acts of the Apostles, it soon becomes evident that imperial power is the greater danger to believers in the Book of Revelation. Just as in the case of Jesus, just as in the case of Nero, when empires or nations become involved, there is a tendency for state powers to act with violence and justify it as due punishment for treason. Times may have changed but tragedy remains. Although there are difficulties in separating religious from nationalistic motives, the use of Turkish armed forces to bring about the deaths of over a million Armenian Christians in 1915 remains a terrible episode in Ottoman history and constitutes possibly the most bloody persecution suffered by any church. Too soon after, the various anti-religious pogroms of the Soviet Union and the murderous actions of the Nazi party demonstrated the depth of animosity that Christianity could arouse in a totalitarian context. Though the heroic resistance to such tyranny is a study in itself, the particular case of Dietrich Bonhoeffer stands out as one which left a mark on twentieth-century spirituality and Christian approaches to political resistance.

Born in Breslau in 1906, Bonhoeffer's early life was that of a privileged Lutheran intellectual whose journey towards ordination included study under some of the most renowned theologians in the world and a garnering of enviable international contacts across Europe and in America. By 1933, however, the anti-Semitism of the Nazi régime had stirred his humanitarian and theological sensibilities in equal measure, compelling him to broadcast his opposition to Hitler and write an essay on *The Church and the Jewish Question*. With German Christianity in turmoil and unable to stem the tide of Aryan supremacist views, Bonhoeffer could be forgiven for pursuing his next phase of ministry in England where he networked support for the Confessing Church, which had come into being in opposition to Nazi policies. Adopting the famous *Barmen Declaration* penned by Karl Barth, it was based on the principle that Christ, not the Fuhrer, was the Head of the Church. Barth himself chided Bonhoeffer to return home to lend his strength to the movement which he did by organizing an underground seminary to train its pastors.

Theologically and spiritually, Bonhoeffer could not have been more suited to explore the dilemma faced by his fellow pastors and countrymen since he had come to the conclusion that the pre-eminence of the individual in modernity had 'invidious consequences for the task of understanding Jesus Christ, community and self-hood' (Marsh, 1997, p. 42). He worked hard at his tasks, and in 1937 published the *Cost of Discipleship*. In dismissing any notion of 'cheap grace' he articulated a Christian incarnational anthropology that at once undermined ego and empowered identity:

> Since the coming of Christ, his followers have no more immediate realities of their own, not in their family relationships nor in the ties with their nation nor in the relationships formed in the process of living. Between father and son, husband and wife, the individual and the nation, stands Christ the Mediator, whether they are able to recognize him or not. We cannot establish direct contact outside ourselves except through him, through his word, and through our following of him. To think otherwise is to deceive ourselves. ([1937] 1959, p. 96)

In other words, Christ delivers people from an immediacy with the world to an immediacy with himself. Hence in a language both similar and different to legendary forebears such as Ignatius of Antioch, he is able to contemplate the consequences of discipleship as a search for the treasure in the field, *expensive* rather than *cheap* grace:

> Costly grace is the gospel which must be *sought* again and again, the gift which must be *asked* for, the door at which a man must *knock*. Such grace is *costly* because it calls us to follow, and it is *grace* because it calls us to follow Jesus Christ. It is costly because it costs a man his life, and it is grace because it gives a man the only true life. It is costly because it condemns sin, and grace because it justifies the sinner. Above all, it is *costly* because it cost God the life of his Son: 'Ye were bought at a price', and what has cost God much cannot be cheap for us. Above all, it is *grace* because God did not reckon his Son too dear a price to pay for our life, but delivered him up for us. Costly grace is the Incarnation of God. ([1937] 1959, p. 45)

In 1939, following visits to Europe and a lecture tour in the United States, he once more returned to Germany and eventually became implicated with his brother in a plot to assassinate Hitler. Though his own role and complicity in the plans remain unclear, he was executed in 1945. Thereafter, his reflections from the time were posthumously published as *Letters and Papers from Prison* (1951). An instant classic, his call that Christians must be witnesses to 'ultimate honesty' in an epoch where *God is not a given* seems eerily prophetic. Marsh summarizes thus:

> Living in view of this recognition is not a concession to the 'godlessness of the world'; rather it enacts a faithfulness to the cross that seems appropriate to a time beyond modernity. The 'godlessness of the world' is not concealed, but 'exposed to an unexpected light'. (Marsh, 1997, p. 47)

It is impossible to read such thoughts and not be reminded of the light/dark/ truth/witness motifs so evident in John's Gospel which testifies there is no greater love than to lay down your life for your friends (15:13). By doing exactly that, Bonhoeffer crystallizes the *martyr paradigm* in a modern way, typifying the challenge faced in so many places by Christian disciples, who in making a choice for truth, confront evil such that their prayer becomes a life offering.

d) The monastic paradigm

As recent inter-religious turmoil in the Middle East, Africa and elsewhere has led to a new phase of persecution for many Christians, *the martyr paradigm* continues to define the era as a century of witness. Yet just as not every believer was called to martyrdom in the Early Church, so in contemporary devotion, believers have found other ways of witnessing to life by means of symbolic worldly death. As noted above, this was first expressed in Christian history by the classic monastic paradigm of 'white martyrdom' – embracing the vows of poverty, chastity and obedience to be free from the jealous earthly gods of greed, lust and power. Foregoing autonomy to embrace freedom is a classic case of Christian paradox and while the choice for monastic life is undoubtedly weaker than it once was in the Northern Hemisphere, its typical features including the call to solitude, reflection and sacramental imagination have remained attractive themes in Christian prayer. The fact that so many monasteries, abbeys, churches and remote retreats have constructed parking spaces for tour buses tells its own story – modern believers want 'to taste' the nectar of monastic life, even if their various circumstances mean they can't embrace it fully.

So what is the 'secret' of monastic prayer? John Cassian, often regarded as *the* Father who straddles the East–West traditions in the Patristic period, reflected that

> The end of every monk and the perfection of his heart direct him to constant and uninterrupted perseverance in prayer; and as much as human frailty allows, it strives after an unchanging and continual tranquillity of mind and perpetual purity. ([c.426] 1997, p. 329)

Some fifteen hundred years later, it was in the quest for such 'tranquillity and purity' that Thomas Merton joined the strict Trappist monastery of Gethsemane in Kentucky in 1941. Following a difficult childhood and hedonistic youth, which included the fathering and loss of a child, there was little to suggest as he stepped across the threshold that the would help to renew a global fascination for the contemplative life. Yet his extraordinary literary talent and willingness to engage with both Christian and non-Christian traditions meant he quickly became something of a poster boy for the monastic lifestyle. Within two weeks he had written:

> Your brightness is my darkness. I know nothing of You and, by myself, I cannot even imagine how to go about knowing You. If I imagine You, I am mistaken. If I understand You, I am deluded. If I am conscious and certain I know You, I am crazy. The darkness is enough. (2002, p. xiii)

In his first phase of religious life, Merton journeyed *inwardly* and in 1948 he published a minor classic, *The Seven Storey Mountain,* which introduced readers to the confessional drama of his *inward* 'contemplation journey'. Tellingly, however, he recalls a visit from Baroness Catherine de Hueck

Docherty whose stirring testimony leaves a deep impression ([1948] 1990, p. 339). In some ways it foreshadows Merton eventually moving *outward* and travelling the world stage as his contemplation led him inexorably into action. Intimately autobiographical, his various publications such as *Raids on the Unspeakable, Solitude and Love of the World, Conjectures of a Guilty Bystander*, and *New Seeds of Contemplation* enabled readers to participate vividly in the joys *and* struggles of his prayer life expressed in pithy aphorisms, poetic metaphors and feisty frustration:

> What I wear is pants. What I do is live. How I pray is breathe.
>
> > I will travel to you through a thousand blind alleys.
> > You want to bring me to You through stone walls.
>
> > You have got me walking up and down all day under those trees, saying to me over and over again: 'Solitude, solitude.' And you have turned around and thrown the whole world in my lap. You have told me, 'Leave all things and follow me,' and then You have tied half of New York to my foot like a ball and chain. You have got me kneeling behind that pillar with my mind making a noise like a bank. Is that contemplation? (2002, pp. 1, 23, 15)

This ability to articulate common experience with uncommon genius is evident in one of his most famous prayers:

> My Lord God I have no idea where I am going.
> > I do not see the road ahead of me. I cannot know for certain where it will end. Nor do I really know myself and the fact that I think I am following Your will does not mean that I am actually doing so. But I believe that the desire to please You does in fact please You. And I hope I have that desire in all that I am doing. I hope that I will never do anything apart from that desire. And I know that if I do this, You will lead me by the right road, though I may know nothing about it. Therefore I will trust You always though I may seem to be lost and in the shadow of death. I will not fear, for You are ever with me, and You will never leave me to face my perils alone. (2002, p. vii)

And face perils he surely did. Increasingly involved in the politics of non-violence and engagement with Orthodox and Non-Christian contemplative traditions, Merton's international profile grew enormously but in 1965, he died suddenly – electrocuted in his hotel during a speaking tour of Asia. Thus ended a life which had witnessed vividly to a paradox of the monastic paradigm. The quest for solitude *away* from the world, leads to a sense of unity with all people and all things *in* the world, and a compelling desire to take a stance *against* the sins of the world. Notwithstanding the untimely manner of his passing, he was and remains extraordinarily popular. Like a latter-day Augustine whose early life his own uncannily mirrored, he fulfilled an 'iconic role in a time of massive cultural and religious transition. In a sense, Merton is a paradigm of the late twentieth century spiritual quest' (Sheldrake, 2007, p185).

e) The pilgrim paradigm

BY THE GRACE OF GOD I am a Christian man, by my actions a great sinner, and by calling a homeless wanderer of the humblest birth who roams from place to place. My worldly goods are a knapsack with some dried bread in it on my back, and in my breast-pocket a Bible. And that is all.

If the journey metaphor could be implicitly applied to Merton's very public devotional quest, it was explicitly applicable from the opening lines of the *Way of the Pilgrim*, a vivid prayer diary attributed to an unknown nineteenth-century Russian. Only becoming available to Westerners in the 1920s, it was instantly recognized as a classic exemplar of the *hesychast* or 'inner stillness' tradition of Eastern Orthodoxy and by introducing the 'Jesus Prayer' to the world, schooled Christians everywhere in what has become a popular form of meditation.

The idea of the Christian life as a prayer journey is deeply rooted. Besides the epic Old Testament journeys of Abraham, Moses and the Exiles, it is captured in the story of Jesus as he set his face towards Jerusalem (Luke 9:51). Perhaps even more significantly, it is also implied by the first name by which the Jesus movement was known – 'Followers of the Way' (Acts 9:2 & 11:26). The journey outlined in the *Way of the Pilgrim* begins when he hears the urgent call of St. Paul to 'pray constantly' (1 Thess 5:16). He starts his quest with a tour of local preachers who can't seem to help him and the plot involves the reader in a series of 'nearly moments' as he searches for a solution. Soon, however, he alights on two classic treasures of the Eastern tradition, guidance from a *staretz* (a spiritual mentor) and guidance from the *Philokalia* (a collection of ascetical and mystical texts from saints of the Eastern tradition).

The word *philokalia* translates as 'love of the beautiful' and its title perfectly captures something of the central aesthetic yearning of the Eastern prayer tradition. Broadly speaking, this is more typified by the vision of Mount Tabor and the dazzling transfiguration of love and light than Western spirituality, where the 'disfiguration' of a darkened Calvary dominates the imagery (cf. Matt 17:1-13 & 27: 45-53). Through his *staretz* the Pilgrim is then introduced to the writings of St. Simeon the New Theologian who teaches 'the Jesus Prayer' in the *Philokalia*:

> Sit down alone and in silence. Lower your head, shut your eyes, breathe out gently, and imagine yourself looking into your own heart. Carry your mind, that is, your thoughts, from your head to your heart. As you breathe out, say 'Lord Jesus Christ, have mercy on me.' Say it moving your lips gently, or simply say it in your mind. Try to put all other thoughts aside. Be calm, be patient, and repeat the process very frequently. (1989, p. 19)

For the Pilgrim, although it brings initial consolation, he is soon challenged by distraction and distaste for the task. Again he is guided by the combination of *staretz* and *philokalia* – such things are to be expected since 'to the world, nothing is worse than heartfelt prayer'. At first instructed to say this simple prayer three, then six, then twelve thousand times a day, he is soon allowed to say it as much as he likes. The effect is transformative – the prayer starts to wake him in the morning, his lonely hut has the feeling of a splendid palace. The Pilgrim starts to *become* the prayer as his heart takes over from his volition:

> After no great lapse of time I had the feeling that the prayer had, so to speak, by its own action, passed from my lips to my heart. That is to say, it seemed as though my heart in its ordinary beating began to say the words of the prayer within at each beat. Thus for example, one, 'Lord', two, 'Jesus', three, 'Christ', and so on. I gave up saying the prayer with my lips. I simply listened carefully to what my heart was saying.

Thereupon, the transformative power of contemplative prayer is vividly brought home:

> Then I felt something like a slight pain in my heart, and in my thoughts so great a love for Jesus Christ that I pictured myself, if only I could see Him, throwing myself at His feet and not letting them go from my embrace, kissing them tenderly, and thanking Him with tears for having of His love and grace allowed me to find so great a consolation in His Name, me, His unworthy and sinful creature! (1989, p. 19)

The rest of the narrative unfolds in a series of encounters which are at turns fearful, amusing and consoling. The Pilgrim meets criminals, generals, foreigners, tradesmen, fathers, families and priests. He suffers paralysis and is cured while his own ministrations on occasion also bring healings. He journeys from place to place with the threefold cord of the *Jesus prayer*, *philokalia* and *staretz* acting as a constant thread. Far from being a path of escapism, however, by modelling a prayer method which cultivated detachment, contemplation and concern for others, the *Way of the Pilgrim* once more exemplified in Orthodox style what some regard as the axiomatic paradox of all Christian prayer, identifying it as a transformative dialogue of love involving both God and neighbour.

The 'discovery' of the 'Pilgrim' in the twentieth century had impressive resonance even among non-believers. Because it was written as a kind of spiritual 'road trip', the *Way of the Pilgrim* had an immediate attraction to the post-war 'beat generation', though its rawness made the footloose lifestyles of Jack Kerouac and the later Hippie movement look rather staid by comparison! Indicative of its cultural influence at the time, the novelist J.D. Salinger (1919–2010) weaved the Jesus prayer into his novel *Franny and Zooey*, which considered broad questions of spiritual enlightenment. The mantra-like style of the prayer also caught the *zeitgeist* of spiritual exploration insofar as it exemplified in an authentically Christian fashion, a prayer technique by now more associated with Eastern religions. Lastly, the re-presenting of the *Philokalia* as a treasury of spiritual wisdom stimulated further interest in Orthodox traditions of prayer.

f) Dialogue as paradigm

While entire volumes could (and have) been written on any one of the spiritual paradigms or prayer witnesses considered in this chapter, it is perhaps fitting to end these all too brief reflections on prayer with the Pilgrim and the idea of *journey*. Not only does it capture the ancient sense of pilgrimage which is rooted in the DNA of Christianity, but it also naturally captures a sense of dynamism and purpose, the idea that just as there is a goal of Christian prayer, there is likewise a purpose to life. This is hardly an esoteric secret. Even if one limits a study of Jesus at prayer to his first public appearance at the Baptism in the Jordan, it *can* be argued that the nature and destiny of Christian prayer are immediately revealed as Trinitarian. Just as the humble Jesus is revealed in the Spirit as the Divine Son of the Father, so prayer opens a portal of realization that the believer is also God-beloved. This not only explains the central intimacy of the *Abba/Father* motif in his teaching and practice in prayer (cf. Matthew 6:9 Mark 14:36), but it also explains why the Holy Spirit is the ultimate promise of Jesus and the ultimate desire of human longing (cf. Mark 1:8-11, John 14:16, Gal 4:6 Rom 8:15). Confirming everything that Warren, Bonhoeffer, Merton epitomize, in Christian understanding, this intimacy is not merely 'vertical' (towards God), it is explicitly 'horizontal' (towards one another). In the great priestly prayer of Jesus in John's Gospel, the yearning is 'that they all may be one. As you, Father, are in me and I am in you, may they also be in us' (John 17:21). In short, the 'why' of Christian prayer is to live in the loving intimacy of the Triune God *together*.

But is it the *together* that is the problem? While the twentieth-century luminaries we have reviewed may have been drawn to different paradigms of prayer, their witness has touched hearts across all denominations and in many cases beyond the Christian fold. One of the questions which has therefore remained 'live' in theological discourse is that given such unity in diversity, why have churches remained so *separate*? If the problem is not rooted in prayer, what is it rooted in? Even more fundamentally, if Christian *dialogues in prayer* can find an audience among non-Christian and even non-faith seekers of wisdom, what does that mean for *their* eternal destiny? Are they, also, God-beloved? It is to these most fundamental and final questions of Christian Theology that we now turn.

Summary

Christian prayer may be defined as the raising of the heart and mind to God but it should not be confined either to the public acts of worship of denominational traditions or even vocalized prayer on the part of individuals. From the earliest biblical traditions, Christianity has historically given witness to distinct paradigms of spirituality, which continue to shape the lifestyles, understanding and prayer of believers. Luminaries such as Rick Warren, Dietrich Bonhoeffer, Thomas Merton and the anonymous protagonist of the Way of the Pilgrim epitomize the notion that life as a prayer can be decisively oriented by spiritual dynamics such as mission, martyrdom, monasticism and journey. While all forms of Christian spirituality attest that prayer can be a place of contestation requiring resolve and humility, there is an equally important sense that prayer is never narcissistic, finding its true destiny in divine and neighbourly love.

25

Dialogues in Faith

The long-standing divisions between the great denominations of Christianity operative since the Great Schism of 1054 and the Reformation of the 16th Century are a theological contradiction of the doctrine of Church as Body of Christ. For all the nationalistic tumult and conflict of the twentieth century, it was a remarkable period of rapprochement between Christian Churches. In parallel, a thoroughgoing reappraisal of Christianity's relationship with other religious groupings changed the entire landscape of inter-faith relations. Though not without controversy, consideration of issues such as salvation of those outside the Church and the place of Christ in universal redemption became a focus for a whole sub-set of theologians and lead necessarily to reflection on 'the last things,' the final destiny of humanity.

a) Dialogues in faith

There is an old story of a man being rescued from a desert island, having been stranded there all alone for twenty years. As his rescuers rowed him away from the shore, they noticed that there were two little brushwood chapels built a few hundred yards apart. When they asked the man why he had built two places of worship, he replied: 'Well, there's the one I go to and the one I don't'.

Although Jesus prayed that his disciples 'may all be one' (John 17:21), for centuries, if not millennia, the ecclesiology of belonging has been inevitably defined by choice for and choice against. A disfiguring feature of the different Christian denominations pointed out by critics of religious faith has been their track record of mutual enmity, not to mention their hostility to members of other faiths. The general disappearance over a relatively short time span of the ecclesiological and theological standpoints which gave rise to such pious ferocity needs some explanation.

By its nature, religious faith is all encompassing and is understood to have repercussions far more important than life or death. Moreover, as the sanction for action may be nothing less than a 'divine command', the combination of clear conscience, conviction and utter commitment can make actions in the name of God particularly fanatical. With some justification, the history of Christian violence against individual dissenters, misunderstood mystics, witches, unorthodox sects, minority faiths and indigenous peoples has been cited as the best argument for rejecting the coherence of its theological claims. True, the blurring of the distinctions between national and religious identity which accounted for much of the violence across Europe between the fifteenth and nineteenth century when Protestant England, Holland and Sweden were asserting claims against Catholic Spain, France or Austria makes it difficult to unravel some of the responsibility. Nevertheless, it is significant that when Simon Schama was asked what he had learnt after completing his monumental multi-episode history of Britain for the BBC, he replied: 'The importance of religion'.

The history of the ecumenical (*oikoumene* – 'whole inhabited world') movement is possibly the greatest triumph of twentieth century Christian Theology. Whatever the merits of grappling with atheistic trends in modernity, the fact that grapples between denominations have been replaced by fraternal embraces is remarkable. This has been in no small measure due to the imagination of theologians engaged in constructive dialogues across formerly entrenched ecclesiological divides. By and large, exchanges between churches were more 'you come in -ism' than ecumenism. The dynamic of change can be traced to the development of cross-church interest groups such as the Bible Society and the Student Christian Movement of the nineteenth and the early twentieth century. A turning point was reached when in 1910, the Edinburgh Missionary Conference established the International Missionary Council, which deliberately drew on the resources of member churches for the furtherance of evangelical outreach. A subsequent cross-denominational conference on *Life and Work* in 1925 addressed common concerns regarding social issues, but it was the gathering on *Faith and Order* at Lausanne in 1927 which explicitly began to tackle the theological basis of the Church and its unity. Following World War II, these two streams led directly to the formation of the World Council of Churches in 1948.

Originally a recognizably Protestant initiative, the Eastern and Oriental Orthodox Churches were part of the World Council from the beginning. Increased interaction with Catholic theologians during the 1950s paved the way for highly symbolic meetings in the 1960s. Vatican observers attended the Third Assembly of the World Council of Churches in New Delhi, and the reciprocal invitation by the Pope enabling World Council representatives to attend the Second Vatican Council was highly significant. Pope John XXIII is often credited with being something of a prophetic figure; Vatican II was to be an 'Ecumenical Council for the whole Church . . . to invite the separated Communities to again seek that unity for which so many souls are longing for'. Since as recently as 1928, *Mortalium Animos* had suggested that 'The unity of Christians can be achieved only through a return to the One True Church of Christ of those who are separated from it', there were many who expected little.

They were proved very wrong. Ecclesiological deliberations of universal significance took place at Vatican II. Understanding other Christians as 'separated brethren' rather than 'outside the Church', the 1964 document *Unitatis Redintegratio* – 'The Restoration of Unity' – declared ecclesial reconciliation to be one of the principle concerns of the Council, such that mutual belonging might become a precious lived reality for all Christians. The divisions among Churches are recognized to be scandalous and damaging to the Gospel. Ecumenism is seen to be a work of the Holy Spirit in a brotherhood rediscovered. Using deliberately attractive terminology, it stated:

> It remains true that all who have been justified by faith in Baptism are members of Christ's body, and have a right to be called Christian, and so are correctly accepted as brothers by the children of the Catholic Church. (*UR3*)

With traceable biblical and traditional lines of authority stretching back to the Petrine confession of Matt 16:18, it was important for the coherence of Catholic ecclesiology to square the circle of broader belonging without losing the specificity of its self-understanding as the locus of unity. By articulating that 'this unity *subsists* in the Catholic Church as something she can never lose, and we hope that it will continue to increase until the end of time' (*UR4*), the document managed to affirm strong ecclesial consciousness without being exclusivist. The culmination of the symbolic reconciliations of Vatican II came in December 1965 at the meeting between Pope Paul VI and Patriarch Athenagorus with their revocation of the anathemas of 1054 between Rome and the Eastern Church. Regret was expressed for the offensive words, reproaches without foundation and the reprehensible gestures that marked the sad events of the period.

Since such heady days, there have been continuing friendly relations between all mainstream Churches but frustration in some quarters that full visible Eucharistic communion has not been achieved. Whereas coherent *theological* convergence to an astonishing degree was achieved on doctrinal matters regarding *Baptism, Eucharist and Ministry* at Lima in 1982, things have become less straightforward regarding denominational praxis with regard to ministry (Thurian, 1984). For the Catholic and Orthodox Churches, the issue of demonstrable connection with apostolic lines of authority is extremely important. Moreover, the structure of bishop, priest and deacon is key to their understanding of what constitutes a Church in a way that the threefold order and succession are not so universally important within all the Reformed traditions. Due to similar historic self-understanding, Catholic and Orthodox communions tend to be much more sensitive to 'backward compatibility' – honouring the long centuries of Church deliberation in decisions about moving forward. Although Reformed Churches do have their own cherished traditions, their more manageable size, dispersion and the more immediate nature of their deliberative processes mean they have been able to move more quickly towards different models of ministry, including the ordination of female pastors. If flexibility is seen as an upside, theologically, it is difficult to argue with the criticism that the lesser importance placed on Church structure by the Reformed tradition has had problematic consequences for visible Christian unity. Protestant denominations and independent groups which have splintered from the mainstream almost wholly account for the 40,000 or so different ecclesial bodies operating under the banner of Christianity today (Barrett et al., 2001).

b) Dialogues between faiths

Equally as astonishing as the progress of the ecumenical movement, the initiatives undertaken over the past fifty years in pursuit of interfaith dialogue have put an end to even older enmities. Since mutual mistrust between the great religious traditions has characterized almost all of recorded human history, this sea change in attitude may yet prove to be the most significant revolution of the twentieth century. As noted above (Sections 21e-f), scholars such as

James Frazer, William James and Rudolf Otto had explored commonalities among followers of different religions, but a distinct 'interfaith' movement might be best identified with the convening of a 'World Parliament of Religions' in Chicago in 1893. In subsequent years, while it can be claimed that global travel, increased mobility and the scrambling of borders as a consequence of war were part of the picture, it is a tragic truth that a catalyst for a wholesale change of attitude came from the horrific event of the Holocaust or *Shoah*.

While no one disputed that the immediate cause of the *Shoah* was the unfettered application of Nazi anti-Semitic ideology, it was widely recognized that the pogroms and persecutions of Jews throughout Europe during its professedly Christian epoch had helped to sow poisonous zyklon seeds. The recurrent persecution of Jews was based on theological standpoints of separation, exclusivity and a dangerous interpretation of Matt 27:25 which literally claimed the right to inflict punishments for the death of Christ upon the descendents of the Jerusalem mob. Adorno perhaps captured the mood by saying, 'there can be no poetry after Auschwitz' and the sentiment demanded equal pause for thought within Christian Theology which had signally failed to prevent its occurrence. Taking the Catholic Church as an example, the lessons of those horrors can be heard in the sentiments of Vatican II. Making the fairly obvious point that Christ went to his death by choice, the document takes a universal stand prompted by its rejection of anti-Semitism:

> In her rejection of every persecution against any man, the Church, mindful of the patrimony she shares with the Jews and moved not by political reasons but by the Gospel's spiritual love, decries hatred, persecutions, displays of anti-Semitism, directed against Jews at any time and by anyone. (*Nostra Aetate* 4)
>
> We cannot truly call on God, the Father of all, if we refuse to treat in a brotherly way any man, created as he is in the image of God. Man's relation to God the Father and his relation to men his brothers are so linked together that Scripture says: "He who does not love does not know God" (1 John 4:8). (*Nostra Aetate* 5)

This same document took time out to completely recast relations with Hinduism (noted for its mystery), Buddhism (noted for its asceticism) and Islam (worshippers of the One God). At a time when materialistic Marxism was the ideological option governing half the globe, the document began to map out the contours common to all religious meta-narratives:

> Men expect from the various religions answers to the unsolved riddles of the human condition, which today, even as in former times, deeply stir the hearts of men: What is man? What is the meaning, the aim of our life? What is moral good, what sin? Whence suffering and what purpose does it serve? Which is the road

to true happiness? What are death, judgment and retribution after death? What, finally, is that ultimate inexpressible mystery which encompasses our existence: whence do we come, and where are we going? (*Nostra Aetate* 1)

It was this kind of recognition of the common cause of religions which engendered across all traditions a spontaneous flowering of various interfaith organizations in the Post-war era. Theological conferences and symbolic gatherings took place, which in terms of Christian history were pretty unique. The papal convocation of faith leaders from all corners of the earth at Assisi in 1986 which allowed those of their different traditions to pray in Christian Churches was unprecedented. The choice of Assisi was deliberate, since St. Francis, by meeting with the Sultan of Egypt, Malik al-Kamil in 1219, had fairly uniquely endeavoured to seek a non-violent solution to the Crusades. For some, however, this was all a bit too much. It was one thing to be friendly, but another to join in prayer, or to give off the classic Enlightenment impression that all religions were basically the same and it didn't matter what you believed. Within the Catholic Church the traditionalist Lefevbre movement caused a minor schism due to the syncretism of it all, and in the broader context of worldwide Christianity, ancient theological concerns re-presented themselves. What was God's relationship to all of humanity? How does Jesus fit into the global religious context? What is Christian theological opinion regarding the salvation of non-believers?

c) Salvation and interfaith dialogue

With regard to the salvation of non-Christians, the New Testament seemed to oscillate between two incompatible 'axioms' ('governing principles'). On the one hand, 'God wishes all to be saved and come to the full knowledge of the truth' (1 Tim 2:4) which seems to imply an open-ended approach to dialogue. On the other, 'there is no other name by which we are saved' (Acts 4:12) which seems fairly exclusivist. Although the Gospels present Jesus himself involved in 'proto-interfaith' discussions, for example, the Syrophoenician woman (Mark 7:25-30), the Samaritan woman (John 4) and the Roman Centurion (Matt 8:5-13), his example remains enigmatic. He seems surprised to find himself dealing with the Syrophoenician woman, but is very impressed by the Centurion. Jesus is astonished by the faith of the latter and chides his co-religionists for not having the same degree of conviction. It is a profound liturgical paradox that the words of the Centurion, 'Lord, I am not worthy to receive you under my roof, say but the word and my servant will be healed', form the basis of a prayer recited in Anglican and Catholic rituals *immediately before* reception of communion (Matt 8:8). Since there is no suggestion that the man gave up the military, nor that he left all and followed Jesus, it is perhaps an interfaith pause for thought that the words of a pagan abide at the heart of Christianity and that many 'from the East and the West' will be in on the eschatological feast at the expense, perhaps, of the insiders (Matt 8:12).

Paul is the obvious paradigm of New Testament interfaith dialogue (Acts 17:16-32), but it is the early Christian apologists such as Justin Martyr, Irenaeus and Origen, who are the forebears of the tradition. Because the concept of *Logos* was present in Greek Philosophy and parts of the Oriental religious tradition, these early theologians tended towards the possibility of an implicit relationship with Christ being sown by the Word throughout the world. The more general tradition was that those belonging to God born *before* the time of Christ could be saved, (for example Abraham and Moses), but that those who *left* the Christian faith (apostates), were damned. In between, there was general confusion about those who had never heard about the faith, but the idea of how the Church worked began to coalesce around Origen's idea of the Church as Noah's Ark, floating on the stormy waters of life. The invitation aboard was an invitation of rescue, an offer of salvation.

Like many things, the conversion of Constantine changed the discourse. The assumption that everyone had now received access to the Good News and was therefore culpable if they did not acknowledge Christ meant that effectively, the doctrine of *extra ecclesiam salus non est* – 'outside the Church there is no salvation', became the theological assumption. There were some exceptions allowed. As noted above, both Augustine and Aquinas spoke of the possibility of a 'Baptism of Desire' whereby someone not yet sacramentally in communion could be saved. That said, the more obvious viewpoint was expressed by Lateran Council IV in 1215, 'One indeed is the universal Church of the faithful, outside which no one at all is saved' (Canon 1). The events of the Reformation, obviously, threw the situation into some confusion but it was the perplexing lot of indigenous peoples of the newly discovered lands of East and West that reopened the debate. One option, simply, was to take the command in Matt 28:19 literally, and assume the absolutely urgent task of missionary endeavour. Francis Xavier, who baptized so many he needed help to raise his arm to perform the ritual, exemplifies the fire of the missionary heart:

> Would to God that these divine consolations, which God gives to us in the midst of our labours might not only be related by me but also some experience of them be sent to our European universities to be tasted as well as heard of! Then many of those young men given up to study would turn all their cares and desires to the conversion of infidels. (Coleridge, 1874, p. 349)

This straightforward understanding was and remains a key driver behind the prodigious efforts of linguists to translate the Bible into every language such that every tribe and tongue can hear and speak the Word of God. It is also a tenet of Evangelical Theology that until this has been accomplished, the Lord will not return:

> Then I saw another angel flying in mid heaven, with an eternal gospel to proclaim to those who live on the earth – to every nation and tribe and language of people. He said in a loud voice, 'Fear God and give him glory, for the hour of his judgement has come; and worship him who made heaven and earth, the sea and the springs of water.' (Rev 14:6-7 cf. Matt 24:14)

While this clarity is attractive, part of the softening in the attitudes of the mainstream denominations was that from the perspective of common sense, it seemed fundamentally unfair that innumerable human beings made in the image of God should be damned to eternal fire through no fault of their own. As Thomas Jefferson said, such teaching is a 'demoralizing dogma', a 'counter-religion' taught by 'usurpers of the Christian name' (Johnson, 2005, p. 156). Indeed, by 1854 in *Singulari Quadam*, Pope Pius IX could assert that 'it must be held as certain that those who live in ignorance of the true religion, if this ignorance is invincible, are not subject to guilt in this matter before the eyes of the Lord'. During the twentieth century, a reconceptualizing of the 'problem' by the likes of Tillich and Rahner seemed almost to reverse the theological question anyway. On a cursory reading of their conclusions, it could be construed that since God was potentially present to everyone through their 'ultimate concern' or through the 'holy mystery' of reflective knowing, anxiety regarding salvation was something that really only affected Christians! In fairness, although such theologians are accused of doing away with the very concept of missionary activity, the motive for reviewing the tradition was essentially pastoral, and based on scriptural wisdom (cf. Rom 2:15). Rahner opined:

> There must be a Christian theory to account for the fact that every individual who does not in any absolute or ultimate sense act against his own conscience can say in faith hope and love 'Abba' within his own spirit and is on these grounds a brother to Christians in God's sight. (Hunt, 2005, p. 145)

d) Salvation and the role of Christ

It was with this sort of conviction that well-known monastic figures such as Thomas Merton (1915–1968) and Bede Griffiths (1906–1993) engaged experientially with Buddhist and Hindu religious counterparts. Likewise, contemporary scholars such as Jacques Dupuis, Raimon Panikkar, John Hick, Paul Knitter, Gavin d'Costa and numerous others have sought to theologize concerning the role of Christ in other faiths. There tends to be a classification of approaches, 'exclusivism', 'inclusivism' and 'pluralism', but like many 'isms', they perhaps needlessly categorize an area of theological enquiry that is still developing. At the risk of over-simplification, it might be helpful, given the introductory nature of this book, to take just two theological standpoints to illustrate a contrast in approaches to the matter.

Instead of taking the generic religious experience of other faiths as a starting point, Jacques Dupuis is keen to emphasize as a Christian theologian the 'apex' of revelation that is the Incarnation. That said, he seeks to 'Trinitarianize' (my word) the history of salvation by pointing out that from the beginning of creation and throughout the drama of the human story, God has been revealing Godself through the prophetic Word and the active Spirit. This means that the action of God in the world is not limited to the moment of the Jesus event. It allows him to propose that not only are the Word and Spirit present in the illumination of worldwide faiths *before* the time of Christ (such as the mystical traditions of Hinduism), but also *afterwards* in the wisdom of later prophetic figures such as Mohammed. All these manifestations of wisdom are part of the action of the Trinitarian God, while vouchsafing the revelation in Jesus as the absolute climax of its shining intensity:

> This means that God's saving action, which always operates within the framework of a unified plan, is one, and at the same time multifaceted. It never prescinds from the Christ event, in which it finds its highest historical density. Yet the action of the Word of God is not constrained by its historically becoming human in Jesus Christ; nor is the Spirit's work in history limited to its outpouring upon the world by the risen and exalted Christ. (Dupuis, 1997, pp. 249–50)

The astute reader can see where this argument is going; it seems to be allowing 'salvation systems' to be happily operative in other faiths, which don't just happen to be there, they are in fact all part of God's plan. The Church, on this view, is a sacrament pointing beyond itself in the service of the Kingdom (p. 341). Religious pluralism isn't a problem, it is based on the immensity of a 'God who is love' (p. 387). Harnessing his own reasoning with that of Teilhard de Chardin, he can then conclude:

> Such eschatological convergence does not in any way overshadow the historical event of Jesus Christ: he is the end (omega) because he is the beginning (alpha), the central 'axis' . . . The eschatological fullness of the Reign of God is the common final achievement of Christianity and the other religions. (Dupuis, 1997, p. 390)

Such optimism regarding other religions may be surprising to the reader, but not half as surprising as it is to some of Dupuis' fellow theologians. Allowing what seems to be a sharing of the *soteriological* 'saving' role of Christ is problematic to English theologian Daniel Strange, who has a radically different view. Following the tradition of Hendrik Kraemer, one of the original Reformed commentators on interfaith matters, Strange begins with a strong Karl Barth-style view of biblical revelation which is definitive because it is guaranteed by the 'triune God who speaks authoritatively'. He is more than aware that his position may seem like a 'relic' of a bygone age, but he argues that non-Christian religions are essentially 'an idolatrous refashioning of divine revelation', which are antithetical and yet parasitic on Christian truth, and of which the Gospel of Jesus Christ is this 'subversive fulfilment' (Strange, 2011, p. 93).

Now although all this might sound politically incorrect, and almost designed to shock, by clearing the decks it does allow Strange to begin his argument from precise principles. His reading of the biblical tradition begins with the core revelation of YHWH, not just as a religious option or one God among many, but the Is-God, the 'undefined by any other thing' God, the from within God who actually creates the category. 'The God *is* the living God of the Bible, the self-revealing, self-contained ontological Trinity: YHWH. There is no ultimate reality behind this God. It is this God or no God . . . there is the worship of the Christian God, or the worship of idols, which are nothing at all' (p. 107). *Soli Deo Gloria* – the famous Reformation slogan, only to this God is glory to be given, and it has been the privilege of Israel and the Church to do this. The problem is that human nature is a 'perpetual factory of idols' (p. 113). The injunctions not to create a false image of God are first and earnest in the commandments because they are so necessary. What befuddles the clarity of the situation is that in practice, people of other faiths do good works, their religious systems exhibit similarities, they uphold similar values. This is perfectly understandable not as a result of there being any truth in the patterns and prayers of their faith, but because they are made in the image of God and what Calvin called the *semen religionis* 'the seed of religion' within them is actively seeking expression. In this context, other religions are related to the true faith, but only imperfectly because they are human constructs. As such they function as substitutes for the truth and are thus idols by any other name. They are created things made to replace the maker (p. 120). While this might seem confrontational, understood from within, it is liberational. Idolatry harms us and it is only 'in the person and work of Jesus Christ' we reach the Omega point of biblical revelation and redemptive history (p. 122).

e) Salvation and eschatology

So, both Dupuis and Strange can agree about an 'Omega point', but exactly how the nations are gathered thereunto is still moot. It can be argued that the approach of Strange at least respects the integrity of other faiths by not presumptuously claiming them as ersatz Christianity in some kind of diluted form. Strange is not dismissive of dialogue. Indeed he calls for earnest engagement with other traditions, and a necessary 'trialogue' of respect between interlocutors, while attentive always to the voice of the Spirit already present (Strange, 2011, pp.135-6).. But what will become of non-Christians? Well the fiery passages of Rom 1:18-2:16 which threaten wrath and offer hope in equal measure will have to suffice. There is no excuse for humanity, because what can be known about God is plain, and in the end, even those who do not possess the revelation, can through conscience 'do instinctively what the law requires' (Rom 2:14). On that day, 'God, through Jesus Christ, will judge the secret thoughts of all' (Rom 2:16).

And what happens then? Well – that's a good question! Quite recently, a fairly conservative preacher known for his long sermons caused shock and awe in equal measure with the following brief homily which began reassuringly but ended abruptly:

> There's a common belief these days that when we die,
> we're all going to end up in the same place.
> Well we are . . .
> the judgement seat of *GOD!*

He then sat down. To get folk thinking, you probably don't have to say anything else. Thoughts of the 'end' often focus the mind. The *LXX* writer known as Sirach may be said to have introduced 'eschatology' into the lexicon when recommending that 'In all you do, remember your *eschata* – "last things" – and then you will never sin' (Sir 7:36). Often translated as 'the end of your life', the Christian tradition soon formulated four particular 'last things' which when contemplated would be a good incentive not to sin, namely 'Death, Judgement, Heaven and Hell!' With the balance of those three being 3:1 in the negative, it is no wonder that the topic is not easily dwelt upon. All of these are part of the broader understanding of the term 'eschatology' which means 'the discourse of the last things'. As a subsection of Christian Theology, eschatology includes both the destiny of the individual and the destiny of the whole Creation.

The picture of the cosmic end in Revelation is that God will make all things new (Rev 21:5). Although Christian denominations disagree on the detail of 'End Time' events, there is a general acknowledgement that it will be pretty spectacular and cosmically definitive. The more pressing question for the average Christian arising since the dawn of the kerygmatic proclamation is 'what happens to those who die before then?' Paul goes into overdrive answering this in 1 Cor 15:1-58, and he doesn't seem to want to be interrupted. I particularly like *The Inclusive Bible* translation: 'Perhaps someone will ask, "How are the dead raised? What kind of body will they have?" What a stupid question!' The seed you sow does not germinate unless it dies' (15:35-6). The message is pretty clear, unless you are lucky enough to be around for the Last Trumpet, death is the necessary portal to New Life. The resurrection mystery includes the refashioning of mortal bodies in the imperishable deathless body material of the risen Christ. In arguing thus, Paul expresses the tenacious importance maintained by the Christian tradition that bodily nature is part of the transformation of each individual into who they truly are (1 John 3:2).

And arguably, that is what eschatological salvation is. As one of the most familiar terms in Christian Theology, it is nonetheless one of the most intriguing to explore. Perception of what personal salvation consists in varies greatly among Christians which is partly explicable by denominational differences. However, it is also because the connection of personal salvation with divine judgement and eternal life in God necessarily takes human imagination beyond its limits. Although Paul seems to have had some heavenly glimpses, most Christians have to make do with glimpses of salvation on earth (cf. 2 Cor 12:1-10). The key idea is that eternal life begins when the Christian enters the new life of faith, whether that is described as being 'baptized', 'born again', 'saved', etc. This 'already present but not yet fulfilled' experience parallels the notion that the Reign of God inaugurated by Christ is already partially realized now, but not fully. The destiny of the Christian is the 'Beatific Vision', the unmediated encounter with God, when 'I will know fully, even as I have been fully known' (1 Cor 13:12).

While speculation regarding the 'Last Things' was to reach a peak in the Middle Ages, the very personal tone of Christian conceptualizations of the afterlife was affirmed by Augustine, as he pondered in his famous 'Confessions' the death of his dear friend, Nebridius:

> And now he lives in Abraham's bosom. Whatever is meant by that bosom, there my Nebridius lives, my most beloved friend, Your son by adoption and no longer a freed-man only. There he lives, in the place of which he asked me, an ignorant poor creature, so many questions. He no longer puts his bodily ear to my lips, but the lips of his spirit to Your fountain, drinking his fill of wisdom, all that his

thirst requires, happy without end. Nor do I think he is so intoxicated with the draught of that wisdom as to forget me, since You, O Lord, of whom he drinks are mindful of us. (*Conf.* IX, iii, 6)

It has to be some consolation, dear reader, that even Augustine struggled to answer questions about the heavenly places and that he is (perhaps naturally) confused by the image of Abraham's 'bosom'. That said, understood as an expression of 'intimate belonging', this image of his friend Nebridius matches the picture described by Jesus in the Parable of the Rich Man and Lazarus whereby the poor man who has died is in a place of blessing, held in Abraham's 'bosom' (Luke 16:23). It is also significant that John's Gospel, struggling to convey the intimacy of the revelation present through the Word made flesh, also uses the same maternal, heavenly imagery: 'No one has ever seen God. It is God the only Son who is in the *bosom* of the Father who has made him known' (John 1:18). The NRSV translates this as 'closest to the Father's heart', which only serves to confirm that ultimately, cherished intimacy is the context of eternal God belonging.

f) Dante. Last word on the last things?

Since some of the wildest shores and most poetic peaks of eschatological speculation were trespassed best in the Middle Ages, it might be good to conclude this chapter with a brief look at the mystical theologian Joachim de Fiore and the poet, Dante Alighieri. Anticipating Hegel, Joachim (c.1135–1202) divided the span of history into phases manifesting the pattern of the Trinity. The first age of the Father whereby union of God's people was forged under the Law, the second under the Son was whereby union was forged by the Church, and the third of the Spirit whereby a new union would be forged through the fervour of new religious movements. Joachim calculated a date (1260) for the inauguration of the next phase, which, though it did not explicitly entail the disappearance of the Church, was unsurprisingly a little troubling to those who did not feel that their phase of importance was over just yet. As one of the more famous examples of 'millenarian' thinking (an expectation of End Times/God's direct intervention), he was still considered to be a holy man, so his works rather than his sanctity were condemned at Arles in 1260 and Phase III avoided! (cf. Schmidt-Biggemann, 2004, pp. 381–92).

Dante Alighieri (1265–1321) was a Florentine poet and part-time political activist and philosopher. Thunderstruck with love on seeing the young Beatrice Portinari, his personal crisis when she died led him to a poetic, theological meditation on the after-life. Through the remarkable popularity of the work and its subsequent diffusion throughout European culture, its imagery continues to influence the eschatological imagination and theological discourse of the West. His *Divina Commedia* is in three phases, Hell, Purgatory and Heaven. Despite the fact that to this day, the Catholic Church, for example, has never confirmed that anyone is actually in it, Dante had no trouble filling the circles of his *Inferno* not just with miscreants from the distant past but with several of his near contemporary political and ecclesial enemies. His tortures are memorable; the vain, for example, can't make up their mind what to wear and so are weighed down with clothes and condemned to trudge around disconsolate. In case you're wondering what should be especially avoided, Dante saved circles seven, eight and nine for the Violent, the Fraudulent and the Treacherous.

The central third of his trilogy is the purifying experience of *Purgatorio*, envisaged as the ascent of a seven terraced mountain. As noted previously, the idea of post-mortem sanctification arose from the traditional practice of praying for the dead and the mysterious line in 1 Pet 3:18-20, taken up in the Apostle's Creed, that Christ had descended among the dead to preach to them. This mysterious world of 'Holy Saturday' has been opened up in recent decades through the work of the influential Swiss theologian, Hans Urs Von Balthasar (1905–1988) which has led to a re-evaluation of Purgatory in some quarters. The well-known interfaith theologian, Gavin d'Costa, insists that since this traditional doctrine implies a preparation for the fullness of the vision of God, it may be a key to understanding how 'salvation only through Christ' could be effective in terms of people from other faiths. He argues that the possibility of a redemptive encounter with Christ beyond death solves an awful lot of interfaith conundra and is supported by the tradition (D'Costa, 2009, pp. 174–7).

It needs to be said, however, that though Dante clearly has a soft spot for non-Christians like Aristotle and Plato, they didn't quite make it this far and he finds them consigned to the shades of the fairly benign first circle of Hell. Meanwhile, in the final part of the trilogy, *Paradiso*, Dante's guide through heaven is at first his beloved Beatrice. She may serve as a symbol of 'faith' in contrast to his guide hitherto, the poet Virgil, who may represent 'reason', which can only take him so far. Yet even Beatrice, fair as she may be, steps aside as St. Bernard presents Dante to the Blessed Virgin who allows him a glimpse of the sacred *Empyrean* – the holy firmament of inaccessible light, the very dwelling of God. In all dimensions and all around, the blessed are arranged as petals of a glorious celestial white rose enfolded in the queenship of Mary.

At this point, Dante's poetic powers famously fail him as he is overwhelmed by a vision beyond dreaming and memory. Substance and accidents are fused by light as for a moment, he glimpses the heart of reality, which, as pure goodness, holds in rapture both desire and will. Before him is Living Light, three circles of one dimension yet in three colours, the ever-changing yet constant *perichoresis* – the eternal dance of the Trinity which is the 'love that moves the sun and other stars' (Dante, *Paradiso*, XXXIII:145).

Summary

The transformation in the mutual attitudes of Churches through the ecumenical movement of the twentieth century has been historic. Though the dream of full eucharistic communion remains far away, the warmth of exchange between ecclesial communities and the joint collaboration of theologians across the denominational divides make a return to former hostilities unthinkable. In like fashion, the whole spectrum of interfaith relations has shifted into kinder light. New syntheses of old questions on faith, salvation and the global dimensions of redemption in Christ have come to the fore. That said, when it comes to an equally old question – 'What can I hope for' – theological speculation has probably still not surpassed the poetic heights of Dante, whose eschatological visions remain among the most vivid in Christian thought.

Dialogue and the Future

Chapter Outline

The end is nigh. In this final chapter the main themes of the book are reviewed, some present developments are considered and some pointers to the future are outlined. Two aspects of method are considered, namely the way that Church traditions frame theological discourse and the very good reasons why the harmony of such communities of belonging is sometimes a counterpoint to the eager new songs of theologians. A last note on literature and a last note altogether summarize the thesis, summarize the question, but definitely don't summarize the conversation.

a) Reviewing the journey

Having traversed a path from Eden to the heavenly heights, the time has come to review the journey, sit down, survey the scene, and think about where to go next. The task at hand has been to investigate and assay the phenomenon of Christian Theology as a 'meta-narrative' or 'matrix of meaning'. Its origins are ancient. Theology, understood as 'thoughtful conversation about God', may well have been among the first talking points of humanity, although the Bible would suggest that the language of love just shaded it (Chapters 1–2).

Although the goodness of Creation is one of its most constant and important themes, Christian Theology is not the discourse of a nature religion, it has its roots in the 'salvation history' of God's interaction with a particular people. If the cosmic human story is the ever-relevant drama of the 'gifted individual learning to choose good', then the repeated invitation to covenant with God in the biblical tradition is the ever-relevant drama of a people *together* trying to live out that challenge. The inner struggle seems to be that humanity, understood as *imago dei* – the image of God, seems forever tempted to think that something else, perhaps a bit more information, a crown or two, maybe riches or the odd pomegranate, is more important to acquire than a dignity already held. YHWH, the One who Is, seems to emphasize that the temptation to idolatry is at the heart of the problem. Despite the deliverance from Egypt, despite the gift of the Law, the Prophets and the Writings, it is as if the chosen people are looking for the wrong thing (Chapters 3–5).

Theologically, what happens next is 'the wrong thing' at the heart of the Christian paradox. Instead of human beings in the image of God, the order of history is interrupted by the Jesus event, God in human image. The alluring enigma whereby Jesus self-presents as 'Son of Man' or 'The Human One' is a puzzle that his followers wrestle with. Theologically, the only language available to them is that of messiahship, but not as they'd known it. To miracles, 'Yes', to Calvary, 'No'. The bewildered conviction arising from the events of Easter and Pentecost permitted the startling identification of the crucified Jesus with the Suffering Servant of Isaiah. The rejected Messiah had been exalted and the longed for restoration of the Kingdom reconceptualized (Chapters 6–8).

To some extent, the adventure that began for the followers of Jesus maps a trajectory experienced by many idealistic movements, with early heroic figures accomplishing marvellous deeds in trying circumstances. The pattern is not one dimensional, however. The failures of the Twelve are writ large and the very different characters that emerge in the contrasting theologies attributable to Paul, Luke, John, James and Peter reflect personal concerns and the varied challenges faced by their communities (Chapters 9–11). This 'unity and diversity' can be traced into the early centuries of the Church through debates about diet, scriptures, creeds, devotions and doctrines. Despite its self-understanding as the mystical Body of Christ, none of these conundra was settled without anxiety, and a divine – human admixture of inspiration, perspiration and exasperation is plain to see. That said, the age of persecution remains of immense importance both theologically and ecclesiologically, as a vibrant combination of martyrs, monks, mothers, medics and morals networked a different lifestyle across the Roman Empire (Chapters 12–15).

The conversion of Constantine created a different set of theological concerns, as a triple force of Imperial, Ecclesial and Gospel dynamics drove Western history onwards for the next fifteen centuries. Within that culture, classic contributions to Christian thought were made by influential theologians such as Augustine, Anselm and Aquinas. Their explorations regarding the nature of grace and sin, the existence of God and the cosmic consequences of Incarnation exemplified the endeavour to synthesize faith and reason. While this period ultimately laid the foundations for modern universities and modern scientific enquiry, an 'economy' of salvation through sacramental ministry was orchestrated by the Church which had immense influence over public and private life. The unity of this pattern was shattered by the Great Schism of 1054 and the Reformation of the sixteenth century. Though the continued interweave of nation, religion and ethnic identity largely endured, the theological symbol of the unified Body of Christ was broken (Chapters 16–18).

The Modern era, which largely began with the rationalistic turn of the Enlightenment, proved a very different environment for the pursuit of Christian Theology. A somewhat contrary period, from a variety of philosophical, scientific and anthropological angles, Theology was called into question, not just in terms of core belief, but in terms of its entire purpose and the legitimacy of its methodology. Schleiermacher's *Religion: Speeches to its Cultured Despisers* captured the tone of the times. The 'Queen of the Sciences' was in the middle of an intellectual revolution which witnessed cosmologists, physicists, philosophers, psychologists, sociologists and biologists holding court. The varied discourses which emerged from this time proved nonetheless stimulating, and theologians of every stripe such as Pascal, Otto, Barth, Newman, Rahner and Tillich made their mark (Chapters 19–21).

The last phase of the journey has considered the consequences of a search for authenticity, which by prioritizing consideration of lived experience in its dialogue with revelation, has led to a proliferation of different 'theologies' of liberation. The challenge to live life authentically inevitably impinges on the whole spectrum of Moral Theology, both personal and societal. Here, sea changes in sociological attitudes, advances in medical technology and consciousness of environmental realities have posed new questions for Christian theological discourse. Greater awareness of such global challenges has added dynamism to the search for greater ecclesiological harmony, spirituality, and a similar growth of interfaith initiatives has revolutionized relationships among religious leaders. The theological consequences of these dialogues in terms of core doctrinal issues such as Trinity, Christ, Salvation and Church could not be more profound (Chapters 22–25).

b) Theological method

By now the reader will be aware that there are many ways to 'do' Christian Theology. Different approaches yield different 'theologies' and though this book has referred to 'three great traditions', such shorthand categorization should be used with some caution. The great denominations of Christianity can be understood as interpretation communities, cohering around key biblical texts that are definitive for their self-understanding, but they are also characterized by broader theological method. The classic Catholic procedure is to hold 'Scripture-Tradition-Magisterium' together as a tri-fold unity in dialogue with the contemporary world, privileging the Bible, Christian custom and Church/papal teaching (see Matt 16:19). Orthodox theologians, meanwhile, might pattern reflection more obviously on 'Scripture-Tradition-Prayer', since the mystical and monastic tradition of *theosis* or 'divinization' is at the heart of its self-understanding (Col 3:10). The classic Calvinistic approach has the Bible in first place, with Church tradition and theological speculation very much under its sovereignty. Though sharing the focus on justification (Rom 5:1-5), Lutheran theologians quite naturally sympathetic to *Sola Scriptura* nevertheless *tend* to accord somewhat more weight to Tradition. The Anglican – Episcopalian methodology is different again, often characterized as Scripture-Tradition-Reason (cf. 2 Tim 3:16-17).

Though theological discourse is possible always and everywhere, Churches themselves are a primary source of God-logic and in this regard, can be considered to be in rude health. The Catholic Church has had unusually gifted occupants of Peter's office in recent times. Through profound reflection on his own experience, his deeply personalistic approach and his 'Theology of the Body', John Paul II moved Catholic thinking strongly towards a pacificist position on warfare and towards a renewed ethic of embodiment. Likewise, in his first encyclical, *Deus Caritas Est* (2005), Benedict XVI firmly identified love as the focus of his theological discourse. John Zizioulas, Eastern Orthodox Metropolitan of Pergamon and Chair of the Academy of Athens, has made contributions to ecclesiology and anthropology that have had impact across denominational divides. While the Reformed tradition has nourished some of the most outstanding theologians of recent times, such as Jürgen Moltmann, Wolfhart Pannenberg and Miroslav Volf, the Anglican Church has had in its recent leader, Rowan Williams, a gifted and original thinker.

The great majority of Christian theologians do tend to operate 'across divides' and there are often tensions with 'official stances'. As briefly noted already (Section 25a), one problem that Christianity has is 'backward compatibility'. Unlike the great computer giants or mobile phone manufacturers, it is very rare for ecclesially minded theologians to declare a traditional belief or practice to be 'out of date, overnight'. From whatever denomination, they tend to look for what Joseph Ratzinger (Benedict XVI) calls a 'Hermeneutic of Continuity' – interpretation coherent with life as it has been lived by Christians in their own tradition and that of the wider Church. This perhaps explains why 'official' Christianity can seem predominantly conservative, and permanently behind the times. Although this may be a source of frustration, there can be positives. At the risk of stating the obvious:

- 'New' does not always mean 'good'. Do all developments in medical or military technology ennoble humanity? Gender pregnancy tests are causing huge imbalances in birth rates since males are preferred children in large parts of the world. Neutron bombs kill people and leave buildings standing. Are these good things? Conversely, it is evident that Christians have let fall into abeyance an injunction that their Islamic cousins have maintained, namely, a disavowal of the practice of 'usury' – the charging of interest on loans. This is at the heart of the worldwide banking system, which, until it veered towards total collapse in 2010, was immune to criticism. Rescued by elected governments, a renewed awareness that the worldwide monetary system is *entirely based* on mutual *trust* seems to place its rationale back squarely within the discourse of Theology, Philosophy and the Common Good (cf. Section 1g).
- 'New' can just be a passing phase. It is difficult to imagine now, but in the 1960s, when Communism controlled half the world, an eager student asked his professor when the Church was going to open up to Marxist ideas and affirm the brilliance of the socialist vision. Raising a lizard eye, the professor languidly pronounced: 'It won't last, it is inhuman'. In 1989, the student, by then in his 50s, only remembered the comment as the Berlin Wall fell. There are fashions in human thinking that do wither rather quickly when viewed over a span of centuries rather than decades.
- 'New' can include restoration. The wise scribe is someone who brings forth from his store house 'what is new and what is old' (Matt 13:52). This place between the past and present reminds theologians that the tension of 'already and not yet' is a lived reality. A Church communion may be feeling its way to a new configuration or self-expression, but it is not yet fully present.
- Lastly, 'new' challenges are *exactly* what theologians have to address. The historic role of theologians in every denominational tradition has involved engagement with the 'signs of the times' to reinterpret and re-present cherished wisdom to a new generation. Rightly or wrongly, sanctioned or not sanctioned, many theologians see their role very much in the biblical prophetic line which perhaps also explains why they can get a bit passionate about things. Theology is an agency for change.

Withal, theologians, and indeed Churches, have a duty to stimulate and engage congregations in 'thoughtful conversation about God' if the discipline is to survive and thrive. Theology is not just what happens when the excitement dies down – so where is the 'buzz' right now?

c) Dialogues on the event horizon

Well, one buzz comes from those singing the funeral dirges for Postmodernism. In earlier chapters, we have already outlined the tentative, controversial but always interesting dialogue between Theology and other theoretical disciplines. Indeed, by its very nature, Theology is interdisciplinary. However, it seems that after the advent of Postmodernism, with its denial of objective truth, Theology has had to be humble, and realize that it is merely one discourse among a multiplicity of other discourses.

Or does it? From a quite unusual source on the Old Continent, it looks like the 'Queen of the Sciences' is being lured on new adventures by some unusual suitors. Characterized by a rejection not just of Modernity, but Post-modernism too, philosophers such as Alain Badiou, Slavoj Žižek and others are making a case for the return to a quest for universality. In part they are following through the insights of Jacques Lacan (1901–1981), who combined Freud's theories with linguistic philosophizing, and concluded that far from being a barely fathomable swirl, the subconscious is a highly structured set of social linguistic signs or 'signifiers' which form the matrix for our consciousness. In a reversal of Descartes, not only are we 'out there' before we're 'in here', but in Lacan's drama of discovery, our use of language becomes an indication of our lost, original *jouissance* – 'enjoyment'. To make matters worse, it helps us invent a type of fake satisfaction based on imitation of others to help us get through the day, which becomes our *persona* – 'mask' – 'ego' – 'image'. Whatever we might call it, Lacan thinks it is a block to contentment. The best we can hope for is to be reacquainted with our desiring nature. Much to our chagrin, we have to be satisfied being dissatisfied (cf. Chiesa, 2007).

Now, as noted above (Section 25e), the stripping away of self-delusion is at the heart of what Jesus seemed to be about and is arguably the core idea of salvation, namely Christ saves you from sin, that is, saves you from yourself. It has also been noted that desire is at the heart not just of faith, but of the moral life too, (Section 23g). Yet in Lacan's system, it is discovery of the wordless *Real*, the lost event of our originality that provides the breakout moment. Reminiscent of Kierkegaard, this 'event' is constitutive, it is neither the product of fake imagination nor of linguistic delusion and provides the point of departure for

Alain Badiou (b. 1937). A multi-talented intellectual, Badiou is arguably the most influential philosopher in France today, he is also a mathematician, atheist Maoist Communist and a student of Lacan. Nothing has annoyed Badiou more than the constant focus on language in Postmodernism, which by giving up the search for reality, has given up on the basic task of Philosophy. Badiou proposes that it is only through the interruptive 'event' that the *Real* can be disclosed. It is something which surfaces out of what seems like nowhere in a given situation, but which we usually struggle to recognize. A revolutionary example might suffice (he is a Maoist after all), so who better than St Paul?

Badiou is interested in St Paul as a subject who adheres to the interruptive Easter 'event' and afterwards builds *a universal community* from the singular *interruptive quality* of *resurrection*. Badiou does not have a vested interest in the objective reality of Christ's resurrection, but he is fascinated by Paul and the community he builds. Though Paul's truth is subjective and personal, the distinction Badiou wants to make is that the transformative nature of an 'Interruptive Event' has *social* consequences. It is easy to see that if such an event becomes the source of the *objective real,* then suddenly, Badiou, from a completely atheistic start point, has reasserted the prime importance of conversion which is so much a feature of Christian Theology. I'm not sure if he would have sat down all that comfortably with St Paul or Martin Luther, but if his argument holds, then faith-events are classic start points for encountering reality (cf. Hallward, 2003, xxiv and Eagleton, 2009, pp. 117–19).

Another contemporary thinker making religious waves is the Slovenian Slavoj Žižek (b. 1949). Something of a theoretical gadfly and far less systematic than Badiou, his works are more cultural interventions than philosophical treatises. While he agrees with Badiou on the significance of Paul for radical theory, Žižek thinks that Badiou misses the full effect of this 'interruptive event' on the subject since Paul first has to die to the Law (Rom 7:6). In other words, someone has to undergo what Lacan calls 'subjective destitution' before being able to become a desiring being, freed from the demands of their false self. From a theological perspective this has startling consequences, as it highlights the missing theological factor in Badiou's work – the Cross. In other words, if Badiou is a theologian of *Glory*, then his radical counterpart Žižek is a theologian of the *Cross* (Kotsko, 2008, p. 79).

Meanwhile, more recognizably mainstream theologians such as Lieven Boeve resonate with many of these themes. 'God interrupts history' is for him the shortest definition of religion (Boeve, 2007, p. 203). Theology in a time of upheaval must be aware that the very concept of salvation history bears witness to this – in Walter Brueggeman's evocative phrase, YHWH is an 'unsettling

God' (Brueggemann, 2009). Boeve acknowledges the concern among believers in Western Europe, that for a variety of reasons, the transmission of the Christian tradition has been interrupted, and it is no longer handed down automatically from generation to generation.

The first step is being aware of this: Recognition is part of the process, since faith is always caught up in a particular historical moment, and *constantly demands* recontextualization. This is a never ending task, (and presumably keeps theologians in demand), but the key point is to realize that God *is* the boundary and crisis. God is the Event and does not stand outside the process. In theological terms, this means that far from desiring a return to the nice cosy times of Church-State agreement, so that a quiet and ordered life might be had by all, there is a need to accept that faith implies menace, danger, turmoil and tension:

> After all, Christians are bearers of the subversive memory of the suffering, death and resurrection of Jesus Christ. That is why they actively seek out the boundaries of life and coexistence, moved as they are by the human histories of suffering, that compel them toward a preferential option for the poor, the suffering, the oppressed. By its very nature, the Christian faith disrupts the histories of conqueror and vanquished, interrupting the ideologies of the powerful and the powerlessness of the victims (2007, pp. 203–4).

It is important to emphasize that this short selection of 'new views' is not meant to imply that Theology needs vouchsafing from any other subject discipline. Indeed this point is specifically made by 'Radical Orthodoxy', an originally British school of theological reflection which confidently views the current intellectual context as 'Post-secular'. Associated with John Milbank, Catherine Pickstock and others, their point of departure is thus that Theology as the Queen of the Sciences must once more take centre stage as the reference point for other disciplines which must doff their hats in her direction! (cf. Smith, 2004, pp. 167–8). Suffice to say, these pitifully few examples are given to indicate that central Christian ideas such as cross and resurrection are being explored by a whole variety of thinkers in what may well prove to be the aftermath of Postmodernity. Through transformative *event* and encounter with the *real*, they may in turn bear fruit in new syntheses of hallowed theological truths.

d) Dialogues in new directions?

So if events are the trigger for new horizons, what meteorites of change are heading towards the academy? To some extent, it might be argued that in the

Anglo-Saxon world a recent asteroid threatening extinction to religion and the species of theologians has already landed in the form of the 'New Atheists'. While the socialist sensibilities in continental Europe allow common cause between theists and atheists, the Anglo-Saxon world retains a somewhat narrower, 'right or wrong' tone. In truth, this is not a 'new direction' but it is at least a vibrant version of an old one. That God has returned as a commonplace topic in public debate owes much to the activities of the 'New Atheists' such as Richard Dawkins, Daniel Dennett, Christopher Hitchens et al. Between them, they have successfully raised the issue of religious faith as an important if not *the* most important question facing the world today.

Part of their concern reflects an anxiety among non-religious people in the West regarding fundamentalisms of the kind which led to the attacks in New York 2001, Madrid 2004, London 2007 and Paris 2015. Despite the overwhelming evidence of the twentieth century which demonstrated the genocidal dangers of atheistic worldviews and nationalistic excess, 'organized religion' is held to be a source of violence and danger. Given that atrocities such as 9/11 were precisely attributable to *non-organized* religion and that fundamentalism is relatively rare among students of Christian Theology, this may be seen as a case of the New Atheists knocking down a 'straw man' that doesn't really exist. The astringency of the charges made against religion and theological standpoints has generated a new strand of Christian apologetics, somewhat reminiscent of the first impassioned endeavours of Justin Martyr and Irenaeus. Yet away from the stormy vortex of the polemic, there is a need for theologians to open new avenues of debate at the interface of Atheism – Theism. Fostering profitable dialogue here is precisely the kind of thoughtful engagement necessary for Theology to thrive (cf. Bullivant, 2012 and Rowan, 2010).

Looking ahead (and this is always risky), I think that one of the ironies about the current Atheist – Theist debate is that its original 'foundation' based on presumed scientific disagreements will disappear. The number of 'Theology loves Science' and 'Science, friend of Theology' books that appear in the catalogues is truly staggering. Cosmologists proposing multiple universe theories which can never be empirically proven, and string theorists composing mathematical poems in the unseen skies, are bound to make friends late at night with theologians wandering with Dante through the heavenly spheres. Materialist views on consciousness as presented by Gerald Edelman are very interesting, but it is impossible not to raise an eyebrow at the description by just about everyone of the Hadron Collider experiments in Switzerland as the search for the 'God Particle'. Since its 'discovery' confirms the centrality of relationship and universal connectedness, it affirms rather than contradicts the God hypothesis. The related news that the speed of light still holds as the ultimate cosmic velocity, is just as well – Physics would have died, not Theology. 'Intelligent Design' is often mistaken for 'Creationism', but as a basic proposal, it is the restatement of the ancient Design Argument with a bit of evolutionary theory thrown in. As a theologian, it still disturbs me that the project to build the first atomic bomb at Los Alamos was codenamed 'Trinity'. Insofar as it successfully explored the triple relationship of protons, electrons and neutrons at the heart of all reality, I like the ready theological parallel. Insofar as it split the atomic relationship and caused the death of thousands in a flash of unapproachable light . . . there are no words.

Meanwhile, in the houses of the faithful, it could be that a nuanced understanding of *koinonia* – 'communion' will help to express spiritually what is not yet possible sacramentally between denominations who are nonetheless likely to continue to make common cause on ethical issues. The instrumentalization of the human body for the purposed use of others via cloning is not far away and it may well be the sort of thing that leads to practical unity *vis a vis* society even if ecclesial shapings remain distinct. The environment, too, is a cause for common concern. It will be interesting to see whether developments in the design of sustainable cities reformulate not only notions of nationality in terms of cross-border energy agreements but also of locality and communal solidarity. I predict 'Eco-Theology' will be sustainable! The permeability of churches in terms of mutual membership may also increase as may the number of self-help/therapy groups such as Alcoholics Anonymous. Commencing with a non-specific abandonment to faith, these 'Twelve-step' programmes have been a remarkable grace to millions and seem to thrive 'in between' denominational affiliations.

In terms of interfaith futures, the experience of the Orthodox Church in relation to Islam may prove significant, with mutual wisdom drawn from over a thousand years of shared history. Elsewhere the explosion of Christian faith in China, worldwide Pentecostalism, the election of Pope Francis I and the growing influence of the Indian Church may create other interfaith possibilities, mission issues and nudge Christian theologizing away from its gravitational centre in the West. At the centre of so much that is symbolic, Jerusalem the 'Tower of Peace' may yet live up to its name, since it will inevitably be a key factor in any reconciliation between the three faiths that claim it as holy.

Lastly, with wider purview, it is likely that the strong mystical traditions in all the major world faiths will continue the kinds of exchange started decades ago by Thomas Merton and others. Mysticism is sometimes pilloried – 'starts in mist, with I at the centre and ends in schism'. More generally, though, the contemplative dimension of faith traditions has a mutual receptivity not so evident in more formal exchanges. Popular as piety and a means of cultivating a more godly disposition in many traditions, 'mindfulness' is attracting much attention among educationalists in mental training of pupils and as an aid to discipline. Hence the call to 'Stay Awake!'

e) Theology is everywhere

So in case you might have fallen asleep, it could be important to correct any notion that the adventure of theological discourse is limited to books like this. The most natural milieu of Theology is story, and true to the ancient heritage, brilliant theological insights have been deliberately woven into the dramatic works of Leo Tolstoy, Fyodor Dostoevsky, G. K. Chesterton, Evelyn Waugh, C. S. Lewis, J. R. R. Tolkien and Flannery O'Connor. In poetry too, William Blake, Gerard Manley-Hopkins, R. S. Thomas, Walt Whitman, E. E. Cummings, Elizabeth Barrett-Browning, T. S. Eliot – all genius magicians of syllables who demonstrate a gift for expressing the transcendent. Although comparisons can be invidious, it goes without saying that such writers have generally been more subtle communicators of theological truth than those entrusted with technically minded works of scholarship. The argument can easily be made that Shakespeare is the most important English theologian of all time, since his lucid, acutely religious insights into the human condition before God are almost without parallel. If the supreme religious question is 'How do I love?', then he is the master of enquiry. If it is an understanding of mercy, his Portia will provide the answer. Ten lifetimes of wisdom in one imagination. Story allows Theology to breathe, and there is no one better than Shakespeare for exploring the subtle dramas inherent in the 'gifted individual learning to choose the good' (cf. May, 2005).

Art in all its forms can mediate mystery and meaning which theological discourse attempts in words. There is a permanent brilliance about sculpture, music and architecture that can tell stories where words fail. Modern media such as film, television and the internet can all be showcases for the conversation that is Theology. There is no restriction on how or where theological triggering can take place, its vocabulary is Alpha to Omega, A–Z, there is no limit. At a recent gathering of the American Academy of Religion, a section of the conference was given over to Zombie Theology where the depiction of the zoned out hordes was presented as a parable of Western consumerism, dead from the banality of its desires, in need of the transcendent. If the core hypothesis of Christian theological discourse is true – that *Reality is in relationship with God*, then it stands to reason that anything can be a moment of disclosure. In *Auguries of Innocence*, William Blake famously observed the world in a grain of sand (Marsh, 2001). With similar genius, skilful music and well chosen words, the film *American Beauty* took a discarded plastic bag, tossed by the wind, and made of it a meditation on God such that 'there's no need to be afraid, ever.' (Ball, 1999). From Genesis to Revelation, once the light shines, it is the way we look that counts.

f) Last word or first conversation?

And maybe this is the clue. For Jesus, healing the blind was one thing, getting people to see was another (Mark 8:18 cf. Jer 5:21, Ez 12:2). The preaching of Jesus is tantamount to a 'Glance Theology' and Christianity becomes a religion of recognition. The *imago dei* in the face of humanity is signifier and dignifier and explains all the injunctions to love in the New Testament. Every form of genocide begins with a refusal to recognize this while every act of kindness does so (Matt 25:45). Insofar as Christian Theology helps humanity to recognize itself, its meaning, its dignity and its destiny, that seems to me a conversation worth having.

As a last point, in case you're still not persuaded that Theology is a worthwhile adventure, it might be appropriate to return to the beginning. John 1:1 is normally translated, following Jerome's *In principio erat Verbum* – as 'In the Beginning was the Word'. Interestingly, Erasmus preferred to understand 'Logos' in a different way (Jarrott, 1964). By translating it as *In principio erat Sermo* – 'In the beginning was the conversation', he leaves us with an intriguing notion that the first thing, the primordial occurrence, was a God conversation.

Theology?
From the beginning. . . . .?

Part 6
Customer Support: References and Readings

References, Extracts, Further Readings

Introduction

These sections are meant to help and to complement the main text. You may well have read enough by now and that's fine, but if you fancy a taster of some thoughts from different angles they will contain some sample readings from the wide and wonderful world of theological conversation. These are arranged chapter by chapter along with the reference lists and some select bibliographies. If you're stuck for what a word meant or you've lost track of whether Elijah comes before Moses or Luther before Aquinas, you'll find a glossary, maps and a non-linear timeline at the end. I hope that you will find something or someone intriguing in here so that this book becomes what it is meant to be, a way 'in' not a way 'out' of Theology!

Referencing of biblical passages, Primary sources & Secondary texts

Bible: The chapters and verses that are found in the contemporary Bible were devised by Stephen Langton (c.1160–1228) and for the abbreviations for the books – see the list towards the front of the book. The Chapter number precedes the verse or verses being quoted: e.g. Gen 1:1-3 indicates 'Genesis Chapter 1, verses 1 through 3.' If a selection of verses is referenced it will be indicated thus: Gen 1:1-3, 6 & 8. 'Genesis Chapter 1, verses 1 through 3, verse 6 and verse 8.' Sometimes in the text, the abbreviation 'cf.' is used to indicate a comparison - from the Latin *conferre* – 'bring together.'

Primary sources: Ancient texts and indeed any subject matter about which other books have been written can be considered a 'primary source.' I mention this because there are a variety of conventions regarding the referencing of primary texts, especially since the advent of the internet has opened up access to ancient writers so wonderfully. By and large, the procedure here will be to outline published works in the traditional manner, but be assured, these days you don't have to break the bank to access the wisdom of the sages anymore. Check out sites like http://www.gutenberg.org/ and http://www.earlychristianwritings.com/.

Secondary sources: Books that are referred to in the text will be indicated in the following manner: Author, date of publication, page number. The idea then is that you can refer to the reference lists below and find the full title and publishing details. Where possible, if there is a wide time discrepancy between the first edition published and the one referred to in this text, the first date in square brackets will refer to the original. Hence by using the main text reference (Chesterton, [1908] 1996, p. 63) you should be able to find in the alphabetical reference list, the details of G. K. Chesterton's 1908 book *Orthodoxy*, where in my 1996 version, published by Hodder & Stoughton, the relevant quotation can be found on page 63.

Chapter 1

References

Aquinas ([1274] 1947), *Summa Theologica* (translated by the Fathers of the English Dominican Province). New York: Benziger.

Buber, M. ([1923] 2004), *I and Thou* (translated by W. Kaufmann). London: Continuum.

Chesterton, G. K. ([1908] 1996), *Orthodoxy*. London: Hodder & Stoughton.

Dawkins, R. (2006), *The God Delusion*. New York: Bantam Press.

Flew, A., Varghese, R. A. (2007), *There Is A God: How the World's Most Notorious Atheist Changed His Mind*. New York: HarperCollins.

Newman, J. H. ([1870] 1979), *An Essay in Aid of a Grammar of Assent*. London: University of Notre Dame Press.

Pannenberg, W. (1991), *An Introduction to Systematic Theology*. Grand Rapids: W. B Eerdmans.

Russell, B. ([1946] 1984), *History of Western Philosophy*. London: Routledge.

Whitehead, A. and Russell, B. (1927), *Principia Mathematica*. Cambridge: CUP.

Extracts

1. St Anselm

As noted in the main text, St Anselm [1033–1109], bequeathed one of the classic definitions of Theology in his phrase *fides quaerens intellectum* ('faith seeking understanding'). The scholastic thinkers are sometimes accused of being a bit boring and dry, but there is real passion behind their hunger to learn. Here is an example of Anselm at work in the art of silent reasoning as his faith seeks understanding:

How and why God is both seen and not seen by those who seek him

O my soul,
Have you found what you were looking for?
I was seeking God,
And I have found that he is above all things,
And that than which nothing greater can be thought.
I have found him to be
Life and light, wisdom and goodness,
Eternal blessedness and the bliss of eternity,
Existing everywhere and at all times.
If I have not found my God,
What is it that I have found and understood
So truly and certainly?
But if I have found him,
Why do I not experience what I have found?
Lord God,
If my soul has found you,
Why has it no experience of you?

If I have not found you,
What is this light and truth that I have found?
How did I understand all this,
Except by your light and your truth?
So if I see the light and the truth
I have seen you.
If I have not seen you
I have not seen the light and the truth.
Or is it that I both saw light and truth,
And also did not see you,
Because I only saw you in a certain degree, and not as you are?

O Lord my God,
My creator and my Re-creator,
My soul longs for you.
Tell me what you are, beyond what I have seen,
So that I may see clearly what I desire.

I strive to see more,
But I see nothing beyond what I have seen,
Except darkness.
Or rather I do not see darkness
Which is no part of you,
But I see that I cannot see further

Because of my own darkness.
Why is this, Lord?
Are my eyes darkened by my weakness,
Or dazzled by your glory?
The truth is,
I am darkened by myself
And also dazzled by you.
I am clouded by my own smallness
And overwhelmed by your intensity;
I am restricted by my own narrowness
And mastered by your wideness.
How great is that light from which shines out
Every truth that lightens the reasoning mind!
How wide is that truth
In which is everything that is true
And outside which is nothingness and falsehood!

Source: *The Prayers and Meditations of Saint Anselm with the Proslogion*, edited and translated by B. Ward (London: Penguin, 1973), pp. 254–6.

2. Pannenberg on Theology

Wolfhart Pannenberg (1928-2014) was one of Europe's leading theologians. Schooled in the Lutheran tradition, he was an innovative thinker and writer for over 50 years. In this extract, which begins his famous three volume *Systematic Theology*, he first looks at how 'Theology' emerged as a discipline among Greek thinkers. He then goes on to argue that the distinction between 'Natural' Theology – derived from contemplation of creation – is in fact, dependent on 'Revealed' Theology, since it depends on God, letting Godself be known.

Section 1 Theology

The word 'theology' has many meanings. In today's usage it denotes an academic discipline or at least a human concern for knowledge. In its original Platonic meaning, however, it signified the *logos* in the speech and song of the poet that announces deity (*Rep.* 379a.5-6). It did not denote the philosopher's reflection on the *logos*. In contrast Aristotle described one of the three disciplines of theoretical philosophy, i.e., the one later called 'metaphysical,' as 'theological' (*Meta.* 1025a.19; 1064b.3), since it takes as its object the divine, the all-embracing founding principle of all being. The Stoics then differentiated a philosopher's 'theology,' which is in keeping with the nature of the divine, from the mythical theology of the poets and the political theology of the state cults. Here theology was no longer simply an object of philosophical inquiry but the inquiry itself.

Similarly ambiguous is Christian usage. It arose in the second century A. D. and had a philosophical inclination . . . The theologian is the divinely inspired proclaimer of divine truth and theology is the proclamation. The idea lived on in later Christian usage.

In this sense, all the biblical authors could be called 'theologians,' but especially the OT prophets and John the Evangelist, the 'theologian' of the deity of Jesus.

The founding of theology on divine revelation is not a determination that is foreign to its nature, as the later distinction between natural and revealed theology might seem to imply. Instead, that the knowledge of God is made possible by God, and therefore by revelation, is one of the basic conditions of the concept of theology as such. Otherwise the possibility of the knowledge of God is logically inconceivable; it would contradict the very idea of God.

To say this is not yet to decide the question in what way creatures can attain to the knowledge of God. Nor is it to presuppose that only believing Christians can share in theological knowledge. Already in Clement there is talk of a pagan share, albeit fragmentary and distorted, in the true theology of the divine Logos. But in any case, whether inside the Christian church or outside it, and even in the so-called natural knowledge of God, no knowledge of God and no theology are conceivable that do not proceed from God and are not due to the working of his Spirit.

Source: *Systematic Theology,* Vol. I., translated by G. W. Bromiley (Edinburgh: T&T Clark, 1991), pp. 1–2.

Further reading

The bold claim of this book is that it is trying to introduce the reader to four separate streams of Christian theological enquiry, but here are some recommendations that might help your navigation should you want to pursue the seven seas of the discourse.

The Bible

Obviously indispensable – you may have one already. There are strong opinions not just about its content but also about its translation (see next section). My view is that for your own personal edification, you should use whichever translation speaks your language, stirs your soul or pleases your mind. Just recently there has been the 400th anniversary of the King James Version, and many people are still enthralled by its wonderfully evocative style. Generally, however, for the purposes of analysis or scholarship, you are well advised to stick to modern but prestigious renditions of the text since they have been able to take into account later manuscript discoveries and linguistic discussions. This text will use the *New Revised Standard Version* which has the merit of modern diction combined with close reference to the grammatical structure of the original texts.

NRSV – The New Revised Standard Version Bible (1989). Division of Christian Education of the National Council of the Churches in Christ in the United States of America. London: HarperCollins.

Introductions to the Bible

The 'white-water ride' through the Old and New Testaments (Chapters 2–11) is a bit quick, and the following texts may help you – all these authors are experienced communicators of biblical technicalities with accessible, informative styles.

Benton White, J., Wilson, W. T. (2006), *From Adam to Armageddon* (5th edn). Belmont, CA: Thomson Wadsworth.

Brueggemann, W. (2003), *An Introduction to the Old Testament*. Louisville, KY: Westminster John Knox.

Johnson, L. T. (2010), *The Writings of the New Testament* (2nd edn). Minneapolis, MN: Fortress.

Rogerson, J. W. (2012), *An Introduction to the Bible* (3rd edn). Sheffield: Equinox.

Introductions to Theology

There are several excellent introductions to Christian Theology which will take you into more detail regarding a number of the topics covered in this book, particularly in relation to the classical and modern formulations (from Chapter 12 onwards). I hereby include just some of the books that I have found useful and hope you will too:

Guarino, T. G. (2005), *Foundations of Systematic Theology*. New York and London: T&T Clark.

McGrath, A. E. (2011), *Christian Theology: An Introduction* (5th edn). Chichester: Wiley-Blackwell.

Migliore, D. (2004), *Faith Seeking Understanding: An Introduction to Christian Theology* (2nd edn). Grand Rapids, MI: W. B. Eerdmans.

O'Collins, G. (2009), *Christology: A Biblical, Historical and Systematic Study of Jesus* (2nd edn). Oxford: OUP.

Readers

This is a welcome growth area whereby those beginning theological study don't just have to take the word of their lecturer/ pastor/ mentor on the topic. It is a thrill to 'hear the voice' of some of the greats of the past, and the present!

Anderson, W. P. (ed.) and Diessling, R. L. (illustrations) (2010), *A Journey through Christian Theology* (2nd edn). Minneapolis, MN: Fortress.

Gunton, C., Holmes, S. R., Rae, M. (eds) (2001), *The Practice of Theology: A Reader*. London: SCM.

McGrath, A. E. (ed.) (2011), *The Christian Theology Reader* (4th edn). Chichester: Wiley-Blackwell.

Weaver, C. D., Roldán-Figueroa, R., Frick, B. (eds) (2012), *Exploring Christian Heritage: A Reader in History and Theology*. Waco, TX: Baylor.

Dictionaries

Lastly, I would heartily recommend the following reference tools:

Cross, F., Livingston E. A. (eds) (2005) *The Oxford Dictionary of the Christian Church*. Oxford: Oxford University Press. (Also available in a concise version).

Powell, M. A. (ed.) (2011) *HarperCollins Bible Dictionary*. New York: HarperOne.

Chapter 2

References

Campbell, J. ([1949] 1993), *The Hero With a Thousand Faces*. Princeton: University Press.

Gray, J. (1992), *Men are From Mars Women are From Venus*. New York: HarperCollins.

McClain Carr, D. (1996), *Reading Fractures of Genesis: Historical and Literary Approaches*. Louisville: WJK.

Pritchard, J. B. (2011), *The Ancient Near East: An Anthology of Texts and Pictures*. New Jersey: Princeton University Press.

Ska, J. L. (2006), *Introduction to Reading the Pentateuch* (translated by P. Dominique). Winona Lake: Eisenbrauns.

Excursus

1. In the beginning?

Consider the following translations – which do you prefer?

Genesis 1:1-3 (King James version)
In the beginning God created the heaven and the earth. And the earth was without form, and void; and darkness was upon the face of the deep. And the Spirit of God moved upon the face of the waters. And God said, Let there be light: and there was light.

Genesis 1:1-3 (Young's Literal translation)
[1]In the beginning of God's preparing the heavens and the earth – [2]the earth hath existed waste and void, and darkness [is] on the face of the deep, and the Spirit of God fluttering on the face of the waters, [3]and God saith, 'Let light be'; and light is.

Genesis 1:1-3 (New Life version)
[1]In the beginning God made from nothing the heavens and the earth. [2]The earth was an empty waste and darkness was over the deep waters. And the

Spirit of God was moving over the top of the waters.[3] Then God said, 'Let there be light', and there was light.

Genesis 1:1-3 (New Revised Standard Version)
In the beginning when God created the heavens and the earth,[2] the earth was a formless void and darkness covered the face of the deep, while a wind from God swept over the face of the waters.[3] Then God said, 'Let there be light'; and there was light.

Genesis 1:1-3 (Word on the Street - Rob Lacey)
First off, nothing. No light, no time, no substance, no matter. Second off, God starts it all up and WHAP! Stuff everywhere! The cosmos in chaos: no shape, no form, no function– just darkness . . . total. And floating above it all, God's Holy Spirit, ready to play. Day one: Then God's voice booms out, 'Lights!' and, from nowhere, light floods the skies and 'night' is swept off the scene.

Genesis 1: 1, 3-5: TSV (Technical Slang Version by David Carey)
At time t = 0, Elohiym implemented the heavens and Earth. Now Earth had low information content, . . . And Elohiym said, 'Let there be electromagnetic radiation, and there was electromagnetic radiation.'

All of the above, in their own way are attempting to translate this:

בְּרֵאשִׁית בָּרָא אֱלֹהִים אֵת הַשָּׁמַיִם וְאֵת הָאָרֶץ
וְהָאָרֶץ הָיְתָה תֹהוּ וָבֹהוּ וְחֹשֶׁךְ עַל־פְּנֵי תְהוֹם וְרוּחַ אֱלֹהִים מְרַחֶפֶת עַל־פְּנֵי הַמָּיִם:
וַיֹּאמֶר אֱלֹהִים יְהִי אוֹר וַיְהִי־אוֹר

Although some might find this array of translations bothersome or even irreverent, the fact of the matter is that these are just some of the thousands of versions of the Bible that are 'out there' and inform the way this key source of revelation is read. In fairness, all the above translations evidence the core and common idea of God's creative action but it can be difficult to strike the balance between being accurate and being readable. A 'spot the difference exercise' on the texts above shows that, for example, the *New Life* and Rob Lacey versions indicate that God made everything 'from nothing' – both ignoring the Hebrew watery *tehom* which God divides with light. They have effectively inserted later theologizing into their translation of the text. Note also that the word for 'Spirit' and 'Wind' (*ruah*) is identical in Hebrew and hence there are differences reflected in translations as to whether the Spirit is part of the solution to the chaos or the Wind is part of the primordial mayhem.

Confused? Well yes . . . but don't be dispirited. Most scholars will have their 'favourite' translation and as noted, in this text I will tend to use the *New Revised Standard Version* which follows the word patterns of the original languages fairly closely without being too old fashioned. Also, language exploration, solving the riddles of the origins of words and their parallels in other languages has always been an exciting and constituent part of biblical scholarship. For example, it *used to* surprise students that Biblical Hebrew was originally written without vowels since they thought it could not possibly be understood. Nowadays, the text message generation has acquired the same ability and everyone is writing things like THLGY-GR8 SBJCT without a problem. Nevertheless, confusion about language remains part of the conundrum of being human which the Bible itself is aware of in the famous story of the Tower of Babel in Genesis 11:1-9. There the languages of humanity are confused and co-operation between humans is hampered evermore. That this is true even in everyday life is confirmed by consideration of the English word 'fine.' This can mean nice things (as in a 'fine day' or 'fine silk tie') but it can also be problematic (as in a traffic or library fine) and sometimes very scary – as when a woman tells a man that things are 'fine.'

Sources

The Bible: Authorized King James Version with the Apocrypha, with introduction and notes by R. Carroll and S. Prickett (Oxford: Oxford University Press, [1611] 1997).

Young's Literal Translation of the Holy Bible, translated by Robert E. Young (Greater Truth Publishers, [1862] 2005).

New Life Translation (Carol Stream: Tyndale, 1969).

The New Revised Standard Version Bible, Division of Christian Education of the National Council of the Churches in Christ in the United States of America (London: HarperCollins, 1989).

The Word on the Street, edited and translated by Rob Lacey (Grand Rapids: Zondervan, 2004).

The Bible, Technical Slang Version, edited and translated by David Carey, available at *http://david. carybros.com/html/tsv.html.*

Biblica Hebraica Stuttgartensia, edited by K. Elliger and W. Rudolph (Peabody: Hendrickson, 2006).

Extracts

1. Creation in *Enuma Elish*

As noted in the main text, many civilizations have their own creation epics and one such is the *Enuma Elish* from Mesopotamia. The work, consisting of seven tablets was known by the opening words of Tablet I in Akkadian as *Enūma eliš* – 'When on High.' This epic poem may date from the early part of the second millennium BCE and came to be traditionally recited on the fourth day of the New Year's festival in Babylonia. Tablet V, from which the following extract is taken, describes cosmic creation by Marduk. Note the mention of *šapattu* which clearly has resonances of the Hebrew *sabbath*, likewise the emphasis on the role of the moon for the calendar. One thing that might seem weird is the reference to *Tiamat* the preternatural 'Chaos Monster of the Ocean.' Though we can all be chaos monsters at times (every home should have one), Tiamat is so big that Marduk establishes the 'zenith' by splitting it open in an action which echoes the conquering of the dark watery chaos of Genesis 1.

TABLET V

He constructed stations for the great gods,
Fixing their astral likenesses and constellations.
He determined the year by designating the zones:
He set up three constellations for each of the twelve months.
After defining the days of the year [by means] of (heavenly) figures,
He founded the station of Nebiru to determine their (heavenly) bands,
That none might transgress or fall short.
Alongside it he set up the stations of Enlil and Ea.
Having opened up the gates on both sides,
He strengthened the locks to the left and the right.
In her [Tiamat's] belly he established the zenith.
The Moon he caused to shine, the night (to him) entrusting.
He appointed him a creature of the night to signify the days:
'Monthly, without cease, form designs with a crown.
At the month's very start, rising over the land,
Thou shalt have luminous horns to signify six days,
On the seventh day reaching a [half] crown.
At full moon [*šapattu*] stand in opposition in mid-month.
When the sun [overtakes] thee at the base of heaven,
Diminish [thy crown] and retrogress in light.
[At the time of disappearance] approach thou the course of the sun,
And [on the twenty-ninth] thou shall again stand in opposition to the sun.'

Source: *The Ancient Near East: An Anthology of Texts and Pictures*, edited by James B. Prichard (Princeton and Oxford: Princeton University Press, 2011), pp. 32–3.

2. Flannery O'Connor: Is original sin necessary for good literature?

In the main text, the proposal was made that the narrative at the centre of the biblical drama turns on the 'gifted individual learning to choose good.' Flannery O'Connor was among America's most talented writers of the twentieth century, who, despite her personal piety, in stories such as *A Good Man is Hard to Find*, managed to pen some of the darkest shards of modern literary narrative. Then again, maybe her ability to do so was *because* of her piety. She opines:

> The serious writer has always taken the flaw in human nature for his starting point, usually the flaw in an otherwise admirable character. Drama usually bases itself on the bedrock of original sin, whether the writer thinks in theological terms or not. Then, too, any character in a serious novel is supposed to carry a burden of meaning larger than himself. The novelist doesn't write about people in a vacuum; he writes about people in a world where something is obviously lacking, where there is the general mystery of incompleteness and the particular tragedy of our own times to be demonstrated, and the novelist tries to give you, within the form of the book, a total experience of human nature at any time. For this reason, the greatest dramas naturally involve the salvation or loss of the soul. Where there is no belief in the soul, there is very little drama. The Christian novelist is distinguished from his pagan colleagues by recognizing sin as sin. According to his heritage, he sees it not as sickness or an accident of his environment, but as a responsible choice of offense against God which involves his eternal future. Either one is serious about salvation or one is not. And it is well to realize that the maximum amount of seriousness admits the maximum amount of comedy. Only if we are secure in our beliefs can we see the comical side of the universe . . .
>
> The novelist and the believer, when they are not the same man, yet have many traits in common – a distrust of the abstract, a respect for boundaries, a desire to penetrate the surface of reality and to find in each thing the spirit which makes it itself and holds the world together. But I don't believe we shall have great religious fiction until we have again that happy combination of believing artist and believing society. Until that time, the novelist will have to do the best he can in travail with the world he has. He may find in the end that instead of reflecting the image at the heart of things, he has only reflected our broken condition and, through it, the face of the devil we are possessed by. This is a modest achievement, but perhaps a necessary one.

Source: *Flannery O'Connor: Spiritual Writings.* Edited by R. Ellsberg (New York: Orbis, 2003), pp. 71–2.

Further reading

The following books vary in complexity, but may prove useful:

Cook, J. E. (2011), *Genesis*. Collegeville, PA: Liturgical Press.

Kass, L. (2006), *The Beginning of Wisdom: Reading Genesis*. Chicago, IL: University of Chicago Press.

Ska, J. L. (2006), *Introduction to Reading the Pentateuch* (translated by P. Dominique). Winona Lake, IN: Eisenbrauns.

Wenham, G. J. (1987, 1994), *Genesis 1-15* & *Genesis 16-50*. Nashville, TN: Thomas Nelson.

Chapter 3

References

'*Dei Verbum* – Dogmatic Constitution on Divine Revelation', in Flannery, A. (ed.) (1996), *The Basic Sixteen Documents: Vatican Council II: Constitutions, Decrees, Declarations*. New York: Costello Publishing Company.

Bright, J. (2000), *A History of Israel* (4th edn.). Louisville, KY: Westminster John Knox.

Collins, J. J. (2004), *Introduction to the Hebrew Bible*. Minneapolis: Fortress.

Davies, G. (2004), 'Was There An Exodus?', in J. Day (ed.) *In Search of Pre-Exilic Israel*. London: T&T Clark.

Larsson, G. (1999), *Bound for Freedom: The Book of Exodus in Jewish and Christian Traditions*. Peabody, MA: Hendrickson.

Kille, D. A. (2002), 'Psychology and the Bible: Three Worlds of the Text' in *Pastoral Psychology*, Vol. 51(2), 125–134.

Van Kooten, G. H. (2006), *The Revelation of the Name YHWH to Moses: Perspectives from Judaism, the Pagan Graeco-Roman World and Early Christianity*. Leiden: Brill.

Waskow, A. (1996), *Godwrestling – Round 2: Ancient Wisdom, Future Paths*. Woodstock, VT: Jewish Lights.

Extracts

1. The Code of Hammurabi

The main text refers to the 'Ten Commandments' or 'Ten Words' of God to Moses in Section 3h. If you think they are a bit tough, you might want to have a glance at the Code of Hammurabi who was the sixth of eleven kings in the old Babylonian Dynasty. He ruled from 1728 to 1686 BCE. Below are just a selection of clauses, the first, the last and one or two from in between. Besides detecting parallel concerns with the commandments and the 'eye for an eye' section of Ex 21:23-25, it might be worth contemplating the test for sorcery in clause 2 – trial by drowning! Like many codes from all eras, it has a particular class in society as its focus – *awēlum*. Since this can refer to anyone from a king to a slave, but normally means a 'free man of some standing' the translator has used the Italian – Spanish style term *seignior* to retain some of the ambiguity. It becomes pretty clear that there is a pecking order anyway.

> 1: If a seignior [*Awēlum*] accused a[nother] seignior and brought a charge of murder against him, but has not proved it, his accuser shall be put to death.
> 2: If a seignior brought a charge of sorcery against a[nother] seignior, but has not proved it, the one against whom the charge of sorcery was brought, upon going to the river [Euphrates], shall throw himself into the river, and if the river has then overpowered him, his accuser shall take over his estate; if the river has shown that seignior to be innocent and he has accordingly come forth safe, the one who

brought the charge of sorcery against him shall be put to death, while the one who threw himself into the river shall take over the estate of his accuser.

3: If a seignior came forward with false testimony in a case, and has not proved the word which he spoke, if that was was a case involving life, that seignior shall be put to death.

195. If a son has struck his father, they shall cut off his hand.

196. If a seignior has destroyed the eye of a member of the aristocracy, they shall destroy his eye.

197. If he has broken another seignior's bone, they shall break his bone.

198. If he has destroyed the eye of a commoner, or broken the bone of a commoner, he shall pay one mina of silver.

200. If a seignior has knocked out a tooth of a seignior of his own rank, they shall knock out his tooth . . . .

282. If a male slave has said to his master, 'You are not my master,' his master shall prove him to be his slave and cut off his ear.

Source: *The Ancient Near East: An Anthology of Texts and Pictures*, edited by James B. Prichard (Princeton and Oxford: Princeton University Press, 2011), pp. 155–6, 174 and 179.

2. N. T. Wright on Covenant, Creation and God's action.

Nicholas Thomas Wright is a well-known biblical scholar who besides publishing numerous books has also held the office of Bishop of Durham. In this extract, he argues that there is a 'deep implicit narrative' which connects 'Covenant and Creation' as two sides of the same coin. Do you agree?

[T]he creator God is the covenant God, and vice versa; and his word, particularly through his prophet and/or servant, will rescue and deliver his people from the enemy. This combination constituted the deep implicit narrative within which the multiple other narratives of second-Temple Judaism find their coherence and meaning. We could put it like this, in a double statement which might seem paradoxical but which carried deep meaning through ancient Judaism.

First, the covenant is there to solve the problems within creation. God called Abraham to solve the problem of evil, the problem of Adam, the problem of the world. (That, incidentally, is why accounts of the problem of evil which fail to incorporate covenant theology are doomed before they start; but that is another story.) Israel's calling is to hold fast by the covenant. Through Israel, God will address and solve the problems of the world, bringing justice and salvation to the ends of the earth – though quite how this will happen remains, even in Isaiah, more than a little mysterious.

But, second, creation is invoked to solve the problems within the covenant. When Israel is in trouble, and the covenant promises themselves seem to have come crashing to the ground, the people cry to the covenant God precisely as the creator. Israel goes back to Genesis 1, and to the story of the Exodus, in order to pray and trust that YHWH will do again what, as creator, he has the power and the right to do, and what as the covenant God he has the responsibility to do, namely, to establish justice in the world and, more especially, to vindicate his people when they cry to him for help. In both cases, we should note carefully, it is assumed that something has gone badly wrong. Something is deeply amiss with creation, and within that with humankind itself, something to which the covenant with Israel is the answer. Something is amiss with the covenant, whether Israel's sins on the one hand or Gentile oppression on the other, or perhaps both – and to this the answer is a re-invoking of creation, or rather of God as creator.

Source: *Paul: Fresh Perspectives* (London: SPCK, 2005), p. 24.

Further reading

Anderson, B., Bishop, S., Newman, J. (2006) *Understanding the Old Testament* (5th edn). New Jersey: Prentice Hall.

Brueggeman, W. (2009), *The Unsettling God: The Heart of the Hebrew Bible*. Minneapolis, MN: Fortress.

Meyers, C. (2005), *Exodus*. Cambridge: CUP.

Mills, M. (1998), *Images of God in the Old Testament*. London: Cassell.

Chapter 4

References

Birch, B. C., Brueggemann, W., Fretheim, T. E. and Petersen, D. L. (2005), *A Theological Introduction to the Old Testament* (2nd edn.). Nashville: Abingdon.

Croatto, J. S. (2005), 'Jesus, Prophet Like Elijah, and Prophet-Teacher Like Moses in Luke-Acts' in *Journal of Biblical Literature*, Vol. 124(3) 451–65.

Herodotus ([c.425BCE] 1998), *Histories* (translated by R. Waterfield). Oxford: OUP.

Poirer, J. C. (2009), 'Jesus as an Elijanic Figure in Luke 4:16-30' in *Catholic Biblical Quarterly*, Vol. 71(2) 349–63.

Pritchard, J. (2011), *The Ancient Near East: An Anthology of Texts and Pictures*. New Jersey: Princeton University Press.

Renz, T. (1999) in Ness, R. S. and Wenham, G. J. (eds). *Zion, City of our God*. Grand Rapids: W.B. Eerdmans.

Ska, J. L. (2006), *Introduction to Reading the Pentateuch* (translated by P. Dominique). Winona Lake, IN: Eisenbrauns.

Vogt, P. T. (2006), *Deuteronomistic Theology and the Significance of Torah*. Winona Lake, IN: Eisenbrauns.

Extracts

1. An ancient covenant

Chapter 4 of this book reflects on various aspects of *covenant*. In the Old Testament 'covenant' from the Hebrew word '*Berith*' is used some 286 times.

Its etymology is disputed but is generally understood to incorporate the idea of binding, often signified by a ritual meal. It was a solemn agreement between two parties, either between two equals or between an overlord and a vassal. The first extract gives us an example from the Ancient Near East. It is a fugitive slave treaty between Idrimi of Alalakh and Pilliya of Kizzuwatna. It is written in little triangular or 'cuneiform' script on a clay tablet currently kept in the British Museum. From the wording of the treaty it looks like a covenant between equals. To be noted below is the absolute seriousness of the agreement. Are covenants reassuring *because* they are also a matter of life and death?

TREATY BETWEEN *IDRIMI* AND *PILLIYA*
Tablet of Agreement.

> 2: When Piliya and Idrimi took an oath by the gods and made this binding agreement between themselves: they will always return their respective fugitives (i.e.) if Idrimi seizes a fugitive of Pilliya, he will return him to Pilliya, and if Pilliya seizes a fugitive of Idrimi, he will return him to Idrimi. Anyone who seizes a fugitive, and returns him to his master, (the owner) wil pay as prize of capture 500 (shekels of) copper if it is a man, one thousand as prize of capture if it is a woman. However, if a fugitive from Pilliya enters the land of Idrimi and nobody seizes him, but his owner seizes him, he need not pay a prize of capture to anyone. In whatever city (it is suspected that) they conceal a fugitive, the mayor and five elders will make a declaration under oath. From the very day on which Barattarna has sworn (this) by the gods together with Idrimi, from that day on it is decreed that fugitives have to be returned.
>
> Whoever transgresses this agreement, IM, Shamash and Ishhara, and all the (other) gods will destroy him.

Source: *The Ancient Near East: An Anthology of Texts and Pictures*, edited by James B. Prichard (Princeton and Oxford: Princeton University Press, 2011), p. 210.

2. Jeremiah and new covenant

Jeremiah was the prophet who seems to have most keenly lived the drama of events in Jerusalem leading up to the Exile of 587 BCE. Unpopular because of his prophecies – he was thrown down a well for his troubles – his oracles were sliced up and burnt by a grumpy King Jehoiakim, fed up of the negativity (Jer 38:6 and 36:23). In the midst of all this despair, he famously voiced a vision of hope: a glorious rebuilding of Jerusalem and a new covenant written not on stone but on hearts:

> The days are surely coming, says the LORD, when I will make a new covenant with the house of Israel and the house of Judah. It will not be like the covenant that I

made with their ancestors when I took them by the hand to bring them out of the land of Egypt – a covenant that they broke, though I was their husband, says the Lord. But this is the covenant that I will make with the house of Israel after those days, says the Lord: I will put my law within them, and I will write it on their hearts; and I will be their God, and they shall be my people. No longer shall they teach one another, or say to each other, 'Know the Lord', for they shall all know me, from the least of them to the greatest, says the Lord; for I will forgive their iniquity, and remember their sin no more.

Thus says the Lord,
who gives the sun for light by day
and the fixed order of the moon and the stars for light by night,
who stirs up the sea so that its waves roar—
the Lord of hosts is his name:
If this fixed order were ever to cease
from my presence, says the Lord,
then also the offspring of Israel would cease
to be a nation before me for ever.
Thus says the Lord:
If the heavens above can be measured,
and the foundations of the earth below can be explored,
then I will reject all the offspring of Israel
because of all they have done,
says the Lord.

The days are surely coming, says the Lord, when the city shall be rebuilt for the Lord from the tower of Hananel to the Corner Gate. And the measuring line shall go out farther, straight to the hill Gareb, and shall then turn to Goah. The whole valley of the dead bodies and the ashes, and all the fields as far as the Wadi Kidron, to the corner of the Horse Gate towards the east, shall be sacred to the Lord. It shall never again be uprooted or overthrown. (Jeremiah 31:31–40)

Source: *The New Revised Standard Version Bible* (1989). Division of Christian Education of the National Council of the Churches in Christ in the United States of America. London: HarperCollins.

Further reading

Esler, P. F. (2011), *Sex, Wives and Warriors Reading Old Testament Narrative with its Ancient Audience.* Eugene: Wipf & Stock.

Gaffney, W. (2008) *Daughters of Miriam: Women Prophets in Ancient Israel.* Philadelphia, PA: Fortress.

Hayes, J., Maxwell Miller, J. (2006) *A History of Ancient Israel and Judah* (2nd ed). Philadelphia, PA: Westminster Press.

Hutton, R. (2004), *Fortress Introduction to the Prophets.* Minneapolis, MN: Fortress.

Romer, T. (2007), *The So-called Deuteronomistic History.* London: T&T Clark.

Chapter 5

References

Boss, J. (2010), *Human Consciousness in the Book of Job*. London: T&T Clark.

Cox, D. (1978), *The Triumph of Impotence: Job and the tradition of the Absurd*. Rome: PUG.

Crenshaw, J. L. (2010), *Old Testament Wisdom: An Introduction* (3rd edn). Louisville, KY: Westminster John Knox.

Fox, M. V. (1999), *A Time to Tear Down, A Time to Build Up: A Re-Reading of Ecclesiastes*. Grand Rapids: W.B. Eerdmans.

Knibb, M. A. (2009), *Essays on the Book of Enoch and Other Early Jewish Texts and Traditions*. Leiden: Brill, pp. 271–7.

Mays, J. L. (1994), *Psalms*. Louisville, KY: John Knox.

Murphy, R. E. (2002), *The Tree of Life: An Exploration of Biblical Wisdom Literature* (3rd edn). Grand Rapids: W.B. Eerdmans.

Myers, E. M. and Rogerson, J. (1997), 'The World of Apocalyptic' in Chilton, B. (ed.) *Cambridge Companion to the Bible* (2nd edn). Cambridge: CUP.

Reardon, P. H. (2000), *Christ in the Psalms*. Ben Lomond, CA: Conciliar Press.

Extracts

1. Psalm 151? One more for the hymn book?

As mentioned in Chapter 5, the classification *Ketubim* includes a mixture of writings comprising books of historical type (Ezra, Nehemiah and Chronicles), poetry (Psalms, Lamentations and Song of Songs), wisdom (Job, Proverbs and Ecclesiastes) and more fabulous stories (Ruth, Esther and Daniel). In the canonical scriptures there are 150 Psalms, but as the Qumran sect shows, there were other hymns in use apart from the 150 in our Bible. This excerpt is one example. Its original language is Hebrew. Originally it was two separate psalms, 151A and 151B. As noted, many of the psalms are ascribed to David, since he was a musician and something of a dancer too (1 Sam 16:23, 2 Sam 6:16). This one is different, it is *about* David, and the situation it refers to is the account of the anointing of David as King of Israel in 1 Sam 16:1-13.

> 1: I was the smallest among my brothers,
> And the youngest among the sons of my father;
> And he made me shepherd of his flocks,
> And the ruler over his kids
> 2: My hands made a flute,
> And my fingers a lyre;
> And I shall render glory to the Lord,
> I thought within myself.

3: The mountains cannot witness to him,
Nor the hills proclaim (him);
The trees have elevated my words,
And the flocks my deeds.
4: For who can proclaim and who can announce,
And who can recount the deeds of the Lord?
Everything God has seen,
Everything he has heard and he has listened.
5: He sent his prophet to anoint me,
Samuel to make me great;
My brothers went out to meet him,
Handsome of figure and handsome of appearance.
6: (Although) their stature was tall,
(and) their hair handsome,
The Lord God
Did not choose them.
7: But he sent and took me from behind the flock,
And he anointed me with holy oil,
And he made me leader of his people,
And ruler over the sons of his covenant. (11QPs.151)

Source: *The Old Testament Pseudepigrapha* (Vol. 2), edited by J. H. Charlesworth (London: Darton, Longman & Todd, 1985), pp. 612–3.

2. Daniel: The end of the world as they knew it?

Although the Book of Daniel appears in the *Ketubim*, it is very much *sui generis* – 'unique'. In the Christian Bible, it is found among the prophets, a classification that rendered its interpretation problematic. It is much better understood as apocalyptic literature, a type of writing common between 200 BCE and 100 CE and written at times of great crisis in the history of Israel. Its purpose was to give hope and courage to a nation under persecution. The genre is written in secret symbolic language, hence the reader needed to decode it in order to appropriate its meaning. This excerpt from the book of Daniel is one of the most famous passages in the Old Testament, due in part to the presence of the title 'Son of Man' later appropriated by Jesus of Nazareth. In a style scholars refer to *vaticinium ex eventu* (prophecy after the event), the author of Daniel is writing as if he is referring to the events of the Babylonian captivity but he is actually referring to a later period during the reign of Antiochus IV Epiphanes, who ruled the Seleucid Empire from 175 to 164 BCE. Many in the past have misinterpreted apocalyptic literature as being primarily about *the end of the world*, but for the apocalyptic writers it was about *the end of empires* – the end of persecution and suffering under evil rule such as that of the Greeks or later the Romans. In this extract, note how the battle will be between the Holy Ones and the oppressive beast. Exactly the same sort of imagery will be present in the last scroll of the New Testament, the Book of Revelation.

As I watched,
thrones were set in place,
   and an Ancient One took his throne;
his clothing was white as snow,
   and the hair of his head like pure wool;
his throne was fiery flames,
   and its wheels were burning fire.
A stream of fire issued
   and flowed out from his presence.
A thousand thousand served him,
   and ten thousand times ten thousand stood attending him.
The court sat in judgement,
   and the books were opened.
I watched then because of the noise of the arrogant words that the horn was speaking. And as I watched, the beast was put to death, and its body destroyed and given over to be burned with fire. As for the rest of the beasts, their dominion was taken away, but their lives were prolonged for a season and a time.
As I watched in the night visions,
I saw one like a son of man
   coming with the clouds of heaven.
And he came to the Ancient One
    and was presented before him.
To him was given dominion
   and glory and kingship,
that all peoples, nations, and languages
   should serve him.
His dominion is an everlasting dominion
   that shall not pass away,
and his kingship is one
   that shall never be destroyed.
As for me, Daniel, my spirit was troubled within me, and the visions of my head terrified me. I approached one of the attendants to ask him the truth concerning all this. So he said that he would disclose to me the interpretation of the matter: 'As for these four great beasts, four kings shall arise out of the earth. But the holy ones of the Most High shall receive the kingdom and possess the kingdom for ever—for ever and ever'.
This is what he said: 'As for the fourth beast,
there shall be a fourth kingdom on earth
   that shall be different from all the other kingdoms;
it shall devour the whole earth,
   and trample it down, and break it to pieces.

As for the ten horns,
out of this kingdom ten kings shall arise,
   and another shall arise after them.
This one shall be different from the former ones,
   and shall put down three kings.
He shall speak words against the Most High,
   shall wear out the holy ones of the Most High,
   and shall attempt to change the sacred seasons and the law;
and they shall be given into his power
   for a time, two times, and half a time.
Then the court shall sit in judgement,
   and his dominion shall be taken away,
   to be consumed and totally destroyed.
The kingship and dominion
   and the greatness of the kingdoms under the whole heaven
   shall be given to the people of the holy ones of the Most High;
their kingdom shall be an everlasting kingdom,
   and all dominions shall serve and obey them.'
Here the account ends. As for me, Daniel, my thoughts greatly terrified me, and
my face turned pale; but I kept the matter in my mind (Dan 7:9-28)

Source: *The New Revised Standard Version Bible* (1989). Division of Christian Education of the National Council of the Churches in Christ in the United States of America. London: HarperCollins.

Further reading

Alter, R. (2010), *The Wisdom Books*. New York: W. W. Norton.

Crenshaw, J. L. (2010), *Old Testament Wisdom: An Introduction* (3rd edn). Louisville, KY: Westminster John Knox.

Hunter, A. G. (2008), *An Introduction to the Psalms*. London, New York: T&T Clark.

Murphy, R. E. (2002), *The Tree of Life: An Exploration of Biblical Wisdom Literature* (3rd edn). Grand Rapids: W. B. Eerdmans.

Chapter 6

References

Bauckham, R. (2006), *Jesus and the Eyewitnesses: The Gospels as Eyewitness Testimony*. Grand Rapids, MI: W. B. Eerdmans.

Bultmann, R. K. (1951), *Theology of the New Testament*. New York: Charles Scribner's Sons.

Davies, G. (2004), 'Was there an Exodus?', in J. Day (ed) *In Search of Pre-Exilic Israel*. London: T&T Clark.

Fitzmyer, J. A. (2007), *The One Who Is To Come*. Grand Rapids, MI: W. B. Eerdmans.

Keith, C. and Hurtado, L. (eds) (2011), *Jesus among Friends and Enemies: A Historical and Literary introduction to Jesus in the Gospels*. Grand Rapids: Baker Academic.

Pines, S. (1971), *An Arabic Version of the Testimonium Flavianum and Its Implications*. Jerusalem: Israel Academy of Sciences & Humanities.

Extract

1. The other Servant songs

Chapter 6 already contains a generous helping of the fourth *Ebed* YHWH song. As Acts 8:26-40 shows, the *Ebed* YHWH songs lent themselves to application to the sufferings of Jesus of Nazareth. The idea of a crucified Messiah was, to say the least, problematic. Below, I present a medley of the other three songs of the *Ebed* YHWH.

Isaiah 42

¹ Here is my servant, whom I uphold, my chosen one in whom I delight; I will put my Spirit on him and he will bring justice to the nations.

² He will not shout or cry out, or raise his voice in the streets.

³ A bruised reed he will not break, and a smouldering wick he will not snuff out. In faithfulness he will bring forth justice;

⁴ he will not falter or be discouraged till he establishes justice on earth. In his law the islands will put their hope.

(Isa 42:1-4)

Isaiah 49

The Servant of the LORD

¹ Listen to me, you islands; hear this, you distant nations: Before I was born the LORD called me; from my birth he has made mention of my name.

² He made my mouth like a sharpened sword, in the shadow of his hand he hid me; he made me into a polished arrow and concealed me in his quiver.

³ He said to me, You are my servant, Israel, in whom I will display my splendour.

⁴ But I said, I have laboured to no purpose; I have spent my strength in vain and for nothing. Yet what is due to me is in the LORD's hand, and my reward is with my God.

⁵ And now the LORD says – he who formed me in the womb to be his servant to bring Jacob back to him and gather Israel to himself, for I am honoured in the eyes of the LORD and my God has been my strength.

⁶ he says: It is too small a thing for you to be my servant to restore the tribes of Jacob and bring back those of Israel I have kept. I will also make you a light for the Gentiles, that you may bring my salvation to the ends of the earth.

(Isa 49:1-6)

Isaiah 50

[4] The Sovereign LORD has given me an instructed tongue, to know the word that sustains the weary. He wakens me morning by morning, wakens my ear to listen like one being taught.

[5] The Sovereign LORD has opened my ears, and I have not been rebellious; I have not drawn back.

[6] I offered my back to those who beat me, my cheeks to those who pulled out my beard; I did not hide my face from mocking and spitting.

[7] Because the Sovereign LORD helps me, I will not be disgraced. Therefore have I set my face like flint, and I know I will not be put to shame.

[8] He who vindicates me is near. Who then will bring charges against me? Let us face each other! Who is my accuser? Let him confront me!

[9] It is the Sovereign LORD who helps me. Who is he who will condemn me? They will all wear out like a garment; the moths will eat them up.

(Isa 50:4-9)

Source: *The New Revised Standard Version Bible* (1989). Division of Christian Education of the National Council of the Churches in Christ in the United States of America. London: HarperCollins.

2. Fitzmyer on Messiah

Joseph Fitzmyer is one of the most significant American scripture scholars of recent times. At the conclusion of his meticulous survey of messiahship in biblical and extra-biblical literature, he contrasts the eventual rabbinic understanding of the concept with the theological conclusions of the Jesus movement.

> To sum up, first, the Jewish belief, one must stress that the expectation of a Jewish Messiah was not of one form, for we have seen that the expectation envisaged at times a kingly and priestly figure, A Messiah of Aaron and a Messiah of Israel, a Messiah of David and a Messiah of Joseph (or Ephraim). Moreover, it even cast the prophet Elijah, who was thought to return, as an awaited High Priest. The dominant expectation, however, was one that awaited a human kingly figure who was (and is) to bring deliverance, at once political, economic, and spiritual, to the Jewish people, and through them peace, prosperity, and righteousness to all humanity. Moreover, in the Babylonian Talmud such a figure was also said to be among the seven things created before the world came to be. That means that at times the Messiah was thought of as a pre-existent being. He was also considered eventually as the King Messiah destined to fulfil the role of the child of whom Isaiah spoke and described as "Everlasting Father, Prince of Peace" (Isa 9:5). For in his day all peoples would be gathered to worship the God of Israel, who was regarded as the sole deliverer and redeemer of humanity. This aspect of redemption varied at times when some Jewish sages understood the Messiah as a corporate personality or believed that redemption would take place without a personal Messiah – a form of messianism without a Messiah. In all of this Jewish belief the expectation was (and is) still focused on the future . . .

Fitzmyer then contrasts this perspective with a theological and confessional view of the messianism of Christianity:

> How different that Jewish Messiah is from the Christian Messiah, who has already come. He has not only been identified with Jesus of Nazareth, who was crucified as a criminal and rebel, but he bears in human history the name Jesus Christ (= Jesus the Messiah), both among those who are his followers and among those who are not. His mission differed too, because it was no longer deliverance in a political or economic sense, but solely in a spiritual sense; and because it was aimed directly at all human beings, it no longer was considered as coming through a chosen people. Moreover, his death by crucifixion was understood in a vicarious sense, intended to deliver all who would accept him from evil, sin, and suffering. The Christian Messiah, then, is known as the one who fulfils the role of Deutero-Isaiah's Suffering Servant of God (Isaiah 53), who has not only suffered and died for humanity, but was also raised by God to give it hope of sharing a blissful afterlife with Him in the Father's glorious presence. The Christian Messiah is also known to be the Son of God in a transcendent sense, the Word (*Logos*) of God, and the Second Person of the Triune God. In this, he is the God-Man. In these respects, the Christian Messiah differs radically from the awaited Jewish Messiah, without whom, however, he would not be known in human history as "Jesus Christ, the Son of God" (Mark 1:1).

Source: *The One Who Is to Come* (Cambridge: W. B. Eerdmans, 2007), pp. 182–3.

Further reading

Bockmuel, M., Hagner, D. A. (2005), *The Written Gospel*. Cambridge: CUP.

Fitzmyer, J. A. (2007), *The One Who Is To Come*. Grand Rapids: Eerdmans.

Graffy, A. (2002), *Trustworthy and True: The Gospels Beyond 2000*. Dublin: Columba.

Marsh, C. Moyise, S. (2006), *Jesus and the Gospels*. London: T&T Clark.

Platt, E. (2004), *Four Portraits of Jesus*. New York: Paulist Press.

Senior, D. (2002), *Invitation to the Gospels*. New York: Paulist Press.

Stanton, G. (2002), *The Gospels and Jesus* (revised edn). Oxford: OUP.

Chapter 7

References

Ashley, E. (2010), 'The Miracles of Jesus' in Harding, M. and Nobbs, A. (eds) *The Content and Setting of the Gospel Tradition*. Cambridge: W. B. Eerdmans.

Dunn, J. G. D., McKnight, S. (2005), *The Historical Jesus in Recent Research*. Winona Lake: Eisenbrauns.

Esler, P. F. (2000), 'Jesus and the Reduction of Intergroup Conflict: The Parable of the Good Samaritan in the light of Social Identity Theory,' *Biblical Interpretation*, Vol. 8, 325–57.

Horsley, R. A. (2001), *Hearing the Whole Story: The Politics of Plot in Mark's Gospel*. Louisville, KY: Westminster John Knox.

O'Collins, G. (2006), *The Lord's Prayer*. London: DLT.

Oden, T. (ed.) (1978), *Parables of Kierkegaard*. New Jersey: Princeton University Press.

Prior, M. (1999), 'The Liberation Theology of the Lucan Jesus' in *Studii biblici francescani liber annuus*, Vol. 49, 79–99.

Snodgrass, K. (2004), 'Modern Approaches to the Parables' in McKnight, S. And Osborne, G. R. (eds) *The Face of New Testament Studies: A Survey of Recent Resources*. Grand Rapids: Baker Academic.

Voorvinde, S. (2010), 'The Kingdom of God in the Proclamation of Jesus' in Harding, M. and Nobbs, A. (eds) *The Content and Setting of the Gospel Tradition*. Cambridge: W. B. Eerdmans.

Extracts

1. Robert Farrar Capon on the parables of the kingdom

Few would doubt the idiosyncratic way that Jesus preached – through the medium of parables. Hence if we need to find out what he thought about the Kingdom of God, the parables are not a bad place to start. In this first extract, Robert Farrar Capon, the American Episcopalian minister and exegete, reflects on the Parable of the Sower. Capon works on the theory that while most of our straightforward logical thinking comes from 'left-brain/ right hand' approaches to life which are great for fixing broken furniture and map reading, our more intuitive 'right-brain/left hand' thinking is what proves to be best when solving more complex things like broken relationships. Reconciliations are rarely achieved by a forensic 'I said-you said, you did-I did' arithmetic of blame. Capon suggests that the Gospels must be understood as Jesus' attempt to change the way we think, to become more intuitive – hence his use of parables, hence his enigmatic messiahship.

The Sower: The Watershed of the Parables

The parable of the Sower, therefore, seems to be yet another of the Gospel 'flags'. Take, for example, the matter of the 'messianic secret'. Prior to the Sower, Jesus' reluctance to come right out and declare his messiahship in plain terms was mostly a matter of occasional warnings – both to demons and to the beneficiaries of his signs – not to reveal who he really was. Subsequently, though, it becomes a kind of intentional mystification that he incorporates into his teaching as a deliberate principle. To see that, all you have to do is note the words of Isaiah that Jesus interposes between the Sower and its interpretation: He says that he speaks to the people in parables in order that 'seeing they might not see and hearing they might not understand'. Till now, in other words, he has been aware in a general way that his kind of messiahship is not what people have been expecting; but from here on he takes this preliminary, mostly negative perception and turns it into a positive developmental principle of his thinking. 'Well', he seems to say 'since they've pretty well misunderstood me so far, maybe I should capitalize on that. Maybe I should start thinking up examples of how profoundly the true messianic kingdom differs from their expectations. They think the kingdom will be a parochial, visible proposition – a militarily established theocratic state that will simply be handed to them at some future date. Hm. What if I were to stand every one of those ideas on its head? What if I were to come up with some parables that said the kingdom was catholic, mysterious, already present in their midst, and aggressively demanding their response? Let me see . . . .'

Whatever his thoughts, their outcome was what we have in Matthew 13 and its parallels: the proclamation of exactly such a paradoxical kingdom. Furthermore, these passages show Jesus giving not only a new substance but also a new style to his proclamation – a style that will turn out to be the most important single development in his teaching technique. For the first time (in the Sower and the Weeds), he goes beyond mere comparisons and produces parables that are actually stories.

Source: *Kingdom, Grace, Judgment: Paradox, Outrage, and Vindication in the Parables of Jesus* (Grand Rapids: Wm. B. Eerdmans, 2002), pp. 55–6.

2. Bultmann on the Kingdom

One of the most controversial exegetes of the twentieth century, Rudolf Bultmann was convinced that the key to the Gospel message lay in the 'crisis' excited by the preaching of Jesus which forced people to make a decision for God or otherwise. This enabled Bultmann to dispense with most of the other elements of the accounts, particularly anything supernatural – a project he called 'demythologization'. An active missioner, Bultmann's view was that such things got in the way of the modern mind, and very much rooted in his own tradition, the idea that the 'word of God' was present in preaching meant he saw his project as pastoral. Though his many and varied views on all sorts of New Testament topics are not now widely held, the directness of his approach can be 'heard' in this extract from his *Primitive Christianity*, which discusses the 'Reign of God'.

The Eschatological Preaching of Jesus

The preaching of Jesus is controlled by an imminent expectation of the Reign of God. In this he stands in a line with Jewish eschatology in general, though clearly not in its nationalistic form. He never speaks of a political Messiah who will destroy the enemies of Israel, of the establishment of a Jewish world empire, the gathering of the twelve tribes, of peace and prosperity in the land, or anything of that kind. Instead, we find in his preaching the cosmic hopes of apocalyptic writers. True, he never indulges in learned or fantastic speculation such as we find in their works. He never looks back upon the past epochs of world history or attempts to date the End. He never invites his hearers to look for the signs of the end in nature or history. Equally, he eschews all elaboration of detail as regards the judgement, resurrection and future glory. All these elements are absorbed in the single all-embracing thought that God will then reign. Only a few apocalyptic traits appear here and there and characterize the present as the time of decision . . .

This sense of crisis in human destiny expresses itself in the conviction that the hour of decision has struck. So it is with Jesus. He is convinced of God's will and determination, and that it is his business to proclaim it, that he feels himself to be standing on the frontiers of time. His eschatological preaching is not the outcome of wishful thinking or speculation, but of the sense of the utter nothingness of man before God. The understanding of human life implied thereby clearly does not stand or fall with his expectation of an imminent end of the world. In other words, it sees the world exclusively sub *specie Dei*. His claim that the destiny of men is determined by their attitude to him and his word was taken up by the early Church and expressed in their proclamation of Jesus as 'Messiah' – particularly in their expectation that he was to come on the clouds of heaven as the 'Man', bringing judgement and salvation. His preaching was thus taken up in a new form, thus becoming specifically 'Christian' preaching. Jesus proclaimed the message. The Church proclaims *him*.

Source: *Primitive Christianity in its Contemporary Setting*, translated by R. H. Fuller (London: Collins Fontana Library, 1960), pp. 102–3 and 110.

Further reading

Harrington, D. J. (2006), *What Are We Hoping For: New Testament Images*. Collegeville, MN: Liturgical Press.

Howell, J. C. (2006), *The Beatitudes For Today*. Louisville, KY: Westminster John Knox.

Getty-Sullivan, M. A. (2007), *Parables of the Kingdom*. Collegeville, MN: Liturgical Press.

Longenecker, R. N. (2000), *The Challenge of Jesus' Parables*. Cambridge: Eerdmans.

Schottroff, L. (2007), *The Parables of Jesus*. Minneapolis, MN: Fortress.

Snodgrass, K. R. (2008), *Stories with Intent: A Comprehensive Guide to the Parables of Jesus*. Grand Rapids, MI: Eerdmans.

Chapter 8

References

Archer, J. and Moloney, F. (2007), *The Gospel according to Judas*. London: Macmillan.

Dylan, B. (1963 and 1991), *With God on Our Side* ©Warner Bros. & Special Rider Music.

Hanson, K. C. and Oakman, D. E. (2009), *Palestine in the Time of Jesus: Social Structures and Social Conflicts*. Minneapolis: Fortress.

McCaffrey, J. (1988), *The House With Many Rooms: The Temple Theme of John 14.2-3*. Rome: PIB.

Pitre, B. (2011), *Jesus and the Jewish Roots of the Eucharist*. New York: Doubleday.

Setzer, C. (1997), 'Excellent Women: Female Witness to the Resurrection' in *Journal of Biblical Literature*, Vol. 116(2) 259–72.

Stuhlmacher, P. (2005), 'Jesus' Readiness to Suffer and His understanding of His Death' in Dunn, J. D. G. and McKnight, S. (eds) *The Historical Jesus in Recent Research*. Winona Lake, IN: Eisenbrauns.

Wright, N. T. (2003), *The Resurrection of the Son of God*. Minneapolis: Fortress.

Extracts

1. Josephus on Pontius Pilate and Jesus Christ

Josephus (c.37–100 CE) is our best 'third party' literary source for information regarding Palestine during the Graeco-Roman period. A Judean by birth from a priestly line, he was general-in-command of the Jewish forces of Galilee in the Great Revolt against Rome (66–73 CE) and his first-hand accounts of the braveries and tragedies of the events include his own garrison's decision to commit suicide rather than surrender. Josephus survived, and after receiving a revelation which included the prophecy that Vespasian would become emperor, the latter spared his life. While Pontius Pilate is somewhat exonerated in the Gospels for the death of Jesus, this extract describes the kind of violent environment of the time and how vicious Pilate could be when he felt his position was under threat. I have also included a fuller version of Josephus' reference to Jesus referred to in the main text Section 6d, which as you can see, is almost a confession of faith and hence is generally thought to have been altered by a later Christian editor.

> [Pilate] spent money from the sacred treasury in the construction of an aqueduct to bring water into Jerusalem, intercepting the source of the stream at a distance of 200 furlongs. The Jews did not acquiesce in the operations that this involved; and tens of thousands of men assembled and cried out against him, bidding him relinquish his promotion of such designs. Some too even hurled insults and abuse of the sort that a throng will commonly engage in. He thereupon ordered a large number of soldiers to be dressed in Jewish garments, under which they carried clubs, and he sent them off this way and that, thus surrounding the Jews, whom he ordered to withdraw. When the Jews were in full torrent of abuse he gave his soldiers the prearranged signal. They, however, inflicted much harder blows than Pilate had ordered, punishing alike both those who were rioting and those who were not. But the Jews showed no faint-heartedness; and so, caught unarmed, as they were, by men delivering a prepared attack, many of them actually were slain on the spot, while some withdrew disabled by blows. Thus ended the uprising.
>
> About this time there lived Jesus, a wise man, if indeed one ought to call him a man. For he was one who wrought surprising feats and was a teacher of such people as accept the truth gladly. He won over many Jews and many of the Greeks. He was the Messiah. When Pilate, upon hearing him accused by men of the highest standing amongst us, had condemned him to be crucified, those who had in the first place come to love him did not give up their affection for him. On the third day he appeared to them restored to life, for the prophets of God had prophesied these and countless other marvelous things about him. And the tribe of the Christians, so called after him, has still to this day not disappeared.

Source: *Antiquities*, 18.60-64 in *Josephus*, translated by L. H. Feldman (London: Heinemann, 1969), Vol. IX, pp. 47–51.

2. O'Collins on Resurrection appearances

The well-known Australian theologian, Gerald O'Collins is a brilliant communicator and has spent much of a long lifetime exploring the mystery of the resurrection. The main text has alerted the reader to the 'ordinary' nature of the post-mortem appearances of Jesus and O'Collins takes up that theme. In the following extract, he points out that they seem almost contrarily unexcited, no lights, no dazzle, the unspectacular side of Easter?

> But the witnesses never recall, or at least explicitly recall, the risen Jesus as betraying any emotions. He never expresses any satisfaction at what he has achieved, no radiant joy at his intimate experience of resurrection, no deep happiness at being reunited with Mary Magdalene, the male disciples, and his other friends. No feelings were shown through his testimony provided by the Gospels . . .
>
> They are likewise *silent about any bodily transformation* of Jesus and the way he looked. There is a remarkable, albeit mysterious, 'ordinariness' about him. The resurrection stories lack the traits of apocalyptic glory found in the narratives of the transfiguration (Mark 9:2-8). According to Luke's account of the walk to Emmaus, for several hours two disciples entertain Jesus unawares. As C. F. Evans comments 'the story is the furthest possible remove from the category of heavenly vision of the Lord in glory. Bewitched by the luminous phenomenon Luke associates with Paul's Damascus road encounter, by the conviction that the transfiguration is a misplaced Easter appearance, by the apocalyptic language of Revelation 1:12-20 and, at times by alleged Gnostic parallels to the resurrection stories, some have attempted to smuggle glorious features into the Easter appearances. But the only glorious figure in the Gospels accounts of the appearances is the 'angel of the Lord' whose appearance terrifies the guard at Jesus' tomb and causes the two holy women some fear (Matthew 28:2-5). None of the Gospels ever describes the risen Jesus himself like that angel. St Paul writes about 'the glory of God in the face of (the risen) Christ' (2 Corinthians 4:6). But in their Easter Chapters the Gospels maintain a sober silence about the glorious transformation that Jesus' resurrection from the dead entailed.

Source: *Jesus A Portrait* (London: Darton, Longman & Todd, 2008), pp. 187–8.

Further reading

Bauckham, R., Hart, T. (1999), *At The Cross: Meditations on People Who were There*. Illinois: InterVarsity Press.

Carter, W. (2003), *Pontius Pilate: Portraits of a Roman Governor*. Collegeville, MN: Liturgical Press.

Charlesworth, J. H. (2006), *Resurrection*. London: T&T Clark.

Gilbert, J. (2000), *The Passion and Death of Jesus*. Nashville, TN: Abingdon Press.

Levenson, J. (1993), *The Death and Resurrection of the Beloved Son*. New Haven, CT: Yale University Press.

Longenecker, R. N. (ed.) (1998), *Life in the Face of Death: The Resurrection Message of the New Testament*. Cambridge: W. B. Eerdmans.

O'Collins, G. (2012), *Believing in the Resurrection*. Mahwah, NJ: Paulist.

Chapter 9

References

Finger, R. F. (2007), *Of Widows and Meals: Communal Meals in the Book of Acts*. Cambridge: W. B. Eerdmans.

Johnson, L. T. (1998), *Religious Experience in Earliest Christianity*. Minneapolis, MN: Augsburg.

Nietzsche, F. ([1885] 1969), *Thus Spoke Zarathustra* (translated by R. J. Hollingworth). London: Penguin Books.

Pilch, J. (2004), *Vision and Healing in the Acts of the Apostles*. Collegeville, MN: Liturgical Press.

Seccombe, D. (1998), 'The New People of God' in Marshall, I. H. and Peterson, D. (eds) *Witness to the Gospel*. Cambridge: W. B. Eerdmans.

Shillington, V. G. (2007), *An Introduction to the Study of Luke/Acts*. London: T&T Clark.

Witherington III, B. (1998), *Acts of the Apostles: A Socio-Rhetorical Commentary*. Cambridge: W. B. Eerdmans.

Extracts

1. Josephus on Pharisees, Sadducees and Essenes

When reading about the development of the Church in the Acts of the Apostles, it is easy to get carried away with its unique picture of the life of the early Christian community. However, it cannot be stressed enough that the Jesus followers were only one of several movements extant at the time. In this extract, Josephus pens a portrait of three others, and it is no secret which is his favourite. Note the similarities between his description of the Essenes and some of the life-pattern aspirations depicted in Acts 2-5.

> Jewish philosophy, in fact, takes three forms. The followers of the first school are called Pharisees, of the second Sadducees, of the third, Essenes.
>
> The Essenes have a reputation for cultivating peculiar sanctity. Of Jewish birth, they show greater attachment to each other than do the other sects. They shun pleasures as a vice and regard temperance and the control of the passions as a special virtue. Marriage they disdain, but they adopt other men's children, while yet pliable and docile, and regard them as their kin and mould them in accordance with their own principles . . .
>
> Riches they despise, and their community of goods is truly admirable; you will not find one among them distinguished by greater opulence than another. They have a law that new members on admission to the sect shall confiscate their property to the order, with the result that you will nowhere see either abject

poverty or inordinate wealth; the individual's possessions join the common stock and all, like brothers, enjoy a single patrimony . . .

Of the first-named schools, the Pharisees, who are considered the most accurate interpreters of the laws, and hold the position of the leading sect, attribute everything to Fate and to God; they hold that to act rightly or otherwise rests, indeed, for the most part with men, but that in each action, Fate co-operates. Every soul, they maintain, is imperishable, but the soul of the good alone passes into another body, while the souls of the wicked suffer eternal punishment.

The Sadducees, the second of the orders, do away with Fate altogether, and remove God beyond, not merely the commission, but the very sight of evil. They maintain that man has the free choice of good or evil, and that it rests with each man's will whether he follows the one or the other. As for the persistence of the soul after death, penalties in the underworld, and rewards, they will have none of them.

The Pharisees are affectionate to each other and cultivate harmonious relations with the community. The Sadducees, on the contrary, are even among themselves rather boorish in their behaviour, and in their intercourse with their peers are as rude as to aliens. Such is what I have to say on the Jewish philosophical schools.

Source: Josephus *The Jewish War, II:7* in *The New Testament Background* (revised edn). Edited by C. K. Barrett (London: SPCK, 1989), pp. 158–9.

2. Ben Witherington III on the links between Luke and Acts

Ben Witherington III is a prolific contemporary New Testament commentator. As an argument for common authorship, in the following extract he is underlining the complementarity of the Gospel of Luke and the Acts of the Apostles, both in their emphasis on universalization and their geographical design:

Even the geographical orientation of the Gospel of Luke is in part caused by the concern about salvation. Jesus must go up to Jerusalem, for it is the center from which Jews looked for salvation (Luke 9:51; 13:22, 33, 35; 17:11; 18:31; 19:11, 28). Jesus must accomplish or finish his earthly work there so that salvation and its message may go forth from Jerusalem to the world as the Hebrew scriptures had always suggested . . .

The universalization of the gospel will embrace not only all ethnic diversity within the Empire but also people up and down the social scale, including both the oppressed and the oppressor. Furthermore, a concern will be shown in both Luke and Acts for the physical as well as the spiritual welfare of humankind, so that the gospel's liberation is not merely to come to all people but is to affect every aspect of their lives. Such a total salvation requires a total response of discipleship. One must be prepared to leave *everything* and follow (Luke 5:11), renounce all (14:33), take up one's cross *daily* (9:23), and put one's hand to the plow and not look back (9:62) – agendas reiterated in Acts 3-6 and elsewhere. The whole gospel must be proclaimed to the whole person in the whole world, for there is one, all-sufficent Savior for all, and therefore all must be for this one.

There is a sense in which, if the main figure in Luke was Jesus, in Acts it is not any human being, but the Holy Spirit, so that some have called this document the Acts of the Holy Spirit. Yet the focus is actually on events, not on persons or personalities, even of God. Clearly Luke intends us to see movement in this story from Jerusalem to Rome, and it is possible that we should see Jerusalem as the center of Jewish Christianity and Rome as the center of Gentile Christianity. The book then develops as the Church did, away from Jewish Christianity to Gentile Christianity and in a sense away from Peter to Paul. Yet Peter and Paul are simply vehicles for God, who speaks and acts in the same way through both men.

Source: *Acts of the Apostles: A Socio-Rhetorical Commentary* (Cambridge: W. B. Eerdmans, 1998), pp. 70–2.

Further reading

Johnson, L. T. (2006), *The Acts of the Apostles*. Collegeville, MN: Liturgical Press.

Fitzmyer, J. (1998), *The Acts of the Apostles*. New York: Doubleday.

Peterson, D. (2009), *The Acts of the Apostles*. Grand Rapids: Eerdmans.

Shillington, V. G. (2007), *An Introduction to the Study of Luke/Acts*. London: T&T Clark.

Chapter 10

References

Campbell, W. S. (2008), *Paul and the Creation of Christian Identity*. London: T&T Clark.

Ehrensperger, K. (2009), *Paul and the Dynamics of Power*, London: T&T Clark.

Horrell, D. (2000), *An Introduction to the Study of Paul*. London: Continuum.

Johnson, L. T. (2010), *The Writings of the New Testament*. Minneapolis, MN: Fortress.

Longnecker, R. N. (1997), *The Impact of Paul's Conversion on His Life, Thought and Ministry*. Cambridge: W. B. Eerdmans.

Maccoby, H. (1986), *The Mythmaker: Paul and the Invention of Christianity*. London: Weidenfeld.

Morton A. Q., McLeman, J. (1966), *Paul: the Man and the Myth*. London: Hodder & Stoughton.

Smith, D. A. (2010), *Revisiting the Empty Tomb: The Early History of Easter*. Minneapolis: Fortress.

Towey, A. M. G. (2010), 'Damascus in Pastoral Ministry' in *The Pastoral Review*, Vol. 5(4) 22–9.

Extracts

1. Stegman on Paul and Christ's saving act.

One of the most distinctive aspects of Paul's theological approach is the priority he puts on the attitude of faith rather than religiosity, trust in God rather than trust in your own good deeds being the key to salvation. To an extent, however, this could be understood to have the strange effect of making human faith the key to salvation. But does this do justice to Paul's argument? By contrast, the leading American scholar, Thomas Stegman, demonstrates that the faith that saves is precisely not a 'work' of human beings but a grace effected by Christ.

> In contrast to the first Adam, Jesus' life was marked by *obedience* to God's will. And whereas the first Adam's disobedience unleashed on all people the enslaving powers of sin and death (Rom 5:12-14), Christ's obedience (Rom 5:19) – an obedience that culminated with offering his life on the cross – has led to the possibility of acquittal and life for all. In fact, Paul insists on the centrality of Jesus' role in the revelation of God's righteousness. Observe that, in 5:18, it is Christ's 'righteous act' of offering his life in obedience to God that has brought about salvation: there is no mention here of the human response of faith.
>
> This point is critically important because reading *pistis Christou* as 'Christ's faithfulness' puts the emphasis on Paul's 'gospel of God' precisely where it belongs, on Christology. Indeed, this emphasis should be obvious from the opening verses of the letter where he describes the gospel of God as 'the gospel concerning his Son, who was descended from David according to the flesh and established as Son of God in power according to the Spirit of holiness' (Rom 1:3-4). Jesus is Messiah and Son of God, the one through whom God has acted to manifest his saving righteousness by his own faithful obedience to God, an 'obedience unto death' (Phil 2:8). And in doing so, he not only revealed God's love for us, he also showed what it means for human beings to live as created in God's image (Gen 1:26-27).
>
> We are now in position to fully set forth what Paul meant by the expression 'out of faith to faith [or for faith].' As we have seen, the phrase 'out of faith' refers to the faithfulness of Christ. Now while it is true that Paul places Jesus at the center of the gospel of God, this gospel is ultimately 'good news' *for us* because God has acted on our behalf for our salvation. The proclamation of what God has done in and through Christ has a goal or end, namely that people respond to it with faith. This is what Paul signifies with the phrase 'to faith' or 'for faith.' Indeed, in Rom 3:22 he makes explicit that God's righteousness has been manifested 'through the faithfulness of Jesus Christ for all those who have faith.'

Source: 'What's in a phrase? A look at two key Pauline concepts' in *The Pastoral Review*, Vol. 4, Issue 5 (2008), 13–14.

2. Esler on Abraham and ethnic identity

Philip Esler, Bruce Malina, Wayne Meeks and many other leading scholars are engaged in what is called 'social-scientific' criticism of the Bible. The premise is that without proper attention to the 'world-view' and contextualized experience of the characters who inhabit the texts under discussion, the unwary reader will be insensitive to many of the nuances of passages that they are considering. Religious and ethnic identity rank among the major concerns of exegetes in this theoretical approach, which, along with notions of more specific group belonging can be seen to explain many of the tensions in given narratives or other scriptural exchanges. Nowhere is this more evident than in the Letter to the Galatians. While many see the 'peak' moment in this letter as Paul's cry in 3:28 that there is no longer Jew nor Greek, male nor female, slave nor free, Esler sees the peak moment as the *next* verse! His reason? Paul's whole argument is not about dissolving differences, but appropriating Abraham as properly belonging to *his* group – the *true* heirs to the covenant promise made to his seed in Genesis 15.

> Having cited Genesis 15:6, (Abraham 'put his faith in God') and prior to any argument in support, he dares in Galatians 3:7 to assert that the 'sons of Abraham' are 'those of faith.' To interpret: Christ-followers are the descendents of Abraham. He is establishing an ingroup identity that embraces Abraham and Christ-followers on the basis that they are both typified by faith. It is the extremely fortunate predication of faith to Abraham in Genesis 15:6 before he was circumcised that allowed Paul to wrest Abraham from the Judeans. Thus, at a stroke, he attaches Abrahamic descent and the high status identity that went with it, to Christ-followers. This categorical way of stating the positions allows, quite remarkably, no room for anyone else to share such status and identity. Paul is not suggesting that there are various ways to manifest Abraham's lineage and that being a Christ-follower is one of them. No, faith in Christ is the only way he will allow. This sentiment, which is extraordinarily anti-Judean to the extent it denies them Abrahamic descent but nicely illustrates how far someone contesting a dominant memory may go, is confirmed in the way Paul proceeds to mount his defense of this proposition . . .
>
> This brings Paul to his magnificent conclusion to this section of the text dealing with Abraham (Galatians 3:26-29). Here he paints an exalted picture of identity-in-Christ. He begins with a statement of the current status and identity of his addressees; they are sons of God through faith in Christ Jesus (v26). Then he moves to the mechanism and process by which they acquired this identity – by baptism: those who have been baptized into Christ have put on Christ (v27). This leads, in turn, in v28, to the great exultation of unity in Christ Jesus (a unity of Judean and Greek, slave and free, male and female), yet this is not some isolated statement, for all the while the argument is pushing on to its summative conclusion: 'If you are of Christ, surely, you are the seed of Abraham, heirs according to the promise' (3:29) . . . This represents the fullest pitch of Paul's mnemonic socialization of this converts. He has contested the memory of Abraham to such a degree as to remove Abrahamic descent entirely as an element in Judean identity and lodge it firmly in among the ranks of the Christ followers of Galatia.

Source: 'Paul's Contestation of Israel's (Ethnic) Memory of Abraham in Galatians 3' in *Biblical Theology Bulletin*, Vol. 36 (2006), 23–34.

Further reading

Campbell, D. A. (2005), *The Quest for Paul's Gospel*. London: T&T Clark.

Dunn, J. D. G. (2003), *The Cambridge Companion to St. Paul*. Cambridge: CUP.

Hayes, M. (ed.) (2009), *In Praise of Paul*. London: St. Paul's Publishing.

Murphy-O'Connor, J. (2004), *Paul: His Story*. Oxford: OUP.

Wright, N. T. (2005), *Paul: Fresh Perspectives*. London: SPCK.

Chapter 11

References

Bauckham, R. (2006), *Jesus and the Eyewitnesses: The Gospels as Eyewitness Testimony*. Grand Rapids, MI: W. B. Eerdmans.

Eusebius ([c.325] 1989), *The History of the Church from Christ to Constantine* (translated by Williamson, G. A) London: Penguin Books.

Hengel, M. (2008), 'The Prologue of the Gospel of John as Gateway to Christological Truth', in Bauckham, R. and Mosser, C. (eds), *The Gospel of John and Christian Theology*. Grand Rapids, MI: W. B. Eerdmans.

Marcus, J. (2009), 'Birkat Ha-Minim Revisited' in *New Testament Studies*, Vol. 55(04), 523–51.

Martyn, J. L. ([1968] 2003), *History and Theology in the Fourth Gospel*. Louisville, KY: WJK.

Extract

1. St Augustine on John

I'm aware that by highlighting the contentious background to the Gospel of John in the main text, I may have partly distracted the reader from the sweeping brilliance of many of its passages. As noted above, Sections 16a-c, St Augustine of Hippo was a giant of a theologian and his words may serve as an antidote. He bore high regard for the beloved disciple (who is symbolized by an eagle) as is evident in the following extract from one of his homilies on the Gospel of John.

> **John the Evangelist was high above the Mountains**
>
> 5: So then, brothers and sisters, John was one of these mountains, and he said, *In the beginning was the Word, and the Word was with God and the Word was God*. This mountain had received peace, and he was contemplating the divinity of the Word. What was this mountain like? How high was it? It had soared above all the peaks of the earth, soared beyond all the plains of the air, soared beyond the dizzy heights of the stars, soared beyond all the choirs and legions of angels. For, unless he soared above and beyond all these created things, he would never reach the one *through whom all things were made* (Jn 1:3). You can only have a sense of all that he surpassed if you notice where he ended up.

Are you asking about heaven and earth? They were made. Are you asking about the things in heaven and on earth? Obviously, even more clearly were they made. Are you asking about spiritual creatures, about angels, archangels, thrones, dominions, powers and princedoms? They too were made. In fact, once the psalm listed all these things, it finished in this way: *He spoke and they were made; he gave the command, and they were created* (Psalm 148:5). If *he spoke and they were made*, then they were made through the Word; but if they were made through the Word, then the only way John's heart could have arrived at what he said, In the beginning was the Word, the Word was with God and the Word was God, was by soaring above all things that were made through the Word. What a mountain this man was, how holy, how high among those mountains which received peace for the people of God so that the hills might receive justice.

Source: Fitzgerald, A. D. et al. (eds), *St Augustine: Homilies on the Gospel of John 1-40* (New York: Augustinian Heritage Institute, 2009), p. 42.

2. Richard Bauckham: John as eyewitness?

In every generation, a scholar produces a book which stops the clocks and causes academics to think again. In *Jesus and the Eyewitnesses*, the British exegete Richard Bauckham has caused a considerable stir in New Testament studies. There has long been a puzzle about the Fourth Gospel insofar as it demonstrates detailed knowledge of the topography of Judea and customary practices known to have been part of socio-religious life at the time of Jesus. Yet, while it carries the kind of details that an eyewitness might have, it is swathed in highly theologized interpretations of events and discourses that are hard to reconcile with the more modest recollections found in the Synoptic tradition. Bauckham manages to square this circle by pointing out that the very claim to be an eyewitness entitles the author of the Fourth Gospel to be more 'interpretative' than those, like Luke, expressly dependent upon the testimony of others. This is in keeping with protocols of Greco-Roman historiography and explains the highly selective nature of John's Gospel.

There is at least one sense in which the Gospel of John resembles Greco-Roman historiography more closely than the Synoptic Gospels do. All scholars, whatever their views of the redactional work of the Synoptic Evangelists and of the historical reliability of the Gospel of John, agree that the latter presents a much more thoroughly and extensively interpreted version of the story of Jesus. Though the writers of the Synoptic Gospels incorporate and fashion their sources into an integrated whole, a biography *(bios)* of Jesus, they remain close to the ways in which the eyewitnesses told their stories and transmitted the sayings of Jesus. They are collections of such stories and sayings, selected, combined, arranged, and adapted, but with only a relatively small degree of freely created interpretative comment and addition. They have preserved the formal character of their sources to a much greater extent than most Greco-Roman historians did. The latter generally assimilated their sources into seamless, comprehensive narratives strongly expressive of their own developed interpretations of the history they related.

Bauckham then points out that John's Gospel is just such a 'developed interpretation of the history' before offering an overall conclusion regarding the historical nature of the four-part 'Good News'.

The eyewitness claim justifies this degree of interpretation for a context in which the direct reports of the eyewitnesses were the most highly valued forms of testimony to Jesus. In the case of the other Gospels it was important that the form of the eyewitness testimonies was preserved in the Gospels. The more reflectively interpretative Gospel of John does not, by contrast, assimilate the eyewitness reports beyond recognition into its own elaboration of the story, but is, as it stands, the way one eyewitness understood what he and others had seen. The author's eyewitness status authorizes the interpretation. Thus, whereas scholars have often supposed that this Gospel could not have been written by an eyewitness because of its high degree of interpretation of the events and the words of Jesus, by contrast with the Synoptics, in fact the high degree of interpretation is appropriate precisely because this is the only one of the canonical Gospels that claims eyewitness authorship.

Conclusion

In all four Gospels, we have the history of Jesus only in the form of testimony, the testimony of involved participants who responded in faith to the disclosure of God in these events. In testimony, fact and interpretation are inextricable; in this testimony, empirical sight and spiritual perception are inseparable. If this history was in fact the disclosure of God, then to have the report of some uncommitted observer would not take us nearer the historical truth but further from it.

Source: *Jesus and the Eyewitnesses: The Gospel as Eyewitness Testimony* (Cambridge: W. B. Eerdmans, 2006), pp. 410–11.

Further reading

Brodie, T. (1997), *The Gospel according to John: a Literary and Theological Commentary.* New York: Oxford University Press.

Edwards, R. (2003), *Discovering John.* London: SPCK.

Keener, C. S. (2003), *The Gospel of John: a Commentary.* Peabody, MA: Hendrickson.

Lincoln, A. (2005), *Gospel according to St. John.* London: Continuum.

Chapter 12

References

Bauckham, R. (2006), *Jesus and the Eyewitnesses: The Gospels as Eyewitness Testimony.* Grand Rapids, MI: W. B. Eerdmans.

Bettenson, H. (ed.) (1963), *Documents of the Christian Church*, (2nd edn.). Oxford: Oxford University Press.

Chesterton, G. K. ([1908] 1996), *Orthodoxy.* London: Hodder & Stoughton.

Crossley, J. G. (2004), *The Date of Mark's Gospel.* London: T&T Clark.

Hurtado, L. (2003), *Lord Jesus Christ: Devotion to Jesus in Earliest Christianity.* Grand Rapids, MI: W. B. Eerdmans.

James M. R. (ed.) (1924), *The Apocryphal New Testament Translation and Notes.* Oxford: Clarendon Press.

Johnson, L. T. (2010), *The Writings of the New Testament.* Minneapolis, MN: Fortress.

Ulrich, E. (1999), *The Dead Sea Scrolls and the Origins of the Bible.* Grand Rapids, MI: W. B Eerdmans

Extract 1

1. Eusebius

Eusebius of Caesarea (263–339) was a bishop of Caesarea in Palestine around the year 314 but was also a biblical scholar of note and a historian. His *Historia Ecclesiastica*, c.325, is a wonderful repository of memories, comments and anecdotes. Despite the fact that he is a man of strong opinions which can cloud some issues, his *History* is an invaluable resource for deriving a picture of those early centuries of Christian thought and action. In the following extract, he comments on the books he regards as 'canonical', that is, belonging to the authentic collection of scriptures that are suitable to be read in Church. Note his reasonings for and against acceptance.

> **The Eusebian Canon**
>
> It will be well, at this point, to classify the New Testament writings already referred to. We must, of course, put first the holy quartet of gospels, followed by the Acts of the Apostles. The next place in the list goes to Paul's epistles, and after them we must recognize the epistle called I John; likewise I Peter. To these may be added, if it is thought proper, the Revelation of John, the arguments about which I shall set out when the time comes. These are classed as Recognized Books. Those that are disputed, yet familiar to most, include the epistles known as James, Jude, and II Peter, and those called II and III John, the work either of the evangelist or of someone else with the same name.
>
> Among Spurious Books must be placed the 'Acts' of Paul, the 'Shepherd', and the 'Revelation of Peter'; also the alleged 'Epistle of Barnabas', and the 'Teaching of the Apostles' [Didache], together with the Revelation of John, if this seems the

right place for it; as I said before, some reject it, others include it among the Recognized Books. Moreover, some have found a place in the list for the 'Gospel of Hebrews', a book which has a special appeal for those Hebrews who have accepted Christ. These would all be classed with the Disputed Books, but I have been obliged to list the latter separately, distinguishing those writings which according to the teaching of the Church are true, genuine, and recognized, from those in a different category, not canonical but disputed, yet familiar to most churchmen; for we must not confuse these with the writings published by heretics under the name of the apostles, as containing either Gospels of Peter, Thomas, Matthias, and several others besides these, or Acts of Andrew, John, and other apostles. To none of these has any churchman of any generation ever seen fit to refer to his writings. Again, nothing could be farther from apostolic usage than the type of phraseology employed, while the ideas and implications of their contents are so irreconcilable with true orthodoxy that they stand revealed as forgeries of heretics. It follows that so far from being classed even among Spurious Books, they must be thrown out as impious and beyond the pale.

Source: Eusebius, *The History of the Church from Christ to Constantine*, translated by G. A. Williamson (New York: Penguin, 1989), pp. 88–9.

2. The acts of Paul: Example of Christian Apocrypha

The Acts of Paul is one of the numerous texts that 'never made it' into the final collection of the New Testament. It is named by Eusebius as one of the major pseudepigraphal and non-canonical books on the apostle Paul, perhaps dated around 185–195 CE and probably composed by a presbyter in Asia Minor (cf. Barnstone, 2005, p. 445). The Acts were first mentioned by Tertullian who found it heretical because it encouraged women to preach and baptize. The Acts were considered orthodox by Hippolytus, but were eventually regarded as heretical when the Manichaeans started using the texts. The author does not show any dependency on the canonical Acts, but uses oral traditions of Paul's missionary work. Note the description of Paul – not a pretty sight, but still angelic. Note too the contrasts of attitude between the guests, the old problem of 'holiness as a competition' comes through in texts like this.

Acts of Paul and Thecla

As Paul went up to Iconium after his flight from Antioch, his travelling companions were Demas and Hermogenes, the coppersmith, who were full of hypocrisy and flattered Paul as if they loved him. But Paul, who had eyes only for the goodness of Christ, did them no evil, but loved them greatly, so that he sought to make sweet to them all the words of the Lord, of the doctrine and of the interpretation of the Gospel, both of the birth and of the resurrection of the Beloved, and he related to them word for word the great acts of Christ as they had been revealed to him.

And a man named Onesiphorus, who had heard that Paul was come to Iconium, went out with his children, Simmias and Zeno, and his wife, Lectra, to meet Paul that he might receive him to his house. Titus had told him what Paul looked like for hitherto he had not seen him in the flesh, but only in the spirit. And he went along the royal road which leads to Lystra, and stood there waiting for him, and looked, at all who came, according to Titus' description. And he saw Paul coming, a man small of stature, with a bald head and crooked legs, in a good state of body, with eyebrows meeting and nose somewhat hooked, full of friendliness; for now he appeared like a man, and now he had the face of an angel.

And when Paul saw Onesiphorus he smiled and Onesiphorus said: 'Greeting, servant of the blessed God!' And he replied: 'Grace be with you and your house!' But Demas and Hermogenes grew jealous, and went even further in their hypcocrisy so that Demas said: 'are we then not servants of the Blessed, that you did not greet us thus?' And Onesiphorus said: 'I do not see in you any fruit of righteousness; but if you are anything, come also into my house and rest yourselves!' And when Paul entered into the house of Onesiphorus there was great joy, and bowing of knees and breaking of bread, and the word of God concerning continence and resurrection, as Paul said: 'Blessed are the pure in heart, for they shall see God. Blessed are they who have kept the flesh pure, they shall become a temple of God. Blessed are the continent, for to them will God speak.'

Source: *The Other Bible: Jewish Pseudepigrapha, Christian Apocrypha, Gnostic Scriptures, Kabbalah, Dead Sea Scrolls,* edited by W. Barnstone (New York: Harper San Francisco, 2005), pp. 447–8.

Further reading

Jenson, R. (2010), *Canon and Creed.* Louisville, KY: Westminster John Knox.

Lienhard, J. T. (1995), *The Bible, the Church and Authority.* Collegeville, MN: Michael Glazier.

McDonald, L. M. (2011), *The Origin of the Bible: A Guide for the Perplexed.* London: T&T Clark.

Metzger, B. (1987), *The Canon of the New Testament: Its Origin, Development and Significance.* Oxford: Oxford University Press.

Chapter 13

References

Bettenson, H. & C. Maunder (eds.) (2011), *Documents of the Christian Church.* Oxford: OUP.

Jenson, R. (2010), *Canon and Creed.* Louisville, KY: Westminster John Knox.

Kelly, J. N. D. (1972), *Early Christian Creeds.* London: Longman.

Neuner, J., Dupuis, J. (1983), *The Christian Faith in the Doctrinal Documents of the Catholic Church.* London: Collins Liturgical Publications.

O'Collins, G. (1999), *The Tripersonal God.* New Jersey: Paulist Press.

Roberts, A. & J. Donaldson (eds) (2007), *The Writings of Justin Martyr*. Berkeley: Apocryphile Press.

Skarsuane, O. (2008), 'From the Jewish Messiah to the Creeds of the Church,' *Evangelical Review of Theology*, 32(3), 224–37.

Stevenson, J. (1987), *A New Eusebius: Documents Illustrating the History of the Church to AD 337*. London: SPCK.

Extracts

1. Didache: Thomas O'Loughlin

The *Didache* is the better known title of the document which describes itself as *The Teaching of the Lord to the Gentiles through the Twelve Apostles*. Discovered as recently as 1873 in a monastery in Constantinople, it caused great excitement among scholars of Christian antiquity because it gave an insight into Church order from an early period of its development. Thomas O'Loughlin, whose translation is used below, situates the text around the time of the Gospel formation – perhaps as early as 50 CE or maybe nearer 80 CE. The selection of verses here give a glimpse of the pattern of worship expected of an early community and the sense of messianic expectation that was pulsing through the *ekklesia* – 'the called out ones'. At the heart of this early community of Jesus followers is their adherence to the *Kerygma* preached by the apostles and their successors and in this sense, it reflects the kind of whirly world of faith that Paul and the other New Testament authors were writing in.

14.1 On the day which is the Day of the Lord gather together for the breaking of the loaf and giving thanks. However, you should first confess your sins so that your sacrifice may be a pure one;

14.2 and do not anyone who is having a dispute with a neighbour, join until they are reconciled so that your sacrifice may not be impure.

15.1 Select for yourselves bishops and deacons: men who are worthy of the Lord, humble, not greedy for money, honest, and well tested, because these too carry out for you the service of the prophets and teachers.

16.1 Watch over your lives. You must not let your lamps go out, nor should you let your loins be ungirded, rather you should be ready because you do not know the hour at which our Lord is coming.

16.2 Gather together frequently and seek those things that are good for your souls. Otherwise what use will having faith over all the time of your life be to you, if at the end of time you are not made perfect.

16.3 For in the last days there are going to be many false prophets and those who would corrupt you, then the sheep will turn into wolves and love will turn into hate.

16.4 Then when lawlessness is increasing, people will hate and persecute and be treacherous with one another. Then, indeed, the Deceiver of this world will appear as if a son of God and will do signs and wonders and the earth will be delivered into his hands and he will commit lawless acts such as have never been seen since the world began.

16.5 Then all people will be brought through the trial of fire. Then many will fall away and perish; but those who stand firm in their faith will be saved by the Cursed One himself.

16.6 And then, the signs of the truth will appear:

The first sign will be the heavens opening;

Then [second,] the sound of the trumpet;

And third, the resurrection of the dead -

16.7 but not of everyone, but as it has been said: 'the Lord will come and all his saints with him.'

16.8 Then the world will see the Lord coming upon the clouds of heaven.

Source: *The Didache: A window on the earliest Christians* (Grand Rapids, MI: Baker Academic, 2010), pp. 170–1.

2. The Apostolic Tradition of Hippolytus third-century CE?

In a similar vein to the *Didache* but perhaps a century or three later, the *Apostolic Tradition of Hippolytus* gives us a glimpse at early liturgical life. It is disputed as to whether it is an Egyptian or a Roman church order and it is given a variety of datings. For our purposes, the importance is that the document shows the baptismal context of faith confession. In preparation for the ceremony, the candidates gather at cockcrow, disrobe and enter the water. The bishop gives thanks over the oil of the sacrament and a presbyter then asks a series of questions which mirror creedal formulae.

21 At the hour set for the baptism the bishop shall give thanks over oil and put it into a vessel: this is called the "oil of thanksgiving". And he shall take other oil and exorcise it: this is called "the oil of exorcism". A deacon shall bring the oil of exorcism, and shall stand at the presbyter's left hand; and another deacon shall take the oil of thanksgiving, and shall stand at the presbyter's right hand. Then the presbyter, taking hold of each of those about to be baptized, shall command him to renounce, saying:

I renounce thee, Satan, and all thy servants and all thy works.

And when he has renounced all these, the presbyter shall anoint him with the oil of exorcism, saying:

Let all spirits depart far from thee.

Then, after these things, let him give him over to the presbyter who baptizes, and let the candidates stand in the water, naked, a deacon going with them likewise. And when he who is being baptized goes down into the water, he who baptizes him, putting his hand on him, shall say thus:

Dost thou believe in God, the Father Almighty ?

And he who is being baptized shall say:

I believe.

Then holding his hand placed on his head, he shall baptize him once. And then he shall say:

Dost thou believe in Christ Jesus, the Son of God, who was born by the Holy Ghost of the Virgin Mary, and was crucified under Pontius Pilate, and was dead and buried, and rose again the third day, alive from the dead, and ascended into heaven, and sat at the right hand of the Father, and will come to judge the quick and the dead? And when he says:

I believe,

He is baptized again. And again he shall say:

Dost thou believe in the Holy Ghost; in the holy church, and the resurrection of the flesh?

He who is being baptized shall say accordingly:

I believe,

And so he is baptized a third time.

And afterward, when he has come up, he is anointed by the presbyter with the oil of thanksgiving, the presbyter saying:

I anoint thee with holy oil in the name of Jesus Christ.

And so, each one, after drying himself, is immediately clothed and then is brought into church.

Source: *The Apostolic Tradition of Hippolytus,* translated by B. S. Easton (Cambridge: Cambridge University Press, 1934), pp. 45–7.

Further reading

Ashwin-Siejkowski, P. (2010), *Early Christian Doctrines and the Creeds.* London: SCM.

Campbell, T. (2009), *The Gospel in Christian Traditions.* Oxford: Oxford University Press.

Johnson, L. T. (2003), *The Creed: What Christians Believe and Why It Matters?* New York: Doubleday.

Lash, N. (2003), *Believing Three Ways in One God: A Reading of the Apostles' Creed.* London: SCM.

Milavec, A. (2004), *The Didache: Faith, Hope and Life of the Earliest Christian Communities, 50-70 CE.* New York: Newman Press.

Chapter 14

References

Arius 'Letter to Alexander'and'Thalia' in Stevenson, J. (1987), *A New Eusebius: Documents Illustrating the History of the Church to AD 337.* London: SPCK.

Bettenson, H. (1982), *The Later Christian Fathers: A Selection of the Writings of the Fathers from St. Cyril of Jerusalem to St Leo the Great.* London: Oxford University Press.

Neuner, J., Dupuis, J. (1983), *The Christian Faith in the Doctrinal Documents of the Catholic Church.* London: Collins Liturgical Publications.

O'Collins, G. (1999), *The Tripersonal God.* New Jersey: Paulist Press.

Stevenson, J. (1987), *A New Eusebius: Documents Illustrating the History of the Church to AD 337*. London: SPCK.

Sparks, J. (ed.) (1978), *The Apostolic Fathers*. Nashville, TN: Thomas Nelson.

Tanner, N. (2011), *A Short History of the Catholic Church*. London: Burns & Oates.

Velimirovich, Nikolai (2008), *The Prologue from Ohrid: Lives of Saints* (2nd edn). Alhambra: Serbian Orthodox Diocese of Western America.

Extracts

It is often said that the Holy Spirit is the 'forgotten member' of the Trinity. The 56-year gap between the Council of Nicaea and that of Constantinople was a period dominated theologically by the fall-out from the Arian heresy, but it also was a period where *pneumatology* – the 'God-logic' of the Holy Spirit was a matter for debate. Here, one of the Spirit's titles, 'giver of life', is examined by a modern writer:

1. Thomas Smail on the Holy Spirit

The comprehensive summary of the work of the Spirit offered by the creed is captured in the single Greek word *zōopoioun,* usually rendered in English as 'giver of life.' It would be in line with the Trinitarian understanding that we have been outlining to understand the Spirit's characteristic function in giving life as being its communicator rather than it source. Life has its source in the Father, it becomes incarnate in the Son, and it is imparted to us in the Spirit.

It is also instructive that the word used for life here, *zōē*, is used in the Johannine tradition to describe in a forward-looking way the eschatological new life of the age to come. To describe the created life of the present age, John prefers *bios*. Whether a similar distinction was being drawn by the compilers of the creed we have no way of knowing, but for the New Testament witness as a whole, the Spirit is viewed eschatologically rather than protologically. The involvement of the Trinity in the original creation is viewed christologically rather than pneumatologically, in terms of the Logos rather than in terms of the Spirit. The brooding of the Spirit over unformed chaos and God's breathing of his life into Adam in Genesis are certainly not denied, but the defining context of the work of the Spirit is the inbreaking of the first fruits and first instalment of the life of the age to come that is inaugurated at Pentecost as a result of the finished work of Christ. In the New Testament the Spirit is the Spirit of the future rather than the Spirit of the past, and although the God of the end is also the God of the beginning, in the Spirit we are people whose concentration is directed far less to where we came from than to where we are going.

On the uncontroversial periphery of its confession the creed proclaims the Holy Spirit as the divine agent through whom God incorporates us into the life of the age to come, which the Father has opened to us through the incarnation, death and resurrection of the Son.

Source: *Nicene Christianity: The Future for a New Ecumenism* ([edited by C. Seitz], Grand Rapids, MI: Brazos, 1999), p. 153.

2. Jürgen Moltmann on the Spirit and friendship

It is one thing for a Council to get together and decide a doctrine, but what difference does it make? According to the Gospels, the demons who recognized Jesus were spot on with their theological understanding, even if they weren't too keen on him being around. By defining God as Triune, the Councils of Nicaea and Constantinople were making bold theological moves – but how can they be understood in normal language and experience? Moltmann (b.1926) is convinced that the Trinity is key to understanding the riddle of the Kingdom, that participation in the life of God is at the heart of the mystery. Towards the end of his groundbreaking *Trinity and the Kingdom of God*, he outlines the specific relational efficacies of Father [creatures to servants], Son [servants to children] and Spirit [children to friends] . . .

> In the kingdom of the Spirit the sovereign freedom towards the world of God's servants, and the intimate freedom of his children are both preserved; but again the inward quality of these things is changed. The servants of the Lord and the children of the Father become God's friends; 'No longer do I call you servants, for the servant does not know what his master is doing; but I have called you friends, for all that I have heard from my Father I have made known to you' (John 15:15). By virtue of the indwelling of the Holy Spirit, people enter into this new 'direct' relationship with God. The freedom of God's friends does not evolve out of the freedom of God's children. It only becomes possible when people know themselves in God and God in them. That is the light of the Holy Spirit.
>
> Friendship with God finds its pre-eminent expression in prayer. In obeying God's command a person feels himself to be the Lord's servant. In faith in the gospel he sees himself as being the child of his heavenly Father. As God's friend he talks to God in prayer, and his prayer becomes a conversation with his heavenly friend. Friendship with God means the assurance that his prayer is heard. Of course 'praying' and hearing are still expressions belonging to the language of servants and children. In friendship the distance enjoined by sovereignty ceases to exist. The friend knows that his friend is listening to him. God 'can be conversed with'. God listens to his friends. By virtue of friendship with God in the Spirit, we have the chance to influence God and participate in his rule. God does not want the humility of servants or the gratitude of children forever. He wants the boldness and kindness of friends who want to share his rule with him. Kant said that friendship combines affection with respect. God makes men and women his friends by inclining affectionately towards them and by listening to them . . . Friendship is 'the concrete concept of freedom.'

Source: *The Trinity and the Kingdom of God: The Doctrine of God*, translated by M. Kohl (London: SCM, 1981), pp. 220–1.

Further reading

Bellito, C. (2002), *The Councils of the Church.* Mahwah: Paulist.

Davis, L. D. (1983), *The First Seven Councils: 325-787.* Collegeville, MN: Liturgical Press.

Tanner, N. (2000), *The Councils of the Church: A Short History.* New York: Crossroad.

Young, F., Teal, A. (2010), *From Nicea to Chalcedon: A Guide to the Literature and its Background* (revised edn). Grand Rapids, MI: Baker Academic.

Chapter 15

References

Arnold, E. (1972), *The Early Christians After the Death of the Apostles.* New York: Plough Publishing House.

Athanasius. ([c.360] 1980), *The Life of Anthony and the Letter to Marcellinus,* translation and introduction by R. C. Gregg, preface by W. A. Clebsch. New York: Paulist Press.

Bettenson, H. & C. Maunder (eds.) (2011), *Documents of the Christian Church.* Oxford: OUP.

Brown, R. (1970), *Priest and Bishop: Biblical Reflections.* London: Geoffrey Chapman.

Clarkson, J. F. (ed.) (1960), *The Church Teaches: Documents of the Church in English Translation.* St Louis: Herder.

Eusebius. ([c.325] 1989), *The History of the Church.* London: Penguin Books.

Esler, P. (2011), 'Judean Ethnic Identity and the Purpose of Hebrews' in McGowan, A. and Richards, K. H. (eds), *Method and Meaning: Essays on New Testament Interpretation in Honour of Harold W. Attridge.* Atlanta, GA: Society of Biblical Literature.

Gregory the Great ([c.600] 1974), *Homilies on Ezekiel,* this translation in *The Divine Office III.* Glasgow: Collins, p. 233*.

Lieu, J. M. (2002), *Neither Jew Nor Greek?* London: T&T Clark.

Sparks, J. (1978), *The Apostolic Fathers.* Nashville, TN: Thomas Nelson Publishers.

Stark, R. (1996), *The Rise of Christianity.* New Jersey: Princeton University Press.

Extracts

1. Nice one Cyril?

In tracing the development of the early *Kerygma* into the later creeds the role of the Roman Emperor, beginning from Constantine, was crucial. The following excerpt is a letter by Cyril of Jerusalem to the Emperor Constantius in which he describes a miracle that occurred in the city whereby a vast luminous body appeared in the form of a cross. It may be recalled that Constantine had seen a vision of the Cross 'by which he would conquer'. Cyril may well be calling this to mind, but in any case, is he just being a bit *too* gushing? What do you think?

A Cross in the Heavens (351)

3: For, in the days of Constantine your father, most dear to God and of blessed memory, there was discovered the wood of the cross fraught with salvation, because the divine grace that gave piety to the pious seeker vouchsafed the finding of the buried holy places. But in your time, your majesty, most religious of Emperors, victorious through a piety towards God greater even than that which you inherited, are seen wonderful works, not from the earth any more, but from the heavens. The trophy of the victory over death of our Lord and Saviour Jesus Christ, the only begotten Son of God, I mean the blessed cross, has been seen at Jerusalem blazing with refulgent light!

4: For in these very days of the holy feast of Pentecost, on the seventh of May, about the third hour a gigantic cross formed of light appeared in the sky above holy Golgotha stretching out as far as the holy Mount of Olives. It was not seen by just one or two, but was most clearly displayed before the whole population of the city. Nor did it, as one might have supposed, pass away quickly like something imagined, but was visible to sight above the earth for some hours, while it sparked with a light above the sun's rays. Of a surety, it would have been overcome and hidden by them had it not exhibited to those who saw it a brilliance more powerful than the sun, so that the whole population of the city made a concerted rush into the Martyry, seized by a fear that mingled with joy at the heavenly vision. They poured in, young and old, men and women of every age, even to maidens hitherto kept in the seclusion of their homes, local folk and strangers together, not only Christians but pagans from elsewhere sojourning in Jerusalem; all of them as with one mouth raised a hymn of praise to Christ Jesus our Lord, the only-begotten Son of God, the worker of wonders. For they recognized in fact and by experience that the most religious creed of Christians is *not with enticing words of wisdom, but in demonstration of the Spirit and power*, not merely preached by men, but having witness borne to it by God from the heavens.

Source: *Creeds, Councils and Controversies: Documents illustrating the History of the Church, AD 337-461* (revised edition), J. L. Stevenson & W. H. C. Frend (London: SPCK, 1989), pp. 28–9.

2. Leonardo Boff on Constantine

Living with the sharp end of inequality during the 1980s, the South American theologian, Leonardo Boff never minced words with regard to the duties of the Church to the poor. This extract from his *Church, Charism and Power,* notes the problems arising from the conversion of Constantine which turned the alternative nature of the Christian vision into the official ideology of the Roman Empire, with detrimental effects even to the present.

This situation changed radically with the conversion of Constantine. From a *religio illicita* (illicit religion), Christianity became both the official religion and the sacred ideology of the empire. This was an opportunity for the church to cease being a ghetto church and become a true *ecclesia universalis*. The Church thus embarked upon its great cultural and political adventure. It took on great power, with all of the risks that such power implies. Would it be able to use the historical *kairos* in order to exercise power in the gospel sense, as opposed to the power of the pagans, giving rise to another form of human sharing, another humanism, another meaningful activity?

Everything happened too fast. The Church, in spite of persecutions, was not prepared to face the challenges of power from an evangelical perspective. It did not abolish the existing order. Rather, it assumed it and adapted itself to that order. It offered the empire an ideology that supported the existing order and even blessed the pagan cosmos. One scholar has concluded his study of the origin of Christianity's rule as the religion of the state by remarking that 'the religion that marked the West was not properly the Christian message.' When the leaders of the empire joined the Church, a paganization of Christianity took place, and not a christianization of paganism. The Church, which until A.D. 312 was more of a movement than an institution, became an heir of the empire's institutions: law, organization by diocese and parish, bureaucratic centralization, positions, and titles. The Church-institution accepted political realities and assumed inexorable uniformity. It began on a path of power that continues today and that we must hasten to end.

Source: *Church, Charism and Power: Liberation Theology and the Institutional Church* (London: SCM, 1985), pp. 50–1.

Further readings

Chadwick, O. (1998), *A History of Christianity*. Macmillan: St Martin's Press.

Gonzalez, J. L. (2010), *The Story of Christianity: The Early Church to the Dawn of the Reformation* (revised edn). New York: HarperCollins.

MacCulloch, D. (2009), *A History of Christianity*. London: Allen Lane.

Mursell, G. (ed.) (2001), *The Story of Christian Spirituality: Two Thousand Years from East to West*. Oxford: Lion.

Tanner, N. (2011), *A Short History of the Catholic Church*. London: Continuum.

Chapter 16

References

Anselm ([c.1098] 1974), 'Cur Deus Homo' in *Basic Writings* (translated by S. N. Deane). La Salle: Open Court, pp. 177–288.

Aristotle ([c.350BCE] 2001), 'Metaphysics' in *The Basic Works of Aristotle* (edited and translated by R. McKeon). New York: The Modern Library.

Augustine ([c.397] 1984), *The Confessions of Saint Augustine* (translated by F. J. Sheed). London: Sheed and Ward.

Augustine ([c.428] 2003), *City of God* (translated by H. Bettenson). London: Penguin Books.

Aquinas ([c.1274] 1947), *Summa Theologica* (translated by the Fathers of the English Dominican Province). New York: Benziger Bros.

Cross, R. (1999), *Duns Scotus*. Oxford: Oxford University Press, pp. 127–8.

Horan, D. P. (2011), 'How Original was Scotus on the Incarnation?' in *The Heythrop Journal*, Vol. 52, 374–91.

Mulholland, S. (2011), *A Gasp of Love. Duns Scotus. Franciscan Theologian and Mystic.* Canterbury: FISC Press.

Russell, B. ([1946] 1984), *History of Western Philosophy*. London: Routledge.

Stevenson, J., Frend, W. H. C. (1989), *Creeds, Councils and Controversies: Documents Illustrating the History of the Church AD 337-461* (revised edn). London: SPCK.

Weisheipl, J. A. (1983), *Friar Thomas d'Aquino: His life, thought and Work*. New York: Doubleday.

Extracts

This chapter has looked at the theological contribution of the three As (Augustine, Anselm and Aquinas). Since the first named was supremely influential, here his legacy is further examined.

1. St Augustine on Philosophy and Theology

In this extract from St Augustine's *De Doctrina Christiana* (On Christian Doctrine), written around 397, Augustine tackles a hitherto hotly debated question of the relationship between Christian Theology and Philosophy. He argues in much the same way Thomas Aquinas would have utilized Aristotle, that there is no reason why one should not extract all that is good from pagan thinking and put it at the service of true religion, no doubt contributing to the medieval idea that Philosophy is the 'handmaid' of Theology.

> If those who are called philosophers, particularly the Platonists, have said anything which is true and consistent with our faith, we must not reject it, but claim it for our own use, in the knowledge that they possess it unlawfully. The Egyptians possessed idols and heavy burdens, which the children of Israel hated and from which they fled; however, they also possessed vessels of gold and silver and clothes which our forebears, in leaving Egypt, took for themselves in secret, intending to use them in a better manner (Ex 3:21-22; 12:35-36) . . . . In the same way, pagan learning is not entirely made up of false teachings and superstitions . . . . It contains also some excellent teachings, well suited to be used by truth, and excellent moral values. Indeed, some truths are even found among them which relate to the worship of the one God. Now these are, so to speak, their gold and silver, which they did not invent themselves, but which they dug out of the mines of the providence of God, which are scattered throughout the world, yet which are improperly and unlawfully prostituted to the worship of demons. The Christian, therefore, can separate these truths from their unfortunate associations, take

them away, and put them to their proper use for the proclamation of the Gospel . . . . What else have many good and faithful people from amongst us done? Look at the wealth of gold and silver and clothes which Cyprian – that eloquent teacher and blessed martyr – brought with him when he left Egypt! And think of all that Lactantius brought with him, not to mention Marius Victorinus, Optatus and Hilary of Poitiers, and others who are still living! And look at how much the Greeks have borrowed! And before all of these, we find that Moses, that most faithful servant of God, had done the same thing: after all, it is written of him that 'he was learned in all the wisdom of the Egyptians' (Acts 7:22).

Source: *The Christian Theology Reader*, edited by A. E. McGrath (Oxford: Blackwell, 2001), p. 9.

2. John Hick: Augustine on evil

Although the problem of evil is addressed in the main text (cf. Section 20d), it is perhaps useful to note yet another hugely influential aspect of Augustine's thought. The idea that evil is an absence of good is not an immediately apparent notion, but as John Hick explains, by combining it with the tradition of a preternatural angelic fall, Augustine manages to maintain the idea that Creation is good, but that sin has brought disorder to proceedings.

The main traditional Christian response to the problem of evil was formulated by St Augustine (354–430 A.D.) and has constituted the majority report of the Christian mind through the centuries, although it has been much criticized in recent times. It includes both philosophical and theological strands. The main philosophical position is the idea of the negative or privative nature of evil. Augustine holds firmly to the Hebrew-Christian conviction that the universe is *good* - that is to say, it is the creation of a good God for a good purpose. There are, according to Augustine, higher and lower, greater and lesser goods in immense abundance and variety; however, everything that has being is good in its own way and degree, except insofar as it has become spoiled or corrupted. Evil - whether it be an evil will, an instance of pain, or some disorder or decay in nature - has therefore not been set there by God but represents the going wrong of something that is inherently good. Augustine points to blindness as an example. Blindness is not a 'thing.' The only thing involved is the eye, which is in itself good; the evil of blindness consists of the lack of a proper functioning of the eye. Generalizing the principle, Augustine holds that evil always consists of malfunctioning something that is in itself is good.

As it originally came forth from the hand of God, then, the universe was a perfect harmony expressing the creative divine intention. It was a graded hierarchy of higher and lower forms of being, each good in its own place. How, then, did evil come about? It came about initially in those levels of the universe that involve free will: the free will of the angels and of human beings. Some of the angels turned from the supreme Good, which is God, to lesser goods, thereby rebelling against their creator; they in turn tempted the first man and woman to fall. This fall of angelic and human beings was the origin of moral evil or sin . . . Thus Augustine could say, 'All evil is either sin or the punishment for sin.' (*De Genesi Ad Litteram, Imperfectus liber, 1.3.*)

Source: 'The Augustinian Theodicy' in *Philosophy of Religion,* 4th edn (New Jersey: Prentice-Hall, 1990), pp. 41–2.

Further reading

It would probably be good for the soul to read a biography of any of these characters and if you've never tried Augustine's autobiography, *The Confessions,* it is definitely worth a go. Meanwhile, here are three good reads.

Chesterton, G. K. ([1933] 2009), *St. Thomas Aquinas.* New York: Dover.

O'Donnell, J. (2005), *Augustine: A New Biography.* New York: HarperCollins.

Southern, R. W. (1990), *Anselm: A Portrait in a Landscape.* Cambridge: Cambridge University Press.

Chapter 17

References

Aquinas ([1264] 2003), 'Adoro te devote' (translated by G. Manley-Hopkins) in *Laudate.* Brandon: Decani.

— ([1274] 1947), *Summa Theologica* (translated by the Fathers of the English Dominican Province). New York: Benziger Bros.

Fatula, M. A. (1993), *Thomas Aquinas: Preacher and Friend.* Collegeville, MN: Liturgical Press.

Hippolytus ([c.250?] 1962), *The Apostolic Tradition* (translated with introduction and notes by Burton Scott Easton). Cambridge: Cambridge University Press.

Macy, G. (1992), *The Banquet's Wisdom: A Short History of the Theologies of the Lord's Supper.* New Jersey: Paulist Press.

Lombard, P. ([c.1150] 2006-10) *The Sentences I-IV* (translated by Giulio Silano) Toronto: PIMS

Rosemann, P. (2004), *Peter Lombard.* Oxford: Oxford University Press.

Towey, A. M. G. (1995), *Amicitia as the Philosophical Foundation and the Principal Analogy of the Eucharistic Theology of Thomas Aquinas.* Rome: PUG.

Extracts 1

1. Calvin on Sacraments

The main text places the sacramental section before the events of the Reformation, for the simple expedient that it is easier to discuss them in an evolutionary way. Part of the 'theo-logic' of the 'Seven Sacraments' entailed a belief both that they were *instituted by Christ* and that *Church Tradition* supported the septiform nature. Calvin was not impressed.

> **That the sacraments are seven in number was unknown in the ancient church**
>
> If they would like to press us with the authority of the ancient church, I say that they are deceiving. For nowhere among ecclesiastical writers is this number 'seven' found, and it is uncertain at what time it first crept in. I indeed admit that they are sometimes quite free in their use of the word 'sacrament'; but what do they mean by it? They mean all ceremonies and outward rites, and all exercises of piety. But when they speak of those signs which ought to be testimonies of divine grace toward us, they are content with these two. Baptism and the Eucharist.
>
> Lest anyone think I am falsely claiming this, I shall refer here to a few testimonies of Augustine. He says to Januarius: 'First, I want you to grasp what is the chief point of this discussion, that our Lord Christ (as he himself says in the gospel) has laid upon us a gentle yoke and a light burden [Matt. 11:29-30]. Accordingly, he has bound together the society of the new people by sacraments very few in number, very easy to observe, very excellent in meaning. Such are baptism, consecrated with the name of the Trinity, and the communion of the Lord's body and blood, and any other that is approved in the canonical Scriptures' Again, he says in *On Christian Doctrine:* 'Since the Lord's resurrection, the Lord himself and the teaching of the apostles have authorized some few signs instead of many, ones very easy to perform, most exalted in meaning, most chaste in observance. Such are baptism and the celebration of the Lord's body and blood.' Why does he make no mention of this sacred number 'seven'? Is it likely that he would have omitted it if it had then been established in the church, especially since he is otherwise more bent on observing numbers than is necessary? Indeed, when he names Baptism and Supper, and says nothing of the rest, is he not sufficiently implying that these two mysteries excel in singular dignity, and the other ceremonies sink to a lower place? Therefore, I say that these sacramentary doctors are destitute not only of the Lord's Word but also of the agreement of the ancient church, however greatly they boast of this pretense.

Source: *Institutes of the Christian Religion,* edited by J. T. McNeill, translated by F. L. Battles (Philadelphia, PA: Westminster Press, 1973), Vol. II, pp. 1450–1.

2. John Zizioulas – Ecclesial personhood – substructure of sacrament

From the calmer ecclesial seas of the twentieth century, it may be helpful to hear a view from the East. John Zizioulas (b.1931) is the Orthodox Metropolitan of Pergamon. A noted academic, his 'breakthrough' work was *Being as Communion,* in 1985, a study of personhood understood through the lens of Church. Taking seriously the New Testament theologizing of believers into one Body of Christ, Zizioulas challenges Western identity instincts – 'I' will join 'that' Church. Instead, Zizioulas notes the priority of 'ecclesial being' which constitutes the believer in the image of God.

> The Church is not simply an institution. She is a 'mode of existence', *a way of being*. The mystery of the Church, even in its institutional dimension, is deeply bound to the being of man, to the being of the world and to the very being of God. In virtue of this bond, so characteristic of patristic thought, ecclesiology assumes a marked importance, not only for all aspects of theology, but also for the existential needs of man in every age.
>
> In the first place, ecclesial being is bound to the very being of God. From the fact that a human being is a member of the Church, he becomes an 'image of God,' he exists as God Himself exists, he takes on God's 'way of being.' This way of being is not a moral attainment, something that man *accomplishes*. It is a way of *relationship* with the world, with other people and with God, an event of *communion*, and that is why it cannot be realized as the achievement of an *individual*, but only as an *ecclesial* fact.
>
> However, for the Church to present this way of existence, she must herself be an image of the way in which God exists. Her entire structure, her ministries etc. must express this way of existence. And that means above all else, that the Church must have a right faith, a correct vision with respect to the being of God. Orthodoxy concerning the being of God is not a luxury for the Church and for man: it is an existential necessity . . .
>
> The *ecclesial* experience of the Fathers played a decisive role in breaking ontological monism and avoiding the gnostic 'gulf' between God and the world. The fact that neither the apologists, such as Justin Martyr, nor the Alexandrian catechetical theologians, such as the celebrated Clement and Origen, could completely avoid the trap of the ontological monism of Greek thought is not accidental: they were above all 'doctors,' academic theologians interested principally in Christianity as 'revelation.' By contrast, the bishops of this period, pastoral theologians such as St Ignatius of Antioch and above all St Irenaeus and later St Athanasius, approached the being of God through the experience of the ecclesial community, of *ecclesial being*. This experience revealed something very important: the being of God could be known only through personal relationships and personal love. Being means life, and life means *communion*.

Source: *Being as Communion* (London: Darton, Longman & Todd, 1985), pp. 15–17.

Further reading

Kelly, L. (1998), *Sacraments Revisited.* London: Darton, Longman & Todd.

Mcquarrie, J. (1997), *A Guide to the Sacraments.* London: SCM.

Schmemann, A. (1995), *For the Life of the World: Sacraments and Orthodoxy.* Crestwood, NY: St. Vladimir's Seminary Press.

Thompson, R. (2006), *The Sacraments.* London: SCM.

Thurian, M. (1986–88), *Churches Respond to BEM*, Vols. I-VI. Geneva: World Council of Churches.

World Council of Churches (1982), *Baptism, Eucharist, Ministry*. Geneva: World Council of Churches.

Chapter 18

References

Caraman, P. (1990), *Ignatius Loyola*. London: Collins.

Calvin, J. (1973), *The Institutes of the Christian Religion*. Philadelphia, PA: Westminster Press.

Johnson, M. D. (2005), *The Evolution of Christianity: Twelve Crises that Shaped the Church*. London: Continuum.

Luther, M. ([1517] 1957), 'The Ninety-Five Theses' in *Luther's Works*, Vol. 31. St. Louis: Concordia.

—. ([1520] 1966), 'Address to the Christian Nobility of the German People' in *Luther's Works*, Vol. 44. Philadelphia: Fortress.

—. (1520] 1959), 'The Babylonian Captivity of the Church' in *Luther's Works*, Vol. 36. Philadelphia: Fortress.

—. ([1520] 1957), 'On Christian Liberty' in *Luther's Works*, Vol. 31. St. Louis: Concordia.

Extracts

1. Luther and Zwingli on the edge

Religious feelings were running high throughout the first decades if not the first centuries following the events in Wittenberg. In the exchange below, Luther and Zwingli are attempting a consensus regarding the Eucharist. The kind of passion that Luther and Zwingli demonstrate gives some sense of the profundity of what was/is at stake around the 'table of the Lord' in a straight talking exchange reminiscent of St Paul (check Phil 3:8 in the Greek). Not for the faint-hearted, if you prefer syrup in your theological discourse, give this one a miss.

> *Luther*
> Your argument boils down to this: because there is a spiritual meal there is no need for a physical one. My answer is that we aren't denying the spiritual meal, in fact we insist that it is necessary. But this doesn't mean that as a direct result the physical meal is useless or unnecessary. I don't ask whether it is necessary or not, that isn't why we're here. It is written, 'Take, eat, this is my body'. Because of this one has to obey and believe no matter what the cost. One has to do this! One has to do this! Without this I could not believe in Christ! He gives Himself to us in many ways; in preaching, in baptism, in consoling our brethren, in the sacrament. Over and over again Christ's body is eaten just as He ordered us to do. If He were to order us to eat shit I would do it and be convinced that it was good for me. Servants don't sit around questioning their lord's commands. You just have to close your eyes . . .

Zwingli

You yourself admit that it is the spiritual meal which is worthwhile. Since we agree on this, the most important point, I beg you for Christ's love not to label someone a heretic for these [other] differences. The [Church] fathers disagreed without condemning one other . . . You mentioned taking the Bible literally. Some of that I can agree with but other bits I reject because they were completely silly, for example: 'If God told us to eat shit'. What God tells us to do is for our good. God is truth and light. He doesn't lead us into darkness. Thus he doesn't mean 'This is my body', literally, actually, physically because that contradicts the Bible. Satan's words are hard to understand, not Christ's. That isn't how God works. The soul is spiritual, the soul doesn't eat flesh. The spirit eats spirit.

Don't be offended by what I've said. I want your friendship, not enmity. I disagree with you willingly Doctor Luther, and with you Master Philip.

Luther

Out of respect to God and our gracious lord and prince I will keep control of myself. The past is the past. Let's look forward! We may not be able to agree on everything but we can still have fellowship.

Source: *Documents on the Continental Reformation,* edited by W. Naphy (Basingstoke: Macmillan, 1996), pp. 96–8.

2. Trent on Eucharist

Equally passionate, in formal tones, the Council of Trent prescribed the canons on the Sacrifice of the Mass:

Canon 1. If anyone says that in the mass a true and real sacrifice is not offered to God; or that to be offered is nothing else than that Christ is given to us to eat, let him be anathema.

Canon 2. If anyone says that by those words, *Do this for a commemoration of me,* Christ did not institute the Apostles priests; or did not ordain that they and other priests should offer His own body and blood, let him be anathema.

Canon 3. If anyone says that the sacrifice of the mass is one only of praise and thanksgiving; or that it is a mere commemoration of the sacrifice consummated on the cross but not a propitiatory one; or that it profits him only who receives, and ought not to be offered for the living and the dead, for sins, punishments, satisfactions, and other necessities, let him be anathema.

Canon 4. If anyone says that by the sacrifice of the mass a blasphemy is cast upon the most holy sacrifice of Christ consummated on the cross; or that the former derogates from the latter, let him be anathema.

Canon 5. If anyone says that it is a deception to celebrate masses in honour of the saints and in order to obtain their intercession with God, as the Church intends, let him be anathema.

Canon 6. If anyone says that the canon of the mass contains errors and is therefore to be abrogated, let him be anathema.

Canon 7. If anyone says that the ceremonies, vestments, and outward signs which the Catholic Church uses in the celebration of masses, are incentives to impiety rather than stimulants to piety, let him be anathema.

Canon 8. If anyone says that masses in which the priest alone communicates sacramentally are illicit and are therefore to be abrogated; let him be anathema.

Canon 9. If anyone says that the rite of the Roman Church, according to which a part of the canon and the words of consecration are pronounced in a low tone, is to be condemned; or that the mass ought to be celebrated in the vernacular tongue only; or that water ought not to be mixed with the wine that is to be offered in the chalice because it is contrary to the institution of Christ, let him be anathema.

Source: *The Canons and Decrees of the Council of Trent*, translated by H. J. Schroeder (Rockford: Tan, 1978), pp. 149–50.

Further reading

There isn't enough ink in the world to capture the tumult. A few thoughts below:

Duffy, E. (2001), *The Voices of Morebeth: Reformation and Rebellion in an English Village*. New Haven: Yale University Press.

Herrin, J. (2007), *Byzantium*. London: Allen Lane.

McCulloch, D. (2004), *The Reformation*. New York: Viking.

McKim, D. (ed.) (2003), *The Cambridge Companion to Luther*. Cambridge: Cambridge University Press.

— (2004), *The Cambridge Companion to Calvin*. Cambridge: Cambridge University Press.

Mullett, M. (1999), *The Catholic Reformation*. London: Routledge.

Chapter 19

References

Lumen Gentium, Dogmatic Constitution on the Church, 21st November 1964. in Flannery, A. (1996), *Vatican Council II; The Basic Sixteen Documents*. New York: Costello Publishing.

Anderson, W. (ed.) (2010), *A Journey Through Christian Theology*. Minneapolis, MN: Fortress Press.

Barth, K. (1957), *Church Dogmatics II*. Edinburgh: T&T Clark.

Hume, D. ([1748] 2007), *An Enquiry Concerning Human Understanding*. Cambridge: CUP.

Kant, I. ([1781 & 1788] 1952), *The Critique of Pure Reason, The Critique of Practical Reason and other Ethical Treatises* (translated by T. Kingsmill Abbot). Chicago: Benton.

Pascal, B. ([1662] 1966), *Pensées* (translated by A. J. Krailsheimer). London: Penguin.

Rahner, K. (1982), *Foundations of Christian Faith*. (translated by W. V. Dych). New York: Crossroad.

Schleiermacher, F. ([1799] 1996), *Religion: Speeches to its Cultured Despisers* (translated by R. Crouter). Cambridge: Cambridge University Press.

Tyler, P. (2011), *The Return To The Mystical*. London: Continuum.

Extracts

As noted in the main text, David Hume is a witty writer. Here he takes a pot shot at presumptions inherent in the Design Argument for the existence of God.

1. Hume on the Design argument

> But were this world ever so perfect a production, it must still remain uncertain, whether all the excellencies of the work can justly be ascribed to the workman. If we survey a ship, what an exalted idea must we form of the ingenuity of the carpenter, who framed so complicated, so useful, and beautiful a machine? And what surprise must we entertain, when we find him a stupid mechanic, who imitated others, and copied an art, which, through a long succession of ages, after multiplied trials, mistakes, corrections, deliberations, and controversies, had been gradually improving? Many worlds might have been botched and bungled, throughout an eternity, ere this system was struck out: Much labour lost: Many fruitless trials made: And a slow, but continued improvement carried on during infinite ages in the art of world-making. In such subjects, who can determine, where the truth; nay, who can conjecture where the possibility, lies, amidst a great number of hypotheses which may be proposed, and a still greater number which may be imagined?
>
> And what shadow of an argument, continued Philo, can you produce, from your hypothesis, to prove the unity of the Deity? A great number of men join in building a house or ship, in rearing a city, in framing a commonwealth: Why may not several Deities combine in contriving and framing a world? This is only so much greater similarity to human affairs. By sharing the work among several, we may so much farther limit the attributes of each, and get rid of that extensive power and knowledge, which must be supported in one Deity, and which, according to you, can only serve to weaken the proof of his existence. And if such foolish, such vicious creatures as man can yet often unite in framing and executing one plan, how much more those Deities or Daemons, whom we may suppose several degrees more perfect?

Source: Peter Tyler, *Philosophy of Religion - a Guide and Anthology*, edited by B. Davies (Oxford: Oxford University Press, 2000), pp. 265–6.

2. Tyler on Wittgenstein

Ludwig Wittgenstein (1889–1953) retains a unique mystique among twentieth-century philosophers. In his recent ground-breaking work on language and mysticism, English theologian, Peter Tyler explores the connection between Wittgenstein's theories and the work of Theresa of Avila (1515–1582), a pre-eminent Christian spiritual writer. Anticipating the subject matter of Chapter 25 below, Tyler makes the theological connection between, 'seeing and acting' which is not always facilitated by talking about it!

A Concluding Unscientific Postscript: A 'Life Question' or 'Empty Chatter'?

If you and I are to live religious lives, it mustn't be that we talk a lot about religion, but that our manner of life is different.

(Wittgenstein to Drury quoted in Rhees 1987:114)

It is now time to draw together the main arguments of this book and to highlight its conclusions. We began with a quote from Wittgenstein's conversation with Drury and we begin these conclusions with another together with some recollections of Wittgenstein's friend and fellow architect Paul Engelmann. Together the two quotes encapsulate some of the key arguments of the book, namely:

1. That we find in Wittgenstein's writings a method of looking at 'the mystical' by means of employing his essential division between 'saying and showing'. The mystical for Wittgenstein is unutterable, but, it can however *be manifest through showing.*

2. The 'perspicuous view' suggested by Wittgenstein enables us to 'see connections' in discourse as we relate them to a 'form of life'. We shall, in his words, 'see a new aspect'.

3. Consequently, if we look at religious texts and life we are as much concerned with *acting* as with *thinking*. For Wittgenstein, 'a religious form of life' *must* be embedded in action.

The argument of this book has been that both Wittgenstein and the medieval mystical writers covered, by similar means, challenge conventional ways of seeing to open up a new 'creative, relational space' where new 'connections and relations between aspects of our lives' may be opened up. Wittgenstein uses the tools of linguistic philosophy to subvert that very genre into a 'new way of seeing', whereas the Christian medieval writers use the tools of the venerable tradition of *theologia mystica* (ultimately derived from their interpretation of Dionysius) to present an equally subversive 'way of looking' that changes our way of viewing, our way of being and ultimately our way of acting in the world.

Source: *The Return to the Mystical: Ludwig Wittgenstein, Teresa of Avila and the Christian Mystical Tradition* (London: Continuum, 2011), pp. 227–8.

Further reading

To some extent, this massive area is perhaps better approached by consulting sections of one or two of the compendious readers (e.g. Davies and Ford) listed below. As well as these more general works, the eager may choose to grapple with the original writings of some luminaries of the age:

Davies, B. (2000), *Philosophy of Religion – A Guide and Anthology.* Oxford: Oxford University Press.

Descartes, R. ([1637] 1999), *Discourse on Method* (translated by D. M. Clarke). London: Penguin.

Hume, D. ([1779] 1990), *Dialogues Concerning Natural Religion.* London: Penguin.

Ford, D. F. (ed.) (1997), *The Modern Theologians.* 2nd edn. Oxford: Blackwell.

Griffiths-Dickson, G. (2005), *The Philosophy of Religion*. London: SCM.

Harrison, V. (2007), *Religion in Modern Thought*. London: SCM.

Kant, I. ([1788] 1997), *Critique of Practical Reason* (translated by M. Gregor). Cambridge: CUP.

Strauss, D. ([1840] 1994), *Life of Jesus, Critically Examined*. (translated by G. Eliot). Pennsylvania, PA: Sigler Press.

Chapter 20

References

Darwin, C. (1872), *On the Origin of Species by Means of Natural Selection, or the Preservation of Favoured Races in the Struggle for Life*. London: John Murray. NB. For comparisons of editions of Darwin's Works see: http://darwin-online.org.uk/Variorum/1859/1859-490-c-1872.html.

Einstein, A. ([1941] 2010) *Ideas and Opinions*. New York: Crown Publishing.

Hawking, S. W. (1988), *A Brief History of Time*. New York: Bantam Press.

Hoyle, F., Burbidge, G., Narliker, J. V. (2000), *A Different Approach to Cosmology: From a Static Universe through the Big Bang towards Reality*. Cambridge: CUP.

Jastrow, R. (1978), *God and the Astronomers*. New York: W. W. Norton.

Knight, D. (ed.) (2003), *The Evolution Debate 1813-1870 (8 Vols)*. London: Routledge.

Kuhn, T. (1962), *The Structure of Scientific Revolutions*. Chicago, IL: Chicago University Press.

McGrath, A. E. (1999), *Science and Religion: An Introduction*. Oxford: Blackwell.

Nietzsche, F. ([c.1873] 1962), *Philosophy in the Tragic Age of the Greeks* (translated by M. A. Cowan). Washington: Regnery.

Popper, K. (1959), *The Logic of Scientific Discovery*. London: Hutchinson.

Extracts

In the United Kingdom, following the death of Bertrand Russell, the torch of atheistic contestation was taken up first by the philosopher Anthony Flew and subsequently by the scientist Richard Dawkins. Flew spent many years arguing that the Design Argument was flawed (see main text, Section 20g), but in later life became a Deist, compelled by a combination of Big Bang considerations and the Anthropic principle. Dawkins, as a zoologist, argues from a Darwinian viewpoint. For him, the geometric potentialities of life as it reproduces make our appearance far less surprising than some would suggest and render 'Intelligent Design' unnecessary.

1. Dawkins on Evolution

> We have all dealt with the alleged alternatives to the theory of natural selection except the oldest one. This is the theory that life was created, or its evolution

master-minded, by a conscious designer. It would obviously be unfairly easy to demolish some particular version of this theory such as the one (or it may be two) spelt out in Genesis. Nearly all peoples have developed their own creation myth, and the Genesis story is just the one that happened to have been adopted by one particular tribe of Middle Eastern herders. It has no more special status than the belief of a particular West African tribe that the world was created from the excrement of ants. All these myths have in common that they depend upon the deliberate intentions of some kind of supernatural being.

At the first sight there is an important distinction to be made between what might be called 'instantaneous creation' and 'guided evolution'. Modern theologians of any sophistication have given up believing in instantaneous creation. The evidence for some sort of evolution has become too overwhelming. But many theologians who call themselves evolutionists, for instance the Bishop of Birmingham quoted in Chapter 2, smuggle God in by the back door: they allow him some sort of supervisory role over the course that evolution has taken, either influencing key moments in evolutionary history (especially, of course, human evolutionary history), or even meddling more comprehensively in the day-to-day events that add up to evolutionary change.

We cannot disprove beliefs like these, especially if it is assumed that God took care that his interventions always closely mimicked what would be expected from evolution by natural selection. All that we can say about such beliefs is, firstly, that they are superfluous and, secondly, that they must *assume* the existence of the main thing we want to *explain*, namely organised complexity. The one thing that makes evolution such a neat theory is that it explains how organized complexity can arise out of primeval simplicity.

Source: *The Blind Watchmaker* (London: Penguin Books, 1991), p. 316.

2. Flew: Did something come from nothing?

Anthony Flew starts this section in his book recalling the famous song in *The Sound of Music* – when Maria von Trapp, feeling the first stirrings of love, muses that 'Nothing comes from nothing, nothing ever could' which brings him on to the 'Big Bang'.

In the Beginning

When I first met the big-bang theory as an atheist, it seemed to me the theory made a big difference because it suggested that the universe has a beginning and that the first sentence in Genesis ('In the beginning, God created the heavens and the earth') was related to an event in the universe. As long as the universe could be comfortably thought to be not only without end but also without beginning, it remained easy to see its existence (and its most fundamental features) as brute facts. And if there had been no reason to think the universe had a beginning, there would be no need to postulate something else that produced the whole thing.

But the big-bang theory changed all that. If the universe had a beginning, it became entirely sensible, almost inevitable, to ask what produced this beginning. This radically altered the situation. At the same time, I predicted that atheists were bound to see the big-bang cosmology as requiring a physical explanation - an explanation that, admittedly, may be forever inaccessible to human beings. But I admitted that believers could, equally reasonably, welcome the big-bang cosmology as tending to confirm their prior belief that 'in the beginning' the universe was created by God.

Modern cosmologists seemed just as disturbed as atheists about the potential theological implications of their work. Consequently, they devised influential escape routes that sought to preserve the nontheist status quo. These routes included the idea of the multiverse, numerous universes generated by endless vacuum fluctuation events, and Stephen Hawking's notion of a self-contained universe.

Until a Beginning Comes Along

As I have already mentioned, I did not find the multiverse alternative very helpful. The postulation of multiple universes, I maintained, is a truly desperate alternative. If the existence of one universe requires an explanation, multiple universes require a much bigger explanation: the problem is increased by the factor of whatever the total number of universes is. It seems a little like the case of the schoolboy whose teacher doesn't believe his dog ate his homework, so he replaces the first version with the story that a pack of dogs – too many to count – ate his homework.

Source: *There is a God: How the World's Most Notorious Atheist Changed His Mind* (New York: HarperOne, 2007), pp. 136–7.

Further reading

Just a small selection from a booming market . . . Hannam is intriguing.

Deane-Drummond, C. (2006), *Wonder and Wisdom: Conversations in Science, Spirituality and Theology.* London: Darton Longman & Todd.

Hannam, J. (2009), *God's Philosophers: How the Medieval World laid the Foundations of Modern Science.* London: Icon Books.

Kennedy, J. B. (2003), *Space, Time and Einstein: An Introduction.* Chesham: Acumen.

O'Murchu, D. (1998), *Quantum Theology: Spiritual Implications of the New Physics.* New York: The Crossroad Publishing Company.

Peters, K. E. (2002), *Dancing With The Sacred: Evolution, Ecology and God.* Pennsylvania: Trinity Press International.

Southgate, C. (ed.) (2005), *God, Humanity and the Cosmos.* London: T&T Clark.

Stannard, R. (2004), *Science and the Renewal of Belief.* London: Templeton Foundation Press.

Teilhard de Chardin, P. (1959), *The Phenomenon of Man.* New York: Harper and Row.

Chapter 21

References

Feuerbach, L. ([1854] 2008), *The Essence of Christianity* (translated by George Eliot), New York: Cosimo.

Frankl, V. E. (1964), *Man's Search for Meaning: An Introduction to Logotherapy* (translated by I. Lasch). London: Hodder & Stoughton.

Guthrie, W. K. (1971), *A History of Greek Philosophy: Volume 3, The Fifth Century Enlightenment.* Cambridge: CUP.

Jung, C. G. ([1933] 2001), *Modern Man in Search of a Soul* (translated by W. S. Dell and C. F. Barnes). London: Routledge.

Marx, K. ([1843, 1845, 1867] 1988), *Selected Writings* (edited and translated by D. McLellan). Oxford: OUP.

Newman, J. H ([1870] 1979), *An Essay in Aid of a Grammar of Assent.* London: University of Notre Dame Press.

— (1875), *Letter to the Duke of Norfolk.* London: Catholic Publication Society.

Otto, R. ([1923] 1968), *The Idea of the Holy.* (translated by J.W. Harvey). Oxford: OUP.

Tillich, P. (1951), *Systematic Theology Vol. I.* Chicago, IL: Chicago University Press.

Extracts

1. Durkheim – Theology as Sociology

As noted in the main text, Durkheim was convinced that far from being a by-product of some individual mystical moment, the patterns of religious ritual and thinking are a by-product of the socialization of humanity. I sometimes think of religion as 'organized wonder' but in a passage entitled *Concerning the Definition of Religious Phenomena*, Durkheim is more inclined to think of it more as 'socialized sentiment'.

> Therefore it is not in human nature in general that we must seek the determining cause of religious phenomena; it is in the nature of the societies to which they relate, and if they have evolved in the course of history it is because their social organization has been transformed. From now on, the traditional theories which pointed to the source of religiosity as being in the feelings of individuals, like the awe inspired in each one of us by such things as great cosmic forces at work, or the spectacle of certain natural phenomena like death, must be viewed with more than suspicion . . . The problem presents itself in sociological terms. The powers before which the believer prostrates himself are not simply physical forces. They are the direct product of collective sentiments which have clothed themselves in material covering . . .
>
> This is how the distinction between sacred and profane things to be found in all religions takes on its full meaning. Sacred things are those whose *representation* society itself has fashioned; it includes all sorts of collective states,

common traditions and emotions, feelings which have a relationship to objects of general interest, etc.; and all those elements are combined according to the appropriate laws of social mentality. Profane things, conversely, are those which each of us constructs form our own sense data and experience; the ideas we have about them have as their subject matter unadulterated, individual impressions, and that is why they do not have the same prestige in our eyes as the preceding ones. We only put into them and see in them what empirical observation reveals to us. Now, these two sorts of mental states constitute two kinds of intellectual phenomena, since one type is produced by a single brain and a single mind, the other by a plurality of brains and minds acting and reacting on each other. This duality of the temporal and the spiritual is not an intervention without reason and without foundation in reality; it expresses in symbolic language the duality of the individual and the social, of psychology proper and sociology. That is why for a long time the initiation into sacred things was also the operation by which the socialization of the individual was completed. At the same time, as a man entered into the religious life, he assumed another nature and became a new man.

Source: *Thinking about Religion - A Reader,* edited by I. Strenksi (Oxford: Blackwell Publishing, 2006), pp. 206–7.

2. Peter Morea – Psychology of Salvation?

In 2004, after 25 years of lecturing in Psychology, Peter C. Morea collated a series of thoughtful reflections on different aspects of the discipline. Taken individually, none of the topics under review (personality, self-actualization, transcendence etc.) offer a case for God's existence, but by the time Morea has woven seventeen strands of thinking together, the rope is a bit thicker and, if not compelling, then at least capable of tugging the mind in his preferred direction. Here, Morea makes the case for eternal life from our dissatisfied desire!

A secular psychology might regard the idea of eternal life as pure projection of human personality into some ideal future, motivated by present deprivation. Though elements of projection will almost certainly influence how we perceive any life after death, we might expect increased material and bodily satisfaction to reduce any such projection. But this appears not to happen. Even when human needs are more than adequately satisfied, there never seems any diminishment in human longing for a qualitatively superior future; we continue to desire some unknown goal. This again suggests that programmed into personality is the search for a satisfaction beyond the realm of the material world that we know . . .

Such intimations are a kind of mild ecstasy, an attenuated mystical experience which go beyond just a pleasurable response. But what becomes known never becomes fully known. Intimations elevate us to a degree of experience that we had not realised we were capable of; we enjoy for a moment the fulfilment of our potential for happiness. I suggest that the experience of the intimation further provides basis for belief in an eternal life with God - not in the sense that the actual experience causes belief, though this may happen for some, but the experience provides an argument for belief. The longing for God and the longing for eternal life are inextricably entwined both in our experience - and in our argument for their existence.

The intimations of eternal life that we experience in ciphers of transcendence, moments of being, epiphanies and peak experiences, are often wonderful moments; but they are transient and leave us satisfied but still longing. For our happiness to be complete, there would have to be no such transience; eternal life would be the experience of God outside time, the fullness of God experienced in one never-ending and ever-present now. In this life there are only particular moments and experiences, elevated or seemingly ordinary, which appear to be an intimation - a promise even - of a reality beyond our present experience.

Source: *Finding God in Human Psychology* (London: St Pauls, 2004), pp. 145–7.

Further reading

Insofar as the hot topic in this zone has moved away from classic sociological positions to the outworkings of various 'intelligent design' versus 'social' or 'neural' Darwinian discussions, here are a few samples, but there will be more along in a minute. Sociologists might want to check out Wilson and also the radical theories of René Girard via Michael Kirwan's introductory work.

Ayala, F. J. (2006), *Darwin and Intelligent Design*. Philadelphia: Fortress.

Dembski, W. A. (ed.) (2006), *Darwin's Nemesis: Philip Johnson and the Intelligent Design Movement*. Downers Grove: Inter Varsity Press Academic.

Dennett, D. C. (1996), *Darwin's Dangerous Idea*. New York: Simon & Schuster.

Durkheim, E. (1975), *Durkheim on Religion: A Selection of Readings With Bibliographies* (edited by W. S. F. Pickering). London: Routledge & Kegan Paul.

Edelman, G., Tonnoni, G. (2000), *A Universe of Consciousness: How Matter Becomes Imagination*. New York: Basic Books.

Freud, S. ([1927] 2008), *The Future of an Illusion: Religion is the Universal Neurosis* (translated by J. A. Underwood and S. Whiteside). London: Penguin.

James, W. ([1902] 1997), *The Varieties of Religious Experience*. New York: Simon & Schuster.

Kirwan, M. (2009), *Girard and Theology*. London: T&T Clark.

Lennox, J. C. (2009), *God's Undertaker: Has Science Buried God?* (revised edn). Oxford: Lion.

Wilson, E. O. (2006), *The Creation: An Appeal to Save Life on Earth*. New York & London: W. W. Norton.

Chapter 22

References

Barnstone, W. (ed.) (2005), 'The Infancy Gospel of James' in *The Other Bible*. New York: Harper San Francisco.

Cady-Stanton, E. ([1898] 1999), *The Women's Bible*. New York: Prometheus Books.

Clark-King, E. (2006), 'Mary: A Revolutionary Virgin' in *The Expository Times,* Vol. 118(2), 85–6.

Grey, M. (2004), *Sacred Longings*. Minneapolis, MN: Fortress.

Gutiérrez, G. (1983), *The Power of the Poor*. London: SCM.

Hinfelaar, H. F. (1994), *Bemba-Speaking Women of Zambia in a Century of Religious Change (1892–1992)*. Leiden: E.J. Brill.

Hirsch, E. (1976), *The Aims of Interpretation*. Chicago, IL: Chicago University Press.

Kierkegaard, S. ([1843] 1986), *Fear and Trembling* (translated by A. Hannay). London: Penguin.

— ([1845] 1967), *Journals and Papers* (translated & edited by H. V. Hong and E. H. Hong). New York: Harper & Row.

— ([1848] 1997), *Christian Discourses: The Crisis and A Crisis in the Life of an Actress* (translated & edited by H. V. Hong and E. H. Hong). New Jersey: Princeton.

McDonagh, E. (ed.) (1990), *Faith and the Hungry Grass: A Mayo Book of Theology*. Dublin: Columba.

Muggeridge, M. (1983), *A Third Testament*. New York: Plough Publishing House.

Mullin, C. (2011), *Decline and Fall: Diaries 2005–2010*. London: Profile Books.

Nietzsche, F. ([1882] 1974), *The Gay Science* (translated by W. Kaufman). New York: Vantage.

Prior, M. (1997), *The Bible and Colonialism: A Moral Critique*. Sheffield: Sheffield Academic Press.

Radford Reuther, R. (2011), *Women and Redemption: A Theological History*. Minneapolis: Fortress.

Rowland, C. (ed.) (2007), *The Cambridge Companion to Liberation Theology*. Cambridge: CUP.

Sugirtharajah, R. (2012), *Exploring Postcolonial Biblical Criticism: History, Method, Practice*. Oxford: Wiley-Blackwell.

Trible, P. (1973), 'Eve and Adam: Genesis 2-3 Reread,' *Andover Newton Quarterly,* Vol. 13, 251–58.

Van Biema, D., Magg, C. et al. (2005), 'Hail Mary' in *Time* 3/21/2005, Vol. 165(12), 60–69.

1. Mary Grey – digging deeper wells

Long before Postmodernism dominated the arena, the existentialist turn in exegesis led noted hermeneutical scholar, Ed Hirsch to express the concern that commentaries risked becoming 'works of fiction' (Hirsch, 1976, p. 157). At first glance, this may be precisely your reaction to the following extract from Mary Grey's book, *Sacred Longings* – an imaginative reconstruction of thoughts and conversations between Zipporah and Miriam (Ex 2:21, 15:20) which are absent from the biblical text. But think again. Quite apart from perhaps overlooking the application of political, economic, social and religious knowledge which underpins feminist hermeneutics, it might be worth pondering the last time you were anxious about the availability of water? For how long and for how many nameless women has the search for water been the nodal point of the day? And in terms of understanding the significance of water in the desert stories of Exodus, who is better equipped, Mary Grey who has taken time out to work with the charity *Wells for India* in Rajasthan, or Anthony Towey – occasionally found grumbling about hosepipe bans in London?

Miriam's Well

[Miriam] stood alone by the waters, trying to understand her role in the struggle of her people for survival. Already she saw that in the depths of the waters lay many meanings . . .

But it was not as bitterness that she experienced the night of escape from slavery and the crossing of the Sea of Reeds (Exodus 14). This was the night when her prophetic powers emerged into their fullest expression. They had reached the shore, scarcely believing that they were alive – the walls of water had been so huge and terrifying. Moses and her brother Aaron were leading the men into their ancient warrior chant of freedom (Ex 15.1-18). But Miriam looked around at the weary, tearful women, with the exhausted children they were carrying, hungry, thirsty and fearful. 'Come!' she cried, 'It is freedom we celebrate . . .' These women had no strength . . . Backbreaking labour, death and murder of their children – and struggle for the most basic necessities of life had been their lot. But, looking at Miriam's radiant face, they put down their infants in the sand, they took up timbrels, remembered ancient melodies – of who they had been, of lands which delivered harvests, vineyards that yielded flowing wine, of flocks and herds with rich milk, cheese and butter . . . – and they danced with Miriam into a long forgetting of the hope-crushing suffering in Egypt, into the possibility that visions and dreams would be re-kindled.

But they did not know about the desert. They could not imagine that they would wish for Egypt once again, that an existence only of forgotten dreams and lost hopes stretched out before them . . . So Miriam stood with Zipporah . . . 'Lord God of Israel,' she pleaded, 'Hear the cries of your people . . . You led us out of bondage to suffer even more cruelly the vanishing of the waters that give life.' . . . And slowly the miracle happened. The water began to bubble out of the parched earth beneath them. It bubbled up from a spring far beneath the earth, to form a pool, and from the pool a river began to flow. And Miriam knew that God's compassion was flowing through her and that the children of Israel would drink their fill. She was filled with confidence in this compassionate God and she knew that as long as she lived she would call for the wellsprings that would arise to heal the thirst of the people.

Source: *Sacred Longings* (Minneapolis: Fortress, 2004), pp. 23–6.

2. Sugirtharajah on conquest, Christianity and colonialism

One of the most famous contributions to interpretation theory of the twentieth century came from Hans Georg Gadamer (1900–2002), who pointed out, among other things, that with the best will in the world, we engage with texts such as the Bible with accumulated prejudice which conditions what we are able to hear or 'see'. This he called our 'horizon'. Some things go swishing away off screen because (to mix metaphors) they are not on our radar. If you want to have a glance at what might be beyond your own personal bifocals, may I recommend the work of Rasiah Sugirtharajah. In this extract, he quizzes the connection between Christian Theology and colonization.

> The Christian Bible, for all its sophisticated theological ideals like tolerance and compassion, contains equally repressive and predatory elements which provide textual ammunition for physical and spiritual conquest. It provides confidence and justification for invading the lands of other peoples and bringing non-Christians into the Christian fold. To rephrase the epigraph, conquest is a bible thing. The Bible records examples of occupation and invasion. A well-known case is the conquest of Canaan by Israel, a land which did not belong to her. This has provided a cue for modern colonizers who project themselves as a latter-day Israel, and a charter for conquering other peoples' lands. A classic example of biblical texts put to this sort of use was Oliver Cromwell's campaign in Ireland in 1649. In the words of the late Robert Carroll, himself an Irishman,: 'In the massacres of the Irish towns of Drogheda and Wexford, Cromwell played the biblical Joshua against the Irish as imagined Canaanites. Cromwell invited the Irish towns to surrender and annihilated the occupants when they refused to give themselves up to the invading English forces.' The biblical accounts of Joshua's mass murder of the Canaanites and the destruction of their towns provided Cromwell with legitimation and validation for his military strategy of extirpation of the native Irish.
>
> Enshrined in the pages of the bible is the notion that the heathen should hear the gospel as a sign of the end of the world. Many early colonial pioneers such as Christopher Columbus and Bartolomé de las Casas made use of this biblical idea as a way of justification for conquering other peoples' lands . . . [Columbus] was equally spurred on by the twin eschatological goals of the time – the recovery of Jerusalem and the conversion of the heathen. Both these tasks, seen as signs of the end of the world, Christians were expected to fulfil before Christ returned . . . Columbus was unequivocal about where he got his inspiration:
>
> 'I am not relying on my lifetime of navigation and the discussions I have had with many people from many lands and religions, or on the many disciplines and texts that I spoke of previously. I base what I say only on holy and sacred Scripture, and the prophetic statements of certain holy persons who through divine revelation have spoken on this subject.'

Source: *Exploring Postcolonial Biblical Criticism: History, Method, Practice* (Chichester: Wiley-Blackwell, 2012), pp. 32–3.

Further reading

In addition to the works referenced above, it might be useful to glance at

Boff, L. (1995), *Ecology and Liberation*. New York: Maryknoll.

Cooper, T. (2007), *Controversies in Political Theology: Development or Liberation?* London: SCM.

Ellsberg, R. (2006), *Blessed among all Women: Women Saints, Prophets and Witnesses for Our Time.* London: Darton, Longman & Todd.

Fry, H., Montagu, R., Scholefield, L. (eds) (2005), *Women's Voices*. London: SCM.

Nietzsche, F. ([1883] 2003), *Thus Spoke Zarathustra* (translated by R. J. Hollingdale). London: Penguin Books.

Ringe, S. H. (1985), *Jesus, Liberation, and the Biblical Jubilee*. Philadelphia: Fortress.

Schüssler-Fiorenza, E. (1996), *In Memory of Her: A Feminist Theological Reconstruction of Christian Origins*. London: SCM.

Vanhoozer, K. (ed.) (2003), *The Cambridge Companion to Postmodern Theology*. Cambridge: Cambridge University Press.

Chapter 23

References

Humanae Vitae 'On Human Life' ([1968] 1998), in *Vatican Council II: Vol 2 - More Post Conciliar Documents*, edited by A. Flannery. New York: Costello.

Aquinas ([c.1274] 1947), *Summa Theologica* (translated by the Fathers of the English Dominican Province). New York: Benziger Bros.

Aristotle ([c.350BC] 1976), *Nichomachean Ethics* (translated J. A. K. Thomson). London: Penguin.

Bentham, J. ([1789]1962), 'Introduction to the Principles of Morals and Legislation,' in *Utilitarianism*. London: Collins Fontana.

Cameron, N. M. (2001), *The New Medicine: Life and Death after Hippocrates* (revised edn). Chicago & London: Bioethics.

Dawkins, R. (1976), *The Selfish Gene*. Oxford: Oxford University Press.

Capon, R. F. (2002), *Kingdom, Grace, Judgment: Paradox, Outrage, and Vindication in the Parables of Jesus*. Grand Rapids, MI: W. B. Eerdmans.

Fletcher, J. (1966), *Situation Ethics: The New Morality*. Louisville, KY: Westminster John Knox.

Giubilini, A. and F. Minerva. (2013), 'After birth Abortion: Why should the baby live? *Journal of Medical Ethics* 39/5:261.

Hauerwas, S. (1981), *A Community of Character*. Notre Dame: Notre Dame Press.

Kant, I. ([1797] 2002), *Groundwork for the Metaphysics of Morals* (translated A. Zweig, edited by T. Hill and A Zweig). Oxford: Oxford University Press.

McCoy, A. (2004), *An Intelligent Person's Guide to Christian Ethics*. London: Continuum.

McFague, S. (2008), *A New Climate for Theology*. Minneapolis, MN: Fortress.

Mill, J. S. ([1860] 1962), *Utilitarianism*. London: Collins Fontana.

Singer, P. (1996), *Animal Liberation* (2nd edn). London: Pimlico.

— (2011), *Practical Ethics* (3rd edn). Cambridge: Cambridge University Press.

West, C. (2003), *Theology of the Body Explained*. Leominster: Gracewing.

Wojtyla, K. (1992), *The Jeweller's Shop* (translated by B. Taborski). San Francisco, CA: Ignatius Press.

Extracts

1. Karl Barth on human life and the will to live

As noted in the main text, one of the main distinctions between traditional Christian approaches and secular, more utilitarian arguments in ethical discourse centres on personal autonomy in relation to life. It is evidently the case that many people find life has become intolerable, but in this extract, Karl Barth makes an argument for *resolve* in the face of suffering.

> But this whole consideration is only defeatist thinking, and not at all Christian. It overlooks the fact that the command of God is not withdrawn but still in force, namely, that man must will to live and not die, to be healthy and not to be sick, and to exercise and not neglect his strength to be as man and the remaining psycho-physical forces which he has for this purpose, and thus to maintain himself. This command has not been revoked even for sinful man forfeited to the judgment of God, and it is not for him to counter God with speculations whether obedience to it is possible or offers any prospects. Unquestioning obedience is his only option if he is not to bring himself into even greater condemnation. Again this consideration overlooks the fact that the realm of death which afflicts man in the form of sickness, although God has given it power and it serves as an instrument of his righteous judgment, is opposed to His good will as Creator and has existence and power only under His mighty No. To capitulate before it, to allow it to take its course, can never be obedience but only disobedience towards God. In harmony with the will of God, what man ought to will in face of this whole realm on the left hand, and therefore in face of sickness, can only be final resistance. Again and supremely, this consideration overlooks the fact that God Himself is not only Judge but faithful, gracious and patient in his righteous judgement, that He Himself has already marched against that realm on the left, and that he has overcome and bound its forces and therefore those of sickness in Jesus Christ and His Sacrifice, by which the destroyer was himself brought to destruction. Those who know this . . . can only reply to the faithfulness of God with a new unfaithfulness if they try to fold their hands and sigh and ask what help there is or what more they can will . . . with God they must say No to it without asking what the result will be or how much or how little it will help themselves . . . A little resolution, will and action in the face of that realm and therefore against sickness is better than a

whole ocean of pretended Christian humility which is really perhaps the mistaken and perverted humility of the devil and demons.

Source: *Theological Issues in Bioethics: An Introduction with Readings,* edited by N. Messer (London, Darton Longman & Todd, 2002), pp. 111–12.

2. Paul VI on Human Life (*Humanae vitae*)

This declaration by Paul VI (Giovanni Battista Montini) marked a particular moment in Catholic thinking on sexual ethics. There had been an expectation that the Catholic Church, still glowing with the excitement of developments at Vatican II, would move to a more liberal attitude to birth control and allow the use of artificial contraception within marriage. Although the specially convened advisory committee seems to have found in favour of change, Paul VI decided not to break with traditional teaching. In this extract, note the emphasis on the unitive dimension to marital intercourse and the combination of Natural Law and Divine Command ethical reasoning:

Respect for the Nature and Purpose of the Marriage Act

11. The sexual activity, in which husband and wife are intimately and chastely united with one another, through which human life is transmitted, is, as the recent Council recalled, 'honourable and good.' It does not, moreover, cease to be legitimate even when, for reasons independent of their will, it is foreseen to be infertile. For its natural adaptation to the expression and strengthening of the union of husband and wife is not thereby suppressed. The facts are, as experience shows, that new life is not the result of each and every act of sexual intercourse. God has wisely ordered the laws of nature and the incidence of fertility in such a way that successive births are already naturally spaced through the inherent operation of these laws. The Church, nevertheless, in urging men to the observance of the precepts of the natural law, which it interprets by its constant doctrine, teaches as absolutely required that in any use whatever of marriage there must be no impairment of its natural capacity to procreate human life.

Teaching in Harmony with Human Reason

12. This particular doctrine, often expounded by the Magisterium of the Church, is based on the inseparable connection, established by God, which man on his own initiative may not break, between the unitive significance and the procreative significance which are both inherent to the marriage act . . . And if each of these essential qualities, the unitive and the procreative, is preserved, the use of marriage fully retains its sense of true mutual love and its ordination to the supreme responsibility of parenthood to which man is called . . .

Faithfulness to God's Design

13. For men rightly observe that to force the use of marriage on one's partner without regard to his or her condition or personal or reasonable wishes in that matter, is no true act of love, and therefore offends the moral order in its particular application to the intimate relationship of husband and wife . . . But to experience the gift of married love while respecting the laws of conception is to acknowledge that one is not the master of the sources of life but rather the minister of the design established by the Creator . . . human life is sacred - all men must recognize that fact., Our Predecessor, Pope John XXIII, recalled, 'since from its first beginnings it calls for the creative action of God.'

Source: *Vatican Council II: Vol 2 – More Post Conciliar Documents,* edited by A. Flannery (New York: Costello, 1998), pp. 404–5.

Further reading

There's really almost no limit to what could be read – here are just a few works I have found both useful and interesting. Bowie is a great introduction to theory and issues, Gill is a bit more specialized, Jones and Meilander technical but accessible. Midgley – memorable!

Bowie, R. A. (2004), *Ethical Studies* (revised edn). Cheltenham: Nelson Thornes.

Gill, R. (ed.) (2001), *The Cambridge Companion to Christian Ethics*. Cambridge: Cambridge University Press.

Jones, D. A. (2004), *The Soul of the Embryo*. London: Continuum.

Meilander, G. (2005), *Bioethics: A Primer for Christians* (2nd edn). Grand Rapids, MI: W. B. Eerdmans.

Midgley, M. (2003), *Heart and Mind: The Varieties of Moral Experience* (revised edn). London: Routledge.

Chapter 24

References

Anon. ([c.1860] 1993), *The Way of the Pilgrim and the Pilgrim continues his Way* (translated and adapted by R.M. French and F.A. Sand). Pasadena: Hope Publishing House.

Burgess, S. and E. Van der Maas (eds.) (2002), *The New International Dictionary of Pentecostal and Charismatic Movements*. Grand Rapids: Zondervan.

Bonhoeffer, D. ([1937] 1959), *The Cost of Discipleship* (translated by R.H. Fuller). London: Macmillan.

Cassian, J. ([c.426] 1997), *The Conferences* (translated by B. Ramsey). New York: Newman Press.

Farley, L. (2007), *Let us attend: A Journey through the Orthodox Divine Liturgy*. Ben Lomond CA: Conciliar Press.

Marsh, C. (1997), 'Dietrich Bonhoeffer' in *The Modern Theologians* (2nd Ed.) (edited by D. Ford). Oxford: Blackwell.

Merton, T. (1990), *The Seven Storey Mountain*. London: SPCK

Merton, T. (2002), *Dialogues with Silence: Prayers and Drawings* (edited by J. Montaldo). London: SPCK.

Sheldrake, P. (1987), *Images of Holiness*. London: DLT.

Sheldrake, P. (2007), *A Brief History of Spirituality*. Oxford: Blackwell

Warren, R. (2002), *The Purpose Driven Life*. Grand Rapids, MI: Zondervan

Extracts

1. Eric Doyle on the Creation Paradigm

Creation as a prism for prayer is another classic paradigm of Christian spirituality. It can be argued that the Bible begins with a 'Cosmic prayer' and throughout history, what Christians might call the *sacramentality* of creation has literally offered common ground for human reflection on transcendence. While Celtic Spirituality and the work of Hildegard of Bingen (1098–1179) have particular potency in this regard, perhaps the most famous example from the tradition is the *Canticle of Brother Sun* of Francis of Assisi. Also known as *Laudato Sii* – it is translated and introduced here by a lyrical theologian of the Franciscan tradition, Eric Doyle OFM (1938–84).

> The *Canticle of BrotherSun* gives St. Francis a sure place among poet-mystics. It is a prime example of mystic poetry which reveals his experience of the fundamental unity and coherence of reality. Francis did not understand himself as an isolated subject facing objects in the world. He saw himself as one love-centre in a universal brotherhood and he expressed this in *The Canticle*. Indeed, as the key to Einstein's universe is contained in the devastatingly short statement that time is relative, so is the key to Francis's universe found in the tremendously simple belief, the grace of brotherhood in Christ, which is given to every creature. The vision of the universe which *The Canticle* presents is as fresh and relevant today as it was when Brother Pacificus first sang it.
>
> Most high, all powerful, good Lord.
> Yours are the praise, the glory and the honour and every blessing.
> To you alone, Most High, they belong
> and no man is worthy to pronounce your name.
> Be praised, my Lord, with all your creatures,
> especially Sir Brother Sun,
> who is day and by him you shed light upon us.
> He is beautiful and radiant with great splendour,

of you, Most High, he bears great likeness.
Be praised, my Lord, through Sister Moon and the Stars,
in the heavens you formed them clear and precious and beautiful.
Be praised, my Lord, through Brother Wind
and through Air and Cloud and fair and all Weather,
by which you nourish all that you have made.
Be praised, my Lord, through Sister Water,
who is very useful and humble and precious and pure.
Be praised, my Lord, through Brother Fire,
by whom you light up the night;
he is beautiful and merry and vigorous and strong.
Be praised, my Lord, through our Sister Mother Earth,
who sustains and guides us,
and produces diverse fruits with coloured flowers and herbs.
Be praised, my Lord, by those who pardon for love of you,
and endure sickness and trials.
Blessed are they who shall endure them in peace,
for by you, Most High, they shall be crowned.
Be praised, my Lord, through our Sister Bodily Death,
from whom no man living can escape.
Woe to those who die in mortal sin.
Blessed are those whom she will find in your most holy will,
for the second death will do them no harm.
Praise and bless my Lord
and give him thanks and serve him with great humility.

In much the same way as Rublev's icon of the Trinity, but in words, *The Canticle* holds out an invitation to participate in what it is communicating. While reading it I have felt myself to be part of a total unity. It is an affirmation of being and so it confirms one's sense of the value of one's own existence. It brings reality to a fine point at which it is revealed that all beings are held in unity through a vast and intricate network of love relationships. And because the potency to love all creation is in every one of us, so too is the power to create. By love and creativity the self and the world blend into ever finer unity. In loving we create and by creating we discover pathways to the future.

Source: *St. Francis and the Song of Brotherhood,* (London: Allen & Unwin, 1980) pp. 39–40

2. Dorothy Day on the Paradigm of Poverty
While *The Canticle of the Sun* is perhaps the most famous prayer of Francis of Assisi, it should not be forgotten that it was 'Lady Poverty' who transformed his life, when, counter to all his instincts, he felt compelled to embrace a leper. Seeing Jesus in what Mother Theresa of Calcutta has called 'his most

distressing disguise' is one of the recurring themes in Christian spirituality and was exemplified in the twentieth century by the life and legacy of Dorothy Day (1897–1980). A non-believing journalist attracted to Communism, one failed love affair led to her having an abortion but a second pregnancy found her inexplicably wishing to have the child baptized. Thereafter, her own choice for faith estranged her from the child's father and quickened within her a desire to serve the poor. It is beyond startling that a single-mum with Communist leanings could go on to found 'The Catholic Worker Movement' with Peter Maurin in 1930's America, but her direct action and plain speaking disarmed both politicians and prelates alike. In fact the 'Houses of Hospitality' founded by the Movement were less about work than about the unemployed, and less about faith than food. Or were they? Ultimately, her stance for the poor, so deeply rooted in the Gospel, made her an international symbol of Christian service. In this extract she reflects on the 'pearl of great price' – her work with those living in 'the cheap flophouses, the benches of the parks, the holes and corners of the city.'

The Pearl of Great Price

When we began the Catholic Worker, we first thought of it as a headquarters for the paper, a place for round table discussions, for learning crafts, for studying ways of building up a new social order. But God has made it much more than all this. He has made it a place for the poor. They come early in the morning from their beds in cheap flophouses, from the benches in park across the street, from the holes and corners of the city. They are the most destitute, the most abandoned.

It is easy for people to see Jesus in the children of the slums, and institutions and schools are built to help them. That is a vocation in itself. But these abandoned men are looked upon as hopeless. 'No good will come of it.' We are contributing to laziness. We are feeding people who won't work. These are the accusations made. God help us, we give them so little: bread and coffee in the morning, soup and bread at noon. Two scant meals.

The reason for our existence is to praise God, to love Him and to serve Him, and we can do this only by loving our brothers. This is the great truth that makes us realize God. Great crimes, it is true, have been committed in the name of human brotherhood; that may serve to obscure the truth but we must keep on saying it. We must keep on saying it because Love is the reason for our existence. It is what we all live for, whether we are the hanger-on in Times Square or the most pious member of a community. We are seeking what we think to be the good for us. If we don't know any better, often it is because radio, newspapers, press and pulpit have neglected to inform us. We love what is presented to us to love, and God is not much presented. It is as hard to see Jesus in the respectable Christian today as in the man on the Bowery. And so 'the masses have been lost to the Church.'

We must try hard, we must study to be poor like Lazarus at the gate who was taken into Abraham's bosom. The Gospel doesn't tell us anything about Lazarus' virtues. He just sat there and let the dogs lick his sores. He would be classed by any social worker of today as a mental case. But again, poverty, and in this case destitution, like hospitality, is so esteemed by God, it is something to be sought after, worked for, the pearl of great price.

Source: *Dorothy Day: Selected Writings*, edited by Robert Ellsberg (New York: Orbis, 2005) pp. 112–14.

Further reading

Holder, A. (2009), *Christian Spirituality: The Classics*. London: Routledge.

McGrath, A. (1999), *Christian Spirituality: An Introduction*. Oxford: Wiley-Blackwell.

Malone, M.T. (ed.) (2006), *Praying with the Women Mystics*. Dublin: Columba.

Sheldrake, P. (2007), *A Brief History of Spirituality*. Oxford: Blackwell.

Smith, A (ed.) (2012), *The Philokalia*. Woodstock, VT: Skylight Paths.

Thompson, R. (2008), *Christian Spirituality*. London: SCM.

Tyler, P., and R. Wood (eds.) (2012), *The Bloomsbury Guide to Christian Spirituality*. London: Bloomsbury.

Chapter 25

References

Nostra Aetate, 'The Declaration on the Relation of the Church to Non-Christian Religions', in Flannery, A. (1995) *Vatican II: The Basic Sixteen Documents*. New York: Costello.

Unitatis Redintegratio, 'The Decree on Ecumenism', in Flannery, A. (1995) *Vatican II: The Basic Sixteen Documents*. New York: Costello.

Augustine ([c.397] 1984), *The Confessions of Saint Augustine* (translated F. J. Sheed). London: Sheed and Ward.

Coleridge, H. J. ([1874] 2009), *The Life & Letters of Francis Xavier*. Charleston: Nabu Press.

Barrett, D. B., Kurian, G. T., Johnson, T. M. (2001), *World Christian Encyclopedia: A Comparative Survey of Churches and Religions in the Modern World*. Oxford & New York: Oxford University Press.

Dante Alighieri. ([c.1321] 2006-7), *The Divine Comedy* (3 vols) (translated by R. Kirkpatrick). London: Penguin.

D'Costa, G. (2009), *Christianity and World Religions: Disputed Questions in the Theology of Religions*. Chichester: Wiley-Blackwell.

Dupuis, J. (1997), *Theology of Religious Pluralism*. Maryknoll: Orbis.

Hunt, A. (2005), *Trinity*. New York: Orbis.

Johnson, M. D. (2005), *The Evolution of Christianity: Twelve Crises that Shaped the Church*. London & New York: Continuum.

Schmidt-Biggeman, W. (2004), *Philosophia Perennis: Historical Outlines of Western Spirituality in Ancient, Medieval and Modern Thought*. Norwell: Springer.

Strange, D., D'Costa, G., Knitter, P. (2011), *Only One Way?* London: SCM.

Thurian, M. (ed.) (1984), *The Churches Respond to Baptism Eucharist & Ministry*. Geneva: Faith and Order.

Extracts

1. The Qur'an on Mary and Jesus

As noted in the main text, Islam shares much of the theological heritage of Judaism and Christianity. Uniquely, Mary is given her own book and in this extract, the story of the miraculous conception and birth of Jesus is told:

> And mention in the Book Mary
> when she withdrew from her people
> to an Eastern place,
> and she took a veil apart from them:
> then We sent unto her Our Spirit
> that presented himself to her
> a man without fault.
> She said, 'I take refuge in
> the All-merciful from thee!
> If thou fearest God . . . .'
> He said, 'I am but a messenger
> Come from thy Lord, to give thee
> A boy most pure.'

> She said, 'How shall I have a son
> Whom no mortal has touched, neither
> have I been unchaste?'
> He said, 'Even so thy Lord has said:
> 'Easy is that for Me; and that We
> May appoint him a sign unto men
> And a mercy from Us; it is
> a thing decreed."
> So she conceived him, and withdrew with him
> to a distant place.
> And the birthpangs surprised her by
> the trunk of the palm-tree . . .

Then she brought the child to her folk
carrying him; and they said,
'Mary, thou hast surely committed
a monstrous thing!
Sister of Aaron, thy father was not
a wicked man, nor was thy mother
a woman unchaste.'
Mary pointed to the child then;
but they said, 'How shall we speak
to one who is still in the cradle,
a little child?'

He said 'Lo, I am God's servant;
God has given me the Book, and
made me a Prophet.
Blessed He has made me, wherever
I may be; and He has enjoined me
to pray, and to give the alms, so
long as I live,
and likewise to cherish my mother;
He has not made me arrogant,
unprosperous.
Peace be upon me, the day I was born,
and the day I die, and the day I am raised up alive!'

That is Jesus, son of Mary,
in word of truth, concerning which
they are doubting.
It is not for God to take a son
unto Him. Glory be to Him! When he
decrees a thing, He but says to it
'Be,' and it is.
Surely God is my Lord, and your
Lord; so serve you Him. This is
a straight path.

Source: Book XIX 'Mary' in *The Koran Interpreted*. Translated by A. J. Arberry (Oxford: Oxford University Press, 1982), pp. 303–5.

2. Rowan Williams on Interfaith dialogue

Rowan Williams has enjoyed a distinguished theological career. In his role as Archbishop of Canterbury, he was the spiritual leader of the many millions of Anglican and Episcopalian Church members throughout the world. In this extract, he speaks thoughtfully about conducting dialogue beyond fear.

Hindus, Sikhs and others are afraid of 'Abrahamic' universalism. Christians and Muslims are afraid of each other's universalism. Everyone is afraid of secular universalism. That's rather a lot of fear, and we ought to be starting by now to think of how we can move beyond this, not only into friendship but into some sort of positive discourse of human solidarity. Because that is, after all, the immensely creative aspect of universalism – the belief that human beings ultimately have the same dignities, the same possibilities, that the good of any one part of the human family is bound up with that of all others . . .

In Christian terms, one focal aspect of what is already bestowed is the self-identification of God with every person through the assumption of human nature by the divine Logos. Christ's incarnation creates a universal solidarity; and its healing effect is at work whether or not it is recognized and celebrated. The Church is, absurdly, both necessary and unnecessary. It cannot help being there because the response of the tenth leper is an uncontrollable outpouring of thanks and a desire to be where thanks is given to God in Christ. And at the same time, the Church is 'unnecessary' in the sense that it is not the cause of God's healing action, God's solidarity. It simply announces that God is already healing all and in solidarity with all, and that here is a space in which that solidarity can be embraced and imagined and woven into the texture of a healed and healing life. Conversion is not the cause of healing, but the response to it. If healing is not embraced in this way, it does not stop (the nine lepers do not have their leprosy back as a punishment), but we do not know how it works itself out in the transformation of particular lives. We have to be agnostic about how exactly this might work; and it is important not to talk about this as if healing were impersonal, automatic, unconnected in its outworking with the specific graces given in the community of belief, the community that is both necessary and unnecessary.

Source: *Fear and Friendship: Anglicans Engaging with Islam.* Edited by F. Ward and S. Coakley (London: Continuum, 2012), pp. 148–9.

Further reading

Cassidy, E. I. (2005), *Ecumenism and Interreligious Dialogue*. New York: Paulist Press.

De Chirico, L. (2003), *Evangelical Theological Perspectives on Post-Vatican II Roman Catholicism*. Oxford: Peter Lang.

Kärkkäinen, V. M. (2004), *Trinity and Religious Pluralism: The Doctrine of the Trinity in Christian Theology of Religions*. Aldershot: Ashgate.

Hick, J., Knitter, P. (eds) (2005), *The Myth of Christian Uniqueness: Toward a Pluralistic Theology of Religions*. Eugene: Wipf & Stock.

Murray, P. (2010), 'St. Paul and Ecumenism: Justification and All That' in *New Blackfriars*, Vol. 91(1032), 142–70.

O'Collins, G. (2008), *Salvation for All: God's Other Peoples*. Oxford: Oxford University Press.

Von Balthasar, H. (1990), *Mysterium Paschale*. (translated by A. Nichols). San Francisco, CA: Ignatius Press.

Chapter 26

References

Ball, A. (1999), *American Beauty*. Directed by S. Mendes, Dreamworks.

Boeve, L. (2007), *God Interrupts History*. London: Continuum.

Brueggemann, W. (2009), *The Unsettling God: The Heart of the Hebrew Bible*. Minneapolis, MN: Fortress.

Bullivant, S. (2012), *The Salvation of Atheists and Catholic Dogmatic Theology*. Oxford: Oxford University Press.

Chiesa, L. (2007), *Subjectivity and Otherness: A Philosophical Reading of Lacan*. Cambridge, MA: MIT Press.

Eagleton, T. (2009), *Reason, Faith and Revolution*. New Haven: Yale University Press.

Hallward, P. (2003), *Badiou: A Subject to Truth*. Minneapolis, MN: University of Minnesota Press.

Jarrott, C. A. L. (1964), 'Erasmus' "In Principio erat Sermo:" A Controversial Conversation' in *Studies in Philosophy*, Vol. 61(1), 35–40.

Kotsko, A. (2008), *Žižek and Theology*. London: T&T Clark.

May, L. (2005), 'Shakespeare for the Soul' in *The Pastoral Review*, Vol. 1(5), 22–5.

Marsh, N. (2001), *William Blake: The Poems*. New York: Palgrave.

Rowan, P. (2010), 'G. K. Chesterton and the Court of the Gentiles' in *The Pastoral Review*, Vol. 6(6), 59–65.

Smith, J. K. A. (2004), *Introducing Radical Orthodoxy: Mapping a Post-Secular Theology*. Grand Rapids: Baker Academic.

Extracts

1. Terry Eagleton on Reason, Faith and Revolution

Lest anyone think that only continental philosophers harbour Marxist-Theist syntheses, perhaps the foremost British literary critic and theorist, Terry Eagleton, has also contributed to the recent 'God-debates' that have eddied around in public life over the past decade. In *Reason, Faith and Revolution*, Eagleton has astringent words for Churches who have betrayed their radical heritage and for secularists who do not know the provenance of their values. In this extract, he pillories the notion that God and freedom stand in opposition:

> This, then, is what it means to say that God has created us in his own image and likeness, since he himself is pure liberty. It follows also that he is the ground of our ability to reject him-which is to say that in a splendidly big-hearted gesture, he is the source of atheism as well as faith. He is not a censorious power that prevents us from being good middle-class liberals and thinking for ourselves. This is simply the primitive, Philip Pullman-like view of those who cannot wean themselves off

the idea of God as Big Daddy. The poet William Blake would have had nothing but scorn for this naïve misconception. What writers like Pullman do not see is that the liberal doctrine of freedom derives among other sources from the Christian notion of free will, rather as the liberal belief in progress has a distant resonance of Christian ideas of Providence. As John Gray writes, 'The key liberal theorists of toleration are John Locke, who defended religious freedom in explicitly Christian terms, and Benedict Spinoza, a Jewish rationalist who was also a mystic.'

To highlight such affinities between liberalism and Judeo-Christianity (and there are many more) is in no sense to disparage the great liberal or Enlightenment heritage. Some Marxists are churlishly reluctant to acknowledge that Marx owes a good deal to the Judaic tradition; but why should they have such a low opinion of that lineage as to regard this claim as somehow devaluing his work? Liberalism (or radicalism) and religious faith are not necessarily at odds with each other . . .

The non-God or anti-God of Scripture, who hates burnt offerings and acts of smug self-righteousness, is the enemy of idols, fetishes and graven images of all kinds gods, churches, ritual sacrifice, the Stars and Stripes, nations, sex, success, ideologies, and the like. You shall know him for who he is when you see the hungry being filled with good things and the rich being sent empty away. Salvation, rather bathetically, turns out to be not a matter of cult, law, and ritual, of special observances and conformity to a moral code, of slaughtering animals for sacrifice or even of being splendidly virtuous. It is a question of feeding the hungry, welcoming the immigrants, visiting the sick, and protecting the poor, orphaned and widowed from the violence of the rich. Astonishingly, we are saved not by a special apparatus known as religion, but by the quality of our everyday relations with one another. It was Christianity, not the French intelligentsia, which invented the concept of everyday life.

Source: *Reason, Faith and Revolution: Reflections on the God Debate* (New Haven & London: Yale University Press, 2009), pp. 17–19.

2. Leonard May on Shakespeare for the soul

The brilliance of the bard from Stratford is known throughout the world. In this extract, Leonard May, a well-known spiritual guide and seasoned observer of the human condition borne of 60 years of priestly ministry, takes a look at the literary master.

Is Shakespeare a religious poet? He does not deal with religious issues directly, although the society in which he lives was alive with religious controversy; . . .

It seems to me that as he explores the darker depths of human characters, he is inevitably a religious poet, for every person is caught up in the drama of love: love accepted, love rejected, love corrupted, love abused. And this is surely the ultimate religious question: how do I love, and can there be life and hope without compassionate forgiveness? . . .

Long before modern versions of the nature v nurture debate we hear Hamlet acknowledging the destructive dispositions of some:

So oft it chances in particular men,

That for some vicious mole of nature in them,

As in their birth- wherein they are not guilty . . .

Oft breaking down the pales and forts of reason . . .

In Hamlet then, the dry bones of a few facts have become a destructive tragedy of a noble humanity torn apart by strange and dark emotions, breaking through the pales and forts of reason. Fallen man cannot save himself. He must look for divine compassion to heal his darkened mind and hurting heart- *'O, the mind has mountains, cliffs of fall frightful, hold them cheap he who n'ere hung there!'* The true hero of the human tragedy hung there, and saved us from the heat of the storm. And how often in this harsh world do we need the divine compassion to redeem so much that began as splendid promise.

The great, tragic figures that began as Hamlet, Lear and Othello die without hope, victims of uncontrollable forces tearing away at their minds and emotions. As St Paul told us,

'But I see another law at work in my body, making war against the law of my mind and making me a prisoner of the law of sin at work within my members. Wretch that I am, who will deliver me from this body of death?'

These tragic characters find no way out of their prison, and this is the tragedy of fallen Man who seeks redemption from within himself. Only in the drama of Divine Love, which in itself is a triumphant tragedy, can the human spirit find the place and power of redemption . . .

The tragedy of humankind is that either by betrayal, cold custom or death, lovers must part. The boundless beauty that is as deep as the ocean, the infinite well reaching out for the divine, is bounded by time and death, and can therefore live only in memory and hope. This is how the playwright shows humankind to itself. He reveals its infinite longings and finite limits . . .

Shakespeare knew the heart of Man and clearly knew the heart of God, and in that compassionate heart, he must surely have found his peace.

Source: 'Shakespeare for the Soul' in *The Pastoral Review*, Vol. 1(5) (Sept. 2005), 22–5.

Further reading

Over to you!

Glossary

Overview of biblical and theological terms

Don't let the jargon put you off!
If you can't remember a word, it should be in here somewhere.

Aetiology

Stories designed to explain why things are the way they are. The study of causation or origination, rooted in the Greek *aitiologia* – meaning 'to give a reason for'.

Agnostic

From the Greek *a-gnosis*, meaning 'one who does not know'. A 'convinced' agnostic holds that it is impossible to prove whether there is a God or not.

Allegory

A form of symbolic storytelling or interpretation which fosters imaginative engagement.

Anamnesis

'Remembrance' – a theological concept frequently associated with sacramental ritual.

Annunciation

The announcement by the angel Gabriel that Mary would conceive and become the mother of Jesus.

Anthropic principle

The theory that the entire organization of the cosmos was geared to produce humanity.

Anthropology

The study of human life and how social relations among humans are organized.

Anthropomorphic

Having a human form or characteristics.

Aphoristic

Sayings-based writings somewhere between poetry and prose that make allusions and distinctions to illuminate or define something.

Apocalyptic

A genre of symbolic writing that developed in post-Exilic Judean culture. The primary examples in the Bible are the books of Daniel and Revelation. Apocalyptic literally means 'un-veiling' or 'revealing' literature.

Apollinarianism

The theory that Jesus did not have a human mind or soul, therefore, he could not be considered to be fully man.

Apokatastasis

From the Greek word meaning 'restoration' – the ultimate reconciliation of all things in God.

Apologetics

Giving a reasoned explanation for a position. In a Church context – the discipline of defending a position in Christian Theology and aiming to present a rational basis for the Christian faith.

Apophatic

Sometimes called 'denial' or 'negative' theologizing – effectively describing God in terms of what God is not.

Apotheosis

The glorification or elevation of a subject to a divine level.

Assumption (of Mary)

The body of the Virgin Mary was taken up (assumed) into heaven at the end of her life.

Atheist

Takes a negative standpoint on God's existence – the rejection of belief in the existence of deities.

Axiom

Universally accepted or governing principle.

Contextualization

To put an event or an idea into a historical or theoretical framework to assist understanding.

Canon

The collection of scriptures – commonly termed as the Bible, containing inspired writings that have been gathered over many centuries.

Canon law

Ecclesial/Church legal system.

Catechumen

Someone not yet initiated into the church and who is preparing to be baptized.

Causality

Links one event with another or an action with a series of consequences.

Charisms

A Greek word meaning God given gifts bestowed for the good of the Church by the Holy Spirit.

Communism

A Marxist revolutionary socialist movement which aims to create a classless, moneyless and stateless society.

Concupiscence

Human tendency towards sexual lust or sin in general.

Consubstantial

A Latin word meaning 'of the same substance/nature/being'.

Correlation

A measure of the relation between two or more variables.

Cosmology

Considers the explanation of nature and of the universe as a whole.

Covenant

In a biblical context, this means a solemn agreement between God and humanity but can more widely include any mutually binding agreement.

Creeds

A creed is technically a statement of beliefs – usually that describes those shared by a religious community. Some originated out of the context of prayer while others were formulated at the great councils in the early Christian centuries.

Creationism

The religious belief that all of humanity and the whole of the universe are created by God.

Crusades

A series of religious expeditionary wars sanctioned by the Western Church in the Middle Ages which aimed to reclaim the Holy Land for Christendom.

Deconstructionist

A method of textual analysis which argues that the meaning of a text is endlessly open to further interpretation.

Deism

Deists believe that there is a supernatural Creator but are sceptical of the notion that God intervenes in human affairs or suspends the natural order of the universe.

Deontological

'Duty ethics' based on inherently good ethical actions

Diakonia

To minister or be of service to the community.

Dialectical materialism

A Marxist interpretation of reality – advocating revolutionary action to trigger the next stage of human development.

Diaspora

From the Greek meaning 'scattering' or 'dispersion'. In biblical terms, it refers to the Jewish faithful living outside of the Promised Land.

Didache

An early church document of liturgical and moral instruction reputedly to be based on the 'teaching' of the Twelve apostles.

Docetism

An early heresy – the belief that Jesus was a spirit being/avatar and not really human.

Ekklesia

From the Greek meaning 'the called out' 'assembly' or 'Church'.

Empiricism

The view that all concepts or knowledge arise from experience.

Enlightenment

Sometimes referred to as the 'age of reason', it was a cultural movement that started in the mid-seventeenth century – aimed at reforming society and furthering knowledge.

Episkopos

An 'overseer, 'supervisor' or 'bishop'.

Epistemology

The logic of knowing – the basis of Philosophy – it concerns the nature, scope and limitations of what we can know.

Eschatology

From the Greek meaning 'last things'. It can refer to the four last things (death, judgment, heaven and hell) or 'End Times' – cosmic judgement and the restoration of all things in Christ.

Essenes

A Jewish sect which flourished around the time of Jesus who lived ascetic lives. The 'Dead Sea Scrolls' are associated with this community.

Etymology

The study of the history of words, their origin and meaning and how their form and use have changed over time.

Eucharist

From the Greek meaning 'thanksgiving' – commonly called Holy Communion or the Lord's Supper.

Exegesis

Usually used with reference to the Bible – the critical interpretation of a text.

Existentialism

A type of philosophizing that places an emphasis on individual existence, freedom and choice. Kierkegaard is commonly regarded as the father of existentialism.

Ex Nihilo

A Latin phrase meaning 'out of nothing'.

Ex opere operato

An aspect of sacramental thinking meaning from the 'doing of the action'. Sacraments are understood as graced actions of Christ and are not dependent on the worthiness of the person conferring the sacrament.

Fundamentalism

Strict adherence to specific doctrines often linked to biblical literalism.

Glossolalia

Speaking in specific tongues as in Acts 2:4 or a gift of praise as in 1 Cor 14:2.

Gnostic

From the Greek word *gnosis* meaning 'knowledge' or 'insight'. Gnostics were 'in the know' and held a wide range of religious/cosmic theories. Their writings were disputed by mainstream Christian thinkers, particularly because they downplayed the human dimensions of the Gospel.

Haggadah and *Halakah*

Rabbinic forms of interpretation emphasizing story and law respectively.

Hegelianism

Ideas based on Hegel's philosophical views – in this text mainly relevant for the notion of historical 'epochs' and the evolution of human consciousness important for Marxist theory.

Hellenization

A term used in reference to the spreading of ancient Greek culture, for example, the 'Greek-ifying' of the original Judean *Kerygma*.

Hermeneutics

The theory and practice of interpretation.

Homoousios

A Greek word meaning 'of the same substance/nature/being'.

Hypostasis

In Christian Theology, this eventually came to mean a 'particular way of being' – especially relevant to Christological and Trinitarian thinking.

Iconoclasm

The intended destruction of religious paintings and other sacred artistic images and artefacts.

Incarnation

The Christian belief that Jesus was the divine pre-existent Word of Love, 'enfleshed' in the womb of the Virgin Mary, becoming both God and Man.

Infallibility

The doctrine whereby the Pope, as the successor of Peter, in consultation with his fellow bishops and the *sensus fidelium* (sense of the faithful), can make binding declarations regarding Christian faith and morality.

Jouissance

In the theories of Lacan – Original joy/pleasure/delight.

Kerygma

A Greek word used in the New Testament – meaning the apostolic proclamation and preaching of the Christ event.

Ketubim

Writings that form the third major subdivision of the Old Testament – priestly, poetic and wisdom literature. The central theme running through these writings is the hunger for understanding or 'wisdom'.

Kyrios

Greek word meaning 'Lord'.

Lex Orandi Lex Credendi

From the Latin 'the law of prayer is the law of belief' – the idea that the reasoned propositions of doctrine follow on from the experiential expressions of prayer.

Liberation Theology

Originating in South America, Christian interpretation of the Gospel aimed at bringing about social change and justice for the poor and marginalized.

Literalism

Biblical literalism is a simplistic 'face value' reading of a text which does not take into account subtleties of meaning, context and translation. It can often be associated with Fundamentalism.

Logical positivism

A philosophical movement which regarded most theological assertions as meaningless according to its famous 'Verification Principle'.

Logos

From the Greek originally meaning 'word', 'thought', 'principle' or 'speech'. In the New Testament, the 'Word (*logos*) of God' found in John 1:1 poetically expresses God's desire to speak to humanity through his Son, 'the Word made flesh'.

Logotherapy

Viktor Frankl's psychological treatment which emphasizes the importance of meaning in life.

Manicheism

Dualistic 'spirit good – flesh bad' religious system associated with the Gnostic thinker Mani (216-c.277 CE).

Maranatha

An Aramaic word-phrase meaning 'Our Lord – Come!' associated with Early Christian worship.

Messiah

From the Hebrew term *Mashiah* – meaning 'anointed one'.

Meta-narratives

The 'great stories/great symbolic worlds' which influence the direction of our lives. Religions, nations and cultures all generate meta-narratives which imbue meaning, values and purpose.

Metanoia

A 'turning around' – 'change of mind/heart'. Associated with Jesus' preaching about the Kingdom of God, often translated as 'conversion' or 'repentance'.

Modalism

Modalism claims that God is a single person revealed through history in three forms – thus a denial of the essential distinctions of the Trinity – in that the Father, Son and Holy Spirit never all exist at the same time, just one after another.

Modernity

The post-Medieval and post-Renaissance epoch associated with the Enlightenment of the seventeenth century and the subsequent quest for certainty in philosophical and scientific enquiry. Modernity in this book is analysed in Chapters 19–21.

Monotheism

The belief in the existence of one God.

Natural Philosophy

Until the early Modern period, this was the name for Science – the study of nature in all of its various forms.

Natural Theology

Theology based on reason, creation and ordinary experience, which is distinguished from *Revealed Theology* – God's direct self-disclosure/intervention through word and spirit.

Nihilism

The philosophical belief that all values are baseless and nothing can be properly known or communicated.

Occasionalism

The idea that God is the only guarantor of the correspondence between experience and the mind.

Oikoumene

A Greco-Roman term referring to the 'whole inhabited world' or universe. In the twentieth century, the word has been employed to refer to *Ecumenism* – the dialogue seeking unity between different Christian Churches.

Omnipotent/Omniscient/Omni-benevolent

All powerful. All knowing. All loving.

Ontological argument

Anslem's famous argument for God: 'That greater than which cannot be thought'.

Pantheism

God is not just everywhere – God is identical with everything.

Parables

A Greek term meaning 'to throw alongside'/juxtapose. Parables were Jesus' preferred method of teaching – using succinct stories to start discussions or illustrate one or more instructive principles, often using familiar items or experiences to connect with his audience.

Paradigm

A term describing a generally accepted benchmark or point of reference. 'Paradigm shifts' are when ways of thinking alter drastically because of new theories or discoveries.

Parousia

The second coming of Christ and the reconciliation of all things in him.

Patriarch

Generally, the male who is at the head of a family lineage e.g. Abraham, Isaac and Jacob are referred to as the three patriarchs of the people of Israel.

Patristics

The study of the early Christian theologians or 'Fathers' of the Church.

Perichoresis

The Trinitarian 'eternal dance of love' of the Father, Son and Holy Spirit.

Personalism

A tendency to focus on individuality and the uniqueness of a human person in the world of nature.

Pesher

From the Hebrew word meaning 'interpretation'. A Jewish-Christian way of reading scriptures that is sensitive to hidden meanings and fulfilment at a later time.

Philosophy

Literally 'love of wisdom'. The study of general and fundamental problems connected with existence, knowledge, values and reason.

Platonism

'Plato-type Philosophy' – often shorthand for thinking which favours ideas over experience.

Pluralism

A diversity of views rather than one understanding or interpretation of reality.

Postmodernism

Conceptual frameworks and ideologies that are defined in opposition to the certainties of Modernity, emphasizing the elusiveness of objective truth and prioritizing personal meaning.

Pneuma

Greek – 'Breath', 'Wind', 'Spirit'. In the biblical context (especially the New Testament), often referring to the Holy Spirit.

Pneumatomachi

Members of a fourth-century sect who did not believe in the equal dignity or divinity of the Holy Spirit.

Postmodernity

The much less coherent economic and cultural condition of society said to exist after the debunking of the presumed certainties of political scientific and philosophical worldviews.

Purgatory

After death, a place/period of purification for the imperfect soul before it enters heaven.

Recontextualization

The process that extracts texts or signs from their original context in order to introduce them to another framework, which usually involves a change in their significance.

Reflexivity

Reflection on the way that research is carried out – understanding how the process of doing research shapes its outcomes.

Religion

Rooted in the Latin word *re-ligare*, which means 'to bind together'. Religion is a collection of cultural systems, sacred practices and worldviews containing narratives, symbols and traditions. Religion by its nature differs from private belief in that it has a public aspect.

Reformation

The Protestant Reformation was the sixteenth-century schism within Western Christianity – some of the key protagonists were Martin Luther, John Calvin and Huldrych Zwingli. The English Reformation developed as the Church in England broke away from the authority of the Pope in the course of the sixteenth century. See Chapter 18d-g.

Revelation

The 'un-veiling' or disclosure about the nature of God. Divine truth that can only be known through God's self-communication.

Sacraments

Sacraments are rituals continuing the sanctifying work of Christ through the Church. Since the Middle Ages, the traditionally recognized seven have been Baptism, Confirmation, Eucharist, Reconciliation, Marriage, Holy Orders and Anointing of the Sick. Despite Reformation controversies, Baptism and Communion remain the common ritual signs of Christian identity and belonging.

Scholasticism

A method of teaching and critical thinking dominant in the Middle Ages.

Secularism

In general terms, the concept that government and public life should be conducted separately from religion and/or religious beliefs.

Septuagint

The translation of the Hebrew Bible (or Old Testament) into Greek – sometimes known as 'The Seventy' or the 'LXX'.

Shekinah

God's holy presence among the chosen people.

Situation ethics

The idea that moral principles can sometimes be put aside if 'agape' (selfless love) is to be best served.

Sitz im Leben

In biblical criticism, this is a German phrase roughly translating as 'life context'.

Stoicism

Philosophical/religious system linking humanity and the cosmos. The wisdom of the stoics involved a 'love of fate' – acceptance of what might happen and bravery in the face of it.

Sukkoth

The Feast of 'Booths' or 'Tabernacles' – in Judaism, a type of harvest celebration remembering the shelters the Jewish people used at the time of the Exodus from Egypt.

Syllogism

A type of logical argument whereby conclusions are drawn from two or more propositions.

Symbiosis

A 'living together' – 'mutually beneficial thriving'.

Synderesis

The basic human moral instinct to do good and avoid evil as an endowment of nature.

Synoptics

From the 'same-view' – it refers to the first three canonical Gospels – Matthew, Mark and Luke. Much of the material in these three books is similar.

TaNaK

'Torah, Neb'im, Ketubim' – Law, Prophets, Writings. This is a shorthand term for the Hebrew Bible, the sacred writings of Judaism known to Christians as the core elements of the 'Old Testament'.

Teleology

Associated with Aristotle – the idea that everything has an 'end' or 'final purpose'.

Theocracy

'God rule' – used to describe societies where priests or religious authorities are in charge.

Theodicy

Theories explaining why an all powerful benevolent God allows suffering and evil.

Theology

Rooted in the Greek *Theos* meaning 'God' and *logos* which signifies 'word,' 'reason' or 'meaning'. Theology may be understood as 'thoughtful conversation about God'.

Theophany

The appearance or manifestation of God.

Theotokos

A popular devotional title of Mary meaning 'God-bearer' which became a contentious point of dispute in the fifth century.

Torah

Also understood as 'The Law of Moses', it is the collective name for the first five books of the Hebrew Bible (Genesis, Exodus, Leviticus, Numbers and Deuteronomy).

Tradition

Handing on of beliefs and customs from generation to generation. In the Christian context, this dimension of 'lived faith' is of vital importance since it encompasses patterns of worship, behaviour and essential theological considerations.

Theandric

Human and divine attributes at work in the person of Christ.

Transubstantiation

A way of explaining how in the Eucharist, the bread and wine become the 'real presence', changing into the body and blood of Jesus.

Trinitarian

This word is used in conjunction with ideas or things pertaining to the Holy Trinity (the doctrine that defines God as three divine persons – the Father, the Son (Jesus Christ) and the Holy Spirit.

Uncertainty principle

Heisenberg's quantum 'Uncertainty Principle' relates to particular subatomic perplexities such as the fact that it appears impossible to determine both the speed and the location of a particle at the same time. It implies a more holistic view of the universe and in theological terms, it is perhaps most relevant in terms of freedom and biblical interpretation (see Section 19f). If you aren't outside nature, you're in it and life-truth is discovered by participation rather than detached observation.

Utilitarianism

An ethical theory teaching that the key to moral choice and the best way forward for society is to maximize the overall happiness for the greatest number of people.

Zeitgeist

The 'spirit of the time' – the mood of an era.

Timeline

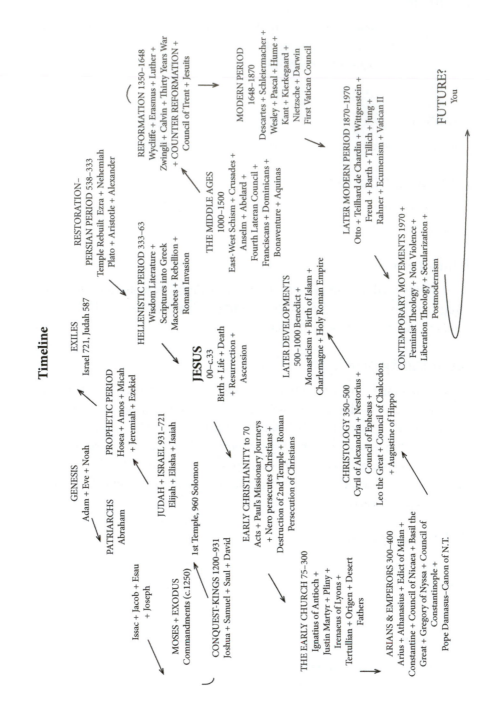

GENESIS
Adam + Eve + Noah

PATRIARCHS
Abraham

Issac + Jacob + Esau
+ Joseph

MOSES + EXODUS
Commandments (c.1250)

JUDAH + ISRAEL 931–721
Elijah + Elisha + Isaiah

1st Temple, 960 Solomon

PROPHETIC PERIOD
Hosea + Amos + Micah
+ Jeremiah + Ezekiel

EXILES
Israel 721, Judah 587

RESTORATION–
PERSIAN PERIOD 538–333
Temple Rebuilt Ezra + Nehemiah
Plato + Aristotle + Alexander

HELLENISTIC PERIOD 333–63
Wisdom Literature +
Scriptures into Greek
Maccabees + Rebellion +
Roman Invasion

REFORMATION 1350–1648
Wycliffe + Erasmus + Luther +
Zwingli + Calvin + Thirty Years War
+ COUNTER REFORMATION +
Council of Trent + Jesuits

MODERN PERIOD
1648–1870
Descartes + Schleiermacher +
Wesley + Pascal + Hume +
Kant + Kierkegaard +
Nietzsche + Darwin
First Vatican Council

THE MIDDLE AGES
1000–1500
East-West Schism + Crusades +
Anselm + Abelard +
Fourth Lateran Council +
Franciscans + Dominicans +
Bonaventure + Aquinas

LATER MODERN PERIOD 1870–1970
Otto + Teilhard de Chardin + Wittgenstein +
Freud + Barth + Tillich + Jung +
Rahner + Ecumenism + Vatican II

JESUS
00–c.33
Birth + Life + Death
+ Resurrection +
Ascension

CONQUEST-KINGS 1200–931
Joshua + Samuel + Saul + David

EARLY CHRISTIANITY to 70
Acts + Paul's Missionary Journeys
+ Nero persecutes Christians +
Destruction of 2nd Temple + Roman
Persecution of Christians

LATER DEVELOPMENTS
500–1000 Benedict +
Monasticism + Birth of Islam +
Charlemagne + Holy Roman Empire

CONTEMPORARY MOVEMENTS 1970 +
Feminist Theology + Non Violence +
Liberation Theology + Secularization +
Postmodernism

FUTURE?
You

THE EARLY CHURCH 75–300
Ignatius of Antioch +
Justin Martyr + Pliny +
Irenaeus of Lyons +
Tertullian + Origen + Desert
Fathers

CHRISTOLOGY 350–500
Cyril of Alexandria + Nestorius +
Council of Ephesus +
Leo the Great + Council of Chalcedon
+ Augustine of Hippo

ARIANS & EMPERORS 300–400
Arius + Athanasius + Edict of Milan +
Constantine + Council of Nicaea + Basil the
Great + Gregory of Nyssa + Council of
Constantinople +
Pope Damasus–Canon of N.T.

Index